## 8—Issues for Further Study: Where Does the Researcher Go from Here?

## Appendices

D1153730

# Industrial Concentration: The New Learning

*Edited by:*

## Harvey J. Goldschmid
*Professor of Law*
*Columbia University*

## H. Michael Mann
*Professor of Economics*
*Boston College*

## J. Fred Weston
*Professor of Business Economics and Finance*
*University of California, Los Angeles*

*Columbia University Center for Law and Economic Studies*

Little, Brown and Company
Boston    1974    Toronto

LIBRARY OF CONGRESS CATALOG CARD NO. 74-15993

THIRD PRINTING

Cover design by Ellen Clancy

Published simultaneously in Canada
by Little, Brown & Company (Canada) Limited

PRINTED IN THE UNITED STATES OF AMERICA

# Table of Contents

## 4—The Concentration and Profits Issue

## 5—Market Concentration and Innovation

## 6—Inflation and Concentration: The Theory and Evidence

## 7—Public Policy Implications of the New Learning

# Director's Preface

A traditional theme in antitrust enforcement is the undesirability of industrial concentration. It is said to be neither a technological imperative nor primarily dictated by economic efficiencies. Market concentration is alleged to chill innovative instincts, produce excessive profits, fuel inflation, and generally cause a serious misallocation of resources. Thus, monopoly has long been an antitrust concern, and acts that have the purpose or effect of reducing the number of competitors in a market have usually been condemned.

Recently, a structuralist approach to antitrust enforcement has gained new prominence with the introduction of Senator Philip A. Hart's Industrial Reorganization Act and the filing of so-called structural suits against IBM, Xerox, the leading cereal manufacturers and the oil industry, to name only a few. All of these are designed to break into smaller units the large corporations in concentrated markets.

But, also within the past few years, assumptions underlying the structuralist approach have come under significant attack. Empirical and theoretical challenges have come from respected segments of the academic community.

At issue are questions such as: Is market concentration primarily dictated by economic efficiency? Is concentration conducive to product and process innovation? Is it an important inflationary force? Do present antitrust statutes adequately deal with instances where concentration results in economic costs? What are the likely costs and benefits of an industrial deconcentration policy?

In the fall of 1973, the Faculty of Law at Columbia decided to organize a conference to probe these issues deeply. This volume grew out of the Columbia Law School Conference on Industrial Concentration which was held at Airlie House, in Virginia, on March 1 and 2, 1974. While planning the Conference, we set forth two fundamental goals:

> first, to provide an impartial forum for free discussion and debate on one of the paramount issues of our day; second, to assemble papers and excerpts from the Conference's proceedings which will form the nucleus of an important book.

This volume, we hope, demonstrates that our ambitions did not exceed our reach.

The volume contains a number of unusual features. First, it brings together an extraordinary group of economists and lawyers who carefully marshaled the evidence on key issues of industrial concentration and prepared papers which are, in my view, first-rate. The Conference's format provided for the exchange of drafts and for direct oral confrontations. Protagonists, with sharply differing views, who had previously dueled only sporadically and at a distance in journals, now grappled hand to hand. Removed was the opportunity to blur a hard issue or decimate a straw man.

Second, the book is comprehensive *and comprehensible* — it is written at a level that intelligent noneconomists can understand. While we expect it to be used widely in economics courses and at business schools, law students, for example, should find only a few papers where the going is rough for them. Each of the chapters will richly reward a careful reading.

Third, the "dialogues" to be found in each of the major chapters represent a striking interdisciplinary success. In attendance at Airlie House were most of the nation's leading thinkers on industrial concentration. Approximately seventy-five lawyers, law professors, economists, judges, and government policymakers took part in what at times were heated debates.* Questions often produced answers which significantly clarified, modified, or added to an author's point of view. The editors selected excerpts from the Conference proceedings and condensed them to provide what we believe is an invaluable pedagogical and policymaking resource. While, for the sake of readability, connectives have been added and many words deleted (all without ellipses or other warnings to the reader), the substance of discussions has not been changed.

Finally, as director of the Conference, I would like to express Columbia's gratitude to Ira Millstein, Esq., senior partner of Weil, Gotshal & Manges in New York City, and Robert M. Estes, senior vice president and general counsel of General Electric Company, for their indispensable assistance in establishing the Conference and obtaining support. On a similar plane, our thanks go to the Conference sponsors (listed in Appendix F) who made grants "without reservation or qualification"; we could not have gone forward without them.

I am also in debt to my coeditors, H. Michael Mann and J. Fred Weston, to Michele Corash and to Dean Michael I. Sovern of Columbia Law School. Each helped to organize and plan the Conference program and offered sage advice every step of the way.

I must add a special word of thanks to Ellen Hartwell, the Conference's associate director. Both while organizing the Conference and assembling this book, she displayed great patience, care, skill, dedication, and inexhaustible good cheer. In a real sense, she made everything work. A substantial share of the credit for what is valuable herein should be attributed to her.

This volume provides no "clear final solutions." The issues related to industrial concentration are simply too complex. But it does pin down, more precisely than I have ever seen before, *where* and *why* leading authorities agree or disagree. While the focus of the book is on economic and legal issues, some political and social values (properly, to my mind) often thrust themselves to the fore. In the end, I hope the reader will agree with me that what is offered sheds far more light than heat.

Harvey J. Goldschmid
Fall, 1974

---

* Appendix D gives biographical information on authors, chairmen, and editors; Appendix E identifies the Conference participants.

# Industrial Concentration:
# The New Learning

# An Introduction to the Issues

## The New Learning: One Man's View

### Donald J. Dewey*

### 1. TWO PROPOSITIONS

In the hope of stimulating thinking about the policy implications of industrial concentration, let me offer two important propositions for your consideration. They are not advanced merely for the purpose of heating up the discussion, though I hope that they will have this effect. I believe both of these propositions to be true.

My first propostion is this. Let us suppose that the legal framework of any economy is a close approximation to laissez-faire, that is, to the legal framework of the United States before 1890 or Great Britain before 1956.[1] Then, given the wide scope to freedom of contract allowed by such a system of laws, in the manufacturing sector of a mature capitalist economy — to borrow one of the more useful terms in the Marxist vocabulary — production will ultimately be concentrated in a relatively small number of firms. In such an economy our expectation is that in such industries as steel, machinery, food processing, aluminum, petroleum refining, etc., no more than four firms will usually control

---

* Professor of Economics and Chairman of the Department, Columbia University. For further biographical information, see Appendix D.

1. In the United States and Britain the end of laissez-faire, so far as industrial structure is concerned, may reasonably be dated from the first anticartel statute — that is, in the United States, from the Sherman Act, 26 Stat. 209 (1890), and, in Britain, from the Restrictive Trade Practices Act of 1956, 4 & 5 Eliz. 2, c. 68.

at least 50 percent of output. Moreover, the conglomerate firm will be a very prominent part of the economic landscape. In other words, one expects that a laissez-faire legal environment will sooner or later, produce an economy very like that of modern Japan.

I doubt that many of you will find anything controversial in the idea that the end product of laissez-faire is a highly concentrated economy. After all, who can cite a mature capitalist economy that is not highly concentrated? Your reaction is more likely to be that of a veteran New Yorker — "So what else is new?"

Hopefully, my second proposition has a greater claim to novelty. It is that, within wide limits, a mature capitalist economy can have whatever levels of concentration that it desires without the social fabric being seriously strained. Please accept that in framing this proposition I have tried to choose my words carefully. Almost any type of structural change in an economic system is conceivable if high enough costs are to be imposed upon some people. If Stalin could collectivize Russian peasants, it is certainly possible to break General Motors up into a hundred smaller units — and at a much lower human cost. Rather, my proposition says that the social costs of altering industry concentration ratios by changing public policy are small enough to be seriously contemplated by sensible people.

At this point I believe that a digression is in order. Economists, who from their training and experience should know better, sometimes assert that the economic impact of antitrust policy on concentration is so negligible that it need not be taken seriously. As we know, J. K. Galbraith[2] implies the antitrust case is like a nightly arrest for prostitution in the town's red-light district. It is a sop to silly reform opinion and a virtual guarantee to wrongdoers that they have nothing to fear in the normal course of business. Essentially the same view of antitrust is taken by some disillusioned supporters. In the tiredest of all clichés, they hold that it is a perfectly good idea that has never been tried.

Now certainly there are excellent reasons for doubting whether antitrust has had more than negligible effects on economic variables that really matter — the distribution of personal income, the rate of economic growth, the level of unemployment, the kinds of race and sex discrimination practiced, and the distribution of political influence. But the assertion that antitrust has not affected concentration ratios in the American economy is simply wrong. It would be tedious to list all of the industries whose structures, over the last seventy years, have been changed by dissolution and divestiture, all of the mergers discouraged by the possibility of prosecution, and all of the consent decrees that placed competitive handicaps on large firms. If antitrust does not matter, it follows, of course, that a repeal of the antitrust laws and the dismantling of enforcement machinery would have no effects worth mentioning on the structure of the economy. Surely no informed person really accepts this inference. We know perfectly well, from the experience of other countries and from what went on in the American economy in the closing years of the nineteenth cen-

2. John K. Galbraith, *Economics and the Public Purpose* (Houghton Mifflin 1973), p. 121.

tury, that the end of antitrust would see wholesale mergers and/or rapid cartelization in most industries. The kinds of guessing games that oligopolists play
when constrained by the antitrust laws have no raison d'etre in other contexts.
There is, after all, no point in speculating about the probable reaction of a
business rival to a change in your price policy when the law allows you to negotiate a cartel agreement with him. And, if the cartel is difficult to arrange or
enforce, there is always the alternative of a merger in a world of laissez-faire.
(It seems worth mentioning yet again that the mergers which produced the
United States Steel Corporation in 1901 resulted directly from the industry's
difficulties in operating cartels in the 1890s.)

Personally, I would not rule out the possibility that the consolidation and
cartelization that would follow the elimination of antitrust might result in a
more efficient and progressive economy. After all, the view that antitrust promotes economic efficiency and progress rests more upon faith than evidence —
and the view is probably held by a minority of economists outside the United
States. It is easier to be precise about the ways in which the antitrust laws
reduce the efficiency of the American economy than about the ways in which
they improve it. One can show in detail how the antitrust laws make it impossible to realize economies of scale in production, finance, and marketing
in many industries. The benefits that allegedly follow from a policy that limits
market share and/or firm size are, almost without exception, nebulous and un-
measurable. To repeat, it is by no means certain that the antitrust laws operate,
on balance, to improve economic performance. But that the end of antitrust
would produce a rapid change in the structure of the American economy I can
see no reason to doubt.

From the above observations it follows that, since this country has had more
than eighty years of antitrust, there is nothing "natural" about the present
structure of the American economy. On the contrary, I submit that the present
level of concentration, especially in the manufacturing sector, is unnaturally
low; and, indeed, that the ubiquity of oligopoly is a tribute to the effectiveness
of antitrust. Further, I submit that the end product of laissez-faire is not oligopoly but rather the dominant-firm pattern that was emerging in many industries before 1911 and is so common in Europe. This is not to say that the
end product of laissez-faire is monopoly — only that it is "something that looks
like monopoly but really isn't." Unless a sole producer enjoys legal protection
against possible entry into his market by other firms, it is an abuse of language
to describe him as a monopolist.

If I am correct in assuming that, given a world of free contract, high concentration ratios are inevitable in most mature industries in manufacturing, our
first task would seem to be obvious: it is to explain why laissez-faire ultimately
leads to high concentration. Now our difficulties begin. Offhand, it would
seem that we are faced with a scientific problem. A quick sampling of the literature of industrial organization suggests that the study of concentration has
traditionally had much in common with evangelical theology. One influential
dogma asserts that concentration occurs because it creates scale economies
in production and research. We have it on Professor Galbraith's authority that
"most of the cheap and simple inventions have, to put it bluntly and unpersua-

sively, been made." [3] The other major contending dogma asserts that industrial concentration comes about because it creates monopoly power and so makes possible the collection of economic rents. In the unambiguous prose of Henry Simons:

> Few of our gigantic corporations can be defended on the ground that their present size is necessary to reasonably full exploitation of production economies: their existence is to be explained in terms of opportunities for promoter profits, personal ambitions of industrial and financial "Napoleons" and advantages of monopoly power.[4]

Many economists of an earlier day, in common with a great many of their contemporaries, desperately wanted to believe that the economies of multiplant ownership were slight or nonexistent. If this were true, there was nothing natural or inevitable about the large corporation which had to be explained in the classroom and possibly contained by public policy. The dogmatists have been doing battle for many years now without, so far as I know, producing any new arguments or facts that are worthy of our attention.

Surely we can all agree that the time has come to break out of the theological mold and start thinking about industrial concentration as a scientific problem. Still, we might begin by considering why so many able economists of the past never managed to escape the clutches of evangelical theology. I offer the following thoughts.

First, in explaining industrial concentration, economists were up against a problem which could not be easily tackled with conventional statistical techniques. It is, of course, a relatively simple matter to measure scale economies in a particular industrial plant at some particular time and place. Engineers do it every day. But measuring the scale economies that result from the creation of a multiplant firm in an industry, or a conglomerate firm across different industries, is far more difficult. If I understand Professor McGee correctly, he claims that such measurement is virtually impossible.

To say the obvious, the percentage of the labor force that is employed in manufacturing, retail, or wholesale establishments having more than 5,000 employees is very slight. The large firms of this world — say, those that are large enough to be listed in anybody's compilation of the 500 largest — are, almost without exception, multiplant firms. It is the multiplant firm (usually the multiplant conglomerate firm) that one must deal with in order to explain industrial concentration. We can easily identify many possible economies of scale in multiplant operations. We can just as easily identify many possible diseconomies of scale in multiplant operations. Each specific individual economy or diseconomy of scale is usually very small in relation to total cost; and hundreds of specific economies and diseconomies can be identified. Hence, measurement of the net impact of an increase in the size of the multiplant firm on

3. John K. Galbraith, *American Capitalism* (Houghton Mifflin 1956), p. 86.

4. Henry C. Simons, *Economic Policy for a Free Society* (Univ. of Chicago Press 1948), p. 61.

average total cost is very difficult. And when measurement is very difficult, economists, like other people, succumb to a very human temptation: they believe what they want to believe because there is no good reason to believe otherwise.

There is, I believe, another and more parochial reason why economists had difficulty in thinking clearly about industrial concentration. From his earliest training, the economist has had drummed into his consciousness the image of the firm's curve of average total cost. And it is U-shaped. Such a cost curve dictates an optimum size of the firm. And given the way the curve is drawn in all basic textbooks, i.e., as rising steeply in the area of its minimum, any significant change in the firm's output will cause average total cost to change significantly.

In the tight little world of microeconomic theory, the U-shaped cost curve plays a most important role. It makes possible a competitive equilibrium and, with the aid of additional assumptions that need not trouble us here, it insures the existence of such an equilibrium. If there were no U-shaped cost curve to provide an optimum size for the firm, economists would have to find something to replace the idea of competitive equilibrium. And to economists this is a very frightening prospect. All good textbooks in microeconomic theory note somewhere that an industry will ultimately be taken over by a single firm if it contains at least one firm that can always cut average total cost by increasing output.[5] But this point ("natural monopoly") is generally treated as an interesting curiosity rather than an important — not to say a profound — truth.

In the real world, multiplant firms need not have U-shaped cost curves. Only in the very shortest run does a firm expand output by making greater demands on its existing productive capacity. Rather, it expands output by increasing productive capacity which usually means acquiring another plant; and there is no good a priori reason to suppose average total cost will increase when the additional plant is acquired. Since multiplant firms exist, economies of multiplant ownership must also exist. This inference is so patently reasonable that I blush to mention it in public.[6]

Once we have broken free from the tyranny of the U-shaped curve of average total cost, we have also taken a long step toward discarding the hold of unprofitable dogma. We can then accept with equanimity the possibility that, over a wide range of output, the multiplant firm has decreasing average total cost and hence that the equilibrium condition of the industry may be the concentration of output in a single multiplant firm.[7] It should be emphasized

---

5. One of the better treatments of "natural" monopoly is Gary S. Becker, *Economic Theory* (Univ. of Chicago Press 1971), pp. 95-98.

6. Donald Dewey, *The Theory of Imperfect Competition: A Radical Reconstruction* (Columbia Univ. Press 1969), pp. 42-59.

7. Strictly speaking, it is not necessary that the multiplant firm have decreasing average total cost over the relevant range of output in order to emerge as the only producer in the market. It is only necessary that average total cost not increase over this range. That is, this outcome is possible whenever average total cost is approximately constant, because the firm's efficiency is not affected by adding or subtracting

that such total concentration need not rest upon "great" scale economies. Strictly speaking, the merger of two or more firms is an "either/or" proposition when the complications of an uncertain future can be ignored. Either it pays to combine two independent enterprises or it does not. If a scale economy can be realized through the merger, then the merger pays. The magnitude of the cost saving made possible by combination is irrelevant. It is sufficient that the saving be positive. Therefore, "small" savings in finance, advertising, and management suffice to bring into existence highly concentrated industries.

The actual magnitude of economies of scale is, of course, a problem for empirical investigation. By my reading, the weight of the evidence indicates that, over a wide range of output, scale economies in the multiplant firm are usually very small. Thus those economists who argue that the scale economies of multiplant firms are exaggerated by the uninformed and credulous are probably correct. Economists who hold that there are no scale economies in the multiplant firm are clinging to a faith, not appraising evidence.

In short, the "fact" of industrial concentration is easily explained. The causes of concentration are to be found in the economies of multiplant operation (also in the economies of multiproduct operation). Arguments to the contrary will, upon close examination, be found to contain errors of logic or to rest on unacceptable assumptions. However, our main concern is not really with the causes of industrial concentration. It is rather with the costs that we must incur, and the benefits that we might obtain, by doing something about it. No feat of high-powered economic analysis is needed to explain why the country has four automobile producers rather than forty. What we want to know is what the net change in economic welfare would be if we created another one, three, or ten automobile producers (presumably through a dissolution of divestiture decree). There may be obstacles to splitting each of the 500 largest industrial firms into, say, four equal parts. But if my conjectures are correct, they are to be found in law and politics — not in technology. And this cost-benefit analysis, of course, is what the economics of antitrust should be all about. For reasons to be noted presently, this is not what the economics of antitrust has been about in the past.

My second proposition was that a mature capitalist economy can, within wide limits, choose its concentration ratios without incurring heavy social costs. This proposition implies that such a choice will be exercised by placing limits upon the size of multiplant firms. It follows directly from the assumption that average total cost is approximately constant over a wide range of output.

---

plants when every plant is operated at an output at which average total cost is at its minimum.

The formal proof of the above proposition is somewhat involved, but the idea behind it is simple enough. To discourage the entry of potential rivals, the multiplant firm with approximately constant costs need only keep its profit at a very modest level by practicing limit pricing. It has the power to insure that, although it earns a modest profit, the market will become unprofitable for both itself and a rival if a potential rival enters. For details on limit pricing see Dewey, *supra* n. 6, at 42-86.

Therefore, trust-busting of the cautious sort traditionally sanctioned by the
federal courts will not produce startling losses of technical efficiency.

## 2. INDUSTRIAL CONCENTRATION AS A POLICY PROBLEM

Let us assume, if only for the sake of argument, that the American economy
can be restructured in accordance with a master plan to be drawn up jointly
by Professor Blair, Senator Hart, and Justice Douglas. What arguments can be
advanced for believing that it should be so restructured? There is no scarcity
of advocates who will come forward to urge that such a blow for decentralization is desirable because it will increase economic welfare by making the
economy more competitive. In order to appraise the validity of this argument,
we must inform ourselves about the connection (if any) between monopoly
power and industrial concentration. Is a high concentration ratio in any industry, or a high market share in any firm, associated with an above-average
rate of return on capital? Or with a more efficient use of resources in research
and development (which may or may not be associated with an above-average
rate of return on capital)?

Other commentators included in this volume will have much to say on this
matter — perhaps more than the reader wishes to know. Here, I will only cite
what I believe to be the majority opinion of specialists, namely that the connection between profitability and technical progress on one hand, and industrial concentration on the other, appears to be quite weak. It is, of course, all
too easy to quibble over words. And since highly concentrated industries do
have somewhat higher rates of return on capital, economists do quibble. However, I believe the following generalization holds: over the last fifty years the
only firms that have averaged a rate of return on capital of more than 15
percent for long periods are those that the government protects against the
entry of competitors. The rate of return on capital invested in New York City
taxicabs is now well over 100 percent per annum. But then, the number of
permits to operate taxicabs issued by the city has not increased in over thirty-
five years. One shudders to think of the rate of return on capital invested in
the typical metropolitan TV station.

## 3. A DIGRESSION ON MONOPOLY

Personally, I have never been one to depreciate the concern of so many
economists with the problems of monopoly power. However, I have always
been puzzled by the tendency to search for monopoly in concentration ratios
rather than in the myriad of entry restrictions embodied in federal, state, and
local legislation. I will let Professor Demsetz speak for me on this point.

I am not sure what the friends of antitrust will make of the argument developed so far. On the one hand, it implies that any gains in economic welfare
from a restructuring of the American economy will be modest at best and quite
possibly nonexistent. On the other hand, it implies that most multiplant firms
have neither much monopoly power nor important scale economies that will be
destroyed by the typical dissolution decree. Therefore, few individuals will be

much hurt by restructuring, and few will have a vested interest in opposing it. This is one of the ironic features of American antitrust: the spectacular remedies of dissolution and divestiture decrees are most frequently employed in those cases where they have the least economic impact for either good or ill.

As we know, the legal fiction is that a monopolist must be deprived of his monopoly power (unless its possession is specifically sanctioned by law — by patents, exclusive franchises, etc.) whenever it can be identified. But, of course, courts do not really translate this fiction into legal remedies, and their refusal to do so is quite sensible. In a world where monopoly rents are capitalized, the only beneficiaries of monopoly are those who get in on the ground floor. Whenever public policy comes up against unmistakable monopoly power which it wishes to eliminate quickly — for example, the privately owned toll bridges of my youth or the jobs of railroad workers in the 1970s — it pays compensation to the monopolist. And it is right to do so.

Whenever the state has tolerated a course of events that allows monopoly rents to be capitalized and purchased by Johnny-come-latelies, it has, so to speak, pursued a policy of entrapment. There may be nothing in the federal or state constitution to stop the city of New York from increasing the number of taxicab permits and so wiping out the life savings of hardworking drivers who have bought their cabs for sums of $15,000 or more. Obviously, it would be quite immoral for the city government to do such a thing. When faced with undoubted monopoly, public policy has only three alternatives: to live with it, to buy it back (presumably for elimination) from its present owners, or to proceed to diminish it over a period of time by means that give owners time to adjust. The massive shuffling of stock certificates that has often accompanied a major dissolution or divestiture decree (*Standard Oil,*[8] *Pullman,*[9] *du Pont–General Motors,*[10] for example) has had the unfortunate effect of disguising this truth.

## 4. ECONOMISTS AND ANTITRUST

I think it fair to say that most economists who are interested in industrial organization, and have kept up with the professional literature, would decline to endorse most of the economic arguments which, in the simpler intellectual world of Frank Fetter,[11] Justice Brandeis,[12] William Ripley,[13] and Henry Simons,[14] were thought to justify measures designed to discourage industrial concentration. My impression is that disaffection is rapidly spreading to the antitrust and regulation courses of our law schools. And yet, while the new

8. Standard Oil Co. of New Jersey v. United States, 221 U.S. 1 (1911).
9. United States v. Pullman Co., 330 U.S. 806 (1947).
10. United States v. E. I. du Pont de Nemours & Co., 353 U.S. 586 (1957).
11. Frank Fetter, *The Masquerade of Monopoly* (Harcourt Brace 1931).
12. Louis D. Brandeis, *The Curse of Bigness* (Kennikat Press 1934).
13. William Z. Ripley, *Main Street and Wall Street* (Little, Brown 1927).
14. Henry C. Simons, *Economic Policy for a Free Society* (Univ. of Chicago Press 1948).

light in industrial organization has led to the discarding of many long-held views, and to much carping criticism of antitrust, it has not led to a mass re- pudiation of the policy. The time has not yet come when most economists (or, for that matter, most industrial organization specialists) will endorse the senti- ment expressed by Professor Armentano in his recent attack on antitrust that the policy is — and always has been — a ghastly mistake rooted in economic ignorance.[15] Why do economists persist in a loyalty which they are no longer prepared to defend with the traditional arguments?

One reason may be simple time-lag. That is, maybe the implications of the new learning in industrial organization have not yet been fully grasped. Econ- omists were slow to rally to the idea of antitrust in this country; perhaps the slowness of their defection should cause no surprise.[16]

Another possible explanation is that the past achievements of antitrust have saved our generation from the need to make difficult choices. Only a very few economists in this country would give an affirmative answer to the question: should the antitrust laws be repealed in their entirety? This is true, I believe, for several of the distinguished participants in this discussion who have not had a good word to say for an antitrust prosecution in twenty-five years. However, the present level of industrial concentration is one thing; what the level might be today had there been no antitrust in the past is another thing. Thus one may believe that no good purpose would be served by breaking up a major oil company in 1974, and still give thanks that we no longer have to face a situation where one oil company has 85 percent of the national market.

The above thought can be put another way. A great many American econo- mists take an industrial structure shaped by the antitrust laws so much for granted that they have difficulty in imagining an economy without them. I confess to getting a wry pleasure from discovering that some young economic theorists can, without difficulty, rattle off five different theories of oligopoly and yet have trouble analyzing a simple cartel problem. This is understandable and pardonable given the content of their graduate training. It is not their fault that they view oligopoly as somehow more natural than cartelization. They have never been moved or compelled to think through the implications of laissez-faire for market structures.

---

15. D. T. Armentano, *The Myths of Antitrust: Economic Theory and Legal Cases* (Arlington House 1972).

16. In the 1890s most American economists greeted the passage of the Sherman Act with at best indifference and at worst hostility. The indifference was traceable to the suspicion (not unfounded) that the legislation was a congressional bow in the direction of populist discontent that sensible courts would not take too seriously. The hostility was traceable to the fear that the Sherman Act represented a potentially serious restriction on freedom of contract which economists, then as now, were dis- posed to view as both necessary for economic efficiency and a good thing in itself. It would be an interesting exercise in intellectual history to trace the steps by which economists gradually shifted their allegiance from laissez-faire to antitrust. Some fea- tures of the change are discussed in Letwin, "Congress and the Sherman Antitrust Law: 1887-1890," 23 *U. Chi. L. Rev.* 221, 235-240 (1956); and Hans B. Thorelli, *The Federal Antitrust Policy* (Stockholm, P. A. Norstedt & Söner 1954), pp. 108-127.

Again, economists may continue to support the idea of antitrust because they believe that it helps to save the economy from a worse fate; that is, it is possible to view antitrust as a second-best policy. Most economists who hold this view probably prefer a legal framework that is closer to laissez-faire. A few economists who would like to be socialists may support antitrust only because government ownership is not viewed as a politically viable alternative at the present time.

I will admit to having considerable sympathy with the view that antitrust, whatever its shortcomings, is attractive as a second-best policy. For reasons that we cannot explore today, in the United States there is not going to be a policy turn in the direction of laissez-faire in the near future. Consequently, the alternatives to antitrust are now, as they have been for many years, public utility type regulation and government ownership. Among economists the disdain and contempt for regulation is nearly universal; if effective, it is thought to be pernicious, and if ineffective, a waste of resources. While the hostility to public ownership as an organization alternative to antitrust is not so marked among economists, hostility is still the dominant attitude. Few would claim that direct public production of goods and services has worked well in this country. This is so even if we allow for the fact that it is usually invoked only as a measure of last resort (urban transit, etc.). The case for public ownership among economists is generally made to rest upon the assumption that, once we are prepared to take this alternative seriously, we should be able to devise forms that will be superior to anything yet seen — certainly superior to the United States Postal Service, the Long Island Railroad, and the Port of New York Authority.

Does antitrust really act as a buffer against pressures pushing the economy in the direction of more government ownership and more public utility type regulation? Socialists who view antitrust as a diversionary fraud have often brought this charge over the years. I suspect that they are more right than wrong. My impression is that industrial concentration acts as a lightning rod that concentrates and draws down all sorts of political discontents and frustrations. In an old story, the rabid supporter of William Jennings Bryan blames his wife's adultery on the Union Pacific Railroad. He has plenty of modern counterparts. Are we really surprised that Ralph Nader attacks General Motors rather than a random sample of southern textile mills? By keeping down concentration ratios in major industries, antitrust dissipates the political force of dissatisfactions with the economic system by spreading it over a greater number of targets.

## 5. THE DISGUISED GOALS OF ANTITRUST

So far we have cited time-lag, lack of imagination, and willingness to settle for the second best to explain the persisting loyalty of economists to the idea of antitrust. None of these reasons is very flattering to my profession. A possibly more honorable reason for the attachment can be cited. We are made uneasy and suspicious by great corporate size in the private sector of the economy for the same reason as our fellow citizens. We react in this way because we believe that great corporate size concentrates discretionary authority in the hands of too few people. Objectively, we may accept that such concentration is necessary for the efficient production of goods and services. American economists, at any rate, have never doubted that hierarchical organization, especially when fueled by the profit motive, is superior to all other forms for achieving economic efficiency.[17] And objectively, we may know that discretionary authority and monopoly power are two different things.[18] The management of a bankrupt railroad may be utterly unable to obtain a positive return on its capital and still have the power to affect the lives of thousands of individual workers, shoppers, and commuters by its decisions. Unfortunately, we — this time I mean both economists and lawyers — seem to believe that there is something discreditable in admitting our distrust of discretionary authority. One result is that, in antitrust policy, whenever we act on the basis of this fear, we feel obliged to play elaborate word games to conceal the fact. I submit that much of what passes for economic analysis in antitrust litigation is perilously close to window dressing, in the sense that it has little effect upon the outcome of the case. (In Robinson-Patman cases the truth of this proposition is virtually self-evident.) I draw back from asserting that most antitrust economics is window dressing, but only because this term has a connotation of cynical calculation which is not applicable.

A case that wonderfully illustrates the reasons for my doubt that the quality of economic analysis has much to do with shaping antitrust policy is *du Pont–General Motors,* decided in 1957.[19] Incidentally, I think that the decision was a good one. I think it would have been even better if the Court had not attempted to use economic arguments to justify what was done. Here the Supreme Court compelled the du Pont company to divest itself of a substantial stock interest (about 23 percent) in General Motors Corporation that it had acquired in the early 1920s. Effective voting control of the du Pont company itself rested with a family holding company.

The ostensible economic issue in this case was whether du Pont, as a consequence of the stock acquisition, was able to sell more of its paints, varnishes, and fabrics to General Motors. If so, other manufacturers of these products were injured. The question that occurs to an economist is whether there is any reason to believe that the injury sustained by those others was not in the public

17. For the most recent elaboration of this faith, see A. Alchian and H. Demsetz, "Production, Information Costs, and Economic Organization," *American Economic Review,* 62 (1972), pp. 777-795.

18. Perhaps the asserted distinction between monopoly power and discretionary authority should be elaborated. Discretionary authority is essentially power to make decisions that affect the lives of other people; it is, of course, more closely associated with the size of an organization than with its power to affect price by varying output. The sophomore who, in a basic economics course, has trouble seeing the difference between a firm which is merely large and a large firm which has a large market share may not be quite so obtuse as his instructor believes. It is probable that "economic power" to the sophomore signifies power over people, which is exercised by the higher management of A&P just as surely as by the higher management of General Motors.

19. United States v. E. I. du Pont de Nemours & Co., 353 U.S. 586 (1957).

interest. Presumably an injury to competitors is not the same thing as an injury to competition, and, to say the painfully obvious, competition as a dynamic process requires losers as well as winners. The answer to this question depends upon why the stock acquisition resulted in du Pont selling more paints, varnishes, and fabrics to General Motors — assuming, for the sake of argument, that this change really did occur.

There would seem to be two possibilities (not mutually exclusive). First, the stock acquisition may have allowed the du Pont family to perpetrate a near-fraud on the other stockholders of General Motors. The family had, in fact, a greater equity interest in the du Pont company than in General Motors; hence it was to their advantage that some earnings be diverted from General Motors to the du Pont company. This possibility was not explored in the case. In any event, it is the sort of problem that is best handled by stockholders' suits or an investigation by the Securities and Exchange Commission.

The second possibility is that the stock interest of the du Pont company in General Motors somehow made possible some economies of vertical integration somewhere in the process of producing paints, varnishes, and fabrics and applying them to automobiles. Now if General Motors willingly bought more du Pont materials, then the price of automobiles was presumably lowered. If it bought more du Pont materials because it was ordered to do so by guardians of the du Pont family interests, then the price of automobiles was presumably raised. In short, the significant economic issue in the *du Pont–General Motors* case was: had the stock tie raised the price of automobiles over a period exceeding thirty years? Suffice it to say, this issue was never placed before the Court. Even if it had been, it is unlikely that econometric technology of the 1950s would have proved equal to providing an answer worthy of the Court's respect. Most economists would, I think, have simply shrugged and said that, whether positive or negative, the impact of the du Pont's stock acquisition on the price of automobiles was probably negligible.

Actually, most of the economic analysis in the *du Pont–General Motors* case was devoted to trivia, e.g., to a breakdown of GM's purchases of paints, varnishes, and fabrics over the years, the degree of autonomy enjoyed by the purchasing agents of GM's divisions, how automobile varnishes differed from household varnishes, etc. In the end the Supreme Court decided that there was a reasonable possibility that, in the early 1920s, du Pont's buying into General Motors tended to reduce competition in paints, varnishes, and fabrics. Admittedly, the economic analysis supplied by the government was pretty shoddy; still I cannot believe that the Court's decision would have been different even had it received the benefit of economic analysis which was positively brilliant.

Do we really think that the stock tie between General Motors and du Pont was cut by the Court because of its possible impact on markets for the paints, varnishes, and fabrics in the 1920s? Surely not. The games that lawyers play often puzzle other people; however, every professional group has ways of conducting its business that seem quaint and surprising to outsiders. I have no wish to attribute cynicism or opportunism either to the Justice Department or the courts. Nevertheless, I think the following inference is justified and will be drawn by future historians of antitrust: the ostensible issues in this case provided a convenient pretext for eliminating a corporate arrangement that makes many of us uneasy. More specifically, the target of the *du Pont–General Motors* case was the discretionary authority of certain members of the du Pont family; the principal consequence of the case was the transfer of some part of this authority to the higher management of General Motors. Similar generalizations can be made about many of our most famous antitrust cases.

To repeat, this country has an antitrust policy not because it fears the economic consequences of industrial concentration (which, in any event, are difficult to identify and probably small). Nor even because industrial concentration is thought to be a useful, if crude, proxy for monopoly power. For this reason, a more accurate estimate of the economic consequences of industrial concentration, while a good thing in itself, is not likely to have much impact on public policy.

If the country does not really fear the economic consequences of industrial concentration, then what is antitrust all about? The answer that I would give has already been suggested: it is about discretionary authority in the private sector of the economy. Admittedly, if we tried to infer the goals of antitrust from the manner in which antitrust laws have been interpreted and enforced over the years, the list would be a long one. (Among other things, the antitrust laws have been used to punish income tax evasion and labor racketeering.) Nevertheless, I submit that the greatest common denominator in antitrust decisions is a commitment to smallness and decentralization as ways of discouraging the concentration of discretionary authority. Since the antitrust decisions of the courts are hardly ever overruled by subsequent legislation, it seems a fair inference that this commitment is widely approved. One argument frequently used to justify hostility to corporate size and concentration is that owners and managers of large firms derive an unfair amount of political influence from their positions. Indeed, Harlan Blake of the Columbia Law School has maintained that the large conglomerate firm is objectionable mainly because it makes possible economies of scale in lobbying. (Somewhere, of course, there is an economist who will maintain that any innovation that economizes on the use of scarce resources in lobbying cannot be all bad.) Personally, I favor a more simple-minded explanation of the hostility to corporate size and concentration. It is that many of us fear that, at some time in our lives, we may find ourselves opposing its owners and managers in an unequal contest. No doubt there are also other reasons for distrusting great corporate size and concentration. Some, I suspect, are so deeply buried in our subconscious that they could be revealed only by a psychiatrist with an MBA degree.

## 6. A FINAL THOUGHT

Since I do not believe that antitrust is mainly about the economic consequences of industrial concentration, I think it appropriate to close by emphasizing both the promise and limitations of this Conference. Our commentators will demonstrate that we know much more about industrial concentration — its causes, magnitudes, and strictly economic consequences — than we did twenty years ago. But this demonstration will, I suspect, have mainly negative value so far as policy alternatives are concerned. Our commentators will show that much of what was formerly asserted about the economic consequences of industrial concentration is, at worst, wrong and, at best, incapable of being proved or disproved. It will, I think, be a good thing if they manage to impart some of their skepticism about the traditional arguments for antitrust to men of the law. Still, the skepticism that a federal judge brings to an antitrust case will not make his job easier when a decision must be written and a decree framed; indeed, it may make his job even more difficult. Perhaps the most valuable lesson that a lawyer can gain from an introduction to the new thinking about industrial concentration is a clearer view of what help he can — and cannot — expect from economists.

Within a few years the Antitrust Division, if only to maintain its self-respect, will bring a dissolution suit against General Motors — provided, of course, that management miscalculations or foreign automobile imports have not seriously eroded its ability to generate an impressive rate of return on capital. When the suit is brought, I trust that the courts will find that the economists who are consulted will speak with far more caution and unanimity than in past cases. Very likely the government will win some sort of a "victory" whatever the economists have to say about competition in the automobile industry. This is because the case will really be about the discretionary authority of General Motors management and not about the firm's monopoly power. Is it Utopian to hope that, in accepting that General Motors must be split into $n$ pieces, the Supreme Court will say simply: "Since the best professional opinion is that this restructuring will do little harm to the company's workers and stockholders, or to the general public, we see no reason for not ordering it"?

# 2

# Economies of Scale
# as a Determinant

## Editors' Note

The Industrial Reorganization Act proposed by Senator Philip A. Hart (see Appendix B) seeks the breakup of dominant firms in concentrated industries if certain specified conditions hold. Like other proposals with the same objective, it permits an exception if significant economies would be sacrificed by the creation of a larger number of firms. This is sensible because even a large increment to consumer welfare arising from the reduction in price and the expansion of output as concentration decreased could be negated by only a mild increase in costs occurring from production by smaller, less efficient firms.

The exact dimension of the trade-off is an empirical issue, a crucial part of which is the extent to which high levels of concentration are based upon economies of scale. Professors Scherer and McGee address this question. Scherer, reporting on the results of a thorough investigation of twelve industries, finds little reason to believe that dominance of a few is generally the outcome of a full realization of economies of scale. Therefore, he doubts that reductions in concentration threaten serious losses in efficiency. Scherer's results are consistent with the findings of other studies, though many of the previous undertakings are considerably less well-grounded than his.

McGee argues that studies of economies of scale inevitably produce unreliable estimates because they are based upon flawed data and very restrictive assumptions which prevent taking into account such critical dimensions as the quality of management and the degree of risk-bearing. McGee suggests that the actual sizes of firms, in fact, result from a correct accommodation to the requirements of efficiency. Dismantling a large firm would, therefore, inevitably sacrifice economies.

The disagreement between Scherer and McGee is fundamental. If large size and market concentration are the consequence of substantial economies, deconcentration and decreases in firm sizes would be expensive. In such a circumstance, we would have to calculate most carefully whether the social benefits of deconcentration are worth the cost.

# Economies of Scale and Industrial Concentration

## F. M. Scherer*

My assignment is to summarize what economists know about the extent to which attaining economies of scale necessitates industrial concentration. To keep an impossibly large task within barely manageable bounds I shall deal only with manufacturing industry, neglecting such admittedly important and interesting sectors as retailing, mining, financial institutions, power, intercity transportation, and communications, among others. Even with this constricted focus, it will not be possible to survey the sizeable empirical literature exhaustively. Individual industry studies will be ignored to emphasize multi-industry comparative works. And even then, certain substantive topics must receive only cursory attention, and some minor interpretational liberties must be taken on matters which in a longer scholarly work would be treated more cautiously.

### WHAT SCALE ECONOMIES ARE

In the most common usage, economies of scale are defined as reductions in cost per unit of product manufactured and sold associated with the operation of large as compared to small production, distribution, and merchandising entities. An "entity" in this context may be a production line, a plant, a complex of integrated plants, or a still broader aggregation of more or less loosely integrated plants — i.e., a "firm." The existence of scale economies is conceptualized graphically by means of the "long-run unit cost curve," as illustrated in Figure 1. Entities geared to produce relatively large volumes, e.g., one million tons per year (read up from the horizontal axis), have lower unit costs (read from the curve to the vertical axis) than entities with low production volume, all else equal. To the extent that unit costs are indeed lower for larger entities, economies of scale are said to prevail. It is possible that beyond some scale (e.g., 1.5 million tons per year in Figure 1) further size brings no additional unit cost savings. Then the unit cost curve becomes horizontal. An entity might also be too big to manage or to sustain efficient internal mate-

* Director, Bureau of Economics, Federal Trade Commission. For further biographical information, see Appendix D.

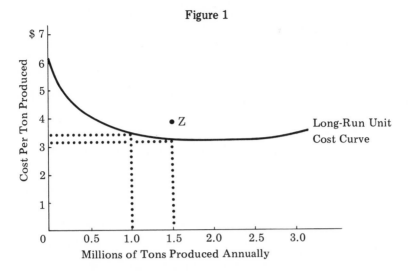

Figure 1

rial flows, so that its unit costs are higher than those of smaller entities, ceteris paribus. Then, as beyond a volume of 2.5 million tons in Figure 1, diseconomies of scale are said to prevail.

An important simplification made in conceptualizing the long-run unit cost curve is that the entities of varying size are all assumed to be adapted optimally to the opportunities and constraints associated with their size. That is, they operate "on" the curve rather than "off" it. One cannot, however, rule out the possibility that, say, an entity producing a million tons per year will not be adapted optimally to its size and will therefore incur costs of $3.80 per ton (i.e., at point Z) instead of the minimum feasible $3.25. This poses no serious problems if nonoptimal behavior is rare and unsystematic, but if there is a systematic tendency for many entities in certain size ranges to depart further from their respective cost minima than larger or smaller entities, it may be necessary to modify the concept of scale economies to reflect *representative* rather than *optimal* behavior.

Unit costs are not the only economically interesting magnitude varying systematically with entity size. The scale economy notion can be extended to encompass systematic relationships involving product quality, service, image, innovation, and similar variables. There may be no feasible way that, for example, a 10-million-gallon-per-year paint plant can provide customer service as personalized as the one-man shop turning out 50,000 gallons per year.[1] For the small paintmaker, achieving a brand image equivalent to that of Kem-

1. "No feasible way" can be translated back to a two-dimensional framework by saying that the cost per unit would be prohibitively high for the larger paint-maker. But it is often more enlightening to observe the direct relationship between size and such attributes as service or image than to attempt converting everything to a common cost denominator.

Tone or Lucite is equally infeasible. Each such size-correlated advantage may be exploited by entities in the favored size-class, and it is commonplace for entities of quite diverse sizes to coexist and survive profitably, each serving some subset of the market to which its special attributes are best adapted. This is an important point. We must not forget it, even though the bulk of the analysis which follows will be devoted to the narrower issue of cost–scale relationships.

We shall in fact begin our survey of the evidence on scale economies by considering unit *production* cost relationships, first in the context of individual plants and then in a broader multiplant framework. Other relationships between unit costs and scale, such as in materials procurement and capital raising, will then be taken up. We hold until last the more complex questions associated with sales promotion, product image, innovation, and the quality of management.

## SOME METHODOLOGICAL PRELIMINARIES

Before confronting the evidence, some methodological issues must be considered briefly. One concerns the method by which scale economies, and especially production scale economies, are measured. There are three main alternatives: statistical cost studies, the so-called survivor method, and the engineering analysis method.

In a statistical cost study, the analyst assembles data on costs, outputs, and other characteristics of plants varying widely in size. He then uses standard statistical techniques to estimate the cost–scale relationship, holding other variables such as equipment age, rate of capacity utilization, and wage levels constant. The main advantage is amenability to high-powered analytic techniques; the main disadvantage is the difficulty of getting adequate data on costs (subject to, inter alia, accounting convention biases) and on such variables as product mix. Among other things, the more compelling the scale economies tend to be, the fewer plants — and hence, statistical observations — one is likely to have for analysis. Also, relatively few plants are likely to be found operating where the cost penalties of too small or too large a scale are prohibitive, so one obtains little insight into the extreme ranges of the unit cost curve. Statistical cost studies work best for industries like electric power generation, where the product is simple and regulatory agencies require the compilation of extensive, fairly uniform accounting data.[2]

Survivor studies analyze the ebb and flow of activity over time in various entity size-classes. Entities in classes with declining activity are inferred to be of suboptimal or excessive scale; those with increasing or constant activity are

2. For excellent surveys of the statistical cost study literature, see Joel Dean, *Managerial Economics* (Prentice-Hall 1951), pp. 296-313; Caleb A. Smith, "Survey of the Empirical Evidence on Economies of Scale," in the National Bureau of Economic Research conference report, *Business Concentration and Price Policy* (Princeton Univ. Press 1955), pp. 213-238; and A. A. Walters, "Production and Cost Functions: An Econometric Survey," *Econometrica*, 31 (January-April 1963), especially pp. 39-52.

presumably of optimal size. Advantages of the survivor technique include its ability to use abundant data from periodic *Censuses of Manufactures* and its tendency to relate the "optimal" size range to any characteristics which are important to survival. These are simultaneously its disadvantages — the *Census* data (arrayed according to employment) are often ill-suited to measuring changes meaningfully over time, and one never knows what underlying phenomenon one is observing when one sees that entities of a certain size are proliferating at the expense of smaller or larger units. Inconsistent and even erratic inferences are not uncommon.[3]

With the engineering approach, economists exploit the expert knowledge of industrial engineers and other industry insiders responsible for making actual plant-size choices, querying how costs vary in facilities (usually newly constructed) of diverse sizes, holding other cost-influencing variables constant. Since firms repeatedly make such comparisons for their own internal decision-making, it is often possible to obtain carefully controlled, highly detailed estimates. Drawbacks include the considerable amount of time required to interview widely dispersed sources, the dangers of small sample and interviewer-induced bias, and the likelihood that in stagnant industries few firms have seriously thought about building new plants and, hence, about the unit cost consequences of alternate size decisions.

Each technique has its advantages and disadvantages. The most comprehensive multi-industry comparative plant scale economy studies have, for the most part, been based upon engineering analyses, and therefore that method will be emphasized here when the evidence is surveyed.

A second problem concerns how one reports what one has learned in scale economy studies. Curves — even cost curves — may be a thing of beauty, but they are also hard to describe succinctly and compare analytically. A standard solution is to invoke the concept of the "minimum optimal scale" (MOS) or sometimes "minimum efficient scale." The MOS is conventionally defined as that scale at which scale economy opportunities are first fully exhausted and the unit cost curve becomes horizontal — e.g., at an annual volume of 1.5 million tons per year in Figure 1. One can then work from this benchmark to evaluate the cost consequences of building suboptimal scale entities — e.g., by determining the percentage elevation in unit cost relative to MOS unit costs in an entity producing only, say, one-half or one-third the MOS volume.

Unfortunately, there are some serious pitfalls dotting the path of those who employ this ostensibly simple convention. What costs, for instance, are to be included in ascertaining the smallest minimum-cost scale? Professor Bain, who pioneered the MOS concept, included in his estimates not only materials and in-plant production costs but also outshipment and other physical distribution costs where "they have a significant effect on the net advantages of increasing the size of plant."[4] Yet this convention makes it impossible to say there is any such thing as *the* minimum optimal scale. The higher the transportation costs

3. See W. G. Shepherd, "What Does the Survivor Technique Show About Economies of Scale?" *Southern Economic Journal*, 34 (July 1967), pp. 113-122.

4. Joe S. Bain, *Barriers to New Competition* (Harvard Univ. Press 1956), p. 71.

per unit are (on a shipment of given size and distance), the more difficult it is to justify expansion of production volume by increasing the geographic radius served. That is, while production scale economies motivate building large plants, high transport costs exert a countervailing pull. Unit transport costs vary not only with the nature of the product (i.e., value per pound and bulk-to-weight ratio) but also with the density of demand in surrounding potential markets. A 10-million-gallon-per-year paint plant located in the New York City area may be able to sell its entire output within a fifty-mile radius. But a plant of similar size located in Denver or Winnipeg would have to ship hundreds of miles to utilize its capacity fully, and the shipping cost may be sufficiently high that such a large plant is simply uneconomical and will not be built, even though unit *production* costs are lower than in smaller plants. What is optimal in one region can be economically disastrous elsewhere. He who sets out to measure *the* MOS in terms of combined unit production and shipping costs under these circumstances will, unless he is careful to restrict his assumptions, end up with (at best) imprecise and quite possibly confused estimates.

It appears preferable therefore to define the MOS in plant scale economy studies as that output or capacity at which unit materials plus production costs first attain a minimum value. Even then there are methodological difficulties. Materials costs may be sensitive to plant location, the availability of transportation media, and the quantity of input used. Thus, a prairie petroleum refinery receiving its crude oil by rail or by tapping a nearby transcontinental pipeline probably exhausts all crude in-shipping and storage economies at a throughput volume of 80,000 barrels per day, while opportunities for reducing unit crude in-shipping and storage costs at a coastal refinery served by deep-draft tanker persist out to throughputs of at least 500,000 barrels per day. Labor cost–scale relationships may also vary with location. A big-city plant can usually obtain either small or large supplies of labor at a constant (but perhaps high) wage level, whereas a small-town plant must count on bidding up wages to lure workers from afar or from alternate jobs if it wants to increase its size. Differences in wage levels affect incentives for automation and hence, in some industries, the optimal plant size. Labor market conditions may govern the attractiveness of working second and third shifts, and thus significantly influence the output of a given optimally equipped plant. Optimal scales are also highly sensitive to differences in assumed product mix. A least-cost operation for weaving cotton-synthetic-blend sheetings, for example, is likely to produce two to four times as much square yardage per year as an optimal plant oriented toward style-sensitive quality dress goods. To secure meaningful MOS estimates under such complex conditions, limiting assumptions must be spelled out with great care. Precision is an unavoidable casualty.

Technological change complicates matters further. Scale economies are not something there for the taking; difficult technical problems must be solved before they can be exploited. In many industries the consequence of technical developments, often inspired by rising labor and energy costs, has been a steady increase in the minimum optimal scale. Figure 2 illustrates the dynamics, assuming wage and other input costs to be held constant. As time passes, new larger-scale processes are developed which both reduce unit costs and increase

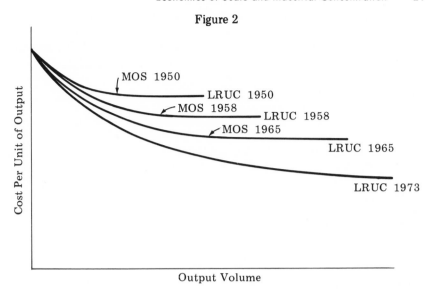

Figure 2

the scale required to take full advantage of the cost reduction potential. In such cases, any estimate of *the* MOS must be a snapshot of a perhaps rapidly moving scene. The result is some blur. Also, at any given moment in time, little operating experience will have been accumulated with plants exploiting the latest scale economy developments. Consequently, there may be considerable uncertainty concerning both the optimal size of the most advanced plants and the magnitude of their cost advantage. Often the unit cost curve is believed to continue falling out to plant scales larger than any yet built, but no one is sure exactly where the curve actually bottoms out. One means of resolving such MOS estimation uncertainties is to define the MOS, as I have in my recent work, as the capacity of those plants with the lowest unit costs on which significant operating experience has been accumulated — i.e., of "best current practice" plants.

A different tack has been taken by the Pratten-Silberston-Cockerill scale economies research group in England.[5] Given uncertainty concerning the exact location of the least-cost scale and the fact that only very minor unit cost savings may be realized by probing the last increments of volume before the least-cost scale is attained, they have benchmarked their MOS estimates to that scale "above which any possible subsequent doubling in scale would reduce total average unit costs by less than 5% and above which any subsequent doubling in scale would reduce value added per unit . . . by less than 10%."[6] Needless to say, good information on the shape of the unit cost curve

5. See especially C. F. Pratten, *Economies of Scale in Manufacturing Industry* (Cambridge Univ. Press 1971).

6. *Id.* at 26.

in its lowest reaches is essential in order to make reliable MOS estimates using this criterion.

Several observations relevant to our further analysis follow from this examination of methodological issues. Estimates of the MOS are apt to be sensitive to the assumptions made. My associates and I and British researchers, unlike Professor Bain, have excluded outbound transportation costs in determining the MOS, in part because only by so doing could some degree of consistency be achieved across regions. This does not imply that minimization of production costs alone is a proper goal. To the contrary, if industrial structures are to be efficient, firms must take transportation costs into account in their plant size and location decisions. This in turn means that different plant sizes will be optimal under different conditions and, in particular, that unit produc-duction-plus-transportation cost minimizing plants will be smaller, the higher the unit transport costs are in relation to product value and the less dense the demand is in the market served. Those who ignore such complexities do so at the peril of serious error.

## OPTIMAL PLANT SIZES AND MARKET SIZE

We turn now to the evidence, considering first the structural implications of scale economies at the *plant* level. That plant economies of scale exist is indisputable. Unit production costs fall with increasing scale for many reasons:[7] because equipment and special skills often come in indivisible lumps whose cost is advantageously spread over a relatively large output; because equipment can be scaled up at less than a proportional increase in capital cost, at least up to some critical capacity level;[8] because larger volume permits increased specialization of machinery and labor; and because a relatively large plant can maintain smaller reserves of equipment and repair personnel to cope with randomly occurring breakdowns; and so forth. The central question for industrial structure policy is not whether such scale economies exist, but whether they persist out to such large plant sizes that production efficiency can be achieved only by accepting high levels of seller concentration. In other words, to what extent do production economies of scale necessitate plants of such large capacity or output that only a very few minimum-cost facilities can be accommodated within a market?

Professor Bain was the first to address this question systematically for a substantial sample of American industries.[9] Using the engineering analysis method implemented through questionnaires and interviews, he compiled MOS

7. The classic discussion of the sources of scale economies continues to be E. A. G. Robinson, *The Structure of Competitive Industry* (rev. ed., Univ. of Chicago Press 1958).

8. For impressive statistical evidence on this point covering 221 production processes, see John Haldi and David Whitcomb, "Economies of Scale in Industrial Plants," *Journal of Political Economy*, 75 (August 1967), pp. 373-385.

9. Bain, *supra* n. 4; and Joe S. Bain, "Economies of Scale, Concentration, and the Condition of Entry in Twenty Manufacturing Industries," *American Economic Review*, 44 (March 1954), pp. 15-39.

estimates for twenty relatively large, concentrated manufacturing industries, assuming 1951 technology and market conditions. The first numerical column of Table 1 summarizes his estimates of the percentage of 1951 *national in-*

TABLE 1

Estimated Relationship of MOS Plant Capacities to U.S. National Market Volume in the 20 Bain Industries, Circa 1951

| Industry | | MOS Plant Capacity as Percent of National Capacity | 1947 Four-Firm Concentration Ratio |
|---|---|---|---|
| Meat Packing | Fresh | 0.10 | 41 |
| | Diversified | 2.25 | |
| Flour Milling | | 0.30 | 29 |
| Canned Fruits & Vegetables | | 0.37 | 26 |
| Distilled Liquors | | 1.50 | 75 |
| Cigarettes | | 5-6 ‒ | 90 ‒ |
| Rayon Yarn and Fibers | | 4-6 | 78 |
| Soap and Household Detergents | | 4-6 ‒ | 79 ‒ |
| Integrated Petroleum Refining (coastal location) | | 1.75 | 37 |
| Rubber Tires and Tubes | | 1.4-2.8 | 28 |
| Shoes (other than rubber) | | 0.32 | 28 |
| Cement | | 1.00 | 30 |
| Gypsum Plaster and Plasterboard | | 2-3 ‒ | 85 ‒ |
| Integrated Steel Works (flat-rolled products) | | 1.0-2.5 | 50 |
| Copper Refining | | 10 | 92 |
| Metal Containers | | 0.3-2.0 | 78 |
| Farm Machinery, except Tractors | | 1.25 | 36 |
| Tractors | | 10-15 | 67 |
| Typewriters | | 10-30 | 79 |
| Integrated Auto Component Production and Car Assembly | | (5-10) | (90) |
| Fountain Pens | | 5-10 | 58 |

Source: Joe S. Bain, *Barriers to New Competition* (Harvard Univ. Press 1956), pp. 72 and 84.

dustry capacity required for the smallest plant or integrated plant complex achieving minimum unit production and (where significant) physical distribution costs.[10] Only in copper refining and in the manufacture of tractors, typewriters, automobiles, and fountain pens did production scale economies require a plant to possess as much as 10 percent of national capacity, and hence only in those five industries would a national concentration ratio of

10. Most of Bain's estimates covered a range of possible sizes, taking into account the possibility of measurement error. The data have been simplified here so that only the midpoint is given when the range of possible error was less than one percentage point. Industries in this table and all others are listed in the order of their appearance in the U.S. Standard Industrial Classification.

40 or more (i.e., approaching loose oligopoly) be necessitated if the four leading sellers each operated one plant at the upper end of Bain's MOS estimate ranges. Single-plant scale economies appeared potentially to justify complete dominance of the national market by four sellers only in the typewriter industry. The last numerical column of Table 1 shows the four-firm concentration ratios actually prevailing in 1947. In all industries except typewriters and tractors, seller concentration had reached a level considerably higher than that which would exist if each Big Four member operated a single MOS plant. In flour, shoes, canned fruits and vegetables, tin cans, and distilled liquors, actual national concentration levels exceeded this minimum threshold by ten times or more.

Two more recent studies in the same tradition as Bain's were undertaken by C. F. Pratten, Aubrey Silberston, R. M. Dean, and others at Cambridge University in England (hereafter Pratten et al.),[11] and by Alan Beckenstein, Erich Kaufer, R. D. Murphy, and myself (hereafter SBKM).[12]

Pratten et al. developed engineering estimates of the MOS for some twenty-six British industries, assuming 1969 technology and market conditions and defining the MOS in terms of production and material costs only. Their choice of industries was apparently biased somewhat in favor of branches with relatively important scale economies.[13] In relating MOS estimates to national market size, they naturally focused on United Kingdom conditions, but in Table 2 we have put their data into a U.S. perspective by assuming conservatively that the U.S. market was uniformly five times larger than the corresponding U.K. market.[14] For only seven of the twenty-nine estimates presented — i.e., about the same fraction as for Bain's quite different sample — does achieving the MOS as defined by Pratten et al. appear to require a

11. Pratten, supra n. 5; C. F. Pratten and R. M. Dean, The Economies of Large-Scale Production in British Industry: An Introductory Study (Cambridge Univ. Press 1965); and (for a concise summary) Aubrey Silberston, "Economies of Scale in Theory and Practice," Economic Journal, 82 (March 1972 Supplement), pp. 369-391.

12. F. M. Scherer, Alan Beckenstein, Erich Kaufer, and R. D. Murphy, The Economies of Multi-Plant Operation: An International Comparisons Study (hereafter, SBKM) (Harvard Univ. Press, forthcoming in 1975). The underlying research was supported under National Science Foundation Grant GS-2809 and a Ford Foundation Grant to the University of Michigan Comparative Economics program. Other largely overlapping empirical studies include H. C. Eastman and S. Stykolt, The Tariff and Competition in Canada (Macmillan 1967); and Gunnar Ribrant, Stordriftsfordelar inom Industriproduktionen (Stockholm, Statens Offentiliga Utredningar 1970).

13. Cf. Silberston, "Economies of Scale in Theory and Practice," Economic Journal, 82 (March 1972 Supplement), p. 379.

14. A comparison of 1965 population counts, times an index of 1965 national income per capita derived for the SBKM book, chapter 3, indicates that the U.S. market was 5.24 times as large as the U.K. market. The simple average of the ratios of 1967 U.S. to U.K. output for the twelve industries in the SBKM sample was 5.59. Thus, taking 5.0 as the divisor for the Pratten MOS plant share estimates tends to err on the side of exaggerating U.S. national market concentration imperatives, all else equal.

TABLE 2

Estimated Relationship of MOS Plant Sizes to U.S. National Market Volume
for Industries in the Pratten Sample, Circa 1969

| Industry | | MOS Plant Output as Percentage of 1969 U.S. Production* | U.S. Four-Firm Concentration Ratios, 1967 or 1963 |
|---|---|---|---|
| Bread | | 0.2 | 24 |
| Beer Brewing | | 0.6 | 40 |
| Cotton Textile Spinning and Weaving | | 0.4 | 35 |
| Warp-knitted Stockings | | 0.6 | 28 |
| Newspaper Publication | | 6 | 16 |
| Book Publishing | | 0.4 | 20 |
| Ethylene | | 5 | 49 |
| Sulphuric Acid | | 6 | 60 |
| Synthetic Fibers | Polymer Production | 6.5 | 84 |
| | Yarn Extrusion | 3 | |
| Synthetic Detergents | | 4 | 88 |
| Petroleum Refining | | 2 | 33 |
| Injection-molded Plastic Products | | 0.2 | 8 |
| Shoes | | 0.04 | 27 |
| Cement | | 2 | 29 |
| Bricks | | 0.1 | 13 |
| Steel | BOF Raw Steel Plant | 6.5 | 48 |
| | Wide Strip Rolling Works | 18† | 55 |
| Iron Foundries | Large Castings | 0.2 | 27 |
| | Small Castings | 0.04 | |
| Machine Tools | | 0.1 | 21 |
| Diesel Engines | | 2 | 72 |
| Turbogenerators (range of designs) | | 10 | 100 |
| Electric Motors | | 12 | 57 |
| Refrigerators or Washing Machines | | 10 | 73 |
| Electronic Data Processing Equipment | | 20 | 63 |
| Automobile (range of models) | | 10 | 99 |
| Aircraft (one type only) | | > 20 | 69 |
| Bicycles (range of models) | | 0.8 | n.a. |

Source: C. F. Pratten, *Economies of Scale in Manufacturing Industry* (Cambridge Univ. Press 1971), pp. 269-277.

* Pratten's U.K. output share estimated divided by 5.0.

† Percent of wide strip output, unlike Tables 1 and 3, which relate to output of all primary steel mill products.

plant producing 10 percent (or more) of U.S. national demand. In more than half the cases, 3 percent (or less) of U.S. output sufficed to capture the principal economies of scale. Needless to say, this translation to U.S. market dimensions alters significantly what to Pratten et al. was a crucial conclusion: that in a market the size of the United Kingdom, even if not in the United

States, simultaneously achieving all important plant scale economies and a fragmented national industry structure may be quite difficult.[15]

Minimum optimal plant scale estimates, assuming 1965 technology and market conditions, were obtained for the twelve manufacturing industries in the SBKM sample through interviews with 125 companies in six nations — the United States, Canada, Germany, France, Sweden, and the United Kingdom. Unlike the Bain and Pratten samples, the SBKM sample was not intentionally biased toward highly concentrated or scale-economy-prone industries. Its main conscious bias was toward industries in which the leading firms exhibited fairly high levels of multiplant operation. Since the extent of multiplant operation and the share of national output contributed by an MOS plant tend to be inversely correlated, this may imply some bias toward low scale economy industries. This in turn may explain why, as the first numerical column in Table 3 reveals, achieving minimum unit production costs required a plant output

TABLE 3

Estimated Relationship of MOS Plant Sizes to U.S. National Market Volume
in the 12 SBKM Industries, Circa 1967

| Industry | MOS Plant Size as Percentage of 1967 U.S. Consumption | 1967 Four-Firm Concentration Ratio | Percentage Elevation of Unit Costs at One-Third MOS |
|---|---|---|---|
| Beer Brewing | 3.4 | 40 | 5.0 |
| Cigarettes | 6.6 | 81 | 2.2 |
| Broad-Woven Cotton and Synthetic Fabrics | 0.2 | 36· | 7.6 |
| Paints, Varnishes, and Lacquers | 1.4 | 22 | 4.4 |
| Petroleum Refining | 1.9 | 33 | 4.8 |
| Shoes (other than rubber) | 0.2 | 26 | 1.5 |
| Glass Containers | 1.5 | 60 | 11.0 |
| Cement | 1.7 | 29 | 26.0 |
| Integrated Wide Strip Steel Works | 2.6 | 48 | 11.0 |
| Ball & Roller Bearings | 1.4 | 54 | 8.0 |
| Household Refrigerators and Freezers | 14.1 | 73 | 6.5 |
| Storage Batteries | 1.9 | 61 | 4.6 |

Source: F. M. Scherer, Alan Beckenstein, Erich Kaufer, and R. D. Murphy, *The Economics of Multi-Plant Operation: An International Comparisons Study* (Harvard Univ. Press, forthcoming in 1975), ch. 3.

exceeding 10 percent of 1967 U.S. consumption in only one industry — refrigerators and freezers — rather than the three which would be expected if the Bain and Pratten fractions were duplicated. As with both the Bain and Pratten samples, actually prevailing 1967 national market four-firm concentration

15. See especially Pratten, *supra* n. 5, at 313; and Silberston, *supra* n. 13, at 389.

(given in the second numerical column) was characteristically much higher than it would need to be if each Big Four member operated a single MOS plant. Only in refrigerators and freezers — where four MOS plants would supply 56 percent of 1967 U.S. consumption, and the four-seller concentration ratio was 73 — is anything like parity approached.

The final column of Table 3 offers additional insight into the significance of plant scale economies. It contains rough estimates of the percentage by which unit production costs (including materials) are elevated in plants designed to operate at only one-third the MOS output, as compared to unit costs in an MOS plant. In other words, the relative steepness of the long-run cost curve (Figure 1) is described. In some industries like cement and steel, the cost implications of suboptimal scale operation are substantial. In cigarettes, on the other hand, unit costs (excluding excise taxes) would be elevated only slightly if plants were built to supply 2 percent of national consumption, and what could be a force compelling moderate levels of four-firm concentration (e.g., 26 percent for single MOS plant Big Four members) appears to have less potency than one might at first suppose.

There are six overlaps between the industries included in the Bain and Pratten samples, five between the Bain and SBKM samples, and six between the Pratten and SBKM samples. Although benchmark dates and MOS definition assumptions differed widely among the three studies, the estimates of MOS plant volume as a percentage of U.S. consumption or capacity are generally similar. The largest absolute differences appear for steel — where (as we shall elaborate) technological change has been dramatic, and Pratten related MOS plant output to narrowly defined product market volume — and for refrigerators — where, however, Pratten's 10 percent figure and the SBKM estimate of 14 percent do not differ much in relative terms. The most striking relative difference is for the brewing industry, with Pratten et al. estimating the MOS at 0.6 percent of U.S. consumption and SBKM at 3.4 percent. This divergence, deeper investigation reveals, is due in part to Pratten's inability to get cost estimates for U.K. breweries having a capacity larger than 1.5 million U.S. barrels per year, and partly to Pratten's assumption that pegged the MOS at a still-falling point on the long-run cost curve.

For the twelve SBKM industries, additional information on changes in optimal scales over time was obtained. Six of the twelve — brewing, paints, cement, steel, refrigerators, and batteries — exhibited distinct MOS increases during the 1950s and 1960s, and in cigarettes a weaker upward trend was observed. In steel, for example, Bain's estimate for the early 1950s put the MOS of a fully integrated flat-rolled steel works at a capacity of 1.0 to 2.5 million ingot tons per year — a judgment consistent with the historical information gathered by the present author in interviews conducted during 1970. By 1965, changes in blast furnace, steel converter (BOF), and rolling mill technology had raised the MOS capacity to 4.0 million tons. By 1972, major blast furnace advances pioneered by Japanese companies had pushed the least-cost scale to a capacity of 10 or perhaps even 20 million tons per year. Likewise, dramatic increases in optimal size for cement kilns raised the capacity of a least-cost cement works from roughly 3 million U.S. (376-pound) barrels per year in the mid-1950s to 7 million barrels in 1965, and 12 to 15 million barrels in 1972. The only industries experiencing (generally modest) decreases in MOS outputs over time were weaving, shoemaking, and antifriction bearings. The principal reasons for these decreases were a growing product line complexity, calling for a tighter span of control by plant managers; plus a flight to rural areas in search of low-wage labor typically available in quantities too small to staff plants of traditional scale.

The Bain, Pratten, and SBKM studies together cover a total of forty-four nonoverlapping industries encompassing approximately 26 percent of 1967 value added in the U.S. manufacturing sector. Only in ten of the forty-four is MOS plant volume sufficient to justify four-firm national concentration ratios of forty or more under U.S. conditions if each Big Four member operated a single efficient plant. In the vast majority of the industries, actual concentration is much higher than it would be if each leading firm operated one MOS plant. Thus, the three studies all point toward the same conclusion: that nationwide oligopoly and high seller concentration cannot be viewed primarily as the inevitable consequence of production scale economies at the plant level.

To this conclusion two qualifications must be added at once. First, the MOS plant market share estimates have assumed that the relevant market is *nationwide*. This is often not appropriate. Especially when transportation costs are high in relation to product value, plants' shipping may be confined to subnational — i.e., regional — markets, and it is *within* such fractionalized markets that the main opportunities for competition among multiple independent suppliers must normally be evaluated. The more geographically fractionalized the markets are, the more the estimates in Tables 1, 2, and 3 understate the compulsion of scale economies toward oligopoly. Second, industry product lines might also be subdivided into numerous products which may (although need not always) be manufactured in separate specialized and essentially noncompeting plants. To the extent this is so, the Table 1, 2, and 3 estimates again view the possibility of securing structural competition too optimistically. Each complication warrants more careful analysis.

One indication of the extent to which U.S. markets are regionalized can be drawn from Professor Weiss's study of average shipping distances for 283 three- and four-digit manufacturing industries.[16] Basing his estimates upon the shipping radius within which 80 percent of an industry's outbound tonnage was distributed, with certain judgmental adjustments for industries potentially able to ship substantial distances economically but constrained by geographic concentration of actual customers' demand, he classified his sample industries (as shown in Table A) according to the number of relevant markets within the continental United States. Nearly two-thirds of the 283 industries were found to be nationwide or nearly nationwide — i.e., with only one or two identifiable segments. Twenty-two, or 8 percent, were fractionated into twelve or more shipping regions. For the vast majority of all U.S. industries, it would appear, taking regionalization into account does not require radical revisions in one's

16. Leonard W. Weiss, "The Geographic Size of Markets in Manufacturing," *Review of Economics and Statistics,* 54 (August 1972), pp. 245-266.

TABLE A

| Number of Continental U.S. Markets | Number of Industries | Percent of All Industries |
|---|---|---|
| 1 | 111 | 39 |
| 2 | 76 | 27 |
| 3 | 31 | 11 |
| 4 | 17 | 6 |
| 5-11 | 26 | 9 |
| 12 or 16 | 2 | < 1 |
| 24 | 5 | 2 |
| 48 | 2 | < 1 |
| More than 48 (city markets) | 13 | 5 |
| | 283 | 100 |

estimates of how many competing MOS plants the national market — as opposed to appropriately adjusted regional markets — can accommodate.

In Table 4 the implications of regionalization are explored more fully with respect to the twelve SBKM industries. It must be noted at the outset that the sample probably includes disproportionately many multiregion industries, compared to the population of all U.S. manufacturing industries. A bias toward industries with high levels of leading-firm multiplant control was effected deliberately, and high transportation costs are positively and significantly correlated with the incidence of multiplant operation, all else equal.[17] The first column of Table 4 reveals that five of the twelve industries, or 42 percent, had average unit transportation costs of five cents or more per dollar of F.O.B. mill product value, using an average mix of transport media over a standardized 350-mile haul — e.g., between Chicago and Cleveland. For a broader and more representative sample of 155 four-digit U.S. manufacturing industries, only about 14 to 18 percent of the industries had comparably high unit shipping costs.[18] Interviews and computer analyses disclosed that the pull toward regional markets is generally quite strong when transportation costs exceed 5 percent of product value on a 350-mile haul.

Column (2) of Table 4 gives the number of continental United States markets estimated by Weiss, and Column (3) divides that number into an estimate of the number of MOS plants accommodated by the total U.S. market in 1967, to

17. F. M. Scherer, "The Determinants of Multi-Plant Operation in Six Nations and Twelve Industries," *Kyklos*, No. 1, Vol. 27 (1974), pp. 34-44.

18. This estimate is based upon data in Appendix Tables 5.1 to 5.3 of *SBKM*. The range of possible error is given because low-cost shipping media such as barges and pipelines were not taken into account for the broader sample and because direct transportation cost estimates were available for only 101 of the 155 industries. Among the excluded industries were a disproportionate number of branches with low unit-transportation costs.

TABLE 4
Market Regionalization Indicators for the 12 SBKM Industries

| Industry | (1) Transport Cost per Dollar of Product Value on Standard Haul | (2) Number of Regional Markets: Weiss | (3) Number of MOS Plants per Average Weiss Regional Market | (4) Corrected Number of Regional Markets | (5) Corrected Number of MOS Plants per Average Regional Market |
|---|---|---|---|---|---|
| Beer Brewing | 7.8 cents | 6 | 4.8 | 6 | 4.8 |
| Cigarettes | 0.7 | 1 | 15.2 | 1 | 15.2 |
| Broad-woven Fabrics | 0.7 | 1 | 451.7 | 1 | 451.7 |
| Paints | 2.2 | 2 | 34.9 | 5 | 14.0 |
| Petroleum Refining | 8.9 | 1 | 51.6 | 5 | 10.3 |
| Shoes | 0.4 | 2 | 261.5 | 1 | 523.0 |
| Glass Containers | 9.9 | 9 | 7.3 | 9 | 7.3 |
| Cement | 44.6 | 24 | 2.5 | 24 | 2.5 |
| Steel | 7.5 | 6 | 6.5 | 4 | 9.8 |
| Bearings | 0.9 | 3 | 24.0 | 1 | 72.0 |
| Refrigerators | 1.7 | 1 | 7.1 | 1 | 7.1 |
| Storage Batteries | 2.4 | 6 | 8.9 | 6 | 8.9 |

indicate how many competing MOS plants were attainable per *average* regional market. We observe that in six of the twelve industries, regional four-firm concentration ratios of forty or more (i.e., with fewer than ten MOS plants per region) are implied. In Column (4) the Weiss market-count estimates, derived largely from historical shipping pattern data, are adjusted judgmentally for five industries in which interviews and computer simulations suggested that the forces encouraging regionalization were stronger or weaker than the Weiss figures implied. The resulting estimates of MOS plant per region in Column (5) require no fundamental alteration of conclusions based directly upon Weiss's calculations. For six industries the average regional market holds fewer than ten MOS plants; in two more (paints and petroleum refining) the adjusted estimates approach ten. Only in fabrics, shoes, and antifriction bearings is no tendency toward national or (where appropriate) regional oligopoly discernible.

To this conclusion three qualifying comments must be appended. First, to repeat, the SBKM sample is biased in the direction of more regional market fragmentation than would be found for all manufacturing industries. In this sense the compulsions toward oligopoly are exaggerated. Second, even though markets defined as regional here may have sufficient demand to hold only a few MOS plants, the pricing discretion of those plants could be constrained by actual and potential fringe competition from plants in other regions. This is especially likely if the increased transportation cost due to interregional shipping is offset significantly by unit production cost savings due to scale economies or increased capacity utilization during slack periods. Computer analyses embodying a rich array of realistic data showed that in industries like paints, combined unit production and transportation costs were relatively insensitive to wide variations in the regional specialization patterns adopted by plants.[19] Thus, when the continental U.S. paint market could be served at *minimum* production plus transportation cost if divided into seven regions, the increase in total cost would be only 2.7 percent if the whole national market were served from plants in a single centrally located region, while dispersing production among sixteen regions would lead to a 1.2 percent cost rise. The cost premium that assumes centralized production provides an upper-bound estimate of the extent to which prices might be raised without stimulating interregional competition. Finally, any estimate of the average number of MOS plants a region can hold ignores the wide variation existing between regions. Thus, the amount of structural competition attainable is underestimated for densely populated regions like the Northeast Seaboard, while it is overestimated for sparsely populated regions such as the Plains and Northwest states.

Analogous market fragmenting propensities exist when an industry's overall product assortment includes a substantial number of noncompeting items manufactured in different plants so specialized that they cannot easily shift from one product type to another. Steel-making is an important example. Although the blast furnaces and converters of a steel works are flexible, the rolling mills

19. See *SBKM* ch. 8.

with which those hot metal facilities are often physically integrated are almost always limited to a certain class of products — e.g., wide strip, plate, structurals, bars, or rods. When, in addition, such a rolling mill must produce a substantial output to achieve minimum unit costs, the efficient organization of production may require high concentration. Thus, the minimum optimal scale for a mill producing hot-rolled wide strip, enjoying the highest tonnage demand of any product class in the United States, is an output of at least 3.2 million short tons per year, and perhaps more. Even the Chicago-Detroit area, the leading regional wide strip market, cannot fully utilize any more than seven or eight such mills.[20] And there is apparently only enough demand *nationwide* to support two mills capable of rolling 36-inch flange I-beams. Similarly, cotton and synthetic cloth mills typically specialize in weaving only a very narrow subset of the industry's product array; shoe plants specialize in women's dress, women's casual, children's, men's dress, men's work, or other footwear types; and bearing plants seldom combine the production of ball, roller, tapered roller, and miniature precision types under the same roof. To the extent that the opportunities for substitution between such products are limited both on the demand and supply sides, the "number of MOS plants per market" estimates for those industries in Table 4 exaggerate the scope for atomistic but efficient market organization. In fact, however, much of the equipment and know-how in weaving, shoemaking, and bearing plants is highly adaptable, so that production could be shifted over from one line to another fairly rapidly — i.e., in not more than a year or two — if the incentive were to arise. This substitution potential means that the competitive benefits of unconcentrated market structure may be compatible with production efficiency at least over the long run, even if not at any particular moment in time. Considerations of this sort greatly complicate the task of judging how many MOS plants can be accommodated in relevantly defined product markets.

    To sum up a long and complex chain of analysis — integrated consideration of plant scale economy imperatives, the decentralizing pull of transportation costs, and plant specialization patterns leave us less sanguine about the opportunities for simultaneously enjoying minimum production costs and atomistically structured markets. Although concentration approaching oligopoly threshold levels on a *nationwide* four-digit industry plane appears mandated by scale economies in only a small minority of cases, the threshold may be breached in perhaps as many cases as not, when regional market fragmentation and plant specialization forces intrude. The compulsion toward oligopoly is weaker when measured in terms of aggregate economic activity than in numbers of markets, it should be stressed, because the densely populated markets least affected by regional fragmentation account for a disproportion-

20. This plant specialization aspect of market fragmentation is taken into account explicitly in Pratten's relatively high estimate of the narrow product market share required by an MOS hot strip works in Table 2. Indeed, many of Pratten's market definitions are drawn sufficiently narrowly to minimize concentration-imperative estimate errors due to the neglect of specialization.

ate share of total manufacturing activity. A more exact enumeration is difficult to compile without richer data, especially for the industries studied solely by Bain and Pratten. The implications for the vigor of competitive performance, taking into account (inter alia) regional market interpenetration and plant reconversion potentialities, are even harder to assess. Two conclusions are nevertheless warranted. First, at least in the huge U.S. market, plant scale economies alone seldom mandate extremely high seller concentration — i.e., with four-firm concentration ratios exceeding 80 — even in the typical appropriately defined regional or product-class market. If there is a plant scale imperative toward oligopoly, it is for the most part an imperative toward loose oligopoly. Second, the levels of *nationwide* four-digit concentration observed in U.S. industries can rarely be attributed solely or even primarily to the need for large plants. Concentration ratios exceed the market shares which would be held by single-MOS-plant Big Four members so often and by such large multiples that multiplication of plants — on either a regionally decentralized or product-specialized basis — must carry heavy weight in explaining actual U.S. industry structure. We shall confront the question of multiplant operation squarely after a brief preparatory digression.

## PRODUCT RUN LENGTH ECONOMIES, MULTIPLANT OPERATION, AND THE EFFICIENT ORGANIZATION OF PRODUCTION

Our concern thus far has been scale economies associated with the overall sizes of plants. For want of a precedent, we seize the initiative and call such plant-size-related cost advantages "plant-specific" scale economies. There is, however, another quite different class of volume-associated cost savings opportunities which arise because the production of individual items frequently involves fixed setup costs and the cumulative growth of operative skills and production engineering know-how as the length of the production run increases. These we call "product-specific" scale economies since they are linked primarily to individual product volume, not overall plant output. The production of ball bearings affords an illustration. Setting up an automatic screw machine to cut bearing races takes about eight hours. Once ready, the machine produces from 80 to 140 parts per hour. An increase in the total number of parts produced in a batch from, say, 5,000 to 10,000 reduces unit costs by more than 10 percent due to the broader spreading of setup time and skilled labor costs. Similar setup economies exist at the cage-stamping, grinding, honing, and assembly stages of bearing production. Also, when an annual volume of roughly one million identical bearings can be sustained, the whole production process can be transformed from job-shop to straight-line methods with automated assembly and work piece transfer, permitting unit cost savings of 20 percent or more. Thus, the larger an item's production volume is, the longer individual production runs will be and the more attractive automation becomes, with unit cost savings as a direct consequence. For products which, unlike most antifriction bearings, have not yet reached mature design and production technology stages — e.g., aircraft, electronic apparatus, new shoe designs, and a new cloth weave — gains in production know-how and operative skill associated with an accumulating production volume are often a very significant source of cost reductions.[21]

For some reason this phenomenon has been ignored almost completely by U.S. industrial organization economists. Yet the neglect of product-specific scale economies is no longer excusable, for the phenomenon is extremely important. Among other things, understanding the nature of product-specific economies is essential to analyzing the efficiency implications of horizontal mergers. While physically merging *plants* is difficult, so that horizontal mergers are unlikely to yield substantial plant-specific economies, the reallocation of production assignments for overlapping products can often be accomplished easily, with an ensuing increase in production run lengths and fall in unit costs. Furthermore, for at least seven of the twelve SBKM sample industries (cigarettes, fabrics, paints, shoes, bottles, bearings, and refrigerators), product-specific scale economies appeared to be more important quantitatively than plant-specific economies, in the sense that a doubling of individual production run lengths from 1970 levels would probably lead to a greater percentage reduction in costs than a doubling of plant sizes, all else equal.

Because of different intellectual traditions and perhaps also because the cost sacrifices resulting from failure to exploit all product-specific scale economies have been particularly high in the historically fragmented European markets, European industrial organization economists have shown greater awareness of the product-specific scale economy phenomenon. The work of Pratten et al. is illustrative. Several of their MOS market share estimates presented (after a U.S. size adjustment) in Table 2 — notably, for aircraft, turbogenerators, electronic data processing equipment, and diesel engines — were influenced more by product-specific scale imperatives than by cost relationships linked primarily to *plant* output.[22] It cannot escape notice that these are prominent among the industries in which an oligopolistic structure is hard to escape if minimum production costs are sought. Moreover, Pratten supplements the more clearly plant-oriented estimates of Table 2 with estimates of how large a U.K. market share *individual product runs* must achieve for costs to be minimized.[23] He found that economies of scale persisted out to annual production volumes exceeding total British demand for many individual machine tool,

21. See, for example, Harold Asher, *Cost-Quantity Relationships in the Airframe Industry* (RAND Corporation report R-291, 1956); Armen Alchian, "Costs and Output," in Moses Abromovitz et al., *The Allocation of Economic Resources: Essays in Honor of B. F. Haley* (Stanford Univ. Press 1959), pp. 23-40; Jack Hirshleifer, "The Firm's Cost Function: A Successful Reconstruction?" *Journal of Business*, 35 (July 1962), pp. 235-255; and L. E. Preston and E. C. Keachie, "Cost Functions and Progress Functions: An Integration," *American Economic Review*, 54 (March 1964), pp. 100-106.

22. My colleagues and I tried hard to keep product-specific effects disentangled from plant-specific relationships in the MOS estimates underlying Table 3. We have been less than completely successful, especially for paints and batteries, where the assumption that plants produce a full line necessarily implies that overall unit costs will be affected by an increase in plant output and hence individual product volumes.

23. Pratten, *supra* n. 5, at 268-280.

diesel engine, and turbogenerator models and for specific extruded plastic products, hard-cover books, and organic dyestuffs.

My own research suggests that a useful way of approaching the product-specific scale economies question quantitatively is to think in terms of the size distribution of demand for an industry's products. A good first approximation is provided by an empirical generalization known as the "80-20 rule." [24] It says that when a firm's (or industry's) physically distinguishable products are arrayed in order of sales, the best-selling 20 percent of the items account for roughly 80 percent of total sales, while the other 80 percent by number — the "cats and dogs" products — contribute only 20 percent of sales. The U.S. manufacturers we interviewed appeared on average to experience little difficulty exploiting the most important product-specific scale economies for products on the best-selling side of this dichotomy, but significant scale economy sacrifices were commonplace in producing the lower-volume items. The exact division point does of course vary among industries and among firms within industries. In bearings, for example, well over 20 percent of total U.S. sales involve items produced in lots of suboptimal size, while in cigarettes all but trivial product-specific economies tended to be exhausted on more than 95 percent of total output. It is probable that our sample, by omitting technically dynamic capital goods industries like airplane and computer manufacturing, failed to uncover really extreme cases in which important product-specific scale economy potential was left unexploited on *most* of the total production volume. Still, for that large segment of U.S. manufacturing industry concerned neither with exotic big-ticket items nor with standard commodities produced by continuous process methods (such as cement and petroleum products), the 80-20 dichotomy provides a tolerable representation of where the product-specific scale economy problem lies.

There certainly exists a substantial set of products for which the demand is so restricted, and/or the product-specific economies are so persistent, that large shares of the total demand must be supplied by one manufacturer if production costs are to be minimized. The implications of this fact for market structure, conventionally construed, are less than obvious. It is quite possible that a tiny textile company might satisfy *all* the demand for some highly specialized fabric, yet that firm will be only an atom in what we normally consider to be the fabric industry or its major product segments. Obversely, a well-balanced broad-line firm with a 35 percent market share in some important industry — enough to evoke close antitrust surveillance — is apt to be producing some low-volume items in quantities well below the minimum optimal scale even though its volume for most products exceeds the MOS by a sizeable multiple. Evidently, market share as measured in most economic analyses and the exploitation of product-specific scale economies are not linked on any one-to-one basis. The pattern of specialization prevailing is equally important.

From the standpoint of public policy the crucial derivative question is this: Is there a systematic tendency for multiproduct firms with large market shares (in the conventional sense) to achieve larger volumes in producing any given nar-

24. See John F. Magee, *Physical Distribution Systems* (McGraw-Hill 1967), p. 38.

rowly defined product, and hence higher degrees of production specialization, than firms with smaller market shares, all else equal? Or, alternatively put, is seller size in a relevantly defined market the result of producing *more* products, or a conventional array of products in greater average volumes?

There is probably no simple, unambiguous answer to these questions. I think I may have collected more evidence on the issue than other U.S. industrial organization economists have to date, but I confess to understanding the empirical relationships far too imperfectly. My systematic knowledge can be organized in terms of two main plant-product specialization pattern cases.

For the first, consider an industry such as paints, steel, or automobile batteries with a broad array of products and with transportation costs appreciable enough to induce some geographic decentralization of production. Assume two firms — a full-line multiplant nationwide operator, and a full-line single-plant regional supplier with the same share of its *regional* market as the nationwide rival but with much smaller total production. Each will manufacture high-volume products in close proximity to the locus of demand. But the nationwide firm can centralize the production of low-demand items, combining the requirements of several regional markets to achieve larger production lots and accepting increased shipping costs to reap a more than compensating gain in product-specific scale economies. Obviously, the regional supplier unable to centralize production in this way must sell its low-volume products at a cost disadvantage vis-à-vis the nationwide firm. Or must it? If it can *buy* its low-demand items outside from centrally located specialists or nationwide manufacturers at competitive prices (i.e., equal to the full cost of production plus transportation), it can continue to supply a full line at no cost disadvantage. Only if the market fails to make low-demand products available to regional specialists at competitive prices does the multiplant nationwide firm enjoy an advantage due to its size. Thus, the question is transformed from one of cost–volume relationships to an inquiry into how well intermediate goods markets are functioning.

In industries with low transportation costs compared to product value, a different multiplant firm specialization pattern is observed. Then each plant is likely to concentrate on producing a narrow subset of the firm's total product array for the entire national (or even a multinational) market. Smaller companies with only one plant, or at least fewer plants, cannot simultaneously cover as broad a product array and enjoy comparable product-specific scale economies. To have equally low costs (other things such as managerial competence and wage levels held equal) they must specialize more narrowly. Whether and to what extent they do so are key empirical questions on which little evidence exists. Real-world patterns are clearly very complex. In five of the ten SBKM sample industries with appreciable product-specific scale economy potentialities — weaving, paints, shoes, bottles, and steel — firms of moderate size in relation to their national or relevant regional competitors adapted by specializing more narrowly and tended, at least in the United States, to do about as well on average product run lengths as the very largest companies. The larger firms were large because they offered *more* products or (in high transport cost industries) served more regional markets, not because their plants achieved higher average volume on given products. In brewing, cigarettes, batteries, and (especially) refrigerators, suppliers of widely varying size all tended to offer full lines, and so the smaller firms experienced shorter average production runs and greater scale economy sacrifices than their larger rivals. The situation in antifriction bearings was too mixed to permit a pointed conclusion, but the industry tended more toward the second (small firm, disadvantaged) category than the first. In nearly all of these industries, it should be noted, there was considerable variation, uncorrelated to size of firm, in product run length experienced among companies.

When relatively small suppliers were perceptibly less successful than larger rivals in realizing run length economies on otherwise comparable products, one or more of three factors was typically responsible: customers manifested preferences for broad-line suppliers; or promotional and other economies of scale (to be discussed later) favored large broad-line firms; or price competition broke down (e.g., due to strong respect for oligopolistic interdependence), with producers lacking either the will or the incentive to increase their specialization by bidding for a larger share of the market on some narrow class of products. About the first and (less clearly) second causes of inadequate specialization, there may be little one can do through, say, governmental policy actions. But the third cause poses an interesting and important policy dilemma. Permitting concentration to rise by tolerating or encouraging mergers can lead to fuller exploitation of product-specific scale economies *if* specialization-enhancing competition is unlikely in any event, but increasing concentration which heightens respect for oligopolistic interdependence makes it all the more unlikely that the price mechanism will function to stimulate specialization. My own impressionistic observation is that the loss of product-specific scale economies has been less serious in the United States than in the western European nations, in part because competition in U.S. markets has historically been much less restrained by cartels and very high concentration.

It seems clear, then, that the links between concentration and the realization of product-specific scale economies in production are quite intricate. Higher concentration *may* permit larger production lots and longer runs; but by paralyzing price incentives for specialization, it can also work in the opposite direction. We need to know much more about the conditions under which one propensity is stronger than the other.

## MARKET POSITION, MULTIPLANT OPERATION, AND THE SCALE OF PLANT INVESTMENTS

We return now to the realm of plant-specific production scale economies, this time emphasizing not the bare technological possibilities but rather how a firm's market position affects the *decisions* it makes. Especially in processing industries like steel, petroleum refining, and cement, and to a lesser degree also in other branches, key capital equipment items tend to be lumpy and durable. The decisions about size that are made when such units are first installed delimit a plant's potential for scale economy realization and hence both its capital carrying costs and operating costs for decades to come. The question is, are these decisions influenced systematically by such structural variables as the level of concentration within a relevant market and the extent of multiplant operation sustained by leading sellers?

Investments are made partly to replace obsolescent plant and partly to serve growing demand. The firm which has a large share of some market must have a relatively large capacity and hence, all else equal, a relatively large amount of equipment falling due for replacement in any given time interval. If the capacity of least-unit-cost capital equipment items is large in relation to total market demand, such a firm should find it easier to phase in new full-scale plants or plant increments than an enterprise with a small market share and replacement requirement. Of course, how plant investments relate to growth of demand is also important. If each firm behaves as if it had a priority claim to a given fraction (presumably related to its historical market share) of any period's demand increase, the firm enjoying a large market share and hence a claim to a large increment of new demand will be in a better position to build big new production units than will the firm with a small share. High concentration, by dividing up the available demand increment among few claimants, facilitates large-scale investment. If, on the other hand, producers are prone to struggle for position in making capacity expansions, the aggressive seller with a small market share may be no less disposed to build at a large scale and push its output onto the market — if need be, through price competition. Whether or not the size of capacity increments is correlated with market shares, and hence (on the average) with the level of concentration, depends upon the behavioral pattern adopted.

My statistical investigation of plant sizes in six nations and twelve industries yielded significant support for the nonaggressive, market-sharing investment hypothesis.[25] The higher concentration was, the larger plants tended to be — other things such as the size of the market, the strength of scale economies, and the decentralizing pull of shipping costs held equal. Yet this tendency was much stronger in the European nations, where respect for spheres of influence among sellers has traditionally been prevalent, than in Canada and the United States. A plausible interpretation seems to be that increases in concentration contribute more to the realization of plant scale economies when concentration and restrictive practices are already deeply entrenched than in situations where workable competition exists.

When moderately high unit transport costs induce regional decentralization of production, the size of plant capacity expansion increments may also be affected by whether or not a firm operates multiple plants — e.g., one in each region. The multiplant firm always has the option of treating each regional plant as if it were an autarkic independent entity; that is, like a single-plant regional specialist. But it has another option too — it can coordinate its plants' investments interregionally. One year the firm's Cleveland plant will be expanded by a large increment, the new capacity being used in part to satisfy growing demands in adjoining portions of the Atlanta and Philadelphia plants' natural market territories. Later Atlanta will be expanded, picking up not only its own supply deficit (previously covered from Cleveland) but also the mount-

25. F. M. Scherer, ''The Determinants of Industrial Plant Sizes in Six Nations,'' *Review of Economics and Statistics*, 55 (May 1973), pp. 135-145.

ing deficit around Philadelphia. At a third stage Philadelphia is expanded, taking full responsibility for demands in its own natural market and also at the periphery of the increasingly taxed Cleveland plant's market. To be sure, such an investment strategy entails higher transportation costs than a strategy of regional autarky. But path-breaking mathematical analyses by Alan S. Manne and associates have shown that when unit transport costs are not prohibitively high — e.g., less than 10 percent of product value on 350-mile shipments — and when certain other conditions are satisfied, such a multiregion investment staging strategy can sharply reduce the average level of excess capacity and make it possible to construct plants or plant additions of considerably larger scale. Total savings as high as 20 percent of total discounted capital, operating costs, and transport costs were found to be attainable, at least in the context of the Indian national economy.[26] This then is a most important potential scale economy attributable to firm size of an explicitly multiplant character.

The cost-saving advantages of coordinated multiplant investment staging dwindle and perhaps disappear unless certain conditions hold. In particular, the Manne analysis assumes that firms are confronted with a set of product demands which they must satisfy from their own intracompany production. Price adjustments to choke off excess demand or absorb excess capacity, and buying deficit supplies from or selling surplus to nearby rivals, are ruled out. If, however, firms can always buy and sell deficit or surplus supplies at competitive prices — that is, at prices equal to long-run marginal cost — optimal multiplant investment staging turns out to confer *no* incremental savings. The multiplant strategy is advantageous only if, and to the extent that, competitive market processes fail to provide an alternate adjustment mechanism. In reality, resort to the market is often an imperfect alternative to intrafirm coordination for various reasons: transfer prices are set above competitive levels; companies are unwilling to help rivals bring a large-capacity increment on-stream, or fear excessive dependence upon rivals during a capacity deficit period; antitrust discourages transactions among competitors, or different sellers' products are too differentiated physically to be substitutable. Therefore many multiplant firms do in fact engage in Manne-type interplant investment coordination and derive benefits therefrom.[27] Still, those benefits must be recognized for what they are — gains attributable to strategies which compensate for competitive market breakdowns, or, in the terminology of modern economic theory, *second-best* gains. If the first-best solution — coordination through competitive market processes — is attainable, as it is to a tolerable approximation in many situations, the incremental second-best benefits of internal multiplant coordination dwindle.

Similar reasoning applies with respect to another potential advantage of multiplant, multiregion operation — the possibility of holding smaller capacity reserves against random regional demand fluctuations when one plant con-

26. Alan S. Manne, ed., *Investments for Capacity Expansion* (M.I.T. Press 1967), especially pp. 229-235; and Donald Erlenkotter, "Capacity Planning for Large Multi-location Systems," discussion paper (U.C.L.A. Graduate School of Management, September 1972).

27. *SBKM* ch. 7.

fronted by booming demand can be helped out by another with excess capacity. Price adjustments and competitive market transactions provide, to the extent that businessmen are willing and able to use them, an equally effective means of solving the same problem. Our interviews with some 125 North American and European companies revealed that this potential economy of multiplant operation was not very important in actual practice because the most pronounced demand troughs and peaks, connected with macroeconomic fluctuations or major strikes, coincided in all regions or because cross-shipping costs frittered away too much of the peak-spreading gains.

Recapitulating and clarifying what has become a pervasive theme, we find that many and perhaps even most of the production and physical distribution economies attributable to large firm size and high concentration are second-best economies — realizable when and to the extent that competitive market processes break down. Single-plant regional specialists are disadvantaged relative to multiplant firms centralizing the production of low-demand items only if the regional sellers are unable to buy those products for their lines at competitive prices. Sellers with large overall market shares have an advantage in exploiting product-specific scale economies when, inter alia, oligopolistic price-matching is the industry norm, so that small firms are motivated to increase their volume by broadening their product lines rather than attempting to win a larger share of some more narrowly specialized product array. The sizes of new plants and plant expansions will be correlated with concentration only to the extent that producers adopt a market-sharing attitude toward demand growth instead of struggling independently to capture sufficient orders to uitilize fully an efficient new capacity increment. Multiplant suppliers can, by coordinating their investments interregionally, bring larger capacity increments on-stream and press further down the long-run unit cost curve than can single-plant rivals with comparable market shares, only to the extent that the single-plant firm lacks access to smoothly functioning competitive markets to absorb the shocks of lumpy capacity changes.

Markets do fail, and to the extent that they do, the second-best economies of investment, production, and physical distribution associated with large market shares and multiplant size can be real and substantial. Nevertheless, the extent of market failure is susceptible to a considerable amount of policy control. The more concentration is permitted to develop, the more likely market failure will be, and hence the more importance the second-best benefits of concentration will assume. Obversely, the more successfully competitive market processes can be maintained, the less valuable will be the second-best benefits of increases in concentration. This paradoxical dualism renders the links between market structure and scale economies extremely complex and difficult to measure. It also poses tough challenges for the choice of appropriate market structure policies.

## OTHER ECONOMIES OF MULTIPLANT FIRM SCALE

Scale-correlated variations in the cost at which products are manufactured and physically distributed have monopolized our attention thus far. The relatively large plants or firms which realize such scale economies may or may not pass the savings on to customers in the form of lower prices; but whether or not they do, the resources saved can (assuming a constant level of aggregate economic activity) be used elsewhere in the economy to produce additional goods or services. Thus, a real increase in material standards of living results when such scale economies are captured. Now we must analyze some advantages of size that have less clear-cut implications for economic welfare. These include advantages of large-scale capital raising, materials procurement, and sales promotion. One characteristic shared by all three is that they may be associated with scale increases continuing into the range of multiplant operation. We shall therefore call them advantages of multiplant operation without necessarily implying that single-plant enterprises are barred from their realization. Under this heading of multiplant scale economies, it will also be convenient to take up two additional issues: the links from firm size to (1) technical innovativeness and (2) managerial efficiency.

### Capital-Raising Economies

Business firms enjoy no special immunity from fate's caprices. But the company serving many geographic markets with numerous products has a better opportunity to average out random ups and downs in the business fortunes of its units than does a smaller enterprise, all else (such as the quality of managerial control and motivation) held equal. Statistical studies, in fact, reveal that profits are relatively less variable in relation to their mean value in large corporations than in small; and that the relative frequency of securities default or bankruptcy tends to decline with increasing firm size.[28] Whether these relationships will survive the age of Penn Central and Litton remains to be seen, yet it seems clear that, within some limits, size confers financial risk-pooling advantages.

Investors, both individual and institutional, appear to have a bias toward risk aversion. They react to the superior stability of large corporations by being willing to pay a somewhat higher price for larger firms' stocks, bonds, and notes, all else (such as industry branch, growth history, etc.) being held equal. The securities of large corporations also enjoy higher price/earnings ratios because they are better known, more widely traded, and (hence) more liquid.[29] The size of loans and stock issues is correlated positively with issuer size, but

28. See, for example, H. O. Stekler, *Profitability and Size of Firm* (Univ. of California Institute of Business and Economic Research 1963), pp. 92 ff.; Geoffrey Whittington, *The Prediction of Profitability and Other Studies of Company Behavior* (Cambridge Univ. Press 1971), ch. 3; and W. B. Hickman, *Corporate Bond Quality and Investor Experience* (Princeton Univ. Press 1958), pp. 499-510.

29. This tendency may have become exaggerated in recent years by the concentration of mutual fund portfolio buyers on a small group of highly visible, widely traded corporations' common stocks. See "Are the Institutions Wrecking Wall Street?" *Business Week*, June 2, 1973, p. 59. On the other hand, Gruber found some statistical evidence that the price/earnings ratio advantage of large firms had been declining over time. Martin J. Gruber, *The Determinants of Common Stock Prices* (Pennsylvania State Univ. Office of Business Research 1971), pp. 57-76.

flotation costs are relatively invariant with issue size, so large companies characteristically experience lower average flotation costs per dollar raised than do small enterprises.[30] For all these reasons, the average cost of capital tends to vary inversely with firm size. There have been many statistical studies of parts of this relationship, but to the best of my imperfect knowledge, no one has done a really thorough study putting all the pieces together to estimate systematically how sizeable the larger corporations' advantage is for a substantial sample of industries. The survey of literature and the limited statistical analyses by my co-workers and me suggests that these capital-raising economies persist at least out to the billion-dollar asset range, and that the average cost of capital advantage of a billion-dollar firm as compared to a $10 million firm under mid-1960s market conditions amounted to nearly one percentage point.[31] Better estimates, I hasten to add, are badly needed.

Assessing the society-wide benefit from such capital-raising scale economies is ticklish. Except with respect to real legal and other flotation or administrative cost savings, it is not clear that size-correlated capital cost reductions would free any resources for use elsewhere in the economy, and in this sense they are different from production and physical distribution economies of scale. Also, and analogously to some production economies, if capital markets could be made to work more perfectly — inter alia, by permitting investors to hedge more effectively against risk across a portfolio of securities rather than within individual issues — the size-correlated capital cost differential would decline. So although large firms derive an advantage from their size, it is not clear whether this benefit accrues to the good of society as a whole.

### Procurement Economies

Large purchasers often pay lower prices for raw materials and for other inputs than do small purchasers. These advantages have three main causes: (1) real savings in order-taking, production scheduling, administration, and shipping costs due to the larger volume purchased; (2) the practicality of shopping around more widely for bargains when one is purchasing in large quantities; and (3) the ability of large firms to wrest better price bargains from suppliers because of the leverage connected with size per se or the ability to threaten more credibly that they will commence or expand their own vertically integrated production unless concessions are forthcoming. In addition to possible legal (e.g., Robinson-Patman) distinctions which will not be belabored, there are sharp differences in the society-wide implications of the different types of procurement scale economies. Those of the first type are directly analogous to production scale economies, freeing resources for alternative uses. The second and third types, on the other hand, involve primarily redistributions of income, not real resource savings: Paul benefits at Peter's expense. The

30. Cf. Glenn Miller, "Long-Term Small Business Financing from the Underwriter's Point of View," *Journal of Finance*, 18 (May 1963), pp. 280-290; and S. H. Archer and L. G. Faerber, "Firm Size and the Cost of Externally Secured Capital," *Journal of Finance*, 21 (March 1966), pp. 69-83.

31. Cf. *SBKM* ch. 7.

desirability of such redistributions cannot be assesed without further information and value judgments. If the concession-granting supplier is a small business and the recipient a powerful oligopolist which pockets (or distributes to its wealthy shareholders) the savings, one may well disapprove. But if the concession grantor is highly profitable and the grantee passes the savings along to consumers by reducing end product prices, society may applaud.

The only known systematic evidence on procurement economies of scale is for the SBKM twelve-industry sample.[32] In paints and refrigerators, such economies were very important; in batteries, brewing, textiles, and shoes, moderately to slightly important. In the petroleum refining and steel industries, better ability to integrate vertically into crude oil, iron ore, and coal production and hence to ensure security of supplies was said to be an important advantage of size. However, except with respect to refiners' crude oil operations, the procurement or internal production of pigments by paint manufacturers, and refrigerator assemblers' procurement or production of compressors, the opportunities for realizing input cost savings could be exhausted almost completely by a company operating only one plant of minimum optimal scale. Multiplant procurement economies tended, in other words, to be negligible in the vast majority of cases. When multiplant size did confer significant advantages, the benefits were largely redistributional in character and nearly always resulted from some breakdown of competitive market processes.

### Sales Promotional and Market Access Advantages

Sales promotional, product image, and market access advantages of size are both important and complex. For one thing, they take myriad forms: spreading the fixed costs of advertisement preparation, or a salesman's between-stops travel, over more product volume; quantity discounts in securing media space or time, and the possibility of reinforcing more consumers' habits with a single broadcast message when one has a large market share; a wider choice of media and less loss of loyal but geographically mobile customers when one's market is nationwide rather than regional; greater ability to establish exclusive relationships with strong retail and wholesale outlets in thinly populated markets where only an outlet of considerable size can earn maximum profits; the brand recognition or loyalty which accrues from having been a substantial element in the market for an extended period; and so on. A second complicating factor is the variety of ways in which the economies of large-scale promotion can be exploited: as price premiums; straight cost advantages reflected in profits; cost savings passed along through lower prices and reflected in deeper market penetration; cost savings plowed back into more intensive promotional effort which enhances price premiums or market penetration; etc. Third, the relationship between input and "output" in sales promotion is more erratic and influenced by mystique than in production, materials procurement, and physical distribution. There is simply no other way of explaining Coors' ability to build and, more recently, maintain a 30 percent share in its eleven-state Western beer market while spending less than 25 cents

32. SBKM.

per barrel on advertising, whereas Schlitz has averaged between $1.40 and $2.00 per barrel in gaining a national market share of 14 percent. Fourth and most important, it is impossible to avoid strong ethical judgments in dealing with the relationship between promotional economies and scale. No one is apt to be greatly upset over the fact that the Reynolds man can visit a retail outlet and tidy up displays which will sell twice as many cigarettes as those the Philip Morris representative services on a call requiring nearly as much time. But a paramount effect of successful promotional activity is discretionary control over price — monopoly power. And one may well be concerned that by cumulated large-scale advertising campaigns, the Schlitz Company can convince millions of consumers that they should pay two cents more per can for a product which by any plausible set of objective standards is no better qualitatively than rival "regional" brands. Lesser injustices have driven sensible men to drink.

Professor Bain, the pioneer here as in other areas, has dealt with the cost-saving–price-premium–volume problem and the fact that product image advantages are built up over time by viewing large firms' promotional advantages not as a conventional economy of scale but as a "barrier to entry." That is, he sought to measure the price discount plus unit selling cost premium suffered by a new entrant as compared to established sellers, assuming that the entrant entered at the MOS plant scale.[33] Not surprisingly, he found that sales promotional or product differentiation barriers to entry were either insignificant or slight in most of the Table 1 producer goods industries, which largely offered standardized products to well-informed buyers. The main exceptions were tractors and typewriters, where established firms were said to enjoy a substantial advantage due to established brand loyalty and well-developed customer service networks.[34] In consumer goods the picture was different, with either moderately or very important product differentiation being the rule, usually because of established firms' accumulated advertising and dealer network loyalties. Altogether, Bain found newcomers to face "great" product differentiation barriers to entry — i.e., involving at least a 5 percent price–cost disadvantage for ten years after entry or a 5 percent handicap for ten years — in six industries: tractors and complicated farm machinery, cigarettes, liquor, quality fountain pens, automobiles, and typewriters. "Moderate" promotional barriers were attributed to specialty canned fruits and vegetables, higher-priced men's shoes, branded flour, tin cans, rubber tires, petroleum refining, and soap. In soap, liquor, cigarettes, tin cans, flour, canned specialties, high-priced men's shoes, complex farm machinery, and tires, significant economies of large-scale promotion were believed to persist out to the size of firms operating multiple MOS plants. Bain observed furthermore that very high overall barriers to the entry of new firms were more likely to be due to the sales promotional advantages of large established firms than to scale economies in production and physical distribution.[35] He cau-

33. Bain, *supra* n. 4, at 122.
34. *Id.* at 124-133.
35. *Id.* at 142, 216.

tioned, however, that his questionnaire respondents showed greater uncertainty concerning the magnitudes of promotional advantages than on production scale economies.[36]

Promotional scale economies received only cursory treatment in Pratten's industry studies, at least partly because of the considerable analytic difficulties posed.[37] Pratten's general conclusion was that there were definite marketing economies of scale in at least some consumer goods industries, particularly soap and automobiles, but that in many situations small firms found effective strategies for avoiding the disadvantages of smallness in their marketing.[38]

My colleagues and I departed from Bain's methodology in our twelve-industry analysis, comparing instead the sales promotional advantages of large and especially large multiplant enterprises relative to small *established* companies. One of our most vivid impressions was that the relationships are highly variegated. Large firms did enjoy significant promotional advantages in many instances, but there are many ways to skin the marketing cat, and smaller sellers displayed considerable ingenuity in developing strategies which minimized or avoided altogether any handicaps associated with their size. To have a complete understanding of the promotional scale economy phenomenon, one must know not only how large a firm must be to enjoy all potential advantages of large-scale marketing, but also how commodious the market niches are in which smaller enterprises can thrive by emphasizing private label sales, vigorous "push" through retail distribution channels, excellent service, trading stamps, innovative product design, or other tactics to which they have access on roughly equal terms. In some consumer goods industries like shoes and paints, these niches are quite sizeable; in others like refrigerators and (at least before the television advertising ban) cigarettes, they are small. It is also clear that the economies of large-scale promotion are culture-bound, so a strategy which is dominant in the United States may be ineffective or legally barred in, say, Germany. Since laws and customs are changeable, this means that if there is a social consensus that large firms enjoy undesirable promotional advantages, the ground rules might be altered.

Three further observations deserve mention. First, accumulated brand image is often more important than the size of a company's marketing effort at any moment in time. There may of course be links between current image and the scale of past promotions, but there are also significant random elements. Second, for many industries the unit with respect to which scale really matters is the brand, not overall firm size. The costs of advertising Doral cigarettes were affected much more critically by the fact that Doral had only a 1.2 percent share of the U.S. market in 1971 than by the fact that Reynolds, Doral's maker, enjoyed a total market share of 32 percent. This implies a likely limitation on the advantages of multiplant size in promotion. Third, in advertising campaigns and the deployment of field sales forces, what matters most is often

36. *Id.* at 120, 121.
37. Pratten, *supra* n. 5, at 284.
38. *Id.* at 288.

one's position in specific compact geographic submarkets. Advertisers commonly find it more profitable to tailor their promotional efforts to particular local markets through spot television and newspaper messages — i.e., a rifle shot approach — than by buying shotgun network coverage, even when their nationwide sales posture makes it completely feasible to pursue the network approach. This means again that the advertising advantages of nationwide multiplant operation, though not negligible, are often not very great; or in other words, that single-plant regional specialists may be able to compete by using the powerful television medium on nearly equal terms.[39]

In Table 5 an attempt is made to assess, for the twelve SBKM industries, the extent to which established sellers operating only a single MOS plant experienced promotional handicaps relative to multiplant firms under mid-1960s conditions.[40] The size threshold at which all significant promotional advantages of scale were realized and its national market share implications are also estimated. For all the producer goods industries but bearings, where customer broad-line preferences are influential, the promotional advantages of multiplant size are slight or negligible.[41] In most of the consumer goods industries, single-plant firms do experience handicaps in competing toe-to-toe in the promotional arena with multiplant enterprises, although the advantages of size are often exhausted at relatively low levels of multiplant operation and national market penetration. Wide margins of uncertainty must nonetheless be indicated for a majority of the consumer goods fields, because strategies exist by which sellers can elude or minimize the handicaps of small scale. A more precise categorization would be unwarranted in view of the underlying complexities. And to repeat, while large firms may benefit due to their size in such heavy advertising industries as beer, cigarettes, and gasoline, it is debatable whether society as a whole derives commensurate benefits.

### Technological Innovation

There no longer seems to be much doubt that industries' success in creating and adopting new product and production process technologies is more important over the long run to material prosperity than is success at any moment in time in exploiting production, distribution, and promotional economies of scale. On this point Joseph A. Schumpeter's cries in the wilderness have gained

---

39. An implication is that the advantages of network television time discounts, if indeed they are correlated with advertiser size at all, are not very compelling. See the debate over this issue in Harlan Blake and Jack A. Blum, "Network Television Rate Practices: A Case Study in the Failure of Social Control of Price Discrimination," 74 Yale L.J. 1339-1401 (1965); David M. Blank, "Television Advertising: The Great Discount Illusion, or Tonypandy Revisited," Journal of Business, 41 (January 1968), pp. 10-38; the comment by William Leonard with rejoinder by Blank in id., 42 (January 1969), pp. 93-112; and John L. Peterman, "The Clorox Case and Television Rate Structures," Journal of Law & Economics, 11 (October 1968), pp. 321-422.

40. The table is taken directly from SBKM ch. 7.

41. In the paint and fabric industry branches catering to industrial customers, single-plant firms also face negligible promotional handicaps.

TABLE 5
Summary of the Promotional Advantages Associated with Multiplant Size

| Industry | How Seriously Disadvantaged Are Efficient Single-Plant Producers? | Main Sources of Multiplant Promotional Advantages | How Many MOS Plants Needed To Achieve All Significant Promotional Advantages in U.S. Market? | Percentage of U.S. Market Required, Circa 1967 |
|---|---|---|---|---|
| Beer Brewing | Slightly to Severely | National Brand Image, Choice of Media | Possibly one, but as many as five | 3-17 |
| Cigarettes | Slightly to Moderately | Sales Force Deployment, Advertising Economies | Two for advertising; up to four for sales force deployment | 12-27 |
| Fabric Weaving | Slightly to Moderately | Broad-line Preferences, Advertising Economies | As many as twenty | Up to 6 |
| Paints (Trade) | Slightly | National Brand Image, Choice of Media | Three or four | 4-6 |
| Petroleum Refining | Slightly to Moderately | National Brand Image, Choice of Media, Broad-line Preferences | One to four | 2-8 |
| Shoes | Moderately | Sales Force Deployment, National Brand Image, Advertising Economies | Four to eight | 1-2 |
| Glass Bottles | Negligibly | None | One | 1.5 |
| Cement | Negligibly | None | One | 1.7 |
| Ordinary Steel | Negligibly | Nationwide Customer Ties | Four | 2.5-10 |
| Bearings | Moderately | Broad-line Preferences, Sales Force Deployment | Four to eight | 6-11 |
| Refrigerators | Slightly to Severely | National Brand Image, Broad-line Preferences, Service Networks | As many as twelve, including other appliances | c. 30 |
| Automobile Batteries | Slightly | Broad-line, National Supply Preferences | Five | 10 |

nearly universal acceptance.[42] More controversial is another Schumpeter assertion: that large, monopolistic firms are a superior vehicle for conceiving and
implementing technological innovations.[43]

I do not know how to improve noticeably upon my survey of the state of
knowledge on this question published four years ago,[44] so perhaps I will be
forgiven for presenting only a superficial summary. Since Professor Markham
has been assigned to explore the issues comprehensively, no gaping lacunae
should remain.

In principle, firms which are large both absolutely and with respect to
specific markets should be able to realize economies of scale in technological
innovation. Large corporations can better afford to support sizeable research
and development laboratories employing specialized scientists and engineers
using costly specialized equipment. By maintaining a diversified portfolio of
R&D projects, they can pool risks and perhaps therefore undertake ventures
whose failure would ruin a small company. To the extent that they enjoy promotional economies of scale, they may be able to bring new products into
widespread use more rapidly and therefore anticipate larger discounted profits from a project than could a smaller enterprise with limited distribution
channels. The costs of conducting an R&D project may be so high that only
firms in a position to gain and/or hold a large share of the relevant market
can anticipate sufficient sales to justify the investment. Profits from existing
monopoly or oligopoly positions may be a prime source of funds for research,
and the security afforded by a strong market position may permit a farsighted
attitude without which long-range research investments might not be made.

Security could, on the other hand, breed complacency rather than vision.
The best spur to action may be the fear of being left behind technically by one
or more of numerous rivals. Large organizations are not always renowned for
their speed in recognizing good ideas, and this sluggishness may drive the
most ambitious creative individuals into smaller firms, where their proposals
have a better chance of receiving personal consideration by the top decision-
maker. A simple willingness to take risks can also do much to offset the small
firm's inability to hedge by amassing a diversified R&D project portfolio.

Whether large firms are in fact superior or inferior innovators depends
upon how these various characteristics balance out, and that is basically an
empirical question. One should not expect completely general answers, how-

42. See his *Capitalism, Socialism, and Democracy* (third ed., Harper 1950), ch. 5.
In an heroic attempt to quantify the causes of growth in U.S. real national income
per worker between 1929 and 1957, Edward F. Denison attributed a 36 percent
share to "the advance of knowledge" and a 21 percent share to growth of markets
leading to enhanced economies of scale. *The Sources of Economic Growth in the
United States* (Committee for Economic Development 1962), pp. 173-181, 217-255,
270. One of the many measurement problems is, as we have noted earlier, that advances in technology are often a prerequisite to achieving production scale economies.

43. Joseph A. Schumpeter, *Capitalism, Socialism, and Democracy* (third ed.,
Harper 1950), ch. 8.

44. F. M. Scherer, *Industrial Market Structure and Economic Performance* (Rand
McNally 1970), ch. 15.

ever, since the activities we categorize under the heading "research and development" vary tremendously in cost, risk, and strategic significance. The most useful way to think about the scale imperatives of R&D is to visualize a spectrum or frequency distribution of potential projects arrayed according to cost. The distribution is highly skewed: a few projects are extremely costly; many are surprisingly inexpensive. Very few companies in the world have the know-how, resources, reputation, and market access to develop a Boeing 747.[45] For every 747, however, there are thousands of projects which could be squeezed without great strain into the budgets of medium-sized and even quite small companies. It is also important to recognize that certain industries like chemicals and electronics enjoy, by virtue of their rich scientific heritage and the logic of specialization, comparative advantage in supplying new technology for other more traditional industries. As a result, a single-plant textile company, though too small to support an R&D laboratory, may have no trouble producing the most up-to-date products (incorporating chemical makers' fibers) on highly efficient machines (imported from specialized Swiss manufacturers). In such cases the size of the technology-*using* firm may have little or no bearing on either the rate of technological progress or the balance of strategic advantage between large and small users.

There have been numerous statistical investigations of the relationship between firm size or market concentration levels and some index of industrial innovativeness such as the number of significant new products and processes introduced, the number of inventions patented, R&D expenditures, or R&D employment.[46] The gist of their findings can be summarized as follows. First, for firms with fewer than 1,000 employees to support formal research and development programs is much more the exception than the rule, while manufacturing corporations with 5,000 or more employees (a population with nearly 500 members during the late 1960s) account for a share of total industrial R&D outlays nearly twice their share of value added. This suggests advantages of size up to the 5,000-employee threshold, although the inventive and innovative contributions of those smaller firms which do engage in R&D

45. It is worth repeating that on such massive projects, product-specific economies of scale in *production* can be so overwhelming that costs may be minimized when only a single firm satisfies the entire market demand. A delicate trade-off between seeking such economies and preserving a competitive stimulus may be required. A statistical analysis of World War II bomber production costs showed that the rate of cost reduction over time tended to be faster when two or more firms competed in production than when one firm produced all orders for a given design. For fighters, however, the "learning curve" slope differences were not statistically significant. F. M. Scherer, *The Weapons Acquisition Process: Economic Incentives* (Harvard Business School Division of Research 1964), pp. 119-126.

46. For a survey and references, see Scherer, *supra* n. 44. Important new contributions include Edwin Mansfield, John Rapoport, Jerome Schnee, Samuel Wagner, and Michael Hamburger, *Research and Innovation in the Modern Corporation* (Norton 1971); and Thomas M. Kelly, "The Influence of Size and Market Structure on the Research Efforts of Large Multiple-Product Firms," unpublished Ph.D. dissertation, Oklahoma State Univ., August 1969.

are by no means negligible. Second, quantitative analyses reveal little or no discernible advantage of size beyond the 5,000-employee threshold. The most vigorous firms in terms of significant innovations or patents generated per billion dollars of sales, R&D employment per thousand employees, subjectively evaluated research program effectiveness, and other indices of innovative performance appear to be the medium-sized organizations. A possible exception to this generalization could be the chemicals industry (excluding pharmaceuticals), where the largest firms (du Pont in particular) have historically exhibited a slight but fading innovative edge over medium-sized rivals. Third, with respect to market concentration, no really strong statistical relationships exist once differences in the richness of the technological opportunities confronting diverse industries are properly taken into account. Two studies investigating quite different data samples found that R&D employment per thousand employees was positively but loosely correlated with the four-firm concentration ratio up to concentration levels of 50 or 55, after which the relationship turned negative. The positive segment of the "innovative activity–concentration" correlation appeared to be stronger in industries with limited as compared to rich technological opportunities and also (but less clearly) in industries with meager as compared to rich product differentiation potential. It bears repeating that it is the rich technological opportunity industries, where the concentration links were weakest, which contribute a lion's share of technological improvements for both their own internal exploitation and the use of less well-endowed branches.

A perspective only slightly different is provided by my analysis of the size thresholds above which firms in the twelve SBKM industries experience "no significant research, development, and innovation scope or size handicaps."[47] In some industries — notably fabrics, shoes, bottles, cement, bearings, and batteries — the threshold at which all such handicaps were avoided entailed the operation of from four to fifty MOS plants. Yet only in industrial paints, bottles, and antifriction bearings were the adverse strategic consequences of being large enough to operate only one MOS plant more than "slight," and in both paints and bottles a firm with three MOS plants could exhaust the main R&D advantages of multiplant operation.

In sum, there are advantages of scale in research and innovation. They appear, however, to be fully realized (in the vast majority of cases) at firm sizes and concentration levels well below the upper size and concentration ranges of existing U.S. industrial structure. Exceptions to this generalization can be found, but they must be recognized as such.

### Management

I have saved until last the sub-section where I must breach my contract with the conference sponsors. I cannot review "the economic evidence on economies of scale . . . in managerial factors" because I have found nothing that

47. SBKM ch. 7. It should be noted that the sample includes no industries heavily involved in the most dynamic chemical, electronic, and aerospace technologies.

would qualify as "evidence" under any reasonably tough-minded definition of that term.

Theory, as usual, is not scarce. Large firms are better able to afford managerial super-stars and a rich complement of specialized talent in such areas as tax law, labor contract negotiations, and market research. They may also enjoy "massed reserves" economies, focusing their top brains first on one problem and then on another, and thus achieving fuller "utilization" than would a small company with fewer deserving problems. Still smaller firms may be able to compensate for in-house talent gaps by hiring outside consultants as the occasion demands. More important, the problems of monitoring, motivating, and guiding a business organization multiply as the size of the organization increases, so staffing levels and communications costs may rise more than proportionately with scale, and those at the top of the organizational pyramid may need every ounce of their superior talent just to keep the whole enterprise from sinking into the sand.

One facet of the managerial scale economies question — whether staffing levels increase more or less than proportionately with organizational size — might be subjected to quantitative tests. The data currently available are scant, however, and as a result no really conclusive studies exist.[48] Systematically relating the quality of management to organization size poses even more formidable analytic difficulties, especially if one correctly measures "quality" in terms of ability to cope with problems whose magnitude may increase simultaneously with scale. The most we have are subjective impressions. My own, based upon personally participating in 86 of the 125 SBKM company interviews, is that there is no obvious association between firm size and such dimensions of managerial quality as dynamism, intelligence, awareness, and skill in interpersonal relations. On the basis of my interview experience, I am inclined toward the view that the unit costs of management, including the hidden losses due to delayed or faulty decisions and weakened or distorted incentives as well as more tangible staff salary costs, do tend to rise with organizational size. Indeed, the rise may be sufficient to neutralize what otherwise would be compelling economies of scale in production, capital raising, and sales promotion. But impressions are not hard evidence, so the issue must remain open.

## CONCLUSION

Those who expect simple, precise generalizations from this survey are bound to be disappointed. Clearly, important scale economies exist. Equally clearly, they are exhausted at relatively modest concentration levels in many manu-

---

48. For a survey of the literature, see William H. Starbuck, "Organizational Growth and Development," in James G. March, ed., *Handbook of Organizations* (Rand McNally 1965), especially pp. 495-519. The latest "nice try" award goes to L. R. Pondy for "Effects of Size, Complexity, and Ownership on Administrative Intensity," *Administrative Science Quarterly*, 14 (March 1969), pp. 47-61.

facturing industries of a nation as large as the United States. The variance from industry to industry is great, however, and even in industries where the most-advantaged plant or firm must be large in relation to the market, there are apt to be niches where much smaller units can sustain a profitable existence.

For the twelve SBKM industries, a more explicit (though not necessarily more exact) set of judgments can be rendered. Table 6 attempts to evaluate the

TABLE 6

Summary of Single-Plant Firm's Overall Relative Disadvantage
and the Firm Size Required to Experience Not More Than Slight Price/Cost Handicaps:
Twelve SBKM Industries

| Industry | (1) Overall Disadvantage of Representative General-Line Single MOS Plant Firm | (2) Number of MOS Plants Needed To Have Not More Than "Slight" Overall Handicap | (3) Share of U.S. Market Required in 1967 | (4) Average Market Share per U.S. Big Three Member, 1970 |
|---|---|---|---|---|
| Beer Brewing | SLIGHT TO SEVERE, depending upon inherited brand image | 3-4 | 10-14 | 13 |
| Cigarettes | SLIGHT TO MODERATE (borderline) | 1-2 | 6-12 | 23 |
| Fabric Weaving | VERY SLIGHT TO MODERATE, depending upon product line | 3-6 | 1 | 10 |
| Paints | SLIGHT | 1 | 1.4 | 9 |
| Petroleum Refining | VERY SLIGHT TO MODERATE, depending upon regional market position and crude oil access | 2-3 | 4-6 | 8 |
| Shoes | SLIGHT TO MODERATE, depending upon product line | 3-6 | 1 | 6 |
| Glass Bottles | SLIGHT TO MODERATE, depending upon location and products | 3-4 | 4-6 | 22 |
| Cement | SLIGHT | 1 | 2 | 7 |
| Ordinary Steel | VERY SLIGHT | 1 | 3 | 14 |
| Bearings | SLIGHT TO MODERATE, depending upon product line | 3-5 | 4-7 | 14 |
| Refrigerators | MODERATE | 4-8 (incl. other appliances) | 14-20 | 21 |
| Storage Batteries | SLIGHT | 1 | 2 | 18 |

overall disadvantage of a main-line firm with only one MOS plant compared to firms realizing *all* the benefits of multiplant size. It also estimates how many plants an enterprise must operate to experience, at most, only a "slight" disadvantage — defined as not much more than 1 percent in terms of unit cost premiums incurred or price premiums sacrificed.[49] It adheres consistently to several assumptions — e.g., that the technological frontiers and market environment are those of the United States in the mid- to late 1960s; that the firms compared operate in an industry's mainstream rather than in offbeat market niches; that multiplant scale economy opportunities are in fact exploited fully by the largest companies and not foregone due to organizational sluggishness; and that the various advantages of large scale are weighted according to their strategic importance in the market without regard to social desirability. Even with such a homogenization of assumptions, the advantages of size are sufficiently sensitive to environmental and hereditary variables that a range of estimates must be presented for seven industries.

Column (3) translates the multiplant figures of Column (2) into estimates of how large a percentage share of 1967 U.S. production a general-line supplier needed to experience, at most, slight cost and/or price handicaps. In effect, they summarize the combined scale economy imperatives for national market concentration. In most instances, realizing the principal advantages of multiplant size did not necessitate high concentration at the nationwide level. Only in the refrigerator, brewing, and (less certainly) cigarette industries did scale economies compel anything approaching moderately tight oligopoly. Consideration of regional and product divisions could, however, lead to less sanguine conclusions. Oligopoly may be mandated by the interaction of scale economies and high transport costs in sparsely populated cement markets, in markets for gasoline and fuel oil lacking good pipeline or water transport connections, and in all glass bottle markets except those with a high concentration of demand.[50] For important steel products such as hot-rolled strip, heavy plates, and large structural members, fairly tight oligopoly is also implied, since optimal rolling mills are sizeable and specialized and it is difficult to serve much more than a fourth of the continental United States economically from a single site. The bearings industry estimates of Column (2) assume a firm specializing in ball, roller, or tapered roller bearings; not all three. With multiplant firms so specialized, there would be middling oligopoly levels in the ball and roller market segments, and high levels in such segments as tapered and needle bearings. Similar market segmentation occurs in textiles, but equipment and skills are sufficiently transferable that the Column (3) estimates reflect the long-run structural imperatives better than upward-adjusted variants would. The national market share estimate for brewing is also unchanged when regionalization is taken into account, because the Column (2) range assumes a multiplant firm deployed spatially to serve the national market.

When these complications are recognized, we find moderate or tighter oligopoly to be unwarranted for the vast bulk of production in four industries — shoes, batteries, paints, and fabrics; and for substantial fractions of two more

49. Table 6 is taken without substantive change from Chapter 7 of *SBKM,* and the discussion which follows here is in part drawn from *SBKM* with only minor abridgements.

50. Compare also the last two columns of Table 6.

— petroleum refining and cement. For steel, glass bottles, and bearings, the multiplant scale economy threshold estimates imply four-firm concentration ratios of 50 or more in most significant regional or product submarkets. In brewing and refrigerators, *national* market concentration ratios of 50 to 70 are indicated. In no covered U.S. industry or major subsegment is anything like natural monopoly or total dominance by two or three firms compelled.

Column (4) reports the actual average 1970 national market shares (that is, the average per company) of firms counted among each industry's Big Three. In only three industries — brewing, refrigerators, and petroleum refining — are the observed leading firm market shares of about the same magnitude as the "required" estimates of Column (3). In weaving and storage batteries, actual shares exceed "required" shares by approximately ten times; in paints, shoes, bottles, and steel, by four to six times; and in cigarettes, bearings, and cement, by two or three times. Thus, national market seller concentration in most industries appears to be much higher than it needs to be for leading firms to take advantage of all but slight residual scale economies.

One final element of perspective must be added. It is at least arguable that the estimates in Table 6 overstate the *social* compulsion toward concentration. The advantages of multiplant size in brewing and cigarettes stem preponderantly — and in petroleum refining, partly — from large-scale advertising exaggerating brand differences or cynically exploiting consumers' yearning for peer group approval. One might, with justification, believe that however more successfully this promotion is conducted by the largest corporations, it deserves no positive Brownie points. In petroleum refining, another key advantage of multiplant firms has been greater ability to secure crude oil supplies through vertical integration, but integration would be much less advantageous if artificial barriers to the importation of foreign crude oil were dismantled (as they have been to a considerable degree in 1973) and if special tax provisions making it attractive to shift as much profit as possible to crude production were eradicated. Society might well conclude, furthermore, that it is willing to accept production, physical distribution, and other cost penalties well above 1 percent to secure the greater dispersion of power and other benefits associated with less concentrated industrial structures. And finally, because we have almost no systematic knowledge on the question, nothing has been said here about the possibility that blue- and white-collar-worker alienation rises with increased plant and firm size. Yet if that were indeed the case, society could be paying a prohibitively high price for the ostensible economies of large-scale operation. Here, as in many other areas, we need to dispel our ignorance through penetrating further research.

# Efficiency and Economies of Size
## John S. McGee*

## I.    INTRODUCTION

Economists do not always agree. Among other things, they disagree about the causes and significance of industrial concentration, as this Conference demonstrates. What one hears depends significantly upon whom one listens to, which — one would think — might retard the tendency to cook up hasty policies.

Some of economists' disagreements stem from differences in their theories, which, in turn, have influenced their perceptions of reality. Such differences in theory also lead to requests for different kinds of "facts"; different appraisals of the feasibility and relevancy of various kinds of empirical studies; and to different predictions, explanations, and appraisals of observed economic outcomes. In addition, economists' theories also differ because the economists have had different kinds and amounts of experience in the world outside.

These kinds of differences make it tedious even to summarize what economists think they know about economic efficiency and business size. Unfortunately, the relevant task is more formidable than that. What passes for knowledge about this subject is in general extremely skimpy, and it is sometimes wrong. Simple summary of such stuff will not do. The only decent alternative is first to summarize, then critically to evaluate, and finally to propose. We shall also need to review and develop some economic fundamentals as we go. I hope to keep these to the minimum necessary to explain why I have come to my conclusions.

The main body of this essay is divided into five parts. Part II is a brief digression on what "economies of scale" really means and why the notion has gotten us into trouble. The third explores why unit costs fall with larger size. The fourth shows ways in which costs differ amongst firms. In the fifth part I summarize and evaluate the methods and findings of several "empirical" studies. Part VI restates where things have gone fundamentally wrong in economists' treatment of the efficiency question; it develops, then applies, the economics of trade to notions of efficiency, and offers an alternative view.

## II.    "ECONOMIES OF SCALE"

It is conventional to associate the efficiency question with something called "economies of scale." For two reasons, I think that rubric misdirects excursions

* Professor of Economics, University of Washington, Seattle. For further biographical information, see Appendix D.

into the real world, and perpetuates a set of mind that interferes seriously with analysis and diagnosis.

First, in theoretical economics a change in "scale" means any proportionate change in the rate at which a plant or firm uses *all* inputs, which are commonly imagined to be homogeneous and as finely divisible as sand. "*All*" inputs obviously must include entrepreneurship, management teams, elbow room, and each and every other relevant production factor and input service. If the rate of output from such an imaginary producing unit expands strictly proportionally with any proportionate expansion in the rate of inputs of all factors of production, we have a case of "constant returns to scale." Doubling the *rate* of factor inputs doubles the *rate* of output, for example.

Given all the underlying assumptions, and the kind of imaginary world they imply, it would be a little odd to expect that returns to scale could be anything *but* constant.[1] If all factors were supplied at unchanging prices, the firm's long-run average costs would then also be constant: doubling the rate of output would double the rate at which costs are incurred, and unit costs would be equally low irrespective of the size of firm. To avoid certain unwanted implications of the assumptions and logic (including that the number and sizes of firms would be indeterminate), economists have sometimes contrived ad hoc escapes. Among the more graceful and sophisticated is to assume that something called "entrepreneurship" is not priced in the market and that only one "unit" of it is held by each firm.[2] But, under those circumstances, we can not talk about returns to "scale" anymore, since the quantity of at least one factor is constant, and *all* factors simply could not be varied proportionally.

In a sense, then, economists have had it both ways. To bring out certain distributional results that were historically welcomed largely on equity grounds, and to ease certain statistical and computational tricks of which they are fond, constant returns to scale simplified economists' academic life. For some other purposes the implications were embarrassing, and were then bent into better fit. Almost all economists learn these tricks early in their training. I suspect that most of us carry some corrupt version of this constant-returns-to-scale game with us when we look at, or pontificate about, the real world. But few, if any, real-world problems are "scale" problems.

Second, with few exceptions economists have ignored total model volume as an important dimension of size and output, and have thought of "size" exclusively in terms of output rate, as the traditional "returns to scale" analysis implies. One million VW Beetles *per year* is a *rate* of output. If they are produced at that rate for twenty years, 20 million is the model *volume*. It is one thing to produce one million Beetles per year, for *one* year, at which point the plant is converted or sold off. It is quite another to produce one

1. For a compact proof, and a profound analysis of some things that happen when the arithmetic outruns understanding, see Nicholas Georgescu-Roegen, "The Economics of Production," *American Economic Review*, 60 (May 1970), pp. 1-2.

2. For example, see Milton Friedman, *Price Theory: A Provisional Text* (Aldine 1962), pp. 96, 140.

million per year for twenty years. The organization of the firm, the tooling, and the costs, will be very different. Yet the *rates* of output are the same, and typical textbook theory does not distinguish between these profoundly different output programs. This fixation is not only troublesome logically; it leads to profound misunderstandings when one talks to engineers and businessmen, or otherwise attempts to understand how specific firms and industries work in the real world.[3]

## III.   BUSINESS FUNCTIONS AND SOURCES OF ECONOMIES

Although we talk about it all the time, economists actually know very little even about what a "firm" *is*.[4] Even so, it is sometimes useful to classify and discuss some of the things that businesses obviously do. These clearly include things like production, finance, marketing, research, management, and risk-taking.[5] It is in production that what economists call "technical economies" most obviously arise, and it is these technical or "nuts-and-bolts" economies that seem easiest to understand.

The classic discussion of technical production economies is found in Adam Smith, *The Wealth of Nations*.[6] His most famous example is an eighteenth-century pin factory. It is a simple case that seems to rely primarily upon economies from labor specialization. If there is little or no market for pins, each person or family must make for itself such pins as it wants. If there is a broad market, it pays to "divide" the process into many subprocesses, each completed by one or more men. In Smith's words,

> a workman not educated to this business (which the division of labour has rendered a distinct trade), nor acquainted with the use of the machinery employed in it (to the invention of which the same division of labor has probably given occasion), could scarce, perhaps, with his utmost industry, make one pin in a day, and certainly could not make twenty. But in the way in which this business is now carried on, not only the whole work is a peculiar trade, but it is divided into a number of branches, of which the greater part are likewise peculiar trades. One man draws out the wire, another straights it, a third cuts it, a fourth points it, a fifth grinds it at the top for receiving the head; to make the head requires two or three distinct operations; to put it on, is a peculiar business, to whiten the pins is another; it is even a trade by itself to put them into the paper; and the important business of

3. See also the discussion in John S. McGee, *In Defense of Industrial Concentration* (Praeger 1971).

4. Two important advances, which also show the primitive state of our knowledge, are R. H. Coase, "The Nature of the Firm," *Economica*, New Series Vol. 4 (November 1937), pp. 386-405 (reprinted in G. J. Stigler and K. E. Boulding, eds., *Readings in Price Theory* (R. D. Irwin 1952), pp. 331-351; and Armen A. Alchian and Harold Demsetz, "Production, Information Costs, and Economic Organization," *American Economic Review*, 62 (December 1972), pp. 777-795.

5. One familiar and influential treatment is E. A. G. Robinson, *The Structure of Competitive Industry* (Univ. of Chicago Press 1959).

6. Adam Smith, *An Inquiry Into the Nature and Causes of the Wealth of Nations* (Modern Library 1937), pp. 3-21.

making a pin is, in this manner, divided into about eighteen distinct operations, which, in some manufactories, are all performed by distinct hands, though in others the same man will sometimes perform two or three of them. I have seen a small manufactory of this kind where ten men only were employed, and where some of them consequently performed two or three distinct operations. But though they were very poor, and therefore but indifferently accomodated with the necessary machinery, they could, when they exerted themselves, make among them about twelve pounds of pins in a day. There are in a pound upwards of four thousand pins of a middling size. Those ten persons, therefore, could make among them upwards of forty-eight thousand pins in a day. Each person, therefore, making a tenth part of forty-eight thousand pins, might be considered as making four thousand eight hundred pins in a day. But if they had all wrought separately and independently, and without any of them having been educated to this peculiar business, they certainly could not each of them have made twenty, perhaps not one pin in a day; that is, certainly, not the two hundred and fortieth, perhaps not the four thousand eight hundredth part of what they are at present capable of performing, in consequence of a proper division and combination of their different operations.[7]

Even in such a simple example, there are several potential sources of economies. Men's interests and talents differ, and fuller play and better place for these peculiarities can be had if one man need not do it all. Less time is lost setting down one task and tools to take up others. Learning and improved physical skill are acquired when one concentrates on a smaller range of tasks. And — even when technology is primitive — a relatively simple and efficient machine may be designed to take over one or more subtasks, whereas there may be no machine that can economically undertake them all. As a consequence, said Smith, a relatively small, specialized *team* work force was able to turn out many times more pins than a corresponding number of isolated workers, each forced to perform all the tasks himself.

But there is much more to size economies than the specialization and division of labor. There are also economies of the "large machine" (which often has as its real-world counterpart the absolutely expensive, durable, or highly productive machine or process). Engineering and economic literature are filled with examples showing that, in general, productive capacity increases faster than cost.[8]

On the basis of logic and his own experience, Armen A. Alchian long ago concluded that costs of producing a given product are influenced by a number of variables, in addition to factor prices and the state of technology.[9] These

7. Id. at 4-5.

8. For example, see John Haldi and David Whitcomb, "Economies of Scale in Industrial Plants," *Journal of Political Economy,* 75 (August 1967), pp. 379-385; Frederick T. Moore, "Economies of Scale: Some Statistical Evidence," *Quarterly Journal of Economics,* 73 (May 1959), pp. 232-245.

9. Armen A. Alchian, "Costs and Output," in M. Abramovitz et al., *The Allocation of Economic Resources: Essays in Honor of Bernard F. Haley* (Stanford Univ. Press 1959); A. A. Alchian, "Reliability of Progress Curves in Airframe Production," *Econometrica,* 31 (1963), pp. 679-694; A. A. Alchian and William R. Allen, *Exchange and Production Theory in Use* (Wadsworth 1969), pp. 287-312; A. A. Alchian, "Cost,"

include the *rate* of output (say, the number of a specific kind of automobile produced per year); the total *volume* of a model produced before its production is stopped for good; and the amount of *time* available for planning and preparation before any production is actually begun. The total *volume* produced is the average *rate* of production per unit time multiplied by the time period of production (say, 1 million VW Beetles per year, *times* twenty-six producing years).

For typical industrial processes, Alchian asserts that: (1) For a given total *volume* (say, 1 million cars of a given model), total costs will generally rise at an *increasing* rate as the *rate of production* rises: it will be cheaper — or, at all events, not more expensive — to build 1 million cars in two years than in one year; in one year than in six months, and so on. Among other things, this rate effect is said to occur because of planning, control, and congestion: these are costs of haste. (2) For a given *rate* of production (1 million cars per year) the cost *per car* will fall if the total volume to be produced rises: if you plan to produce 4 million VW Beetles at 1 million per year, the cost per car will be lower than if you were to produce only 2 million identical cars at 1 million per year. He gives two main reasons: (a) Some techniques, tools, and organizations will be best for small volumes and others will be best for large volumes. But those best suited for large volumes cost less per unit. If one plans for it, the best techniques for producing 2 million cars will be less than twice as costly as those for producing 1 million cars (*rate* of production being the same in both cases). My own experience and research support this result. (b) Even if the best techniques were the same for small and large volumes, management and labor actually *learn* during production, which also lowers unit costs for large volumes.

The logic and facts are more complex when *both* rate and volume are varying in the same direction — proportionally, for example. For there are now two opposing tendencies: The increase in *rate* of production tends to drive up average cost; but the increase in *volume* tends to lower average cost. The net effect, over given ranges of volume and rate, may differ amongst industries and amongst firms within the same industry. But, in any case, costs are meaningful only when associated with a precisely defined "production program," which necessarily has a time dimension.

Once one is aware of the problem, Alchian's volume effects can be seen most places one looks.[10] A much-simplified version of auto body production

*International Encyclopedia of the Social Sciences,* Vol. 3 (Macmillan and Free Press 1969), pp. 404-414; McGee, *supra* n. 3, and McGee, "Economies of Size in Auto Body Manufacture," *Journal of Law & Economics,* 16 (October 1973), pp. 239-273; Walter Y. Oi, "The Neoclassical Foundations of Progress Functions," *Economic Journal,* 77 (September 1967), pp. 579-594. That Alchian's theory may be useful for a surprisingly wide variety of industries is suggested by Jack Hirshleifer, "The Firm's Cost Function: A Successful Reconstruction?" *The Journal of Business,* 35 (July 1962), pp. 235-255.

10. For example, consult Jack Hirshleifer, "The Firm's Cost Function: A Successful Reconstruction," *The Journal of Business,* 35 (July 1962), pp. 235-255.

will do for an example.[11] For a fixed production period, the total volume of any model varies directly and proportionally with production rate. For a five-year production period, and a rate of, say, 350 metal bodies per year, the cheapest way to do the job is to make the bodies by hand, using highly skilled men with hammers. For certain vehicle designs to be produced at higher rates and volumes, molded fiberglass bodies make sense. Alternatively, to produce metal bodies at still higher rates and volumes, soft dies of lead- or zinc-alloy and one or a few presses come into play. For intermediate rates and volumes, cast-iron dies and heavy press-lines supersede alternative techniques, though — given the rates and volumes wanted and costs and characteristics of available presses — each major die will spend only a short time mounted in a press: there will be considerable "cycling" of dies. For still higher rates and volumes, mechanical handling devices will substitute for labor in moving sheets and parts between presses, and each die stays in the press for a longer period. For extremely high rates and volumes — as for VW's Beetle — some dies will even be permanently mounted in more ideally matching presses, and expensive and highly specialized machines will be used in assembling the panels (as with VW's amazing roof-fitting-and-welding machine). The remarkable thing is that, as rates and volumes expand in this way, average production cost falls. The same phenomenon can be observed in *many* processes.

In some processes the appropriate shifts in technique — as rates and volumes change — are technologically even more dramatic and complete. A frequently encountered production "hierarchy" starts, at the low-rate-and-volume end, with the hand-filing of bars; it shifts, at higher rates and volumes, to forging and milling; then to investment casting; and ultimately to cold-or-hot forming. Another hierarchy runs from sand-casting to permanent molding to die-casting. Still another, from machining to drawing to casting, and finally to stamping, which — as we have seen — has its own subhierarchy.

Alchian's view of costs is very helpful in understanding a wide variety of processes and functions. It is not confined to manufacturing or other technical processes. Volume effects extend to management, procurement, contracting, selling, financing, researching, billing, and so on. Unfortunately, however, many economists seem to have been unaware of all this. Ignoring volume is a well-established tradition. Neoclassical economics makes little or no explicit mention of it and seems couched either in terms of rate of production alone, or in terms of unspecified mixtures of changes in both rate and the period of production.

Any serious study of costs in the real world simply must consider volume as well as rate of production and must try to keep them straight, which, judging from most studies I have seen, is not as easy as it sounds.

One must be very careful about what all this means. High-rate and high-volume techniques are often highly specialized and highly risky. There is nothing automatic about actually achieving the lower unit costs that such

11. John S. McGee, "Economies of Size in Auto Body Manufacture," *Journal of Law & Economics*, 16 (October 1973), 239-273.

techniques afford. It is necessary to plan significantly ahead (risking catastrophe if the plan is wrong), and to design and offer products that people will actually buy at the higher rate and volume for which production is planned. To prosper, the firm must do a good job of planning, designing, and financing; organizing and tooling appropriately for the rates and volumes actually achieved; controlling the production process; selling the products; and so on. There is no reason to believe that all firms will be equally good at everything that is involved.

## IV.   COST DIFFERENCES AMONGST FIRMS

Apart from data problems and measurement errors, costs differ amongst firms in a variety of ways and for a variety of reasons. First, suppose that two firms could manufacture *roughly* comparable products at identical costs for physically equal rates and volumes. Suppose that they both adopt practically identical production programs. This does not mean that they will actually incur equal unit costs; their *realized* output rates and volumes may differ. One of several possible reasons is that one of the firms sells more, because most consumers prefer the product it offers.

Second, suppose that two firms could in principle produce identical products at the same unit cost *if* they should choose identical production programs. Suppose, however, that they choose *different* production programs, because of different sales forecasts, for example. Depending upon the precise circumstances, both firms may end up with identical realized unit costs; or the first firm may have lower unit costs than the second; or the second may have lower unit costs than the first. Such differences arise even though both firms could, in principle, produce identical products equally cheaply. The rub is that they made significantly different choices. Some economists would say that firms are equally "efficient" if, in principle, they could all climb onto the same cost function. That is not enough. Actual results also crucially depend upon whether the firms in question were also equally efficient in making choices: choosing the right product designs and timing, the right sales forecasts, the right tooling, the right plant and firm sizes, and so on. Those who make better choices in these respects are more efficient, no matter what the putative cost curves for identical choices might look like.

Economists — including Scherer — have done a good deal of theorizing about whether there are economies of size because larger firms are better able to cope with risk. Although this is fine so far as it goes, it distracts us from another aspect of the risk problem, and it leads the unwary to improper tests of "riskiness." It is conceivable that a firm may try very hard to start life large, on the conviction that risk demands it. I say "try," because to get large, of course, it has somehow first to sell a lot of stuff that people want. On the other hand, and I think more typically, some firms start small, prosper, and grow large simply because over the years they have adjusted better to such risks as there are.

I have mentioned that low-cost mass-production techniques are very risky, because, among other reasons, they commonly involve long-term commitments to apparatus and organization that are highly specialized. If the plans prove to be wrong, highly specialized techniques are expensive to convert and very burdensome.

In the real world, then, how well a firm does is partly determined by the degree and kind of risk it faces, and partly by how well it adjusts to such risk as it faces. It is, to put it mildly, very difficult to separate these factors empirically. Some economists infer that some larger firm has not been exposed to much risk because its earnings have been relatively stable and high over time. That will not do. Such studies do not provide body-counts of those who failed, and it is impossible to count those who never even tried because they feared what faced them.

Furthermore, even if a firm has higher unit costs, it may nevertheless be *more* efficient. It can earn higher profits and serve consumers better, because, among other reasons, superior products fetch higher prices, and superior location is valuable in a world in which freight is not free. *Total* results are what count for consumers and sellers, not whether some engineer or economist postulates that costs would be equal for identical plans.

Third, some factors of production, some firms, and some people are simply more competent than others to do identical things; some are better at one thing and worse at another. Such differences are commonplace in business and, for example, amongst dancers, painters, lawyers, novelists, and bullfighters. Early in the history of economics they were also observed in agriculture.

Farms with lower costs do better, and may also be much bigger. One reason for such superiority is that not all farmers or farm managements are equally good, whether at hiring and using workers, guessing about future prices for various crops, deciding what and how much to plant, or reading weather signs. Still other reasons are that land itself differs in fertility, location, and the like.

Whereas most would agree that such cost differences *arise,* there is considerable confusion about whether and to what extent they will *persist.* Much depends upon what causes the difference; whether whatever causes it can be quickly and cheaply identified; and, then, upon how cheaply it can be bought and effectively transferred. Suppose that the superior performance of a specific farm is due to the skills and talents of the farm owner. If, in the large, such situations are not recognized (and not correctly appraised for as little as the difference between what these skills are worth and what must be paid to hire them), such a farmer stays where he is, makes money, and no change occurs.

The business of inquiring into just how well different farms are doing, discovering why, then appraising the precise worth of different peoples' talents, all costs something and is subject to error. Such costs reduce the amount that can profitably be offered to acquire the services of superior farmers. As a result, unless someone makes a mistake, such farmers cannot systematically be induced to move to other farms identical to their own. To make business sense, the necessary inquiry, appraisal, and other transactions costs must be taken out of the net contributions such farmers could make on other identical farms. That reduces feasible offers to less than they make by staying where they are. If such (inadequate) offers were nevertheless to be made, some economists might tell the talented farmers to incorporate them into their present cost curves, since they represent the alternative or "opportunity" cost of their resources. Others might urge that these amounts be counted as scarcity "rent" accruing to superior resources.

To anyone but an economist it is a matter of comparative indifference whether such farmers take the advice, since they will still earn just as much in total whether they call all or any part of it "profit," "wages," or "rent." If a farmer chooses to call such offers "costs," his cost curve will rise, though not by enough to wipe out all the "profits."

Another theoretic possibility is to have someone buy such a farm and retain the farmer by hiring him to work it; but this produces the same result. Unless his performance would actually improve as a hired hand (which raises some questions about why he has not hired-out already), a purchaser qua simple investor cannot pay the farmer as much as the discounted value of the "rents" he now earns, and he has that much already.

Under the circumstances, the only way to move such a farmer would be to find or create another different kind of farm on which his qualities would be so much more valuable as to exceed the transactions and other costs needed to discover and move him. Of course, in principle, the farmer would have liked to find such a farm himself, a process which would also cost something. If his costs of finding it are less than those of an independent enterpriser, there is no room for our talent broker.

Suppose, alternatively, that the superiority of a farm is attributable wholly to qualities of the land itself. Subject to the costs of identifying and precisely appraising such cases, and contracting for and effectuating new ownership, none, little, or much of these superiority "rents" may explicitly be incorporated into the cost functions. But, in the real world, it is hard to see why ownership would change unless there are different appraisals of the facts (including futurity), or unless other better factors could be found to operate on the superior land. Present owners now have more than the amount — net of such inquiry and transactions costs — that prospective owners could profitably offer, unless, for example, by bringing in other factors (more suitable organization, management, labor, etc.), they could increase the net product by more than the costs of setting them to work on the superior land.

Even such simple examples reflect that, in the real world, there are substantial costs of discovering cases of superiority, discerning and evaluating their cause, and arranging transfers of rights. The amount of these information and transactions costs will influence the precision with which bundles of factors are brought together, the identity of those who retain the fruits of unusual efficiency, and the precision with which even economists' (let alone accountants') "costs" come to capitalize the value of superior resources. *This is not a question of monopoly or "market failure." It is not temporary "disequilibrium." It is real-world equilibrium, given the costs of information, evaluation, and change.*

These examples also illuminate some other crucial matters. It is in the interests of consumers as well as factory owners that all participants in the economic process be given a great deal of freedom to better their own positions. It is clearly desirable to permit net reductions in the costs of bringing the appropriate bundles of production factors together in appropriate ways at appropriate times and places. Under freedom to contract, all concerned will be striving to reduce the costs and increase the precision of discovering and increasing efficiency, and acquiring rights to efficiency. Some people and organizations may be better at it than others. For this reason alone, consumers should be extremely suspicious of harsh laws penalizing mergers, large firms, and freely contracted changes in the organizational forms and other characteristics of firms.

Although the modern farm is not nearly so simple as economics textbooks make it seem, many manufacturing concerns are even more complex. It is also well known that some firms produce better results than others. Assume, contrary to fact, that we have good measures of the costs of several different firms. In such a case, theory and common sense suggest that it is in the interest of each firm to produce each output and product quality as efficiently as it can. But there is nothing to suggest that the best performance of different firms must be equally good.

Superiority can take several forms. So far as cost-superiority goes, some firms can produce more cheaply than their rivals for some ranges of output, but not for all. Some others may be able to produce more cheaply over all output ranges so far observed. Such partial or full cost-superiority can occur even when there are not economies of size in the conventional sense: unit costs of such firms may be lower whether the relevant cost functions are U-shaped, decreasing, or constant.

Another way in which a firm can be superior is in estimating or discovering what the so-called long-run cost curve is really like, whatever the engineers may be saying. One management rightly concludes that unit costs can be lowered drastically by producing much larger outputs. Another concludes, wrongly, that there is no such advantage. The performance of the first firm proves to be vastly superior. One reason for the success of Messrs. Rockefeller (oil), Carnegie (steel), and Ford (autos) seems to have been just that. They were also superior at estimating how demand was shifting through time, and in understanding how proper incentives lower costs.

Some firms are superior in offering products that consumers value more highly relative to what they cost to produce.

If it were obvious or cheap to discover what really causes superiority and how great it is, it would tend to disappear. Other firms would emulate the leader, if they could, or try to hire away some or all of the factors accounting for its success. The first course would close the gap by lowering the costs of the hitherto inferior firms; the second would raise the costs of the superior firms and/or lower those of the others, and raise the incomes of the factors on which differential efficiency depended.

As we have seen, life is not that simple, even in parables about farms. For there are substantail costs of inquiry, evaluation, contracting, and change.

And, in the case of mass-production manufacturing operations, things are more complicated by orders of magnitude.

In a sizable manufacturing concern there are a number of more or less specialized functional parts (general administration, research and development, product design, tool design, manufacturing, finance, marketing, and so on), all interdependent and each operating several or many teams. Consumers, and the markets in which their preferences are expressed, routinely evaluate the qualities of whatever the firm manages to produce, and the sum of these market evaluations appraises the performance of the whole concern taken together. But there is no such routine external assessment of which functional parts, which teams, and which team members are responsible for superiority, and in what degree. Indeed, the highest degree of practical efficiency does not require that any single person or small number of people even *within* the organization be able to make such detailed and precise assessments. Superior success and efficiency, in any useful real-world sense, demand only that whatever the parts, teams, and team members accomplish adds up to a better result than is provided by other organizations. If so, all is well.

But from the standpoint of talent brokers, other firms in the industry, or prospective entrants, the socially necessary costs of inquiry, evaluation, negotiation, contract, and transfer are formidable. Thus, in a complex firm, it is even more likely that much of the returns attributable to special qualities and talents of specific factors, and all or most of the greater returns from superior meshing of teams and functions, will remain with the superior firm in the form of "profits" and not be bid away. Part or most of this will probably be reflected in a high "going-concern" value not easily attributable to anything in the firm that can be transferred, certainly nothing that is transferable piecemeal.[12]

## V.  EMPIRICAL STUDIES

We come now to empirical studies that purport to reveal the relationship between firm size and efficiency. I will divide my discussion of them according to the basic methods they employ: (1) statistical cost studies; (2) engineering studies; (3) survivorship studies; and (4) profit studies. Each section deals briefly with the peculiar problems and findings involved.

### 1. Statistical Cost and Production Function Studies

Since the nation is rich in statistics and accounts, it no doubt seems reasonable to expect that questions about business size and cost, and a lot of other things, could readily be answered by direct statistical assault. There have been

12. This is the sort of analysis that underlies the brief remarks in McGee, *supra* n. 3, at 42. For a fuller analysis, see Harold Demsetz, "Industry Structure, Market Rivalry, and Public Policy, *Journal of Law & Economics,* 16 (April 1973), pp. 1-9; and Armen A. Alchian and Harold Demsetz, "Production, Information Costs, and Economic Organization," *American Economic Review,* 62 (December 1972), pp. 777-795.

hundreds of attempts to do so.[13] Unfortunately the problems they tackle are tougher than they look, and the data available are a good deal weaker. In my opinion, the general result is extremely disappointing. Many of these studies use accounting data that were prepared for routine business reporting. Accounting-cost studies are not likely to be highly relevant as guides to the present or future, and all suffer from arbitrary asset valuations and a host of other technical difficulties. Furthermore, quite different production programs (so far as different total volumes, product types, etc.) are often being compared.

Some statistical studies attempt to estimate the physical relationships between inputs and outputs, to establish whether there are constant or increasing "returns to scale." From such estimates, some have tried to infer what the resulting cost functions would probably look like.

A. A. Walters introduces his thorough — and pessimistic — review of the subject in these words:

> Production processes can be studied empirically in terms of either production functions or cost functions. . . . The central questions relating to technology are (1) whether production processes display decreasing, constant, or increasing returns to scale; (2) how technological progress affects the parameters of production processes; and (3) at what rate technological progress has occurred. Estimation and interpretation of the estimates is complicated by the fact that observations on inputs, outputs, and costs reflect not only the state of technology but also the economic decisions made by producers and factor suppliers. Assumptions regarding economic behavior and competition in input and output markets often play a crucial role in the statistical analyses, and it is not always easy to determine whether the results reveal the nature of technology or serve instead to test the validity of the economic assumptions.[14]

One technique employs monthly, quarterly, or annual accounting data for one firm or a group of firms, and notes how costs vary with size as time passes. Whereas many such studies generate an estimated marginal cost that is declining or constant over the output ranges studied,

> [t]he main difficulty with this type of study is that it samples a dynamic adjustment process — a mixture of factor price movements, technological changes, and exogenous shocks. One cannot be sure that one has identified the static production function or cost function.[15]

13. See, for example, the bibliographies shown in A. A. Walters, "Production and Cost Functions: An Econometric Survey," *Econometrica*, 31 (January-April 1963), pp. 1-66; A. A. Walters, "Production and Cost Analysis," *International Encyclopedia of the Social Sciences*, Vol. 12 (Macmillan and Free Press 1968), pp. 519-523; A. A. Walters, *An Introduction to Econometrics* (Norton and Wiley & Sons 1970); and J. Johnston, *Statistical Cost Analysis* (McGraw-Hill 1960).

14. A. A. Walters, "Production and Cost Analysis," *International Encyclopedia of the Social Sciences*, Vol. 12 (Macmillan and Free Press 1968), p. 519.

15. *Id.* at 521.

Cross-section estimation is still another technique. It compares cost and size of a number of *different* firms in, say, a given year. The results are sometimes interpreted as a "long-run" relationship, which they most assuredly are not. According to Walters:

> The main difficulty with cross-section analysis . . . is that in a competitive market there is no separate and quantitatively different stimulus for each firm. . . . [Any] observed differences in factor inputs are caused by differences in production functions (or accidents) and the observations do not identify a *particular* production function. Similarly, the cost function of a perfectly competitive cross section shows that average costs, as measured by price, are constant over the sample. . . . Constant cost curves in cross sections may be evidence of competition rather than of constant returns to scale.[16]

There are still other troubles. Using the recorded costs of two or more different firms is a treacherous game, even if they happen to be on — or are adjusting from different points on — the same long-run cost curve. Partly, this is a matter of letting enough time run (which may also get us into trouble: the technologies themselves may change); partly, a matter of confusing the results of mistakes or "disequilibrium" with the long-run cost differences.

As far as I can see, the statistical inferences can be wrong in all kinds of ways: one might infer that there are constant long-run costs when they are really rising or declining; falling long-run costs when, in fact, they are constant or rising. In addition, as Milton Friedman long ago pointed out, cross-section cost studies often embody the regression fallacy; they are more likely to tell us something about managerial mistakes and the precision with which accountants and capital markets reevaluate assets, than about long-run cost functions.[17]

Though they are not worth much, such studies have often shown average costs declining rapidly with increased output, starting from small outputs, and more or less constant for large firms: there is no evidence that large firms suffer high costs.[18] Walters concludes that, if they show anything, findings of that type are consistent with the hypothesis that small firms produce specialized products at high prices; whereas, as a group, medium-sized and large firms produce similar products at about the same (lower) price.[19]

Statistical studies of some industries — railways, pipelines, power generation, banking, and so on — are consistent with the hypothesis of economies of size; but, like the other studies, they have their problems.[20]

In the case of estimates of production functions — rather than cost curves —

16. *Ibid.*

17. Milton Friedman, "Comment," in George J. Stigler, ed., *Business Concentration and Price Policy* (Princeton, National Bureau of Economic Research 1955), pp. 230-238.

18. Walters, *supra* n. 14, at 521.

19. *Id.* at 521-522.

20. *Id.* at 522. See also Benston, *infra* n. 24, who had added another to the list of industries showing "economies of scale."

other serious objections apply. Among other things, it is questionable whether the findings are evidence of constant returns to scale of a "representative" production function, or evidence of the workings of the marginal productivity law or some such principle of factor compensation.[21]

There are also lots of interindustry cross-section studies that purport to measure some kind of production function. If anything, these studies show how input and output relationships vary with the size of industries, not firms. They shed no light on economies of scale for a firm.[22]

Walters also has an opinion about statistical measures of technological progress. As he sees it, the methodology applied in them has tended to divert our attention away from such economies of scale as there are.

> This outcome is partly due to labeling as "technical progress" the increase in output which one cannot statistically attribute to other causes. When the basic model has taken into account returns to scale, it seems that a substantial fraction of the progress is in fact due to economies of scale.[23]

Where does all of this leave us? Pretty much where I started. When I began to study economics, I had high hopes that statistical analysis would solve these and other mysteries. Such a hope was naive then; it is naive now. Apart from expense, there are intractable problems involving accounting data; the determination and allocation of administration, planning, and other crucial costs to the outputs being measured; the interdependence of costs from one production period with those of others; and so on. All in all, such studies are at least as likely to mislead as to inform. At best, they would inform only about the irrelevant past.[24] Furthermore, as I shall argue later on, costs are only part of the story. Finally, there are other ways.[25]

### 2. "Engineering" Studies

As an alternative to digging into accounting records, a number of economists have attempted to make, or — more often — have asked others to make,

21. Walters, *supra* n. 14, at 522.

22. *Ibid.*

23. *Id.* at 522-523.

24. For a recent attempt — on a relatively simple industry having relatively "clean" and standardized data and fairly homogeneous outputs — see George J. Benston, "Savings Banking and the Public Interest," *Journal of Money, Credit, and Banking*, 4 (February 1972), pp. 133-266; and G. J. Benston, "Economies of Scale of Financial Institutions," *Journal of Money, Credit, and Banking*, 4 (May 1972), pp. 312-341.

See also J. Johnston, *Statistical Cost Analysis* (McGraw-Hill 1960), for a fuller treatment of problems and methodology, and a canvass of findings.

25. Walters notes, "One real test of economies of scale is, of course, the historical experience of industries — to see whether small firms either grow or go bankrupt, or whether the large firm is just a transitory phenomenon; but this research is outside the scope of production function analysis." A. A. Walters, *An Introduction to Econometrics* (Wiley & Sons 1970), p. 338. So far at least as this aside, Walters can be put into the "survivorship" group.

engineering cost estimates for new and "most efficient" plants or processes. This approach has advantages and disadvantages.

If the cost estimates arrived at were forward-looking, which they seldom really are, on that count they would appear to be closer to economists' notions about long-run or "planning" cost curves. Such estimates also can avoid some of the pitfalls of accounting data, which embody differing and arbitrary asset evaluation procedures. And, depending upon the knowledge, skill, and imagination of the economists and engineers involved, the pure production aspects of the problem can be made to include any production dimensions thought to be relevant; for example, the number and detailed specifications of models, and the precise rates and volumes to be produced.

Unfortunately, however, as Stigler, Walters, and others have pointed out, there are also crucial disadvantages. For one thing, there really is no way to include managerial and entrepreneurial qualities and capacity in such estimates. And, as we have seen, firm teams differ in the real world. Some may be absolutely better at everything they do than are others; some may be better in some respects, worse in others. Real-world *choices* of "plants" and "processes" reflect these differences; engineering estimates cannot. Implicitly, then, some specific present (or some speculative "average" or "ideal") production management, organization, and control is partly embodied in the estimates; then, some unspecified overall management is imagined to choose and use the production processes on which the estimated costs were based.

Engineering data and estimates can cover only technical processes, which leaves out much of the real problem: recruitment, evaluation, and promotion; product design; research; planning; administration; cost and quality control; finance; marketing, and so on. As Stigler puts it, "much of the problem is solved only in the unhappy sense of being delegated to a technologist." [26] There are any number of variables, estimates of and decisions with respect to which are management-team and not engineering matters, including location, factor costs and factor cost changes, fluctuations in demand and changes in what is being demanded — which influence the judgment of how long models are to be produced, in what total volumes, and precisely how tooling and the like can best be accommodated to the runs.

Furthermore, as I myself have observed, engineers differ in experience, flexibility, and vision. For these and other reasons, so will their estimates. I have also observed that engineers, like most of us, understand and estimate best when they deal with hypothetical programs very close to their recent experience. Most of them break down utterly when they are asked, but not paid very well to answer, questions about a "plant" whose production rate and volume will be, say, twice as large as anything they have personally seen.

I have spent a fair amount of time with industrial engineers, and greatly respect good ones. Nevertheless, most engineers are not in the business of teaching economists the facts of life. Some have been known to give poor answers to poor questions, especially when they are not being paid very well either to answer, demolish, or reconstruct the questions. Some engineers, as

26. George J. Stigler, *The Organization of Industry* (R. D. Irwin 1968), p. 71.

well as some economists, realize that "cost" can only be associated sensibly with a *definite output program* which spells out the specifications of each product, the number of different products, outputs per time period, the total period of production and total model output, and so on.

Other difficulties face anyone who asks (or answers) questions about "costs" and "plant size." For example, there is the question of what the "product" really is, and it applies both to firms and the industry as a whole. This problem is solved by definition in the usual models of perfect or atomistic competition: each firm sells only one product, and all firms make precisely the same product, for which there is a given and fixed total industry demand. But price theory and governmental policies are not always concerned with atomistic industries, and much of manufacturing is undertaken by large, multi-product firms, no two of which sell identical lines of products. To *which* products, and to *which* product mixes do the relevant "costs" then refer?

It appears that we have a variety of choices and a broad field for misunderstanding both the questions and the answers. In principle we could standardize output characteristics and mixes, and enquire of our engineer friends how the average cost of producing *that* mix of products would differ for different output rates and total volumes. We could, for example, prepare detailed specifications for a hypothetical family of automobiles (four-door sedans, two-door sedans, four- and two-door hardtops, convertibles, station wagons, etc.) to be produced in certain proportions. We could then enquire how average production costs of such a package would differ for widely different total output rates and volumes.

Second, we could enquire of each firm how average production costs would differ if it produced the same *proportions* of whatever products it *now* makes, but produced widely different *total* amounts of that same mix. Third, we could enquire about the costs of producing a *single* product (say, a red VW Beetle with certain standard equipment and no options) at a wide variety of rates and total volumes.

Although there are doubtless many other approaches, these are enough to indicate that — in terms of product specification alone — there are various ways to explore relationships between "size" and "cost." What is worse is that they all ask fundamentally different questions. Each answer might conceivably be useful for something; but they are very different.

In addition to the problem of defining the relevant *product,* is that of measuring *output* and, therefore, the "size" of plant or firm. I have already discussed that issue in connection with Alchian's volume-effect, and will have more to say about it later.

In addition to the difficulties of defining "product" and "size" there are problems with "plants." I have indicated that economists are still unclear about just what a "firm" is. Unfortunately, there is also a good deal of confusion about what a "plant" is. The simplest, but still dominant, economic theories deal with imaginary "firms" that operate one "plant," so that "the plant" is the sum total of bricks, machinery, and such that the firm owns. Commodity and industry statistics compiled by the Census Bureau are based on reports from individual "establishments," each of which is generally a physical facility that performs technologically distinct operations at one specific geographic location. Although terminology in industry varies, it is common to refer to separate buildings or processes as "plants" no matter how interdependent, specialized, or close they may be. A foundry may be called "Plant No. 1," while thirty feet away, under a separate roof but connected by conveyor, sits "Plant No. 2," in which parts cast in the first building are machined and assembled. Similarly, various establishments performing broadly similar technical functions may be called different "plants" even though the components or finished products they make are not interchangeable; that is, even though the establishments are not duplicates. For example, in 1972, a number of automobile producers each had several stamping establishments. In each case, such establishments were specialized parts of a single articulated plant-complex and were not duplicates. As far as I could find out, no producer had more than one stamping "plant" in an economically meaningful sense. The same thing occurs for many processes and products.

These ambiguities in concept and language cause real trouble for researchers who try to cover a lot of ground too fast. In much of manufacturing, even engineers of relatively high rank are typically attached to, or know most about, one establishment. No matter how good they are, in the time they have to give, engineers are also often reluctant to answer questions that are *not* asked, and reluctant to try to lay out the whole realistic picture with all of its complications. If economists ask them about "plants" in a one-week (or one-day) interview, some very competent engineers I know can and will give a simplified picture of what goes on in "Plant No. 2," and speculate superficially about what might happen if it grew. But few engineers will be able and willing to explain how "Plant No. 2" fits in with all the others, or what is likely to happen to specialization and costs if still another, and another, "plant" were added on to those already in the complex. That is something else.

Although there are hundreds of engineering studies of specific tools and processes, there is space here briefly to examine only four: those of Haldi and Whitcomb; Bain; Pratten; and Scherer.[27]

Haldi and Whitcomb attack the problem by explicitly trying to exclude everything but *production* costs and economies. They use two basic sources of data. First, they derived estimated relationships between costs and output capability from 687 observations of catalog purchase prices for various kinds

27. John Haldi and David Whitcomb, "Economies of Scale in Industrial Plants," *Journal of Political Economy*, 75 (August 1967) (Part I), pp. 373-385; Joe S. Bain, "Economies of Scale, Concentration and the Condition of Entry in Twenty Manufacturing Industries," *American Economic Review*, 44 (1954), pp. 15-39, reprinted in R. B. Heflebower and G. W. Stocking, eds., *Readings in Industrial Organization and Public Policy* (R. D. Irwin 1958), pp. 46-68; J. S. Bain, *Barriers to New Competition* (Harvard Univ. Press 1956); C. F. Pratten, *Economies of Scale in Manufacturing Industry* (Cambridge Univ. Press 1971); F. M. Scherer, "Economies of Scale and Industrial Concentration," in this volume.

of new "basic industrial equipment." Second, using 221 so-called "long-run cost curves" from the engineering literature, they derived distributions of the apparent scale coefficient for "plants" in a variety of industries.

For industrial equipment, they conclude, productive capacity rises much faster than price: a machine that costs twice as much will typically produce much more than twice as much. Their "plant" data yielded similar results. As they saw it,

> in many basic industries, such as petroleum refining, primary metals, and electric power, economies of scale are found up to very large plant sizes (often the largest built or contemplated). These economies occur mostly in the initial investment cost and in operating labor cost, with no significant economies observed in raw material cost. Scale economies can also result from learning curve effects, spreading of set-up costs, and certain stochastic processes associated with inventories. . . . Evidence that there are economies of scale in plant production cost is not inconsistent with the observation that in the United States most industries have at least several plants, often differing in size. This is explained both by historical development and by the other elements of total cost which we have excluded. Average transportation costs rises with the output of a single plant, since average distance to market rises, ceteris paribus. Furthermore product differentiation may place an ultimate demand constraint on expansion, with market diseconomies appearing as that constraint is approached.[28]

For several reasons, I will not spend much time on Bain. For one thing, apart from differences in the specific industries sampled, later studies do virtually everything that Bain did, and do much of it better, or at least more understandably. Because they also share certain deficiencies with Bain's work, it will save time to consider those together at a later point. Furthermore, Bain's estimates apply to 1950-1952, which means that however good they may have been when fresh, they are certainly quite stale, and probably downright poisonous for 1974 consumption. My brief remarks refer to Bain's more accessible reprinted article rather than to his book. For eight out of twenty-one industry categories (for this purpose he split meat products into two parts), Bain offered no estimates of multiplant economies at all. For six, he found that multiplant economies reduced "total costs" by amounts ranging from "small" or "slight" to 5 percent; for seven there were no reported multiplant economies at all.

What did Bain conclude that he had found?

> [T]he following popular horseback observations are apparently not true: that economies of scale of plant are never or almost never important in encouraging oligopoly or impeding entry, and that such economies always or almost always are important in these ways. The picture is not extreme in either direction and not simple. . . .
> The economies of large multiplant firms are left in doubt by this investigation.[29]

28. John Haldi and David Whitcomb, "Economies of Scale in Industrial Plants," *Journal of Political Economy*, 75 (August 1967) (Part I), p. 373.

29. J. S. Bain, "Economies of Scale, Concentration, and the Condition of Entry in Twenty Manufacturing Industries," reprinted in R. B. Heflebower and G. W. Stock-

Pratten collected various kinds of estimates for some 25 U.K. industries. His basic sources were interviews with and estimates made by engineers, staff, and management in the industries analyzed. As he notes, the methodology and measurement methods differed amongst industries, e.g., in whether all-new or vintage plants were involved, and with respect to procedures used to estimate capital costs. He inquired more deeply than Bain did into nontechnical firm functions, which would not be hard. He also at least acknowledges the importance of length of run, product line, and volume.

Although he systematically discusses the problem, in only a few cases does he actually present any quantitative information about economies of multiplant operation or present estimates for efficient *firm* sizes.

Naturally enough, Pratten tried to compare his findings with Bain's. This could be done only in the case of six industries, and there were complications even then. Pratten claims to have "placed more emphasis on measuring the economies of scale for [specific] products," which would be a strength; and in three of the six cases (shoes, soap and detergents, motor vehicles) "comparisons are difficult because of differences in the dimension of scale to which the estimates relate," which is also a symptom of Pratten's superiority: it has never been clear to me *what* dimensions Bain used. But for steel and cement, even Pratten's MES, which does not exhaust all economies, is more than three times as large as Bain's "most efficient size," and Pratten's estimate for oil is also higher.[30]

Pratten's emphasis is basically on plant sources of economies, with some qualitative judgments about large firm economies tacked on. I have noted elsewhere[31] that Pratten underestimated even the purely technical size economies in auto manufacture, although his estimates are much larger than others currently fashionable amongst academics. People who really know something about the other industries would do well to examine closely the estimates he gives for them. Whereas Bain claims to have measured the "most efficient size" of plant, Pratten claims to have measured the "minimum efficient scale," which is not what it sounds like. In Pratten's words, "In many industries some economies of scale would be expected for plants larger than those we have defined as the MES . . ."[32]

He also concluded that economies of scale are increasing over time and that "the achievement of the maximum economies of scale is not, on our evidence, compatible with the existence of competition of many firms for a large number of products within the U.K."[33] Pratten's estimates are for the

ing, eds., *Readings in Industrial Organization and Public Policy* (R. D. Irwin 1958), p. 68.

30. I am not sure whether, in making these comparisons, Pratten used his original or amended — and much increased — estimates for cement and oil.

31. John S. McGee, "Economies of Size in Auto Body Manufacture," *Journal of Law & Economics,* 16 (October 1973), pp. 239-273.

32. C. F. Pratten, *Economies of Scale in Manufacturing Industry* (Cambridge Univ. Press 1971), p. 304.

33. *Id.* at 313.

United Kingdom, and as Scherer shows, looks rather different if they are casually dropped into markets as large as those in the United States. Even if I believed in what Pratten did, I would be reluctant to import and consume his findings without a more thorough repackaging. Anyone attempting that job should note that in at least two cases (oil and cement), Pratten's addenda and revisions substantially increase the "efficient" sizes shown in his basic tables.

In summary, let Pratten speak for himself:

> There has been a theme underlying some of the past work dealing with economies of scale, that there is a general, or typical, shape for the long run average cost curve, or, as we have called it, the scale curve. Throughout this paper we have emphasized the diversity of the firms operating within industries, and the differences between industries. The effects of scale vary for each type of plant over different ranges of scale, for plants and firms in different industries, and for firms following strategies within an industry. Nevertheless our estimates show that there are substantial technical economies of scale for the production of many products. Also, where two firms have different sales of a similar range of products, the firm with the larger sales can achieve economies by spreading certain marketing and management costs, and in some cases by spreading expenditure on research. Although there must be qualifications to any conclusions, we would emphasize the sources of economies of scale which generally apply to producing a constant range of products on a large scale.[34]

This brings us to the paper Scherer prepared for this Conference. It is apparently related to a larger unpublished work, which I have not seen. Methodologically, Scherer's paper is in the Bain-Pratten tradition.

*Unlike* Bain, Scherer eschews outbound freights as part of his "costs" since there *is* no unique "efficient" size if they are left in. He does seek, somehow, to include "materials" costs, which seems to me to cause comparable ambiguity: the quality and prices of water supplies, rights to use air, land, labor, and of other important "materials" also vary geographically in enormously complicated ways. That may be a minor trouble as compared with some of the others.

As we have seen, most economics textbooks still picture plant and firm size in terms of output *rates* per unit time. "Market share" expresses plant (or firm) output *rate* per time period as a fraction of the total *rate* at which such stuff is demanded. As I see it, the quantity demanded in a market in each time period, and the total number of such periods, result from the "consumption programs" of all relevant buyers. These consumption programs are analogous to Alchian's production programs, among other ways because they incorporate various volume effects and operate through time. So far as I know, no published work systematizes this notion of consumption programs and derives its implications. No wonder: it is a very tough problem. Although this is not the place to solve it, it *is* an appropriate place to recognize it.

The main point is simple. Since all sorts of numbers can be used to derive ratios, it is obvious that we can divide someone's output rate by the rate at

34. *Id.* at 302.

which total market quantities are demanded. But the trouble is that both the production rate and sales rate — and therefore, the ratio — observed at any point in time are determined by cost and demand relations that have *volume* and time dimensions, among others.

Like Pratten, Scherer recognizes at least some forms of Alchian's cost-reducing volume effects on the production side, which is all to the good.[35] Although he *recognizes* some of such effects, I am not convinced that he successfully reconciles them with his estimates of the so-called minimum optimal size ("MOS") of plants. Indeed, he tells us in a footnote, he has tried hard to ex-clude these volume effects from his "MOS" estimates. I don't think he should have tried.

In my opinion, there is really only one way to do what he says he tried to do. If, in a particular case, Alchain's volume effects are to be "removed" from a cost curve, volume must be held constant at some specified level as we move along the curve. If, for example, we double the *rate* of output, the period of production must be halved. A cost curve derived in this way would incorporate pure *rate* effects for a given, fixed volume. It would also exag-gerate how high the relevant costs actually are, and how quickly they turn up, as compared with permitting a firm to adjust both rate and volume — as the real world does. In principle, there will be a whole family of such cost curves, each one defined for a different volume. Different firms have different de-grees of success in designing their products, services, and terms, all of which means that different firms face different cost curves of this kind. Even if we should want one of these cost curves, which one is it? Alternatively, which, if any, have Scherer's engineers served up to us?

One alternative is to define cost curves so that, along any such curve, rate and volume are varying proportionally. For example, one could hold the period of production constant at some specified level, and ask the engineers to guess what the costs would be at various rates (and corresponding vol-umes). By specifying some period of production, we have put a different artifi-cial constraint on the problem; but at least we know what we have got.[36] Nevertheless, there is no reason to believe that the relevant period of produc-tion will be the same for all firms. Ford's Model T sold for eighteen and a half years; VW's Beetle for more than twenty-six. If we judge by volume as well as period of production, no one else has come close. In the real world, one crucial determinant of success is how well the different firms' choices of prod-ucts, rates, periods of production, and volumes pan out when they are judged by consumers. One of the important choices a firm can make is the period of production.

I do not think Scherer should have tried to exclude these volume effects, though (except for paints and batteries) he thinks he largely succeeded in

35. Be careful: volume is not really integrated into Scherer's analysis; he intro-duces it in a "preparatory digression." When Scherer uses the word "volume" in tables or texts, he usually really means *rate* of output. He sometimes refers to Al-chian's volume in terms of "length of run."

36. This formulation underlies the costs shown in McGee, *supra* n. 3, at 28.

doing so. It is from such a formulation that he derives his estimates of "MOS."

Scherer agrees that, in the real world, volume significantly influences unit cost. I applaud Scherer both for observing the phenomenon and for explicitly recognizing its importance. I am considerably less enthusiastic about what he does with it. I think that some of his problems stem from the way he implicitly defines "plants." I discussed this definitional issue in detail, above.

According to Scherer, for some unspecified mix of products, "MOS" is a size of "plant" for which average production cost is minimized. "MOS" is, thus, some sort of "overall size" that exhausts what he calls "plant-specific" economies. But he concedes that, in at least seven of the twelve industries he studied, such a size does *not* exhaust something called "product-specific" economies. Indeed, in such cases, these economies seem to be larger than the other kinds of economies that determine the "MOS" itself. No matter how many times I look at it, I do not see how a "size" that does not exhaust major economies can be called a least-cost size. He says that the economies he excludes are attributable to "setup" costs and to learning, and he uses bearings production to illustrate them. In my opinion, a great deal more than setup costs and learning is involved. What is involved is that high-volume techniques are systematically different from low-volume techniques, as I explained earlier.

The economics of multiple products, which applies to the "width" of a product line, is complicated. Often, and perhaps always, variety costs something. For several processes that I have studied carefully, a widened product line *increases* the "overall" size at which unit production cost would be lowest. For many production processes, the largest "plants" yet seen do not exhaust even the purely technical economies available. Partly this is a matter of balancing tools and plant in general. Partly it is because several products share management, or share one or more tools and processes that must be compromised for the smaller outputs. Many important production and assembly lines deal with two or more heterogeneous products. And the use of multiple-purpose tools, which must be reset as different products are run, is very common. For much larger outputs, specialized tools could be used.

Although there are obvious measurement problems involved, we can find simple cases in which, for an individual firm, the unit cost for a varied product line exceeds that of a line consisting of any one of those products put out at crudely comparable "overall" rates and volumes. This does *not* mean that a given degree of product variety could be produced more cheaply by two or more utterly *independent* managerial-production teams. There are good reasons why a single firm produces two or more different products. One reason is that the products are favorably related, either on the cost or demand side. Under good management, and with properly designed products and tools, an auto body plant complex, for example, can significantly share management, designs, tools, and parts to produce a whole family of related cars. And it does this more cheaply than several independent firms could accomplish the same result. I do not see that Scherer has taken this common occurrence into account.

What Scherer does with his "product-specific" economies seems peculiar to me. For he says that such economies, as large as they are, would not matter if only the world were completely different. This seems to be an example of what Demsetz calls the "nirvana" fallacy.[37] In this connection, what disturbs Scherer about the world he sees is that markets have "broken down." By this he does not mean that there are no markets, or that there are no transactions in such markets as there are, or that the population is primarily engaged in stealing one another's rags. He means, rather, that some markets are not perfectly or even atomistically competitive, which is not surprising given his estimates; that markets are not in full long-run equilibrium at all times; that transport is not free; that there are uncertainties and risks; that all industrial products are not homogeneous; and that there are costs of information, buying, selling, and contracting. No doubt. But if this be market failure, some sort of market failure accounts for the very existence of firms in the first place. It is equally useful to say that markets exist whenever firms "break down." [38]

Scherer's work has other virtues. He recognizes that there is a lot more to manufacturing concerns than purely technological functions. To explore what size has to do with the efficiency with which the various functions are performed, engineers aren't much help. Scherer looks for what he calls multiplant economies, and, in a variety of sources, finds some. He has seen, heard, or read about economies in sales promotion, raising capital, purchasing, investing in plant, selling, inventing and innovating. He is suspicious of them all. He also does not admire some of, or at least some degrees of, such economies, for various reasons. They include, again, that in the real world it costs something to find buyers and sellers, and to make and enforce deals; and that atomistic competition is not ubiquitous. That is, real-world markets do not operate "perfectly" and at zero cost. In the real world, of course, nothing does. He seems also to object that some of these economies look as though they may favor large, succesful and prosperous firms.

I have elsewhere[39] analyzed some theories and facts about economies in raising capital, inventing and innovating, and advertising. Others at this Conference will also explore some of these matters in detail. Even so, in the light of Scherer's treatment, I must add some brief notes.

Although Scherer finds substantial size economies in raising capital, he doubts whether this is really a good thing. This attitude points up a profound difference between Scherer and me. It is also the basis of difference between the Soviet faith that only "nuts and bolts" matter, and a free market's emphasis upon individuals' preferences. I infer from Scherer's paper and his textbook that he sees little or no merit in allowing investors to express a

---

37. "In practice, those who adopt the Nirvana approach seek to discover discrepancies between the ideal and the real and if discrepancies are found, they deduce that the real is inefficient." Harold Demsetz, "Information and Efficiency: Another Viewpoint," *Journal of Law & Economics*, 12 (April 1969), p. 1.

38. Coase, *supra* n. 4.

39. McGee, *supra* n. 3.

preference for lower risk.[40] According to my economics, a state of mental anguish is not a preferred position, and reducing anguish is as real and respectable an economic good as is production of pig iron or ball bearings. Furthermore, capital is also a resource, and the total amount of it generated, as well as its allocation, are surely not independent of the risks and terms to which it will be exposed. Taken to its logical conclusion, Scherer's attitude would compel people to lend their own money at rates lower than they think risk demands, and to lend to people whom they do not trust. In my opinion, this is not only tyranny; it is a tyranny that will distort the generation and allocation of capital as well.

There is considerable evidence that invention and innovation have been important to us all. They have significantly changed our personal lives; they have also changed the size of firms and influenced the existence and structure of whole industries. Over the years, many economists have also tried to measure a quite different thing: how invention and innovation are statistically related to the size of firms. Elsewhere, I have chronicled the ambiguities and failures of this work,[41] and Professor Markham is to bring us up to date. I will, however, add a few remarks in the light of Scherer's paper. Since it is not inherently desirable simply to maximize the number of people hired to invent or innovate, we should be wary of those who — like Scherer — measure *results* in terms of the quantities of *inputs* engaged. We are interested in results. But how to measure them? Individual economists often either count patents or subjectively rank or grade inventions and innovations, much like an academic grading term papers. Not all inventions and innovations are alike, and different subjective judgments even of the same ones also differ. That is not a highly satisfactory way to evaluate. Of course the capital and products markets do make daily evaluations, which is another story to be picked up later.

This brings us to managerial efficiency, another important topic to which engineering studies do not contribute. Scherer candidly admits that he has no evidence about the relationship between management quality and the size of firms. I would have been happier if he had left it at that. Instead, he offers "subjective impressions" based on interviews. Scherer says that the managers of big and little firms seemed equally dynamic, intelligent, aware, and skillful. Although I am sympathetic, I am not impressed. Babe Ruth didn't look like much to me until he hit the ball. The great Jim Brown looked thoroughly moribund between plays. Off the field, the Gas House Gang looked to me a good deal like they sound, and Jim Dickey doesn't look or talk much like a poet. If anything, this proves only that appearances are deceiving, and that Scherer and I are better off as economists than we would be as talent brokers, executives, and recruiters. Professionals are to be judged by how well they do what

---

40. "Obviously, large firms offer something extra — greater security — in obtaining capital at lower costs from investors. Still the real resource savings are elusive; at best, investors save some subjective anguish by knowing their capital is in steady, time-tested hands." F. M. Scherer, *Industrial Market Structure and Economic Performance* (Rand McNally 1970), pp. 100-101.

41. McGee, *supra* n. 3, ch. 7.

they are paid to do, not by how impressive they seem in interviews with economists and engineers. God help economists if executives are permitted to evaluate *us* in interviews.

In the Bain-Pratten tradition, Scherer somehow combines his engineering estimates with his nonengineering judgments to arrive at a notion of the minimum firm sizes required to minimize overall unit cost. Atomism is not implied. But, like Bain, Scherer concludes that, in the twelve industries he sampled, actual concentration was much higher than is "warranted" or can be "justified" by what he concluded were the overall economies of size.

On scientific principle, rather than sentiment, I would prefer him to say "explained" rather than "warranted" or "justified." For this is where such studies really lead us: using engineers' estimates with respect to "plants," whose output and size are curiously defined, they arrive at "plant" sizes claimed to be lowest cost, although they do not exhaust much or even most of the production cost-savings available. They then tack on findings with respect to capital-raising and some other essential functions. But, according to Scherer, we have no evidence about managerial quality. As I showed, differences in the quality of managerial choices and decisions are compatible with high concentration, even in the complete absence of economies of size in the traditional sense. Firms can grow big *because* they are efficient; that is different from cases in which a firm must be big before it can be efficient. With evidence of managerial quality lacking or unpalatable to them, and using doubtful evidence about other things, such studies attempt to explain on paper how *big* firms or "plants" would have to be in order to be "efficient." When they find that leading firms or plants are, in fact, much bigger than what they read in their papers, they conclude that the difference is "unwarranted." That is serious methodological bias. The plain fact is that, with their methods and opinions, they have simply failed to *explain* the difference. "Unwarranted" and such terms are really just misleading names for our own ignorance.

Let's sum up. First, none of these studies has satisfactorily measured "minimum optimal size" even in the very limited sense in which the authors set out to do it. But even if the engineering parts of these studies had been done impeccably, they would still be engineering studies and nothing more. Second, as I shall show later, no study of "costs," no matter how well done, is sufficient for policy or normative judgments about the "proper" size of firms. Third, Pratten and Scherer both claim that "efficient" size, as they perceive and measure it, has generally and dramatically increased over time. If nothing else, this suggests that estimates delivered to us this year are likely to be wrong for the next. And, it appears, we shall never catch up. Scherer's recipes, for consumption in 1974 and after, were designed for 1965 kitchens and ingredients. It is understandable that engineers and economists are reluctant to print arithmetic that is based on *future* technology, demands, and factor costs — for that treads on what Scherer calls terra incognita. But those are precisely the sorts of judgments that businessmen are really making, and on which their survival and success depend. It is such past business judgments that today's and tomorrow's markets evaluate.

Besides keeping economists and engineers in cakes and ale, other good has come out of the Bain tradition. If nothing else, it shows that atomism is not a practical alternative in much of manufacturing. That may be some help the next time someone suggests making steel in the backyard or turning everything back to handicraft industry. It may also help the next time someone tries to offer perfect competition as a structural benchmark against which reality is unfavorably to be compared.

### 3. The "Survivorship" Technique

In an ingenious and influential 1958 paper, George J. Stigler succinctly shows the irrelevancy of making, and the difficulties of interpreting, statistical cost and engineering studies as they relate to economies of size.[42] He also develops and uses a quite different technique.

> The survivor technique proceeds to solve the problem of determining the optimum size as follows: Classify the firms in an industry by size, and calculate the share of industry output coming from each class over time. If the share of a given class falls, it is relatively inefficient, and in general is more inefficient the more rapidly the share falls.
>
> An efficient size of firm, on this argument, is one that meets any and all problems the entrepreneur actually faces: strained labor relations, rapid innovation, government regulation, unstable foreign markets, and what not. This is, of course, the decisive meaning of efficiency from the viewpoint of the enterprise. Of course, social efficiency may be a very different thing: the most efficient firm size may arise from possession of monopoly power, undesirable labor practices, discriminatory legislation, etc. The survivor technique is not directly applicable to the determination of the socially optimum size of enterprise, and we do not enter into this question. The socially optimum firm is fundamentally an ethical concept, and we question neither its importance nor its elusiveness.[43]

Stigler recognized that "various firms employ different kinds or qualities of resources," as a result of which "there will tend to develop a frequency distribution of optimum firm sizes." [44] By applying the technique to the steel and auto industries, Stigler concludes that long-run average cost in steel apparently declined for firm sizes up to about 5 percent of total industry capacity, was flat up to about 25 percent, then rose (because of the declining *share* of U.S. steel). In autos, apart from periods of price controls, long-run average cost declined over the whole range of firm sizes.[45]

---

42. Among other difficulties with those approaches, "it is almost as if one were trying to measure the nutritive values of goods without knowing whether the consumers who ate them continue to live." G. J. Stigler, "The Economies of Scale," *Journal of Law & Economics,* 1 (October 1958), p. 54, reprinted, with valuable addenda, as Chapter 7 in Stigler, *The Organization of Industry, supra* n. 26.

43. Stigler, *supra* n. 26, at 73.

44. *Id.* at 74.

45. Others have applied Stigler's techniques to a variety of industries. See, for example, T. R. Saving, "Estimation of Optimum Size of Plant by the Survivor Technique," *Quarterly Journal of Economics,* 75 (November 1961), pp. 569-607; L. W. Weiss, "The Survival Technique and the Extent of Suboptimal Capacity," *Journal of Political Economy,* 72 (June 1964), pp. 246-261; *id.,* 73 (June 1965), pp. 300-301.

Using somewhat different measures of optimum size, Stigler concludes that in many industries long-run average and marginal cost are relatively constant over a wide range of firm sizes; that advertising has no general tendency to lead to large firms; and that good statistical explanations of the size of firms are plant size and technological complexity, as measured by the proportion of engineers and chemists employed. These specific uses of Stigler's theory are very impressive. His theory and technique have scientific application: they help predict and explain how firm or plant sizes respond to changes in various economic conditions.

In an addendum, Stigler spells out in greater detail some analytical and procedural problems encountered in the empirical determination of economies of scale.

> The difficulties we encounter in defining a minimum optimum size arise, not from the survivor principle, but from the fact that a frequency distribution of resources (and possibly of markets) underlies the argument. The conventional cost theory, with its single minimum long-run average cost, must assume resources [and markets] which are identical for every firm. Where this is true, there will of course be either a single observable size of firm or (with constant returns to scale) a rectangular distribution of sizes.[46]

If the object is to infer how firm size influences costs, the firms being compared should be in reasonably similar product and geographic markets. Even so, one must also be careful in interpreting what he finds. Suppose, for example, that several sizes of firms hold stable shares of industry output over time. An inference that there is an approximately flat long-run cost curve does *not* mean that the smaller of such firms can expand at constant average cost. Nor does it mean that large firms could be shrunk, whether by spin-offs or governmental policy, without suffering higher average costs. Assuming that the analysis is cleanly done, it may simply mean that the best that everyone does, with what he has, turns out to be about equally good. The smaller firms — with their techniques and resources — are holding their own as well as the larger firms — with their techniques and resources. It does *not* mean that the size of either could be changed without affecting the costs. In short, we are not really measuring the abstract effect of *size* on cost, for size depends on how efficiently organizations utilize their own peculiar teams, factors, and resources.

If firms from basically different product or geographic markets are being lumped together, we are liable to get misleading readings on both "costs" *and* efficiency. A small firm may be doing extremely well, even though its unit cost is very high compared with a larger firm, and even if it could never successfully grow large. For it may be producing a different product, at higher cost; but it is getting a price higher than its "costs," and providing substantial consumer satisfaction. Furthermore, perhaps no one else could figure out how to produce comparable quantities of that same highly valued product at as low a unit cost. On the other hand, it is entirely possible that the firm could not

46. Stigler, *supra* n. 26, at 91.

organize and manage the team and other resources which it would require in order to grow large.

Both the larger and smaller firms would be viable because they are doing a good job for consumers. A casual use of the survivorship test might then show "constant costs," which would be wrong by the conventional standards. It would correctly show that both firms are viable and worthwhile; but they are not on the same product or cost function. Whether they are equally efficient depends upon the criteria applied: the larger firm is likely to be producing an absolutely larger stream of consumer benefits.

There are additional ambiguities whose interpretation calls for care. For example, in the U.S. steel industry during the period 1880-1900, there were surely economies up through the largest firm size.[47] Stigler's survivorship measure would show this, since firms were growing, in part through merger. But after 1901 — when U.S. Steel was formed — a careless appraisal of Stigler's measures leads to the inference that there are *diseconomies* of the largest size of firm! What happened was, of course, that the largest firm continued to grow, but not as fast as the market. What Stigler would say is that the largest optimum size of firm has fallen *relative* to the market, and that his technique shows it. I nevertheless find this troublesome. Even though the literature is full of assertions that U.S. Steel was relatively inefficent, other studies, including some of Stigler's,[48] cast doubt on the assertion. If, as legend has it, U.S. Steel set high prices that its smaller friends followed, it could be expected to show a *lower* rate of return on investment than its smaller followers, even if it produced at as low costs in each facility. In fact, U.S.S. was apparently even *more* profitable! This is consistent with *superior* cost efficiency; or superiority in product mix, location, or other dimensions.

Take another example. Suppose, in some industry, that there is a unique optimum firm size, which at the first date equals 25 percent of industry capacity, and that, because of superior judgment, one firm is exactly that size. The other firms are all smaller than that. Suppose, now, that the market starts growing substantially. The largest firm does *not* grow, since it correctly believes that it would suffer diseconomies. The smaller firms *are* growing, some by merger. In the process, of course, the market share of the largest and most efficient firm is falling — leading, if one is not careful, to a false inference that it is inefficent. The shares of the smaller firms are growing — leading, if one is not careful, to the false inference that the smaller firms are more efficient. Stigler would probably say that his index properly shows that the optimum firm size *is* falling relative to the size of market, and — if one waits long enough and something *else* does not change — the ultimate distribution of firm sizes will show what happened.

There is also the problem that law may not be neutral with respect to firm size. In some instances, law favors *larger* firms, especially in regulated in-

47. For example, see D. T. Armentano, *The Myths of Antitrust* (Arlington House 1972), pp. 99-106.

48. Stigler, *supra* n. 26, ch. 9, "The Dominant Firm and the Inverted Umbrella," and ch. 8, "Monopoly and Oligopoly by Merger."

dustries. On the other hand, antitrust and other laws discourage larger firms even though "economies," as normally construed, persist beyond present firm sizes. Of course, Stigler would say that his test measures efficiency in terms of the ability of firms to adjust to *everything,* including law, and that is so. But it may not coincide perfectly with the long-run average cost curve that textbooks picture. The point is that few if any economists are as skillful and careful as Stigler, and that we should carefully evaluate the results they get using his technique. Finally, Stigler's test leaves open the question of whether *within* a size class, firms are turning over, and what *that* means.

Bain and Shepherd have not been enthusiastic about Stigler's survivorship technique.[49] Shepherd, for example, voices various objections to survivorship measures. In his words,

> what *is* is by no means necessarily what *ought to be*. One might almost as well use trends in actual market structure as a basis for prescribing the optimum structure, rather than merely predicting the natural structure. Survival of a size group of plants or firms may reflect pure pecuniary advantages or any number of socially dubious activities, instead of technical efficiency. This defect is most severe in just those industries where market power is greatest (such as automobiles, computers, telephone equipment, drugs, and aircraft), for which normative estimates of scale [economies?] are needed as a guide for public policy. A financially robust, dominant firm may or may not be technically superior; that is precisely the question which cannot be assumed away.[50]

Since "technical superiority" is in my view not a dominant objective, governmental inquisitors and people like Shepherd should in each case be compelled to point out, explain, and defend precisely what "pecuniary advantages" and "socially dubious activities" really mean. In the meantime, intelligent use of some form of survivorship test may be one of the better things we can practice, especially if one regards it as reflecting overall adaptability rather than "cost" advantage alone.

### 4. Profitability Studies

There are serious conceptual and mechanical problems involved in using accounting numbers in statistical investigations. Nevertheless, some economists have argued either that measured profits *are* the evil, or that they're a good proxy for it. They may be astounded to see profits used to indicate efficiency. These important issues can better be analyzed if we lay to one side the

49. For example, see J. S. Bain, "Survival-Ability as a Test of Efficiency," *American Economic Review,* 59 (May 1969), pp. 99-104; Lester Telser, "Comment," *id.,* p. 123; W. G. Shepherd, *Market Power and Economic Welfare* (Random House 1970), pp. 168-170.
One of Bain's criticisms is that a fair fraction of a typical industry's output is commonly supplied by what *he* considers inefficiently small firms, which nevertheless survive for a variety of reasons, and that Stigler's analysis incorrectly counts them as efficient simply because they *do* survive.
50. Shepherd, *supra* n. 49.

question of whether reported "profits" really measure profit in an economically relevant sense. Suppose they do. I previously argued that, as a general rule, well-measured profits are *part* of an appropriate measure of efficiency.[51] Some measure of consumer benefits — such as consumer surplus — is the rest.[52] Put in this way, the question becomes whether, in a particular case, the sum of profit (properly measured) plus consumer surplus is higher than it would be under achievable alternatives, after attributing to the alternatives the costs of achieving them. Under what, if any, circumstances would properly measured profit be a *proxy* for greater efficiency? When would profit precisely *measure* efficiency?

There are several theoretic possibilities. First, suppose that for some industry, unit cost is significantly lower under the present concentrated industry structure than it would be under a less concentrated one that some economist or engineer says is theoretically achievable. Suppose, further, that price under the present structure is precisely the same as it would be under the less concentrated structure, i.e., is significantly above present unit costs. Consumers are equally well off under either structure. Producers are better off under the present structure. Costs are lower under the present structure, which is what accounts for that structure and generates the profits. In such a case, profit *precisely* measures the superior efficiency of the present structure, since it simultaneously measures the value of resources saved, and the increased income of shareholders. Consumers of the product are just as well off.

Suppose, alternatively, both price and unit cost are *lower* under the present structure than under the alternative posed. In such a case, profit *understates* the efficiency of the present structure. Resources are saved, consumers are better off, and firms prosper.

Different theoretical constructs bother the structuralist reformers. The classic formulation, for example, postulates that unit costs are the same under the present industry structure and some posited alternative; price is asserted to be higher with the present structure. In such a case, profit would neither indicate nor measure efficiency. But this theoretical formulation makes no logical or empirical sense unless entry to the industry is absolutely closed, as by *law*. Otherwise, entry will force price down to cost, since smaller newcomers can produce as cheaply as anyone else. It is interesting to note assertions that, in the cases of at least some of the early "trusts" (including sugar, Northern Securities, Standard Oil (N.J.), tobacco, steel) costs *and* prices *fell,* not rose.[53]

So much for logic. What, if anything, do empirical "profits" studies contribute?

For many years there has been some evidence of a positive statistical association between rates of reported profits and the absolute or relative size of firm. Subsequent research, whether directed to that issue or some other, some-

51. McGee, *supra* n. 3.

52. In the case of most things we buy, the amounts we pay nowhere near exhaust the total benefit we derive from having them. The dollar value of this difference is traditionally called "consumer surplus."

53. D. T. Armentano, *supra* n. 47, at 56-106.

times revealed such a relationship (at least over some ranges of firm sizes) and sometimes not.[54] Such studies are subject to various alarming statistical and conceptual problems, including whether (and how well) firms are classified into broader or narrower "industry" categories; the time periods involved; the measure of profitability; the fact that some owners of relatively smaller companies reduce reported profits by withdrawing inflated salaries; and problems with measuring firm size.

I will concentrate here on three more recent sources: work by J. M. Blair, W. G. Shepherd, and H. Demsetz.[55]

Blair's analysis is based on 1966 data from the FTC's annual *Rates of Return for Selected Manufacturing Industries,* which shows after-tax profits on equity for large firms classified into three-digit industries. Firm size is measured in terms of book *assets.* According to Blair's scatter-diagrams, in six out of thirty "industries" (motor vehicles and parts, textiles, business machines, paperboard boxes, malt liquors, iron and steel foundries) the larger firms tended to earn higher profits. Blair infers that this superior performance of larger firms is a result of greater "efficiency," or greater efficiency plus "monopoly power." In eight "industries" (blast furnaces and steel mills; distilled liquors; primary aluminum; meat packing; nonferrous metals other than aluminum; plumbing fixtures; pulp, paper, and paperboard; ball and roller bearings) the larger firms tended to earn lower profits. From this Blair infers that the larger firms were *less* efficient. In the sixteen remaining industries — which Blair does not name and for which he does not show scatter-diagrams — there was "no clear relationship, either direct or inverse, between size and profitability. . . . In most cases the absence of a relationship stemmed from widespread variations in the profit rates of the smaller companies, particularly those less than one-fifth the size of the industry leader."[56]

Apart from the usual conceptual and statistical problems invovled in comparing book profit rates amongst different kinds of firms classified more or less arbitrarily into broad industry classes, using these kinds of numbers in statistical work can lead to something called spurious correlation. For the size

---

54. For example, see W. L. Crum, *Corporate Size and Earning Power* (Harvard Univ. Press 1939); N. Collins and L. Preston, "Price-Cost Margins and Industry Structure," *Review of Economics and Statistics,* 51 (August 1969), pp. 271-286; M. Hall and L. Weiss, "Firm Size and Profitability," *Review of Economics and Statistics,* 49 (August 1967), pp. 319-331; P. Asch and M. Marcus, "Returns to Scale in Advertising," *Antitrust Bulletin,* 15 (Spring 1970), pp. 33-42.

55. John M. Blair, *Economic Concentration* (Harcourt Brace, Jovanovich 1972), pp. 177-185; W. G. Shepherd, "The Elements of Market Structure," *Review of Economics and Statistics,* 14 (February 1972), pp. 25-37; H. Demsetz, "Industry Structure, Market Rivalry, and Public Policy," *Journal of Law & Economics,* 16 (April 1973), pp. 1-9.

56. Blair, *supra* n. 55, at 184. Blair also presents a table comparing, for the average of 1959-1963, the number of industries showing direct, inverse, and zero relationships with the number he attributed to each class for 1966. For the earlier average period, 7 of 30 industries show a direct relationship, and 15 a zero relationship.

measure of firms — i.e., assets — enters into the denominator of the profits measure. If this denominator is correlated with firm size, as measured, measurement error alone would tend to produce a spurious relationship between profit rate and firm size.

It might be an interesting exercise to follow Brozen's procedure:[57] if Blair's results *truly* show an efficiency–size relationship, one would expect to find *increasing* market share of larger firms in those industries showing a positive relationship between efficiency and size, and declining shares in those industries for which the relationship is negative.

The methodology used by Shepherd and Demsetz differs from Blair's: they use multiple regression analysis;[58] Blair used scatter-diagrams. Shepherd's data are for a sample of 231 large firms, over several years. I leave to others the important questions arising from sample size and possible sample bias. Like many others, Shepherd tries to explain profit differences in terms of several variables. And he adds some new wrinkles. First, in some regressions, and in two different ways, Shepherd uses an interperiod (*not* intraindustry) estimate of "risk" for each firm.[59] Second, Shepherd employs a market share (variously measured) for each firm. Third, he uses a "group" share variable, a rather mysterious "approximation" of the difference between the concentration ratio and individual firm's market share.[60]

His key result is that "market share emerges as the main element [explaining profitability], independent of the leading-firm group and entry barriers." [61] The explanatory power of advertising is very small. Industry growth matters. Shepherd's "risk" variable, which seems to me to be misconceived, doesn't contribute anything.

Given these results, Shepherd observes that "the market share–profitability association may stem from scale economies in production or innovation, rather than (or in addition to) the effect of market power." Of course, as I argued earlier, superior profits may just as well reflect a lower *level* of costs, or superior products, whether there are economies of pure *size* or not. Shepherd does not like an explanation that rests on economies of large size. As he puts it, "the pervasiveness of constant-cost conditions in manufacturing industries (Bain, 1956; Stigler, 1968; Shepherd, 1970) suggests that market power is indeed the main root." Nothing of the sort, for at least two reasons: first, for the firms he is analyzing, the sources he cites are probably not even as good

---

57. Yale Brozen, "Bain's Concentration and Rates of Return Revisited," *Journal of Law & Economics,* 14 (October 1971), pp. 351-369; "The Antitrust Task Force Deconcentration Recommendation," *Journal of Law & Economics,* 13 (October 1970), pp. 263 ff.

58. This applies various statistical techniques to sample data. The object is to estimate how different values of several variables, as defined and measured, were associated in the sample. Such analysis does not measure or imply causality.

59. W. G. Shepherd, *Market Power and Economic Welfare* (Random House 1970), p. 28. But see his footnote 15.

60. *Id.* at 26 and footnote 6.

61. *Id.* at 35.

evidence as what he found himself; second, some firms have *lower* costs than others, or produce better products for equal costs, even in the complete absence of "economies of scale."

Subject to caveats about data and sample, Shepherd just may have found evidence of something important: firms grow large because they have low costs relative to consumers' appraisal of what their goods are worth, a circumstance that also brings profits. If their superiority persists, so do their market share and profits. If not, their shares decline. Shepherd's findings suggest that, on average, "High initial-year profitability is associated with later declines in market share;" [62] and, "cases of persistent high profitability at market shares above 50 percent are unusual . . ." Unfortunately, he immediately concludes that such "unusual" cases "especially invite an anti-trust evaluation of the competitive and technological trade-offs," which I think is generally quite backwards. For if such superiority is temporary, the market erodes share and profits when superiority fades. If the superiority endures, the market does not cut the firm down. Nor — so far as I can see — should any man.

At this point, Demsetz's contribution seems especially appropriate. It is highly relevant to whether efficiency and firm size are related, and in what way. As Demsetz puts it:

> Under the pressure of competitive rivalry, and in the apparent absence of effective barriers to entry, it would seem that the concentration of an industry's output in a few firms could only derive from their superiority in producing and marketing products or in the superiority of a structure of industry in which there are only a few firms. In a world in which information and resource mobility can be secured only at a cost, an industry will become more concentrated under competitive conditions only if a differential advantage in expanding output develops in some firms. Such expansion will increase the degree of concentration at the same time it increases the rate of return that these firms earn. The cost advantage that gives rise to increased concentration may be reflected in scale economies or in downward shifts in positively sloped marginal cost curves, or it may be reflected in better products which satisfy demand at a lower cost. New efficiencies can, of course, arise in other ways.[63]

An increase in the size of superior firms may or may not result in "monopoly power." But two things seem reasonably clear to me: First, the world is highly uncertain, and the risky and economically beneficial experiments of firms require a prospect of profit. If any profit gotten from such success is to be wrenched away by antitrust or other policy, the incentive to experiment, change, and grow is much reduced. Second, whether an industry is "competitive" or "monopolistic," superior firms can be expected to earn higher profits. This is also true even under collusion, as Demsetz points out.

62. *Id.* at 34.
63. Harold Demsetz, "Industry Structure, Market Rivalry, and Public Policy," *Journal of Law & Economics*, 16 (April 1973), p. 1.

If one size of firm earns a higher rate of return than another size, given any collusive price, then there must exist differences in the cost of production which favor the firm that earns the higher rate of return. Alternatively, if there is no single price upon which the industry agrees, but, rather a range of prices, then one firm can earn a higher rate of return if it produces a superior product and sells it at a higher price without thereby incurring proportionately higher costs; here, also, the firm that earns the higher rate of return can be judged to be more efficient because it delivers more value per dollar of cost incurred.

A deconcentration or antimerger policy is more likely to have benign results if small firms in concentrated industries earn the same or higher rates of return than large firms, for, then, deconcentration may reduce collusion, if it is present, while simultaneously allocating larger shares of industry output to smaller firms which are no less efficient than larger firms. But if increased concentration has come about because of the superior efficiency of those firms that have become large, then a deconcentration policy, while it may reduce the ease of colluding, courts the danger of reducing efficiency either by the penalties that it places on innovative success or by the shift in output to smaller, higher cost firms that it brings about. This would seem to be a distinct possibility if larger firms in concenrated industries earn higher rates of return than small firms.[64]

Demsetz performs ingenious statistical tests of these propositions. In general, it appears that larger firms earn more than their smaller rivals, and that the superiority of their performance *increases* with industry concentration. Both findings are consistent with the superior efficiency of large firms, and not with collusion or monopoly. In Demsetz's words:

> The data do not seem to support the notion that concentration and collusion are closely related, and, therefore, it is difficult to remain optimistic about the beneficial efficiency effects of a deconcentration or anti-merger public policy. On the contrary, the data suggest that such policies will reduce efficiency by impairing the survival of large firms in concentrated industries, for these firms do seem better able to produce at lower cost than their competitors.[65]

## VI.   BUSINESS SIZE AND EFFICIENCY: RESTATEMENT

On my reading of both theory and the evidence, statistical cost and engineering studies teach us precious little about even the relationship between business size and cost. If he likes, an optimist can await the day when we *will* have learned a lot about costs. I think he will have a very long wait.

Whether that wait is long or short, costs are not enough. Any useful definition of efficiency involves a great deal more than "cost." For example, it is *cheaper* to put a pound of flesh on a human frame, or to sustain a given level of physical activity, by eating soy beans or grains directly instead of using them to feed livestock that are then consumed as meat. The indirect method results in technical conversion losses, which might carelessly be called "inefficiencies." But there is more to life and economics than technical or engineer-

---

64. *Id.* at 4-5.
65. *Id.* at 6-7.

ing standards. Many people like meat. For a given technical effect, they have to pay more for it and are glad to do so. In *any* question of economic "efficiency," consumers' satisfactions are at least as important as costs. Some of us also believe that ignoring what consumers want is tyranny.

Some economists apparently believe that it is desirable to have in any industry only "efficient-sized" firms and to have as many of them as "possible." The roots of this belief are not hard to find. In the usual textbook model of atomistic competition, swarms of firms produce one identical product, and generally are conceived to have identical cost functions as well. In such a simple model, the total cost of producing a homogeneous product at a given annual rate is minimized when each firm produces at the minimum point of its long-run average cost curve, when — as textbooks have it — each is of the "optimum size." Furthermore, in spite of little or no logical or empirical support, the naive structuralist theories assert that competition increases with the number of firms. Thus — the story goes — the "right" number of firms produces the "competitive" results at the "right" cost.[66]

My own research into a few real-world manufacturing processes convinces me that, in at least some cases, even purely technical economies are a long way from being exhausted, and that there are also economies of size in other business functions besides manufacturing. But the point I want to make now is that, *even if some firm or firms had actually grown past the output rate and volume for which unit cost is minimum, this does not support breaking them up or otherwise inducing them to shrink.* Experience abundantly demonstrates that in a specific case it is not easy to quantify the relevant cost curves, and that most economists have virtually no idea of what is really going on. But, in addition to the costs, difficulties, and mistakes involved in discovering what costs are, the really basic problem is that the naive view is based upon a misconception of what an economy should be minimizing and what it should be maximizing. Consumers are often not indifferent to various characteristics of products, and there is no reason why they should be.

Suppose that we were actually able to find that, for a certain fixed period of production, firms' unit costs are minimized at an annual output rate of say, 1 million, then rise for larger outputs. If we sought artificially to minimize the industry's unit costs, each firm would have to be that size. But surely it is not desirable to minimize the costs of stuff that consumers do not want, since the object of economic efficiency is presumably to maximize individuals' satisfaction. At any point in time, consumers have not been equally attracted to all of the products of all producers, and consumers' preferences have been subject to significant revision over time. Suppose that the unit costs of shirts could be minimized by forcing all producers to make only one size and one model of shirt: undyed and unbleached cotton, no buttons, and all size 15½, 33. A commissar's pride in the "minimum costs" thereby achieved would be small comfort to those whom the shirts do not fit and to whom they do not otherwise appeal. Indeed, it is not even clear that enough of these shirts could be sold

66. For a fuller explanation and evaluation of these contentions, see McGee, *supra* n. 3.

to cover the costs, minimum or not. It makes no sense to "minimize costs" of stuff consumers do not want, or to prevent consumers from buying stuff not produced at "minimum costs."

Suppose that there is a producer who sells many fewer than 1 million units per year. His unit costs could be lower if only his customers could be induced to buy more. To minimize costs, do we say he must make and sell none? That he must make and sell more? How would we compel either result? We could compel some consumers who prefer something else to buy what the smaller producer offers. This would lower his unit costs; but it would reduce consumers' satisfaction.

Note the obverse. If a firm is currently selling substantially more than 1 million units a year, the naive view is that it is too large to minimize unit costs. By assumption, if it could somehow be shrunken to 1 million units, unit costs could be reduced. How could that result be accomplished? The firm could be forced to turn the additional business away, by rationing; or to raise prices or lessen the attractiveness of its product so as to induce enough customers to do without or to switch to its competitors. None of these schemes makes much sense if we are interested in individuals' satisfaction. For they, and the firms that seek to serve them, have already weighed the trade-offs between cost, price, and quality. Consumers are perfectly content to pay at least the additional costs required to get additional output of what they want. They like it better than the alternatives.

Similar analysis governs cases in which unit costs reach a minimum value and remain constant for larger outputs. Cost minimization in the naive, limited sense is not a dominant objective.

Additional insights can be gotten by reviewing the economics of trade.[67] Imagine the position of Robinson Crusoe before Friday arrives. He possesses his own personal skills and knowledge, some nonhuman resources from the outside world, and some local resources. Like everyone else, he also has a variety of wants. His resources are scarce, relative to his wants. Scarcity compels choice. Like all the rest of us, he must choose amongst competing uses of his skills, time, and other resources. He uses what he has to best advantage, given his tastes. He allocates resources so as to minimize the cost of all results. He maximizes his net benefits. Given his accessible alternatives, which are obviously the only ones that are relevant to him, Crusoe is both "production efficient" and "utility efficient." "Production efficient," because the cost of what he does will be as low as possible. "Utility efficient," because, with the resources he has, he cannot increase his satisfactions by altering the kinds or amounts of the various goods and services he produces. Though they are generated by only one man who is both producer and consumer, these results meet the same criteria as evolved from the theory of atomistic competition.

67. For an exemplary and full treatment, see A. A. Alchian and W. R. Allen, *Exchange and Production Theory in Use* (Wadsworth 1969), or their larger counterpart volume, *University Economics* (Wadsworth, 2nd ed. 1967, 3rd ed. 1971). Of special interest are the chapters "Basis of Exchange" and "Production, Exchange, Specialization and Efficiency."

Nevertheless, Crusoe is liable to be rather badly off as compared with consumers in larger societies that have lots of "monopoly."

To improve their lot, individuals have historically abandoned self-sufficiency in favor of trade, often with "monopolistic" outsiders. People do not trade unless it makes them better off. Benefits from trade arise under several conditions. These include differences in individuals' tastes, skills, and endowments. If there are economies of large-scale production, specialization also pays on that account, and trade emerges.

In a complex economy, there are *many* producers, traders, and consumers. And, within the limits of differing tastes, and differing competence of different firm-teams and bundles of production factors, there is continuous pressure on costs and on prices. Nevertheless, since tastes and competence differ, there will *never* be enough of the right kind of resources to drive *all* prices to the level of "costs" for all producers. In any real world it is absolutely inevitable that the demand for different things, relative to the array of competencies of firms and factors to produce them, will not everywhere produce the same relationship of price to cost.

Gains from specialization and trade exist, and may be very substantial, *because of,* not in spite of, the "profits" either or both traders earn. Indeed, as Alchian and Allen put it, "profit is *part* of the product." The only "costs" relevant to traders and consumers are the costs of doing things themselves and the various *prices* offered in the marketplace. Enormous "profit" is perfectly consistent with the very best that is achievable, given all the real alternatives. If markets are "open" in the sense that present and potential producers are free to offer the products and terms they wish, and consumers are free to accept what they regard as the best offers going, there is a very strong presumption that the benefits from trade will be as high as realistically can be. Freedom to trade and the desire to do the best one can are extremely powerful forces. Firms occupy a piece of the market by providing, on good terms, what consumers want.

It must now be recognized that, within limits, the real trading alternatives can be influenced by State action. Although precisely what a State is and how it behaves are not yet settled, one distinguishing feature is that the State asserts a monopoly of the legal supply of coercion and violence. State rules can exclude from the marketplace specific traders or particular kinds and sizes of traders, and have often attempted to limit the number of traders or the quantities and qualities they are permitted to offer.

Without complete specification, it is impossible to indicate *all* of the different kinds of State action that will occur. Nevertheless, both the history and logic of State licensure, franchising and regulation, and the sale of privilege, are rich enough to deserve our attention. Under cost, demand, and constitutional conditions that are evidently not rare, accomplishing and keeping monopoly through State action has been very attractive to some teachers, doctors, lawyers, unionists, businessmen, utilities, and many others. The precise outcomes, of course, depend not only upon product demands and costs. The details of the governmental apparatus and mechanisms for determining who has what power also apparently matter. However, for our present purpose they are not crucial; I am not interested here in precisely how much is paid to whom, and in what coin.

Suppose someone effectively monopolizes an industry under a State franchise that permits him to choose output and price, and otherwise to manage his business as he likes. Under these circumstances, I would expect that the business will come to produce each output as cheaply as can be managed, although it is possible to write into the franchise some constraints that significantly alter the sense in which that is true. Suppose that the monopoly is "production efficient" in the usual sense. As always, consumers adjust as best they can.

Economists of liberal persuasion historically opposed such arrangements for various reasons. One is that such a franchise would not be valuable, and therefore would not be sought, unless it excludes from the market those resources, traders, and offers that would otherwise appear. An artificial "scarcity" is contrived and, then, is not permitted to be ameliorated. As a consequence, the argument goes, consumers are hurt by more than the franchise earns, and this is perverse.

If all of that is so, some reason for granting the franchise, or for operating it in such a way, must be found. Possibilities are that the hurts are diffused over many consumers, whereas the gains are relatively concentrated; and that it is too costly for consumers effectively to confederate. If it were costless for consumers to confederate, they could obtain a better result all around, either by preventing the franchise, by buying and operating it themselves, or inducing the present owner to produce and price appropriately.

Such costs of confederating and transacting, rather than the fact that there is a single seller, may be the heart of the matter. If there were only one consumer, he would bear all of the loss; but he would not have the cost of identifying and coalescing with other customers to do something about it. Instead, he could independently negotiate with the franchise monopoly to produce the "right" amount of the good in question; buy out the monopoly; or, alternatively, bargain with the State to prevent the franchise at the start, or to rescind it. It is true that the franchise, or its prospect, will cost the consumer; but under negotiation it will not then cost him more than the monopoly gains. There will have been a straightforward transfer of wealth. Those who love the consumer more than they love whoever benefits from the franchise, can, of course, still choose to oppose the franchise.[68]

Under at least some circumstances, therefore, franchise monopolies — and the closed markets they imply — cause mischief. Following the same line, under these kinds of State exclusions, there is no clear general presumption that overall efficiency obtains in the traditional sense. Accordingly, there is a lesser or no presumption that the size and structure of an industry under State franchise monopoly is to be explained by traditional notions of superior effi-

68. Some economists (e.g., Gordon Tullock and Yoram Barzel) believe that this line of argument is dangerously incomplete. If there is a good prospect for valuable monopoly franchises, substantial resources will be spent on acquiring them, which some might believe to be "wasteful."

ciency. For example, under State monopoly, there will be people on the out-side who are competent and willing to offer as good or better terms; but the artificial requirement of the franchise (not the evaluation of consumers) keeps them outside, looking in.[69] It is artificial in that crucial sense. When markets are open, sellers gain a place by offering *consumers* a better deal. To close markets, a seller (or buyer) offers what an *authority* considers to be a better deal. An authority often can get a better deal for itself by closing markets and excluding traders and trades, as history shows.

Although this is an essay about economics, it is fair to point out that many economists of the liberal persuasion have also decried the immediate and prospective tyrannies such arrangements generate, not to mention corruption and the sale of privilege.

In contrast, examine the case of a new open market, occupied at first by only one seller, but free of State closures. If you like, call the first seller a "monopolist." New sellers, if their costs are lower than the "monopolist's" prices, come into the market or bid to do so. On net balance, each such chal-lenger benefits consumers, and hurts the "monopolist," more than he benefits himself. But apart from offering the best terms, there is really no way the monopolist can keep them out. For several reasons, he cannot effectively bribe the newcomers to go away.[70] One reason is that no one can be sure whom and how many he would have to bribe, only partly because a threat is known to be genuine only when it is effectuated. Another is that some promises, includ-ing promises not to enter, are unenforceable.

For all of these reasons, in the absence of artificial strictures there is a strong presumption that the *existing* structure of industry is the *efficient* struc-ture. Open markets are an environment within which powerful and appraising evolutionary forces are at work. The kind of competition often overlooked is that between different ways of doing things, including technologies and tech-niques, and the organization of firms; different products; and different services. There is competition, selection, and choice *within* firms as well as between firms; there is competition within and amongst fields, and both inside and outside competition to displace inferior performers from their places in the field. Never have consumers had so many real options. The options that we have, have made their way on the basis of how efficiently they serve con-sumers' wants.

Hundreds of huge firms, and millions of large and small ones, are continu-ously searching for profitable fields. The prices consumers pay are not only bids to the present suppliers; they are also bids to anyone who thinks he can

---

69. As always, one must be careful in attempting to design empirical tests. It is difficult for anyone to admit that he is responsible for his own failures. No matter how open and competitive markets may be, in taverns, parks, and courthouse squares one can always find discontented failures who blame "the system," "market," "govern-ment," "Big Business," or someone else.

70. As cartel histories show, a splendid situation for any seller is to have *some-one else* reduce output and raise prices. If he suffers no cost disadvantage, the "inde-pendent" will then sell more goods and make more money per unit of investment.

do better for the consumers. Market research, compilations of potential customers, and informal discussions with buyers are daily tests of whether it would pay for new or old suppliers to bid for consumers' custom by offering better terms. The capital markets churn away daily, funneling capital from low-return to high-return areas. Firms daily choose whether to make or buy — and large firms often have large customers. Firms in any particular field are constantly appraising prices and prospective costs in other fields. If prices significantly exceed the costs of a prospective entrant, he enters. If different product qualities yield a higher difference between revenues than between costs — that is, would produce higher net benefits — different products will be offered. If different techniques or forms of organization show promise, someone is likely to try them.

The market is an enormous information network that signals when opportunities exist, and moves resources to take advantage of them.[71] In the process, consumer benefits are *really* maximized, within the real-world constraints of the amount and qualities of resources, information, and the competence of different teams.

If any firm should be larger than efficiency requires, and charges higher prices than the costs of its present and prospective competitors, they and the market will shrink it. If any firm should innovate better techniques, or offer a superior product at the same costs as its competitors, the market will respond and it will grow. If any firm offers the same product as its competitors at lower costs, it will prosper and grow. If any firm is so large as to be inefficient, there will be internal and external challenges to put things right; if they are not righted, its present and prospective competitors will outstrip it.

Of course, as Stigler rightly pointed out, evolutionary processes produce survivors that are well adapted to their total environment. In my view, this raises three very different kinds of questions. First, some critics seem to think the kinds and sizes of firms that survive are not in fact well adapted to the environment we have. Such criticisms range from possible internal inefficiency to charges that consumers are badly catered to. In general, such deficiencies imply that it would pay someone to do something about them. Apparently the critics believe they know enough about efficiency, costs, and revenues in specific industries to conclude that results are "bad." They must also believe they have a durable monopoly on the information, which *is* strange of them: the critics have for a long time been pretty free in giving it out. For, unless there are absolute legal closures, such "bad" performance cannot persist if others have that information. A state of information sufficient to discern the "bad" performance should be sufficient to guarantee that the "bad" performance will not persist. The fact is that millions of firms and people who know what they are doing are constantly looking for places in which the present economic adjustments can be improved. Anyone who believes he has found

71. Much of recent economic analysis ignores the indispensable role that markets play in producing information. As a partial corrective, see F. A. Hayek, "The Use of Knowledge in Society," *American Economic Review*, 35 (September 1945), pp. 519-530.

one can bet against the market. If he is right, he may become rich, and deserves to.

A second issue is whether something is correctably wrong with the legal, business, and industrial environment itself, and whether and in what sense it pays to correct it. It goes without saying that, by some standard, no real environment is perfect. Suppose that certain successful survivors got where they are through, say, fraud, arson, mayhem, or theft, and that — by economic standards — it clearly pays to somewhat reduce the amount of such activities. One way to do it is to make such activities relatively more expensive in a variety of ways. Punishment is one way; but in tolerable societies it is imposed because of bad things that specific people can be proved to have done.

It is all too easy to get agreement about things like mayhem and theft. But I am afraid that there are grave dangers if this environmental reform approach is applied too broadly and too fast. A great many governmental policies were allegedly developed to help consumers by improving the business and professional environment. Many of them — including franchising, licensure, allocations, and other market closures — frustrate consumers and competitors, and they concentrate enormous power in the State. In every field there are those who would benefit from slowing the pace, by either excluding or taxing the efficient.

There may be a good case for discouraging cartels — although it is well to recognize that not everyone agrees what a cartel is, and where to draw the line between cartels and beneficial organizations. Similarly, many oppose massive mergers that would mop up an entire industry and all of the better resources used to perform in it.

But I think we are now clearly in danger of confusing the possible changes in such "rules of the game" with penalties against beneficially superior performers, which brings us to the next problem. It involves the propriety of striking directly at the characteristics of successful survivors — like size and profitability — rather than at bad things they can be shown to have done. This is an especially hazardous confusion in dealing with things like industrial structure, for there is much logic and fact to suggest that, in open markets, beneficially superior performers do rise to the top. Law that strikes at the characteristics of the best discourages the good performance by which they earned those very characteristics. I do believe that law has, in several respects, already gone way too far with conduct rules — Robinson-Patman, to take only one example. Nevertheless, I am tolerant of continuing, full, and fair debate about specific kinds of identifiable conduct asserted to have antieconomic consequences. That seems better by far than penalizing characteristics that are largely or wholly associated with good performance.

In my view, some of what passes for economic analysis would, if it were widely believed, threaten a system of law and economics that has served us well. Look first at law and politics. Substituting a principle of guilt by characteristic for that of guilt by deed is, if history can be believed, liable to produce generally unhappy consequences. Furthermore, there is the issue of concentrated economic and political power, with which the structural reformers claim they will help us. On the contrary, I think they would bury us. They would compel firms to *justify* their size and existence to tribunals on the basis of what some engineers or economists assert is efficient. Apart from the economics, this creates serious difficulties. First, in open markets, successful large firms have *already* justified themselves to millions of consumers and to potential competitors who have decided against competing for consumer dollars. Unless an efficiency tribunal ratifies market results, it substitutes its decisions for those of millions of free individuals. If that does not increase the concentration of economic and political power, nothing does. This would be bad enough even if it produced better results in other respects. In my view, however, market forces can be expected to take care of present and changed conditions with better accuracy, flexibility, and balance of costs and tastes than seems likely to be accomplished through policies based on badly measured, partial, out-of-date, ill-conceived, and generally irrelevant estimates of "costs" made by some outside observer or policymaker.

Second, we might as well recognize the facts of self-interest. Economists, lawyers, and politicians — like everyone else — try to do as well as they can. In my view, a thoroughgoing policy of industrial deconcentration would hurt us as consumers. But some of us could make it up in what we sell: new laws of this kind would increase the demand for the services of lawyers and economists, not to mention those who would actually run and man the tribunals. Imagine the position of a politician under a constitution that permits very little policy other than letting markets run. For this reason, when economists pontificate about "policy" they can always find some sympathetic audience pursuing its own self-interest.

Third, a policy of forced industrial deconcentration is curiously discordant with the basic spirit of antitrust law itself. When a law case or a statute breaks up a firm, it denies a particular firm-team and bundle of resources access to the market. If this were attempted by private parties, it would be called monopolizing. Indeed, the total result is likely to be much worse than Sherman Law monopolizing: denying a firm access to, say, some geographic market segment would be illegal and (presumably) bad enough. But the same teams could still serve the rest. "Deconcentration" destroys that organization without correspondingly increasing the capability of others to serve.

Let us conclude. Some Americans emphasize cutting apart firms that they think are larger than minimally necessary to be "efficient." They do not usually favor inducing or compelling smaller firms to merge into the putative "efficient" size. On the other hand, with their implicit or explicit admiration for the accomplishments of large-scale American enterprise, many in Europe, Africa, and Asia are enthusiastic about State programs for "rationalization," which usually means pushing or pulling smaller firms into fewer and larger units.

In addition to being unfair, either policy has more important drawbacks. In the first place, the number, kinds, and costs of firms that will even *enter* an industry likely to be systematically subjected to such policies cannot be expected to be the same. For there is now a tax on firms whose size differs from that acclaimed as "optimal" by some engineer, economist, or tsar. This will influence the number, kinds, and amounts of products as well as firms; and consumers' preferences will not be permitted to determine the outcome.

Another crucial problem is *incentive*. The shock of such policy by surgery — whether it takes the form of grafting-on or cutting-off — can be expected to shift the costs and drives not only of those directly affected by the operation, but also of others in the industry as well. Trauma influences those who observe as well as those who suffer. Unless a law that forces dissolutions guarantees that it will be used just once in any industry — a promise that is not enforceable — there is a reduced incentive to excel. Performance may therefore be very poor indeed, no matter how the superior teams are dispersed.

There are various reasons why we cannot generally specify just how ruinous forced "deconcentration" would be to efficiency. It is tempting to guess that cutting a firm with an 80 percent market share into four equal-sized bits will produce the same costs and performance as are observed in the firm that now serves 20 percent of the market. In some cases this might conceivably be true, as for example when economies of pure size are the whole story. But one should ask why the 80-percent firm was able to design and sell enough more units to *achieve* the economies, and what will happen to the teams that made this result possible. The 20-percent firm may in fact be better at what it does, and more efficient for the size it is, than any single bit that would survive when the leading firm is atomized. In that case, costs for the 20-percent firm would *underestimate* the probable costs of the new bits. On the other hand, if the essential teams that initially produced the superior results were somehow transfered to *one* surviving bit, its performance would be better — and the performance of the other three bits, worse — than that of the original 20-percent firm. It could also be expected to grow to a very considerable market share as time moves on.

Apart from governmental interferences, the only way a firm can hold or improve its position is by offering consumers equal or greater value per dollar, with respect both to what consumers pay and what the firm expends. If there are differences in the competence of firms in regard to qualities of product or cost of providing it, some firms will be bigger and do better than others. This seems to me to be both fair and efficient. It provides an incentive to excel, which serves both consumers and those who achieve the superior performance.

Apart from the very serious problems of correctly estimating or measuring even average relationships, such policies ignore differences in the qualities and talents of different people and different firms, and tax the important incentives to serve and succeed as best one can. If people are worried that business size may no longer be "justified" by efficiency, I think the worry is misplaced.

# Commentary

## F. M. Scherer

Granted, the problems in measuring scale economies are tough. I believe, however, that my colleagues and I have found ways of coping with them.

Before summarizing the results of our investigations, I would like to focus on one fundamental issue. The logic is rather intricate, but it is important to get it straight.

By way of introduction, there is disagreement or confusion between Professor McGee and me over what is meant by a "plant." My definition is very close to the Census definition of an "establishment." I mean a physically and managerially integrated facility or set of facilities contiguous in geographic space, producing some more or less broad range of products generic to the industry in question. McGee clearly has a broader definition. He views as a single plant, say, all of Ford's several facilities for stamping metal auto body parts, one at Dearborn, one at Chicago Heights, one at Buffalo, and so forth. This difference is extremely important, because some scale economies are uniquely associated with the size of a plant in my sense, some with the size of a geographically dispersed but technically similar set of facilities in McGee's sense, some with the still broader concept of a firm, and some with the very narrow concept of the volume of a single physically homogenous product. Unless these different dimensions of the problem are kept separate, confusion will arise.

It is normally (but not always) possible to distinguish what I call plant-specific economies, associated with the rate of production at which a *plant* is designed to operate, from product-specific economies, associated with the rate of production, the length of production runs, and the planned and actually realized production volume (over all time) of some specific product. Over-simplifying a bit, I would argue that the profit-maximizing firm will seek to build a plant, in my sense, with a production rate capacity at least large enough to minimize its unit costs. To find out how large that plant must be is the principal problem of plant-specific scale economies estimation.

Firms whose rate of production exceeds that minimum optimal plant scale may choose to build additional geographically separated plants. To any given plant, in my sense, product assignments must be made. Some products may be demanded in sufficient quantities that all the conceivably attainable product-specific scale economies can be exploited by a particular firm. If, in this instance, the minimum optimal product-specific production rate is less than the minimum optimal plant-specific output rate, plants are likely to produce multiple products.

If the minimum optimal product-specific production rate exceeds the minimum optimal plant-specific output, and if the product demand is sufficiently strong, the size of the optimal plant in my sense will be raised, complicating the scale economy measurement problem. I will come back to that in a moment.

For some products, on the other hand, the minimum optimal product-specific output rate may be less than the minimum optimal plant-specific output, but the firm's demand is insufficient to warrant producing that product volume. Once again, plants will be assigned multiple products. But on such products, not all product-specific scale economies will be exploited. Ignoring some complications related to transport costs and risk-spreading, no firm will divide the production of such low-demand products between two or more plants in my sense, because to do so would be to forego even more scale economies.

It is true that if, in this situation, the output rate of the plant could be doubled without changing the product mix, further scale economies could be realized. That is to say, lower costs would be achieved. But such an output doubling is inconsistent with the demand weakness responsible for the scale economy sacrifices. Because the demand for many narrowly defined products is in fact weak, most firms do have some plants manufacturing some items in quantities which fail to exhaust all the product-specific scale economies. This situation is by no means incompatible with the realization of all *plant*-specific scale economies.

McGee's failure to understand this point in his paper reflects his failure to grasp the distinction between plant-specific and product-specific scale economies. For him to imply that plants in such a situation must be larger so that individual product volumes can be larger, flies in the face of demand limitations, committing the sin of commissarism with which he tries to tar others. And even if, by some magic, the demand for all products could be doubled, it is by no means necessary that plant sizes will be increased when production settles down into a new optimal pattern. It is entirely possible that instead the number of plants will be raised, with each plant in my sense specializing more intensively on a smaller range of products.

With this conceptual background in mind, let me now summarize what my co-workers and I discovered about the relationships between scale economies and concentration in twelve major manufacturing industries.

Considering first the scale imperatives at the plant level, it is worth noting that in no case did we find the optimal product-specific production rate to exceed the plant-specific optimum. Thus, our optimal plant scale estimates are for the most part free of biases due to ignoring product-specific economies.

Given these estimates, we found that in every industry of the twelve but refrigerators, the annual output of an optimal plant was less than 7 percent of nationwide demand. Thus, if every firm operated only one plant of minimum optimal scale, national four-firm seller concentration would be less than 28 percent, except for refrigerators, where the concentration ratio would be roughly 56 percent. Actually observed ratios are in every industry considerably higher.

The case for big business hinges, then, as Professor Dewey has already intimated, on whether there are compelling economies of multiplant scale. McGee seems to be arguing in his paper that production economies will continue into the multiplant size range if the firm's product array is so broad that exploiting all the product-specific scale economies requires a total volume greatly exceeding the output of a single optimal plant. This is an important insight, but we must be wary of circular reasoning. Multiplant size may be necessary for efficiency if firms must produce a broad line. But why must they produce a broad line? Is society any worse off if production is divided up among single-plant specialists, some making, say, cemented-sole fashion shoes in optimal quantities, some loafers, some boots, and so on? The answer may be yes, if either of two conditions holds:

First, single-plant size will be disadvantageous if competition breaks down and fails to stimulate specialization. By this, I do not mean that competition must be atomistic. That is a straw man introduced by McGee to confuse the issue. Rather, I mean merely that producers must strive vigorously to increase their sales of those items on which they can achieve a potential cost advantage.

Second, multiplant size can yield production cost economies if there is a strong interaction effect between broad-line production and other advantages of size, for example, because broad-line firms can promote their products more successfully and hence sell more of any given product, all else equal, or because buyers simply prefer dealing with broad-line suppliers.

My colleagues and I worked very hard to pinpoint such specialization breakdowns and broad-line interactions. We found that they do indeed exist, but that at least under market conditions in the United States they are typically either weak or exhausted at relatively low levels of multiplant operation. If very large broad-line multiplant firms were broken up into smaller, appropriately specialized groups, the loss of product-specific scale economies would in most instances be quite small.

We observed other economies of multiplant size, too, for example, in investment coordination, peak-load spreading, and parts procurement resulting from breakdowns in competition, not in McGee's straw man atomistic sense but in the sense that market prices failed to approximate costs. Others, such as advantages of size in advertising, are real enough, but one can argue that society's benefits are by no means proportional to the benefits realized by the large-scale advertisers, and that there may indeed be a direct conflict between the parties concerned.

Thus, strong value judgments are required. Even when all such value judgments are resolved in favor of the firms, without any discounting for social acceptability, as in my summary Table 6, one finds that the advantages of multiplant size are either modest or largely exhausted at relatively low levels of multiplant operation.

When all such advantages are taken into account, atomistic market structures seldom prove feasible. But high levels of concentration are also not mandated in the vast majority of cases, and actual concentration levels appear in many industries to be much higher than they need to be if all but slightly residual economies of single-plant size, plus multiplant size, are to be realized.

If society shares a value consensus in favor of decentralizing economic power and discretionary authority much more than it is presently decentralized, our study suggests, the efficiency losses would be finite but small. In my judgment, Professor McGee greatly exaggerates the costs and dangers of a deconcentration program.

# Commentary

## John S. McGee

Some contemporary thinkers ask whether modern business firms can justify their size and existence on the basis of nuts-and-bolts economies that are due purely to size. Apart from questions about what "size" and "economies" mean in this connection, there are other fundamental issues. There are many reasons why firms within one industry differ in size, and many reasons why, on average, firms in one industry are larger than those in another. Concentrating solely upon something called "economies of size" ignores much of the problem; it colors the rest.

We live in a complex and uncertain world. Individuals are not all alike. The teams that make up business firms are not alike, and the effectiveness of firms differs. In the usual textbook analysis of economies of size, costs are determined by a firm's size. In the real world, it is often the other way around: the size of a firm is determined or strongly influenced by the cost level that it manages to achieve.

This leads to differences in the sizes and effectiveness of firms whether there are or are not any economies of size in the usual sense, in part because the things they sell offer consumers different values relative to the costs incurred in providing them. Whether one actually tries to measure and attribute these differences to differences in managerial quality, or simply infers differences in managerial quality from the different performance resulting, surely makes no difference to the results the firms accomplish.

There are cases in which two or more firms would have identical costs for a given output program, but only if they made identical choices, and only if consumers value their products equally. Costs differ amongst firms partly because some actually manage to achieve different sales and outputs under roughly comparable output plans; or because some chose significantly different output and organizational plans, for better or worse. In an uncertain and changing world, differences in efficiency result even from different appraisals of what the relevant techniques and best long-run cost function really are.

Similarly, it is extremely difficult, if not impossible, to avoid confounding several other things. The degree of risk to which a firm subjects itself, and that risk to which it is necessarily subject, at minimum, are in the result commingled with any special ability it may have devised in coping with whatever kind and degree of risk it faces. Much of the literature on economies of size is naively mechanical, and it abstracts from, or casually denies, such important differences. That is too bad, since both logic and history suggest that they account for some outstanding industrial successes, as well as some outstanding industrial failures.

A large chunk of my paper summarizes and critically evaluates significant examples of each of four different types of studies, all of which purport to shed light on the size–efficiency question.

The first group of studies with which I dealt are the statistical cost studies. There is a little for everybody in them. However, the data are flawed, the statistical tools brittle, and the assumptions all too powerful. Ambiguities are considerable, to put it mildly. In my opinion, little help can be expected here.

Over the past twenty years or so, several multi-industry engineering studies have been made, including one introduced at this conference by Professor Scherer. There are a number of general and specific objections to the technique and to uses made of it. Among them are that such estimates cannot be forward-looking and are stale when done. They must implicitly embody some unspecified but homogeneous quality of production management, organization, and control, and must assume that some unspecified but given quality of overall management is imagined both to choose and to use the hypothetical physical plant that someone constructed on paper. Also, business problems are not solely engineering problems — which partly explains why not all successful businesses are run by practicing engineers.

Furthermore, even very good engineers differ in vision, experience, and willingness to donate the time required to teach that part of the facts of life they know to whoever comes in off the street. I also noted that such studies run into trouble with respect to definitions and measurement of plant, product, and size.

I now come to a delicate issue, the mishandling of which could put me out of the guild. Fortunately for us academic economists, much good work can be done in classrooms and in general economic analyses, even though we do not know much about specific industrial processes, techniques, and technology, let alone about the more complicated nontechnical business functions.

Most economists, I believe, actually have very little firsthand knowledge about such things relative to even one present-day industry, although they may have read several industry studies that were prepared as Ph.D. theses. A few know a little about a handful of industries, and still fewer know a fair amount about perhaps one or a very few.

I have already said that one of the failures of the engineering studies is that they attribute to all other management teams some particular level of competence, skill, and understanding. I do not want to make that same mistake myself, in this case by assuming that those who have done the studies are no more talented and energetic than I am.

In my paper, I refer to a recently published study that I did on auto bodies. In it, I discovered massive economies of mass production. What I can say in all candor is that it took me an embarrassingly long time to begin to understand how to analyze even the major technical factors involved in manufacturing automobile bodies, which is only one part of a larger and enormously more complicated undertaking. Furthermore, some others who have written about that very subject have clearly got it wrong. As a consequence, I hope I may be pardoned for wondering how deeply the ground is likely to have been tilled by those who deal with the complex technologies and economics of several industries, and who sum up for each the actual, as well as the proper, state of affairs with one or two numbers. Scherer and company may be much better, which would deflate my ego but confirm my view: competencies do differ.

According to Scherer, there are two sorts of technical size economies. The first derives from some kind of overall size of plant, which I suppose means some unspecified mixture of a variety of unspecified products. This size, whatever it is, is expressed as a proportion of some industry size, whatever that is.

The second kind of economies he calls product-specific, and they apparently arise from producing specific products in long runs. As I understood him, in seven out of his twelve cases the product-specific economies seem to be more impressive than the other kind, but he tried hard to exclude them from his study.

My perception of what he said today is that he excluded them simply because including them would have done nothing to his estimates so far as enlarging them. If that be so, I can only submit on the basis of very modest experience that the twelve industries are either a peculiar set or he may have got that wrong.

He gives two reasons for this procedure, neither of which I think is wholly satisfactory. First, for one reason or another, some firms do not find it advantageous fully to exploit the economies potentially available in that dimension. That may be so. But if his mission was to show the effects of size upon costs, he has not done it. A so-called minimum optimum size that does not exhaust all of the economies is simply not a minimum-cost size. His second reason is that however large such economies are, they would not matter, or would matter in different ways, if only he could reconstruct the world according to his own private and unachievable design.

It is very easy in conferences and classrooms to ask for a system of industrial organization such that prices conform to costs. That is not so easy to get, and it is not even so easy to specify, as a number of us have learned to our sorrow.

There are also troubles with Scherer's treatment of efficiencies in management and other nonengineering business functions. With respect to management, he concedes, he has only subjective impressions from interviews. I am sympathetic with Scherer's predicament: can anyone conceive how to evaluate business management apart from how well the enterprise does? But sympathy is not enough. Many firms grow large simply because they are efficient and well-managed, which is different from the thing that he says he wants to measure.

As I see it, Scherer is trying to find out whether and to what extent firms must be large in order to achieve some level of technical efficiency. To the issue of managerial efficiency, he contributes nothing. In short, differences in the efficiency with which firms make their plans and choices, and administer the enterprise, simply do not appear in Scherer's arithmetic.

Like some others who have used such a methodology, Scherer concludes that many firms are larger than his figures and impressions say is necessary to achieve minimum costs. From this, he infers that their actual size is not warranted, is not justified. I shall later indicate briefly why this inference would be improper even if his figures showed what he claims. For now, it is enough to say that Scherer's arithmetic simply does not explain actual firm sizes, in either direction, and that his lack of explanatory power should not cost us sleep.

I also summarized and commented on various survivorship and profit studies. With some cautions about interpretations, I conclude that, in several respects, they are about the best we have.

In the end, one of my conclusions was that, for most industries, we do not have reliable estimates even of the purely technical economies of size, let alone for the more crucial nontechnical business functions.

Readers may expect that, following the statement that "We do not know very much," there will be a plea that more research on the subject is urgently needed. They will not hear it from me. I see little reason to spend much more time estimating optimum plant or firm sizes except, perhaps, in a completely centralized and governmentally controlled economy in which the State tries hard to keep markets from working and consumers from expressing preferences. When property and markets are at work, and consumers are permitted to choose what and from whom to buy, it is, as far as I am concerned, a trivial matter what the facts of technical economies are, or what economists and engineers have to say about them. Consumers will choose products and firms that offer what is, to their tastes, the best deal. Consumers will make the trade-off between prices and product qualities. The prices they pay for the qualities they buy are signals to anyone who would do better by them. Such economies as there are will assert themselves, and no one need be concerned how large or small they are.

In a property and market system, I am neither surprised nor disturbed to hear that some firms are much smaller, and indeed some are much larger, than someone's estimate of the minimum optimal size, or that some firms have much higher costs than others. The fact is that we do not know very much about costs, which is no cause for mass lamentation. In any case, costs are only a part of the story. Unless we are dealing with industries into which the State blocks entry, industrial reorganization schemes have very much the same results as simply dictating to consumers what and from whom they can buy. In my view, this is both antieconomic and, to use an old-fashioned word, tyrannical.

In sum, I conclude that, apart from those industries dominated by State controls, there is the strongest presumption that the existing structure is the efficient structure.

# Dialogue*

*Leonard Ross:* I wonder if Professor Scherer will elaborate on the reasons why he says that some capital market economies may be economies of the firm but not social economies.

*Scherer:* That is a tough question. I am reluctant to get into it and take a lot of everybody's time. But basically, this observation comes out of portfolio theory, which says that if one could put together an optimal portfolio of securities, one could achieve a given amount of risk aversion either by combining the securities of numerous independent firms, each single-plant, or by buying the securities of a multiplant firm. And so there are various ways of getting the same result.

Now, it is true that the capital markets frequently do not function perfectly, and therefore it is not always possible to put together the first type of portfolio. I think John McGee makes a good point: individual investors do save some anguish, if the market fails in this way, by being able to create a portfolio within the bounds of a single corporation. But it is a difficult value judgment to say whether society as a whole, as opposed to those particular investors, derives a commensurate benefit.

I do believe McGee's criticism here is the most telling blow he scores on me in his whole paper.

*Ross:* It seems to me one of the main economies that may be going on is simply an economy of producing information about the firm and not simply diversification, and that high-quality information about management may require large-scale firms even if management itself doesn't require large-scale firms.

But secondly, I am still a little bit confused on why individual investor preferences for portfolio diversification are less worthy of being considered social gains than any other individual preferences, a lot of them not particularly esthetic.

*Scherer:* I must say, I am confused too. As McGee correctly points out, I have vacillated on this question. It is quite clear that there is a utility created for individual investors by being able to diversify their risks in this particular way. A class of people in society does benefit. It is, however, much less clear that society as a whole benefits. That is point number one.

Point number two is that the phenomenon is de minimis. I have measured it in my forthcoming book. The size of the capital cost advantage of the largest firm in an industry over an efficient single-plant firm turns out to range somewhere between, as I recall, one-tenth of 1 percent of unit costs and 1 percent of unit costs, depending upon a number of variables, including the capital intensity of the production processes.

Going back to the more fundamental issue, I really don't know the answer.

---

* The session was chaired by Morris A. Adelman, Professor of Economics, Massachusetts Institute of Technology. For further biographical information, see Appendix D.

There are some strong value judgments involved. I do believe that the character of the benefits created in this case is distinctly different from the character of the benefits created when goods are produced using fewer inputs.

*Yale Brozen:* There is a missing element, it seems to me, in this discussion of capital economies, and that is a consideration of the size of issues and flotation costs. The bigger the size of the issue, according to some studies, the lower the flotation cost, and certainly that is a very real social economy as well as a private economy, to reduce flotation costs.

Similar looks have been taken at sizes of bank loans and interest rates. They indicate it is cheaper, per dollar, to make large bank loans than small bank loans. This may relate back to the information costs suggested by Leonard Ross. Why are these private economies not equally social economies?

*Scherer:* In my book, I draw precisely that distinction. The book says this is the one area where economies seem to persist out to the largest size of firm we have been able to observe. Let's be very clear on this. If you want to pick out the one area where economies of scale continue out to very large firm sizes, this is it. But let's get into perspective also the size of this advantage. I have just stated that it ranges between one-tenth of 1 percent and 1 percent of unit costs, moving from an efficient single-plant firm to the largest firms we actually have in the economy.

*Brozen:* One percent of a trillion dollar economy amounts to something on the order of $10 billion. That is appreciable.

*Scherer:* That is the maximum. The average was something like .25 percent. That is still a big number, but we may have to make some trade-offs, and let's find out what they look like.

*Brozen:* Let's come back to the packaging-of-risks notion, putting together securities versus a single security.

*Scherer:* Please recall one of the main analytic points of my paper, namely, that there are several ways of skinning this cat. One can say, "Okay, let's have big business to protect investors from risk." I argue that there is an alternative approach, namely, let us try to perfect the working of capital markets. And if capital markets work more effectively, than the portfolio problem could be solved in an alternative way and the capital-raising advantages of size would be even less than they presently are.

*Brozen:* Isn't that one of the ways of perfecting the working of capital markets, precisely by this packaging of risks?

*Scherer:* It is one way, but there are alternative ways.

*Warren Schwartz:* One difficulty that I, as a simple lawyer, have with even the degree of disagreement that you people have, is that you talk about plant and multiplant efficiency, and sort of sub silentio translate that into the size of the firm.

It is not obvious to me why the plant efficiencies of scale could not conceivably be achieved by plants owned by more than one firm, and why some of the technical multiplant efficiencies of scale could not result from competition which would produce a configuration of plants in which these scales were achieved. In other words, how do you move from the technical economy of scale to the size of the firm, since, as I understand it, the theory still needs to be worked out.

*Scherer:* Your understanding of the problem is very good indeed. The evidence we have developed suggests that most of the multiplant economies that may be realized by a firm with numerous plants can, if markets are working well, be realized equally well by a set of properly specialized single-plant firms. One of the main reasons why multiplant firms may achieve scale economies associated with their multiplant status is the fact that markets don't always work well.

*Schwartz:* Doesn't that suggest that the explanation may exist centrally where McGee puts it — that is, efficiency of utilizing and generating information, the very thing you can't measure?

*Scherer:* It is much more complicated than information. I do have trouble dealing with your concept because I am not imbued in the University of Chicago ideology, where information means everything. There are a lot of reasons why markets don't work well, and I suppose you could call all of those reasons ''information'' if you wanted to define ''information'' in a certain way. But there are many actual reasons. For example, in our steel industry and ball bearing industry, firms are simply unwilling to try to undercut one another in price in order to achieve longer runs of certain products.

There are many very complex reasons why the processes of competition may break down, and why therefore the multiplant firm *may* have some advantage in scale economies over the single-plant firm. As Mr. McGee points out, it is a very complex problem.

*McGee:* I couldn't myself formulate the issue any better than Warren Schwartz did. The theory of the firm is somewhat in disarray in spite of two or three important bits of progress. I like his formulation of the question, in fact the implicit answer to it, better than I like Scherer's. Maybe I should go into the practice of law.

*Milton Handler:* Am I correct in interpreting Professor Scherer as favoring a program of deconcentration? If I am correct, he is telling us that in a program of deconcentration we would not lose plant efficiency, and if we lose some multiplant efficiency, the loss to society would not be very great.

Well, to me that is like saying that you can take a drug, a medicine, and it is not going to do you any harm. But I haven't heard him expound what good would flow from a program of deconcentration.

*Scherer:* Well, I have been asked to do a job as an economist at this Conference. It is a narrowly constrained job. If one tries to do everything, one ends up doing nothing well. All I have tried to do in my paper, and indeed in the much longer book on which it is based, is measure the scale economies associated with various kinds of size. The conclusion to which I came is that if we were to move toward an economy of efficient-sized single-plant firms, we wouldn't lose a lot in terms of scale economies relative to the present economy.

Now, your question goes further: Should we in fact try to do that? This involves two additional issues. One is the sort of question on which the economist presumably has some expertise, namely: What are the economic effects of size, market power, and so on? We will deal later with these questions. I am certainly on the record in an earlier book as to how I believe those relationships work out.

I think, however, the issue goes a good deal further than that. Professor Dewey has nailed it on the head. We may like deconcentration for a variety of sociological and political reasons. I happen to share that value judgment, but I don't think it is my business to be telling society what its value judgments should be.

My role as an economist is to say, "Look, Society, if you want this kind of world, here is what it is going to cost." But I am not willing to say, "Do it." I think that is the business of the legislative bodies.

*Harold Demsetz:* Professor Scherer, if we are really interested in what the costs of deconcentration would be, I presume that as economists, especially in the modern terminology, we ought to be concerned with what the social costs of deconcentration would be, and not what the cost of producing a particular product would be.

So let me confront you with an example and see how you respond to it. Suppose we have a given state of technology in which the price charged for the product, the competitive price, is one dollar a unit. A new technology is developed by one firm; and at that one-dollar price, that one firm finds it practical to expand out beyond the point at which your estimates of average cost are at the lowest. All right?

*Scherer:* All right.

*Demsetz:* According to your statement as I read it or heard you, if we break that firm apart and therefore move closer to the low point of its average cost curve, we will not suffer any great cost disadvantages. But I put it to you that the social cost of doing so, because of the effect it has on the incentive to develop a new technology, can be very great. And those kinds of costs are nowhere contemplated in your scheme; is that correct?

*Scherer:* Yes. Given the way you have put the question, it is correct. I haven't, in fact, advanced any scheme for deconcentrating industries. I haven't said that we should deconcentrate in Situation A and concentrate in Situation B.

*Demsetz:* I was not referring to a scheme for deconcentration. I was referring to your scheme for estimating what costs we would bear if we do deconcentrate.

*Scherer:* But if you state this as a universal generalization you are saying, as Professor McGee has sometimes alleged, that all firms are the sizes they are because at one time or another they reduced costs below the costs of everyone else and therefore advanced to very large size. That is a factual assumption. I think you will find there are some firms that are indeed large because they have done just that. But there are other firms that are large for quite different reasons.

If I were trying to design a policy of deconcentration, I would surely take into account the differences between these two kinds of cases. I fully agree with you — if you go around ruthlessly breaking up any firm that happens to have achieved large size because of its superior innovativeness, yes, you will indeed cause a high social cost. I haven't advocated any such policy.

*Demsetz:* Okay, my question is much narrower. My question is: Do your estimates attempt to take account of such potential cost? And the answer is no. That is your estimate of the cost of deconcentrating. Is that not correct?

*Scherer:* I have not estimated any costs of deconcentrating. I have simply compared the costs of a large multiplant firm with the costs of a firm operating a single efficient plant.

*Demsetz:* I'm sorry. I thought you said that as an economist you were prepared to answer the following question: If we choose to deconcentrate, what costs will we bear? And I thought your answer was, "slight."

*Scherer:* Okay, that is a fair statement. There would be an additional cost — an incentive cost — if deconcentration follows in a highly correlated way with the achievement of size through superior efficiency.

*Demsetz:* I'd like to repeat a question that John McGee asked. And that is: If firms are larger than the optimal size — in the narrow sense that you are discussing it, not in the sense that I have just broached the subject — why is it that they don't spin off?

*Scherer:* Well, there are some pretty simple answers to that. One, I have said that at least in some cases minor economies do persist out to substantial multiplant sizes.

Second, I have not alleged that unit costs necessarily *increase* with more multiplant operation. Therefore, it is six of one and half a dozen of the other, whether you have a single-plant firm or a firm with twelve plants.

Third, during interviews in which we discussed with firms how and why they attained their multiplant size, it came out clearly that there is a kind of "expansion to fill the universe" motive among managers. All else equal, a manager would prefer to have a whole lot of plants and cover the whole geographic market, product spectrum, and what have you, than be a single-plant specialist.

*Walter Adams:* Couldn't Mr. Demsetz's question be answered with: "Because they have power"?

*Demsetz:* Power to do what?

*Adams:* Power to insulate themselves from the market discipline, either in the marketplace or through their control of the political mechanism, which we assume is neutral, acting on society's behalf. In other words, can we assume that there is a hermetically sealed compartment in society called government, and can we assume that there is a hermetically sealed compartment called the economy? It seems to me if we want to be relevant to the questions of our time, we have to answer that kind of question.

*Scherer:* Well, what I have observed on the basis of our research would suggest a slight amendment to Walter Adams's statement. I would say firms become large because they *want* power. They may not achieve it. Many are disappointed. They reach their multiplant size and may find they have relatively little power, but nevertheless they are there. Should we do anything about it?

*John Blair:* Members of the legal profession should not go away with the impression that the sole issue in this technological size and efficiency debate is whether reductions in the size of multiple-plant companies down to the level of concentration indicated by existing single-plant firms is the only issue with which economists working in this field are now concerned, or have been concerned for some time.

On that point we have here two speakers, one representing a more conservative point of view, namely Professor McGee; and one who on the whole, in this broad spectrum, represents a more or less centrist point of view, although the questions he has been receiving sort of indicate that he is rather far out on the left. Well, he isn't.

Now, there *is* a somewhat radical or extreme or leftish point of view on this issue, and it is not easily to be dismissed. And its premise departs from the premise of Professor Scherer in that it does not accept existing technology as given data. It presumes — and its ideas are based upon the presumptions — that new technology is greatly reducing the size of plant required for efficient production, so that the size of plant existing today is increasingly obsolete, and that it makes no sense (to use an example from Professor Scherer's study) to study the economies of scale in making a glass bottle — that is, a nineteenth-century technology — or steel beams, another nineteenth-century technology.

What is relevant and what this group should be primarily concerned with is whether having bottles made of glass, which lends itself to a fairly high degree of concentration on both the plant and company basis, is not itself an obsolete technology since today more and more bottles are made not of glass but of plastics; and the technological requirements and capital investments for making bottles out of plastic are in the order of 1 or 2 percent of the capital investment required to make bottles out of glass.

So the real issue that is rapidly developing in the economy is replacement of the existing technologies by newer, capital-saving technologies. It is the issue to which antitrust activities should be directed, not in the sense of trying to break up the glass-bottle-making companies, but rather in seeing to it that the new companies, with new technologies, are not driven out (to die in their infancy) as a result of the application to them of the variety of predatory practices that have been developed over a long period of time, and for which the present law is adequate if it is enforced.

*Louis Schwartz:* Have the diseconomies of large scale been explored? Are you talking about net economies? Many of us who have worked in a large organization are keenly aware of the delays in decision, to take one example, which constitute a diseconomy in large scale. What about diseconomies?

What account has been given to the kind of self-fulfilling prophecy or the mythical character of the efficiency and reliability of large organizations? I perceive, for example, that the lower capital costs which might be found for large organizations are attributable to a mass belief that General Motors is dependable, will not die.

Now, this may be quite independent of the facts of General Motors' technical proficiency. And if it is attributable in a manner somewhat comparable to the former belief in the divine right of kings, to the magic of these institutions, we may be at work dispelling that belief and the capital cost differences might disappear.

It was pointed out that there were real, if not substantial, economies of scale which would account for the pattern of four or five firms dominating principal industries. Nothing was said about whether those economies, if a justification for four or five firms, are equally a justification for a single firm. If costs continue to decline as a multiplant firm grows ever larger, does this imply that there ought to be a merger of Ford, General Motors, and Chrysler, and maybe American Motors?

*McGee:* There has been a great deal of free negative advertising against size in this country for a long, long time, certainly as long as I have been around, which is too long. And everybody can freely engage in it to his heart's content. You can tell people the major firms are not reliable and will die next week, but I wouldn't be at all surprised if people with good judgment wouldn't believe you. And ultimately the test that appears appropriate to me is the market test.

*Scherer:* We were concerned with the problem of diseconomies of large scale. As I point out in my paper, that is the area where our evidence is perhaps weakest. The estimates in my Table 6 involve, among other things, the assumption that large multiplant firms can in fact manage their operations. We found many examples to the contrary. There is, however, so much randomness in this process of coping with large size that we weren't able to reach any clear systematic judgments as to whether on balance there are these diseconomies of size.

*William Baxter:* Let me accept Professor Scherer's general contention that the net economies of very large size are small, and the question then becomes what gains, if any, we would receive from abandoning those very small economies.

If what he says is true, the one kind of power that I really think sometimes exists as a result of monopoly must also be sharply limited; because, if those economies are as slight as he says, then the monopolistic position can be exploited only to the point where it will invite entry at those very minor cost penalties which he says follow.

Although I take his case as proven for the moment, it also goes a long way to eliminate what some have argued are the penalties that go with it.

*Scherer:* I agree with Professor Baxter that the economic losses attributable to monopoly are not very great. I happen to think it is the social consequences of size that are more important than the economic consequences. It is not just a matter of political clout. I think it makes a difference, for instance, if you are working in a battery plant, whether the boss is right there in that plant or whether he is sitting somewhere in Philadelphia.

*Baxter:* I suppose we are in the realm of psychology now, but my perception is that life would be no different on the assembly line if there were ten aluminum companies in America rather than five, and life in the secretarial pool would go on pretty much as before, and the lives of the truck drivers and the maintenance crews would not change much. Life changes for those middle-management groups who suddenly become chief executives instead of middle managers. My perception is that a very large fraction of antitrust is this kind of excise tax we levy on consumers by forsaking these minor economies in order to subsidize the free spirit and lifestyle of middle-class, would-be entre-preneurs. And that is not a welfare program that I, individually, would be willing to vote for in Congress.

*Donald Turner:* If you have a preference for deconcentration for some rea-son and there is no economic cost, why not do it? Cannot there be some in-dustries of that sort?

One answer is that they would spin off. But, they wouldn't spin off if there were no efficiency gain. If you suppose a sort of level of efficiency — if you get efficient to a certain point and the bigger you get there is no change at all — they may not spin off voluntarily for a variety of reasons.

*McGee:* I think the problem is that efficiency has, as we are unfortunately coming to see, at least two major meanings. One has to do with costs. That is a troublesome question. The second has to do with streams of benefits which those plants are providing to different kinds of people. The reason, presum-ably, they don't spin off, if we posit that costs would not be changed if they did, is that those plants are generating a net stream of benefits. They pay, in short, under that style of organization.

*Turner:* But they may pay because of market power; and if you have 50 per-cent of the markets in five plants, of course they are not going to spin off.

*Demsetz:* Could I just add a comment on this question. If we set aside the market power thing, the answer is that they would spin off if there were no cost differences, if only you people who would those social preferences would pay them one dollar to do so.

*Louis Schwartz:* I would like to press the question which Mr. McGee did not answer earlier, which is: Believing as he does in the economy of progressively larger scale, and reinforced in that respect by the fact that on a multiplant basis they may go up to 100 percent of the market, he sees no reason to prevent the merger of our three or four big companies.

I think Dewey did present a reason. He said he felt that ultimately there ought to be divestiture to multiply the number of decision-making centers, to prevent the vesting of discretion in progressively fewer hands.

That may be a noneconomic view of it, but at any rate I want to test your view of it, Mr. McGee, by asking whether you see any objection to the merger of all the automobile companies. In other words, would you support some kind of antimerger program?

*McGee:* I think I would, even with Scherer's arithmetic, or a like kind, if it were studiously done and not casually done.

## SELECTED BIBLIOGRAPHY

Bain, Joe S. "Economies of Scale, Concentration, and the Condition of Entry in Twenty Manufacturing Industries." *American Economic Review,* 44 (March 1954), 15-39.
———. *Barriers to New Competition.* Harvard University Press, 1956, Chapter 3.
Esposito, Louis; Noel, Norman R.; and Esposito, Francis F. "Dissolution and Scale Econ-omies: Additional Estimates and Analysis." *Antitrust Law and Economics Review,* 5 (Fall 1971), 103-114.

McGee, John. "Economies of Size in Auto Body Manufacture." *Journal of Law and Economics,* 16 (October 1973), 239-273.

Moore, Frederick T. "Economies of Scale: Some Statistical Evidence." *Quarterly Journal of Economics,* 73 (May 1959), 232-245.

Pratten, C. F. *Economies of Scale in Manufacturing Industry.* Cambridge University Press, 1971.

Pratten, C. F., and Dean, R. M. *The Economies of Large-Scale Production in British Industry: An Introductory Survey.* Cambridge University Press, 1965.

Scherer, F. M. "The Determinants of Industrial Plant Sizes in Six Nations." *Review of Economics and Statistics,* 55 (May 1973), 135-145.

Scherer, F. M.; Beckenstein, Allen; Kaufer, Erich; and Murphy, R. D. *The Economics of Multi-Plant Operation: An International Comparison.* Harvard University Press, forthcoming in 1975.

Schwartzman, David. "Uncertainty and the Size of the Firm." *Economica,* 30 (August 1963), 287-296.

Shepherd, W. G. "What Does the Survivor Technique Show About Economies of Scale?" *Southen Economic Journal,* 34 (July 1967), 113-122.

Subcommittee on Antitrust and Monopoly. *Economic Concentration.* U.S.G.P.O., 1965, Part 4.

# 3

# Advertising as an Impediment to Competition

## Editors' Note

Advertising is viewed by some as an important cause of concentration. It allegedly erects barriers to entry and thus performs an important role in the structure-conduct-performance paradigm. This paradigm holds that small numbers of firms, other things being equal, facilitate overt or tacit collusion. The alleged collusion results in restricted output and higher prices. In the absence of barriers to entry, new firms and potential entry would cause prices to move back to competitive levels. However, if advertising (or any other factor) operates as a significant barrier to entry, higher prices and profits could be maintained.

A basic issue is the mechanism by which advertising may produce or sustain concentration. A related issue is how advertising could function as an entry barrier. One view is that there are economies of scale in advertising causing barriers. Another possible explanation offered is that the good will built up through advertising (and possibly product quality) would require substantial outlays by a new firm. In this respect, advertising is a capital-requirements barrier. Of course, existing firms would at one time also have had to overcome the good will of rivals.

Another view is that advertising is a means of entry, i.e., it destroys brand loyalties. There is some evidence, for example, that new products are advertised more intensively than old, the firm with the largest market share is not always the most intensive advertiser in its industry, and customer brand loyalty is lower in markets with heavy advertising than in markets with less intense advertising.

The discussions to date, as evidenced by the papers of Professors Brozen and Mann, have been mostly empirical, dominated by controversies on whether advertising is related to concentration ratios or excess profit rates. Another issue is whether the direction of the influence is from advertising to concentration to profits, or from profits to concentration to advertising. The evidence suggests that advertising intensity is associated with higher profits. However, some argue that when the good will investment built up by advertising is taken into account, the adjusted profit rates are no longer positively associated with advertising intensity.

A number of public policy questions are raised by the advertising issues. One is whether the amounts spent on advertising should be limited because of the barriers argument and because advertising is said to lead to competitively wasteful efforts. A counterargument is that advertising is in this regard no different from other methods of competitive striving. Another proposal is to reduce the amount of advertising expenses that can be taken as a tax deduction. A further suggested remedy is to abolish legal trademarks and brands, which would reduce incentives to advertise. Still another possibility is to develop product information sources other than the sellers, who are not regarded as objective.

The papers by Brozen and Mann go into these matters in great detail, but reach diametrically opposite conclusions. Brozen finds advertising is a basis for new entry; it permits firms to grow and yields high volume, low price, and good quality. Advertising, in Brozen's view, promotes competition and the efficient allocation of resources. Mann concludes the opposite: advertising stifles competition and new entry, leads to a misallocation of resources (with the effect that firms produce too few goods at too high a price), and results in excess profits.

# Entry Barriers: Advertising and Product Differentiation

## Yale Brozen*

To anyone who has noticed the use of advertising by any business to woo the customers of other firms, it must seem a bit surrealistic to be considering the evidence for and against the view that advertising is a means of monopolizing. To any casual observer, it would seem that advertising is a means of competing. Most importantly, advertising is much more a means of entry than a barrier to entry.

Much of the behavior we observe fits the view that advertising is a means of entry and impeaches the view that it is a barrier. New products are adver-

* Professor of Business Economics, Graduate School of Business, University of Chicago. For further biographical information, see Appendix D.

The author is indebted to Professors Sam Peltzman, Phillip Nelson, Peter Pashigian, and Lee Benham for helpful comments and criticisms.

tised more intensively than old products.[1] Many firms which are not the biggest in their industries advertise more intensively than the firm with the largest market share.[2] Customers in markets with heavy advertising are less loyal to any one brand than are customers in markets where advertising is less intense.[3] (Loyalty to a brand seems to be a function of experience with the brand rather than the advertising of the brand.[4]) Within any one product category, the more heavily advertised brands are more uniform and of higher average quality than the less-advertised brands.[5] "Search" goods (those whose important characteristics can be determined by observation) are less heavily advertised than "experience" goods (those whose important characteristics can be tested only by use).[6] None of these data fits the view that advertising is a barrier to entry or is used to create a barrier to entry.

## HOW DID THE BARRIER VIEW OF ADVERTISING ARISE?

Given these observations, how did the entry-barrier view of advertising become so pervasive among economists after the 1930s? Part of the answer appears to lie in the nature of the attack on the pre-1930s paradigm used by most economists. Authors in the 1930s, such as Joan Robinson, attempting to inflate the importance of their works, labored diligently to discredit the realism or usefulness of the perfectly competitive model of markets.[7] In doing so,

1. National Commission on Food Marketing, *Studies of Organization and Competition in Grocery Manufacturing,* Technical Study No. 6 (1969), pp. 37-38; David Schwartzmann, "Size of Firm, Research and Promotion in the Drug Industry," (unpublished, New School of Social Research 1972), p. 15; Lester G. Telser, "Advertising and Competition," *Journal of Political Economy,* 72 (December 1964), p. 551; Jules Backman, *Advertising and Competition* (NYU Press 1967), pp. 26-27.

2. James M. Ferguson, "Advertising and Liquor," *Journal of Business,* 40 (October 1967), p. 426; Douglas F. Greer, "Product Differentiation and Concentration in the Brewing Industry," *Journal of Industrial Economics,* 19 (July 1971), p. 214; Yoram Peles, "Economies of Scale in Advertising Beer and Cigarettes," *Journal of Business,* 44 (January 1971), pp. 32-37; "100 Leaders' Advertising as Per Cent of Sales," *Advertising Age,* August 27, 1973, p. 28; National Commission on Food Marketing, *supra* n. 1, at 206, 210.

3. National Commission on Food Marketing, *supra* n. 1, at 198. Yale Brozen, "New FTC Policy from Obsolete Economic Doctrine," *Antitrust Law Journal,* 41, No. 3 (1973), pp. 480-481.

4. Lester Telser, "The Demand for Branded Goods as Estimated from Consumer Panel Data," *Review of Economics and Statistics,* 44 (August 1962), pp. 300-324.

5. Federal Trade Commission, *Chain Stores: Quality of Canned Fruits and Vegetables* (1933).

6. Phillip Nelson, "Advertising as Information" (unpublished, S.U.N.Y. at Binghampton 1972), p. 32.

7. Lack of realism is an irrelevant consideration in determining the applicability of a theory. See Milton Friedman, "The Methodology of Positive Economics," *Essays in Positive Economics* (Univ. of Chicago Press 1953), pp. 16-29.

they made a number of unverified assertions about the uses and effects of advertising — assertions which attained the status of axioms.[8]

Prior to the mid-thirties, most economic theorists argued that the world could be well understood by viewing it "as if" markets operated in a perfectly competitive fashion (with an exception for those where a patent of monopoly had been conferred by the monarch — and even these could be understood in terms of the fact that markets had to be prevented from behaving "as if" they tended to become perfectly competitive, and therefore those holding patents of monopoly had to constantly call on the monarch to apply force to shut out swarms of would-be competitors).[9] This was a view with eighteenth-century roots well expressed in *The Wealth of Nations*.

Viewing the world "as if" it were perfectly competitive for purposes of understanding, prognosticating, or prescribing was practiced and thoroughly accepted by most economists. The only exception was the monopoly case in which the firm was faced by the less than perfectly elastic industry demand curve. Then came Mrs. Robinson, claiming to have described an important set of tools for analyzing an intermediate case — imperfect competition — in which only a few believed. Mrs. Robinson feared her book would receive little attention unless she established the importance of the intermediate case in which firms were faced with a downward-sloping curve as were monopolists but, nevertheless, the demand curve facing them was not their industry's demand curve. The demand facing these firms would be more elastic than industry demand, but would not be perfectly elastic as it would be under perfect competition.[10]

Mrs. Robinson speaks of "emancipating economic analysis from the tyranny of the assumption of perfect competition,"[11] and she tells us that "Every in-

8. "Does advertising in practice promote industrial concentration, restrict the entry of newcomers and unnecessarily raise prices above the level they would be at in its absence? The question is a matter of fact. . . . Nevertheless, since the work of Professor E. H. Chamberlin and Mrs. Joan Robinson in the 1930s most economists have inclined to the belief that advertising does have these adverse effects." H. Gray, "Economics of Advertising: A Summary of Sources," *The Advertising Quarterly,* 11 (Spring 1967), pp. 9-15.

9. "Before the Great Depression, that chasm between darkness and light, economists had generally looked upon the economy as a mixture of industries that approximated conditions of perfect competition and industries that were 'monopolies.' The competitive industries, it was believed, were satisfactorily analyzed by the theory of competition." George J. Stigler, "Monopolistic Competition in Retrospect," *Five Lectures on Economic Problems* (Macmillan 1949); reprinted in G. J. Stigler, *The Organization of Industry* (R. D. Irwin 1968), p. 309.

10. The elasticity of demand facing a firm is treated by economists as a measure of the monopoly power possessed by the firm (and as a measure of product differentiation).

11. Joan Robinson, "What is Perfect Competition?" *Quarterly Journal of Economics,* 48 (1934), p. 105.

dividual producer has the monopoly of his own output." [12] To further assert the relevance of her analytics, Mrs. Robinson informs us that "The traditional assumption of perfect competition is an exceedingly convenient one for simplifying the analysis of price, but there is no reason to expect it to be fulfilled in the real world." [13] She offers arguments for expecting the demand curve facing the firm to be less than infinitely elastic.[14] Mrs. Robinson asserts that "the customer will be influenced by advertisement, which plays upon his mind with studied skill, and makes him prefer the goods of one producer to those of another because they are brought to his notice in a more pleasing or more forceful manner." [15] And just in case the market does become perfectly competitive, making her analytics irrelevant, she tells us that "when a firm finds the market is becoming uncomfortably perfect it can resort to advertisement and other devices which attach customers more firmly to itself." [16]

In her discussion of the impact of advertising on the character of markets, Mrs. Robinson herself seems to remain in the grip of "the tyranny of the assumption of perfect competition." She implicitly assumes that the *natural* state of the economic universe is perfectly competitive.[16a] She then tries to show, by a series of assertions about the effects of various business activities, especially advertising, that the world is actually composed of numerous monopolies — an unnatural but actual state of affairs brought about by deliberate acts designed to produce that result. She seizes on any action by firms such as product improvement or advertising, and asserts that these acts are *the* anticompetitive forces which bring about this unnatural state of affairs. In this, she has followed the same path trod by the Antitrust Division and the Federal Trade Commission. Both have designated competitive actions as monopolizing actions. Economists have joined in this game and have come to believe that upside down is right side up almost as frequently as have the enforcers of the antitrust law. They have been asserting for the last three decades that such means of entry as product differentiation and advertising are barriers. About the only upside-down antitrust doctrines they have not bought wholeheartedly are Judge Hand's assertions that building additional

12. Joan Robinson, *Economics of Imperfect Competition* (Macmillan 1933), p. 5.

13. *Id.* at 88.

14. The view that the forces and circumstances which Mrs. Robinson and Professor Chamberlin believe to be causes of downward-sloping curves will necessarily result in such curves has been strongly contested by Alfred J. Nichols, "The Influences of Marginal Buyers on Monopolistic Competition," *Quarterly Journal of Economics,* 48 (November 1934), pp. 121-135. Warren Nutter, "The Plateau Demand Curve and Utility Theory," *Journal of Political Economy,* 63 (December 1955), pp. 525-528, shows that Professor Nicols makes theoretical sense despite arguments to the contrary.

15. Robinson, *supra* n. 12, at 90.

16. *Id.* at 101.

16a. Economists following Mrs. Robinson often make the same assumption. "Bain's analysis implicitly assumes that the selling costs have appeared in what would otherwise be a fairly *perfect* market." Alfred Nicols, "The Monopoly Basis of Success," *Schweizerische Zeitschrift für Volkswirtschaft und Statistik,* 98 (1962), p. 509.

capacity is an exclusionary practice,[17] that reciprocal dealing and vertical integration are anticompetitive,[18] or that predatory activities financed by cross-subsidization or "deep pockets" are likely activities by conglomerates or large firms.[19]

Part of the confusion which has led economists astray is the mistaking of association or correlation with causation. No advertising would occur under Robinsonian perfect competition or Chamberlinian pure competition. "The very nature of a purely competitive market precludes a selling problem. . . . Advertising would be without purpose under conditions of pure competition." [20] But advertising does not create monopolistic or imperfect competition. It is a consequence of or is profitable under monopolistic competition — a correlate of monopolistic competition, not a cause. Chamberlin has told us that "selling costs cannot be defined without a theory which recognizes the monopoly elements responsible for them." [21]

Professor Chamberlin's definition of pure competition includes perfect knowledge, and no inertia, on the part of buyers. Mrs. Robinson's perfect competition also assumes these same circumstances. Where no knowledge can be added to the buyer's store of information by advertising and there is no inertia to overcome, there is no function for advertising. It follows, then, that the occurrence of advertising is a signal by which we can recognize the existence of monopolistic competition (or nonstationary circumstances arising out of technical progress, population change, additions to resource supplies, or birth, aging, and death). But that does not mean that advertising is the cause of the absence of static pure competition.

17. "One would suppose that . . . the kind of competitive conduct and performance that ordinarily has unquestioned economic merit . . . would also include expansion capacity to meet existing or anticipated demand, which is obviously one of the most important responses that we expect a competitive market to generate. Yet this is precisely the kind of conduct which Judge Hand cited as the principal element in Alcoa's offense." Donald F. Turner, "The Scope of Antitrust and Other Economic Regulatory Policies," 82 *Harvard L. Rev.* 1207, 1221 (1969).

18. Joel E. Segall, "The Conglomerate Phenomenon," *Brittanica Book of the Year 1970*, p. 779; Robert Bork, "Vertical Integration and the Sherman Act: The Legal History of an Economic Misconception," 22 *U. Chi. L. Rev.* 157 (1954); George J. Stigler, *Theory of Price* (Macmillan 1966), p. 207; Sam Peltzman, "Issues in Vertical Integration Policy," in J. F. Weston and Sam Peltzman, eds., *Public Policy Toward Mergers* (Goodyear Publ. Co. 1969), p. 167; J. J. Spengler, "Vertical Integration and Antitrust Policy," *Journal of Political Economy*, 58 (August 1950), pp. 347-352.

19. Kenneth G. Elzinga, "Predatory Pricing: The Case of the Gunpowder Trust," *Journal of Law & Economics,* 13 (April 1970), pp. 223-240; Roland H. Koller II, "The Myth of Predatory Pricing: An Empirical Study," *Antitrust Law & Economics Review,* Vol. 4. No. 4 (1971), pp. 105-123. John S. McGee, "Predatory Price Cutting: The Standard Oil (N.J.) Case," *Journal of Law & Economics,* 1 (April 1958), pp. 137-169.

20. E. H. Chamberlin, *The Theory of Monopolistic Competition,* (Harvard Univ. Press 1933), pp. 10, 72.

21. *Id.* (1946) at 174.

Chamberlin tells us that the existence of monopolistic competition is the cause of advertising, not that advertising is the cause of monopolistic competition as Mrs. Robinson believes. He wrote that "the fact that each producer . . . has a market at least partially distinct . . . introduces forces absent under pure competition. . . . [A]dvertising and selling outlays are invited by the fact that the market of each seller is limited." [22]

## ADVERTISING MAKES MARKETS COMPETITIVE

In Mrs. Robinson's *Economics of Imperfect Competition,* there are observations which could have been used as the foundation for a realistic and useful view of the consequences of advertising. She tells us that "Every individual producer has the monopoly of his own output," [23] and she also informs us that "inertia or ignorance . . . prevents customers from moving instantly from one seller to another, as soon as a difference appears between the prices which they charge. . . ." [24]

These observations tell us that the natural state of affairs absent advertising is the imperfectly competitive (or nonstationary) world which Mrs. Robinson believes to be the unnatural state of affairs. There is no need to prove that an imperfectly competitive world is contrived in some way by corrupting the naturally perfectly competitive (or naturally stationary) world. The imperfectly or monopolistically competitive world would exist absent any activity by business to bring it about, and does exist despite activities by business which make it far less monopolistic than it would be absent the competitive striving for sales through such means as advertising and product differentiation. What advertising does, is to make demand curves facing individual firms more elastic — bringing the world closer to the perfectly competitive situation, as Mrs. Robinson defines perfect competition, than it would be absent advertising.

Chamberlin recognizes this consequence of advertising, despite his forcing the definition of pure competition into an inappropriate two-dimensional mold which corrupts and vitiates much of his analysis.

> Buyers often do not know or are but dimly aware of the *existence* of sellers other than those with whom they habitually trade or of goods other than those they habitually consume; they are ill-informed of comparative prices for the same thing

22. *Id.* at 10. Chamberlin himself becomes confused at a later point, however, when he argues that "an essential part of free enterprise is the attempt of every business man to build up his own monopoly. . . . There is no tendency for these monopolies to be competed out of the picture. . . ." *Id.* at 213-214. He recovers a bit in telling us that "pure competition may no longer be regarded as in any sense an 'ideal' for purposes of welfare economics" (*id.* at 214) but fails to recognize that what he regards as ideal is simply multidimensional pure competition where additional dimensions other than price and quantity are introduced as variables in the competitive market. See Harold Demsetz, "The Welfare and Empirical Implications of Monopolistic Competition," *Economic Journal,* 74 (September 1964), pp. 623-641.

23. Chamberlin, *supra* n. 20, at 5.

24. *Id.* at 89.

sold by different merchants; they are ignorant of the quality of goods, in them-selves, compared with other goods, and compared with prices asked. . . . By spead-ing this knowledge, advertising makes the demand for a seller's product more elastic.[25]

Rather than go through an elaborate derivation of firm demand functions in the presence of advertising and comparing them with those occurring in the absence of advertising — a task already ably carried out by Professors Harold Demsetz and Phillip Nelson[26] — I will use an empirical analysis provided by Professor Lee Benham which demonstrates and verifies the point.

In a landmark study, "The Effect of Advertising on the Price of Eyeglasses," Professor Benham examined markets for eyeglasses in states which completely restricted advertising by suppliers and those in states which had few or no restrictions on advertising. Comparing the most and least restrictive states, he found that the average price of eyeglasses differed by nearly $20 in 1963. Where advertising was completely banned, the price of eyeglasses averaged $37.48. Where there was no restriction on advertising, the price of eye-glasses averaged $17.98.[27]

Professor Benham explains this phenomenon as follows:

In general, large-volume low-price sellers are dependent upon drawing consumers from a wide area and consequently need to inform their potential customers of the advantages of coming to them. If advertising is prohibited, they may not be able to generate the necessary sales to maintain the low price. . . . At the same time, the likelihood that small-volume high-priced retailers survive in the market will in-crease.[28]

Professor Benham also interviewed representatives of a number of com-mercial firms. He reports that "Several said that they would not enter a new market unless advertising were permitted. . . ."[29] Benham's study offers evi-dence consistent with the contention that advertising makes markets more per-fectly competitive (see Appendix II),[30] contrary to what Mrs. Robinson and

25. *Supra* n. 20, at 118. Lester Telser adds that advertising attracts customers with weaker preferences for the brand who are sensitive to price, thus further in-creasing the elasticity of demand. "Advertising: Economic Aspects," *International Encyclopedia of the Social Sciences,* 1 (1968), p. 106.

26. Harold Demsetz, "The Nature of Equilibrium in Monopolistic Competition," *Journal of Political Economy,* 67 (February 1959), pp. 21-30; H. Demsetz, "Do Com-petition and Monopolistic Competition Differ?" *Journal of Political Economy,* 76 (January-February 1968), pp. 146-148; Nelson, *supra* n. 6.

27. Lee Benham, "The Effect of Advertising on the Price of Eyeglasses," *Journal of Law & Economics,* 15 (October 1972), p. 342.

28. *Id.* at 339.

29. *Id.* at 346.

30. Benham's study seems to be strong evidence that advertising makes de-mand more elastic in the eyeglass market (how could price fall so far without de-creasing the ratio of price to marginal cost?), but it is conceptually possible that the marginal cost in the advertising market is proportionately lower relative to price

other economists have asserted. It also indicates that advertising is a means of entry. *Prohibition* of advertising is a barrier, not advertising. Without advertising, the natural state of the eyeglass market is imperfectly competitive.

A study of toy manufacturers' television advertising reveals almost equally startling effects on price. Prior to the mid-1950s, the typical toy with a $5 retail list price tended to retail at $4.95 to $4.98. An occasional sale at $4.49 was advertised by retailers in newspaper ads. After the mid-1950s, toy manufacturers began to use spot TV ads in some cities. In the typical case, the $5 retail list toy that was advertised on TV came down to an everyday price of $3.49. The occasional sale advertised by the retailer became a $2.99 sale instead of a $4.49 sale. But in cities where no TV advertising of the toy was undertaken, the price continued at the $4.98 level with the occasional $4.49 sale.[31]

The manufacturer's advertising evidently created a much more elastic demand for the toy at the retail level, eroded local retailer monopolies, made the market for the TV-advertised toy much more nearly perfectly competitive than it had been prior to the manufacturer's advertising campaign, and permitted sellers to take advantage of scale and distribution economies. The television advertisements of toys, and optical shop advertisements of eyeglasses, destroyed much of the "inertia and ignorance" which Mrs. Robinson told us is a source of imperfection in competition.

Further, the important influence of advertising found in these two studies was not a consequence of including information on prices in the advertisements. In the case of eyeglasses, Professor Benham separated the states which prohibited the appearance of prices in ads from those which allowed unrestricted advertising. He found that "in states prohibiting only price advertising prices are slightly higher than in states with no restrictions, and are considerably lower than in states prohibiting all advertising." [32] In the case of toy advertising, an FTC order resulted in the removal of all price information from toy manufacturer ads on television, but retail prices remained at the lower levels despite this.[33]

Essentially, these studies tell us that instead of advertising making otherwise competitive markets imperfect, it makes otherwise imperfect markets competitive. But these are studies of only two markets which may be exceptional rather than characteristic. However, there are studies of three other markets, less complete than the two just described, which point in the same direction. When

---

than in the no-advertising market. In that case, economists would argue that product differentiation or the degree of monopoly (measured by the ratio of price to marginal cost or the elasticity of demand facing the firm) has increased. But this simply says that the *conventional indexes of competition are not meaningful if the cost structure is changed by advertising.* Consumers would certainly rather buy at $17.98 from a monopolist than at $37.48 from a competitor. (I am indebted to Professor Sam Peltzman for this point.)

31. Robert L. Steiner, "Does Advertising Lower Consumer Prices," *Journal of Marketing,* 37 (1973), p. 24.

32. Benham, *supra* n. 27, at 349.

33. R. L. Steiner, *TV Code News* (1964).

the English Monopolies Commission undertook an investigation of the soap industry, evidence was offered showing that packaging, branding, and advertising of soaps brought about a substantial decrease in retailer markups and in prices.[34] An investigation of the chocolate and cocoa market in England and on the Continent by the Monopolies Commission showed that intensive advertising in England was accompanied by low retailer markups in contrast to high retailer markups on the Continent where chocolate and cocoa were not intensively advertised by manufacturers. And a study of ready-to-eat-cereal marketing in the U.S. showed that intensive television advertising decreased other distribution costs at the manufacturer level, decreased seasonal swings in consumption (thus reducing capacity costs per unit sold), and reduced retail distribution costs.

## ADVERTISING AND PROFITS [35]

An indirect approach to the question of whether advertising serves as a barrier was used by Professors Comanor and Wilson. They put together data on the ratio of advertising to sales by forty-one IRS industry groups, related these to accounting rates of return, and arrived at the following conclusion:

> On the basis of these empirical findings, it is evident that for industries where products are differentiable, investment in advertising is a highly profitable activity. Industries with high advertising outlays earn, on average, at a profit rate which exceeds that of other industries by nearly four percentage points. This differential represents a 50 percent increase in profit rates. It is likely, moreover, that much of this profit rate differential is accounted for by the entry barriers created by advertising expenditures and by the resulting achievement of market power.[36]

There is, however, a major methodological flaw in the regressions used by Comanor and Wilson for organizing their data. They treat outlays for advertising as a current expense. They do this despite their explicit recognition that the current position of a firm in a market — which demands advertising and product jointly — depends upon past advertising outlays. They cite Professor Kristian Palda,[37] who demonstrated that advertising should be treated as an investment, but then disregard this. They even speak of "investment in advertising," but then expense all such outlays in their statistical treatment.

Their conclusion that "Industries with high advertising outlays earn, on average, at a profit rate which exceeds that of other industries by nearly four percentage points" is reached by using understated net worths for the firms in

---

34. G. Polanyi, *Detergents: A Question of Monopoly* (Institute of Economic Affairs Research Monograph No. 24, Transatlantic 1972).

35. For a moderately technical discussion of the studies mentioned in this section, see James M. Ferguson, *Advertising and Competition: Theory, Measurement, Fact* (forthcoming).

36. W. S. Comanor and T. A. Wilson, "Advertising, Market Structure and Performance," *Review of Economics and Statistics*, 49 (November 1967), p. 437.

37. Kristian Palda, *The Measurement of Cumulative Advertising Effects* (Prentice-Hall 1964).

such industries. Since firms do not capitalize their investment in advertising for balance sheet purposes, the omission of this asset leads to an understatement of net worth, which is large for firms with high advertising–sales ratios. As a consequence, the rate of return is overstated for these firms. For example, a firm whose stated equity equals 40 percent of sales, spending 10 percent of revenues on advertising and earning 8 percent on sales, will show a 20 percent accounting rate of return. If this firm's advertising has a ten-year life and its sales and advertising have been level during the past ten years, then current outlays on advertising will be equal to depreciation of past advertising. Its current income will be unaffected by capitalization of current outlays and straight-line depreciation of past outlays. Its equity, however, will be increased by the depreciated value of capitalized past advertising. It will become equal to 100 percent of sales. An 8 percent margin on sales, then, will show an 8 percent return on corrected equity instead of 20 percent on stated equity.

Comanor and Wilson discovered only the fact that the upward bias in accounting rates of return for "industries with high advertising outlays" is four percentage points greater than the upward bias "of other industries." Since they did not use true rates of return, or proportionately biased accounting rates of return, they did not substantiate the presumption that advertising is a barrier to entry.[38]

Professor Leonard Weiss attempted to correct the methodological deficiency of the Comanor and Wilson study. After correcting by capitalizing advertising expenditures over a six-year period, he found that there still remained a positive relationship between advertising and profits.[39] As he points out, however, "It is possible that the net relationship between advertising and profit rates would fall to nonsignificance if ads could be depreciated over more realistic lives (perhaps ten years instead of six)."[40] Professor Weiss used only

---

38. Richard A. Miller, "Market Structure and Industrial Performance: Relation of Profit Rates to Concentration, Advertising Intensity, and Diversity," *Journal of Industrial Economics,* 17 (April 1969), p. 104, also found a positive relationship between profitability and advertising. He argues that this demonstrates the barrier-to-entry effects of advertising. His study, too, may be dismissed as evidence for this view for the same reason as the Comanor and Wilson study, *supra* n. 36. In addition, there is internal evidence in Miller's study that advertising does not erect a barrier. Miller "divides industries into producer and consumer goods industries and runs the same regression for each group. Expecting the coefficient of advertising intensity to be positive only for consumer goods industries, he nevertheless finds this result for both samples. This result suggests that interpreting the advertising variable as a barrier to entry measure is not correct, since advertising is much lower in producer industries." *Supra* n. 35. The similarity of results in the two groups strongly suggests that the positive coefficient of the advertising variable is simply the result of incorrectly measured rates of return with a constant bias toward more greatly overstating the rate of return in the more advertising intensive industries when using accounting rates of return.

39. Leonard Weiss, "Advertising Profits and Corporate Taxes," *Review of Economics and Statistics,* 51 (November 1969), p. 421.

40. *Id.* at 428.

six years of advertising expenditure, for lack of comparable data from the IRS *Source Book* for earlier years.[41]

In attempting to correct the methodological flaw of a study which treated advertising as an expense, Professor Weiss himself committed a major error which influences his results, apart from the limitations imposed by the inadequate data available to him. He assumed that the economic life (rate of depreciation) of the advertising investments by various industries was *identical* (as well as being limited to, in effect, five years). Professor Yoram Peles, in his study of three industries, found rates of depreciation varied, at least among these three.[42] Robert Ayanian found, in a study of six industries, rates of depreciation varying from 5 percent to 46 percent.[43] This variability, which was assumed away by Professor Weiss, could account for Weiss's results as well as the unduly high rate of depreciation used — a rate which exceeded that found appropriate by Ayanian for most of his industries. Estimating the actual rate of depreciation and true profit rates, Ayanian finds no association between advertising intensity and estimated true profit rates.

The FTC staff studied the relationship between advertising and profitability in ninety-seven food manufacturing firms.[44] It found a positive relationship between advertising intensity and accounting profit rates. Again, however, the same methodological deficiency as that occurring in the Comanor and Wilson study was present. In addition, there were data deficiencies.

To see whether or not advertising truly serves as a barrier to entry, if high profitability of intensively advertised products can be taken to mean blockaded entry,[45] Professor Harry Bloch re-did the FTC study, taking account of the fact

41. Professor Harry Bloch finds that Weiss, and Comanor and Wilson, all commit a fundamental error in using industry aggregates. Advertising intensity effects can be appropriately measured only on a firm basis. *Advertising and Profitability: A Reappraisal* (Discussion Paper 81, Dept. of Economics, Univ. of British Columbia 1972). In addition, Robert Ayanian points out that "when a firm grows through acquisition of another firm the value of the acquired firm's advertising capital at the time of acquisition will be included in the purchase price . . . and will thus be included in the acquiring firm's equity. . . . Using acquired firms' past advertising . . . would result in double counting." *Advertising and Rates of Return* (Ph.D. dissertation, UCLA 1974), p. 25.

42. Y. Peles, "Rate of Amortization of Advertising Expenditures," *Journal of Political Economy,* 79 (September/October 1971), p. 1032.

43. R. Ayanian, *Advertising and Rates of Return* (Ph. D. dissertation, UCLA 1974).

44. Federal Trade Commission, *Economic Report on the Influence of Market Structure on the Profit Performance of Food Manufacturing Companies* (1969).

45. It has been argued, and some data point in this direction, that if high profitability were associated with intensive advertising, this would not necessarily mean that the high profits are a manifestation of the success of advertising in serving as a barrier to entry. Intensive advertising could be caused by the high profitability of the product. Sellers find it profitable to advertise their profitable products and do not find it profitable to advertise less profitable products. Richard Schmalensee, *The Economics of Advertising* (Contributions to Economic Analyses Series, No. 80; Humanities 1972).

that advertising has long-lived effects.[46] The fact that it has such effects has been established not only by Professor Palda's work, but also by Professor Telser, Professors Nerlove and Waugh, and other analysts.[47]

Professor Bloch, after correcting the data and methodological deficiencies of the FTC study, found that the firms used in the FTC study do not show a positive relationship between advertising and profit rates. The FTC study did not use actual advertising expenditures of the firms it selected for its work. Rather, it imputed to those firms the same level of advertising as the average level found in their industries. Professor Bloch used their actual advertising expenditures. In addition, he treated advertising as an investment.

With these corrections, the FTC study no longer substantiates the staff view that advertising provides a monopoly shelter; rather, the opposite is substantiated: advertising is a means of entry and an ordinary investment. It is no more a barrier to entry than is any other investment, such as that in plant and equipment. Advertising and competition are compatible — not antithetical. Investment in advertising yields the same return as investment in tangible assets — a result to be expected under competitive circumstances (assuming risks are identical) — and evidence supports the view that advertising is a means of entry, just as the building of production facilities is a means of entry.

A currently underway study by a student of Professor Harold Demsetz has produced preliminary results inconsistent with the hypothesis that advertising is a barrier to entry. When industries find themselves in a disequilibrium situation with above-normal profits, we would expect the rate of return to decline more slowly in industries with high barriers to entry than in those with moderate to low barriers. Comparing industries in such a disequilibrium which are advertising-intensive with those which do little advertising, Professor Demsetz's student can find no significant difference in the rate of decline of profits (rate of entry) between the two sets of industries. Evidently, it is no more difficult to enter the advertising-intensive industries than it is to enter other industries. Advertising is not a barrier according to these data.

## ADVERTISING AND ENTRY

The only industry Professor Bain placed in his group of "industries with very high entry barriers" solely on the basis of advertising and selling costs

46. *Advertising, Competition, and Market Performance* (Ph.D. dissertation, Univ. of Chicago 1971).

47. Lester G. Telser, "Advertising and Cigarettes," *Journal of Political Economy,* 70 (October 1962), pp. 471-499; M. Nerlove and F. Waugh, "Advertising Without Supply Control," *Journal of Farm Economy,* 43 (November 1961), pp. 813-837; Yoram Peles, "Rates of Amortization of Advertising Expenditures," *Journal of Political Economy,* 79 (September-October 1971), p. 1032; Jacques Lambin, "Advertising and Competitive Behavior" (Louvain University, Belgium, Center for Socio-Economic Studies in Advertising and Marketing (CESAM), Working Paper No. 2, 1969); M. L. Vidale and H. B. Wolfe, "An Operations Research Study of Sales Response to Advertising," *Operations Research,* 5 (1957), p. 370; Robert Ayanian, *Advertising and Rates of Return* (Ph.D. dissertation, UCLA 1974).

was liquor.[48] Bain tells us that "Entry on a relatively small scale . . . would encounter overwhelming disadvantages. . . . Large scale entry is not viewed as conceivable. . . ."[49] Since advertising is viewed as producing blockaded entry in the liquor industry by the foremost spokesman for the view that advertising is an entry barrier, an examination of experience in this industry should tell us something about how successfully advertising serves as an entry barrier.

Professor James Ferguson undertook an examination of this industry. He found that "Of seventy-six grain distilled spirit plants authorized to operate July 1, 1965, twenty-two entered in 1944 or later." Ferguson estimates that of the thirty-five companies owning registered distilleries producing whiskey in 1965, twelve were new entrants.[50] The advertising blockage seems to have been ineffective, Bain to the contrary notwithstanding.

The liquor industry was offered by Bain (1956) as a prime example of an oligopoly buttressed by the advertising blockade, yet the share of market sold by the Big Four declined from 75 percent in 1947 to 54 percent in 1967.[51] The share of total consumption of distilled spirits represented by the top twenty brands declined from 1951-1953 to 1960-1962 by more than 14 percent despite an 11 percent rise in their share of distilled spirit advertising in this period.[52]

Since 1970, television advertising of cigarettes has been banned. Experience in this industry before and after the ban casts some light on the advertising-entry-barrier issue. Before the ban, new brands successfully entered the industry, each year being marked by the successful entry of one new brand. Since the ban, no successful new brand has been launched despite the fact that there has been no decline in the number of attempts.[53]

That the cigarette market can be successfully entered despite intensive advertising by established brands was demonstrated in the 1930s. The ten-cent brands launched at that time, and the few already in the market, increased their market share from 0.3 percent to 22.8 percent between 1931 and late 1932.[54] As Professor Lester Telser points out, his study of advertising

48. Joe S. Bain, *Barriers to New Competition* (Harvard Univ. Press 1956), pp. 169-170, 293. It is unclear whether quality fountain pens are also placed in this group solely for this reason, since Bain does not tell us how he ranked this industry in terms of the scale economy barrier, although his discussion at 316 concerning the very small size of the market implies that scale economy is important.

49. *Id.* at 296.

50. James M. Ferguson, "Advertising and Liquor," *Journal of Business*, 40 (1967), p. 419.

51. Bureau of the Census, *1967 Census of Manufacturers, Concentration Rates in Manufacturing* (1970), p. 9.

52. Schmalensee, n. 45, at 424.

53. Studies by students of Professor Peter Pashigian at the University of Chicago.

54. Richard B. Tennant, *The American Cigarette Industry* (Yale Univ. Press 1950), p. 89.

and cigarettes[55] "strongly support[s] the view that one of advertising's main functions is to introduce new products. A large increase in advertising relative to sales occurred during the postwar period as a result of . . . the introduction of many new brands."[56]

If advertising were used to keep customers attached — to increase their loyalty, as Chamberlin and Robinson suggest — and prevent entry, we should expect to find old products advertised as intensively as new products. What we find is exactly the opposite. New products and new models are advertised more intensively than old products and old models.

The fact that new products and new models are advertised more heavily than old products and old models suggests that advertising is a means of entry[57] — a means of informing consumers that a new product, which they may be interested in trying, has appeared on the scene. Without advertising — an inexpensive means of communicating with large numbers of people among whom there may be prospective customers — new and old firms offering new products would have to resort to more expensive means of finding customers. This would increase the cost of entry.

## INTRAINDUSTRY VARIABILITY IN ADVERTISING INTENSITY

If advertising serves primarily to keep customers attached and to bar entry, we would expect firms or brands with the largest market share in each industry to advertise at least as intensively as any other firm or brand in its industry. The consequence would be to make brand demand curves more inelastic, as Mrs. Robinson asserts, if this is the function of advertising. Since firms selling the brand with the largest market share are just as interested as any firm with a smaller share in keeping each buyer attached, or more interested if concentration conveys any market power, we would expect them to spend as

55. Lester G. Telser, "Advertising and Cigarettes," *Journal of Political Economy*, 70 (October 1962), p. 471.

56. Lester G. Telser, "Advertising and Competition," *Journal of Political Economy*, 72 (December 1964), p. 551.

57. The fact that new products are advertised more intensively than old products does not mean that the new product bears a higher expense in order to break into (penetrate) the market than old products, and that this means that advertising is a barrier. If all advertising outlays were a current expense, this would be true. Advertising is an investment, however, and the introducer of a new product must make an investment outlay for this purpose just as he does for production facilities.

Just because current producers have plants for which they have already paid while a new entrant must make outlays for a plant, we would not argue that the necessity for plant outlays by a new entrant constitutes an entry barrier. Professor John Gould has demonstrated that outlays on advertising can be explained in the same way as the accumulation of capital stock in any other form. "Diffusion Processes and Optimal Advertising Policy," in Edmund Phelps, ed., *Microeconomic Foundation of Employment and Inflation Theory* (Norton 1970). Also, see George J. Stigler, *The Theory of Price* (Macmillan 1966), p. 200, and "The Economics of Information, *Journal of Political Economy*, 69 (June 1961), pp. 213-215.

much or more on advertising per unit sold as brands with smaller market shares.

On the other hand, if advertising is directed toward making customers *disloyal*, that is, if it is aimed at attracting the customers of other firms or at entering a market, the firm or brand with the largest market share will spend less per unit sold than many smaller firms. Since it already has the biggest share of the market, there are fewer potential new buyers of its brand among the audience for its advertising than in the case of a smaller firm. If advertising is aimed at creating disloyalty, then, rather than loyalty, we will not find the firm or brand with the largest market share at the top of the list of advertisers ranked by percent of sales spent on advertising or amount of advertising per unit of sales.

Professor Ferguson gathered data on advertising per case for twenty leading liquor brands in the United States.[58] Case sales of the leading brand exceeded case sales of the next brand by more than three times, and its advertising expenditure per case was only about half as great (1960-1962). The leading brand ranked twelfth among the twenty leading brands in advertising per case. The leading advertiser in expenditures per case among the twenty brands ranked sixteenth in sales. None of the top four in sales ranked among the top four in advertising outlays per case. These data do not fit the view that advertising is used to cement loyalty. They fit much better the view that advertising, among other tactics, is used to create disloyalty and is a means of entry.[59]

Professor Douglas Greer provides data on advertising per barrel by nine leading brewers which show similar large variations in advertising expenditures not positively correlated with sales rank. Anheuser-Busch ranked first in sales but eighth out of nine firms in expenditures per barrel (1965-1967). The firm spending the least per barrel ranked third in sales. The range in expenditures was from $0.99 to $1.74 (from $0.84 to $2.02 in 1967).[60] Again the data do not fit the barrier view of advertising.

An examination of a number of other industries from soap to cereals and automobiles shows the largest firm with lower advertising intensity than many smaller firms (with the exception of tires), the most advertising-intensive firm frequently being the smallest among those for whom data could be found.

---

58. Ferguson, *supra* n. 50, at 426.

59. It might be argued that economies of scale in advertising might account for the top four sellers not being among the top four in advertising intensity. Professor James Ferguson's survey of the literature on economies of scale, however, finds no uncontradicted evidence for such economies at the levels of advertising involved here. *Supra* n. 35. Also, the data on sales and advertising in liquor provided by Ferguson do not fit the economies of scale view. The drop in advertising per case with a rise in case sales in several pairings of brands is much too sharp to be accounted for by economies of scale. It might, perhaps, be accounted for by greater efficiency in the advertising of larger-selling brands, but this still leaves the advertising-as-barrier view unsupported.

60. Douglas F. Greer, "Product Differentiation and Concentration in the Brewing Industry," *Journal of Industrial Economics*, 19 (July 1971), p. 214.

This finding may appear to be contradicted by Professor Marcus who, using 1959-1961 data for 32 three-digit IRS consumer goods industries with twelve asset size classes, found advertising intensity increases with firm size in 24 industries (and decreases in 6).[61] However, the study suffers from the fact that there are many firms in each size class, which forces him to use *average* advertising-to-sales ratios. Also, it suffers from the fact that IRS three-digit industries each include many products. Large firms in a given industry may sell different products or have a different product mix than small firms.

It should also be added that the advertising behavior of the "Tobacco Trust" and its successor firms and that of the independent cigarette firms also is consistent with the hypothesis that advertising is aimed at creating disloyalty and is a function of the number of *potential* customers a firm is seeking to reach, not of the customers it already has. In the year before dissolution, American Tobacco, when it produced 83.9 percent of the national output, spent $4.2 million advertising its cigarettes. The successor companies, in the year following dissolution, spent $10.2 million. Advertising per thousand on domestic and blended brands doubled in the successor companies (from $0.37 per thousand in 1909-1910 to $0.82 in 1911-1912) while that of the seven independent companies changed only slightly (from $0.63 per thousand in 1909-1910 to $0.69 in 1911-12). On the other hand, advertising per thousand of Turkish brands, where American's market share was much smaller, increased by only 16 percent in the successor companies from the year before dissolution to the following year.[62]

## CONCLUSIONS

Advertising appears to make the demand curves facing firms more elastic, that is, reduces differentiation, and markets more competitive. We have no studies which show this directly. The one attempt to measure the influence of advertising on firm demand elasticity proved inconclusive,[63] which could mean that price elasticity is independent of the level of advertising. There is indirect evidence whose weight leans toward the conclusion that advertising increases elasticity. There is also evidence which points in the direction that advertising is a means of entry.

First, new products are advertised more intensively than old. Advertising is used more to obtain a market than to hold a market, although there is some evidence showing that it encourages repeat purchases.[64] Even established products must advertise in a nonstationary economy — not to hold a market or to encourage loyalty, but to convey information to uninformed buyers just as a new product must. "A mature product that has gained consumer ac-

61. Matityahu Marcus, "The Intensity and Effectiveness of Advertising," *Oxford University Institute of Economics and Statistics Bulletin*, 32 (November 1970), pp. 339-345.

62. *Supra* n. 54, at 71 and 74.

63. *Supra* n. 49.

64. *Supra* n. 50, at 551.

ceptance requires continuous advertising because there is a turnover of clientele or because of growth in the market so that some new customers are uninformed."[65]

Second, there is less customer loyalty in markets with intensive advertising than in those with less intensive advertising. This would, on the one hand, seem to indicate that customers are not more firmly attached but are attracted by advertising — are informed of products of whose existence they would otherwise be unaware. Advertising is used to create disloyalty, to woo the customers of other firms rather than to keep the loyalty of those the advertiser already has. Of course, heavy advertising occurs in markets where many new brands or models are being introduced; and the appearance of new brands, of which customers learn through advertising, is what results in disloyalty being associated with intensive advertising. On the other hand, it is possible that advertising has a higher payoff where customers are easily detached, so we find high advertising associated with disloyalty not because it causes disloyalty but because it can take advantage of it. But this is still consistent with advertising being a means of entry and a means of attracting rather than attaching customers.

Third, the firm in each industry with the most to protect — the brand with the largest market share — usually does not advertise so intensively as many with much less to protect. This seems to support the view that advertising is used to gain market, not to hold market. If it is used to gain market, then it must be a means of entry. It could be argued that the firm or brand with the largest share is simply the most efficient — that is why it has the largest share, offering more value per dollar of price — and gets more effect with fewer advertising dollars. But this offers no support for the barrier-to-entry view; on this argument, the less intensive advertising of leading brands merely fails to contradict it.

Fourth, the higher uniformity and quality of the more intensively advertised brands suggests that loyalty is created by the product, not by advertising. Higher-quality goods are more intensively advertised because the buyers attracted by advertising are more likely to repeat their purchase than in the case of lower-quality goods. The higher advertising for products where repeat purchase is more likely would seem to mean that advertising is used to gain customers rather than to hold them. If it succeeded in holding customers, thus making demand more inelastic, then lower-quality goods would advertise as intensively as higher-quality brands.

Finally, the fact that "search" goods are not advertised as intensively as "experience" goods would seem to be evidence suggesting that advertising is not used to create brand loyalty. Instead, relative advertising intensities are those expected in terms of the consumer's need for information. Since search goods can be chosen on the basis of inspection, all the consumer needs to know is whether the good has some quality in appearance, size, shape, color, etc. that appeals to him, and the location of a sales outlet. It is fairly cheap to sample by inspection, and he will rely on inspection to give him the informa-

65. *Id.* at 554 n. 14.

tion required to make a choice among alternatives. For an experience good, search is somewhat more expensive since a purchase is usually required to determine its quality (taste of tuna fish, spot removal ability of a cleaning fluid, etc.); advertising will have to provide more information[66] and will be more intensive. If advertising simply creates loyalty, then search goods would be advertised just as intensively as experience goods.

To put these points in general terms — if advertising served only to differentiate products and create loyalty, thereby making firm demand more inelastic, we would not see the large disparities in advertising intensities among brands and product categories that are observed. The disparities are systematically related to customer turnover (durability of advertised information), rate of innovation, growth of market, profitability of product, cost of search, price and age of product, number of prospective customers, and standardization. If advertising plays a role in creating customer loyalty, decreasing firm demand elasticity, and differentiating product, it is a small role and not yet unambiguously detected in any empirical study.

## APPENDIX I
### PRICES OF ADVERTISED AND NONADVERTISED BRANDS

The fact that the prices of advertised brands are frequently higher than the prices of nonadvertised brands is sometimes used as "evidence" that advertising has artificially differentiated the advertised product. Otherwise, why would consumers pay a higher price when the "same good" is available at a lower price? The conclusion does not necessarily follow.

First, is the advertised brand the "same good"? Professor Telser has argued that

> the prices of the more advertised goods might be higher than the prices of less advertised goods because of the higher average quality of the advertised goods. Second, even if the average qualities are the same for both classes, it may be that the advertised goods vary less in quality. Thus the higher price of the more advertised goods may be explained by the stricter quality control exercised over these goods. If one were to choose at random an item from the class of nonadvertised goods, the risk of unsatisfactory performance would be greater than if the choice were restricted to a random selection from the class of advertised goods. The risk is reduced still more if the choice is confined to a class of long-established and advertised products. The evidence of some studies supports this view.[67]

66. "Information" is more than factual data about the good. The fact that a good is advertised is information. The fact that it is advertised frequently is additional information that is particularly relevant in the case of an experience good. P. Nelson, "The Economic Value of Advertising," in Yale Brozen, ed., *Advertising and Society* (forthcoming).

67. *Supra* n. 50, at 542.

We should add that when unadvertised goods have higher quality than advertised items used for comparable purposes, they frequently sell at higher prices than the advertised items. This is a common phenomenon in electronic sound systems.

A recent instance of the inability of advertising to sell low-quality goods at prices comparable to those of high-quality goods, even when assisted by the force of law to prevent the marketing of the high-quality goods, is provided by the experience of the Egg Marketing Board in England. The law specified that all farmers with more than fifty hens had to sell their output to the board and that the board had to buy all eggs offered. The Egg Board marketed fresh eggs under its advertised Lion brand. Unfortunately, many of the Lion trademarked eggs were not so fresh as some illegally marketed, unadvertised eggs. As more and more housewives had unhappy experiences with Lion eggs, they increasingly turned to the unadvertised eggs. Those rose in price from a discount to a premium relative to Lion eggs. The board countered with a stepped-up advertising campaign, raising outlays from $2.2 million to $3.9 million, but sales continued to fall. Unadvertised eggs rose to 56 cents while advertised eggs sold at 48 cents a dozen. Even with the six-cent subsidy provided to the board by the government to assist farmers, they increasingly turned to selling in the unadvertised, illegal market as the premium increased, finally forcing the abolition of the Egg Marketing Board in 1969.[68]

Not only may higher-priced advertised goods be of higher quality than lower-priced unadvertised goods but, second, the cost of a good to a buyer includes not only the price he pays but also the cost of search. In general, products are advertised when the cost of advertising is less than the reduction of the cost of search flowing from the provision of advertising. This means that the cost of the product (cost of search plus price) is reduced by the advertising even when the price of the product is increased to cover the cost of advertising. (Frequently, the advertising is free to the consumer because larger-scale output may reduce unit production and marketing costs enough, or more than enough, to pay for the advertising.) [69]

To illustrate the effect of search costs on a buyer's cost, let us examine some advertising attacked by the FTC's chief economist in 1972. He stated that "once advertising persuades customers, price can be raised and sales not

68. Neil McInnes, "Broken Eggs," *Barron's*, March 17, 1969, p. 9.

69. "[I]n 1958 . . . we decided to run a test television campaign in Cincinnati on some construction sets that had been in our line for several years. We were elated by the roughly tenfold increase in our Cincinnati sales volume and by the equally dramatic retail price cutting that suddenly developed.

"The next year as we rolled out into fifteen markets with our TV campaign, we made another delightful discovery. Though we were spending what seemed like a frightening bundle for advertising, the production economies resulting from the continuing tenfold volume increase covered our TV outlays and maybe then some, so we didn't have to increase our selling price to the trade." Robert L. Steiner, "How Television Advertising Affects Consumer Toy Prices" (unpublished, Univ. of Cincinnati 1973), pp. 2-3.

lost to lower-priced products." He then went on to apply this notion to proprietary drugs, stating that the cost of drugs is high because advertising eliminates competition. Its cost — and more — is added to the price of drugs.

This is a misreading of what makes a drug costly to a consumer. It leaves out the fact that the cost of a product to a buyer includes not only its price but also the cost of search.

To show the effect of advertising on search costs, let us suppose someone wants to get rid of the discomfort of a cough. If he has not been informed about the existence of nonprescription items for cough relief, through advertising, he may have to seek his doctor's counsel on what is available for this purpose. Instead of paying $2 for a cough syrup (including, perhaps, $0.25 for the advertising that informed him of its existence), he will have to pay $10 for the visit to his physician and, perhaps, $3 or $4 for the filling of a prescription.

Perhaps he may simply ask his pharmacist what nonprescription remedy he advises for a cough. Without the availability of advertised remedies (known to consumers) whose prices can be compared in various stores, his pharmacist can advise a $5 remedy (identical, perhaps, to the $2 remedy that would be available with advertising). Without advertising, then, his cost may be anywhere from $5 to $14 for a remedy which, with advertising, he can buy for $2. The cough remedy manufacturer may spend 20 or 30 percent of his revenues to inform him, but that information comes to him far cheaper than from alternative sources.

Third, cheaper nonadvertised products may appear on the shelf alongside more expensive advertised products, but they would not be as inexpensive or might not be available if it were not for the advertising of the more expensive product. Every advertiser is aware of (and concerned about) the "free rider" effect of his advertising. That is, the advertising for Brand X creates additional sales not only for Brand X but also for other brands of the same product. Other brands may choose not to advertise and, instead, offer lower prices, relying on the advertising of Brand X to inform consumers of the utility of the product and its availability.

To take one example, well over 100,000 persons a year die because of hypertension; their lives could be prolonged by a drug which, for the sake of simplicity, we will call Drug A.[70] Let us suppose that the manufacturer of Brand Y of Drug A sets out to inform doctors of the treatment success enjoyed with hypertensive patients. Further, let us suppose that the cost of the product is $1 and the cost of informing physicians is $0.50 per unit of product at the expected volume of sales. By informing physicians of the effectiveness of the product in treating hypertension, a large volume of sales results at $1.50, and 50,000 lives a year are saved.

Because of the large market for this product, a manufacturer may proceed to offer a generic, unadvertised, and unpromoted version of Drug A at $1. Prescriptions of some physicians prescribing the product by generic name will be

70. "Effects of Treatment on Morbidity in Hypertension," *Journal of the American Medical Association*, 202 (December 11, 1967), p. 116.

filled by pharmacists with the unadvertised version. But if the manufacturer of Brand Y had not undertaken his advertising and promotion campaign to doctors, there would be no market for the unadvertised product and it would not have appeared. It can take a free ride on the promotion and advertising done for Brand Y; and only because of the free ride is there an inexpensive, generic version of Brand Y available. The advertising of Brand Y makes its demand more elastic than it would be absent the advertising, by creating the volume which creates a competitor.[71] Absent the competitor, the demand for Brand Y would be more inelastic.

Even without the competitor, the enlargement of the market by advertising in itself makes the demand for Brand Y more elastic. As a product serves more and more users, its market demand grows more and more elastic. Even if the market is served by only a single brand, the demand for the brand grows more elastic as a consequence of the volume generated by the advertising.

## APPENDIX II
### A GRAPHICAL EXPOSITION OF PROFESSOR BENHAM'S STUDY OF ADVERTISING EFFECTS

Using hypothetical cost and demand curves, the graph shown in Figure 3 may be used to illustrate the effects of advertising found by Professor Benham

**Figure 3**

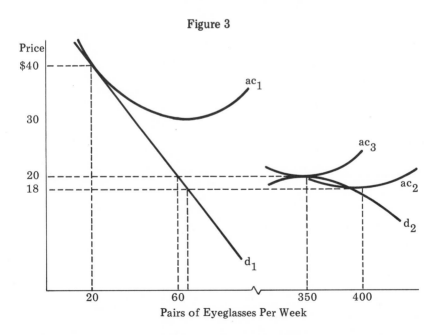

Pairs of Eyeglasses Per Week

71. Harold Demsetz, "The Effect of Consumer Experience on Brand Loyalty and the Structure of Market Demand," *Econometrica*, 30 (January 1962), p. 22.

in the eyeglass market. Let us suppose that $d_1$ represents the demand facing a representative optical shop in equilibrium circumstances in a no-advertising market. Further, let us suppose that $ac_1$ is the average cost curve of the representative optical shop in equilibrium in a no-advertising market. The two curves are tangent to each other and to the no-advertising long-run average cost curve at $40 per pair with sales of 20 pairs per week.

The short-run cost curve of the minimum-cost shop in a no-advertising market is shown as $ac_2$. Such a shop could sell eyeglasses at $18 per pair if it could obtain business amounting to 400 pairs per week. With no advertising, however, it attracts customers for only 64 pairs per week at $18 and is unable to cover capital and other costs. Such a shop would soon be bankrupt.

In a market where advertising is allowed, the equilibrium demand curve becomes $d_2$ (where every different rate of sales shown on the $d_2$ curve has a different and optimum amount of advertising associated with it).[72] The cost curve, including advertising costs, of an optimum-size shop in equilibrium circumstances becomes, let us say, $ac_3$. The demand curve is tangent to the cost curve at 350 pairs per week at $20 per pair of eyeglasses. It is tangent at its minimum average cost rate of output (each different rate of output having a different — optimum for that rate of output — amount of advertising cost).[73] The point on the demand curve at which the shop operates is that point where demand is infinitely elastic. The amount of monopoly power and the measure of differentiation of product is zero in equilibrium.

With no advertising, the elasticity of demand at the price and rate of output at which a representative shop operates is minus 4. Demand is more inelastic without advertising, and the product is differentiated. The introduction of advertising makes the demand more elastic and wipes out any differentiation of product.

If it were costless for buyers to acquire information or for sellers to disseminate information (or, what amounts to the same thing, the economy has long been static), shops would sell eyeglasses for $18 instead of $40. But it is not costless, and the lack of information results in a $40 price. By producing information and presenting it in a way which overcomes inertia, prices are driven down from $40 to $20. Sellers produce the information because it is less costly for them to do so than for buyers to search. Without their production of information, relying only on buyer search, we have demand curve $d_1$. It is seller production of information which creates demand curve $d_2$.

In saying that seller advertising creates demand curve $d_2$, we are not suggesting that advertising creates demand. All that advertising does is move the firm demand curve closer to the industry demand curve and make the firm demand curve more elastic. Even where advertising affects the apparent position of the industry demand curve, it does not create the demand for the

72. George J. Stigler, *The Theory of Price* (Macmillan 1946), p. 263; Harold Demsetz, "The Welfare and Empirical Implications of Monopolistic Competition," *Economic Journal*, 74 (September 1964), p. 623, reprinted in Richard E. Neel, *Readings in Price Theory* (Southwest 1973), p. 341. Demsetz refers to the type of demand curve shown by $d_2$ as a mutatis mutandis average revenue curve.

73. Demsetz, *supra* n. 72, as reprinted in Neel at 349-350.

product but rather moves the effective demand closer to the latent demand for the product in the same way that firm advertising moves the firm demand curve closer to the industry demand.

It should be added that in the paradigm of the non-Robinsonian theorists, advertising is viewed as one of the methods of spreading information in the disequilibrium situation bringing the economy to the long-run competitive equilibrium more quickly under static circumstances (or moving it more rapidly toward the long-run equilibrium or keeping the economy closer to its long-run equilibrium in dynamic circumstances although the long-run equilibrium itself is on the move) than would be the case if only buyer search or the gradual spread of information without investment in spreading information were relied upon. In the non-Robinsonian paradigm, the $ac_1$-$d_1$ tangency is looked upon as a temporary situation and not as an equilibrium, i.e., it will not persist. This view is explicit in the Austrian analysis where the competitive process, rather than the outcome of the process in static circumstances, plays a central role.[74]

# Advertising, Concentration, and Profitability: The State of Knowledge and Directions for Public Policy

## H. Michael Mann*

It is a fundamental proposition of economic theory that oligopolistically structured markets will produce noncompetitive price behavior and thereby interfere with the attainment of allocative efficiency: the optimal allocation of society's resources among alternative uses. The evidence appears to support the theory,[1] although there is not unanimity on this particular consequence,[2]

---

74. Frederick Hayek, "The Meaning of Competition," in *Individualism and Economic Order* (Univ. of Chicago Press 1948), p. 106. Israel Kirzener, "Selling Costs, Quality, and Competition," in *Competition and Entrepreneurship* (Univ. of Chicago Press 1973), p. 135.

* Professor of Economics, Boston College. For further biographical information, see Appendix D.

The author wishes to thank John Henning, Caswell Hobbs, Robert Larner, James Meehan, Jr., and Jack Pearce for their comments on this paper. They do not necessarily subscribe to all the interpretations and policy recommendations contained herein, however.

1. Leonard Weiss, "Quantitative Studies of Industrial Organization," in M. D. Intrilligator, ed., *Frontiers in Quantitative Economics* (Amsterdam: North-Holland Publ. Co. 1971); and "The Concentration-Profits Relationship and Antitrust," this volume, Chapter 4.

2. Yale Brozen, "The Antitrust Task Force Deconcentration Recommendation," *Journal of Law & Economics*, 13 (October 1970), pp. 279-292; Brozen, "Bain's Concentration and Rates of Return Revisited," *Journal of Law & Economics*, 14 (October 1971), pp. 351-369.

or, for that matter, on other alleged consequences of oligopolistic market structures. No one denies, however, that there are industries in the U.S. economy which can be designated as oligopolistic, generally meaning highly concentrated in the sense that a few firms account for most of an industry's output.

It is important to understand what economic forces might create this group of industries. The reasons are two. First, oligopolies may arise because some firms prove to be more efficient, innovative, or adaptive to risk than others. In such cases, there is an obvious trade-off problem for those who believe that an oligopolistic organization leads to undesirable pricing behavior and therefore should be deconcentrated.[3]

Second, and perhaps more significant, is that intelligent consideration of "what kind of remedial action will best defuse any undesirable social results coming from oligopolies" requires knowledge about factors promotive of industry concentration. This permits public policy to act upon the causes of concentration and to mitigate its effects. Otherwise, deconcentration may turn out to be short-lived, for the fundamental forces at work will reconcentrate the market.[4]

## ADVERTISING AND CONCENTRATION: THE THEORY

Expenditures on advertising are only one among several alternative methods a seller may use to differentiate its products, i.e., to develop distinctions between its product offerings and those of other sellers. The more general issue, then, would be the character of the relationship between product differentiation and market concentration. The more modest focus on advertising reflects two considerations.

First, product differentiation is not a well-specified concept. It results from the actions of sellers attempting to heighten inherent traits of a particular product in buyers' minds.[5] The composite of traits, though, may not all influence buyer preferences and thus a producer's sales in the same direction.[6]

---

3. The trade-off issue is raised by Harold Demsetz, "Industry Structure, Market Rivalry, and Public Policy," *Journal of Law & Economics*, 16 (April 1973), pp. 1-9.

4. Some scholars argue that concentration is not important to pricing behavior unless it is in the presence of substantial barriers to entry. Therefore, reduction of entry barriers is more sensible than deconcentration. See, for example, Stanley I. Ornstein, "Concentration and Profits," *Journal of Business* (Univ. of Chicago), 45 (October 1972), pp. 519-541.

5. This notion of "inherent traits" has been called differentiability — that characteristic which somehow permits products seemingly serving the same end use to become distinguished in buyers' minds. John M. Vernon, *Market Structure and Industrial Performance: A Review of Statistical Findings* (Allyn 1972), pp. 67-68.

6. "The dimensions of which product differentiation is to be composed — speed, taste, spatial location, etc. — are not all monotonically related to [consumer] preference, and hence a combination of them cannot be monotonically related to [consumer] preference." Julian Simon, *Issues in the Economics of Advertising* (Univ. of Illinois Press 1970), pp. 298-299.

Therefore, a more manageable inquiry is to single out one way sellers try to exploit the differentiability of a product and determine what predictive statements can be made about its influence on firm-size distributions. Second, sufficient data are available on advertising, as opposed to other means of differentiating, so that the cross-sectional empirical investigations to date have been limited to the role of advertising.

The direct question, then, is why advertising effort and concentration might be related. Whatever a priori theorizing is brought to bear, the predicted relationship would be expected to be confined to consumer goods industries. The reason concerns the two aspects of advertising. Advertising clearly can provide important information about sellers' offerings — price, terms of sale, availability, and the like. Advertising, though, also can try to give a product image — to fix in the buyer's mind some special attribute which connotes superiority over alternative offerings. For some kinds of products, that special attribute appears to be an image of superior quality. This occurrence is most likely for goods purchased for "conspicuous consumption," for which price is a less important consideration than "prestige"; or for goods that are sufficiently complex and expensive, e.g., consumer durables, that consumers cannot evaluate their merits and therefore rely upon product reputation to avoid an unsatisfactory purchase.

Yet, there are some goods, e.g., soap, cigarettes, chewing gum, soft drinks, which are heavily advertised but would seem to be easily appraised and purchased frequently in small amounts, thereby permitting experimentation and comparative judgments among alternatives. It is not clear why advertising seems effective at attracting consumers to certain brands and retaining their custom through repeat purchases. It may be that where there is no obvious basis for choice, consumers treat advertising as a substitute for experimentation. That is, if some seller tells them that its particular brand will improve well-being — e.g., a particular detergent cleans better, a particular cosmetic beautifies more effectively — and a negative experience does not result from the purchase, consumers will stick with the advertised product. Why experiment with alternatives if satisfaction is obtained, especially since repetitive advertising continues to remind and to confirm to the consumer that a positive experience would occur.[7]

It is plausible to argue that advertising can be a means of promoting image for consumer products. The buyer of a producer's good, on the other hand, whose chief concern is with minimization of cost, would be expected to be knowledgeable enough to appraise the available alternatives in order to obtain the lowest price for a given quality. We would expect producers' goods industries to exhibit only that amount of advertising which gives forth perti-

---

7. Michele Corash suggested this reasoning to me. I find it plausible. However, note Joe Bain's comment: "We are at a loss to explain . . . in terms of the preceding arguments [i.e., heavy advertising of prestige and complex goods] the very high level of selling costs that persists in the soap industry. More empirical and theoretical investigation is called for." *Industrial Organization* (Wiley & Sons 1968), p. 460.

nent information, since buyers will not be susceptible to attempts to add image.[8]

Within consumer goods industries, we might predict a positive association between advertising effort and concentration for two reasons. First, the general adoption of advertising by all firms in some initial size distribution is likely to destabilize market shares. Some, those whose messages build image and attract customer patronage, will expand at the expense of others, those whose efforts fail to attract buyers,[9] either because of a rearrangement of shares given industry demand or because of the capture of most of the increment in sales generated by an advertising-induced shift in the industry demand curve. The movement toward increased concentration will be enhanced if there exist economies of scale in advertising.[10] Second, at some concentration level, oligopolistic interdependence should take hold and encourage a nonprice means of competing like advertising. A likely outcome is that advertising expenditures will rise beyond joint profit-maximizing levels because oligopolists fail to coordinate their promotion efforts. The essential reason for this failure lies in what William Fellner calls "inventiveness" — the belief of each firm that it can adopt a nonprice strategy which will increase its relative strength in the group. The outcome of this kind of oligopolistic struggle for market position may be diminished profits for everyone "because the rival firms may copy the measures of the initiating firm, and, the intended benefit at the expense of the rivals may not materialize."[11] The result is waste — higher costs than necessary, in the sense that competing oligopolists would jointly reduce advertising outlays if such cooperation were feasible and permissible. This potential for wasteful escalation is central to any case against levels of advertising expenditure.

This theorizing indicates that advertising and concentration may interact, feeding upon one another, with the result that concentration and advertising will be positively related. Separation of cause and effect, though, is not pos-

8. George Stigler finds that: "The average ratio of advertising expenditures to sales was 1.97 percent in consumer goods industries and 0.57 percent in producer goods industries. . . ." "The Economies of Scale," in *The Organization of Industry* (R. D. Irwin 1968), p. 84. This does not mean that sellers of producers' goods have no latitude for differentiating; only that advertising is not going to be an important means. P. J. Donnelly and R. H. Holton, "A Note on Product Differentiation and Entertainment Expense Allowances in the U.S.," *Journal of Industrial Economics,* 10 (March 1962), pp. 134-138.

9. Nicholas Kaldor, "The Economic Aspects of Advertising," *Review of Economic Studies,* 18 (1949-1950), p. 13.

10. However, neither existing evidence nor theoretical argumentation provides much reason to believe that "the minimum efficient size of the firm is increased by advertising, either in general or in any particular industry." Richard Schmalensee, *The Economics of Advertising* (Contributions to Economic Analyses Series, No. 80; Humanities 1972), p. 237.

11. William Fellner, *Competition Among the Few* (Knopf 1960), p. 186.

sible a priori, since the theory posits a mechanism for advertising to push an industry toward an oligopolistic organization and conversely for high concentration to encourage increases in advertising outlays.

Economic theory also suggests that advertising may contribute to the perpetuation of an oligopolistic market structure. To the extent that advertising stabilizes consumer purchasing habits, potential entrants face a significant obstacle to attracting sales. Recourse to outspending the established firms by some substantial amount, or pricing much below the prices of established products in order to switch customers, may well drop the prospective present value of future earnings in a market characterized by heavy advertising below the entrant's alternative uses of funds.[12]

The potential of intense advertising as a barrier to entry and for reaching wasteful levels in oligopolistic settings can generate social costs, e.g., waste and monopolistic pricing, which are not commensurate with its benefits. This is not to say that other kinds of expenditures made by the firm, e.g., those on labor, cannot have an entry-retarding impact or ever be wasteful.[13] However, advertising attracts special attention because it is one of the important contributors to what Joe Bain's classic study found to be the single most important barrier to entry—product differentiation.[14] Whether it deserves to be singled out turns upon the outcome of other empirical tests concerning advertising's impact upon market structure and performance and the extent to which Bain's finding is corroborated.

An evaluation of the social costs arising from advertising comes later. The next section will examine the empirical tests bearing upon advertising's impact upon market structure and performance.

12. See Vernon, *supra* n. 5, at 93-98, for a presentation of a model, developed by Schmalensee, emphasizing that the slower the consumer responses are to advertising, the less promising entry appears, especially if the entrant heavily discounts future earnings.

Joe Bain notes that industry sources estimated that a new entrant into cigarettes, circa 1950, would need to spend "ten to twenty times [per unit] that of established brands for seven years, in order to gain a market position comparable to that of the largest sellers. This would imply advertising costs running up to several cents per package over a long break-in period, and break-in losses of 100 or 200 million dollars or more in the current market." Joe Bain, *Barriers to New Competition* (Harvard Univ. Press 1956), p. 290. One would expect a potential entrant to attach a low present value to future earnings in such circumstances.

13. Oliver E. Williamson, "Wage Rates as a Barrier to Entry: The Pennington Case in Perspective," *Quarterly Journal of Economics*, 82 (February, 1968), pp. 85-116. When a firm hires factors of production to the point that their incremental contribution to revenue is less than their added cost, it becomes X-inefficient, thereby raising its costs excessively. Harvey Leibenstein, "Allocative Efficiency v. X-Efficiency," *American Economic Review*, 56 (June 1966), pp. 392-415.

14. Bain, *supra* n. 12.

## ADVERTISING, CONCENTRATION, AND PROFITABILITY:
## EMPIRICAL TESTS

There has been considerable controversy concerning whether a significant positive association between advertising and concentration exists. Professor Lester Telser's study, the first on the question, correlated advertising intensity (the ratio of advertising expenditure to sales revenue) and market concentration for forty-two consumer goods industries in the years 1947, 1954, and 1958, and reported a positive but "unimpressive" association.[15] Telser used correlation analysis, a technique familiar to economists, to assess the strength of the positive association. He found that the correlation coefficients[16] were not "high" enough, given his sample size, to conclude that the positive relationship occurred for reasons other than chance. Therefore, one cannot reject the null hypothesis: there is no association between the two variables.

It is important, however, to understand that Telser's results do not establish that the null hypothesis is correct.[17] The only thing the statistical tests permit us

15. Lester G. Telser, "Advertising and Competition," *Journal of Political Economy,* 72 (December 1964), p. 544.

16. The simple or product-moment correlation coefficient, denoted $r$, measures the degree to which two variables move together. Its value can vary from 1.0 (perfect positive correlation) to $-1.0$ (perfect negative correlation); these values obtain if all observations lie on a positively sloped or negatively sloped straight line, respectively. A $r = 0$ means that there is no relationship between the variables, depicted by a horizontal straight line.

The values of $+1.0$ or $-1.0$ for the correlation coefficients are not found in the real world, at least for economic relationships. Rather, observations reveal an imperfect association: values for the dependent variable, e.g., $y$, and values for the independent variable, e.g., $x$, rise (or fall) together, but not in a tightly clustered way along a straight line depicting the relationship, because the value of $y$ is explained in part by the influence of other forces, not just by the variable $x$.

There are two reasons for the computation of a correlation coefficient. The first is to determine whether the value obtained differs from zero in a statistically significant sense. The convention is that if the observed value of $r$ would appear only 5 times in 100, or less if the true $r$ were really zero, the $r$ is statistically significant: the value did not occur by chance and there is a meaningful, systematic relationship between the variables.

The second reason for the computation is that $r^2$ measures "what fraction of the sum of squared deviations of observations on a variable from their mean can be accounted for by the straight line best characterizing that variable's relationship with another variable." F. M. Scherer, *Industrial Market Structure and Economic Performance* (Rand McNally 1970), p. 49 n. 30. In other words, $r^2$ tells us how much of the variation in $y$ is attributable to variation in $x$ and thereby measures what is called "goodness of fit" — how closely the observations are clustered around the upward or downward sloping straight line.

17. "[N]onsignificant evidence quite literally fails to signify *anything;* it leaves us in our original state of ignorance." Daniel Suits, *Statistics: An Introduction to Quantitative Economic Research* (Rand McNally 1963), p. 128. The convention is to use the 0.05 level of significance, i.e., the observed correlation would not have occurred by chance 5 in 100 times if the true correlation was zero.

to claim is: the evidence is unconvincing that the alternative hypothesis, there is an association, is true, i.e., the observed correlation was unlikely to be a chance occurrence. An interpretation that Telser's findings demonstrate that advertising does not diminish competition, at least as measured by the concentration ratio, is illegitimate.[18] There are other hypotheses which may explain the failure of a particular experiment to find convincing evidence by which to reject the null hypothesis and therefore in favor of a positive, statistically significant association between advertising intensity and concentration. Two possibilties follow.

First, Telser's statistically insignificant and "low" r's appear to be related to the existence of a few extreme observations in his sample. Visualize a cluster of observations around an upward sloping straight line relating concentration and advertising intensity. This pattern would indicate a strong positive correlation. However, if a few observations are out of line with the rest of the set of observations, e.g., observations which combine low concentration and high advertising intensity, the computational formula for the simple r will give these extreme observations undue weight and will depress the value of r.

A different kind of correlation analysis than the one employed by Telser, that of rank correlation, which assigns to each observation on concentration and on advertising intensity a number denoting its rank (e.g., in descending order), was applied to Telser's data. The value of the correlation coefficient will vary from 1.0 to −1.0 depending upon how well the orderings of the two variables correspond, either positively or negatively. The advantage of rank correlation is that each observation has equal weight, thereby reducing the influence of extreme observations. Furthermore, since the hypothesis is that concentration and advertising intensity are positively related, i.e., they move upwards together, a rank correlation is a sufficient test of the relationship.

Rank correlation analysis turns up higher and statistically significant coefficients.[19] This strongly suggests that for Telser's own data there is a meaningful positive relationship between advertising intensity and market concentration, which Telser failed to observe because of the presence of extreme observations.

Second, Telser used industry data from the Internal Revenue Service. The IRS industry classifications are very broad, combining many markets which should be separated in terms of their true boundaries.[20] The effect of employ-

18. See Yale Brozen, "Advertising, Competition and the Consumer," *Intercollegiate Review,* Vol. 8, No. 5 (Summer 1973), p. 239.

19. Telser's correlation coefficients were 0.163, 0.165, and 0.169 for the years 1947, 1954, and 1958 respectively, all insignificant at the 0.05 level. The rank correlation coeffcients were 0.292, 0.362, and 0.300 for the same years, respectively, all significant at the 0.05 level or better.

20. For instance, Telser uses an IRS industry called perfumes. This industry combines perfumes, cosmetics, and other toilet preparations, which involves such commodities as hair preparations, mouthwashes, and shaving preparations. These clearly do not fit the definition of a theoretical industry: one in which all sellers produce substitute products and sell them to a common group of buyers and exclude all sellers not fitting this description.

ing such wide definitions is to introduce measurement errors which reduce the confidence one can place in an investigator's statistical findings.[21]

I and two colleagues repeated Telser's experiment, using more narrowly defined industries.[22] The ratio of advertising expenditure to sales revenue of the leading firms in fourteen consumer goods industries was correlated with market concentration in those industries for the years 1954, 1958, and 1963. Two different sets of data were employed to estimate advertising outlays. Of the six correlations, five were statistically significant; the remaining one was not, by the conventional test, although it was quite close.[23] The findings of our experiment led to a debate which raised several statistical issues. I will leave to the reader of the controversy the determination of whether our results emerge unscathed.[24]

An independent test of our findings is to examine what other investigators have found. All studies of which I am aware have found a positive and significant relationship.[25]

21. Edward J. Kane, *Economic Statistics and Econometrics* (Harper & Row 1968), pp. 33-34.

22. Both limitations discussed above apply to the following article: Robert B. Ekelund, Jr. and William P. Gramm, "Advertising and Concentration: Some New Evidence," *Antitrust Bulletin*, 15 (Summer 1970), pp. 243-249. See H. Michael Mann and James W. Meehan, Jr., "Advertising and Concentration: New Data on an Old Problem," *Antitrust Bulletin*, 16 (Spring 1971), pp. 101-104.

23. H. M. Mann, J. A. Henning, and J. W. Meehan, Jr., "Advertising and Concentration: An Empirical Investigation," *Journal of Industrial Economics*, 16 (November 1967), pp. 34-45.

24. "Symposium on Advertising and Concentration," *Journal of Industrial Economics*, 18 (November 1969), pp. 77-100. Participants were: Robert B. Ekelund, Jr. and Charles Maurice, "An Empirical Investigation of Advertising and Concentration: Comment"; H. M. Mann, J. A. Henning, and J. W. Meehan, Jr., "Testing Hypotheses in Industrial Economics: A Reply"; L. G. Telser, "Another Look at Advertising and Concentration"; H. M. Mann, J. A. Henning, and J. W. Meehan, Jr., "Statistical Testing in Industrial Economics: A Reply on Measurement Error and Sampling Procedure."

25. See the following: Bain, *supra* n. 12, at 249-250; P. K. Else, "The Incidence of Advertising in Manufacturing Industries," *Oxford Economic Papers*, 18 New Series (March 1966), pp. 88-110; Federal Trade Commission, *Economic Report on the Influence of Market Structure on the Profit Performance of Food Manufacturing Companies* (1969), Appendix D, p. 48; Louis Guth, "Advertising and Market Structure Revisited," *Journal of Industrial Economics*, 19 (April 1971), pp. 179-200; and S. I. Ornstein, J. F. Weston, M. D. Intrilligator and R. E. Shrieves, "Determinants of Market Structure," *Southern Economic Journal*, 39 (April 1973), pp. 612-625.

Weiss, in a comment on the work of N. Collins and L. Preston concerning concentration and profitability, provides further support. Collins and Preston measure profitability in a way which includes advertising as a part of profit. Weiss states: "[I]f advertising increases with concentration . . . one would expect higher regression coefficients as well." Weiss finds this to be the case. Weiss, "Quantitative Studies . . . ," *supra* n. 1, at p. 367 n. 7.

There is one study which deserves discussion.[26] It claims that the correct specification for a predicted relationship between concentration and advertising is quadratic rather than linear. That is, advertising and concentration are positively related up to some level of concentration and then the relationship turns negative — higher concentration tends to reduce advertising. The theory, in contrast to Fellner's referred to above, is that oligopolists will collude on advertising outlays in order to insure that the temptation to strive for increased market shares does not drive expenditures beyond that amount consistent with joint profit maximization. The investigator, Greer, offers empirical evidence which purports to confirm the theorizing.

It turns out, however, that the statistical results are very sensitive to the presence of one observation. Greer used four different data sets and carried out three correlations for each set, a total of twelve in all.[27] Nine of the twelve correlations pass the conventional standard for statistical significance. However, only three of the twelve retain statistical significance when one observation is dropped from the data sets used by Greer. "Sensitivity of statistical results to one observation hardly constitutes convincing evidence." [28]

Greer advanced some counterarguments in behalf of his quadratic specification. Whether his points are convincing must be left to the reader.[29]

The empirical tests to date convincingly demonstrate, in my judgment, that a positive association exists between advertising intensity and concentration for

26. Douglas Greer, "Advertising and Market Concentration," *Southern Economic Journal*, 38 (July 1971), pp. 19-32.

27. Greer tested for a correlation for three different classifications of consumers goods industries in each of three years, 1947, 1954, and 1957, and for a combined grouping of the three classifications for each of the three years. These last three tests are puzzling. If the three classifications are valid, observations within each class should not be lumped into one group because they are not samples drawn from the same population. In fact, a statistical test, the Chow test, rejects the legitimacy of pooling.

28. H. M. Mann, J. A. Henning, and J. W. Meehan, Jr., "Advertising and Market Concentration: Comment," *Southern Economic Journal*, 39 (January 1973), p. 450. It should be noted that the a priori theory for the quadratic is far from airtight. On balance, the theory and some case-study evidence suggest that effecive oligopolistic collusion on advertising is unlikely. See reference to Fellner, *supra* n. 11, and Scherer, *supra* n. 16, at 334-337.

29. D. Greer, "Advertising and Market Concentration: A Reply," *Southern Economic Journal*, 39 (January 1973), pp. 451-453. One of Greer's contentions makes our point. He states: "What is at issue is the negative relation for moderate-to-high levels of concentration. And the exclusion of a few highly concentrated industries (e.g., sugar and cigarettes) from a small sample, for purposes of regressing the remaining industries of moderate-to-low concentration, does not constitute a fair test of the relation in the moderate-to-high range. It is simply a moderate-to-low range test." *Id.* at 452. But one cannot claim validity for statistical results if they depend upon so few observations in the moderate-to-high range that the removal of one renders a formerly significant relationship insignificant. We need more observations in the moderate-to-high range.

consumer goods industries. This association does not necessarily imply oligopo-listic pricing unless there exist barriers to entry. Professors Comanor and Wilson find that intense advertising does pose a considerable barrier. They discovered that consumer goods industries which spend heavily on advertising earn half again as much as industries for which advertising intensity is low. This conclusion stood up when the analysis was redone to meet the challenge that the treatment of advertising as a current expense rather than as an investment conferring returns over time biases the profitability of heavy advertisers upwards.[30]

Further investigation may find that intense advertisers do not earn rates of return markedly different from modest advertisers.[31] This would not mean that heavy advertising is not an entry barrier. Rather, the meaning is that the tax laws[32] reinforce the oligopolistic tendency to inflate advertising expenditures

30. William S. Comanor and Thomas A. Wilson, "Advertising, Market Structure and Performance," *Review of Economics and Statistics,* 49 (November 1967), pp. 423-430; Leonard W. Weiss, "Advertising, Profits, and Corporate Taxes," *Review of Economics and Statistics,* 51 (November 1969), pp. 421-430.

31. The effect on reported profitability is dependent upon the growth rate of advertising and on the depreciation rate employed. The exact relationship is: $r' - r = (r' - G_A) d$, where $r'$ is the measured profit rate, $r$ is the true profit rate, $G_A$ is the rate of growth of advertising capital, and $d$ is the ratio of advertising capital to total capital. Vernon, *supra* n. 5, at 92. The slower the rate of depreciation as the growth rate falls further below the measured profit rate, the larger will be measured relative to true profitability. Weiss, "Quantitative Studies . . . ," *supra* n. 1, at 423, Table 2. Weiss found little difference between $r'$ and $r$ because $G_A$ tended to be close to $r'$ in most cases.

Weiss points out that if he had used a lower depreciation rate, the observed impact of advertising upon profitability might have been eliminated. Weiss used a depreciation rate which was an average that the studies of the question to that time had found, certainly a conservative procedure.

32. It can be demonstrated that the internal rate of return on a project is higher when the initial outlay is expensed rather than capitalized. Since the internal rate of *return* ($\bar{r}$) is that interest rate which equates the initial cash outlay ($C_0$) to the future stream of returns ($Q_1, \ldots, Q_n$, where $Q = Y$ (profit) + $D$ (depreciation)), it follows that:

(1) $C_0 = Q_1/(1 + \bar{r}) + Q_2/(1 + \bar{r})^2 + \ldots + Q_n/(1 + \bar{r})^n.$

If the cash outlay is expensed, both sides of the equation are reduced by the factor $1 - T$, where $T$ is the tax rate.

(2) $C_0(1 - T) = Q_1(1 - T)/(1 + \bar{r}) + \ldots + Q_n(1 - T)/(1 + \bar{r})^n.$

There is no change in the value of $\bar{r}$ which solves equations (1) and (2). In order to compare the effect of capitalization, (2) can be rewritten:

(2a) $C_0 = TC_0 + Q_1(1 - T)/(1 + \bar{r}) + \ldots + Q_n(1 - T)/(1 + \bar{r})^n.$

With $C_0$ being capitalized, equation (1) becomes:

(3) $C_0 = Q_1(1 - T)/(1 + \bar{r}) + \ldots + Q_n(1 - T)/(1 + \bar{r})^n$

$$+ T(\frac{D_1}{(1 + \bar{r})} + \ldots + \frac{D_N}{(1 + \bar{r})^n}).$$

The difference between (2a) and (3) is that expensing provides an immediate tax deduction, $TC_0$, whereas capitalization provides its tax deductions over time, $T(D_1/(1 +$

excessively. Furthermore, if Comanor and Wilson failed to observe a genuine effect, there is no reason why entry should not occur in industries characterized by intense advertising, at least in cases where other kinds of entry barriers are absent. Some evidence, however, suggests the opposite: industries characterized by high differentiation (advertising-to-sales ratios on the order of 10 percent or more) have experienced significantly greater increases in concentration over the years 1947 to 1970 than industries with moderate or low degrees of differentiation.[33]

The inference to be drawn from the separate tests relating advertising intensity and concentration, and advertising intensity and profitability, is that intense advertising, concentration, and profitability are positively related. Comanor and Wilson's report of a low and insignificant correlation between advertising intensity and concentration does not detract from this conclusion. Their result implies that there are industries with low concentration, intense advertising, and high profitability. This combination, although observable for some of the Comanor-Wilson data, e.g., for perfumes, makes no economic sense and suggests that the observed low concentration ratio does not measure a higher true value. The reasons are two.

First, low concentration should tend to depress profitability toward the competitive rate of return. The Comanor-Wilson analysis suggests that advertising intensity overwhelms any downward impact arising from low concentration. This does not square with any reasonable expectation; why should heavy advertisers, competing with a large number of other sellers, be able to earn half again as much as light advertisers?

Second, an important purpose of advertising is to differentiate — to add image or some similar attribute to the product — so as to reduce substitutability with the offerings of other sellers. To the extent that a seller succeeds in isolating its product from those of competing sellers, it is reducing the number of its competitors or, alternatively, increasing concentration. Heavy advertising, then, should reflect profitable activity — successful reduction in competitors through increased isolation from substitute offerings.

A plausible hypothesis for Comanor and Wilson's failure to find a significant correlation between concentration and advertising intensity is that their data comes from the same source used in Telser. Therefore, the low and insignificant correlation found by Comanor and Wilson probably results for the same reasons as did Telser's.

---

$\bar{r}) + \ldots + D_N/(1 + \bar{r})^n$). Since future dollars are worth less the farther away in time they will accrue, the $\bar{r}$ which solves equation (3) will be lower than the value which solves (1) and (2). The difference will depend upon the depreciation rate applied because the expression $T(D_1/(1 + \bar{r}) + \ldots + D_N/(1 + \bar{r})^n)$ approaches $TC_0$ at the limit — immediate expensing.

I am indebted to my colleague Harold Petersen, for bringing this point to my attention and for the explanation.

33. Willard F. Mueller and Larry G. Hamm, "Trends in Industrial Market Concentration," *Review of Economics and Statistics* (forthcoming).

The accumulated evidence strongly points to the following conclusion: concentration, advertising intensity, and profitability are all positively associated with one another. The combination suggests diminished price competition and the concomitant social loss: misallocated resources.

This conclusion is not controverted by the citation of evidence that vigorous advertising effort fails to protect products from instability in their market positions.[34] We learn nothing about the stability of the market shares of firms, the state of competition, from the fact that heavily advertised products have less stable market shares than do less advertised products. It is arguable that established firms may proliferate brands, periodically introducing new brands in order to restrict the potential sales obtainable by an entrant, thereby forestalling entry.[35] The effect is strengthened if continual new product introduction becomes part of the pattern of competition because buyers may cease to shift randomly, but only in reaction to forceful advertising campaigns attending the introduction.[36] The risk of failure for a new product also rises if consumer response becomes tied to the reaction to the marketing effort rather than the result of random experimenting.[37] This risk is less for a firm with some brands already in the market than for a firm breaking in for the first time.

Intense advertising, then, may reflect strategies to discourage prospective entrants. To the extent that such efforts are successful, it is not surprising that concentration, advertising intensity, and profitability are positively related. An association among variables does not reveal the chain of causation, however. This problem requires brief exploration.

34. Telser, *supra* n. 15, at 547-551.

35. If a certain fraction of customers shift brands periodically on a random basis, a new entrant can expect to pick up a decreasing portion of these switchers as the number of brands offered by the established firms rises. If 20 percent of all buyers switch periodically, a new entrant can attract 5 percent of the market if there are three established firms, each offering one brand (25 percent of 20 percent). If each of the established firms offers five brands, then the new entrant can expect only 1.25 percent of the market, (one-sixteenth of 20 percent). If economies of scale are at all important, the latter market share may preclude successful entry. Richard Lipsey and Peter Steiner, *Economics* (2nd ed., Harper-Row 1966), p. 320.

36. New product introductions substantially inflate advertising budgets. R. D. Buzzell and R. E. M. Nourse, "Product Innovation in Food Processing, 1954-1964" (Graduate School of Business, Harvard 1967). Since advertising intensity is positively related to concentration, and heavy advertising is associated with new product offerings, it follows that the established oligopolists are the chief promoters of the new products, not new entrants. The theory that Lipsey and Steiner offer seems very persuasive.

37. These factors may explain why Procter and Gamble, surely an experienced, successful consumer products firm, decided against entry into the cereals. Sheldon Zalanick, "The Fight for a Place at the Breakfast Table," *Fortune*, (December 1967), p. 130.

## ADVERTISING, CONCENTRATION, AND PROFITABILITY:
## CAUSE AND EFFECT

There are a variety of possibilities which may connect a causal chain among these variables. One is that concentration leads to high profitability which in turn encourages intense advertising. Another is that advertising intensity produces high concentration which in turn generates high profitability. These alternative direct linkages have no a priori claim over more complicated, but possibly more realistic, models indicating interactive, feedback influences among the variables. Furthermore, it may be that all the variables are responding to some exogenous variable not yet incorporated in the analysis.[38]

Little has been done about this important subject. At the theoretical level, Comanor and Wilson argue that intense advertising leads to high profitability. Their argument is: "Firms with high profit rates will not have higher *optimum* advertising expenditures than firms with low profit rates in the same market situation."[39] Interpreting "the same market situation" to mean firms facing the same opportunities for product differentiation and "the same behavior from rivals,"[40] Schmalensee disputes this. He advances a model which shows that, given constant costs for advertising, higher profits per unit of sales will encourage more advertising in order to sell additional units. Thus, any change which "increases the effectiveness of an oligopoly's price policy and raises $P$ [price] increases advertising as well as profits."[41]

Comanor and Wilson advance an empirical argument: "In addition, if high profits lead to high advertising expenditures, we should expect that industries which have high profits for reasons other than product differentiation (e.g., concentration or technical entry barriers) would tend to have high advertising expenditures as well. Yet, as we noted above, advertising is only weakly correlated with the other dimensions of market structure."[42] Schmalensee finds

---

38. Roger Sherman and Robert Tollison argue that the degree to which total costs are variable in the short run will influence both advertising and profitability. If average costs fall rapidly as the firm approaches full capacity in the short run, greater advertising will generate very profitable sales — profitable because, given price, the price-cost margin widens per unit until capacity is reached. The cost structure — high and fixed, relative to total costs — produces intense advertising and high profitability. They purport to show that this presumption is valid. "Advertising and Profitability," *Review of Economics and Statistics*, 53 (November 1971), pp. 397-408.

Comanor and Wilson counter, convincingly in my view, that the Sherman-Tollison findings result from spurious correlation. The definition of cost fixity employed by Sherman and Tollison guarantees their findings, since the measure is composed of those very variables which are supposed to be explained by cost fixity. Comanor and Wilson, "On Advertising and Profitability," *Review of Economics and Statistics*, 53 (November 1971), pp. 408-410.

39. Comanor and Wilson, *supra* n. 30, at 437.

40. Schmalensee, *supra* n. 10, at 223.

41. *Id.* at 226.

42. Comanor and Wilson, *supra* n. 30, at 437.

this contention no more persuasive. Since the independent variables (other than advertising) employed by Comanor and Wilson probably explain less than 40 percent of the variation in interindustry profitability, Schmalensee claims high profitability traceable to variables omitted in the Comanor-Wilson analysis might produce "high optimal and observed advertising–sales ratios." [43]

As an alternative to the Comanor-Wilson attempt to connect advertising as the cause to profitability as the effect, Schmalensee favors the following scenario: concentration is positively correlated with profitability; as concentration increases and raises profitability, marginal units of sales become more profitable, and it pays to advertise to capture these incremental units of sales; therefore, the causal chain runs from concentration to profitability to advertising.

In my view, this is more convincing than Comanor and Wilson, because concentration is omitted from their analysis. As argued above, their emphasis on a positive advertising intensity–profitability relationship with concentration uninvolved is implausible. Schmalensee's model, however, is only hypothesis, and there are other competing theories which can be constructed and suggest a different causal linkage.

There is only one piece of evidence which deals with the issue of causation. Its results are inconsistent with Schmalensee's reasoning, in that advertising is found to precede concentration. [44]

The proposition underlying the empirical analysis is that even if the theory is agnostic in the direction of causation, it may be possible to observe the causal linkage from an empirical experiment. That is, if, say, advertising intensity "causes" concentration, it might be possible to observe this phenomenon.

The procedure is based upon the following conceptual foundation. Suppose a statistical analysis like multiple regression shows that advertising intensity and concentration are both significantly determined by a certain variable, $X$. This tells us that when $X$ varies, both advertising intensity and concentration vary. Suppose further that the same statistical analysis shows that concentration is related to a second variable, $Y$, but that advertising intensity is not: when $Y$ varies, concentration varies, but advertising intensity does not. Thus, the statistical analysis shows that concentration is dependent on all the exogenous variables [45] considered, i.e., $X$ and $Y$, whereas advertising intensity is dependent upon only $X$. This outcome permits the conclusion that advertising intensity must come before concentration in the causal chain. A change in $X$ will induce changes in both advertising intensity and concentration, but a change in $Y$ will induce a change in concentration but not in advertising intensity. This event, if it occurred, would be consistent only with causal priority

43. Schmalensee, *supra* n. 10, at 227.

44. J. A. Henning and H. M. Mann, "Advertising and Concentration: A Tentative Determination of Cause and Effect" (Boston College Working Papers in Economics No. 14, March 1971).

45. These are variables whose values are determined independently of the variable they influence.

for advertising intensity.[46] This follows because if concentration determined advertising intensity or if concentration and advertising intensity were mutually determined, then a variable which affected concentration would have to affect advertising intensity as well. But if Y affects concentration and not advertising intensity, the former cannot be causally prior to the latter.

The results of the one empirical effort made so far suggest that advertising intensity is causally prior to concentration.[47] These findings are, of course, subject to possible revisions if and when data availability permits replication of our experiment and the use of a more complete set of exogenous variables than the few employed in the study.

However, they do run counter to Schmalensee's model which posits concentration coming before advertising intensity. Subsequent to the above work, John Henning added a profits equation to the concentration and advertising equations and found that profitability could be fitted into the chain only at the point between advertising intensity and concentration or after concentration; it could not possibly precede advertising intensity, because all the exogenous variables were significantly related to profitability. Thus, Schmalensee's view is open to doubt at this time because the only empirical evidence on the question places advertising at the beginning, not at the end, of the chain involving advertising, concentration, and profitability.

The issue of causation is unsettled. The demands of public policy will not wait while economists struggle to learn more, to understand the mechanism that lies behind the observed relationships. Does the knowledge that there is a positive association among intense advertising, profitability, and concentration provide any guidelines for policy?

## PUBLIC POLICY, COMPETITION, AND ADVERTISING

It is important to begin this section with the obvious recognition that advertising per se is not undesirable. It can provide significant information which

46. Independence — that is, no relationship between the variables — cannot be ruled out by the kind of empirical investigation suggested in the text. However, no one, to my knowledge, has argued that concentration and advertising intensity are determined independently of one another, although Comanor and Wilson imply such by treating concentration and advertising intensity as independent regressors. My comments on their statistical finding of negligible intercorrelation between concentration and heavy advertising are above; see text at nn. 42-43.

47. In each of the years 1954, 1958, and 1963, three regressions were run: concentration and two different measures of advertising were related to three independent variables: optimal plant size, new products brought forth, and capital requirements. Three significance levels — 10 percent, 5 percent, or 1 percent — were used to identify whether one of the independent variables was "missing" from the concentration or advertising equations. In twelve of a possible eighteen cases, variations in an independent variable did not change advertising intensity, but did change concentration.

When the data was pooled across the years, the causal priority of intense advertising becomes clearer.

reduces the search and transaction costs for consumers; can increase sales and thereby facilitate the realization of production economies of scale; can develop an image which encourages repeat purchases by consumers, thereby rewarding producers who maintain high and uniform quality.[48] All these occurrences are socially desirable.

Advertising, however, is not without costs which, from society's viewpoint, may well not be worth incurring. These instances are where oligopolists indulge in self-cancelling advertising in their struggle for market position, where advertising is deceptive and misleading in regard to reality, where advertising promotes market concentration beyond levels justified by economies of scale, where advertising permits price differences for products which are "alike in every respect but image,"[49] and where advertising creates interdependent utilities among consumers so that unhappiness results whenever one fails to "keep up with the Joneses."

The central issues raised by this catalogue of social costs are whether the social loss can be quantitatively juxtaposed to the social benefit and, if social cost exceeds social benefit, what remedies appropriately address the problem. No estimates, to my knowledge, have been made concerning whether the benefits of advertising exceed the social costs. One study of the costs of the styling rivalry among the automobile producers put the price tag around $5 billion per year between 1956 and 1960. The investigators, however, were not able to make a judgment about whether the costs were worthwhile.[50] The difficulty with evaluation is that the product and the attribute generated by selling costs are frequently a joint product, bought as one by the consumer. There is in such cases no direct market test of whether the image created by advertising is marketable on its own merit: whether consumers would buy the attribute claimed by advertising if it were sold separately from the product.[51]

An indirect test is whether consumers have the option of buying the same physical commodity carrying varying degrees of image at correspondingly varying prices. Application of this standard is hindered whenever the ability to offer alternatives different from those available is impeded by entry barriers. What this means is that the consumption of heavily advertised items at uniform, or nearly uniform, prices does not demonstrate that consumers are

---

48. The Soviet Union apparently realized that there were gains to be had from image differentiation. Marshall J. Goldman, "Product Differentiation and Advertising: Some Lessons from Soviet Experience," *Journal of Political Economy*, 68 (August 1960), pp. 346-357.

49. Scherer, *supra* n. 16, at 331-332.

50. Franklin M. Fisher, Zvi Griliches, and Carl Kaysen, "The Costs of Automobile Model Changes Since 1949," *Journal of Political Economy*, 70 (October 1962), pp. 433-451.

51. Some of the costs of automobile style change meet the market test in the sense that certain options "were separately available and had prices of their own. . . . Thus consumers knowingly purchased more costly cars than those with 1949 specifications, even in the presence of *some* explicit cost differential in favor of the latter." *Id.* at 450.

obtaining exactly that mix of product and image they prefer, because entrants may well not desire to make an expensive, risky investment on the chance that consumers would switch to an alternative which is not currently being offered.[52] Where entry is difficult, then, there may well be a constricted range of choice which gives the consumer more differentiation than he would care to pay for.

The costs of this particular occurrence simply have not been assessed. There has been a guess — estimate of the combined costs of two of the above-listed social costs, "wasteful promotional effort" and "monopolistic interference with the optimal allocation of resources," both of which are to be expected from the observed combination of intense advertising, high concentration, and high profitability. It was 1.9 percent of GNP, circa 1966, or about $15 billion.[53] This amount is, as admitted, arrived at by subjective judgment and should be interpreted as a figure which may understate or overstate the situation by some unknown degree. Even if overstated, however, the sum is not trivial and should be of concern to public policy.

One approach to the public policy issue is to state what would not make good policy. That would be to place a limit on absolute amounts of advertising or on the ratio of advertising to sales. This negative stance, recommending what not to do, is more comfortable for the economist than offering positive recommendations,[54] although I will offer some proposals following the argumentation against placing limitations upon advertising expenditure.

There are three reasons why direct regulation of the absolute or relative amount of advertising expenditure is unwise. First, consumers might be willing to buy the image attached to the product by advertising if it were sold separately with its own price. Since the image cannot be sold separately, curtailment of advertising may reduce some consumers' welfare by providing less image than was available previously.[55] If price remains the same, these consumers are getting less for their money than before. A price decrease would benefit those consumers who were paying more than they would have if

---

52. Even though Fisher and associates are agnostic about the costs of automobile style changes, it is apparent that foreign imports widened the range of choice considerably for consumers by the provision of lower-priced, *less* fancily styled cars. "It is clear that without this competitive prodding, the Big Three would not have offered consumers as wide a choice of automobiles." Lawrence J. White, "The American Automobile Industry and the Small Car, 1945-70," *Journal of Industrial Economics,* 20 (April 1972), p. 192.

53. Scherer, *supra* n. 16, at 408.

54. William J. Baumol, "Informed Judgment, Rigorous Theory, and Public Policy," *Southern Economic Journal,* 32 (October 1965), pp. 137-145.

55. Lester Telser has argued that the joint offering of product plus advertising is more efficient than separate offerings would be. "Supply and Demand for Advertising Messages," *American Economic Review,* 56 (May 1966), pp. 457-466. Even if true, this does not insure that the package price (product plus advertising) would be less than the separate prices in oligopolistic markets, because oligopolists will not pass on to consumers the full cost savings obtained.

they could have had less image, but the consumers who want product plus much image would be denied that alternative. The trade-off among consumers presents an equity issue of unfathomable dimensions.

Second, an advertising limitation raises a difficult question in terms of application. Would we want to control the advertising expenditures for all firms in an industry or just the largest ones? Smaller firms and new entrants will probably need to spend more, absolutely and relatively, even on informational grounds, to make inroads into the market.

Third, advertising is only one means of differentiating. Substitution among kinds of promotional expenditures may be possible which would only shift the problem, not mitigate it.

Besides these three a priori arguments against limiting advertising, there is one experiment which has been undertaken, namely, the banning of cigarette advertising in broadcast media. One analysis strongly indicates that the effects were exactly opposite of those intended: cigarette consumption has increased, not fallen, after the ban, apparently because the formerly concurrent advertising against cigarette smoking on television more than offset the positive impetus of company advertising. "Action based on wishful thinking seldom is as effective as that based on carefully specified models accurately depicting the forces influencing the policy objectives and the connections between forces and proposed policy actions." [56]

If limitations upon advertising are of dubious merit, what policy actions might reduce the social costs inherent in the combination of intense advertising, high concentration, and high profitability; namely, "too much" differentiation and "too great" a departure of price from marginal cost? I suggest three.

First, advertising's treatment as a current, rather than capital, expenditure under the tax laws should be reexamined. The tax favoritism encourages larger amounts of advertising than might otherwise be the case. Forcing firms to consider advertising on the same footing as any other capital expenditure would diminish the role advertising plays in overdoing image differentiation and in contributing to and maintaining high concentration.[57]

---

56. James L. Hamilton, "The Demand for Cigarettes: Advertising, the Health Scare, and the Cigarette Advertising Ban," *Review of Economics and Statistics*, 54 (November 1972), pp. 401-411.

57. Weiss and John Siegfried revised downward the estimates originally presented by Weiss. They estimate that in the thirty-seven industries which Weiss studied in 1963, there was an understatement of profits by $187.6 million because of advertising expenditures. Assuming a tax rate of 52 percent, they estimate that this resulted in a tax avoidance (or subsidy for advertising) of about $97.5 million in the 37 industries. This subsidy was not evenly distributed. They estimate that the ten largest advertisers' profits were understated by $57.1 million, which is equivalent to a subsidy of $29.7 million, or 30 percent of the total subsidy received by all firms in the thirty-seven industries. John J. Siegfried and Leonard W. Weiss, "Advertising, Profits, and Corporate Taxes Revisited," *Review of Economics and Statistics*, 61 (May 1974), pp. 195-200.

Second, easier entry conditions should be encouraged wherever possible. An obvious avenue is to encourage import competition, the effect of which has been salutary for the automobile industry.[58] There are situations in which antitrust may be able to act to diminish the incentives to advertise heavily in image creation. A test case is the litigation involving the cereal industry on the part of the Federal Trade Commission.

Third, possibilities for improving the information available about the alternative offerings of sellers should be explored. Advertising is an important dispenser of information, but it is hardly an objective source, since the seller wants to distinguish his product from those of competitors. *Consumer Reports* makes a commendable effort, but the need is more widespread than *Consumer Reports* now fulfills.

The preceding recommendations all have a common theme, i.e., to encourage an environment which provides as much diversity as possible in the price-product-attribute mix available to consumers. This environment will not usually be consistent with industries characterized by tight oligopoly, heavy advertising, and high profitability because alternatives featuring a low price and little advertising, i.e., unemphasized image, are not likely to be available.[59]

## CONCLUSIONS

Economic theory presents some solid reasons for presuming that intense advertising, oligopoly, and high profitability will be positively associated. The evidence favors the theorizing, although the exact cause and effect linkages among the variables eludes a priori argument at present, and empirical work as a tool for discriminating among alternative theories has barely begun.

The combination of these variables raises a serious issue for public policy because of a potentially substantial social loss, possibly in the neighborhood of $10 to $20 billion. Among the mix of public policies deserving serious attention are: (1) revision of the tax codes which permit advertising to be treated as current expenditure rather than as a capital outlay; (2) use of antitrust or trade policy to ease entry into markets characterized by persistently high levels of heavy advertising, concentration, and profitability; (3) the provision of information about products from sources with a more neutral stake in the products' virtues.

This is a modest set of proposals which would bring us closer to an assurance that the benefits of advertising are commensurate with its costs. This development could change George Stigler's observation that advertising "is treated [by economists] with a hostility that economists normally reserve for

58. See White, *supra* n. 52.

59. If low-priced, little-advertised products are provided by the same oligopolists as alternatives to their heavily advertised, higher-priced brands, we have a case where advertising has separated markets and permitted price discrimination. This result is not socially desirable if consumers believe there are real differences when in fact there are only imagined differences generated by the advertising.

tariffs or monopolists."[60] Advertising which focuses on price, availability, terms of sale, and performance can hardly be faulted by the economist or by anyone else.

# Dialogue*

*Morris Adelman:* I am encouraged, I must say, by one thing. There is progress; the speakers did not address themselves to an issue that a few years ago might have been more prominent: whether advertising makes people spend more money than they would otherwise have spent.

And if I may again mention another former MIT student, Richard Schmalensee, who is abundantly cited on both sides — he was asked to investigate the matter, and I think he quite effectively put the pin to that inflated rubber dragon, such that nobody except J. K. Galbraith believes in it any more.

*Richard Posner:* The question I was mulling for Mike Mann is actually answered by what Professor Adelman just said. It was: does your thinking about the effect of advertising on concentration depend on any assumptions about the degree to which advertising is false? There is a follow-up question, so it is critical how you answer that.

*Adelman:* No entrapment here, please.

*Mann:* It is a good question, to which I have not given much thought, but my response is no.

*Posner:* Well, I think it is the wrong response. Because if advertising is truthful, I don't see how it can be asserted logically that advertising affects the substitutability of goods or the elasticity of demand or anything like that. If advertising is truthful, all it is doing is drawing attention to product characteristics.

Now, if characteristics of products are such as to make consumers prefer a particular product to the substitute, then you might say that the characteristics had reduced substitutability. But I don't see how you could attribute causative force to the advertising.

*Donald Turner:* Unless you mean by "false" everything that is not proved, there are different categories. Something could be true but not tell you anything about the characteristics of the product.

*Posner:* What it seems to me is sufficient for my point is that the advertising be transparent, not be misleading, not create a desire that would not otherwise exist, a desire for a product that is not there, a desire for some imagined characteristic.

I take it Professor Mann doesn't have a view as to whether advertising creates wants rather than simply revealing or pointing people towards products.

---

60. G. J. Stigler, "The Economics of Information," *Journal of Political Economy,* 69 (June 1961), pp. 213-225.

* The session was chaired by Morris A. Adelman, Professor of Economics, Massachusetts Institute of Technology. For further biographical information, see Appendix D.

I did not want to get into the issue of whether the exclusive content of advertising is information. That doesn't seem to be the issue at all. The question is whether the effect of advertising is to direct people to products whose characteristics they can then sample for themselves and decide whether they want to buy that product or some substitute.

*Mann:* It seems to me that there are many areas in which the consumers would have a very difficult time distinguishing the characteristics of goods. All of the attributes you may want or desire may not be obvious by inspection, and therefore the seller of the goods has to try to find a way to distinguish his offering from alternative offerings. And, it seems to me, much advertising directs itself at trying to find some way of attracting attention which is not false, but doesn't reveal anything about performance, availability, or price.

I find it difficult to know why the attribute of being a member of the Pepsi Generation tells me anything significant about Pepsi-Cola. Yet, Pepsi seems to think that this is a message and an attribute it can give to the particular product which will attract sales and hold customers. And if it doesn't, Pepsi will change the message. A lot of advertising is directed at mood in that sense, it seems to me, and to the extent sellers are successful in attracting patronage by serving those moods, they are going to win, and those who are not are going to lose.

*Posner:* Let's stipulate that advertisers, in order to get the attention of the audience, use any attention-getting device that occurs to them, regardless of its relation to any actual characteristic of the product. Nonetheless, it seems to me — and I don't think you are saying anything different — that unless there is some true difference in the characteristics of the product, the result of the consumers being induced to try a product will not be to make the demand for that product less elastic than it would otherwise be. If you try Pepsi and find it is not significantly different from Coca-Cola, why should your demand for Pepsi be less elastic than it would have been in the absence of advertising?

Now, if you want to say that advertising actually attaches false attributes to products, so that the people who drink Pepsi think it has properties that it doesn't have, then you are saying that advertising is, to a significant degree, false. Then you are making a proposition about the cause and effect of advertising on concentration, which, I would think, while empirically incorrect, is intellectually coherent. But I don't see how the fact of advertising gets connected with the elasticity of demands.

*Mann:* Let me first say that it is certainly unclear, I believe, in the present state of knowledge, whether advertising causes concentration, whether there is a reverse flow, or whether there is some interaction.

I accept the evidence that high advertising intensity and concentration are related. Now, why that is so is an intellectual problem on which a lot more work needs to be done. But my connection would be that what happens in a highly concentrated industry is that the few look at the industry demand curve, not their own individual demand curves with respect to their pricing decisions. And to the extent they are successful in coordinating their pricing behavior, they will attempt to exploit the greater inelasticity in the industry demand curve relative to their own demand curves.

*Leonard Weiss:* There has been considerable discussion of my own work and a subsequent work, saying the effect of advertising on profits might diminish considerably if you took into account the investment characteristic of advertising rather than, as is present practice, treating it as a current expense. What I did was to review the studies of depreciation that had been made at that time, and I took a rough average. It came to a depreciation rate of about 33 percent per year.

*Yale Brozen:* But a Ph.D. student at UCLA, Robert Ayanian, did find this range of 5 to 40 percent in his group of industries, and that is an enormous range.

*Weiss:* That is certainly a legitimate point. I can't comment on it. I have never seen it, but I'd hold with the 33 percent depreciation rate.

*Brozen:* I'd certainly agree with you in periods of flat price behavior, but in a period of rapid inflation a low depreciation rate would be appropriate.

*Adelman:* If you treat advertising as a capital outlay, the critical questions become:

One, what is its service life? How long does it last?

Two, what is the appropriate rate of discount whereby you compare present with future expenditures or revenues?

Three, to what extent is this deranged by inflation so that past advertising affords the advertiser a kind of inventory gain?

And, as you can see, this is a fairly complex set of issues, purely on the measurement side.

*Turner:* Professor Brozen, why isn't treating advertising as a current expense correct?

*Brozen:* Because the current satisfied customers are a consequence of past advertising.

*Louis Schwartz:* I'd like to put the following real case into consideration.

Some years ago there was a subsidy proceeding before the CAB involving TWA and Pan Am. Pan Am had just introduced a much more attractive seating arrangement — I forget which model of Boeing plane — and when it came to the question of the allowance for advertising, TWA was given a large additional sum, as a counterpoise to the more attractive seating on Pan Am.

So I ask you to fit that into your informational model of advertising. It is a perfectly rational thing for any private firm to do. If they introduce a better product and you don't have it ready, you'd better increase your advertising budget.

*Brozen:* Unless they have something to offer which consumers are not informed of, then I don't think TWA is going to get any return out of its advertising.

*Schwartz:* This, at least, is a form of advertising expenditure that doesn't fit into an informational model.

*Posner:* I think if you look at rivalry in the airline industry, you will find that the conventional response is: airlines are a peculiar industry where prices are fixed by regulation and where competition takes the form of various types of service change. The usual response to a lounge or a piano bar or the usual form of service rivalry, which is additional flights, is some equivalent form of service competition. I am sure there have been cases where a competitor, caught short, tried to think of some attribute that he could advertise. But again, if you want to look at central tendencies rather than isolated examples, then we find in the airline industry some service rivalry, not merely the attempt to offset genuine service differences with false advertising.

*Schwartz:* At what level of advertising expense do you begin to be concerned, if at all? Would it be 40 percent of the consumer price, 100 percent, or more?

*Brozen:* Well, I wouldn't be concerned at all. I think the market takes its own peculiar vengeance on people who make mistakes in advertising — spending too much or too little, as the case may be. When you talk about ratios of advertising to sales, I can think of new products where they spent 150 percent of the first year's sales trying to teach people they had a new product. Are we going to teach people? The market will do the arguing for us.

*Michele Corash:* The free-rider argument may explain whatever relationship exists between advertising and concentration. It might also explain whatever relationship may exist between profitability and concentration. It seems there would be an incentive for each advertiser in a concentrated market to advertise heavily, knowing that he will reap a share of the rewards. Conversely, there is no commensurate reward for the advertisers in less concentrated markets. Doesn't that suggest that advertising and profitability will be greater in a concentrated market than in a nonconcentrated market?

*Brozen:* I don't see why that will be so. The high profits will attract entry.

*Corash:* You have a limited number of potential competitors —

*Brozen:* If you are going to talk about entry barriers, that is another question. If advertising increases the demand and raises profits, the result will be additional entry into the market.

*John Blair:* There is one type of advertising which has been shown, I think, statistically to be related to increases in concentration. And that is advertising which takes place through a medium with a finite limit, of which there is only so much prime time. This may create substantial barriers to entry.

I am talking about TV advertising. Neither Professor Mann nor Professor Brozen addressed this issue. I wonder whether we could have the benefit of their comments on the studies that have been made of the effect on concentration of TV advertising.

*Brozen:* I don't know what the effect of TV advertising is on concentration versus the effect of any other kind of advertising. I just have not seen any studies that distinguish among varieties of advertising that I find credible.

*Blair:* This is an area where studies have been made; the results are to be found in such unusual places as congressional hearings.

*Mann:* I have to confess ignorance here. I do recall that there have been attempts, as John Blair indicates, to link the intensity of TV advertising to changes in concentration or degree of concentration. And, since I am persuaded that high concentration and advertising intensity are related, I would not find such a relationship unexpected.

My problem goes back to an earlier point. I don't think we yet understand the why of this relationship. And it is important to push research into the why of this relationship, so that we can gain some understanding of the mechanism at work.

*Brozen:* May I add one point here. The way in which TV time is being sold seems to result in greater and greater divisibility of what is available. You have a much greater amount of spot sales in TV advertising. You have a much smaller amount of entire-program sales; you have portions of a program and division of the minutes into 20- and 30-second blocks instead of the 60-second blocks that used to be available. It seems to me there has been increasing division of the time available on television for advertising.

*Jonathan Rose:* The question I'd pose concerns distinguishing between the amount of advertising that a firm engages in to make consumers aware of the existence of a new brand and that which it perceives it must engage in to overcome or respond to the advertising of its rivals. And if that distinction is a valid one, doesn't that have implications for the entry-barrier effects?

*Brozen:* I don't think the distinction is a valid one. I don't think any firm advertises just to overcome the effects of other firms' advertising. It advertises to detach the customers of other firms; and those customers are not there because of the advertising of those firms, but because of whatever product loyalty they have that is created by the product.

What the advertiser is saying is, "I have a product you will like even better"; he is shouting to the world, "Come buy my product." He doesn't have to shout louder because the customers of the other firms are being advertised to. He has to shout louder in terms of how satisfied the customers are with the product. They are not there because of current advertising but because of past advertising and current satisfaction with the product.

*Rose:* In a sense it goes back to the questions raised about informational advertising, noninformational, equivocal, false, that sort of thing.

*Brozen:* Yes.

*Louis Schwartz:* It seems to me, putting the concentration issue aside, there is a considerable case to be made for regulating false advertising and a very serious question as to what might be the right allocation of resources to stopping false advertising. My question is: how much would you spend to stop it?

*Rose:* Another, is it worth trying to stop?

*Mann:* First of all, I don't know how much it is worth to stop false advertising.

*Weiss:* How much do we actually spend?

*Mann:* The Bureau of Consumer Protection has about a $15 million budget, and out of that, I guess, about 10 percent is spent to regulate false advertising.

*Franklin Edwards:* I would like to end by trying to interrelate what went on in the economy-of-scale discussion with this theory of the relationship between concentration and advertising. If advertising expenditures do create an effective barrier to industry, does not that imply substantial capital-fund-raising economies? Otherwise, it seems to me that if we had perfect financial markets in all respects, any small firm could finance the advertising expenditure necessary to detach or combat the attempt to erect an entry barrier.

Earlier, Professor Brozen argued — and I would agree — that because of what I like to call imperfections in the capital account — we could quibble about that word — there are substantial fund-raising economies. Wouldn't it follow a fortiori that advertising could create an effective barrier to entry?

*Adelman:* It seems to me you are saying the capital market creates the barrier to entry.

*Edwards:* And assuming no economies of scale to cloud the issue.

*Brozen:* Well, you are simply saying that wherever there are high costs of entering an industry, there are going to be barriers to entry, in your sense, coming out of the economies of scale in finance. But how far do the economies of scale go? Do they go to one firm encompassing an entire industry, or four firms, or twenty firms?

I don't think we have an answer for that. But yet, if there are economies of scale, sufficient economies of scale in capital raising, it will result in one firm in the industry. So I will repeat what Professor Demsetz argues, however, that in various industries a natural monopolist will not be able to extract the natural monopolist price; it doesn't have to be in the business to bid for the business in the industry. There have been a number of examples: Lockheed didn't even have an airplane designed when it competed with the DC-10; Mack won a bus contract although it was not in the bus-producing business.

## SELECTED BIBLIOGRAPHY

Bain, Joe S. *Barriers to New Competition.* Harvard University Press, 1956.

Bloch, Harry. "Advertising and Profitability: A Reappraisal." *Journal of Political Economy,* 82 (March/April 1974), 267-286.

Comanor, William S., and Wilson, Thomas A. "Advertising, Market Structure, and Performance." *Review of Economics and Statistics,* 49 (November 1967), 423-440.

Dorfman, Robert, and Steiner, Peter O. "Optimal Advertising and Optimal Quality." *American Economic Review,* 44 (December 1954), 826-836.

Doyle, P. "Advertising Expenditure and Consumer Demand." *Oxford Economic Papers,* 20 (November 1968), 394-416.

Greer, Douglas. "Advertising and Market Concentration." *Southern Economic Journal,* 38 (July 1971), 19-32.

Kaldor, Nicholas. "The Economic Aspects of Advertising." *The Review of Economic Studies,* 18 (1949-1950), 1-27.

Mann, H. M.; Henning, J. A.; and Meehan, J. W. "Advertising and Concentration: An Empirical Investigation." *The Journal of Industrial Economics,* 16 (November 1967), 34-45.

————. "Statistical Testing in Industrial Economics: A Reply on Measurement Error and Sampling Procedure." *Journal of Industrial Economics,* 18 (November 1969), 95-100.

Schmalensee, Richard. *The Economics of Advertising.* Amsterdam: North-Holland Publishing, 1972.

Telser, Lester G. "Advertising and Competition." *Journal of Political Economy,* 72 (December 1964), 537-562.

————. "Another Look at Advertising and Concentration." *Journal of Industrial Economics,* 18 (November 1969), 85-95.

Weiss, Leonard W. "Advertising, Profits, and Corporate Taxes." *Review of Economics and Statistics,* 51 (November 1969), 421-430.

# 4

# The Concentration and Profits Issue

## Editors' Note

The concentration–profits relationship plays a central role in the structure–conduct–performance paradigm. The existence of a small number of firms in an industry is said to facilitate collusion which in turn results in higher profits. Thus, a positive association between concentration and profits is held to provide factual proof of the validity of the structural theory.

A competing view is that the profit level of an industry should be regarded as a measure of its health rather than as an indicator of departure from competition. This view would emphasize other factors, in addition to profits, in judging the performance of an industry. Other factors would include: (1) price trends in the industry (e.g., relative to other industries with similar characteristics); (2) trends in product quality improvement; (3) the industry's ability to increase the standard of living of its workers; and (4) the industry's record of innovation. This view holds that a positive concentration–profit relationship may be evidence of superior efficiency. Industries become concentrated for technological and efficiency reasons. The largest firms are the most efficient and thus earn the highest rates of return.

Almost all of the earlier studies showed a positive relationship between concentration and profits. Some recent studies put this finding in doubt. Questions have been posed about both sets of findings with regard to quality of the data, assignment of firms to proper industries, and the specification of the statistical tests.

The concentration–profit relationship, and its behavior over time, is influenced by a number of factors. These include the size of individual firms, the growth rates of the industries, risk, measures of individual firm efficiency, advertising, product differentiation, and research and development activities. These multiple influences must be taken into account and require particular care in the specification of the model tested in the analysis.

The foregoing considerations indicate some of the difficulties in resolving the concentration–profits question. The papers of Professors Demsetz and Weiss attempt to advance our understanding by theoretical discussion and by presenting entirely new empirical evidence. The issue is far from resolved and presents continued research challenges. A particularly penetrating analysis of the complexities was set forth as follows by Professor Coase in introducing the papers:

> There are really two controversies in this area, one relating to the statistics and the other to the analysis. The resolution in one area, either statistical or analytical, doesn't necessarily help one in coming to a resolution of the other.
>
> Now, if we look at the statistics, starting with Bain, there have been a whole series of studies which suggest that there is a relationship, a positive relationship, between concentration and profitability. People point out that this relationship is weak. However, the people who are impressed by this set of statistics say maybe it is weak, but it is really very surprising that so many studies of different sorts get the same results.
>
> It is also very surprising that you get such a result when there are, after all, many disturbing factors which will tend to make it less likely that the relationship becomes apparent, and where, as others including Professor Weiss have argued, many of the disturbing factors lead to a bias towards a zero result. But, of course, others say: "Well, this is an attempt to make a strength out of a weak result, and weak is weak."
>
> But then you have another set of results — which I associate mostly with the work of Professor Brozen, but some others too — which say if you take different time periods, if you extend the sample, this relationship that other people have found tends to disappear. This involves a conflict which really has to be resolved, or so I think.
>
> There are also, of course, people who argue that if one made allowances, for example, for the relationship between advertising expenditures and concentration, research and development expenditures and concentration, that this would also tend to weaken the positive result which the earlier study had shown. Well, these are controversies which exist so far as the statistical analysis is concerned.
>
> But then there are problems of an analytical sort. Many of those who first developed these concentration–profitability studies interpreted a positive relationship as evidence of monopoly. More recently, others have suggested that such results are quite consistent with competition. So you then have the problem that even if you can decide that there is a relationship, it doesn't really tell you whether you have got competition or monopoly.
>
> On the other hand, there are Professor Brozen's results which suggest no relationship at all. And, unfortunately, some people have suggested that you might get this relationship with either monopoly or competition.
>
> So we have this important question on which at the moment there seems to be a great deal of diversity of opinion — diversity which may be less at the end of this session — but, of course, may not.

# Two Systems of Belief About Monopoly

## Harold Demsetz*

### I

The old adage "seeing is believing" contains a double measure of truth, for there also is much merit in the notion that "believing is seeing." Facts must be placed into a system of belief before they yield to interpretation. The same astronomical observations in the Copernican theory convey an entirely different image of the universe in the Ptolemaic theory, and phenomena assume new meaning when we shift from the Newtonian system to the Einsteinian system. Economic facts also require a system of belief before they can be interpreted. There is an impression that economists share a common system of belief about monopoly and competition into which the facts about concentration and profits, whatever they may be, can be fitted neatly. But this is not so, and the illusion of unanimity is now being shattered.

This disillusionment stems partly from the fact that students of monopoly and competition now are being asked to respond to policy alternatives of greater significance than those posed since the decade of the thirties. The renewed attempt to link monopoly to inflation via some type of "cost-push" inflation theory has thrust the monopoly problem into policy areas usually reserved to Keynesians and Monetarists. But more important has been the continuing attempt to incorporate the monopoly model, as that term often is understood or misunderstood, into legislation that would bring about a radical restructuring of industry. Such legislation was recommended by President Johnson's antitrust task force, and, in much stronger form, currently is sought by Senator Hart. These legislative programs already have brought the debate among economists before the public and have forced closer questioning of our beliefs and evidence about the operation of the economic system.

In addition, there recently have been factual findings that are difficult to explain with the accepted doctrine about the relationship between competition and industry structure. These new findings must, at the least, stimulate a reexamination of doctrine and, possibly, a revolution in doctrine. All of this should make the workday of the economist more interesting and that of the policymaker more hesitant.

Two competing theories about monopoly are heading for a showdown. Our understanding of the operation of the economic system depends largely on which of these two systems of belief is adopted. The currently most familiar belief conceives of monopoly power as producible by a firm or an industry without any substantial aid from the government. I shall call this the "self-

* Professor of Economics, The University of California at Los Angeles, and Senior Research Fellow, The Hoover Institution. For further biographical information, see Appendix D.

sufficiency" theory. A second belief, which may be named the "interventionism" theory, sees monopoly power as a derivative of governmental interventions. These two views refer to a difference in belief about the source of *most* monopoly power, not to every instance of monopoly power.

It is true that the government's agreement to provide protection from would-be competitors is secured at least partly through the activities of firms, and therefore, that the interventionism theory of monopoly is a variant of the self-sufficiency theory. Nonetheless it is useful to preserve the substantive distinction of these competing views when we deal with the problem of how we can best cope with monopoly power. Should we try to reduce the degree of government intervention, or should we seek to restructure industries and to modify the competitive tactics used by firms? Those who hold to the belief of self-sufficient monopoly will answer this question by seeking more intervention, while those who see the source of monopoly in government intervention will seek to reduce the role of government in our economy.

This brief description suggests a clearer distinction of these competing beliefs than actually exists. Proponents of either view might see one source of monopoly in explicit agreements to collude, and both groups might consider it desirable to make such agreements illegal. The existence of such agreements might be interpreted as a self-sufficient source of monopoly; or alternatively, the legality of such agreements might be seen as government intervention to help enforce the agreements. Setting aside such problems about specific practices, a correct difference in emphasis is nonetheless captured by this description. The belief in a self-sufficient source of monopoly generates a view of the unregulated economy as one that is monopoly prone, while the belief that government intervention is the prime source of monopoly sees the unregulated economy as essentially competitive. The self-sufficiency theory suggests that political intervention is required; market concentration is seen as an important inhibitor of competition from within the industry, and large capital requirements, intensive advertising, and "predatory" pricing are viewed as important obstacles to competition from outside the industry. The belief that monopoly arises because of government intervention considers these to be relatively unimportant sources of monopoly so long as the government does not use its coercive powers to create and police legal barriers to competition; this viewpoint suggests that the regulation of transport, the imposition of tariffs, the various agricultural programs, the enforcement of licensure, the control of prices, and the legal restrictions imposed on entry and on the use of competitive tactics are the origins of more serious monopoly problems.

II

The intellectual origin of the interventionist theory of monopoly can be traced at least to Adam Smith's attack on mercantilism. In several chapters of *The Wealth of Nations*, Smith explored inefficiencies caused by governmental measures to protect and subsidize industries. This view of the nature of the monopoly problem dominated the thinking of economists until the first quarter of the twentieth century — after which it became quiescent, only to be res-

urrected recently in work dealing with the economic theory of political behavior. The quiescent period began after an important restructuring of industry
had taken place, brought about partly because transport cost had fallen
rapidly (thereby making it feasible for larger firms to sell across obsolete geographic market boundaries), and partly because the laws of incorporation had
been revised in ways that facilitated the massing of large amounts of capital
at low cost through public stock subscription.

Coincidentally with this restructuring, the economic theory of monopoly became increasingly explicit as to its assumptions and narrow as to its applications. The theory contrasted two industry structures and the prices that could
be deduced from each: an atomistic structure comprised of an extremely large
number of firms, and a monopoly structure containing but one firm. The atomistic structure denied any firm the power to control price. The one-firm structure
conveyed complete control over price to the single firm. Increasingly these two
structures were interpreted as descriptions of counterparts in real markets. I
believe this interpretation errs seriously, but, in any case, the search for the
source of monopoly power began to shift from government protection to industry structure.

Although markets had become more concentrated at the turn of the century
(but, in general, not since then), only a very few were so dominated by one
firm that they could be thought to resemble closely the one-firm industry assumed in the monopoly model. Nonetheless, the system of belief had so shifted
that many economists came to view many actual industrial structures as near-
enough approximations to the single-firm structure of monopoly theory. There
was a growing expectation that monopoly was significantly correlated with
market concentration, and this expectation soon hardened into a market concentration doctrine.

No serious theoretical basis yet exists for this doctrine, notwithstanding
Weiss's efforts to demonstrate the existence of such a basis. Weiss does
marshal enough "theories" of oligopoly to make a very convincing case. But
the case he makes is mine.

The essence of monopoly power is the ability to prevent an expansion of
capacity when price exceeds unit cost; yet not one of the oligopoly theories he
described deals with the problem posed for colluding oligopolists by potential
and actual entry; not one tells us how price can be maintained above a competitive level even *if* oligopolists should succeed in eliminating competition
among existing firms. These models thus share a seldom recognized characteristic of the basic monopoly model from which they derive; the monopoly model
assumes that monopoly power exists, it does not explain how monopoly power
is acquired and maintained; the theory then proceeds to show how such power
will be exercised.

The structure of an industry is determined largely by the degree to which
scale economies prevail, or by the comparative efficiencies of firms; but no
good theoretical link has been forged between the structure of the industry
and the degree to which competitive pricing prevails, because no good explanation has been provided for how present and potential rivals are kept

from competing without some governmentally provided restrictions on competitive activities.

What these descriptions of oligopoly behavior attempt to explain is: how oligopolists will act *if* there is no concern about entry. Even at this much more restricted game, these descriptions, with the exception of Stigler's, can hardly be dignified as theories. One theory assumes that each oligopolist believes that his rivals will not change their outputs no matter what he does; another assumes that rivals will keep their prices unchanged no matter what; others reach no definite equilibrium price or fail to explain how the equilibrium price is established. Stigler's theory of oligopoly is the only one that assumes sensible behavior on the part of oligopolists; but even his theory, which is worked out much better than the others, neglects the problems posed by open entry and by the need to discipline firms that compete.

Note that I have been discussing the absence of a well-worked-out theory supporting the link between industry structure and *monopoly power*. The testing of the market concentration doctrine has relied extensively on a search for a correlation between industry structure and *profit rates*. This implies that there is good reason to expect collusion among oligopolists to record higher profit rates as these are measured by accountants. There are, of course, many problems in the use of accounting data as approximations for economic concepts; but even if these measurement problems are set aside, there remain serious theoretical problems which I will discuss later.

Confirmation of the market concentration doctrine was offered first in the work of Professor Joe Bain[1] who, in 1951, published his famous study of the relationship between market concentration and profit rates in 42 selected industries. He found that profit rates were higher for industries in which the largest eight firms accounted for at least 70 percent of industry value added. Table 7 summarizes his results.

Continuing through the decades of the fifties and sixties with the work of Bain and others, there was growing acceptance of the market concentration doctrine. Soon it became the dominant view of economists working in this area. It was taught in economics departments throughout the land at the time that most persons at this conference were attending college. Its influence spread beyond the narrow confines of professional economics and filtered into the world of politics and antitrust law. It has become part of the conventional wisdom of intellectuals and policymakers. "Oligopoly," "shared monopoly," "conscious parallelism in pricing," and "barriers to entry," not yet household words, have become establishment clichés.

When a profession accepts a new system of belief, research is guided by that belief to rationalize observed phenomena in ways that confirm it. The belief in a self-sufficient theory of monopoly power offers no exception. Several studies followed quickly on Bain's and, although a few produced contrary results, most found confirmation of the new paradigm. A weak but gen-

1. Joe S. Bain, "Relation of Profit-Rate to Industry Concentration: American Manufacturing, 1936-1940," *Quarterly Journal of Economics*, 65 (August 1951), p. 293.

TABLE 7

Average of Industry Average-Profit Rates Within Concentration
Deciles, 42 Selected Industries, 1936-1940

| Value Added, Supplied by 8 Largest Firms | Average of Industry Average-Profit Rates | Number of Industries |
|---|---|---|
| 90-100.0% | 12.7% | 8 |
| 80- 89.9 | 9.8 | 11 |
| 70- 79.9 | 16.3 | 3 |
| 60- 69.9 | 5.8 | 5 |
| 50- 59.9 | 5.8 | 4 |
| 40- 49.9 | 8.6 | 2 |
| 30- 39.9 | 6.3 | 5 |
| 20- 29.9 | 10.4 | 2 |
| 10- 19.9 | 17.0 | 1 |
| 0- 9.9 | 9.1 | 1 |

Source: Joe S. Bain, "Relation of Profit-Rate to Industry Concentration: American Manufacturing, 1936-1940," *Quarterly
Journal of Economics,* 65 (August 1951), p. 293.

erally persistent correlation between market concentration and profit rates is
a fairly accurate description of these findings. Alternative explanations for
these data generally were ignored because the market concentration doctrine
had won the imagination of investigators and had given direction to their
thoughts, much as Ptolemaic astronomy provided the signposts for the study
of heavenly bodies during the four hundred years surrounding the life of
Christ.

How did concentrated markets remain concentrated if they yielded above-
average profits and were not protected by the government? Why did Bain
observe lower profit rates for the smaller firms relative to the larger ones that
occupied the same concentrated industries? What distortion is implied when
industry profits are measured primarily by the profits of the larger firms in the
industry? Why did nine industries with concentration ratios between 50 and
70 percent have lower profit rates than the eleven less concentrated industries
contained in Bain's sample? (See Table 7). These matters generally were set
aside during the period when most of the confirmatory studies were produced,
although some attention was given by Bain (and his student H. Michael Mann)
to the problem of why a positive relationship between concentration and profit
rates should be resilient in the face of entry threats. It was decided — largely
by intuition, not analysis — that the use of advertising and capital, as well as
the existence of economies of scale, created what Bain called barriers to the
entry of resources from outside the industry. No clear rationale was given as
to why the use of particular kinds of inputs should create such barriers when
these same inputs are available to firms both inside and outside the industry.

But Bain and Mann did find a stronger correlation between concentration and profits for those industries that used these inputs very intensely.

By 1960, then, collected evidence indicated a weak but generally positive correlation between concentration and profit rates. One large study covering a different time span, by George J. Stigler,[2] did not support these findings nor did a few smaller studies. Nonetheless, the balance of evidence, when measured by a number of studies, clearly favored the market concentration doctrine. In addition, there was the smaller amount of work indicating a potential explanation for this relationship in the intensive use of advertising and capital. Those who believed in the self-sufficient source of monopoly power had found confirmation.

During the middle sixties, development less clearly favored the belief in self-sufficient monopoly. It is true that Stigler[3] did construct a formal rationale for the market concentration doctrine in 1964, and Comanor and Wilson[4] in 1967 presented statistical evidence that higher profit rates were associated with more intensive use of advertising. But both studies really gave less support to the market concentration doctrine than might be supposed. Comanor and Wilson found that after account was taken of advertising expenditures and capital requirements, there no longer existed any correlation between market concentration and profit rates; and Stigler's theoretical analysis indicated that it takes relatively few firms to reduce significantly the gains from a collusive arrangement. Moreover, Stigler's study took no account of the role that entry would play in making such arrangements even less profitable.

Largely unnoticed, there appeared several studies during the late fifties and the decade of the sixties that provided cumulating evidence in favor of the belief that government intervention is a major source of monopoly power. It had always been recognized that tariffs, oil import quotas, the agricultural program, and the legal support of unions constructed impediments to the free flow of resources and created higher returns for small segments of the economy at greater cost to the more dispersed masses. But it generally was believed that government regulation of industry as provided for in the Act to Regulate Commerce, the Maritime Act, the Federal Communications Act, the Air Transport Act, etc., worked to the advantage of consumers. These studies provided arguments and evidence that this was not the case, and that, in general, this type of regulation protected the regulated industries from competition at the expense of consumers. Even at the local level, regulations such as those limiting entry into the taxi business and into housing through zoning requirements were shown to be protective devices creating serious impediments to the efficient use of resources.

2. George J. Stigler, *Capital and Rates of Return in Manufacturing* (Princeton Univ. Press 1963).

3. George J. Stigler, "A Theory of Oligopoly," *Journal of Political Economy*, 72 (February 1964), p. 44.

4. W. S. Comanor and T. A. Wilson, "Advertising, Market Structure, and Performance," *Review of Economics and Statistics*, 49 (November 1967), p. 423.

These studies offered support for the belief that government intervention plays a substantial role in the creation of monopoly power, but they did not undermine the evidence that had been accumulating in favor of the belief in self-sufficient monopoly power, nor did they lead many economists to doubt the market concentration doctrine. The way of looking at economic phenomena remained fairly fixed by the belief in self-sufficient monopoly power. But, beginning with the present decade, new evidence raised doubts about the main statistical supports and theoretical conjectures of the market concentration doctrine.

Yale Brozen[5] attempted to find evidence that would substantiate the rationalization used by President Johnson's Task Force on Antitrust Policy in its call for a Concentrated Industries Act for the purpose of reducing market concentration. The task force based its recommendation on its belief that there existed a large body of evidence showing a *persistent* relationship between concentration and high rates of return. The task force report stated that:

> It is the persistence of high profits over extended time periods and over whole industries . . . that suggest[s] artificial restraints on output and the absence of fully effective competition. The correlation of evidence of this kind with very high levels of concentration appears to be significant.[6]

Brozen found that none of the studies supporting the market concentration doctrine had looked at the question of the persistence over time of the correlation between profit and concentration; their results were based essentially on observations of a cross-section of industries during a given time interval. He examined the question of persistence directly by carrying forward in time three studies that supported the market concentration doctrine. (These were the basic study by Bain, a follow-up study by Mann, and a second, smaller study by Stigler that had found a correlation between profit and concentration for a group of 17 highly concentrated industries.) Brozen found no confirmation of the persistence in these correlations. The correlations degenerated within a few years, and high and low profit rates tended to converge toward a common level.

Why should the period used by Bain, 1936-1940, support the market concentration doctrine when subsequent time periods did not? Brozen[7] answered this puzzle by enlarging the sample used by Bain from 42 to 80 industries, and, in some industries, Brozen also increased the number of firms used to measure profit rates. Bain had used only 42 out of the 340 industries for which census data were available. The information in which Bain was interested was available for only 149 of these, because he relied on profit data

5. Yale Brozen, "The Antitrust Task Force Deconcentration Recommendation," *Journal of Law and Economics,* 13 (October 1970), p. 279.

6. White House Task Force on Antitrust Policy, "Report 1," in *Role of the Giant Corporations* (1968), p. 883.

7. Yale Brozen, "Bain's Concentration and Rates of Return Revisited," *Journal of Law and Economics,* 14 (October 1971), p. 351.

reported by the Securities and Exchange Commission. Another group of industries was omitted because Bain felt that the market definitions used by the census were inaccurate. Brozen was able to enlarge this sample by using information not earlier available to Bain. The enlarged sample, examined for the same time period studied by Bain, failed to reveal any significant correlation between concentration and profits. Apparently Bain's findings were not representative of the population from which he selected his industries.

The undermining of the evidence favoring the market concentration doctrine continued with a recent article by Stanley Ornstein.[8] Ornstein found profit rates to be related significantly to industry and firm growth rates, and to the minimum efficient scale of production, but *not* to market concentration. Meanwhile, other studies have revealed a high degree of temporal instability in correlations between profit rates and market concentration, and some of these correlations are negative.

These new studies constitute a fundamental challenge to the empirical work underlying the market concentration doctrine. Doubts have been raised as to whether there exists a positive correlation between profit rates and concentration, and the proposition that any such relationship holds persistently through time seems to be discredited.

Weiss has provided us with a tabulation of most of the empirical studies bearing on the market concentration doctrine [Table 11]. His detailed critical review of these, however, is limited to those studies whose results are inconsistent with the market concentration doctrine. These he dismisses in some cases because their methodology was poor, because the time period covered was inflationary, or because regional industries were treated as if they had national markets. But almost all of the studies in support of the market concentration doctrine either have methodological problems, or are very heavily influenced by deflationary periods, or treat regional industries as national. If the criteria that Weiss adopts to criticize nonconfirmatory studies are applied to all studies, we are left with very little acceptable evidence about the relationship between profit rates and concentration.

Apparently, we now confront the proposition that successful collusion is practiced only during noninflationary periods by firms that advertise or use capital intensely — unless, of course, market concentration should be less than 70 percent! The theories to which Weiss has appealed tell us very little about oligopoly behavior, and they certainly do not tell us that collusion fails to work when the Consumer Price Index turns upward or when the 8-firm concentration ratio dips below 70 percent.

Brozen's study is selected for special criticism by Weiss. He contends that it was improper for Brozen to classify a few industries as concentrated or unconcentrated. For example, Weiss charges that Brozen was incorrect to include beet and cane sugar among his concentrated industries, because they compete on the same market and "their combined 8-firm concentration ratio was probably less than 70." The reader might suppose from Weiss's discussion that

8. Stanley Ornstein, "Concentration and Profits," *Journal of Business,* 45 (October 1972), p. 519.

these problems were not discussed by Brozen, but the appendix to Brozen's paper [see n. 7 *supra*] discusses the very industries referred to by Weiss, and I recommend a reading of that appendix for those who are curious about why Brozen constructed the sample as he did. For example, Brozen writes:

> Bain excluded the sugar industries (beet and cane) on the ground that the separation of close substitutes "would tend seriously to overstate the true concentration for the theoretical industry within which the outputs in question fell." If we assume that no cane suger refiner produced beet sugar and take the proportion of the output of the leading eight cane sugar refiners of total refined sugar (beet and cane) sales, thus obtaining the lower limit of the possible sugar refining concentration ratio, it exceeds 70 percent and puts the sugar industry in Bain's more concentrated groups.

Brozen did not specially select his sample as seems to be implied by Weiss, but chose to use the complete Federal Trade Commission sample that had been used by the commission to conduct one of the studies quoted by Weiss as support for the market concentration doctrine. Brozen merely shifted the time period to that examined by Bain.

We have already seen that Weiss is simply wrong in saying that the combined 8-firm concentration ratio for the sugar industry was less than 70 percent. Weiss also removed several industries because of their regional character, but it is not proper to exclude an industry from the unconcentrated category merely because it is regional. An accepted procedure is to require regional industries to exhibit very low national concentration measures before they are allowed to enter the unconcentrated category. A national 4-firm concentration ratio less than 20 percent has been found acceptable to other investigators. If we use this criterion, Weiss should not have removed the bread and bakery products industry from the unconcentrated category, nor should he have removed nonalcoholic beverages or malt liquors. The cement industry profits in 1939 and 1940 were below the average for the unconcentrated group, where the industry was placed in Brozen's sample. If it were removed from this category, as Weiss suggests, and placed instead in the concentrated industries category, as was done in Mann's study, the results would have turned out even more favorable to a rejection of Bain's findings. For alcoholic beverages, a strong case can be made that the market was national in scope; for example, most of the beer sold by the top brewers was sold nationwide from single plants. Finally, I am not sure how blast furnace products should be handled, since it is difficult to discover the extent of competition between pig iron producers and integrated steel mills.

Weiss's techniques, of course, can be applied to studies favoring the market concentration doctrine. For example, Bain was not so careful as Weiss implies. Bain did not eliminate all industries with regional characteristics. He used cement and also cast iron pipe. He didn't use the locomotive industry, although it clearly is highly concentrated and manufactures a single product. It earned only 1.7 percent, and its inclusion in Bain's sample would have lowered the concentrated industries' rate of return.

But even after Weiss recasts the FTC sample, he gets a 2.2 percent difference in return between concentrated and nonconcentrated industries for one year — no small reduction from the 4.4 percent difference found by Bain. And in the other year there is no significant difference. The guts of Brozen's study hold their shape very well even when operated on by Weiss.

We have seen that the theoretical basis for the market concentration doctrine is weak at best, and that the empirical work is not clear cut as to results. The situation is much worse when we turn to the notion of self-created barriers to entry. The lack of a theoretical justification for identifying certain types of expenditures as "barriers to entry" is even more glaring than is the lack of a theoretical basis for the market concentration doctrine. The costliness of producing commodities does, of course, limit the amounts that will be made available at particular prices; in this sense cost does create a "barrier" to production, but no pejorative interpretation can be given to such a "barrier to entry." Indeed, it would be wasteful to produce additional units when the cost of doing so exceeds the value of these units to prospective purchasers. Cost, whether incurred to acquire labor or capital or to inform prospective buyers, sets proper limits on the production and marketing of commodities.

What does it mean to say that advertising expenditures and capital outlays constitute barriers to entry? One meaning is that firms must make such expenditures if they are to produce and communicate about the commodities they hope to sell. Such expenditures are no more barriers than are expenditures on labor and material. A second meaning is that existing firms are more efficient in the employment of such inputs than are firms not yet in the industry. If this is so, the existing firms deserve applause, not divestiture. A third meaning is that existing firms have an *undesirable* advantage in the use of these inputs. Since all firms can borrow in the capital markets and can purchase advertising campaigns, it is difficult to see wherein the unfair advantage lies. If large firms are better risks to lenders and, therefore, if they can borrow at lower rates (internally or externally) than can small or new firms, then this element of superiority for the large-scale, older firm is properly recognized by capital markets. Similarly, if buyers have more confidence in, and are more knowledgeable about, well-established products, then this also is a real efficiency not to be denied to firms that have invested in building substantial reputations. Nor should buyers who do not desire to bear the risk of consuming and the cost of searching for *possibly* equally good but less well-known alternatives be denied the advantage of trading with older, larger firms.

Objections based on problems of accounting methods have been raised about the notion that advertising creates a barrier to entry. There is a suspicion that the empirical correlation between advertising intensity and profit rate is an accounting artifact brought about by the fact that accountants treat advertising as a current expense even though the returns from advertising may be earned over several years. Critics have argued that it is this accounting artifact and not barriers to entry that produces this correlation. Two studies have attempted to take into consideration the investment-like quality of advertising. Weiss[9] adjusted Comanor and Wilson's study by introducing a depreciation rate for advertising, but he found that this did not significantly reduce the correlation between profit rates and advertising that had been uncovered by Comanor and Wilson. A doctoral dissertation by H. Bloch[10] using different methods and data, however, concluded that the correlation between these variables disappears when the accounting data are corrected to allow for the investmentlike quality of advertising.

When Weiss modified the Comanor and Wilson study, he applied a uniform advertising depreciation rate to all industries. This is likely to result in a bias if advertising depreciation rates actually differ among industries. R. Ayanian, in a dissertation now being completed at UCLA, has estimated depreciation rates for various industries and found that they do differ. When he uses the different depreciation rates applicable to different industries, he finds no correlation between profit rates and advertising intensity.

The current popularity of "barriers to entry" is puzzling. It is said that existing firms have created a preference for their products through the use of advertising and, therefore, that new competitors need to advertise even more intensely if they are to attract customers. But the firms now in the industry once needed to attract customers away from the established products of other industries, to an unknown new product, so it is not at all clear that new entrants suffer a disadvantage as compared with those who showed the way. Furthermore, the inputs most likely to create a differential advantage for existing firms are those that might make it more difficult for new firms to learn the source of strength enjoyed by old firms. Old firms may have developed particular trade secrets or ways of organizing that are relatively difficult for new firms to learn about. But the use of advertising and large amounts of capital are there for everyone to see and duplicate. Even the particular type of sales pitch used by successful firms can be imitated with relative ease. The use of advertising and capital would seem to me to be the least likely candidates for the role of barriers to entry. One grandfather's clause is worth a very, very large advertising budget.

In summary then, we can conclude that the theoretical support of the market concentration doctrine, including its barriers-to-entry variant, is weak or nonexistent. On the empirical side, it is clear that more studies reveal a positive correlation between profits and concentration than do not. There are enough of those that fail to show such a correlation, however, that the policymaker ought not suppose that conclusive evidence of this statistical relationship exists. What is needed is a thoroughgoing fresh look at the data and methodology. But even if this should reveal a positive correlation, there would still remain a serious problem for policy, for what can be inferred from a positive correlation?

9. L. Weiss, "Advertising, Profits, and Corporate Taxes," *Review of Economics and Statistics,* 51 (November 1969), p. 421.

10. H. Bloch, "Advertising, Competition, and Market Performance" (unpublished Ph.D. thesis, Univ. of Chicago 1971).

III

That any meaning can be given to persistent correlations between profit and concentration is attributable to the fact that accounting measures are necessarily poor approximations to the theoretical concepts they represent. The most important imperfection is their weakness in attaching appropriate values to those assets that are likely to be associated with the preservation of monopoly or the attainment of superior efficiency. If proper economic values were given on these assets, then all firms, whether monopolies or competitive, could be expected to yield the same rate of return. Thus, the trucking industry obtains a grandfather's clause to block entry. This increases the value of the licenses to operate, but accountants are unlikely to value these licenses at anything like their market value; if they were so valued, the rate of return recorded by trucking firms would be no different than that recorded by free-entry industries. A correct evaluation of assets would capitalize monopoly profits into the value of the assets which shield the firms from competition. Similarly, an explicit or implicit agreement to collude, if successful, is an undervalued asset to companies. Hence it is possible to look at accounting returns and form some guess as to the degree of monopoly that is present.

Unfortunately, it is not only sources of monopoly that are undervalued by accountants but also sources of efficiency. For example, General Motors has made a decision to push ahead with a rotary-engine car. No element of monopoly is present in that decision, since Ford and Chrysler also could have adopted the same course of action. But they did not. Let us suppose that GM's decision turns out to be correct, and that it gains both profit and market share, which it holds for many years because of the difficulty of quickly imitating that decision, the uncertainty among all firms as to whether the rotary engine will continue to be successful, and the tendency of consumers in this industry to rate experience highly. Accounting procedures are essentially backward-looking, but the uncertain value of such a decision rests in the future. Hence, for many years GM may record high profits and high market share even though monopoly is absent.

It might be supposed that management wages would reflect the value of a correct decision, but they will do so only imperfectly and with long lags. Indeed, if the full value of such decisions accrued to management, there would be no reason for GM stock to appreciate. Part of the reason that salaries will not capture the full value of such decisions is because some of the reward accrues to shareholders who had a role in selecting a productive (or lucky) team. Another reason is that it is difficult to forecast how long the decision will remain the correct decision. The better the decision turns out in retrospect, the more undervalued (relatively) will have been the management. Finally, the goodness of the decision may not reflect the ability of one man but the ability of an entire management team. No one member of such a team can hope to obtain a salary elsewhere that reflects his value as a member of this team; hence there is no reason for the market to push such salaries to the point where all the gain from the correct decision is exhausted in wages; nor should the market do so, since it is the firm itself, as a team, that has created this value. Similar problems arise in the case of monopoly profits. Since management is "responsible" for the decisions that create monopoly, it might be expected that the monopoly gains will be fully absorbed in managerial salary.

Higher accounting profit rates can arise either for reasons of monopoly or for superior efficiency, because accountants simply cannot appropriately value the assets or the decisions that may give rise to the profits. (Similarly, incorrect or unwise decisions will produce lower accounting profit rates.) Sometimes there will be an element of both efficiency and monopoly. Patent and copyright privileges may deliver to innovative firms some protection from competition and also may lead to higher concentration. To the extent that accounting procedures undervalue such legal protection, there will exist a positive correlation between profit and concentration. But this is cause for alarm only if we believe that the proper workings of the incentive system do not require such protection against easy imitation.

One difference in the implications of the source of high returns should be noted. If firms succeed in colluding to raise price, this may give rise to an increase in accounting profits because this agreement is undervalued by accountants. But these profits and the undervaluing of the agreement will be short-lived if firms cannot control competition in other directions. There will be great incentives to improve product quality and services in order to sell more at the collusive price. Such competition will raise cost towards price and dissipate the profitability of the agreement. This will not be the case if the cause of the higher profits is superior efficiency; there is no reason for a superior firm to dissipate its gains in such a fashion.

We do not yet understand the permanence that can be attached to either source of high accounting rates of return. Collusive agreements, even when enforced by government, do not last forever. The competition for government protection that sometimes creates new monopoly also may do away with old monopoly. Similarly, basic decisions having nothing to do with monopoly sometimes turn out well but other times turn out poorly. The Ford Motor Company acquired a dominant profitable position in the automobile industry by virtue of Henry Ford's decision to produce a standard model with mass-production techniques; but after several years of this, the same decision-maker lost share and profits to GM. In some cases, the effects of monopoly or of superior decisions may be felt for many years, and, in part, this could explain any persistence in high accounting rates of return.

A phenomenon that is likely to generate fairly persistent differences in accounting rates of returns is the fact that some products are more efficiently produced by firms possessing a large share of the market, while in other industries large market shares are not necessary for efficiency. Those firms that first act on the belief that large scale is an advantage, and that invest in the marketing and production techniques prerequisite to executing the move to large scale, will possess a competitively secured advantage in timing and in obtaining early consumer acceptance that will be difficult to overcome in a short time period. The market may not have grown large enough to accommodate more than a handful of such firms. These firms can produce at lower unit cost than smaller firms. They are superior in this respect, and they command an economic rent for achieving primacy. This rent will be measured as profit by accountants. Even though such firms can achieve generally low unit cost, at the margin their capacity may be strained and price will be high enough to allow smaller, higher unit cost firms to accommodate that part of the market not easily serviced by the larger firms. If and when the market grows enough to accommodate additional large firms, such firms will form, perhaps by merger of the smaller firms.

If industries are *persistently* concentrated, the fundamental reason will be the prevalence of large scale advantages. Such firms will record higher profits because the market has not yet grown sufficiently; in order to bring smaller, less efficient firms into production, price will need to be high enough to cover their unit cost, and this means that price will need to be high enough for *accounting* profits to be recorded by the large firms in these industries. Of course, these industries will be the highly concentrated ones.

Since most of the earlier studies of the relationship between profit and concentration relied heavily on the rate of return of only larger firms, it is difficult to know whether monopoly or superior efficiency accounts for the positive correlations frequently found. Does the market concentration doctrine, *unaided by this* "efficient structure" explanation, adequately explain the pattern of profit rates and market concentration? Do higher profits in concentrated industries reflect only monopoly? Or are they in whole or part brought about by the efficiency of large firms in these industries? [11] Some light can be shed on these questions by examining profit–concentration correlations after taking account of firm size. Firms of each size class should have profit rates that increase with concentration if collusion is more successful in concentrated markets. The absence of such correlations for most size classes of firms would be difficult to reconcile with the market concentration doctrine.

Table 8 tabulates the correlation between profit rates and concentration for firms in five different size categories and for each of five years.[12] Each entry shows the size of the correlation (which can vary from $-1$, for a perfect inverse relationship, to $+1$ for a perfect direct relationship) and indicates the level of significance that can be attached to the measured correlation. The most important information in Table 8 is that after the size of the firm is taken into account, *no* significant correlation between profit rate and market con-

---

11. Earlier empirical work exploring this problem can be found in H. Demsetz, "The Market Concentration Doctrine" (AEI-Hoover Policy Studies, August 1973), and H. Demsetz, "Industry Structure, Market Rivalry, and Public Policy," *Journal of Law and Economics,* 16 (April 1973), p. 1.

12. Four size classes were used when this paper was originally presented. At that time the largest class size was $50 million and up, but L. Weiss objected that the three smaller classes did not contain large enough firms. In response to this point, a fifth class size has been added. No cell in Tables 2 and 3 has less than 63 industries represented, and most have over 90.

TABLE 8

Correlations Between Rate of Return and Concentration by Asset Size of Firms

| Asset Size<br>($000) | No. of Industries: | 94 | 116 | 116 | 116 | 76 |
|---|---|---|---|---|---|---|
|  | Year: | 1958 [a] | 1963 | 1966 | 1967 | 1970 |
| $0-500 |  | .29 [b] | —.19 [c] | —.09 | —.01 | —.38 [b] |
| 500-5,000 |  | .11 | —.00 | —.06 | —.07 | —.01 |
| 5,000-50,000 |  | .14 | .11 | .04 | —.05 | —.00 |
| 50,000-100,000 |  | —.01 | .01 | .09 | .10 | —.03 |
| 100,000 and up |  | .03 | .16 | .16 | .16 | .28 [c] |
| All asset sizes |  | .28 [b] | .35 [b] | .28 [b] | .19 [c] | .27 [c] |

Note: Concentration is based on 4-digit census industries weighted by employment to match IRS profit data. The 1958 data were not yet complete, with 14 industries still to be tabulated.

a. Sample coverage for 1958 is small, and the data for 1958 must be interpreted with caution.

b. Significant at 1 percent confidence level.

c. Significant at 5 percent confidence level.

centration is apparent even though the correlations which ignore firm size are positive. It would appear that most, if not all, of the positive correlations between profit rates and concentration uncovered by some earlier studies can be attributed to variations in the size of firms, not the degree to which markets are concentrated. This general pattern of profit rate/concentration correlations cannot be explained by recognized oligopoly or monopoly theory. Indeed, it could be argued, with no more casualness than other arguments surrounding the market concentration doctrine, that the positive correlations should be strongest for moderate- and small-sized firms, since the large firms need to adhere more to the collusive agreement than do moderate-sized firms.

The strongest positive correlations tend to be found in the largest class size; and even though these fail to meet the standard tests of statistical significance, there no doubt will be attempts to link this fact to market power. One such explanation deserves attention. In effect, it is a compromise explanation. Larger firms in concentrated industries have lower cost because there are scale economies in these industries or because of some inherent superiority of the larger firms in these industries. Nonetheless they succeed in colluding so that *their* profit rates are relatively high. The prices they set in this collusion are not so high as to yield high profits for less efficient, more moderately sized smaller firms. Hence we observe a stronger positive correlation between profit rates and market concentration for the largest firms than for other firms.

In this rationalization of the data, the cost of production to moderate-sized firms in concentrated markets apparently sets the upper limit to the prices that are (can be?) set through the collusion of large firms; otherwise, firms of moderate size would exhibit higher profits in concentrated industries than in unconcentrated. Presumably, this limit to profits is effective because higher profits would lead new firms, possibly large new firms, and existing smaller firms to merge or expand capacity in the industry. All of this, of course, implies that existing large firms possess superior characteristics that are difficult to imitate. Their methods of organizing production, of providing service, and of establishing buyer confidence must yield lower cost than can be obtained by newer or smaller firms.

This compromise explanation hardly can justify a call for deconcentration, because considerable economies of large-scale production or other advantages of existing large firms would then be lost with no compensation in the form of lower prices. If the sizes of all firms are limited by deconcentration policies to be no larger than moderate-sized firms in their industries, then it will be the costs of the moderate-sized firms that determine prices. But that is how price is constrained without deconcentration if we accept this rationalization of these data. Since persistent market concentration seems to be associated with economies of scale or other forms of superior performance by existing larger firms in concentrated industries, a move to deconcentrate such industries is very *likely* to increase, not decrease, cost even *if* it were true that collusion is more successful in these industries. Embracing the market concentration doctrine through legislation is thus very likely to penalize the success and superior performance upon which depends the progress and wealth of this nation.

Table 8 reveals that most of the correlation between accounting profit rates and concentration can be attributed to firm size, not market concentration. The remaining correlation might only reflect accounting artifacts or special sources of efficiency other than size. There is a suspicion that the accounting treatment accorded advertising expenditures tends to exaggerate the rates of return recorded by those firms that advertise intensely, because accountants fail to treat advertising as a long-lived asset.

It might well be the case that some of the correlations in Table 8 reflect variations in advertising intensity and not variations in market concentration. It is possible to examine what happens to the correlations shown in Table 8 when variations in advertising intensity are taken into account. Table 9 recasts Table 8 after the effect of variations in advertising intensity are removed from the data. The entries in Table 9 thus isolate to a finer degree than Table 8 the relationship between accounting profit rates and concentration for given size classes of firms. The effect of taking account of advertising intensity is to weaken substantially the correlations between profit rates and concentration.

A closer look at Table 9 is rewarding. For firms with asset sizes larger than $1 million, the correlations prevalent in Table 8 all but disappear. Moreover, the correlations which ignore asset sizes turn out to be insignificant in 1967 and 1970 where before they were significant, and the correlations for 1963 and 1966 are weakened. Only the correlation for 1958 is strengthened, but oddly enough only the smallest firms reveal a significant positive relationship between profit rates and concentration for that year; this hardly can constitute strong evidence of collusion among large firms. The years 1958, 1967, and

TABLE 9

Correlations Between Rate of Return and Concentration by Asset Size of Firms

| Asset Size ($000) | 1958 [a] | 1963 | 1966 | 1967 | 1970 |
|---|---|---|---|---|---|
| $0-500 | .29 [b] | −.18 [c] | −.11 | .00 | −.41 [b] |
| 500-5000 | .12 | −.03 | −.05 | −.11 | −.08 |
| 5000-50,000 | .17 | .02 | −.03 | −.14 | −.12 |
| 50,000-100,000 | −.01 | −.07 | .04 | .04 | −.11 |
| 100,000 and up | .04 | .06 | .06 | .06 | .11 |
| All asset sizes | .36 [b] | .29 [b] | .21 [c] | .09 | .08 |

Note: All data identical to data underlying Table 8, but correlations between profit and concentration are partial correlations derived by taking account of the partial correlation between profit rates and advertising sales ratios.

a. Sample coverage for 1958 is small, and the data for 1958 must be interpreted cautiously.

b. Significant at 1 percent confidence level.

c. Significant at 5 percent confidence level.

1970 no longer yield evidence confirming the market concentration doctrine. The year 1966 yields weak evidence on an overall basis, but not for firms smaller than $50 million in asset size. Only 1963 retains a very significant overall correlation, but even here the smaller firms do not provide confirming data. It happens that 1963 is the year chosen by Weiss to correlate "profit margins" with concentration and advertising intensity. But 1963 appears to be a very atypical year with respect to this correlation, a fact to which I called attention in earlier work.[13] Table 9 does not offer convincing evidence for the market concentration doctrine. This is especially true since the correlations presented in that table are based on "one-tailed" tests of significance. Such tests seek to ascertain the probability that a positive correlation between profits and concentration exists. In view of the severe problems of securing dependable accounting data and the very weak theory underlying the market concentration doctrine, it might be wiser to ascertain whether the correlations differ significantly from zero in either a positive or a negative direction. Such a two-tailed test would cut (approximately in half) the remaining significance of the correlations shown in Table 9.

The role played by advertising in producing the results of Table 9 is still difficult to interpret. In some yet-to-be-described way, advertising might be associated with "barriers to entry." However, much of the correlation between profit rates and concentration found in earlier studies may be due to the inappropriate accounting treatment accorded to advertising; evidence for this exists in other studies referred to above. On the other hand, a true source

13. See Demsetz, "The Market Concentration Doctrine," supra n. 11, at 16.

of superior efficiency may exist in the use of advertising by large firms in concentrated industries.

## IV

Let us now complete the circle, returning to discuss the relative merits of the "self-sufficiency" and "interventionist" views of the monopoly problem. The evidence that has been cumulating in recent years must raise doubts about the importance of self-sufficient sources of monopoly and must increase our estimate of the importance of government intervention to protect industries from competition. It is possible, I think, to give good reasons for believing that this new evidence is indicative of the underlying truth.

The key to sustained monopoly power is the ability of an industry to restrict or retard the expansion and utilization of productive capacity. Government can offer to industry much greater powers of coercion to accomplish this end than can be supplied by the industry itself. Most of the resources supplied by the Department of Agriculture at taxpayer expense have been used to subsidize the policing of output restrictions that never could have been obtained without such aid. Moreover, an industry attempting to restrict capacity by its own efforts would need to rely on much less effective techniques than are available when the laws of the land can be marshaled toward this end. For example, if existing firms attempt to block entry by "predatory" pricing, they must all suffer reductions in their profits. The techniques available to firms without the aid of government are not very specific to penalizing only entrants. But the use of CAB or FCC to restrict competitive entry through the use of licensure or certificates of convenience and necessity specifically penalizes prospective entrants. An investment by an industry to obtain government aid to monopolize is likely to yield much more control than the investment of the same sum without the aid of governmental techniques. Some would argue that without government aid such an investment would generally be unprofitable.

More important than this, however, is the greater ease of securing the funds for such an investment if the restrictions are to be achieved through the government. In the absence of government cooperation there are important incentives for not contributing to an effort to restrict output. First, such an effort might very well run afoul of the antitrust laws. Secondly, to the extent that the agreement to restrict output is likely to succeed, a firm would find it profitable to remain outside the agreement; the firm could then expand its output to take full advantage of any higher prices brought about through the private efforts of other firms. These factors, which undermine the success of efforts to collude, are not as important if restrictions are to be achieved through the good offices of the government.

The government and the courts have been careful to protect the constitutional right of petition. If the firms in an industry cooperate in an in-house *attempt* to restrict output, they are in violation of the antitrust laws; but if they cooperate to obtain the aid of the White House and the Congress in building tariff barriers or in increasing agricultural support prices, they are not in violation of the antitrust laws. The basic conflict between the fundamental right of collective petition and the illegality of attempting to collude has been decided in favor of the right to petition.

The *Noerr* case in 1961[14] dealt explicitly with this conflict. In that case the Court of Appeals for the Third Circuit had held that no violation of the Sherman Act can be predicated upon mere attempts to influence the passage or enforcement of laws even if two or more persons associate in an attempt to persuade the legislature or the executive to take particular action that would produce a restraint or a monopoly. (There was some backing away from this decision in a later case, but this tended to emphasize the illegality of restricting one's competitors from easy access to the judicial or legislative machinery.) The antitrust laws are not violated by agreements to petition the government to restrict competition — but are violated when such agreements do not involve the government, even if those agreements fail to achieve their ends. The legal route of monopoly runs through Washington and the state capitals.

More important than the legality of a collusive agreement, perhaps, is the greater difficulty that would confront a firm which seeks to take advantage of an agreement secured and acted upon by other firms when this agreement works through the law. If such an agreement were to operate outside the law, a firm not joining in the agreement could hope to expand its output in response to the higher price brought about by the output restrictions which other firms imposed on themselves. The propensity to stay out of such an agreement or to secretly break its terms constitutes a serious impediment to collusion outside the law. But if the government is brought into the collusive agreement, then higher powers of coercion can be brought into play to make sure that firms in the industry do not undermine the agreement. How else can individual farmers be prevented from increasing output when prices rise? How else can individual owners of oil-rich land be prevented from increasing crude oil output when oil prices rise or when imports are restricted? In one case the discipline is obtained through the federal government's agricultural program, and in the other through the prorationing programs of state governments.

For these reasons and others, including the statistical evidence that has come to light recently, it is quite plausible to believe that government intervention constitutes the main threat to a competitive economy. It is important  that this threat be recognized, because our belief on this score governs how we deploy resources to ensure that competition will flourish. What is called for is a redirection of our efforts. Government intervention that has created and sustained monopoly should be our primary target.

How such a redirection can be brought about is hardly the province of the economist. I doubt that monstrosities such as the agricultural program can be modified significantly until basic changes in the political makeup of this nation continue for several more years. But I see no basic political beliefs of the

14. Eastern R.R. Presidents Conference v. Noerr Motor Freight, Inc., 365 U.S. 127 (1961).

voters of this nation that predispose them to rejoice when the FCC protects established networks and movie theaters from the competition of pay TV. Nor are there obvious cheers from the electorate when the ICC exercises its control over minimum freight rates, or when it prevents truckers and railroads from competing with each other. John Q. Public does not rise to salute when the SEC cooperates with the attempts of the NYSE to protect itself from competition within and without, nor does he exude great pleasure at the efforts of the CAB to keep airlines from setting lower fares. These regulatory actions have benefited special interests in situations where the typical citizen suffers no great illusion as to where his interest lies.

If we can not do away with such regulation, let us at least make it easier for the Justice Department (or some other agency not beholden to any particular industry) to ask whether the decisions of our regulatory tribunals are in the public interest, and, when it feels that they are not, to bring the issue before the courts of this land. I commend the Justice Department for recent moves that it has made on the question of fixed commissions on our organized exchanges. This is a welcome indirect challenge of the authority of the SEC as the sole arbiter of the public interest in the operation of capital markets. But it should be made easier for some agency to question the merits of regulatory decisions and to represent consumer interests in affairs of these industries.

I do not suggest that we abandon the search for private conspiracy, but I do think that it is time to pay much less attention to the structure of industry and virtually no attention to the notion of nongovernmental barriers to entry. A commitment to the machinery of competitive organization requires that we generally accept the consequences of effective competition. For antitrust, this means that market share and profits can be expected to shift in favor of successful rivals.

Unfortunately, our antitrust laws are being used to protect competitors and penalize efficiency. Competitive pricing policies, effective advertising campaigns, and the efficient management of resources are as likely to run afoul of antitrust as are attempts to collude. To an increasing extent, the *United States Steel* [15] and *Alcoa*[16] cases typify the reasoning in contemporary antitrust cases.

The United States Steel Corporation escaped dissolution by refraining from competitive pricing, thus escaping any charge that it used its power to make life difficult for smaller rivals, but Alcoa was found to violate antitrust laws because it behaved competitively. Alcoa had claimed that it never excluded competitors, but Judge Learned Hand clearly described the source of illegality in his reply: "[W]e can think of no more effective exclusion than progressively to embrace each new opportunity as it opened, and to face every newcomer with new capacity already geared into a great organization having the advantage of experience, trade connections, and the elite of personnel." [17]

---

15. United States v. United States Steel Corp., 251 U.S. 417 (1920).

16. United States v. Aluminum Company of America, 148 F.2d 416 (2nd Cir. 1945).

17. *Id.* at 431.

Those who seek freedom, productivity, and protection through market competition must believe that there is a steady stream of competition that disciplines even those who best their rivals on a given day or during a given decade. The history of market economies provides overwhelming evidence that this belief is based on experience. A public policy based on this belief should cease to be alarmed when effective competition *actually* shifts market share and profits, and certainly should not interfere with competitive processes in *anticipation* of such consequences. Such a cool and unconcerned posture must contemplate the possibility of a modicum of monopoly power for short periods of time in some instances, but this is a small cost to bear in order to avoid the attempt to tune finely the operation of competitive forces. The inadequacies of attempted fine-tuning are readily revealed in contemporary antitrust and in the substitution of regulatory restrictionism and favoritism for market rivalry.

Present trends in antitrust make it difficult to refrain from asking whether present practices encourage more competition than they inhibit. The answer cannot be given yet with any certainty, but there are numerous instances where judicial "cartelization" seems to have taken place. Given these uncertainties, it would seem wise to redirect our efforts to the task of reducing governmentally protected monopolies.

# The Concentration—Profits Relationship and Antitrust

## Leonard W. Weiss*

The concentration–profits literature has something to say in respect to many aspects of antitrust, but its clearest relevance seems to be to the occasional structural monopoly case and the many horizontal merger cases. These will be the main focus of this paper.

The structural monopoly rule prohibits the acquisition or retention of monopoly power by predatory or restrictive practices. The standard definition of monopoly power — "the power to set price or exclude competition"[1] — is hardly precise, but it appears to require a persistent market share of well over half of some significant market, with no close challenger. The underlying assumption in this area is that such dominant firms will follow policies that misallocate resources (e.g., set prices well above cost) and redistribute incomes in favor of those in powerful positions. Conviction for "monopolization" under Section 2 of the Sherman Act seems to require practices well beyond the range of normal business practice, the purpose of which is to attain or maintain a dominant position. The economic concept of pure monopoly is most

---

* Professor of Economics, University of Wisconsin. For further biographical information, see Appendix D.

1. United States v. E. I. DuPont de Nemours Co. (Cellophane), 351 U.S. 377 (1956).

relevant here. Part I of this paper will concern itself with our theoretical analysis and empirical knowledge of the dominant firm.

The horizontal merger rule appears to prohibit mergers between two or more firms of efficient scale that compete directly if the market involved is at all concentrated or shows signs of becoming so. This strict rule seems based on a belief that there is a reasonable probability that increased concentration will substantially lessen competition. The relevant concept here is obviously oligopoly — the effect of concentration on profits. This will be the main concern of Parts II, III, and IV. The same analysis is also relevant to various proposals to deconcentrate industries such as the Neal Task Force's "Concentrated Industry Act" where firms with more than 15 percent of the market where the four largest have 70 percent or more of the market are liable to dissolution[2] or the Hart Bill where firms with market shares of 15 percent are subject to dissolution if the four leading firms have 50 percent of the market [S.1167, 1972]. Some comment on the relevance of our present knowledge about oligopoly to these proposals will also be made.

## I. MONOPOLY AND THE DOMINANT FIRM

The pure monopoly of economic theory involves a single seller with blockaded entry. It is an empirically empty box. Outside of the regulated industries no such firm exists. However, the analysis can be readily extended to cover the cases of the dominant firm with minor rivals or of the monopolist faced with the threat of new entry. The presence of small rivals means that the demand curve facing the dominant firm would be more elastic than the overall demand for the product in question, because the rivals would find it profitable to expand as the price set by the dominant firm rises. If the dominant firm's minimum unit cost were the same as its small rivals', then the strategy that would yield the most value to the stockholders would be to price above cost at first and gradually lose market share as a result of the independents' expansion that this would induce.[3]

The market share of a firm that seeks the stockholders' best interest might persist for any of three reasons. First, its smaller rivals might be unable to expand because they are faced with sharply rising costs if they try to do so. This might be due to some resource that is fixed in supply, or to strong consumer loyalties to present suppliers. Second, the dominant firm might have costs so low compared with the independents that it would find the future flow of income at prices that kept the independents from expanding of greater value to stockholders than the future incomes that would be available if the firm took full advantage of its situation at first and let the independents expand. Finally, the small rivals may collude with the dominant firm to attain prices higher than

2. White House Task Force on Antitrust Policy, "Report," *Congressional Record* (May 27, 1969), pp. S642-S659. See also Appendix C.

3. G. Stigler, "Monopoly and Oligopoly by Merger," *American Economic Review*, 40 (May 1950), pp. 23-34.

it would set if they acted independently. If this occurs, the growth of the small firms at the expense of the dominant firm will be limited.

Where persistent market dominance arises from the low cost of the dominant firm's product, one questions whether dissolution would often be in the public's best interest. It might be, if the cost advantage did not arise from large scale but from superior access to crucial resources (e.g., mineral reserves) or if its persistent market share were due to collusion.

The case of the monopolist faced by potential entry is very close to the case of the dominant firm with small rivals. If the monopolist has no cost advantage over the potential entrants the strategy that would maximize the value of the firm to stockholders would involve prices above minimum costs at first with a gradually declining market share.[4] Where the monopolist has a large advantage over the possible entrants, such as optimal scale that is a large percentage of the market [5] or superior access to inputs or strong consumer loyalty [Bain, *supra* n.4] the strategy that would maximize the value of the firm to its owners might be to set prices that deter entry and preserve the firm's monopoly and more-than-competitive profits indefinitely.

In general, all the analytical cases predict more-than-competitive prices at least for the near term. Where this is associated with a declining market share, dissolution would appear feasible. Whether such costly surgery is worthwhile depends on the speed with which market share falls. The seventy-year relative decline of U.S. Steel seemed more expensive to consumers than a dissolution of the firm early in the century. Where the high market share of the dominant firm persists, dissolution may or may not be useful depending on the source of its advantage.

To my knowledge, no one has attempted a systematic test of the dominant firm hypothesis. Only a suggestive "test" will be presented here. Table 10 contains a list of firms judged to account for half or more of total sales of their primary products, and whose rivals are all much smaller.[6] The average rates of return on sales and on equity for these dominant firms are much higher than are those for all manufacturing corporations. The difference is

4. *Ibid.*; J. Bain, *Barriers to New Competition* (Harvard Univ. Press 1956).

5. Bain, *supra* n. 4; P. Sylos-Labini, *Oligopoly and Technical Process* (2d ed., Harvard Univ. Press 1969). Originally published in Italian in 1956.

6. Firms that are dominant in secondary products — such as General Motors (buses and locomotives), General Electric (light bulbs), Procter and Gamble (toothpaste), DuPont (nylon), or American Metal Climax (molybdenum) — are not included, because their profits would depend primarily on other products. However, these would raise the average rates of return if added to the list in Table 10. The list of dominant firms is based on judgment by approximate market shares estimated by the writer using employment sizes from the *Fortune Plant and Product Directory*. Schwinn and Singer were left off the list because of foreign competition. In addition, sewing machines appear to account for a minority of Singer's sales today. Clorox was left off the list because profit rates were not available for most years. Several of the drug companies probably belong on the list, but the sources used in estimating market shares do not permit identification of particular pharmaceuticals. If they had been included, the average profit rate undoubtedly would have been increased.

TABLE 10
Average Profit Rates of Dominant Firms in 1960-1970

| Firm | Profits After Tax as a Percentage of Sales | Profits After Tax as a Percentage of Equity |
|------|:---:|:---:|
| IBM | 13.0 | 17.6 |
| Western Electric | 4.7 | 10.7 |
| Eastman Kodak | 14.7 | 19.9 |
| Caterpillar Tractor | 8.1 | 17.2 |
| Boeing | 2.0 | 10.6 |
| Xerox | 13.3 | 22.5 |
| Campbell Soup | 6.9 | 12.5 |
| Gillette | 2.4 | 32.4 |
| Ethyl | 7.1 | 18.3 |
| Los Angeles Times Mirror | 6.2 | 13.2 |
| Timkin | 9.8 | 13.4 |
| Joy Manufacturing | 4.2 | 9.3 |
| Knight Newspapers | 6.6 | 13.0 |
| William Wrigley, Jr. | 10.0 | 14.0 |
| Average | 7.8 | 16.0 |
| Average All Manufacturing | 4.8 | 11.0 |

Source: Derived from *Fortune* "500" lists, 1961-1971, and *Economic Report of the President.*

much greater than could occur by chance as often as one time in twenty. Only three firms on the list have rates of return as low as those for all manufacturing. All of these have plausible explanations. Western Electric is part of American Telephone and Telegraph, which is subject to regulation in most of its operations. Boeing faced a number of obvious close potential entrants into commercial aircraft, and its market dominance in the 1960s turns out to have been temporary. Joy Manufacturing faced a stagnant market (for coal mining machinery) over much of the 1960s.

The available data on market shares does not permit any test of the expectation of declining market shares, but to my knowledge most of the firms in Table 10 have been in dominant positions for decades. It would appear, then, that the handful of dominant firms in the American economy are generally quite well protected by high barriers from entry and from the expansion of minor firms.

I can hardly claim that a thorough test of the dominant firm hypothesis has been made here, but at least the simple data available seems to support it. To determine whether the firms on the list are eligible for dissolution suits would require careful examinations of the source of each firm's dominant position and of the conduct of the firm, something that goes far beyond the scope of this paper.

## II.  OLIGOPOLY THEORY

The merger law is much more significant than Section 2 in terms of actual antitrust resources employed. Its theoretical justification lies primarily in oligopoly theory. This is also true of the proposals for some form of "concentrated industry" bill.

The analysis of oligopoly is far less definitive than that of the dominant firm because of the wide range of assumptions possible with respect to the reactions expected from rivals by each oligopolist. This section reviews the major oligopoly theories.

The first in point of time and still one of the most often cited was that of Cournot.[7] He assumed that each oligopolist expects its rivals to keep their outputs fixed. It would choose the most profitable output, given their outputs; each rival would, in turn, adjust its output, again assuming all other firms' outputs remain constant, and the process would continue until they all reach a point where they have no further reason to change. The resulting equilibrium price varies inversely with the number of firms. With two firms the monopoly margin will be halved. It will be halved again with four firms, yet again with eight, and so forth. This theory unequivocally predicts that price will rise with concentration.[8] The theory seems implausible to many, however, because it assumes that oligopolists never learn. They go on assuming their rivals' outputs are fixed, though that assumption is repeatedly proven wrong.

The next major oligopoly theory was that of Bertrand.[9] Here each oligopolist was assumed to expect its rivals' prices to be fixed. As a result, according to Bertrand, each oligopolist, in turn, would cut its price just far enough to capture the market from its rivals. As a result, oligopoly price would decline to the level where it just covered cost, and would stay there. After the adjustment period, oligopoly prices would correspond in the long run to those found in pure competition. This picture of oligopoly seems to have been widely accepted around the turn of the century. One of the great economists of the day, Vilfredo Pareto, concluded on the basis of this theory that the results of competition between two sellers would be the same as if there were many, since either would lower his price until all his supply was sold.[10] Such views may account for Yale Brozen's report that "[i]n the late nineteenth and early twentieth century, the prevailing view seems to have been that even with only

---

7. A. Cournot, *The Mathematical Principles of the Theory of Wealth* (R. D. Irwin 1963). Originally published in French in 1838.

8. It suggests that profits in excess of competitive returns will rise with the Herfindahl index. This index is the sum of the squares of the firms' market shares. If all firms have equal market shares, then the Herfindahl index is equal to $1/N$ where $N$ is the number of firms.

9. J. Bertrand, Review of A. Cournot in the *Journal of Savants* (1883), summarized in W. Fellner, *Competition Among the Few* (Knopf 1949), pp. 77-86.

10. V. Pareto, *Cours d'Economie Politique* (1896), quoted in E. Chamberlin, *Theory of Monopolistic Competition* (6th ed. Harvard Univ. Press 1949). Originally published in 1933; p. 37.

a few firms in an industry, price competition would be persistent and collusion difficult." [11]

Actually, even then some economists were doubtful. Edgeworth amended Bertrand,[12] showing that under Bertrand's assumptions prices were likely to oscillate within the range from the monopoly price to the competitive price. This would yield an average price over a period of oscillations higher than that prevailing in purely competitive markets and therefore a positive effect for concentration once more. The assumptions of the Bertrand theory seem even less plausible than those of Cournot. It seems inconceivable that an oligopolist, after repeated experiences to the contrary, would go on believing his rivals' prices to be fixed. At any rate, continuous oscillations seem hard to detect in real oligopolies. I don't believe that any economist takes this theory seriously today.

A third oligopoly theory that builds on Cournot's is that of Von Stackelberg.[13] Here, each oligopolist assumes that his rivals' patterns of reaction to his moves are fixed, rather than that their quantities or prices are fixed. The results depend on whether all firms are "followers," or one is a "leader" and the others are "followers," or two or more firms strive to be "leaders." The all "follower" case amounts to the Cournot theory. In the second case, the "leader" picks his most profitable policy, given the "followers" reaction pattern. If two or more sellers attempt to be leaders, then a period of "disequilibrium" (roughly, price war) results until all but one abandon their attempts to lead. The first case clearly implies prices inversely proportional to the number of firms and therefore positively related to concentration. The second would also imply higher prices in oligopoly than in competition and therefore a positive effect of concentration on price. The third yields no precise prediction, but one would think that the probability of two firms striving for leadership would increase as the number of firms rises. If so, price wars would be more common the larger the number of firms, and as a result the average price over a period would be lower in less concentrated industries. As with Cournot and Bertrand, this theory requires that oligopolists cling to assumptions about rivals' behavior that are repeatedly proven false. In any event, price wars don't seem all that frequent in real world oligopolies.

A fourth theory was that of E. H. Chamberlin.[14] Essentially, this theory assumes that each oligopolist expects its rivals to meet its price. The result is a price that maximizes the joint profits of the industry and therefore corresponds to monopoly price. This result holds for any number of firms so long as each

11. Y. Brozen, "Concentration and Profits: Does Concentration Matter?," in J. Weston and S. Ornstein, eds., *The Impact of Large Firms on the U.S. Economy* (Lexington Books 1973), pp. 59-70.

12. F. Edgeworth, "La Teoria Pura del Monopolio," *Giornale degli Economisti* (1897), summarized in Chamberlin, n. 10 *supra* (1933 ed.), pp. 37-46.

13. H. von Stackelberg, *Marktform und Gleichgewicht*, summarized in Fellner, n. 9 *supra*, ch. 3.

14. E. H. Chamberlin, *Theory of Monopolistic Competition* (6th ed., Harvard Univ. Press 1949). Originally published in 1933. Ch. 5, part 4.

is large enough to expect its rivals to respond to its moves. At some point, however, the numbers become so large that individual firms need expect no reaction to their moves. At that point, a competitive result is expected. This theory would seem to imply some critical degree of concentration below which an industry would perform competitively and above which it would perform monopolistically. At any rate, the effect on price of a rise in concentration is expected to be positive once more. This is probably the theory most commonly quoted in elementary and intermediate texts today. It should be noted that Chamberlin himself expected *profits* to fall to competitive levels though the monopolistic prices would remain, because the entry such prices induced would result in excess capacity.

Although it is not strictly speaking a separate theory, I would like to suggest a group of amendments to Chamberlin offered by various authors as a fifth alternative. They derive from the notion that the ability of oligopolists to arrive at a price that maximized their joint profit depends on the uniformity of their costs, of their excess capacity, and/or of the elasticities of demand that they perceive (i.e., the extent to which they expect consumers to respond to price changes). If these differ from firm to firm, then oligopoly price will differ from monopoly price. For instance, the low-cost producer would set a price that would be lower than the most profitable price for the industry as a whole, and the other sellers would have no choice but to meet it. Similarly, the firm with the greatest excess capacity or the one that perceived demand to be most elastic would set prices below the optimum for the industry as a whole. These considerations suggest that the greater the diversity among firms, the more the price would fall short of the monopoly price. One would expect such diversity to increase as the number of firms increases. If so, the amended Chamberlin theory would suggest that profits should increase with concentration above the critical level of concentration.

The sixth theory is another variation on Chamberlin, the "kinked demand curve."[15] Here the oligopolists are assumed to expect their rivals to match them on the price reductions but not on price increases. The main result is rigid prices. The effect of concentration on profits is indeterminate except that in the long run prices cannot be less than average cost. The notion of a kinked demand curve was successfully attacked by Stigler.[16] I don't think many industrial organization economists believe it today, but it still appears in some elementary and intermediate texts.

The next major step in oligopoly theory was game theory.[17] In the "zero-sum" game, where one player's gain exactly equals the other's losses, a determinate solution that minimizes the players' losses is derivable. Unfortunately,

15. P. Sweezy, "Demand Under Conditions of Oligopoly," *Journal of Political Economy*, 47 (August 1939), pp. 568-573.

16. G. Stigler, "The Kinky Oligopoly Demand Curve and Rigid Prices," *Journal of Political Economy*, 55 (October 1947), pp. 432-449.

17. J. von Neumann and O. Morganstern, *The Theory of Games and Economic Behavior* (Princeton Univ. Press 1947).

virtually no real oligopoly case fits the zero-sum game mold, so no predictions for oligopoly performance are forthcoming.

Non-zero-sum games, where some combinations of strategies yield higher joint profits than others, do fit realistic oligopoly situations, but the results are much less certain. The two that have received the greatest attention for oligopoly cases are the "prisoner's dilemma" and the "game of survival." The "prisoner's dilemma" refers to a scenario where two suspects are questioned separately. If either confesses he gets a short sentence and the other gets a long one. If neither confesses, they both avoid jail. The comparable situation in realistic oligopoly is where either firm can win a lot at the expense of its rival if it cuts price but the other doesn't, but where they both lose if they both cut price. In both cases the results depend on how cooperative the players are. Ultimately the prediction for oligopoly depends on what the economist thinks contributes to cooperative behavior. One would think that small numbers of firms, uniformity of size, costs, perceived elasticities and capacity utilization, general economic stability, and easy avenues for interfirm communication would make cooperative behavior more likely. Again the theory seems to point to higher prices when there are fewer sellers and hence a more concentrated market.

The "game of survival" refers to the case where one player tries to knock the other out, hoping to benefit from his absence later. It is just new clothing for the old predation idea that has a long history in antitrust. It is easy to criticize. Since the strategy involves near-term losses and later high profits, the present value of the prospective income from such a policy will always be less than the present value of incomes where monopoly is attained by agreement or merger. Even where agreement and merger for monopoly are effectively prohibited, the strategy can't be profitable where entry is easy and quick, because the profits from monopoly in such a situation are at best temporary. Further arguments emphasize that losses are proportional to sales, so that large firms have more to lose than small ones, and that the destruction of a rival is terribly costly because the rival can simply shut down temporarily. The destruction of a rival with substantial assets is particularly costly because his assets, even in bankruptcy, are apt to remain in the market through the acquisition by outsiders, especially large outside firms such as the conglomerates. Altogether, the predation hypothesis is a doubtful one in most settings. In any case, it predicts low prices only temporarily, and high prices and profits when the predation is over. Price wars where some firm could realistically expect to attain dominance are so rare that the game of survival must be an exceptional case if it exists in reality at all.

The latest major addition to the oligopoly theory literature is that of George Stigler.[18] He pictured the goal of oligopolists to be collusion and examined the conditions contributing to the enforcement of effective cartels. The participants in effective cartels must be able to detect secret price cutting. The evidence

18. G. Stigler, "A Theory of Oligopoly," *Journal of Political Economy,* 72 (February 1964), pp. 44-61.

of such "chiseling" is the diversion in sales in excess of what would occur by chance. He concluded that fewness of sellers and disparity of relative seller size both make the detection of chiseling easier, though the effect of additional sellers diminishes rapidly after the second one. He also predicted that the effectiveness of seller collusion would decrease as buyer concentration rose. His theory pointed unequivocally to a positive relation between concentration and price.[19]

Many economists today emphasize the costs of collusion in analyzing oligopoly. They argue that prices above the competitive level require some sort of collusion, tacit or explicit. Whether that collusion is successful or not depends on how costly it is to police the agreement. Where enforcement through the courts or by resort to violence is ruled out, effective collusion requires knowledge of transactions and of changes in market shares plus an effective method for punishing violators. One would think that such knowledge would be harder to come by, the greater the number of firms. Punishment of violators would take the form of price wars, and this would be more costly, the smaller the violators. Both the knowledge and punishment requirements would seem to suggest more effective collusion as concentration increases.

Finally, some mention should be made of theories relating to barriers to entry. The oligopoly theories to this point took the optimal monopoly price as given, and tried to work out how closely oligopoly price would approach it. In fact, barriers to entry vary among industries. As a result, the optimal monopolistic price will vary with them. The main theorist in this area is Bain, who distinguished between the case where barriers are sufficiently high that insiders find it profitable to forgo current profits to keep entrants out and the case where low barriers lead insiders to take temporary profits by charging entry-inducing prices [Bain, *supra* n. 4]. He pictured concentration as leading to higher prices, but the level of prices attainable depending on conditions of entry.

An apology is due to economists for this lengthy review of a familiar subject. It was presented for two reasons. First, some commentators on the concentration—monopoly power relationship have said that there is no theoretical  basis for it [20] — an allegation that is clearly false and should be put to rest. Second, a common statement of economists in general is that oligopoly theories yield an almost limitless range of predictions and are generally inconclusive. I feel that this badly understates the guidance that theory can give in this area. It is, of course, possible to construct theories with yet other predictions, but I believe that I have covered the regularly cited and plausible theories (and some implausible ones as well). Of the theories covered, most predict a positive effect of concentration on profits. None except the doubtful original form of the Bertrand theory predicts continuous competitive prices for

19. As with the Cournot theory and unlike the Chamberlin theory, Stigler's theory suggests that margins should be roughly proportional to the Herfindahl index.

20. H. Demsetz, *The Market Concentration Doctrine* (Washington: American Enterprise Inst. 1973), p. 11.

oligopoly. The later forms of the Bertrand theory, the Von Stackelberg case where two or more firms contend for leadership, and the predation theory, predict low prices some of the time but more than competitive average prices over a long period. The kinked demand curve makes no prediction about the level of price. Moreover, the Bertrand, Von Stackelberg, predation, and kinked demand theories are all largely discredited. In general, the main lines of oligopoly theory point rather consistently to higher prices in more concentrated industries.

Where they disagree is on the precise relation between concentration and prices. Bain and Chamberlin point to some critical level of concentration; Cournot and Stigler suggest that margins rise at an increasing rate with concentration; and most of the other theories might be interpreted to imply that margins rise in a fairly continuous way with concentration. This kind of question can't be resolved by theory. They are issues for empirical study. I have spent a great deal of time and money trying to answer such questions as whether there is a critical concentration ratio, and, if so, where it falls. Also, does the share of the sixth or eighth firm in a market make any difference in market performance? I never really reached a convincing conclusion and I now doubt that we will without much better data. These are important issues. We can probably agree that General Motors shouldn't be allowed to merge with Ford and that a merger among two feed mills is harmless. The real questions have to do with mergers by middle-sized firms in moderately concentrated markets. Unfortunately, I don't think economics can give a definite answer here.

Economic theory does yield a pretty definite answer to the question of whether high concentration involves a lessening of competition. In spite of some uncertainty about the precise functional form, the theoretical answer seems to be a consistent yes.

It should probably be pointed out that both monopoly and oligopoly theories deal primarily with price, not profit. The unequivocal prediction is that price will be high relative to marginal cost. This is consistent with only normal profits if demand is low or if entry results in excess capacity, as in Chamberlin. More than normal profits could be expected in *some* monopolies or oligopolies, however, because of barriers to entry, but the same is true of *some* competitive industries because of short run disequilibrium. The common expectation that profits will be higher in concentrated industries is not nonsense — it is worth testing — but it is not unequivocally predicted by theory either.

## III.  THE DATA

Until World War II the predictions of oligopoly theory were largely untested except for occasional industry studies. Since then there has been a huge outpouring of tests. The concentration–profits relationship must be one of the most thoroughly tested hypotheses in economics by now. The actual tests will be reviewed in Part IV. None of the tests are completely conclusive, however. A major reason for this is that the data available is very imperfect.

### The Concentration Measure

One of the obvious problems is with our concentration data. It is a by-product of Censuses made with entirely different purposes. The Census industries often do not correspond to economic markets. This is obviously true of industries that sell on local or regional markets. In 1958 and 1963 the Census did produce local, state, and regional concentration ratios for certain industries, but it unfortunately abandoned that practice in 1967.

A similar error arises where a Census industry produces a number of non-competing subproducts, such as the many distinct drugs of the pharmaceutical industry. The Census does offer concentration data at both the 4- and 5-digit levels, so some of this distortion can be eliminated by the careful investigator.

A third problem is interindustry competition. For instance, cane and beet sugar are separate Census industries though they surely sell on the same market. There is an ad hoc way of adjusting the Census concentration data in such cases,[21] but it is crude and few have used it.

Finally, foreign trade sometimes makes the Census concentration data incorrect. Where the product is traded on a world market (copper) or a continental market (newsprint) the Census concentration figures based on shipments of American plants only will ordinarily be wrong. The error is apt to be large where barriers to trade are low (newsprint) but small where the domestic market is largely distinct from world markets (automobiles).

Most concentration–profits studies use the crude Census concentration data with all its errors. The result is bound to be a bias in the estimated concentration–profits relationship toward zero, because some markets that appear concentrated in the Census are not really concentrated if economically correct markets are used, and some that do not appear concentrated really are. As a result, any relation between correctly reported concentration and profits will be weakened when crude concentration measures are used.[22]

There are two ways around this problem. One is to limit the study to industries where Census industry definitions correspond closely to economic markets. However, this necessarily involves judgments that are open to question and leaves the results open to the charge that the investigator picked his cases. The other is to try to correct the Census concentration data, for instance by substituting weighted averages of local or regional concentration ratios or of 5-

21. C. Kaysen and D. Turner, *Anti-Trust Policy* (Harvard Univ. Press 1959), p. 297.

22. For instance, the top four pharmaceutical firms made only 24% of pharmaceutical shipments in 1967, according to the Census. This made the drug industry less concentrated than such competitive industries as cotton textiles and shoes, where concentration ratios were 30 and 27 respectively. In fact, however, there are only a few firms — sometimes only one — producing drugs appropriate to many particular treatments. The drug industry is one of the most profitable in America. Using the Census concentration data, this would seem to contradict the concentration–profit hypothesis. In fact, if we had realistic concentration data, it would undoubtedly confirm it.

digit product concentration ratios for the Census national 4-digit figure where appropriate. Studies that use such corrections need not exclude industries, but they are open to question about the judgments involved in making those corrections. Moreover, the corrections themselves are often crude. Altogether, there is no completely satisfactory solution to the concentration measurement problem.

Another difficulty with the Census data is the index used. The Census gives us "concentration ratios," the shares of the top four, the top eight, and the top twenty firms in total shipments. These ratios might be close to the correct index if one envisioned a critical concentration ratio as in the Chamberlin theory, but they are only crude proxies for the concentration measures appropriate to the Cournot or Stigler theories.[23] If the true relationship is of the form suggested by Cournot or Stigler, then the concentration—profits relationship estimated using Census concentration ratios would be further weakened.

Studies that use firms or Internal Revenue Service industries as observations involve another error because of diversification. The concentration ratio of a firm's most important industry will less accurately represent concentration in the markets in which it sells, the more diversified the firm is. Where its most important industry is highly concentrated, its other operations are apt to be in less concentrated markets. A concentration ratio based on its most important industry will therefore exaggerate concentration in the markets in which it sells. Similarly, a firm whose primary industry is unconcentrated is apt to be diversified into more concentrated lines of business. A concentration ratio based on its most important industry will understate concentration in the markets in which it sells. Clearly, diversification will bias the observed concentration—profit relationship toward zero. Since diversification is on the increase, this bias should be getting worse over time.

There are three possible ways around the problem raised by diversification. First, the researcher can limit himself to highly specialized firms. This opens him to the charge of picking his cases again. Moreover, there are not many highly specialized firms left among industry leaders.

Second, he can use a weighted average of concentration in the markets in which a firm sells. This is bound to be rough; we usually don't know the weights with any accuracy.[24] An ordinary weighted average will be inaccurate if the

23. The correct index for these theories would probably be the Herfindahl index. This is equivalent to 1/number of firms if all firms are of equal size. The Census did release some Herfindahl indexes for the 1947 and 1954 Censuses, R. Nelson, *Concentration in the Manufacturing Industries in the United States* (Yale Univ. Press 1963), but has apparently decided not to do so since then. The 1954 figures did not correlate well with profit or margin data, but this may be due to incorrect market definitions.

24. We do know the right weights for IRS "minor industries" for 1958 and 1963 because of the Link Projects in the Census *Enterprise Statistics,* but only a few studies have used them. We also know the correct weights for firms in 1950 because of the FTC's recent report. Federal Trade Commission, *Statistical Report — Value of Shipments by Product Class for the 1000 Largest Manufacturing Companies of 1950,* (U.S.G.P.O., January 1972).

underlying relationship between concentration and profits is not linear.[25] It will also be inaccurate if the weights used are not consistent with the profit measure used.

The third alternative is to finesse the whole problem by using Census establishment data rather than the company data. Then the concentration and other data used clearly apply to the same Census industry.

## THE PROFIT DATA

The profit data available is worse than our concentration data, if anything. The majority of studies have used the rate of return on equity after tax (hereafter, $(\Pi - T)/E$) generally derived from corporate reports or the Internal Revenue Service data. The reported rates of return can vary a great deal depending on which of many alternative accounting conventions are used. Even if the choice of accounting conventions were randomly distributed among firms, such variations would introduce errors that would reduce the correlation between concentration and profits. In fact, the errors are not random. Accounting practices introduce several systematic biases into the reported values of $(\Pi / T)/E$.

First, assets are apt to be written up or down according to their profitability. For instance, plant and equipment that have changed hands since they were installed are apt to be valued at their purchase prices rather than at their original costs, and those purchase prices will reflect their income-earning prospects. Even when assets do not change hands, investments that turn out badly are sometimes written down to reflect their income potential more realistically. The result of such revaluations is to increase the equity of highly profitable firms and reduce it in unprofitable firms, thus biasing all firms toward equal profit rates.

Second, the valuation of assets at their original costs introduces a bias in the presence of inflation. Older assets will be undervalued relative to new ones because of rising prices. The assets of slowly growing firms are older, on the average, than those of rapidly growing firms. This means that their equity will be relatively undervalued and that their rate of return on equity will be exaggerated relative to rapidly growing firms. Since rapidly growing firms are apt to have higher economic profit rates than slowly growing firms, rates of return on equity will be biased toward equality once more. There is little correlation between concentration and growth rates, so this bias merely introduces random errors in tests of the concentration–profits relationship. Studies that control for growth can allow for this bias to some extent.

A third problem has to do with wages and salaries. One would expect wages, salaries, and managerial prerogatives such as expense accounts and palatial offices to be greater in more profitable firms. The clearest case is managerial salaries and prerogatives in small firms where the managers are often the main owners as well. Whether they take their incomes as profits or as

25. The underlying relationship is *not* linear in either the Chamberlin theory or the Cournot or Stigler theories.

salaries and prerogatives is an arbitrary decision likely to depend on tax considerations. This could be important even in large firms if the managerial prerogatives take the form of such things as the location of operations in pleasant but high-cost communities. Moreover, there is evidence that wage rates are correlated with concentration though this correlation can be largely accounted for by the superior "quality" of the labor hired.[26] To the extent that "quality" consists of characteristics that increase productivity, such as education, health, and reliability, the high wages paid by firms in concentrated industries need not mean any lessening of profits; but "quality" also includes such things as race. There is evidence that concentrated industries employ particularly small proportions of blacks.[27] The high wages paid to get a labor force of WASP's has been interpreted as the diversion of profits to a managerial prerogative.[28] Altogether, it seems quite likely that some of the profits of highly profitable firms and especially of firms in concentrated industries are understated because of high wages, salaries, and prerogatives. This will also bias rates of return toward equality in interindustry comparisons.

A less certain bias which has not yet been systematically studied lies in the accounting conventions chosen. One would expect highly profitable firms to be more prone to select accounting rules that understate their profits for both tax and public relations purposes. At the same time, relatively unprofitable firms would want to exaggerate profits to stave off angry stockholders and raiders. Again, this bias, if it exists, would tend to move reported profit rates toward equality.

Finally, the accounting treatment of investment in intangibles such as advertising and research and development also introduces errors. These are usually written off as current expense though they usually have long-lasting value. This results in an understatement of equity and, for firms with growing expenditures on intangibles, an understatement of profits as well. The net effect is the over- or understatement of rates of return on equity depending on whether the reported rate of return exceeds or falls short of $g/(1 + g)$ where $g$ is the percentage rate of growth in expenditures on intangibles.[29] The expensing of intangibles would impart a bias in the concentration–profits relationship if expenditures on intangibles were correlated with concentration. Advertising does seem to rise with concentration when concentration is low, but it falls

26. L. Weiss, "Concentration and Labor Earnings," *American Economic Review,* 56 (March 1966), pp. 96-117.

27. W. Shepherd, "Market Power and Racial Discrimination in White Collar Employment," *Anti-Trust Bulletin,* 14 (Spring 1969), pp. 141-161; R. Straus, "Discrimination against Negroes in the Labor Market" (Ph.D. dissertation, Univ. of Wisconsin 1970); W. S. Comanor, an unpublished paper (1972).

28. A. Alchian and R. Kessell, "Competition, Monopoly and the Pursuit of Money," in Universities-National Bureau, *Aspects of Labor Economics* (Princeton Univ. Press 1960), pp. 70-81.

29. L. Weiss, "Advertising, Profits, and Corporate Taxes," *Review of Economics and Statistics,* 51 (November 1969), pp. 421-430.

when concentration is high.[30] R and D seems to be little affected by concentration where technological opportunity is high, but the two rise together where it is low.[31] In general, the errors due to expensing of advertising and R and D will vary from industry to industry, depending on whether products are sold to consumers or producers, whether technological opportunities are great or small, and whether the growth in advertising and/or R and D is great or small. The errors will vary in a complex way with concentration. The main effect of such a variety of influences will surely be to introduce errors in profits that lessen the correlation betwen profits and concentration once more, but there may also be a bias. The bias seems most likely to result in the overstatement of profit rates in slowly growing consumer goods industries of moderate concentration. This bias should be at least partially eliminated in studies that control for advertising and growth rates.

A number of other profit measures have been used in some studies. These include the rate of return on assets $(\Pi - T + I)/A$ where $I$ is interest, the profit to sales ratio $(\Pi - T)/S$ where $S$ is sales, and various ratios using profits before tax $(\Pi/E, (\Pi + I)/A,$ and $\Pi/S)$. I have argued elsewhere that the rate of return on equity after tax $((\Pi - T)/E)$ was more appropriate because it corresponded more closely to what stockholders seek to maximize [Weiss, *infra* n. 36]. In the long run, in pure competition $(\Pi - T)/E$ would be equalized across industries. The others would not because of interindustry differences in the amount of debt that can be safely incurred, in effective tax rates, and in the capital required per dollar of sale. These other indexes are imperfect proxies for the rate of return on equity. The error in the rate of return on assets probably is not large. The error in using the crude rate of return on sales (unless corrected for capital–sales ratios) or rates of return before tax is likely to be large because capital–sales ratios and effective tax rates differ greatly from industry to industry.

Since my 1971 paper I have been persuaded that other measures might be conceptually superior to $(\Pi - T)/E$. First, there is a good case for the rate of return on sales if some account is taken of the capital–sales ratio.[32] Admittedly competitive industries with equal risk would have the same rate of return on equity in long-run equilibrium. However, two firms with the same degree of monopoly power would not have the same rates of return on equity if the capital they needed per dollar of sale differed. This is because the firm with the higher capital requirement would have more equity and would re-

30. D. Greer, "Advertising and Market Concentration," *Southern Economic Journal,* 38 (July 1971), pp. 19-32; J. Cable, "Market Structure, Advertising Policy, and Inter-Market Differences in Advertising Intensity," in K. Cowling, ed., *Market Structure and Corporate Behavior* (London: Gray Mills 1972), pp. 105-124.

31. F. Scherer, "Firm Size, Market Structure, Opportunity, and the Output of Patented Inventions," *American Economic Review,* 55 (December 1965), Part I, pp. 1097-1125; F. Scherer, "Market Structure and the Employment of Scientists and Engineers," *American Economic Review,* 57 (June 1967), pp. 524-531.

32. This argument was made to me by both Herbert Mohring and William Long independently of one another.

ceive more in "normal profits" (profits needed to attract capital into the business). As a result it would have a lower rate of return on equity. To isolate the pure monopoly profits, we need a measure along the lines of $(\Pi - T - r \cdot E)/S$ where $r$ is the rate of return available in the long run on purely competitive markets. An alternative to this is to let the profit measure be $(\Pi - T)/S$ but to control for $E/S$ when relating profits to concentration.

Taking another tack, what stockholders really want to maximize is the present market value of the company's stock (hereafter $MV$). This suggests as an alternative profit measure the ratio of the market value of the company's stock to its equity or so-called valuation ratio $((MV)/E)$. This should be the same in all firms in purely competitive industries in long-run equilibrium. By the argument in the previous paragraph, this measure would differ for two firms with the same monopoly power but differing capital needs. The correct measure would be something like $(MV)/E - R$ (where $R$ is the valuation ratio that applies in the long run in purely competitive markets).

Finally, studies that try to avoid the diversification problem by using Census establishment (plant) data use as a margin variable something like $(VS - CM - PR)/VS$ where $VS$ is value of shipments, $CM$ is cost of materials, and $PR$ is payroll. This has been referred to as the "price—cost margin." It amounts to the margin over average materials and labor costs as a percentage of price. The numerator includes advertising, central office expenses including research and development, depreciation expense, and taxes, as well as profits. By controlling for $K/VS$ (where $K$ is plant and equipment before depreciation) such studies make rough adjustments for the normal return required to attract capital to the industry and for depreciation. An advantage of this measure is that $VS$, $CM$, $PR$, and $K$ are all available from the Census at the 4-digit industry level. They seem to be much more reliable numbers than the $\Pi$, $E$, and $A$ which appear in the other profit variables (though the $K$ in the control for $K/VS$ is apt to have problems similar to those of $E$ and $A$). This measure also avoids the diversification problem associated with corporate accounting rates of return since it is reported on a plant basis for 4-digit industries. Its obvious defect is that advertising, central office expense, and taxes are included in the margin. Some attempt will be made to allow for these in Part V of the paper.

The price—cost margin has one further advantage over the other profit measures. Oligopoly theory really predicts high prices and not necessarily high profits. If the high prices attract too many resources into the industry, the result will be excess capacity and only normal profits. The "price—cost margin" seems closer to a measure of the relation of price to marginal cost than the other measures used.

All of the profit and margin indexes are likely to reflect irrelevant short-run events at any point in time. Averages of these variables over several years, preferably over an entire business cycle, would wash out many of the short-run aberrations and would therefore provide a superior profit variable. Averaging seems especially important in the valuation ratio $(MV/E)$ because stock prices are so volatile. The valuation ratio on a particular day is particularly suspect. The other ratios suggested at least depend on profits, taxes, interest, and/or sales over an entire year. Studies that depend on profits for a particular year introduce a lot of irrelevant variation and therefore lessen the correlation between concentration and profits once more.

### The Period Covered

One further consideration is the period for which the study is made. There is good evidence that concentrated industries do not raise prices as rapidly as competitive industries do in time of open inflation.[33] One reason is that the prices of large firms in concentrated industries are relatively easy to control when price controls are in effect as they were in 1941 through 1946, 1950 through 1952, and 1971 to the present. Even when no formal controls are in effect, prices seem likely to rise with a lag when tight oligopoly or a dominant firm make price changes the self-conscious decisions of leading firms. In competitive sectors increasing demand or cost leads to rising prices without anyone making an explicit decision, but in highly concentrated industries prices only go up if the leading firm or firms make a decision to raise them. It certainly does not pay for such firms to make price changes for every change in market decisions. Moreover, public relations considerations probably induce them to avoid frequent price increases and to wait for cost justifications when they do make them. At least it appears that concentrated industries raised prices more slowly than unconcentrated industries during the years 1967 through 1969 [MacLaren, *supra* n. 33]. All this suggests that monopoly profits will be relatively low during or right after periods of rapid inflation.

On the other hand, there is also evidence that prices rise more rapidly in concentrated industries than in competitive industries during periods following inflation as powerful firms seek to take full advantage of their positions once more [Weiss, *supra* n. 33].

All this suggests that the concentration–profits relationship would be weakest at the end of periods of rapid inflation (e.g., 1947 through 1948, 1969 through 1971, and probably now and in the next few years). It should be strong a number of years after such an inflation and strongest during a long period of stability or depression. The relationship should show up most clearly in the 1930s and 1953 through 1967.

### Summary

To summarize, there are both conceptual and measurement problems with all the available indexes of concentration and profit. Errors in the concentration indexes reduce the observable correlation between concentration and profits and bias the estimated relationship toward zero. Random errors in the measurement of profits would reduce the correlation further but would not bias the estimated relationship. But in fact, the errors in the profit indexes are not at all random. All of the systematic sources of error, except possibly for the expensing of intangibles, tend to equalize profit rates among firms and therefore to bias the concentration–profits relationship toward zero.

33. L. Weiss, "Business Pricing Policies and Inflation Reconsidered," *Journal of Political Economy*, 74 (April 1966), pp. 177-187, updated in R. MacLaren, Statement Before the Joint Economic Committee in Hearings, July 10, 1970 (U.S.G.P.O. 1970).

In view of the consistent effect of *all* these errors to lessen the correlation between concentration and profits and their almost consistent tendency to bias the observed relationship toward zero, we can be pretty sure that if any positive relationship does appear there is something there and it is understated. On the other hand, if no relationship is detected, one may still exist.

Which of the various, partially erroneous profit or margin variables biases the concentration—profits relationship the least is a matter of judgment. My present preference is for the price—cost margin, $(VS - CM - PR)/VS$, if the study controls for $K/VS$ and somehow allows for advertising and central office expense. It eliminates most of the errors in concentration due to diversification, it minimizes the accounting errors, and it captures a good deal of any excess capacity induced by high prices.

## IV.  EMPIRICAL TESTS

The concentration—profits relationship has been one of the most thoroughly tested hypotheses in economics. Table 11 p. 204 lists many but not all of these tests.[34] It also lists the profit or margin variable and the concentration variable

34. Those left out include: P. Asch, "Industry Structure and Performance: Some Empirical Evidence," *Review of Social Economy*, 25 (September 1967), pp. 167-182; K. George, "Concentration, Barriers to Entry, and Rates of Return," *Review of Economics and Statistics*, 50 (May 1968), pp. 272-275; D. Kamerschen, "The Determination of Profit Rates in 'Oligopolistic' Industries," *Journal of Business*, 42 (July 1969), pp. 293-301; and thesis by Soloman, "Determinants of Interfirm Differences in Profitability among the Largest 500 U.S. Industrial Firms" (Ph.D. dissertation, Univ. of California, Berkeley 1967); R. Arnould, "The Effect of Market and Firm Structure on the Performance of Food Processing Firms" (Ph.D. dissertation, Iowa State Univ., Ames 1968); G. Gambeles, "Structural Determinants of Profit Performance in the United States Manufacturing Industries, 1947-1967" (Ph.D. dissertation, Univ. of Maryland 1969); M. Klass, "Inter-Industry Relations and the Impact of Monopoly" (Ph.D. dissertation, Univ. of Wisconsin 1970); W. Long, "An Econometric Study of Performance in American Manufacturing Industry" (unpublished Ph.D. dissertation, Univ. of California 1971). I have read all of these except Arnould, who told me his results. George and Kamerschen were reworks of Mann. George controlled for growth and estimated entry barriers and still found a significant effect of $CR_8$ on that concentration's effect was significant only when barriers were high. Kamerschen, II — $T/E$. Using interactions between concentration and entry barriers, he concluded using only 25 of Mann's 30 industries, gets a marginally significant positive effect for $CR_8$ ($t = 1.87$ or $t = 2.00$ with 22 degrees of freedom) when estimated barriers to entry are introduced, but the relation drops to near zero when he limits himself to industries where $CR_8 > 70$. Asch and most of the theses must be reported on from memory. I believe they all yielded positive effects of concentration on profit rates or margins in the mid-to-late 1950s and early 1960s, though Gambeles' did not in earlier years. Most of these were significantly positive, but in Long the relation was very weak and largely disappeared when he controlled for the number of trade association employees per firm (which he interpreted as a measure of collusion).

An entire other literature that has been left out of the table has to do with the effect of concentration in local banking markets. I reviewed this literature in 1970

used, the other variables that were controlled for, the period covered, the results, and their significance, using a 5 percent standard. The notes following the table list the most likely sources of error and note some special features not brought out in the table.

Several conclusions can be drawn from this survey. The bulk of the studies show a significant positive effect of concentration on profits or margins. While there is a good deal of overlap in the data (almost half depends on profit rates for American manufacturing in the 1950s), all the studies together reflect a wide range of experience — from 1936 to 1970, and covering Britain, Canada, and Japan as well as the United States.

In the years where there is a great deal of overlap, the wide variety of profit or margin indexes, of concentration indexes, of other variables controlled for, of units of observation, of universes, and of data sources indicates that the relationship was quite robust. It is almost always possible to pick cases or universes or indexes that destroy even an obvious relationship, such as that consumers buy more at lower prices. It is also possible to destroy a relationship by correlating a dependent variable with two almost identical independent variables. For instance, by correlating electric power use with the price at 250 kwh per month *and* the price at 500 kwh per month you can "show" that price has no effect on the quantity consumed. The problem is that the computer (i.e., the regression program) tries to distinguish between the two effects rather than to determine whether the two are important jointly. Of course, it cannot do this, or, more correctly, if it can, the distinction will depend on wild outliers and isn't very trustworthy. By and large the concentration–profits relationship holds up well under a great variety of approaches and survives a good deal of mayhem. I'm sure that the business cycle people or the monetary vs. fiscal policy people would be delighted to see our kind of robustness in their studies.

---

[L. Weiss, Statement in Federal Reserve Bank of Chicago, "Proceedings of a Conference on Bank Structure and Competition" (processed 1970), pp. 71-74] and found at that time that all but one of those studies has shown a significant effect for concentration of the expected sign. The one exception, T. Flechsig, *Banking Market Structure and Performance in Metropolitan Areas* (Washington, D.C.: Board of Governors of the Federal Reserve System 1965), was suspect because of an unusual and complex assignment of cities to "regions." A later study, A. Phillips, "Evidence on Concentration in Banking Markets and Interest Rates," *Federal Reserve Bulletin*, June 1967, pp. 916-926, using similar data but a conventional pair of regions (North and East vs. South and West), got a consistently positive and usually significant effect of concentration on loan interest rates when he controlled for the size of loan. A number of other studies, most of which I cannot cite now, yielded similar results for different samples (e.g., the 99 (largely county) banking markets of Iowa, the local banking markets of New England, and before-and-after study of effects of bank structure in Nassau County, New York, and/or for other variables such as check charges and time deposit interest rates). They all supported the hypothesis that variation in local bank concentration has significant effects of the expected sort on the bank charges or payments that are relevant to local markets. I have not kept track of this literature since 1970.

There are a number of studies on the list that yielded no significant effect of concentration on profits or margins (though most show positive effects). These deserve special attention. They fall into five categories.

First, the weak results of two studies [Singer, *infra* n. 56 and Whittington, *infra* n. 69] are undoubtedly due to poor methodology. Singer took Bain's and Mann's data [Bain, *infra* n. 4, and Mann, *infra* n. 46], arbitrarily excluded some industries, and then tested the hypothesis that profit rates are higher where *four*-firm CRs exceed 70, although Bain's and Mann's results had suggested a critical *eight*-firm CR of 70. One effect of this change was to make automobiles into an "unconcentrated" industry. He relied on weighted averages of the industries included. This put great weight on the large (and misplaced) auto industry and eliminated the effect of concentration on profits. By simply counting autos as concentrated the weighted averages become 20.3 percent for concentrated and 11.1 percent for unconcentrated industries using the industries he selected from Bain's data. The comparable numbers are 14.0 percent and 11.0 percent using the industries he selected from Mann. The unweighted averages with autos treated as concentrated are 16.1 (1.4) vs. 12.4 (1.6) for Bain data and 13.1 (1.0) vs. 11.0 (1.0) (standard errors in parentheses). With this one change, his conclusions are destroyed. Actually, he committed a number of other sins, but I don't feel the paper warrants any more effort to correct them.

Whittington defined "concentration" as the share of firms with more than £4,000,000 in assets in total assets of listed corporation assignable to roughly *two*-digit industries. This is really a size rather than a concentration variable. The number of leading firms involved ranges from none to 39 depending on the industry. He apparently related it to $\Pi/(E + D)$ where $D$ is long term debt — i.e., before tax and after interest — and found no significant effect — not a surprising result in view of the methods used. Miraculously there was a substantial positive effect on large firms' profits in 1954-1960. I do not feel that these two studies do any damage to the hypothesis at all.

A second category contains the studies that yield a weak relationship during periods when the concentration–profits relation was apt to be weak. This was true of Stigler's study [*infra* n. 42] for the years 1938-1941, 1942-1944, 1948-1950, though the study yielded a significant positive effect for the years 1951-1953 and 1954-1957. Similarly, Kilpatrick [*infra* n. 51] in his reconstruction of Stigler found no significant effect in 1950, though he found one in 1956 and 1963. Gambeles' study [*infra* n. 34] showed no significant effect in years before the early 1950s, though he found significant positive effects thereafter.[34a] There seems little doubt that the relationship was weak in the 1940s. The wonder is that one study could yield a significant positive effect even then [Bain, *infra* n. 4, as reworked in Weiss, *infra* n. 36].

With less certainty, the weak positive effects found in Komiya's study [*infra* n. 75] for Japan for 1956-1960 and in Demsetz [*infra* n. 66] for the United States for 1969 may be attributable to the years employed. Uekusa [*infra*

---

34a. The results of the Gambeles study are based on a four-year-old memory. I do not know the precise year in which the relation became significant.

TABLE 11

A Survey of Concentration-Profits Studies

| Study | Profit Measure | Concentration Measure | Other Variables Used | Observation | Universe | Period | Effect of Concentration on Profits | Significance |
|---|---|---|---|---|---|---|---|---|
| Bain 1951[35] | $\dfrac{\Pi - T}{E}$ | 4-digit 8-firm CR | None | Average for leading firms in an industry | 42 manufacturing industries with national markets, no noncompeting subproducts, and profit data for 3 or more firms | 1936-1940 | Positive — profits higher where 8-firm $CR > 70$ | Significant |
| Bain 1956 (reworked in Weiss 1971)[36] | $\dfrac{\Pi - T}{E}$ | 4-digit 8-firm CR for 1935 and 1947 | Estimated barriers to entry | Average for leading firms in an industry | 20 usually 4-digit industries chosen for ease of estimating barriers to entry | 1936-1940 and 1947-1951 | Positive for both periods for each level of barriers to entry | Significant where barriers to entry were substantial or high in 1936-1940 and where they were high in 1947-1951 |
| Schwartzman 1959[37] | $\dfrac{VS}{CM + PR}$ | 4-digit 4-firm 1954 CRs for U.S. and 3-firm 1948 CRs for Canada | Distinguished industries where imports or exports were important | Weighted average for all plants in an industry | 61 4-digit industries similarly defined in U.S. and Canada | 1954 | Positive Margin 7% higher in Canada if $CR \geqslant 50$ in Canada and $CR < 50$ in U.S. Only 2% if $CR < 50$ both places | Significant except for industries where exports were important |
| Levinson 1960[38] | $\dfrac{\Pi}{E}$ and $\dfrac{\Pi - T}{E}$ | Percent of 2-digit shipments where 4-digit $CR \geqslant 50$ | None | Weighted average for all corporations where primary product was in a 2-digit industry (SEC-FTC) | All manufacturing except "Misc." | Each year 1947-1958 | Positive in all years after 1948 | Significant in 1949 and in all years after 1952 |

| | | | | | | | |
|---|---|---|---|---|---|---|---|
| Fuchs 1961[39] | $\dfrac{\Pi+I-T}{A}$ | Weighted average of 4-digit 4-firm CRs | Output growth, regional market dummy. Used percent of value added from multiplant firms as an alternative to CR. Interprets as barrier to entry variable but it's a crude concentration variable | Weighted average for all firms primary to an IRS "minor" industry (roughly 3-digit) | 38 IRS "minor" industries | 1953-1954 | Positive for both CR and multiplant variable | Significant for both variables, but multiplant variable more highly correlated |
| Sato 1961[40] | $\dfrac{\Pi}{S}$ | Weighted average of 4-digit 4-firm CRs in IRS minor industry. Minor industries then classified highly, moderately, and unconcentrated (average CR ≥ 50, 50 > CR ≥ 30, and CR < 30 | Assets ÷ sales, market fragmentation, growth, change in man-hour productivity | Weighted average for all firms primary to an IRS minor industry | 110 IRS manufacturing minor industries (all except those with "Misc." in their titles) | 1948-1951 and 1953-1956 | Positive for high and moderately concentrated industries | Significant for highly concentrated industries but not for moderately concentrated industries |
| Minhas, 1963[41] | $\dfrac{\Pi+I-D}{A}$ | Weighted average of 4-digit 4-firm CRs | Sales growth | All firms primary to an FTC-SEC 2-digit industry | All manufacturing | 1949-1958 | Positive | Significant |
| Stigler 1963[42] | $\dfrac{\Pi-T+I}{A}$ | Weighted average of 1947 or 1954 CR. Minor industries then classified concentrated (CR > 60 and national market), unconcentrated (CR < 50 or CR < 20 and local markets) or ambiguous | None | Weighted average for all firms primary to an IRS minor industry | All manufacturing | 1938-1941 1942-1944 1945-1947 1948-1950 1951-1954 1955-1957 | Positive Negative Negative Positive Positive Positive | Nonsignificant Nonsignificant Nonsignificant Nonsignificant Significant Significant |

| Study | Profit Measure | Concentration Measure | Other Variables Used | Observation | Universe | Period | Effect of Concentration on Profits | Significance |
|---|---|---|---|---|---|---|---|---|
| Weiss 1963[43] | $\dfrac{\Pi - T}{E}$ | Weighted average of "corrected" 1954 4-firm CRs | Output growth | Weighted average for all firms primary to an FTC-SEC 2-digit industry | All manufacturing | 1947-1948 and 1949-1958 | Negative Positive | Nonsignificant Significant |
| Sherman 1964[44] | $\dfrac{\Pi}{E}$ | Weighted average of 1954 8-firm 4-digit CRs | None | Same as Weiss | All manufacturing | 1954 | Positive | Significant |
| Stigler 1964[45] | $\dfrac{\Pi - T}{E}$ $\dfrac{\Pi - T + I}{\bar{A}}$ and market value of stock ÷ book equity | 4-firm 4-digit CR and Herfindahl Index | None | Average of leading firms whose primary product was in a 4-digit industry | 17 4-digit industries where Herfindahl indexes could be constructed | 1953-1957 | Positive highest correlation for market value and H index, lowest for $\dfrac{\Pi - T + I}{\bar{A}}$ and CR | All significant except $\dfrac{\Pi - T + I}{\bar{A}}$ and CR |
| Mann 1966 (reworked in Weiss, 1971)[46] | $\dfrac{\Pi - T}{E}$ | 8-firm 4-digit CR for 1958 classified as concentrated (CR > 70) or unconcentrated | Estimated barriers to entry | Average of leading firms whose primary product was in a 4-digit industry | 30 4-digit industries where barriers to entry could be estimated | 1950-1960 | Positive and Positive for all barriers to entry in Weiss rework | Significant and Significant in Weiss rework where barriers to entry were high |
| Comanor and Wilson 1967[47] | $\dfrac{\Pi - T}{E}$ | Weighted average 4- and 8-firm CRs, dummies for Kaysen and Turner's oligopoly classes and for 8-firm CR > 70 | Average shipment size of plants with top 50% of shipments ÷ industry shipments, capital requirements of such plants, advertising-sales ratio, sales growth, and regional industry dummy | Average for all firms with more than $500,000 assets primary to an IRS minor industry | All consumer goods IRS minor industries | 1954-1957 | Positive by itself, sometimes positive and sometimes negative when plant scale and capital requirements variables used | Significant Nonsignificant when plant scale and capital requirements used |
| Kilpatrick 1967[48] | $\dfrac{\Pi}{E}$ | Various indexes: 4- and 5-digit, 4-, 8-, and 20-firm CRs uncorrected and corrected for imports | Sales growth | All firms primary to an IRS minor industry | All IRS minor industries except those with N.S.K. in their titles | 1952-1954 1954-1957 | Positive for all CRs | Significant for all CRs best fit for 4-firm 5-digit CRs |

| Study | Profit measure | CR measure | Other variables | Sample | Years | Results | Significance |
|---|---|---|---|---|---|---|---|
| Miller 1967[49] | $\frac{II-T}{E}$ | Weighted average of 1958 4-digit 4-firm CR and $CR_8$-$CR_4$, $CR_{20}$-$CR_8$, and $CR_{50}$-$CR_{20}$ | None | All firms primary to an IRS minor industry | 1959-1962 | Positive for $CR_4$ Negative for $CR_8$-$CR_4$ Near zero for $CR_{20}$-$CR_8$ and $CR_{50}$-$CR_{20}$ | Significant Significant Nonsignificant |
| Collins and Preston 1968[50] | $\frac{VS-CM-PR}{VS}$ for 4-digit industries and $\frac{II}{E}$, $\frac{II+I}{E}$, $\frac{II}{S}$, $\frac{II-T}{A}$, $\frac{II-T+I}{E}$, $\frac{II-T+I}{A}$ & $\frac{II-T}{S}$ for 2-digit industries | 4-digit CR and weighted average of 4-digit 4-firm CR for 1958 | Gross fixed assets ÷ sales, and an index of geographic dispersion for 4-digit industries. Assets ÷ sales for 2-digit industries | All plants primary to 4-digit industry. All firms primary to a 2-digit industry | 1958 and 1956-1960 | Positive for 4-digit industries Positive for 2-digit industries | Nonsignificant Significant Significant for all profit indexes except $\frac{II-T}{S}$ |
| Kilpatrick 1968[51] | $\frac{II-T+I}{A}$ | Weighted average of 4-digit CRs for 1954 corrected for imports | Sales growth | All firms primary to an IRS minor industry and all firms with more than $250,000 or $500,000 assets primary to an IRS minor industry | 1950, 1956, and 1963 | Positive in all years | Significant in all years using whole industries; significant in 1956 and 1963 but not in 1950 when small firms are excluded |
| Hall and Weiss 1968[52] | $\frac{II-T}{E}$, $\frac{II-T}{A}$ | Weighted average of corrected 4-firm CRs | Asset size, industry output growth for each of previous 5 years, leverage measured by E/A | All firms in the Fortune "500" Industrials where all data is available | 1956-1962 | Positive | Significant |

| Study | Profit Measure | Concentration Measure | Other Variables Used | Observation | Universe | Period | Effect of Concentration on Profits | Significance |
|---|---|---|---|---|---|---|---|---|
| Sherman 1968[53] | $\frac{\Pi}{E}$, $\frac{\Pi-T}{E}$, and $\frac{\Pi-T-.032E}{S}$ | Weighted average of 4-digit 4- and 8-firm CRs | None | All firms primary to an IRS major industry | All IRS manufacturing "major" industries (roughly 2-digit) | 1955 and 1959 | Positive | Significant |
| Collins and Preston 1969[54] | $\frac{VS-CM-PR}{VS}$ | 4-digit 4-firm CRs for 1958 and 1963 | Same as Collins and Preston, 1968 | All plants primary to a Census 4-digit industry | All Census 4-digit industries | 1958 and 1963 | Generally positive | Significant for consumer goods, not for producer goods; stronger for four leading firms than for other firms |
| FTC 1969[55] | $\frac{\Pi-T}{E}$, $\frac{\Pi-T+I}{A}$ | Weighted average of 5-digit 4-firm CRs corrected for local markets; also 5-digit market shares of a firm | Advertising-sales ratio, output growth, firm diversification, firm size | A firm | All 125 firms primary to food manufacturing in the 1950 FTC report on 1000 largest manufacturers | 1949-1953 | Positive for both CR and market share in same equation | Significant for both |
| Singer 1970[56] | $\frac{\Pi-T}{E}$ (Weighted averages for all industries where 4-firm CR above and below 70) | 4-digit 4-firm employment CR | None | Same as Bain and Mann | 18 of Bain's 20 industries and 24 of Mann's industries | Same as Bain and Mann | No difference between weighted averages; positive difference for unweighted averages in both studies | Nonsignificant Nonsignificant |

| Study | Dependent variable | Concentration measure | Other variables | Unit | Sample | Years | Sign | Results |
|---|---|---|---|---|---|---|---|---|
| Brozen 1970[57] | $\frac{\Pi - T}{E}$ | 4-digit 4-firm and 8-firm CRs | None | Average for leading firms primary to a 4-digit industry | Bain's sample of 42 industries and Stigler's sample of 17 industries | 1936-1940, 1953-1957, and 1962-1966 | Positive in all cases | Bain's sample marginally significant in 1936-1940 ($t = 1.86$), nonsignificant in 1953-1957, and significant in 1962-1966; Stigler's sample significant in 1953-1957 and marginally so in 1962-1966 ($t = 1.73$) |
| Esposito and Esposito 1971[58] | $\frac{\Pi - T}{E}$ | Dummy with value of 1 if 4-digit 8-firm CR > 70 | Ratio of imports to shipments, advertising-sales ratio, average plant size for top 50% of shipments ÷ industry shipments, capital requirements of such plants, sales growth, regional market dummy | Weighted average for all firms primary to an IRS minor industry | 77 IRS manufacturing minor industries | 1963-1965 | Positive in all cases | Significant for all goods except when capital requirements included; significant for producer goods; nonsignificant for consumer goods |
| Imel and Helmberger 1971[59] | $\frac{\Pi - T - .05E}{S}$ | Weighted average of 4-firm CR for 4-digit products, 4- and 5-digit products depending on which is closer to a market, and for refined Census products that correspond closely to markets | Relative firm size (market share ÷ CR), advertising-sales ratio, R&D-sales ratio, and plant scale, growth and diversification variables in unreported regressions) | A firm | 99 firms primary to the food and tobacco industries | 1959-1967 | Positive in all cases | Significant for refined Census products and 4- and 5-digit products, marginally significant for 4-digit products ($t = 1.96$); less significant when plant scale variable was included (not reported); relative firm size always significant |

| Study | Profit Measure | Concentration Measure | Other Variables Used | Observation | Universe | Period | Effect of Concentration on Profits | Significance |
|---|---|---|---|---|---|---|---|---|
| Brozen 1971A[60] | $\dfrac{\Pi - T}{E}$ | 4-firm 4-digit CR for 1935 classified as concentrated if CR ≥ 70 | None | Simple average for firms primary to a 4-digit industry | All industries reported on by the FTC where CR was available | 1939 and 1940 | No difference | Nonsignificant |
| Kessel 1971[61] | Underwriting cost and re-offering less high grade market yields for tax-exempt bonds | Number of underwriting syndicates bidding on new issues of tax-exempt bonds | Issue size, outstanding bonds of borrower, yield and change in yield on highest quality 20-year tax-exempts, maturity, call provisions, rating, trend, general obligation, revenue bond distinction | A tax-exempt issue | 9420 tax-exempt bond issues | 1959-1967 | Both underwriting cost and resale spread decline monotonically with number of bidders roughly in proportion to 1/N | Decline in underwriting costs significant through 8 bidders for general obligation bonds and 5 for revenue bonds; decline in re-offering yield significant through 10 bidders for general obligation bonds and 6 bidders for revenue bonds |
| Keiser 1972[62] | Log (VS − CM − PR) and Log (VS − CM − PR − estimated central office payroll) | 4-digit 4-firm CR and log of number of firms | Logs of gross book value of fixed assets, of inventory, and of payroll, and an index of firm specialization | All plants in a Census 4-digit industry | All Census 4-digit manufacturing industries | 1958 and 1963 | CR positive but log of number of firms also positive | Both significant but the effect of CR only positive for industries where CR ≥ 50 |

| Study | Measure | Concentration/share variables | Other variables | Unit | Sample | Period | Findings | Significance |
|---|---|---|---|---|---|---|---|---|
| Shepherd 1972[63] | $\dfrac{\Pi-T}{E}$ | Weighted averages of corrected 4-firms CR, firm's estimated market shares (MS), and of CR − MS | Firm sales growth, log of asset size, advertising–sales ratio, profit variability | A firm | All firms continuously on Fortune "500" list that were not "excessively diversified," did not have high military sales, and where the primary industry did not have a "major disequilibrium" where MS could be estimated | 1960-1969 | All firms: CR Positive MS Positive (CR-MS) Positive; Consumer goods: same; Producer goods: same except (CR-MS) about zero | Significant Significant Marginally significant ($t = 1.56$); { MS and (CR-MS) both significant MS significant; { (CR-MS) nonsignificant |
| Gale 1972[64] | $\dfrac{\Pi-T}{E}$ | Dummies for high, medium, and low weighted average of corrected 1966 CRs, and interactions between them and weighted average of estimated MSs | Sales size, leverage, industry shipments, growth, firm sales growth | A firm | 106 manufacturing firms where all data was available. Excludes firms where employment data (for MS) includes foreign operations | 1963-1967 | CR has positive effect if MS > 4% in highly concentrated industries or if MS > 6% in medium CR industries | Significant for high CR industries; Nonsignificant for medium CR industries |
| Demsetz 1973A[65] | $\dfrac{\Pi+I}{A}$ | Apparently weighted average of 4-digit CRs for 1963 (not reported) | Asset size | All firms in a size class in an IRS minor industry | Apparently all IRS manufacturing minor industries (not reported) | 1963 | Positive for firms with over $50,000,000 assets, not for smaller ones; difference between large and small firms rises with CR | Not reported but probably significant for firms with over $50,000,000 assets |
| Demsetz 1973B[66] | $\dfrac{\Pi+I}{A}$ | Same as 1973A though CRs used for 1969 may be for a later year (not reported) | Same as above | Same as above | Same as above | 1963 and 1969 | Positive for firms with over $50,000,000 in 1963 and over $35,000,000 in 1969 | Significantly positive for firms with over $100,000,000 in both 1963 and 1969; not significant below that |

| Study | Profit Measure | Concentration Measure | Other Variables Used | Observation | Universe | Period | Effect of Concentration on Profits | Significance |
|---|---|---|---|---|---|---|---|---|
| Rhoades 1973 [67] | $\dfrac{VS-CM-PR}{VS}$ | 4-digit 4-firm CR for 1963 | Specialization ratios for firms primary to the 4-digit industry and for firms not primary to the 2½-digit (Enterprise Statistics) industry, shipments growth, gross book value of fixed assets ÷ shipments, consumer good dummy, and geographic dispersion index | All plants primary to a Census 4-digit industry | All Census 4-digit industries where 8-firm CR ≥ 30 and where growth could be computed | 1963 | Positive | Significant |
| Ornstein 1973 (similar to Ornstein 1972) [68] | Market value of stock ÷ book value of equity, $\dfrac{II-T}{E}$ | 4-digit 4-firm CR | Firm assets ÷ industry value added (offered as a size variable but actually a crude concentration variable). Average plant size for top 50% of shipments ÷ industry shipments, capital requirements for such a plant, firm asset growth, industry output growth, change in labor cost (not defined), capital–labor ratios (not defined), geographic dispersion index, and a dummy for consumer goods | Average for firms primary to the 4-digit industry that are publicly held, have assets of more than $1,000,000, and have at least 50% of sales in the 4-digit industry 1947-1960 | 33 four-digit industries for which data is available | 1949-1950, 1954-1955, and 1959-1960 | Positive without plant size and capital requirements variables; negative with them | Nonsignificant in 1950; significant in 1955 and for market value in 1960; nonsignificant |

| Study | Profit variable | Concentration measure | Other variables | Sample definition | Sample | Period | Sign of relationship | Significance |
|---|---|---|---|---|---|---|---|---|
| Whittington 1971[69] | Apparently, $\dfrac{\Pi}{E+D}$* (not defined in the concentration section — pp. 77-81 — but this is the profit variable most commonly used elsewhere in his book; see pp. 16-17) *D means long term debt. | $E+D$ for firms with more than £4 million assets ÷ total $E+D$ of all listed firms in the industry | None | Weighted average for all firms in an industry or for firms with $>$ £4 million $E+D$ | 21 British roughly 2-digit industries | 1948-1954 and 1954-1960 | Almost zero in 1948-1954; positive for large firms in 1954-1960 | Nonsignificant Nonsignificant |
| Phillips 1972[70] | $\dfrac{VS-CM-PR}{VS}$ | 3-firm CR for roughly 4-digit industries | Average plant employment size ÷ industry employment, advertising–sales ratio, concentration–advertising interaction, number of trade associations attempting to fix price, effectiveness of price-fixing agreements as judged by buyers, producer good dummy, sales growth | All plants primary to a British 4-digit industry | All British manufacturing for which data is available | Average over the three years 1948, 1951, and 1954 | Positive | Significant |
| Shirazi 1974[71] | $\dfrac{VS-CM-PR}{VS}$ | Weighted average of 5-firm CR in roughly 4-digit industries | "Midpoint plant" sales or average sales of plants accounting for top 50% of sales ÷ industry sales, producer good dummy, sales growth, capital–sales ratio for leading firms in relevant 2-digit industry, foreign control of 10% or more of industry, imports as a percentage of sales, exports as a percentage of sales | All plants primary to a British 3-digit industry | All British manufacturing where CR is available for 80% of sales and where specialization ratio $\geqslant$ 80 except margarine where most output under contract to Ministry of Food | 1963 | Positive | Significant in simple regression but nonsignificant in multiple regression |

| Study | Profit Measure | Concentration Measure | Other Variables Used | Observation | Universe | Period | Effect of Concentration on Profits | Significance |
|---|---|---|---|---|---|---|---|---|
| Jones, Lauddio, and Percy 1973[72] | $\frac{II-T}{E}$, $\frac{II+I-T}{A}$ | 4-firm 3-digit CR, Herfindahl index | Advertising-sales ratio, average shipments of plants accounting for top 80% of shipments as a percentage of industry shipments, capital requirements of such a plant, 1965 shipments ÷ 1956 shipments, dummy for regional markets, dummies for high 1961 imports (> 30%) and moderate 1961 imports (15-29.9%), dummy for auto industry | Apparently average for firms assigned to a 3-digit industry | 30 3-digit industries where 50% or more of shipments were consumer goods | 1965 | Positive in all cases | Significant when scale and import variables excluded; nonsignificant when either is in |
| McFetridge 1973[73] | Average $\frac{VA-PR}{VA}$ 1965-1969 | Herfindahl index, $CR_4$, these indexes squared, and 1/(number of firms that account for 80 percent of shipments) for 3-digit industries | Net assets ÷ value added, percent growth in value added 1961-1969; regional market dummy; consumer goods dummy; share of 4 largest plants in industry shipments; advertising ÷ value added; effective tariff rate | All plants in a 3-digit industry | All 43 3-digit industries where all data available, excluding those with "Misc." in their titles | 1965-1969 | Positive for all concentration indexes | Significant for all concentration indexes, strongest using squared Hirfindahl index; significant for consumer goods but not for producer goods when distinguished |
| Komiya 1962[75] | $\frac{II-T}{E}$ | 5-firm CR for roughly 4- to 5-digit industries | None | Average for 5 leading firms primary to an industry | 46 Japanese manufacturing, mining, and service industries | 1956-1960 | Positive | Nonsignificant |
| Niida 1969[76] | $\frac{II-T}{E}$ | 1-, 3-, and 5-firm CR for roughly 4- to 5-digit industries | None | Average for firms primary to an industry | 36 Japanese industries | 1956-1960 and 1961-1966 | Positive in both periods | Nonsignificant in 1956-1960; significant in 1961-1966 |

[Note: All of the following except the last are taken from Uekusa 1973A.[74] Some studies also used $(II-T+I)/A$ and $(II-T)/S$ but these were not reported.]

| Study | Dependent variable | Concentration measure | Other variables | Unit | Sample | Period | Sign | Significance |
|---|---|---|---|---|---|---|---|---|
| Matsushiro 1970[77] | $\dfrac{\Pi-T}{E}$ | 3-, 2-, and 1-firm CR for roughly 4- to 5-digit industries | None | Average for firms primary to an industry | 35 to 37 Japanese manufacturing industries | 1961-1965 | Positive, critical 3-firm CR at 50 | Significant |
| Musashi 1970[78] | $\dfrac{\Pi-T}{E}$ | 3-firm CR for roughly 4- to 5-digit industries | "Rates of growth in demand" | Average for firms primary to an industry | 23 Japanese manufacturing industries | 1956-1965 | Positive | Nonsignificant |
| | | | | | 35 Japanese manufacturing industries | 1961-1965 | Positive | Significant |
| Uekusa 1970[79] | $\dfrac{\Pi-T}{E}$ | 3-firm CR for roughly 4- to 5-digit industries | "Scale economies barriers," "capital requirements barriers," "product differentiation barriers," and "rate of growth in demand" (none of these were defined further) | Average for firms primary to an industry | 38 Japanese industries and 16 Japanese consumer goods industries | 1961-1965 | Positive for both samples | Significant for both samples |
| Musashi 1973[80] | $\dfrac{\Pi-T}{E}$ | 3-firm CR for 4- to 5-digit industries | "Rate of growth in demand" | Average for firms primary to an industry | 23 Japanese industries | 1956-1960 | Positive for both samples | Nonsignificant for 1956-1960 sample; significant for 1961-1965 sample |
| | | | | | 35 Japanese industries | 1961-1965 | | |
| Uekusa 1973B[81] | $\dfrac{\Pi-T}{E}$ and $\dfrac{\Pi-T+I}{E+D}$ | 4-firm CR for roughly 4- to 5-digit industries | Asset size, coefficient of variation of $(\Pi-T)$, sales growth, specialization ratios, percentage of debt from zaibatsu banks, total promotional cost as a percent of sales (not just ads) | A firm | Not reported in work sheets | 1967-1969 and 1961-1970 | Positive | Significant |
| | | | | | | | Positive in all cases | Nonsignificant for $\dfrac{\Pi-T}{E}$ but significant for $\dfrac{\Pi-T+I}{E+D}$ |

35. J. Bain, "Relation of Profit Rate to Industry Concentration, American Manufacturing, 1936-1940," *Quarterly Journal of Economics,* 65 (August 1951), pp. 293-324.

36. See Bain, n. 4 *supra;* reworked by L. Weiss, "Quantitative Studies of Industrial Organization," in M. Intriligator, *Frontiers of Quantitative Economics* (Amsterdam: North-Holland Publ. Co. 1971), pp. 363-403.

37. D. Schwartzman, "Effect of Monopoly on Price," *Journal of Political Economy,* 67 (August 1959), pp. 352-362.

38. H. Levinson, "Post War Movements of Prices and Wages in Manufacturing Industries," Study Paper No. 21 in Joint Economic Committee, *Studies in Employment, Growth, and Price Levels* (U.S.G.P.O. 1960).

39. V. R. Fuchs, "Integration, Concentration and Profits in Manufacturing Industries," *Quarterly Journal of Economics,* 75 (May 1961), pp. 278-291.

40. K. Sato, "Price-Cost Structure and the Behavior of Profit Margins," *Yale Economic Essays,* 1 (Fall 1961), pp. 361-424.

41. B. Minhas, *An International Comparison of Factor Cost and Factor Use* (Amsterdam: North-Holland Publ. Co. 1963).

42. G. Stigler, *Capital and Rates of Return in Manufacturing Industries* (Princeton Univ. Press 1963).

43. L. Weiss, "Average Concentration Ratios and Industrial Performance," *Journal of Industrial Economics,* 11 (July 1963), pp. 233-254.

44. H. Sherman, *MacroDynamic Economics* (Appleton-Century Crofts 1964).

45. G. Stigler, "A Theory of Oligopoly," *Journal of Political Economy,* 72 (February 1964), pp. 44-61.

46. M. Mann, "Seller Concentration, Barriers to Entry, and Rates of Return in 30 Industries, 1950-1960," *Review of Economics and Statistics,* 48 (August 1966), pp. 296-307. L. Weiss, n. 36 *supra.*

47. W. Comanor and T. Wilson, "Advertising, Market Structure, and Performance," *Review of Economics and Statistics,* 49 (November 1967), pp. 423-440.

48. R. W. Kilpatrick, "The Choice Among Alternative Measures of Industrial Concentration," *Review of Economics and Statistics,* 49 (May 1967), pp. 258-260.

49. R. Miller, "Marginal Concentration Ratios and Industrial Profit Rates," *Southern Economic Journal,* 34 (October 1967), pp. 259-267.

50. N. Collins and L. Preston, *Concentration and Price-Cost Margins in Manufacturing Industries* (Univ. of California Press 1968).

51. R. Kilpatrick, "Stigler on the Relationship Between Profit Rates and Market Concentration," *Journal of Political Economy,* 76 (June 1968), pp. 479-485.

52. M. Hall and L. Weiss, "Firm Size and Profitability," *Review of Economics and Statistics,* 49 (August 1967), pp. 319-331.

53. H. Sherman, *Profits in the United States: An Introduction to a Study of Economic Concentration and the Business Cycle* (Cornell Univ. Press 1968).

54. N. Collins and L. Preston, "Price Cost Margins and Industry Structure," *Review of Economics and Statistics,* 51 (August 1969), pp. 271-286.

55. Federal Trade Commission, *Economic Report on the Influence of Market Structure on the Profit Performance of Food Manufacturing Industries* (U.S.G.P.O., September 1969).

56. E. Singer, "Industrial Organization: Price Models and Price Policy," *American Economic Review,* 60 (May 1970), pp. 90-99.

57. Y. Brozen, "The Anti-Trust Task Force Deconcentration Recommendation," *Journal of Law and Economics,* 13 (October 1970), pp. 279-292.

58. L. Esposito and F. Esposito, "Foreign Competition and Domestic Industry Profitability," *Review of Economics and Statistics,* 53 (November 1971), pp. 343-353.

59. B. Imel and P. Helmberger, "Estimation of Structure-Profits Relationships with Application to the Food Processing Sector," *American Economic Review,* 61 (September 1971), pp. 614-627.

60. Y. Brozen, "Bain's Concentration and Rates of Return Revisited," *Journal of Law and Economics,* 14 (October 1971), pp. 351-370.

61. R. Kessel, "A Study of the Effects of Competition in the Tax-Exempt Bond Market," *Journal of Political Economy,* 79 (July 1971), pp. 706-738.

62. L. Telser, *Competition, Collusion and Game Theory* (Aldine-Atherton 1972), ch. 8.

63. W. Shepherd, "The Elements of Market Structure," *Review of Economics and Statistics,* 54 (February 1972), pp. 25-38.

64. B. Gale, "Market Share and Rate of Return," *Review of Economics and Statistics,* 54 (November 1972), pp. 412-423.

65. H. Demsetz, "Industry Structure, Market Rivalry, and Public Policy," *Journal of Law and Economics,* 16 (April 1973), pp. 1-9.

66. H. Demsetz, *The Market Concentration Doctrine* (Washington: American Enterprise Institute 1973).

67. S. A. Rhoades, "The Effect of Diversification on Industry Performance in 241 Manufacturing Industries: 1963," *Review of Economics and Statistics,* 55 (May 1973), pp. 146-155.

68. S. Ornstein, "Concentration and Profits," in Weston and Ornstein, eds., *The Impact of Large Firms on the U.S. Economy* (Lexington Books 1973), pp. 87-102.

69. G. Whittington, *The Prediction of Profitability* (Cambridge Univ. Press 1971), ch. 3, app.

70. A. Phillips, "An Econometric Study of Price-Fixing, Market Structure, and Performance in British Industry in the Early 1950's," in K. Cowling, *Market Structure and Corporate Behavior* (London: Gray Mills 1972).

71. J. Shirazi, "Market Structure and Price-Cost Margins in U.K. Manufacturing Industries," *Review of Economics and Statistics,* 56 (forthcoming in 1974).

72. J. C. H. Jones, L. Laudadio, and M. Percy, "Market Structure and Profitability in Canadian Manufacturing Industry: Some Cross Section Results," *Canadian Journal of Economics,* 6 (August 1973), pp. 356-368.

73. D. G. McFetridge, "Market Structure and Price—Cost Margins: An Analysis of the Canadian Manufacturing Sector," Canadian Journal of Economics, 6 (August 1973), pp. 345-355.

74. M. Uekusa, "Survey of Quantitative Analyses of Industrial Organizations in Japan" (processed 1973).

75. R. Komiya, "Nihon ni okeru Dokusen to Kigyo Riiyun" (Monopoly and Corporate Profits in Japan), in T. Nakamura, Kigyo no Keizai Bunseki (Economic Analysis of Enterprises) (Tokyo: Iwanami Shoten 1962). Reviewed in M. Uekusa, supra n. 74.

76. H. Niida, "Schuchudo no Henka to Riiyunritsu" (Changes in Concentration Ratios and Rates of Return), in Nihon no Sangyo Sochiki (Industrial Organization in Japan) (Tokyo: Iwanami Shoten 1969). Reviewed in Uekusa, supra n. 74.

77. K. Matsushiro, "Wagakuni no Sangyo Schuchudo to Riiyunritsu" (Industrial Concentration Ratios and Rates of Profits in Japan), Sanken Ronshu (Report of the Industrial Study Council) (March 1970). Reviewed in Uekusa, supra n. 74.

78. T. Musashi, "Sangyo Kan Riiyunritsu Kakusa" (Industrial Differences in Profit Rates), Kosei Torihiki (Report of the Antitrust Commission) (December 1970). Reviewed in Uekusa, supra n. 74.

79. M. Uekusa, "Riiyunritsu to Shijo — Nihon to America" (Rates of Profit and Market Structure Elements in the United States and Japan), Mita Gakkai Zasshi (Keio Univ. Assn. Magazine) (July 1970). Reviewed in Uekusa, supra n.74.

80. T. Musashi, "Profits, Growth of Demand and Product Differentiation" (unpublished working paper). Reported on by Uekusa, supra n. 74.

81. M. Uekusa et al., Kasen Sangyo no Shigyo Seika no Keiryo Bunseki (Quantitative Analysis of Market Performance in Oligopolistic Industries) (Japanese Fair Trade Commission 1973).

## Comments on Studies in Table 11

| | |
|---|---|
| Bain 1951 | Accounting II and E; some diversified firms assigned to their primary 4-digit industries; possibly biased sample. |
| Bain 1956 | Same as above plus subjective estimates of barriers to entry; 1947-1951 is a period when CR-profit relation is apt to be weak; biased sample. |
| Schwartzman 1959 | National 4-digit CRs for many industries with regional markets or noncompeting subproducts; possibly biased sample; based on one year only; period when CR-profit relation is apt to be weak; crucial test depends on only a few industries. |
| Levinson 1960 | Accounting II, E, and A; national CRs for many industries with regional markets or noncompeting subproducts. |
| Fuchs 1961 | Accounting II and A; some diversified firms assigned to their primary industries; incomplete barriers to entry variable; based on one year; period when the CR-profits relation is apt to be weak; possibly biased sample. |
| Sato 1961 | Accounting profits; national 4-digit CRs for many industries with regional markets or noncompeting subproducts; profits before tax. |
| Minhas 1963 | Accounting II and A; national 4-digit CRs for many industries with regional markets or noncompeting subproducts; profits before taxes. |
| Stigler 1963 | Accounting II and A; some diversified firms assigned to their primary IRS minor industries; many CRs for industries with noncompeting subproducts; concentration-profits relation apt to be weak in all periods except the last.<br>Note: no significant difference in any period when corrections made for officers' withdrawals, but see Kilpatrick 1968. |
| Weiss 1963 | Accounting II and E; subjective corrections of CRs; first period one when concentration-profits relation apt to be weak. |
| Sherman 1964 | Accounting II and E; profits before taxes; many 4-digit industries where regional markets or noncompeting subproducts; based on one year. |
| Stigler 1964 | Accounting II, E, and A; probably some diversified firms assigned to their primary 4-digit industries; possibly biased sample. |
| Mann 1966 | Accounting II and E; some diversified firms assigned to their primary 4-digit industries; biased sample; subjective estimates of barriers to entry. |
| Comanor and Wilson 1967 | Accounting II and E; some diversified firms assigned to their primary IRS minor industries; national 4-digit CRs in many industries where local markets or noncompeting subproducts. |
| Kilpatrick 1967 | Accounting profits and equity; profits before taxes; some diversified firms assigned to their primary IRS minor industries; many industries with regional markets or noncompeting subproducts. |
| Miller 1967 | Accounting II, E, and A; some diversified firms assigned to their primary IRS minor industries; national 4-digit CRs with many industries with regional markets or noncompeting subproducts; $(CR_i\text{-}CR_j)$ for $i > j$ constrained to be $\leq CR_j$; or $\leq 100 - CR_j$; whichever is smaller. Since most industries have $CR_4 < 50$, this means that $(CR_i - CR_j)$ is positively correlated with $CR_j$. |
| Collins and Preston 1968 | No control for growth, advertising, or central office expense; national 4-digit CRs for many industries with noncompeting subproducts; based on one year; price-cost margin includes tax; control for gross fixed assets includes depreciated value and excludes inventory and financial assets; possibly spurious correlation because VS is a common factor in CR and $\dfrac{VS-CM-PR}{VS}$. |
| Kilpatrick 1968 | Accounting II and A; some diversified firms assigned to their primary IRS minor industries; CR-profit relation apt to be weak in 1950; based on single years.<br>Note: This was an attempt to deal with Stigler's (1963) method of correcting for officers' withdrawals. Kilpatrick shows that Stigler's method involves a bias. By eliminating small firms from the sample or by controlling for the small firms' share in total equity he shows that the CR-profits relation is generally positive and also significant after 1950. |

**Hall and Weiss 1968**

Accounting II, E, and A; no control for capital—output ratios; subjective judgments in corrections of CRs; serious serial correlation problem so probably exaggerates degrees of freedom.

**Sherman 1968**

Accounting II and E; national 4-digit CRs for many industries with regional markets or noncompeting subproducts; based on two single years. Similar to Sherman 1964.

**Collins and Preston 1969**

Same as Collins and Preston, 1968

**FTC 1969**

Accounting II, E, and A; possibly biased sample (but food processing was almost as large a range of industry structures as all manufacturing, unlike other 2-digit industries).

**Singer 1970**

Accounting II and E; some diversified firms assigned to their primary industries; no control for growth or capital—output ratios; biased samples in Bain and Mann; probably further biased by arbitrary exclusion of 2 industries from Bain sample and 6 from Mann sample; reclassifies firms on the basis of whether industry four-firm concentration ratio is greater or less than 70 though both Bain and Mann found that an eight-firm concentration ratio of 70 (roughly a four-firm ratio of 50) was most appropriate; uses unweighted averages of firms though he criticizes Bain and Mann for the same things; uses weighted average of industries— since automobiles are "unconcentrated" by his standard and automobiles are big, the weighted average of unconcentrated industries is almost as high as that of concentrated industries; does not report unweighted averages, though these support the CR–profits hypothesis even with his reclassifications; his rework of Bain occurs in a period when the CR–profits relation is likely to be weak.

**Brozen 1970**

Accounting II and E, some diversified firms assigned to their primary industries — this problem is worse than it was in Bain and Stigler because diversification is increasing rapidly; national 4-digit CRs for many industries with regional markets or noncompeting subproducts; no control for growth or capital-output ratios; biased sample (from Bain) and possibly biased sample (from Stigler); many industry definitions have changed drastically since the earlier studies.

Note: his main emphasis is on the decline in the difference in profit rates between firms in concentrated and unconcentrated markets. He also reworked the Mann (1966) study, but made no comparison between CR and profits in that case.

**Esposito and Esposito 1971**

Accounting II and E; some diversified firms assigned to their primary industries; national 4-digit CRs for many industries with regional markets or noncompeting subproducts; uses critical concentration ratio only, though many industries show an increasing effect of CR well above the chosen critical CRs; possibly biased sample.

**Imel and Helmberger 1971**

Accounting II and E; possibly biased sample (only food and tobacco firms); subjective judgment in defining 4- and 5-digit products and refined Census products; weights and MS data from confidential interviews so the study cannot be replicated.

**Brozen 1971**

Accounting II and E; some diversified firms assigned to their primary industries; national 4-digit CRs for many industries with regional markets or noncompeting subproducts; no control for growth or capital output ratio; based on two single years.

**Kessel 1971**

Alternative hypothesis on re-offer yields is that more syndicates mean a more thorough search for investors. Note that the dependent variable is price, not profits.

**Telser 1972**

National 4-digit CRs used for many industries with regional markets or noncompeting subproducts; no control for growth; based on one year; margin variable is before tax; no control for advertising.

Note: he interprets the positive effect of number of firms to mean that high prices attract entry and protect suboptimal firms.

**Shepherd 1972**

Accounting II and E; possibly biased sample; subjective judgment in correcting concentration ratios; (CR — MS) does not accurately measure the effect of concentration because MS is excluded; moreover, it is negatively correlated with MS; MS estimates probably inaccurate.

**Gale 1972**

Accounting II and E; possibly biased sample; subjective judgment in correcting CRs (he used Shepherd's corrections); uses only two critical CRs though many other studies seem to show CR is a continuous variable; effect of CR without MS not reported; MS estimates probably inaccurate.

**Demsetz 1973A**

Accounting II and A; profits before tax; some diversified firms assigned to their primary 4-digit industries; no control for growth or capital-output ratios; apparently national 4-digit CRs for many industries with regional markets or noncompeting subproducts — if instead he used a single CR for each IRS minor industry the errors would be worse; based on one year only.

Note: the main point to this study was not to test the concentration-profits relationship as such, but to find the effect of concentration on the difference in profits between large and small firms.

Same problems as in Demsetz 1973A; also, 1969 is a year when the concentration–profits relationship is apt to be weak.

**Demsetz 1973B**

Possibly biased sample; national 4-digit CRs for many industries with regional markets or noncompeting subproducts; based on one year; no correction for advertising or central office expense; margin is before tax; possible spurious correlation because VS is denominator of both CR and margin. Note: The main purpose of this study was to find the effect of firm diversification. Diversification had a significant positive effect on margins.

**Rhodes 1973**

Accounting equity in first measure and accounting II and E in the second; some diversified firms assigned to their primary 4-digit industries; possibly biased sample; national 4-digit CRs for industries with regional markets or noncompeting subproducts; both the "size" variable and the plant size variable are highly correlated with CR so serious colinearity problem.

**Ornstein 1973**

Accounting II and E; profits before tax; "concentration" is for a varying number of leading firms (varies from 0 to 39 firms depending on the industry); it is really a measure of size, not concentration; industries are much broader than economic markets; no control for growth or capital–output ratios; 1948-1954 is a period when the concentration–profits relation is apt to be weak; £4,000,000 (about $10,000,000) seems a low value for a "large firm" cutoff.

**Whittington 1971**

Some of the 4-digit industries probably have noncompeting subproducts; price–cost margin is before tax; no control for central office expense; no control for capital–output ratio. Note: the main purpose of this study was to test the effect of collusion. He probably had better information on collusion than we will ever see again. It was based on trade association price-fixing practices and buyers' evaluation of the effectiveness of price fixing at a time when price fixing was not illegal. Nevertheless, the collusion variables were not significant and concentration was.

**Phillips 1972**

Some of the 4-digit industries probably have noncompeting subproducts; based on one year only; no control for advertising or central office expense; possible spurious correlation because price–cost margin, CR, and plant scale variable all have VS as denominator; plant scale variable highly correlated with CR.

**Shirazi 1974**

Accounting II, E and A; some diversified firms assigned to their primary 3-digit industries; 3-digit CRs, so many noncompeting subproducts; high colinearity between CR and other independent variables ($R^2 = 0.682$); single year; possibly biased sample; high imports have a positive effect on profits suggesting a simultaneous equation model where imports depend on profit rates.

**Jones, Laudadio, and Percy 1973**

Three-digit CRs, so many noncompeting subproducts; colinearity between Herfindahl index and plant scale variable ($r^2 = 0.45$).

**McFetridge 1973**

These were all taken from a summary report prepared by Uekusa in 1973. I have not seen the papers themselves so comments are less certain. All the studies seem to use accounting II and E. The concentration statistics are from the Fair Trade Commission of Japan rather than a by-product of a census. Uekusa says they are highly reliable. At least the industry definitions seem to correspond more closely to economic markets than the American Census industries do. Many of the "industries" would be 5-digit in the United States. As a result, the problem of noncompeting subproducts is largely eliminated, but the problem of diversified firms assigned to their primary industries is worsened. Uekusa says that 1956-1960 was a period of exceptionally rapid growth in Japan. Whether this means that the concentration–profits relation would be weakened is uncertain. Komiya, Niida, and Matsushiro apparently did not control for growth, and none appear to have controlled for any other variable except Uekusa. It isn't clear why the samples are so small. The samples could be biased. The scale economy variable used in Uekusa (1970) is reported as close to that used by Comanor and Wilson. If so, it is highly correlated with CR.

**Komiya 1962, Niida 1969, Matsushiro 1970, Musashi 1970, Uekusa 1970, and Musashi 1973**

Accounting II and E; probably many diversified firms assigned to their primary 4- and 5-digit industries; sample unknown but conceivably biased.

**Uekusa 1973B**

n. 74] describes 1956-1960 as a period of exceptionally rapid growth in Japan and attributes the weak relation to that cause. The Demsetz 1969 study certainly covered a year after a considerable inflation when concentrated industries had raised prices relatively slowly [MacLaren, *supra* n. 33]. I would not be surprised to find little or no relationship at present (1973).

The upshot of these studies is that the concentration—profits hypothesis is only strongly supported for normal years of relatively stable price and/or recession — 1953-1967. Hopefully such years will be our normal experience in the future.

Yale Brozen's work constitutes a third category by itself [Brozen, *supra* nn. 57 and 60]. Like a number of other writers [George, *supra* n. 34; Kamerschen, *supra* n. 34; Singer, *supra* n. 56; Weiss, *supra* n. 36], he attempts to reconstruct Bain's pioneering studies, but unlike those others, he turns to other years or other data in doing so. In one study he examined Bain's 1936-1940 [Bain, *supra* n. 35] and Stigler's 1953-1957 samples [Stigler, *supra* n. 45] in subsequent years (1953-1957 and 1962-1966). The Bain sample yielded a weaker, nonsignificant relation in 1953-1957 than Bain found in 1936-1940, but actually a stronger and clearly significant one in 1962-1966 [Brozen, *supra* n. 57, p. 287]. The Stigler sample yielded a weaker, nonsignificant relation in 1962-1966 than Stigler found in 1953-1957 [Id., p. 289]. He interprets the declining effect of concentration over time as due to the fact that the concentrated industries were out of equilibrium when observed by Bain and Stigler. This is surely possible, but it is unclear why concentrated industries as a group should have above-equilibrium profits and unconcentrated industries as a group should have below-equilibrium prices in 1936-1940 [Bain, *supra* n. 35] or 1953-1957 [Stigler, *supra* n. 45]. A plausible explanation might be that concentration fell in the intervals as a result of entry, but Brozen found that the declines in profitability occurred in industries where concentration remained high as well.[83] One alternative explanation for Brozen's findings might be that increasing diversification by firms has attenuated the correlation between their profits and CR in the industries to which they are assigned. A second possibility is that Bain's and Stigler's samples were biased. One thing that seems quite certain to me is that there was a significant positive simple correlation between profits or margins in 1953-1957 and 1962-1966 whether or not Brozen could find it for the samples left him by Bain and Stigler. There are many studies covering these periods that covered *all* manufacturing or all manufacturing except for industries with

83. In any event, the average four-firm concentration ratio for 16 of Stigler's 17 industries did not fall significantly from 1954 — 80.7 (2.3) — to 1963 — 79.0 (2.5). (Standard errors in parentheses.) Sulfur was not included because Census concentration ratios are not reported there, but Brozen says concentration was stable there also. Y. Brozen, "The Persistence of 'High Rates of Return' in High Stable Concentration Industries," *Journal of Law and Economics,* 14 (October 1971), pp. 501-512, at 510. It is impossible to make a similar statement about Bain's sample because of many changes in the industry definition and because Brozen (at 508-509) lists only high stable concentration industries.

n.e.c. or n.s.k. or miscellaneous in their titles that did find significant simple correlations. Showing that the results of two or three studies based on selected industries are weakened at a later date does *not* demonstrate that there is no relation between concentration and profits or that it deteriorates over time. To show that, Brozen would have to work with a broad, unbiased sample such as the all-manufacturing with which many of us have worked. He hasn't done that and I don't believe he can get his results for the periods he used, though he might be able to for a period like 1947-1951 or the years since 1968 when the relationship is apt to be weak.[84]

In Brozen's other paper [*supra* n. 60] he tries to re-examine pre–World War II data to see if the effect that Bain thought he saw holds up. Brozen used a much larger sample of industries than Bain did. In a number of cases the national concentration ratios that he uses are obviously inappropriate. His unconcentrated industries include the following, although they obviously sell on local or regional rather than national markets: nonalcoholic beverages, bread and bakery products, malt liquors, milk and milk products, and cement. In addition he included many industries with obvious noncompeting sub-products such as food preparations, n.e.c. (potato chips, peanut butter, coffee, etc.), drugs and medicines, perfumes, cosmetics and toiletries (toothpaste, hair oil, etc.), electrical machinery and appliances (embracing four *three*-digit industries), and special industry machinery (chemical machinery, foundry machinery, rubber working machinery, petroleum refinery equipment, tobacco industry machinery, cement machinery, glass machinery, shoe machinery, etc. — the top eight firms in this "industry" made only 11 percent of sales though the category included United Shoe Machinery, a pure monopolist).

84. Brozen dismisses the studies based on aggregates such as *all* firms reporting to the IRS or the FTC-SEC classified by 2- or 3-digit industries or *all* plants reporting to the Census classified by 4-digit industries. Aggregation can introduce biases if the wrong weights are used in combining observations or if the true relationship is not linear. On the other hand, these studies do have the great advantage that there is no selection of firms or plants made by the investigator. Moreover, the diversification problem is reduced when broad industries such as 2-digit industries are used, and largely eliminated when the Census plant data is used. Brozen's discomfort with aggregate data may derive from a famous statement of Stigler's: "The disquieting feature is the fact that profitability is better correlated with crude industry measures (food) than with more sharply defined industries (canned fruits and vegetables)." (Stigler, *The Organization of Industry* (R. D. Irwin 1968), pp. 145-146.) This idea has been repeated by J. McGee, *In Defense of Industrial Concentration* (Praeger 1971), and by R. Coase, "Industrial Organization: A Proposal for Research," in V. Fuchs, ed., *Policy Issues and Research Opportunities in Industrial Organization* (New York: National Bureau of Economic Research 1972), p. 69.

The statement seems to be misdirected. Of *all* of the studies listed in Table 11 that used 2-digit industries, only Whittington, *supra* n. 69, attempted to use 2-digit concentration indexes, and of course he got no significant effect. Happily very few investigators have attempted to use such doubtful indexes. What most of them do is to use *weighted averages* of 4-digit concentration within 2-digit industries.

The studies that depend on weighted averages for 2-digit industries do commonly

Another problem is his profit data. It is apparently based on unweighted averages of profit rates for large numbers of firms: for instance 40 in petroleum refining, 23 in motor vehicles (not parts — that is a separate industry with 64 firms), 100 in special industry machinery, 52 in electrical machinery, appliances, and supplies, and 153 in pulp and paper. Many of these must have been clearly suboptimal or specialists in subproducts that did not compete closely with the main products of the industry. In my opinion, such firms do not belong in the study. Marginal firms are very likely to earn only normal profits even when the leading firms of efficient scale are earning very high profits. And the rates of return of small specialty firms are not likely to be affected by concentration in the industry as a whole since that concentration figure depends mainly on the major products of the industry. A weighted average of profit rates would do little harm because the leading firms would dominate such an average. In an unweighted average the suboptimal or fringe market firms would dominate when 40 petroleum refiners or 23 motor vehicle companies are used.

I made an attempt to rework Brozen leaving out overinclusive industries. In general the result was a larger difference in profit rates than he found — average profit rates one to two percentage points higher in industries where the 8-firm CR exceeded 70 than in less concentrated industries — but the difference could have occurred by chance more often than one time in twenty. Further work on his data does not seem warranted because of his inclusion of many suboptimal or specialist firms. Moreover, just which industries to exclude is a matter of judgment which is apt to lead to endless argument. My own judgment is that Bain's effort to limit his study to industries with homogeneous, national markets and to leading firms was more plausible than Brozen's study, but that judgment is unlikely to convince the doubtful.

The fourth group of studies where the concentration—profits relation turns

---

yield higher correlations than those using more narrowly defined industries, but this merely reflects a well-known statistical phenomenon, and has no economic meaning. If you group men by height, you will find a great deal of variation in weight within each group due to varying diet, heredity, etc. This random variation will wash out if you take an average weight for each height. Height will be able to account for a larger percentage of variation among group means (which have eliminated intragroup variation) than among individuals (where it is retained).

The situation is similar when firms are aggregated into 2-digit industries. Intraindustry variations due to differences in luck or management are averaged out. Two-digit industries are fairly homogeneous with respect to concentration [Weiss, *supra* n. 43]. As a result, much of the variation in concentration remains in making comparisons among 2-digit industries, while most of the random variation in profitability has been averaged out. Differences in concentration among 2-digit industries can account for 30 to 50 percent of the variability in profits among them [Levinson, *supra* n. 38; Weiss, *supra* n. 43; Sherman, *supra* n. 44], but seldom more than 10 percent among 4-digit industries. This doesn't mean the 2-digit studies yield better estimates of the relationship. They may well be worse. The case for using aggregates is that the samples are less likely to be biased, not that the correlations are closer.

out to be weak involves some of those that attempt to control for plant scale and capital requirements. The plant scale variable is usually

the average shipments of the top plants
accounting for 50 percent of shipments

÷

industry shipments

This is bound to be closely correlated with the concentration ratio which amounts to

the shipments of this product by plants
of the 4 (or 8) largest firms

÷

industry shipments

The denominators are the same in the two expressions while the numerators are closely related.

The capital requirements variable is usually

$$\text{industry } \frac{K}{VS} \times \frac{\text{the average shipments of the top}}{\text{plants accounting for 50 percent of shipments}}$$

which is also closely correlated with CR. Comanor and Wilson found that in their 42 industry study these two variables accounted for 71 percent of the variation in CR and 81 percent of the variation in Log CR [Comanor and Wilson, *supra* n. 47, p. 435].

When variables are correlated in this way it is usually difficult to distinguish their separate effects. When the computer (the regression program) attempts to do so it is apt to show one or the other or both as having a nonsignificant effect, even where their joint effect is very significant.[85] Moreover, if one is distinguished as the significant variable, that result will depend on the few (often peculiar) cases where variables diverge.

In some of the studies where plant scale and/or capital requirements variables are used along with CR, concentration has a significant effect [Imel and Helmberger, *supra* n. 59; Phillips, *supra* n. 70; McFetridge, *supra* n. 73; and Uekusa, *supra* n. 70]. In others it loses its independent significance in explaining profits or margins.[86] [Comanor and Wilson, *supra* n. 47; Esposito and Esposito, *supra* n. 58; Ornstein, *supra* n. 68; Jones, et al., *supra* n. 72; and Shirazi, *supra* n. 71]. This is the sort of result that might be expected with closely correlated variables. Probably neither group of studies should be trusted in distinguishing between the effects of these variables. What most of

85. It is possible to estimate their joint effect, but none of the studies using these variables do so.

86. Ornstein [*supra* n. 68] found that concentration had a positive but nonsignificant effect in 1950 even without the scale and capital variables, as might be expected in view of the year. It had a significant effect on both profit variables used in 1955 and on the stock valuation ratio in 1960.

them do show is that the three variables together have a significant positive effect on profits or margins.

Perhaps the effects of concentration and economies of scale cannot be distinguished but I suspect they can be. The scale and capital requirements variables used in these studies are really very crude proxies that are definitionally close to the CR index. What we need is direct estimates of optimal scale and of the cost disadvantage of suboptimal plants. Quite a lot of such information is available now, but it has yet to be used in concentration–profits studies. Certainly one of the major determinants of concentration is the scale required for low costs. Yet many other things are also important in determining concentration. Bain found that most of the 20 industries he studied in the early 1950s were much more concentrated than the economies of scale dictated [Bain, *supra* n. 4]. The actual large plants used in most of these studies are often much larger than minimum efficient scale. Moreover, many of them are owned by the leading firms. Direct estimates of minimum efficient scale would be better data and should be less correlated with concentration.

Finally, a number of studies show that the effect of concentration on profits or margins is greatest for large firms [Demsetz, *supra* nn. 65 and 66], or leading firms [Collins and Preston, *supra* n. 54] or firms with high market shares [Imel and Helmberger, *supra* n. 59; Shepherd, *supra* n. 63; Gale, *supra* n. 64]. These studies all point in the same direction, but they are interpreted quite differently by their authors.

Demsetz concludes that the significant positive effect of concentration on the profits of large firms and its weak or even negative effect on the profits of small firms indicate that concentration is not measuring effectiveness of collusion. If it were, he argues, it would raise the profits of small firms as much as those of large ones. He interprets his study as indicating that the high profits of large firms in concentrated industries arise from economies of scale, superior products, or good management which the small firms cannot duplicate. While these last could easily account for a correlation between relative market share and profitability, I see no reason why that should not be true in unconcentrated as well as concentrated industries.

Moreover, the weak or generally insignificant negative effect of concentration on small firms' profits does not undermine the notion that high concentration affects profits by making tacit or explicit collusion more effective. The expectation that high profits will attract inefficient firms that could not survive in a highly competitive industry is an old one. In any case his small firms (under $5,000,000) are terribly small for most important American industries. It seems probable that in many cases they are producing quite different goods from those of the leading firms in the same, quite broadly defined IRS minor industries. When this is so, it is only natural that concentration in the main included product markets should have no effect on the small firms' profitability.

The correct test for the hypothesis that high concentration merely reflects high market shares which derive from the same source as high profits would seem to be a study that takes both market share and concentration into account at the same time. Market share should capture the effect of economies of scale, superior products, or superior management — and then some. At least in the case of dominant firms, it would also show the effect of control over price. If there is any effect left for concentration, this would surely reflect the ability of concentrated industries to act collusively. Indeed, the effect of concentration would probably be understated, since market shares of leading firms and concentration are sure to be correlated.

We have a number of such studies. In two [Imel and Helmberger, *supra* n. 59, and Gale, *supra* n. 64] the effect of concentration remains significantly positive even when market share is introduced. This is also true in Shepherd [*supra* n. 63] for consumer goods but not for producer goods. However, he stacks the deck against concentration by measuring it with (CR − MS), which is surely not right. The ability of leading firms to collude depends on the overall degree of concentration, including the shares of all leading firms. It shouldn't differ from firm to firm in the same industry. I conclude that concentration, if properly measured, would have had a greater effect.

Most authors seem to have thought it quite reasonable that concentration would have its main effect on leading firms in an industry. So do I. I have several reasons.

First, these results are quite consistent with the more plausible oligopoly theories. The leading sellers in an oligopoly would seek prices that maximize their own profits, not those of their smaller rivals. They can certainly overrule smaller rivals that would benefit from higher prices. It would normally pay them to ignore smaller rivals that choose slightly lower prices. The case where a smaller rival's optimal price is substantially lower than that of the leading firms seems certain to be rare because the low costs or superior product that such a case implies would surely turn that "independent" into a "major" in short order. If the leaders do in fact choose prices in their own rather than their smaller rivals' best interests, it should hardly surprise us if they turn out to be the main beneficiaries of high concentration. In less concentrated markets where prices are imposed by competition on the market, the industry leaders would have no such advantage.

A closely related case arises where significant product differentiation exists. Sellers with nationally advertised brands (or brands that elicit strong consumer loyalties for whatever reason) can clearly charge premium prices. It takes only a brief look at the prices of gasoline, beer, liquor, canned goods, or aspirin to realize that sellers of nonpremium brands or of distributors' brands must ordinarily sell at a noticeable discount. It is not inevitable that the leading firms sell a higher percentage of their output under premium labels, but it is difficult to find cases where this is not true. The natural result would seem to be high profits for the leaders where concentration permits them to approach profit-maximizing prices, but little effect in markets too unconcentrated to permit them such control. The premium brand explanation would fit for many consumer goods, but seldom for producer goods where high product differentiation is rare (though aircraft, computers, office equipment, and farm equipment are exceptions). This would imply that concentration should have greater effect on profits or margins in consumer goods industries than in producer goods industries. Collins and Preston [*supra* n. 50],

Shepherd [*supra* n. 63], and McFetridge [*supra* n. 73], do get that result. However, Stigler's prediction that collusion will be more effective when buyers are many and small could also explain this result.

Other reasons for expecting the main effect of concentration to accrue to leading firms are those mentioned in connection with Demsetz above. One is that the smaller firms are apt to be suboptimal producers, attracted or protected by the high prices of concentrated industries, whose high costs prevent them from earning exceptional profits. Indeed, theory would suggest that any firm would enter that could earn as high a return as that available on competitive markets. The marginal firms *should* be earning only normal profits. The presence of such high-cost firms is a socially costly result of concentration, not evidence that concentration has no competitive effect!

My guess is that the true explanation for the fact that leading firms reap the main advantages of concentration is some amalgam of the four interpretations given here. The last three really derive from oligopoly theory. Demsetz' explanation is at least consistent with it. Even if high market shares and, hence, high concentration were derived from low costs, superior products, or superior management, that does not preclude the leading firms from benefiting from an oligopolistic meeting of minds that is made possible by that high concentration. In fact, I cannot see why the same factors would not produce high profits for leading firms in unconcentrated industries if this were the only source of the concentration–profits relationship.

Altogether, I find no reason to reject the conventional interpretation of the effects of oligopoly because of these results.

## V. YET ANOTHER STUDY

The other studies listed in Table 11 generally support the expected relation between concentration and profits quite straightforwardly. However, a glance through the notes at the end of the table will show that none of them is without its faults. In trying to evaluate the relation, we must choose among imperfect alternative expressions of it. In my judgment, the price–cost margin studies minimize the main problems — the inaccuracy of accounting profits, the assignment of diversified firms to their primary industries, and the inaccurate measurement of concentration. Moreover, they reflect prices that are high relative to direct costs even when profits are only normal. I have made an attempt to correct for their major defect — failure to control for advertising and central office expenses. To do this, I took the Collins and Preston 1963 data and inserted advertising–sales ratios from the 1963 input–output matrix [Office of Business Economics, 1969] [87] and central office employment from the Enterprise Statistics [Census, 1970, *supra* n. 24]. I also tried to capture the effect of consumer goods that Collins and Preston observed by introducing the percentage of shipments that were for final consumption according to the 1963 input–output matrix. This seems better than a crude

87. Office of Business Economics, *Input-Output Structure of the U.S. Economy, 1963* (U.S.G.P.O. 1969), vol. 2.

classification of industries into producer and consumer goods categories because many industries have shipments of both sorts. The results for the Collins and Preston data with these additions appear in Tables 12 and 13.

Table 12 shows the results for those 227 4-digit industries that correspond to input–output sectors so that the advertising–shipments ratio is correct. Table 13 shows them for 399 of the 406 industries used by Collins and Preston.[88]

TABLE 12

Determinants of Price–Cost Margins
for 227 Industries that Correspond to
Input–Output Sectors (*t*-ratios in parentheses)

| Variable | (1) | (2) | (3) | (4) | (1) | (2) | (3) | (4) |
|---|---|---|---|---|---|---|---|---|
| | — All Firms' Margins | | | | Four Leading Firms' Margins | | | |
| Constant | .191 † (14.57) | .166 † (14.35) | .166 † (11.01) | .160 (10.25 ) | .206 † (11.40) | .171 † (10.68) | .171 † (8.09) | .164 † (7.45) |
| 4-Firm CR | .0010 † (4.13) | .0007 † (3.30) | .0005 * (2.34) | .0005 (1.83) | .0010 † (3.25) | .0007 * (2.25) | .0004 (1.38) | .0005 (1.23) |
| Geographic Dispersion Index | —.0003 * (—2.13) | —.0003 * (—2.44) | —.0003 * (—2.32) | —.0003 * (2.16) | —.0004 * (—2.03) | —.0004 * (—2.31) | —.0004 * (—2.25) | —.0004 * (—2.10) |
| Fixed Capital–Shipments Ratio | .103 † (4.84) | .131 † (7.04) | .0014 † (7.30) | .0014 † (7.47) | .0011 † (3.73) | .0014 † (5.56) | .0016 † (5.82) | .0016 † (5.93) |
| Advertising–Shipments Ratio | | .017 † (9.16) | .014 † (6.97) | .014 † (6.92) | | .022 † (8.58) | .019 † (6.56) | .019 † (6.48) |
| Central Office Employment ÷ Total Employment | | .0013 (0.75) | .0015 (0.80) | .0020 (1.08) | | .0025 (1.00) | .0029 (1.13) | .0033 (1.29) |
| Inventory–Shipments Ratio | | | —.0004 (—0.77) | —.0003 (—0.30) | | | —.0004 (—0.47) | —.0003 (—0.32) |
| Growth in Output 1954-1963 | | | .0014 (1.23) | .0017 (1.46) | | | .0011 (0.69) | .0014 (0.84) |
| CR × Ratio of Consumer Demand to Total Demand | | | .000008 * (2.26) | .000008 * (2.09) | | | .000011 * (2.11) | .000011 * (1.98) |
| Midpoint Plant Shipments ÷ Industry Shipments | | | | .0013 (0.90) | | | | .0008 (0.40) |
| Fixed Capital and Inventory per Dollar of Shipments × Midpoint Plant Shipments | | | | —.0004 (—1.84) | | | | —.0005 (—1.39) |
| Variation in Margins Associated with These Variables (*R²*) | .177 | .421 | .443 | .452 | .117 | .359 | .376 | .382 |

* Would not differ this much from zero by chance as often as one time in 20.
† Would not differ this much from zero by chance as often as one time in 100.

88. Industry 2819 (inorganic chemicals, n.e.c. [not elsewhere classied]) was excluded because it was split between two sectors in the input–output table. Industry 3943 (baby carriages) does not appear in the input–output matrix for some reason. Industries 2395, 3911, 3912, 3913, and 3914 were excluded because growth figures are not available for those industries.

TABLE 13

Determinants of Price–Cost Margins for 399 Industries Including Some that are Narrower than Input–Output Sectors (t-ratios in parentheses)

| Variable | All Firms' Margins | | | | Four Leading Firms' Margins | | | |
|---|---|---|---|---|---|---|---|---|
| | (1) | (2) | (3) | (4) | (1) | (2) | (3) | (4) |
| Constant | .193 † (18.86) | .174 † (19.31) | .168 (15.34) | .163 † (13.91) | .210 † (14.83) | .187 † (14.43) | .182 † (11.48) | .171 † (10.10) |
| 4-Firm CR | .0011 † (6.04) | .0007 † (3.85) | .0005 (2.76) | .0005 * (2.02) | .0013 † (5.05) | .0007 † (3.03) | .0005 * (2.00) | .0007 * (2.01) |
| Geographic Dispersion Index | −.0003 * (−2.70) | −.0003 † (−2.96) | −.0003 † (−3.04) | −.0003 * (−2.87) | −.0004 * (−2.52) | −.0004 * (−2.67) | −.0004 * (−2.76) | −.0004 * (−2.51) |
| Fixed Capital–Shipments Ratio | .0009 † (5.38) | .0010 † (6.78) | .0011 † (7.26) | .0012 † (7.45) | .0008 † (3.58) | .0010 † (4.54) | .0011 † (5.02) | .0012 * (5.27) |
| Advertising–Shipments Ratio | | .016 † (9.77) | .013 † (7.23) | .013 † (7.07) | | .019 † (8.18) | .016 † (5.91) | .015 † (5.72) |
| Central Office Employment ÷ Total Employment | | .0021 (1.59) | .0020 (1.46) | .0023 (1.71) | | .0024 (1.28) | .0025 (1.27) | .0028 (1.40) |
| Inventory–Shipments Ratio | | | −.0003 (−0.69) | −.0002 (−0.45) | | | −.0004 (−0.64) | −.0002 (−0.36) |
| Growth in Output 1954–1963 | | | .0023 * (2.64) | .0026 † (2.86) | | | .0023 (1.80) | .0026 * (2.01) |
| CR × Ratio of Consumer Demand to Total Demand | | | .000008 † (2.75) | .000008 † (2.78) | | | .000011 * (2.55) | .000011 † (2.63) |
| Midpoint Plant Shipments ÷ Industry Shipments | | | | .0010 (0.73) | | | | −.0002 (−0.11) |
| Fixed Capital and Inventory per Dollar of Shipments × Midpoint Plant Shipments | | | | −.0003 (−1.65) | | | | −.0005 (−1.80) |
| Variation in Margins Associated with These Variables (R²) | .199 | .400 | .422 | .427 | .128 | .284 | .311 | .317 |

* Would not differ this much from zero by chance as often as one time in 20.
† Would not differ this much from zero by chance as often as one time in 100.

The first four columns of each table show the relationship for the margins of all plants in the industry. The last four do so for the margins of plants operated by the four leading firms in the industry. All of the variables other than margins used in either table are for the entire industries.

The columns labeled (1) show the results using the variables in Collins and Preston. Columns (2) include advertising and central office employment variables as well. The effect of advertising on margins is very powerful. The effect of central office employment is much weaker, probably because of the crudeness of the measure used. It refers to employment, not expense, and it is reported for industries broader than 4-digit in most cases. The effect of concentration remains significant in all four cases when these two variables are included. It is notable that the somewhat stronger effect of concentration on margins of the four leading firms falls to industry-wide levels when advertising is taken into account. This suggests that the main reason for the greater payoff to leading firms lies in their control over premium brands.

The columns labeled (3) include the concentration ratio times the ratio of consumer demand to total demand. In these equations the coefficients for 4-firm concentration themselves show the effect of concentration of margins for nonconsumer sales. The effect of concentration on margins for consumer sales is the sum of that coefficient and 100 times the last one in columns (3). The effect on margins for consumer sales is significantly positive in all four cases. It is significantly positive for industrial sales for all-firm margins in both samples, but the effect on leading firms' margins on industrial producer goods sales drops to nonsignificance in the 227 industry sample.

Columns (3) also include two other variables which might be expected to affect margins. The inventory–sales ratio and the average annual percentage rate of growth in physical output are based on Census indexes of industrial production for 1954 through 1963. Inventories are included as part of capital. They have essentially no effect. Growth is included to allow for short-run disequilibria due to unanticipated changes in demand of costs. It has the expected positive effect but it is usually nonsignificant. Finally, in columns (4), plant scale and capital requirements variables are also introduced because of their controversial effects in other studies. A "midpoint" plant scale variable is used. This is the estimated shipment size of a plant at the midpoint in the industry shipments array. Half the industry's output comes from larger plants and half from smaller plants. In virtually all industries for which economies of scale studies have been made, more than half of American output comes from plants of minimum optimal scale or greater.[89] This means that the midpoint plant is at least of minimum efficient scale in virtually all industries. At the same time, it is much less likely to be dependent on the plants of the four leading

---

89. This is true of the 20 industries studied by Bain [*supra* n. 4], the 12 by Scherer [1973], and the 25 for which Pratten gave estimates, C. F. Pratten, *Economies of Scale in Manufacturing Industry* (Cambridge Univ. Press 1971). It is also true of tentative estimates I have made for quite a number of other industries. One probable exception is diesel engines, where I have been told that optimal scale is greater than the total national output.

firms. The variables used are midpoint plant shipments divided by industry shipments and midpoint plant shipments times industry capital–shipments ratios. These variables are still highly correlated with CR (47 percent of the variability in CR can be explained by the first variable and 20 percent by the second). However, concentration retains its significance in Tables 12 and 13 when these variables are introduced. The strange negative effect of the capital requirements variable seems to be due to its correlation with CR, the capital–sales ratio, and the scale variable. The simple relationship between the capital requirements variables and margins is positive, but the other three variables seem to capture its entire effect when they are introduced together.

It might be that the observed concentration–margin relationship is due entirely to dominant firms where theory seems uncontroversial. However, when the industries of the dominant firms listed in Table 10 were left out the results were virtually the same. They support the common prediction of oligopoly theory.

This rework of Collins and Preston still has its faults. Concentration is not accurately measured in some cases. The margin used includes taxes. And the fixed capital variable is derived from accounting measures and excludes financial assets. Nevertheless, I feel that the effects reported in columns (4) are quite meaningful. Concentration did seem to make a substantial difference in determining the ratio of price to direct cost in manufacturing in 1973.

## VI.  CONCLUSION

To summarize, the theory of the dominant firm unequivocally points to high prices and suggests high profit rates for dominant firms. Our assorted oligopoly theories are more equivocal in their details, but all of them that have not been discredited point to higher margins in concentrated industries once more. Our massive effort to test these predictions has, by and large, supported them for "normal" years such as the period 1953-1967, though the concentration–profits relationship is weakened or may even disappear completely in periods of accelerating inflation or directly following such periods. By and large the relationship holds up for Britain, Canada, and Japan, as well as in the United States. In general the data have confirmed the relationship predicted by theory, even though the data are very imperfect and almost certainly biased toward a zero relationship.

In my opinion, the several studies that have seemed to weaken the concentration–profits relation in recent years have not done much damage. Some are blatantly erroneous. Brozen has at best shown that a relationship found for a particular sample was weakened in some subsequent years. Since many studies covering the same years and including all or virtually all of manufacturing show a strong relationship, the most that Brozen may have done is to criticize two or three samples. The studies that show that the main effect of concentration is on large or leading firms' profits or margins merely confirm what most industrial organization economists had expected. The studies that use plant scale and capital requirements variables do seem to indicate that it is difficult to distinguish between the effect of those and that of concentration, but this is probably due to the plant scale data used. At any rate, they certainly do not disprove that concentration makes collusion more effective and margins higher as a result. The most efficient size of plant might dictate the degree of concentration, but this is quite consistent with collusion being the cause of the related high prices.

Altogether, there is still plenty of reason to believe on both theoretical and empirical grounds that high concentration facilitates tacit or explicit collusion. To me this means that the present policy of prohibiting horizontal merger among viable firms whenever significant concentration is present or in prospect is well founded. Even if some of the relationship between profits and concentration (or more likely, market shares) reflects the success of efficient firms, as Demsetz contends, that would be no argument for the creation of other firms with large market shares by merger. It would be an argument for letting firms retain large market shares that they attain by internal growth. By and large, this has been our policy.

Mergers among clearly suboptimal firms should probably not be prevented, and they seldom are in practice. In the 18 horizontal merger cases initiated by the Antitrust Division in calendar years 1968-1970 where market shares were cited in the complaints, the average market share of the *acquired* firm was 14 percent.[90] Market shares are probably exaggerated somewhat in these complaints, but the exaggeration would have to be wild for the average merger attacked to involve clearly suboptimal firms. At any rate, I would oppose an explicit exemption for economies of scale in the merger law or in judicial decisions (except for the failing firm doctrine). I would expect such an exemption to result in a great flowering of legal argument that would make the merger rule much harder to enforce and would probably result in many economically undesirable mergers. The debacle when the ICC admitted economies as an argument in railroad mergers is a blatant example. Every merger proposal carried with it estimates of spectacular economies, few of which seem to have been realized after the mergers were consummated. The present system, where the Antitrust Division and the FTC generally avoid cases against mergers among suboptimal firms but have very powerful precedents when they do bring cases, may permit occasional arbitrary decisions, but it seems to me to be the better of two imperfect alternatives. It probably does prevent an occasional useful merger and some harmless ones, but the social cost of this cannot be great. The main way to attain economies of scale is to build larger plants. Merger may facilitate this in some cases, but if the gains from scale are large, industries can probably be counted on to move to optimal scale plants quite quickly with or without merger.

We can also draw conclusions with respect to structural monopolization cases under Section 2 of the Sherman Act. Dominant firms are expected to have especially high margins in virtually everyone's theory, and my crude tabulation in Table 10 suggests that they generally do. This may be due to

90. L. Weiss, "An Analysis of the Allocation of Anti-Trust Division Resources," in R. H. Haveman et al., eds., *Benefit–Cost and Policy Analysis, 1973* (Aldine 1974), pp. 330-355.

economies of scale or superior business acumen or to a valid patent, or it may derive from long dead patents or from ancient mergers plus high barriers to entry. Monopolization cases may or may not be in the public's interest depending on what the mix of these causes may be. Each case should be examined separately to determine the source of the market power. This seems in fact to be the law.

The critics of the concentration–profits doctrine have oriented their comments toward the "Concentrated Industry Act" proposed by the Neal Task Force[91] or the Hart Bill.[92]

I personally am not terribly enthused about these proposals, especially the Hart Bill, which would establish a prima facie case for dissolution for firms with market shares over 15 percent in markets where the 4-firm concentration ratio persistently exceeds 50 and even in some specified industries less concentrated than that. These numbers are low enough to involve a large proportion of our major firms. The cost of such a law in confusion and litigation would be huge, and the problem of large firms pulling their punches to stay below the magic number would be far more widespread than it is today. The Neal Task Force proposal is less subject to this criticism because the critical concentration ratio is higher ($CR_4 = 70$), so fewer firms would be affected. The probability that either bill will be enacted soon seems low. I doubt that this is the best place for those seeking a more competitive economy to expend their energies. Changes in the rules to make natural gas pipelines and high voltage transmission lines into common carriers, to eliminate minimum rate regulation by the ICC and the CAB, to permit cable TV companies to import unlimited numbers of channels (e.g., from the 10 or 15 other English speaking TV networks in the world), or to require automobile companies to sell cars to all financially competent retailers (e.g., Sears) seem to me to be much more useful places to expend our efforts.

# Dialogue*

*Richard Posner:* Professor Demsetz, I think your theory that the concentration–profits relationship reflects large firm efficiency suffers from the same theoretical problem as the alternative theory of monopoly and collusion.

You point to the market concentration doctrine as failure to deal with the problem of entry and anticipation. Presumably, if the formation of monopolies were anticipated, or if entry were instantaneous, there would be no gains from monopolizing. So if monopolies or cartels would be a problem in the absence of antitrust laws, it must be because of either imperfect foresight or lags in entry.

Now, your theory has the same characteristics. The notion of persistent profits to successful firms implies, it seems to me, lags or imperfections in the capture of efficiency by whatever people in the firm are responsible for their differences in efficiency. It is a standoff between two theories, each of which is incomplete in the sense that neither explains these elements of imperfect foresight or lag.

*Demsetz:* No, it is not a standoff, because until they alter the market concentration doctrine — which I am sure they will do — they do not have a way of explaining the absence of correlation for moderate-sized firms between concentration and profit rates.

*Posner:* I disagree because it seems to me that both theories are capable of predicting the same thing. The reason is that if you have a cartel or monopolized industry where price exceeds cost, that will attract into the industry those firms whose costs are higher than the existing firms' costs. Those firms which have higher costs would tend, I presume, to remain small because by definition they are less efficient. They survive in the industry only because of an excess of price over cost. Now, why isn't that just as good an explanation as your explanation for the difference between profitability of large and small firms?

*Demsetz:* I did explicitly say that the data are consistent with this explanation, although I have some troubles with it that we haven't discussed; but the policy implications are very different than those derived from the market concentration doctrine.

*Posner:* It would be interesting if you were able to show not only that the policy implications of the two theories were the same, but that there was some basis in existing knowledge why we should prefer your theory with its theoretical problems.

*Demsetz:* Would you feel happier if there were no correlation between concentration and rates of return for the large firms, so that prices are always close to cost in all those industries? That is what the data tend to show, that all these correlations are disappearing. This is especially true when the role of concentration is separated from that of advertising.

*Weiss:* There are two other reasons why small firms might show little relationship between concentration and profits. First, in many cases they are in different industries. We are using IRS minor industries, which are very broad. Second, in consumer goods industries the leading firms typically have well-known brands; the minor firms are selling dealers' brands in large part and can't possibly get the same margins.

*Victor Kramer:* Professor Weiss, do you think on the whole the Celler-Kefauver Act has been effectively enforced?

*Weiss:* With respect to the enforcement of it, I have two points.

First, that is the one place in antitrust where you can clearly see that it has made a difference. And I am quoting Stigler again. There has been a sharp drop in horizontal and vertical mergers over time as a result.

Second, you can criticize some cases and some decisions as prohibiting probably harmless mergers and occasionally useful mergers. I think that criticism does not stand up well when you look at the cases actually brought as opposed to some of the decisions that have been made in the courts.

I went through the complaints of the Antitrust Division from 1968 to 1971, and for those that gave market shares, the average market share of the acquired firm was 11 percent. This obviously depends on how you define markets, and they have an incentive to inflate it. The one year I was at the Antitrust Division, 1969 to 1970, I found what I considered sensible decisions being made in this area regularly. So I guess I would say it was effectively enforced.

Mr. Dewey pointed out that an attempt to deregulate the economy would involve the destruction of a lot of capitalized values of innocent bystanders. Here is one area where that is not a problem. In the case of merger, if it's merger for monopoly or has the effect of increasing concentration seriously, such gains as are attained represent a new redistribution of wealth in favor of merging firms.

*Kramer:* Professor Demsetz, if you were a member of the House, would you vote to repeal the Celler-Kefauver Act?

*Demsetz:* Yes, if it continues to be enforced as in recent years. I might say that one of the things that would be interesting to look at, in those industries where mergers have taken place, is what has happened to product prices. In this way we might be able to judge whether there are some advantages to allowing mergers that we currently forbid.

*Donald Turner:* Mr. Demsetz, am I correct in understanding that you would have no antimerger law at all?

*Demsetz:* If I could have an antimerger law that did only what we wanted it to do, I would embrace it. If we have to settle for an antimerger law that prohibits mergers that result in efficiency as well as other kinds of mergers, then my answer is no.

*Turner:* Wouldn't you make some sort of effort to formulate a law that would do this?

*Demsetz:* My answer to that is no, because I do not believe that fine tuning is a good policy, either in macropolicy, that is, in monetary policy, or in micropolicy where the issues really are much more complex than they are in the world of money and inflation.

*Turner:* I would agree with you on the fine tuning. I don't see any possibility of fine tuning any antimerger laws.

*Demsetz:* But that is what you are asking, aren't you?

*Turner:* No, I am not. I am asking if it is not possible to formulate an antimerger law which will not stop efficiency mergers.

*Demsetz:* My answer to that is no, any more than you could formulate a Robinson-Patman Act that would not stop competitive pricing.

*Phil Neal:* Just to complete the record, I want to ask Professor Demsetz whether he would also repeal the Sherman Act.

*Demsetz:* The answer is: as it is presently being carried out, yes.

*Louis Schwartz:* If by fine tuning you mean you disclaim any efforts to assess, on the one hand, the device as a means of colluding, and on the other hand, the device as a means of enhancing efficiency, then it seems to me you do consistently have to advocate a repeal of Section 1 because there are a lot of arrangements which don't involve formal merger which also enhance efficiency — and if that is what fine tuning means, it seems to me it is all gone, isn't it?

*Demsetz:* I think you would get most of the benefits you desire from a policy which made it illegal to enter into explicit contractual arrangements to collude.

*Schwartz:* Is a horizontal merger an explicit contract to collude?

*Demsetz:* In a situation in which you had no legal restrictions on entry? If you had no legal restraint on entry and illegal collusive contracts, I think you would accomplish 90 percent of what you seek in terms of eliminating monopoly without all the costs that arise from fine tuning.

*Schwartz:* Are you calling a horizontal merger an explicit contract to collude?

*Demsetz:* I guess I am not, no.

*Milton Handler:* Putting to one side the imperfections of the data, and assuming that you find a correlation between concentration as you define it and profitability, I wonder whether you could explain to those who are not as well versed as you econometricians *how* you determine, in developing this correlation, that the degree of profitability is something which is economically and socially wrong?

*Weiss:* A theoretical answer would be that the norm would be the opportunity cost of raising capital — what you could get on your capital and your best alternative employment.

*Handler:* How do you determine that?

*Weiss:* In these regression studies, the implicit norm is the profit rates that occur in unconcentrated industries on the average.

*Handler:* How do you know that that may not be too low? Why do you take that as the optimum?

*Weiss:* Well, I could give two answers. One, the unconcentrated industries seem to be able to raise capital. You don't find them continuously pressed for capital, unable to expand, which I would read to mean that they do indeed cover their opportunity cost of capital. Two, the rates of return in those industries — if you take rates of return on equity after tax — run something like 8 percent. And I am not talking about the present inflated period; I am talking about the fifties and sixties. Those are substantial rates of return, compared with the yields that you get on the stock market or the interest rates on long-term securities. And so, by both standards, I would say that on the average it approximates opportunity cost of capital.

*Handler:* How great is the excess over the norm that causes you concern?

*Weiss:* In the studies it is about half again as large. That is, a 50-point increase in the concentration ratio will typically increase profit rates by about half. As I told you, I believe that there is systematic bias that understates high profits and overstates low, and there are also biases in the independent variable. And I would therefore judge that true economic profits in the highly concentrated industries on the average exceed those in the unconcentrated industries by a good deal more than half. This is rate of return on equity.

*Handler:* Let me ask you this: If inflation is going to remain with us over time

— and there is good reason to believe that this is so, and it certainly has been the experience in recent years — then what happens to all of your studies? Because you say it doesn't apply to inflationary periods.

*Weiss:* I am not certain. I would not be surprised to find that if we have a long period of anticipated inflation, the concentration–profits relationship will show up. But we haven't had that experience yet. And so I can't really predict very accurately. It is conceivable that this problem will be weak during a period of long-term anticipated inflation. I suppose something you might want to do would be to look in Brazil or Britain today. I guess I wouldn't believe the Brazilian accounting figures but the British might be credible.

*Mark Green:* I have a comment and a question for Mr. Demsetz on something both speakers mentioned in passing. Mr. Demsetz blamed monopoly power in this country on a city fifty miles away, and I think regulatory commissioners can be monopoly makers. But why do they have this disposition? I don't think they are a small band of willful men from birth, genetically hostile to competition. I think the reason is that most of the industries want to be regulated because they benefit from regulation. The cause of monopoly is the same, corporations seeking monopoly. I don't think you should point to Washington as an abstraction, but to corporations that seek what they can get.

When you urge the dismantlement of regulation, I assume you mean ICC and CAB, and not safety regulations such as DOT over car safety, Health, Education and Welfare, and so on.

*Demsetz:* I was really directing my attention to the regulatory agencies that you describe. I am not prepared now to discuss other agencies such as Health and Welfare. I think those agencies can be used fairly well for the same objective, for example, to keep out foreign competition or make it more costly for foreign automobiles to compete in this country.

I discussed briefly in my paper why I thought it was advantageous to monopolize through regulation as compared with trying to monopolize in the marketplace. I didn't mean to imply that the regulatory agencies were selling monopoly power to these companies, although I don't know any reason to deny that either.

I was arguing that we should make it difficult for the government to sell monopoly power. Whether the impetus comes from the firms or whether it comes from Washington, D.C., I want to stop it.

*James Rahl:* Professor Dewey seemed to agree that the evidence was weak on correlation between profits and concentration. Nevertheless, he concluded that there are some fears about concentration that may be a bit more strongly based because of the fear of discretionary power held by highly concentrated industries. Professor Demsetz, are you saying there are no legitimate concerns about concentration? Or are you limiting your conclusion to the lack of proof on profitability?

*Demsetz:* I am not saying there are no legitimate concerns, whether we look at the broader issue or whether we look at the narrower issue. What I am saying is that the policies we have — and I include antitrust as well as regulation — are not well designed to deal with such problems at a cost that is worth bearing.

I am convinced that antitrust can be used almost as well to protect competitors as can regulatory procedures. When someone comes out with a very successful product and takes markets away from others, he stands a good chance of being sued in the antitrust courts for monopolizing the industry.

Also, what is meant by "discretionary powers" I pass to Mr. Weiss or Mr. Dewey, since I don't know what is meant by the term.

*Rahl:* Harold, are you saying that you are "sort of" in favor of deconcentration?

*Demsetz:* No, I am saying there may be situations in which, in the normal course of market operation, there may be some monopoly power for a period of time. If we could surgically cut out this monopoly power without bearing the costs of frequently penalizing efficiency and competition, I would say, "I am certainly for it." I just don't believe it is possible to do that. The costs of trying would greatly exceed the potential benefits.

*Joseph Brodley:* As I understand it, one flaw in the statistical analyses in the concentration–profits relationship is that the Census data do not necessarily in many cases reflect real markets. I am just wondering what can be done to develop some data which would more precisely indicate true markets.

*Weiss:* I know a couple of possibilities. One that I have thought was desirable for a long time was to try to arrive at a consensus as to what did constitute approximately correct industries among economists.

I once proposed to Mr. Blair that for a selected group of industries, where we could get consensus that there was interindustry competition, we ask for concentration data at a three-digit or even higher level.\*

You could go in the other direction and make a survey of the people who are seriously interested in the field and try to find instances where people can agree that the appropriate concentration measure or the appropriate market measure would be at a seven-digit level, where I am sure it does belong in some instances. I am sure there would be differences of opinion, but on quite a number of these I think that there would be agreement.

One qualification: I'd want to limit it to people who had looked very seriously at the data. There are a lot of people who have pushed this stuff around and not looked seriously at it; we need careful selection of participants.

In Japan, as I understand it, the concentration data are not collected by the census. They are collected by an agency with a function something like that of the FTC. According to Caves and a man from Japan with whom he works, Uekusa, these are economically much more sensible data.

I think for the FTC to collect that kind of data would require them to get market shares from individual firms, and individual firms in this country have

---

\* Industries are defined by the Bureau of the Census in terms of S.I.C. (Standard Industrial Classification) categories. Categories range from broad, where there are few digits (e.g., food and kindred products is a two-digit category), to narrow (e.g., candy and other confectionery products is a four-digit category). See Betty Bock, *Concentration, Oligopoly, and Profit: Concepts vs. Data* (New York: The Conference Board 1972).

resisted that very, very strongly. Only once in history have they been able to get it, and even then it had to be done by the Census definition.

*Demsetz:* It is always difficult to resist an appeal for better data. Yet there may be very legitimate reasons, other than, say, a desire to avoid prosecution under the antitrust laws — legitimate reasons in terms of making the competitive economy work better — for not supplying very private data of one sort or another. There is a real problem in competing of keeping information from competitors. The possible cost of reducing competitive incentives must be taken account of, as must the direct cost of producing additional data.

*Frederic Scherer:* Thus far we have been looking mainly at the relationship between concentration and one kind of monopoly burden — namely the burden of excessively high profits.

It has been mentioned, but largely passed over, that there might be other kinds of burdens that the books simply don't show up — namely the possibility that where there is monopoly power the costs of particular industries might be too high. Indeed, these costs might be so high that any profit relationships disappear.

Now, in the United States context, it is rather difficult to measure this phenomenon. The United States is a very large market in general, and by and large is operated, I think, rather competitively. Our changes in policy also have been for the most part rather gradual, so it is difficult to observe a trend from monopoly to competition under fairly similar circumstances.

One might well ask me what have I been doing. Why did I choose to spend a couple of years in Europe recently? The reason is simple. Europe is a marvelous experimental laboratory for industrial organization. There have been dramatic changes in Europe over the past few years, first of all by the passage and, at least in some countries, the vigorous enforcement of anticartel policies; the opening of the European Common Market and European Free Trade Association has created new winds of collaboration.

My colleagues and I, and Professor Swan and his associates from England, have, among other things, been looking at the effects of sudden changes in competitive conditions on costs. The evidence in general tends not to be nearly as clearly defined, as seemingly precise, as the profit evidence. But there seems to be an overwhelming tendency that when competition has increased sharply, there has been shortly thereafter a major effort by the industries to reduce their costs, and there have been very notable reductions in cost.

To the extent that monopoly persists, to the extent that these winds of competition are not allowed to blow, something may be going on that we simply can't observe in our regression analyses — namely, much higher costs. This is a burden, I suspect, which is much more important than the burden of high profits.

*Yale Brozen:* Professor Weiss sloughs off Demsetz' correlations because they involve three-digit industries. And yet, the correlations on concentrations of profitability for which Weiss seems to have the most respect are three-digit and two-digit correlations. Why does Weiss slough them off in Demsetz' case and take them very seriously in his own context?

*Weiss:* I think there is a good case for using broadly defined industries when your dependent variable is company profit rate, because many firms are diversified out of four-digit industries but not out of two-digit.

*Brozen:* Isn't that a reason for accepting them?

*Weiss:* I'd say that is a case for Mr. Demsetz' work as well. The point I was making is that in a two- or three-digit industry, I think you are seeing firms in different industries. That is, they are in the same two-digit industry, but the large firms are steel companies and the small firms are foundries, or the large firms are primary aluminum and the small firms are secondary aluminum — things like that.

I would guess that much of the difference between the effect of concentration on the profitability of the large firms and the profitability of the small firms is that the concentration figure is approximately right for the large firms, but for many of the small firms it is not.

*Brozen:* But isn't that equally true of your groups of firms in your three-digit and two-digit categories in your other studies?

*Weiss:* That is true. To that extent, the other studies are imperfect; it is the imperfection I mentioned before with respect to diversification in the data.

*William Baxter:* I'd like to come back to the point that Mr. Scherer just made because I think it's a very important one. Other things being equal, I think there is very good reason to suppose that the possession of monopoly power might impact cost consciousness as well as profitability, since it is a much bigger chunk of the income measure.

This seems to me to have very direct connections with Demsetz' reservations about our present antimerger policy. Certainly the most effective social countermeasure to that kind of cost insensitivity is the takeover merger, where the effectiveness of capital markets can come into play in offsetting some of the sluggishness, if indeed there is sluggishness, in product markets; the shares of a badly run company will fall and make it a good takeover target.

In this context, the recklessness with which the preliminary injunction has been used, especially in hotly contested mergers, inhibits proper application of Section 7 standards. I think the overuse of preliminary injunctions impairs the performance of capital markets and is seriously affecting the monopoly problem.

*Ira Millstein:* Professor Weiss, I read your paper with great interest and was disappointed only in the conclusion because it seemed to me inconsistent with everything you had done up to that point. You go through all the statistics and demonstrate satisfaction with them, but in the end you don't seem to have enough confidence in them to base a deconcentration policy on them. You walk away from 80 pages of analysis and state that you don't have enough on which to base a deconcentration policy.

On the other hand, I can't see the logic of being in favor of a merger policy. If your data aren't good enough for a deconcentration policy, why are they good enough for an antimerger policy? What is the distinction? I just don't see the consistency of your position.

I see Demsetz' position as consistent. He is against everything.

I don't quite see your position to be consistent, and I wondered how you explained it. Is there a logical explanation?

*Weiss:* I think I can make one. First of all, my major reason for being ho-hum about vast deconcentration bills is that I am absolutely certain that there isn't a chance in the world of their ever coming about. If there were a good chance of their coming about, I'd have to think about it more carefully. I think I'd still be very skeptical about adopting such a policy.

It is not because I think concentration has no effect on profits or costs. It is because there are costs to a deconcentration policy. There are several of those costs.

One is the famous disruption. You are taking a going concern and tearing it apart. This didn't seem to bother Jimmy Ling, but I sympathize with judges who are uncomfortable about it.

Another is the point that Mr. Dewey made, that where a firm has an established monopoly or where you have established monopoly profits and they have been capitalized, you are confiscating the properties of some innocent bystanders.

A third point is that I can't imagine our adopting such a policy that would not in fact involve enormous litigation costs. I personally am skeptical about small dissolution cases even in the case of dominant firms, partly because of the enormous cost of the very limited antitrust resources we have, a budget of $17 million a year.

And fourth, I believe there is a danger that if you had a rule that a market share of 15 percent or higher established a presumption for dissolution that could only be rebutted by economies of scale or superior product or something like that, then there would just be many, many firms which would have a strong incentive to pull their punches.

It might be in the best interest of the stockholders that such firms would spin off some of their resources voluntarily. But much more likely, it would mean a lessening of competition.

The law we have now in Section 2 applies to a half-dozen firms in the country at the most. There is an old tradition that GM has not taken full advantage of its position, has not fought as hard as it could, because it was afraid of its market share rising. I am not sure if that is true or not. There is so much uncertainty about the application of the law that I doubt whether GM puts much weight on that. But if you had a hundred firms instead of a half-dozen in that position, I think it could be costly to society.

I don't see any of these problems with the merger law.

*Schwartz:* I, too, find an inconsistency between the hard line on mergers and the resistance to deconcentration. I recognize there are costs in a deconcentration program that do not come up when you have a preventive program. But I don't think we should talk about a deconcentration program as if we were just inventing it. There is a deconcentration program in Section 11 of the Public Utility Holding Company Act of 1935, and I would like to ask your views about it.

*Weiss:* I have often used that example in class. Some aspects, such as the elimination of combination utilities in most of the holding companies, clearly had a proper competitive effect. In some instances, the public utility holding companies that were created have become industry leaders in technology. I somewhat agree that the deconcentration program under Section 11 was a healthy development. My major reason for not jumping on the deconcentration bandwagon is that I think it's a hopeless cause.

*Posner:* I think the holding company example is inapposite. As the title of the act suggests, it involved the matter of dissolving holding companies themselves rather than dissolving a firm. Similarly, if you look at the old dissolution of the Standard Oil Trust, the Standard Oil Trust was in the form of a holding company and the act of dissolution was to dissolve the holding company and simply distribute the shares to the stockholders. Now, that didn't deal with any of the problems that should have been faced in trying to restructure the oil industry.

The theoretical question has become positioned as to whether private firms are capable of attaining monopoly power; if the answer is yes, then it seems we should be concerned about concentration on theoretical grounds. I think that is wrong.

I ask Professor Weiss to spell out the theory that connects concentration to profits. You made reference, and Demsetz also, to Stigler's theory. If you go back to that paper, Stigler points out there are a number of factors which are relevant to the gains from tacit collusion. And he points to the conditions on the buying side of the industry and implicitly to the conditions of entry and greater entry, to the nature of the product being sold, whether under standard contract or custom-made. But I don't get from that any strong suggestion that information on a number of firms alone would point you toward those industries in which you expect to find monopolization.

*Weiss:* It is one of the variables. I agree that size and character of the buyer is surely another one of the variables. And it is one that has been largely omitted from our studies, largely because of lack of data.

There are other oligopoly theories. I think in terms of Stigler as one of the competing oligopoly theories today, and both Chamberlin and Stigler picture the effect of concentration to facilitate collusion. But there are certainly other things that facilitate collusion. I certainly don't say that they should be ignored.

*Posner:* But what I was wondering, supposing deconcentration — would you be saying we should be applying it to industries in which the buying side is unconcentrated or in which the rate of entry of new firms seems to be slow? Why is it that policy is fascinated with a number of firms and doesn't look at the other variables at all, or even try to measure the relative importance of the variables?

*Weiss:* If you say deconcentration is costless, then you have to be on the side of deconcentration. But I find it almost impossible to respond to that idea. With respect to the other variables, I guess if I were applying the law, I would be much more concerned about concentration in industries where buyers are many and small than in industries where buyers are large and well-informed. I guess I would be much more concerned about concentration in industries where I perceive entry barriers to be substantial than in industries where I feel entry barriers are minor.

One of my dominant firms was Boeing for the 1960s. Boeing didn't have much monopoly power because right on the edge of the market sat a half-dozen other aircraft manufacturers which were quite capable at any moment, it appeared, of producing aircraft if the opportunity arose. And I guess I don't perceive anybody on the edge of the cigarette market in anywhere near the same position.

*Handler:* I am wondering whether the data that you have studied so carefully would provide any answer to a problem that has always vexed me.

You take four-company concentration ratios, whether they be 70 percent, which will trigger action, or 50 percent. And you are going to do something about it. You are not going to reduce them to 2 or 3 percent. Presumably, if I understand any of these proposals, you would be content if you made eight out of four. My question is this: If you convert four into eight, do you have any evidence that the degree of profitability will be any different when you have eight than when you have four? And if there is a difference, is it a significant difference?

*Weiss:* Over the whole range of concentration, I think all of these studies address what you are talking about. That is, at some point reducing concentration, if you believe the studies, will reduce profitability. But that is not really what I am after. I want to reduce price; profit is merely an index that I can get my hands on.

Over the range of concentration these bills talk about — and especially the Neal Bill, the Concentrated Industry Act, where you are starting off with a concentration ratio of 70 — I just can't answer the question and I don't think anybody can.

That is essentially what I was after when I attempted to distinguish between the critical concentration ratio idea and the Stigler idea. And, as I said, though I produced reams and reams of printout and struggled and struggled and struggled, I was never able to come to a convincing solution, and I don't think I have seen a convincing solution. There are some studies that seem to show critical concentration ratios — a four-firm of 50 or an eight-firm of 70; Bain's original study seemed to show that. There are others where it is almost impossible to determine such a break.

I just don't have any confidence in their details. I do have confidence that, over a wide range, reducing concentration would reduce price–cost margins.

I am equally uncertain as to whether reducing concentration from 70 to 50 — from 70 to 40, I'd be willing to bet, would do something — from 70 to 50 would really change things very much. In Stigler's theory it would. In Chamberlin's theory it might, if we crossed that critical line. I don't even know if that critical line exists. As far as the statistical evidence goes, I am afraid the answer has to be we don't know.

I guess I do believe the country is better off with two firms in an industry instead of one, with four instead of two, and so forth, provided there are no losses in efficiency.

*Handler:* That is based on esthetic instead of economic reasoning.

*Weiss:* I am afraid you're right.

*Demsetz:* We are giving this problem some thought at UCLA. We don't have any definitive answers, but there is some light that can be shed on it.

You can rationalize some of my data in the following way: in concentrated industries the cost to the larger firms is lower. That is why their profit rates tend to be higher than for the smaller firms in those industries.

Let us suppose that the larger firms in concentrated industries are colluding, and that is what keeps the price up. But the collusion keeps price at a low enough level that the next size firms do not make higher profit rates in concentrated industries than they do in unconcentrated industries.

Therefore, the price that is set by the large firms in the concentrated industries is approximately at a level that just covers the cost of the next-size-down firms in those industries. If you break apart the large firms in those industries and convert them into the next-size-down firms, you will not lower price at all. Price will stay where it is. One answer to your question, then, is that there is little to be gained from deconcentration; yet, there will be loss of large firm efficiency.

*Schwartz:* Dick Posner countered my earlier remarks concerning Section 11 by saying: "Well, that was just a holding company business. All that was required was to take the stock and sell it." But to suggest that the desirability of a deconcentration program turns on whether AT&T has separately incorporated Western Electric, or on whether General Motors has separately incorporated its divisions, seems to me the ultimate in legalism. If deconcentration is desirable, all we have to do is to tell these entities to organize their divisions as separate corporations and unload the stock.

*Weiss:* Professor Posner may be right, because what the public utility holding company did was to provide for the division of holdings that were not integral, for instance geographically separate. And so there was more than the legal distinction with respect to dividing electric companies. However, I think Professor Schwartz is right when it comes to electricity and gas. They were typically in the same communities.

*David Martin:* In the process of asking his question, Professor Handler made the assertion, which I have also heard other places, that the industrial reorganization bill that Senator Hart introduced rests in some sense upon the findings that are being debated now — that is, whether profits turn out to be highly correlated with concentration ratios.

I don't know what Senator Hart's position on this question would be, but from my standpoint — and I have had some role in the drafting of the bill — the reason for having a separate profit rebuttable presumption and separate pricing rebuttable presumption is that there is not a perfect correlation between profit and concentration. And if there were, it would be pointless to have both presumptions.

There can be monopoly without profit, for reasons several people have pointed out. There can be high concentration without monopoly. There can be noncompetitive pricing without high concentration and without high profits.

The point of the bill is to shift the burden of proof so that the long litigation, which has always existed in any attempt by any enforcement officials to re-structure, will be simplified.

*Demsetz:* Why do you want to say that the firms are guilty until they prove themselves innocent? Why is that a judicially acceptable precept? We don't use it in other instances.

*Martin:* It is not a criminal statute. It is an amnesty bill. It tries to redress the government interference in the free market of private property and contract that took place when New Jersey liberalized its incorporation laws as a mechanism for legalizing the trusts that Congress had made illegal. It's that bit of government interference that I think brought about a lot of monopoly power, and it is not going to be undone. One way to counteract it is with antitrust.

## SELECTED BIBLIOGRAPHY

Bain, Joe S. "Relation of Profit Rate to Industry Concentration, American Manufacturing, 1936-1970." *Quarterly Journal of Economics,* 65 (August 1951), 293-324.

Brozen, Yale. "The Anti-trust Task Force Deconcentration Recommendation." *Journal of Law and Economics,* 13 (October 1970), 279-292.

―――――. "Concentration and Profits: Does Concentration Matter?" in J. F. Weston and S. Ornstein, eds., *The Impact of Large Firms on the U.S. Economy.* Lexington Books, 1973, pp. 59-70.

Collins, Norman R., and Preston, Lee E. "Price-Cost Margins and Industry Structure." *Review of Economics and Statistics,* 51 (August 1969), 271-286.

Comanor, William S., and Wilson, Thomas A. "Advertising, Market Structure, and Performance." *Review of Economics and Statistics,* 49 (November 1967), 423-440.

Demsetz, Harold. "Industry Structure, Market Rivalry, and Public Policy," in J. F. Weston and S. Ornstein, eds., *The Impact of Large Firms on the U.S. Economy.* Lexington Books, 1973, pp. 71-82.

Hall, Marshall, and Weiss, Leonard W. "Firm Size and Profitability." *Review of Economics and Statistics,* 49 (August 1967), 319-331.

Mann, H. Michael. "Seller Concentration, Barriers to Entry, and Rates of Return in 30 Industries, 1950-1960." *Review of Economics and Statistics,* 48 (August 1966), 296-307.

Ornstein, Stanley. "Concentration and Profits." *Journal of Business,* 45 (October 1972), 519-541.

Shepherd, W. G. "The Elements of Market Structure." *The Review of Economics and Statistics,* 54 (February 1972), 25-38.

Stigler, George J. *Capital and Rates of Return in Manufacturing Industries.* Princeton University Press, 1963.

―――――. "A Theory of Oligopoly." *Journal of Political Economy,* 72 (February 1964), 44-61.

Weiss, Leonard W. "Average Concentration Ratios and Industrial Performance." *Journal of Industrial Economics,* 45 (July 1963), 233-254.

# 5

# Market Concentration
# and Innovation

## Editors' Note

Some hold that concentration and large firm size are necessary to innovation, and that innovation is the most vital of competitive processes. An alternative view is that large firm size and concentration retard technological change. An evaluation of these two opposing views has great significance because a small difference in the rate of innovation may produce substantial differences in the rate of growth of the gross national product.

Much effort has been expended on testing the validity of these diametrically opposed positions. But gathering and analyzing the factual evidence presents substantial difficulties. Candidates for measuring innovational performance include research and development expenditures, the number of personnel engaged in R&D, the number of patents received, the number of inventions, the rating of the importance of inventions, and revenues generated by new products. The measures are inputs which do not indicate performance, or are highly ambiguous, or are subjective output indicators.

With these limitations, the evidence suggests a positive but weak association between concentration and innovation by industry. With regard to firm size, the evidence is mixed. In general, the empirical studies indicate that the ratio of R&D inputs to sales does not increase — and may decrease — in relation to firm size. But these are inputs; the negative association between inputs and size could indicate either efficiency in the use of R&D by larger firms or lack of incentives to make the effort. Studies that used "the most important innovations" in an industry as a measure of output were using subjective measures in which the results differed for individual industries. Of major influence on individual industries is the nature of the technological opportunities for innovation; firms in advanced electronics, chemicals, and metallurgical industries would be expected to be more technically dynamic than firms in the clothing industry.

It is in the context of such conflicting and uncertain findings that the impact of size and concentration on innovation must be evaluated. The following paper by Professor Markham sets forth the theory and evidence; it summarizes a substantial body of literature. His broad coverage of available knowledge provides a basis for formulating public policy. At issue is whether a restrictive merger policy or enactment of deconcentration legislation would have a beneficial or adverse impact on innovational performance in the United States economy.

# Concentration: A Stimulus or Retardant to Innovation?

Jesse W. Markham*

## THE THEORIES AND THE HYPOTHESES

While this paper is principally concerned with the relationships between market structure and technological progress, it will also deal in this context with the related issue of firm size. In part, treatment of the relationships of firm size and technological progress arises out of necessity.

Market structure and firm size are, of course, entirely different concepts and, in fact as well as in theory, may exist independently of each other. For example, several of the large conglomerates high on *Fortune's* list of the largest 500 corporations rank relatively low in terms of their shares of particular markets. On the other hand, a large fraction of the mergers challenged over the past decade on the grounds of the participants' market shares have involved companies of modest size. But while the concepts of market structure and firm size are fundamentally different, students of industrial organization have not always clearly distinguished between the two in generating the literature pertinent to the subject with which this paper is concerned. Hence, an assessment of their research results requires consideraticn of both.

There is yet another and more impelling reason, however, for devoting attention to the role of firm size in an analysis of market concentration and innovation. Even if one could safely assume that the statistical relationship between companies' market shares (concentration level) and innovation is completely independent of that between the mere size of these companies and innovation, firm size and market structure may nevertheless be quite interdependent when it comes to the design and application of appropriate antitrust and/or other policy measures. Suppose, for example, that by applying the best available statistical techniques to the relevant data on the entire cor-

* Clifton E. Wilson Professor of Business Administration, Harvard Business School. For further biographical information, see Appendix D.

porate universe, it was determined that innovational activity was strongly associated with the relative size of companies, but was virtually neutral with respect to the market shares of these companies once the effect of size had been eliminated. However, suppose further that the largest companies also had large market shares. The dilemma such a finding would present to public policy is apparent: the firms with the largest market shares could be broken up in the interests of deconcentration with no adverse effect on innovation; but because dissolution would reduce the size of these same firms, innovation would be adversely affected.[1]

With this introductory caveat, I now turn to the historical evolution of the issue, the results of attempts to subject it to empirical analysis, and its relevance for antitrust policy. Debate among economists on the relationship between market structure and technological progressiveness goes back at least to the initial session of the founders of the American Economic Association in 1886. While most of those in attendance had inherited from their classical forebears a preference for competitive resource allocation, and by implication thought the performance of deconcentrated industries would be superior to that of concentrated ones, dissenters were in evidence even then. Not surprisingly, those who extolled the superiority of monopoly and "bigness" did so on the grounds that it was more efficient.[2] They did not clearly distinguish between the efficiencies of economies of scale and those of technological progressiveness, but often appear to have had both in mind.

The traditional view prompting such early dissents was, and still remains, neither more nor less than the historical rationale for competition generally: the driving forces of the competitive marketplace will assure maximum use of all the means available to business firms to enhance their profits, and in this respect the search for new and better products and more efficient production processes is not fundamentally different from price competition. Additionally, a monopolist will introduce a new and competing process prior to the depreciation of existing capital investment only if the total variable costs under the new process is less than total costs under the old, whereas competition will assure the introduction of such improved processes right away. The stretch-out introduction of the dial telephone — and the suppression of incandescent lamps and nylon hose that last forever and the carburetor that would double the miles-per-gallon for internal combustion motor vehicle engines — have from time to time been offered up as corroborative factual evidence. A more generalized version of the competitive hypothesis is contained in the following observation by Morris Adelman:

1. A similar policy dilemma may be posed by conflicting relationships between size of firm and production scale economies on the one hand, and size of firm and technological progressiveness on the other, i.e., large firms more fully exploit scale economies under existing technologies but are less progressive technologically than are small- and medium-sized firms.

2. Cf. Henry C. Adams, "Relation of the State to Industrial Action," *Publications of the American Economic Association*, Vol. 1, No. 6 (January 1887), pp. 38-39, 42, 49.

The alleged opposition between competition and technological progress is difficult to accept. Where profits on old methods and old products are melted away by competition, the urge is greatest to seek the profits of new products and methods. Conversely, where profits can be maintained by monopolies and cartels, the urge is less. Surely a comparison of Europe with the United States confirms the theory; even more to the point is a comparison with underdeveloped countries. . . . The better record of American industry is more plausibly explained by a more competitive environment than by oligopoly per se. For the other nations have more oligopoly and less progress.[3]

While there were early dissenters to the competitive hypothesis, Professor Joseph A. Schumpeter remains the unchallenged intellectual father of the theory postulating a logical positive relationship between market concentration and technological progressiveness.[4] Professor E. S. Mason, Schumpeter's careful and observant student as well as colleague, had no difficulty in his memorial article on Schumpeter in summing up the theory as follows: "The essence of Schumpeter's position is that market power is necessary to innovation and that innovation is the core of effective competition." [5] But this distills to vial size what originally filled several very large vats. The central thrust of what has come to be called the Schumpeterian hypothesis is that the traditional practice of drawing inferences concerning the state of competition from such parameters as indexes of industry concentration and business size is logically indefensible. Since such statistical measures apply only to a given point in time, they provide no basis for interpreting the dynamic forces that shaped them, or those they in turn set in motion in the future. In brief, such measures divorced from their industrial history are virtually meaningless.

In Schumpeter's scheme of things, however, he singled out innovational activity as among the most important of these dynamic forces. As he put it:

The competition that counts is the competition from the new commodity, the new technology, the new source of supply, the new type of organization (the largest-scale unit of control for instance) — competition which commands a decisive cost or quality advantage and which strikes not at the margins of the profits and the outputs of the existing firms but at their foundations and their very lives. This kind of competition is as much more effective than the other as a bombardment is in comparison with forcing a door, and so much more important that it becomes a matter of comparative indifference whether competition in the ordinary sense functions more or less promptly; the powerful lever that in the long run expands output and brings down prices is in any case made of other stuff.[6]

3. Morris A. Adelman, "Galbraith's 'Concept of Countervailing Power' and Lilienthal's 'Big Business,' " 49 *Nw. U.L. Rev.* 157 (1954).

4. Schumpeter's writings pertinent to this postulation are numerous. However, his works most frequently cited are his two-volume *Business Cycles* (McGraw-Hill 1939); *Capitalism, Socialism and Democracy* (Harper and Bros. 1942), esp. chs. 7 and 8; "Science and Ideology," *American Economic Review*, 39 (March 1949), pp. 345-59.

5. E. S. Mason, "Schumpeter on Monopoly and the Large Firm," *Review of Economics and Statistics*, Vol. 33, No. 2 (May 1951), pp. 139-144.

6. Schumpeter, *Capitalism* . . . , supra n. 4, at 84-85.

Elsewhere, Schumpeter elaborated on his hypothesis concerning the relationship between market power and innovation. The crux of his theory is that the prospects of higher-than-competitive returns were the essential incentive for undertaking risky and uncertain innovational activities, and that accumulated surpluses from past earnings above the competitive level were a necessary condition for firms to react to this incentive. Since a perfectly competitive economy did not fulfill this necessary condition, it can be assumed that Schumpeter viewed market power as a prerequisite to the innovational process. However, since market power (which may be read as high concentration) at any given instant of time is at once a product of the more effective kind of competition of the past *and* sets in motion those forces that will destroy it in the future, it is not simply an irrelevant antitrust target, it is an inappropriate antitrust target.

While more will be said on this point later on, those who have attempted empirical tests of Schumpeter's hypothesis have been confronted with serious analytical difficulties. Schumpeter defined innovation broadly enough to include virtually any new managerial strategy having sufficient impact on the market to disturb a static-state competitive equilibrium, including, among others, new forms of organization, mergers, a new advertising campaign, a new product, or a new process. Only the latter two are logical consequences of technological effort carried on inside the business firm, and for which such quantitative data as R&D expenditures, number and value of patents or important inventions, and so on, might serve as reasonably appropriate measures.

The more fruitful objective, however, is not necessarily to test the Schumpeterian hypothesis according to the precise context in which he formulated it, but rather to test the basic hypothesis as Mason has stated it; i.e., market power is essential to innovation, and innovation is the most socially beneficial form of competition. It is in this form that those who followed Schumpeter have cast their theoretical discourse. For example, Henry Villard has argued that industrial research is most likely to occur "where the firm is not particularly concerned with selling the results of its research but rather hopes to embody them in product or process improvements which will give it at least a temporary advantage over its competition. But this sort of situation is surely most likely to be found in industries which are to a significant extent true oligopolies." [7]

The critical terms in Villard's observation are "at least a temporary advantage" and "true oligopolies." In true oligopolies each firm will eschew competitive tactics readily counteracted by its rivals, especially if after they are counteracted the firm is worse off than before. Hence, overt price competition rarely offers a true oligopolist the opportunity to gain even a temporary advantage. As Professor E. H. Chamberlin put it in his classic treatment of the subject, "When a move by one firm evidently forces the other to make a countermove, he is very stupidly refusing to look further than his nose if he

---

7. Henry Villard, "Competition, Oligopoly and Research," *Journal of Political Economy*, 66 (December 1958), p. 492.

proceeds on the assumption that it will not." [8] Usually, price moves are readily detected and easily counteracted; moves in the form of new products and new processes are not. Hence, innovations of this type hold out to oligopolists the prospects of gaining at least a temporary, often an enduring, advantage over their rivals. This refines the hypothesis, and in a formal sense reduces it to operational dimensions: an appropriately designed factual inquiry should find innovational effort disproportionately centered in truly oligopolistic industries.

The postulations concerning business size and technological effort can be dealt with much more summarily. In the first place, while debate concerning the merits and demerits of Big Business has a long history, it has served more to obscure than illuminate the issue of market power. Second, the debate has failed to generate a hypothesis approaching the elegance of that relating market power to innovational effort. And finally, unlike market power, firm size as such is not a critical antitrust issue. To be sure, the courts emphasized the immense size of the companies involved in the *du Pont–General Motors* case [United States v. E. I. du Pont de Nemours & Co., 353 U.S. 586 (1957)], and it is not entirely accidental that in most of the conglomerate acquisitions challenged so far, the acquiring company ranked high on *Fortune's* list of the largest 500 corporations. And viewed from the positive side, the district court judge applauded du Pont's innovational vigor in his decision in the *Cellophane* case [United States v. E. I. du Pont de Nemours & Co., 351 U.S. 377 (1956)]. But even in these cases firm size was at best a conditioning factor and not the central issue, a point which antitrust officials have publicly emphasized with uncommon unanimity and sensitivity when charged with turning antitrust policy to a crusade against Big Business.

We may infer from all this that the question of how firm size, and nothing more, relates to innovational effort is of relatively little import for public policy, however much that question has aroused the interests and stimulated the efforts of students of industrial organization. When staunch proponents of vigorous antitrust recoil against pronouncements that bigness is essential to technological progress, it is probably because they cannot shake the habit of equating Big Business with market power. But it is market power that counts, and if "mere size is [*still*] no offense," it is a netural factor in antitrust policy. Hence, relationships between firm size and innovational effort do not raise the issue of trade-offs between technological progress and normal antitrust law enforcement.

None of this is to deny the plethora of explanatory hypotheses relating innovational effort to firm size. A strong current running throughout most of Galbraith's economic writings pertinent to this issue is that because R&D is both costly and risky, it can be carried out only by firms of large size. [9] Others

---

8. Cf. E. H. Chamberlin, *The Theory of Monopolistic Competition* (Harvard Univ. Press 1933), p. 46.

9. Cf. J. K. Galbraith, *American Capitalism* (rev. ed., Houghton Mifflin 1956), pp. 86-87; and *The New Industrial State* (Houghton Mifflin 1967), pp. 11-21.

have emphasized the necessity of size to reduce risks; i.e., only large firms can support the number of projects required to assure enough successes to make R&D operations commercially viable. Still others have urged that economies of scale in R&D may be such that only large firms can carry on R&D efficiently. A related hypothesis advanced by Richard Nelson is that R&D is less risky in the large diversified (conglomerate) firm, or alternatively more profitable, than in single-product firms. He reasons as follows:

> Whatever direction the path of research may take, the results are likely to be of value to the sponsoring firm . . . it is the broad underlying techonological base, the wide range of products they produce or will be willing to produce if their research efforts open possibilities.[10]

By now it should be abundantly clear that we suffer from no theory-shortage crisis when it comes to explanatory hypotheses concerning market factors conducive to innovational activity in the private sector of the economy. At the theoretical level, however, the central issue of how market structure relates to innovation remains unresolved. On the one hand, the traditional competitive hypothesis contends that an antitrust policy directed toward deconcentration serves the ends of both allocative efficiency and technological progress. On the other, a very specialized version of the Schumpeterian hypothesis contends that over a significant range these may be mutually exclusive objects. In the face of conflicting and equally appealing hypotheses, the choice as to which is the more valid is ultimately an empirical matter.

Before turning to the pertinent body of factual analysis, however, it may be helpful to clarify the quantitative relationships between allocative efficiency and efficiency attributable to technological change. As Professor Scherer[11] has pointed out, the deadweight welfare loss from monopolistic misallocation of resources is overcome by growth in the GNP from technological change in a surprisingly short time; to wit, "an output handicap amounting to 10 percent of gross national product due to static inefficiency is surmounted in just five years if the rate of output can be raised through more rapid technological change by 2 percent." Clearly, if it should turn out that market power, or oligopoly, is highly conducive to innovative activity, the determination of which of the two competing hypotheses stands up better under empirical scrutiny is not a trivial matter.

This can be illustrated by expanding Scherer's calculations to cover ranges of GNP growth from technological change, and welfare losses from monopolistic misallocation of resources, as shown in Table 14. The values shown are the number of years required for various growth rates to surmount alternative deadweight welfare losses from monopoly. It will be observed that the lower ranges of monopoly welfare losses are offset by even modest growth rates in a very short time. For example, it requires less than 2½ months (0.2 years)

10. Richard R. Nelson, "The Simple Economics of Basic Scientific Research," *Journal of Political Economy,* 67 (June 1959), p. 297.

11. F. M. Scherer, *Industrial Market Structure and Economic Performance* (Rand McNally 1970), p. 346.

TABLE 14

Time Required for Selected GNP Annual Growth Rates from Technological Change to Offset Various Assumed Annual Welfare Losses from Monopoly (expressed in years)

| Average Growth Rate in GNP from Technological Change | Annual Welfare Loss from Monopoly (expressed as percent of GNP) | | | | | |
|---|---|---|---|---|---|---|
| | .05 | .10 [b] | 1.0 [b] | 2.5 [c] | 5.0 | 10.0 |
| 0.50 | 0.100 | 0.20 | 2.0 | 5.0 | 10.0 | 20.0 |
| 0.75 | 0.067 | 0.13 | 1.3 | 3.3 | 6.7 | 13.3 |
| 1.00 | 0.050 | 0.10 | 1.0 | 2.5 | 5.0 | 10.0 |
| 1.20 [a] | 0.040 | 0.08 | 0.8 | 2.1 | 4.2 | 8.0 |
| 1.50 [a] | 0.033 | 0.07 | 0.7 | 1.7 | 3.3 | 6.7 |
| 2.00 | 0.025 | 0.05 | 0.5 | 1.3 | 2.5 | 5.0 |

[a] Derived from Solow-Denison estimates of annual GNP. Growth from technological change.

[b] Derived from upper range of Harberger-Schwartzman estimates of static monopoly welfare loss.

[c] Derived from mid-range of Kamerschen estimates of static monopoly welfare loss.

for a growth rate of 0.5 percent to offset an annual monopoly welfare loss of 0.1 percent of GNP. Stated somewhat differently, if a large proportion of technological change is attributable to oligopoly, the static monopoly welfare loss would have to be fairly large before society could be made better off by making oligopolistic markets into competitive ones.

Of course, if market power *retards* technological change, i.e., injects a negative component into the overall growth rate of the economy, this *multiplies* rather than *offsets* the deadweight static welfare loss, thereby making the total welfare losses from monopoly not only quite large but also cumulative and permanent.

Attempts have been made to estimate the actual values of growth rates from technological change and static monopoly welfare losses for the U.S. economy. Historically, output per man-hour for the nonfarm U.S. economy has grown at an annual rate of 1.5 percent. Robert M. Solow estimated that 81 percent of this annual increase, or about a 1.2 percent annual productivity growth rate, was attributable to technological change and the upgrading of the quality of the labor force.[12] In a later analysis, Edward Denison estimated that 78 percent of the annual productivity growth rate was attributable to these two factors, and that technological change alone accounted for 36 percent.[13]

12. Robert M. Solow, "Technical Change and the Aggregate Production Function," *Review of Economics and Statistics*, 41 (August 1959), pp. 312-320.

13. *The Sources of Economic Growth in the United States and the Alternatives Before Us* (Committee for Economic Development 1962), pp. 271-272.

While these estimates are highly illuminating, they do not isolate and measure with precision the full contribution of technical change and innovation to economic welfare.[14] Most importantly, since they are based on changes in output per man-hour, they measure only the growth attributable to process improvements, omitting altogether the average annual welfare gains from product improvement. As data presented later on will show, more than three-quarters of the annual outlays on R&D by business enterprises are directed toward product improvement and new products. Also, some portion, very likely a large portion, of the upgrading of the quality of the labor force is itself attributable to process and product innovation. Hence, a minimum estimate of the annual average welfare gains from innovation and technical change would appear to fall in the neighborhood of from 1.2 percent to 1.5 percent.

Attempts to measure the deadweight static welfare loss of monopoly have consistently led to the conclusion that this loss is much smaller than it was generally thought to be, but the results obtained rest on fairly heroic assumptions. Since these assumptions greatly affect the calculated loss, there follows a brief description of the methodology used, and the data to which it has been applied.[15]

The methodology generally employed is set forth in Figure 4. Under com-

**Figure 4**
**Welfare Loss from Monopoly**

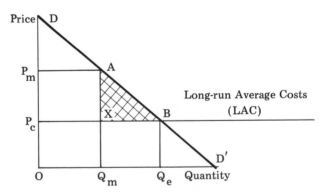

petition price ($P_c$) is assumed to be equal to long-run average unit costs (LAC). At the price $P_c$, total consumer surplus, the total value consumers receive over and above what they would have been willing to pay for it, is represented by the triangle $P_cDB$. By definition, the segment $DB$ of the demand schedule $DD'$ shows that consumers would have been willing to pay more than $P_c$ for all units sold except the marginal (last) unit bought at $P_c$. Similarly, under the monopoly price ($P_m$) total consumer surplus is represented by the triangle

.14. See Scherer, *supra* n. 11, at 346-347.

15. For a more detailed description see *id.* at 401-403; and articles by Harberger and Schwartzman, *infra* nn. 16, 17.

$P_mDA$. The *total* loss in consumer surplus resulting from monopoly is therefore represented by the trapezoid $P_mABP_c$. However, the loss in consumer surplus represented by the rectangle $P_mAXP_c$ is exactly offset by the gain in producer surplus reaped by the monopolist. Hence, the *net* welfare loss from monopoly is represented by the smaller hatched triangle $XAB$. If we conveniently assume the demand schedule to be linear, the area of $XAB$ can be calculated from the rule governing the area of right triangles as

(1)    $A = \frac{1}{2} AX, XB;$

and, since $AX$ equals the difference between the monopoly and competitive price, and $XB$ equals the difference between the monopoly and competitive output,

(1a)    $A = \Delta P \Delta Q.$

By substituting into (1a) the appropriate expression for the price elasticity of demand, $n$, and collecting the rearranging terms, the equation for the net deadweight welfare loss from monopoly $(W)$ can be derived as:

(2)    $W = \frac{1}{2} PQ_{nt}{}^2$

where $PQ$ = total sales;
$\quad n$ = coefficient of the price elasticity of demand; and
$\quad t$ = the relative price distortion of monopoly.

Industry sales $(PQ)$ are available from the *Census of Manufactures*. However, the size of $W$ hangs critically on the values of $n$ and $t$. Various methods have been employed to estimate $t$, the relative price distortion attributable to monopoly, but in all attempts to calculate $W$ it has been necessary to assume a value for $n$. Since $W$ varies linearly with $n$, it is evident that the calculated size of $W$ varies according to the assumed values of $n$ used to solve the equation.

Two independent studies, using different methods for calculating values for $t$, have reached the conclusion that the welfare loss from monopoly in the U.S. manufacturing economy is trivial, amounting to no more than from 0.06 percent to 0.10 percent of GNP. Arnold Harberger, the first to make such a calculation, estimated $t$ from profits earned in excess of the average rate of return.[16] By incorporating these values for $t$ in the equation, and assuming for each industry that $n = 1$, he concluded that the net welfare loss attributable to monopolistic price distortion for all manufacturing amounted to about 0.06 percent of GNP. After making several additional adjustments, he estimated the loss at something less than 0.1 percent of GNP, but offered several reasons why this very likely overstated the loss.

David Schwartzman, using essentially the same model, estimated $t$ by first comparing price/cost ratios in concentrated Canadian industries with the

16. Arnold Harberger, "Monopoly and Resource Allocation," *American Economic Review*, 44 (May 1954), pp. 77-87.

same industries in the United States that were unconcentrated.[17] The comparison provided a basic yardstick for measuring *t*. He then substituted the relevant values in equation (2) and concluded that if the value of *n* were ≤ 2, the welfare loss from monopolistic price distortion was no more than 0.06 percent of GNP.

Critics of Harberger and Schwartzman have pointed out that their computations understate welfare losses by failing to take into account such factors as monopolistic cost distortions, the capitalization over time of monopoly profits, and monopoly in the nonmanufacturing sectors of the economy. Professor Kamerschen, using essentially Harberger's method and estimating the additional social costs of these factors, concludes that monopoly welfare losses may amount to as much as 1 percent to 2 percent of national income; and if different and higher coefficients of price elasticity of demand are assumed, the losses run upwards of two to three times this figure.[18] However, these estimates rest on the questionable assumptions that (1) all (100 percent of) advertising outlays, royalty receipts, and intangibles (e.g., goodwill) represent monopoly cost distortions; (2) all partnership and proprietorship profits (almost equal to corporate profits over the time period Kamerschen used) should be included along with corporate profits in making welfare loss calculations; and (3) national income originating in trade, financial institutions, services, mining and agriculture is as pertinent to the issue of monopoly welfare loss as that arising in manufacturing.

It is not at all obvious that an agricultural proprietorship or a regulated utility reporting a rate of return on investment in excess of the average for its industry, or for the entire business population, should ipso facto be defined as a monopolist for purposes of calculating deadweight welfare losses. But the principal objection to the Harberger and Kamerschen analysis is their reliance on above-average profits rates as a basis for measuring monopoly price distortions. A set of data pertaining to any variable will contain, by definition, values higher than the average for the entire set — in a perfectly normal distribution, exactly one-half. Hence, since rates of return vary by industry and by firms within each industry, the method assures that the calculation will show some welfare loss, and the magnitude of the loss calculated will depend largely on the distribution of the profits rates about the mean. Furthermore, the dispersion of profits rates about the arithmetic mean is a function of differential risks, managerial skills (including successful innovational activity), accounting methods *and*, among others, monopoly power. Perhaps the best way to illustrate the methodological weakness is to point out that in an entirely cartelized economy with each firm earning an identical rate of return, the calculated welfare losses would turn out to be zero.

However, if we accept the above estimates at face value, it becomes readily

17. David Schwartzman, "The Effect of Monopoly on Price," *Journal of Political Economy*, 67 (August 1959), pp. 352-362; and "The Burden of Monopoly," *Journal of Political Economy*, 68 (December 1960), pp. 627-630.

18. D. R. Kamerschen, "An Estimation of the 'Welfare Losses' from Monopoly in the American Economy," *Western Economic Journal*, 4 (Summer 1966), pp. 221-236.

apparent from Table 14 that the calculated growth in GNP of 1.2 percent to 1.5 percent per year attributable to innovation overcomes the deadweight welfare loss from monopoly in a surprisingly short period of time — for the Harberger-Schwartzman estimates, approximately one month! And for the much higher Kamerschen estimates, only two years. However, the shortcomings of these estimation methods, enumerated by those who have critically assessed them, argue strongly against accepting the results at face value.[19] Unfortunately, we have no more reliable estimates to put in their place. But supposing the monopoly welfare loss is twenty times that estimated by Harberger and Schwartzman, the welfare gains from innovation would still overcome the deadweight loss from monopoly in the short span of eighteen months. Obviously, the gains from innovation can be a powerful counteractive force to monopolistic price distortions. It is to the critical question of how much, if any, of these gains can be traced to the existence of oligopoly in the U.S. economy that the empirical analyses taken up below have been directed.

## THE FACTUAL EVIDENCE

Most of the systematic studies of the relationships between market structure and innovational effort have, of necessity, relied on historical data pertaining to various years or time periods over the past two decades. At the outset, it may be helpful to describe the nature of these data.

The most frequently used measure of innovational effort is R&D outlays financed internally by private business corporations. Between 1953 and 1960 these outlays just about doubled, increasing from $2.37 billion to $4.6 billion. By 1970 they had more than doubled again, reaching $10.8 billion.

While R&D financed by private business has become an increasingly larger percentage of total R&D expenditures in recent years, especially since the cutbacks in government outlays on space- and defense-oriented industries, at no time since World War II have they accounted for as much as one-half of the total of such expenditures. In 1953 they accounted for 42 percent; in 1960 for 33 percent; and in 1970 for 40 percent. The remainder was financed by the federal government (well over 50 percent of total R&D) and by non-profit organizations including educational institutions. Obviously, R&D effort is generated by factors besides market forces, such as scientific creativity operating in the framework of nonprofit institutions, national objectives, and the consensus on national needs as perceived by governmental agencies and congressional appropriations committees. However, the issue of market concentration and innovational activity is confined to R&D outlays of business firms.

Considerable debate still attends the appropriateness of using R&D as a

19. Cf. George J. Stigler, "The Statistics of Monopoly and Merger," *Journal of Political Economy,* 64 (February 1956), pp. 33-35; Scherer, *supra* n. 11, at 403-408; Abram Bergson, "On Monopoly Welfare Losses," *American Economic Review,* 63 (December 1973), pp. 853-870.

measure of inventive and innovational effort.[20] Its principal virtues are that it *is* a numerical quantity, and hence lends itself to quantitative analysis, and that, at least in theory, it reflects the extent to which firms commit funds to innovational activities. On the other hand, because it is an input rather than an output, it leaves unanswered some critical questions pertaining to how efficiently the funds were used and the performance record of the firms that used them. Moreover — a point especially pertinent to some of the empirical studies discussed below — R&D outlay comparisons among firms may tend to understate the innovational efforts of small firms and, to the extent such firms are more frequently found in competitively structured industries, overstate the case for concentration.[21]

Other measures of inventive and innovational effort include the number of personnel engaged in R&D, the number of patents received, a nose count of the number of important inventions, and revenues generated by new products. Using the number of R&D personnel as a yardstick has most of the merits and shortcomings of measuring R&D expressed in dollar terms. The remaining measures relate essentially to outputs of R&D effort and — since in the end it is output that counts — have been preferred by some over measures of input. However, they also have their drawbacks. Patented inventions are not only extraordinarily heterogeneous, varying from the trivial to the revolutionary scientific breakthrough, but the number of patented inventions assigned is significantly affected by company policies toward patenting. Additionally, product innovations lead as frequently to trademarks as to patents, although sometimes to both. Since most company-financed R&D is directed toward new products and product improvement, numerical counts of patents by company will bypass much of this activity. Data on the number of important pioneering inventions, and on the amount of revenues from new products, are not available from any of the usual statistical sources and must be developed ab initio for the purpose at hand by tedious processes. They have for this reason been used only selectively and sparingly.

The deficiencies in the conventional measures of oligopoly are at least as serious as those of innovational activity. By this I mean that no single quantitative index identifies the relevant point — along the spectrum of few to many firms — where one can be reasonably certain that firms will act and react as oligopolists. It is generally agreed that the Herfindahl index[22] calculated for well-defined industries is the best single measure of market concentration.

---

20. For a discussion of the various measures of innovational efforts see Scherer, *supra* n. 11, at 357-359.

21. Cf. Jacob Schmookler, "Bigness, Fewness and Research," *Journal of Political Economy*, 67 (December 1959), pp. 629-631. Schmookler offers evidence that in small firms R&D is often conducted even though these firms have not established a formal R&D organization and do not show R&D expenditures in their financial statements.

22. The index is defined as $H = \sum_{i=1}^{n} (p^2)$ where $p =$ share of industry sales, output, or employment for the *i*th firm.

However, since it is based on the sales, output, or employment of each individual firm comprising the industry, it cannot be used for practical reasons. Moreover, while appropriately designed concentration indexes describe the relevant structural aspects of an industry, they are the beginning rather than the end of informative inquiry into oligopoly behavior. Most analyses of concentration and inventive activity have, of necessity, relied on the 4-firm concentration ratio for 4-digit Standard Industrial Classification (S.I.C.) industries periodically compiled by the *Census of Manufactures*. Its deficiencies, even as a structural index, have been belabored in the literature at length and need not be repeated here.

In addition to these conceptual weaknesses in the available measures, the problem is further aggravated by the fact that R&D data are generally available on a company or broad industry group rather than a 4-digit S.I.C. industry basis. Most companies operate in so many 4-digit industries that, in order to use the reported R&D data, they have to be classified into the much broader 3-digit, or even 2-digit, group. It then becomes necessary for purposes of comparability to calculate weighted concentration indexes at this level. In the process of aggregation, the resulting concentration indexes lose much of their relevance to meaningfully defined industries and markets.

To point out these data and conceptual problems is not to say that they utterly frustrate attempts to analyze the relationship between concentration and innovational effort, but it does imply that the results must be viewed with extreme caution — and as, at best, only suggestive of what the "true" relationship would be in a world of perfectly appropriate data tested out under perfectly framed hypotheses. Most of those who have carried out empirical studies on this topic have been cognizant of these problems and, on the whole, have stated their conclusions with appropriate caution.

I should like to turn now to an assessment of the factual evidence itself. Most empirical studies of concentration and innovational activity fall into one of two broad categories: (1) those that simply divide the total amount of innovational activity as measured in terms of R&D expenditures, or one of the other measures discussed above, between firms in oligopoly and in competitive markets, and by inspection of the results form a conclusion as to which group of firms comes out best; this we may call the dichotomous approach, and the one that more closely follows the method pursued by Schumpeter in generating his theory; and (2) the statistical "model" approach, which seeks to ascertain the stochastic laws governing the relationship between concentration indexes and various measures of innovational effort. These models are specified in the form of regression equations, of which the simplest is as follows:

(1)    $Y_i = a + bX_i + E_i$

where $Y$ is some measure of innovational effort, $X$ is a measure of industry concentration, and $E$ is an error term providing for certain random elements. The process, described in simple terms, is to collect R&D expenditures and concentration ratios by industry, which when laid out in graphic form might look like the scatter of plots appearing in Figure 5. By conventional statistical procedures, the line that "best" describes (minimizes the sum of the squares of the deviations about the line) the relationship between R&D and concentration is fitted to this set of points. As a practical matter, of course, the line is not actually fitted; rather, the data are programmed on a computer which solves for the values of *a* and *b*. The numerical value of *a* defines where the line, if drawn, would intercept one of the axes; determination of the numerical value of *b*, however, is the objective of the operation since it tells us how R&D varies in respect to industry concentration. If *b* is positive, R&D increases as the concentration index increases; if *b* is negative, R&D decreases as concentration increases. It is also customary to subject the value of *b* to a statistical significance test; i.e., to determine whether the chances are 5 out of a hundred, or 10 out of a hundred, etc., that the computed value of *b* is wrong. By tradition, statistical analysts are strong risk averters; they tend to abide by

**Figure 5**

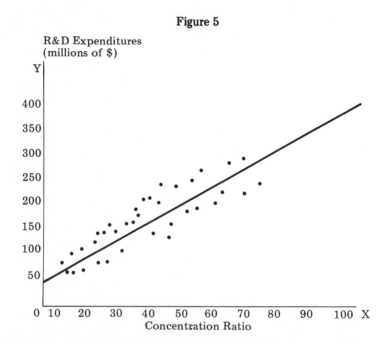

R&D Expenditures
(millions of $)

the rule that if the chances are more than 5 out of a hundred that the computed value of *b* is wrong, it is judged not to have met the test of statistical significance.

Such models can be made vastly more complex and designed to discover whether other variables, either independent of or interactive with concentration, "explain" the intensity of innovative activity. Consider, for example, the following multiple regression computed by Frederic Scherer, which will be referred to later on:

$$log \; (E_i + S_i) = -.03 + .95 \; log \; N_i + .94 \; log \; C_i + .30 \; Elec_i + .44 \; Chem_i$$
$$-.47 \; Trad_i -.05 \; Reg_i + .05 \; DUR_i - .14 \; Cons_i$$

where $E_i + S_i$ = respectively, the number of engineers and
            scientists employed in industry $i$;
    $N_i$ = total employment of the $i$th industry;
    $C_i$ = concentration ratio for the $i$th industry;
    and the remaining are dummy variables to allow for interindustry
    differences in technological opportunity, industry classifications,
    and regional market conditions.

At the last count, at least ten studies, varying in coverage from 4 or 5 to 56 industry groups, and from several dozen to over 300 firms, have analyzed concentration and innovational activity through the application of regression techniques.

The empirical evidence developed in both types of such studies does not point consistently to any striking conclusions. If we view the dichotomous approach as designed simply to answer the question, "Do large firms in oligopolistic industries account for a disproportionately large amount of the business-financial R&D that has taken place over the past twenty years or so?," it answers this question with an unqualified yes, but it reaches this conclusion by an indirect route. All of the National Science Foundation Surveys show that the 400 to 500 largest companies having 5,000 or more employees account for from 80 to nearly 90 percent of all such R&D expenditures. These same companies account for only 25 to 30 percent of total employment and total sales. Many of these companies, but not all, operate under conditions of oligopoly. According to FTC compilations,[23] 100 of these companies are among the top four in at least one 4-digit industry, 20 of which are among the top four in from 4 to over 20 such industries. A large percentage of the remaining 300 or so NSF large companies compete with these industry leaders. All the evidence we have suggests that the R&D conducted by these companies occurs predominantly in industries broadly defined as oligopolistic in character. Five industry groups alone have consistently accounted for nearly 75 percent of all company-financed R&D: chemical and allied products, electric equipment and communications, motor vehicles and transportation equipment, machinery, and aircraft and missiles. If we delete aircraft and missiles and add iron and steel and nonferrous metals, the list becomes virtually identical with the industries identified in the proposed Industrial Reorganization Act as meriting special study because of their presumptive high concentration.

The regression model approach has yielded results that do not, on the whole, refute the above conclusion but do call for some modifications and qualifications. At the risk of sacrificing immense quantums of statistical pro-

23. Federal Trade Commission, *Economic Report on Corporate Mergers* (1969), p. 216.

cedures, analytical refinements, and subtleties of detail in the interest of brevity, a summary of a representative group of these studies follows.[24] Wherever possible the essential conclusions reached in the various studies are restated as their authors originally stated them.

### Daniel Hamberg

This was a study of 340 large firms in which R&D/sales ratios, absolute R&D expenditures, and weighted concentration indexes were organized into seventeen 2-digit and 3-digit S.I.C. manufacturing industries. His least squares and rank correlations between absolute R&D spending and industrial concentration ratios were respectively .56 and .46, both significant at the .05 level; those between R&D/sales ratios and concentration were respectively .54 and .36, with the former but not the latter significant at the .05 level.

Hamberg concluded that "positive association between R&D intensity and industrial concentration apparently exists, [but] it must be described as weak." [25]

### Ira Horowitz

Horowitz, using similar R&D data but from different sources, performed the same analysis as Hamberg, obtaining virtually the same results and reaching the same conclusion.

24. W. S. Comanor, "Market Structure, Product Differentiation and Industrial Research," *Quarterly Journal of Economics,* 81 (November 1967), pp. 639-657; W. S. Comanor and F. M. Scherer, "Patent Statistics as a Measure of Technical Change," *Journal of Political Economy,* 77 (May/June 1969), pp. 392-398; Franklin M. Fisher and Peter Temin, "Returns to Scale in Research and Development: What Does the Schumpeterian Hypothesis Imply?," *Journal of Political Economy,* 81 (January/February 1973), pp. 56-70; Henry G. Grabowski and Nevins D. Baxter, "Rivalry in Industrial Research and Development: An Empirical Study," *Journal of Industrial Economics,* 21 (July 1973), pp. 209-235; D. Hamberg, "Size of Firm, Oligopoly, and Research: The Evidence," *Canadian Journal of Economics and Political Science,* 30 (February 1964), pp. 62-75; Ira Horowitz, "Firm Size and Research Activity," *Southern Economic Journal,* 29 (January 1962), pp. 298-301; Edwin Mansfield, "The Size of Firm, Market Structure, and Innovation," *Journal of Political Economy,* 71 (December 1963), pp. 556-576; Edwin Mansfield, Industrial Research and Development Expenditures: Determinants, Prospects, and Relation of Size of Firm and Inventive Output," *Journal of Political Economy,* 72 (August 1954), pp. 319-340; Jesse W. Markham, "Market Structure, Business Conduct, and Innovation," *The American Economic Review,* 55 (May 1965), pp. 323-332; F. M. Scherer, "Size of Firm, Oligopoly, and Research: Comment," *Canadian Journal of Economics and Political Science,* 31 (May 1965), pp. 256-266; F. M. Scherer, "Firm Size, Market Structure, Opportunity, and the Output of Patented Inventions," *American Economic Review,* 55 (December 1965), pp. 1097-1125; F. M. Scherer, "Market Structure and the Employment of Scientists and Engineers," *American Economic Review,* 57 (June 1967), pp. 524-531; Leonard W. Weiss, "Average Concentration Ratios and Industrial Performance," *Journal of Industrial Economics,* 11 (July 1963), pp. 250-252.

25. D. Hamberg, "Size of Firm, Oligopoly, and Research: The Evidence," *Canadian Journal of Economics and Political Science,* 30 (February 1964), p. 75.

*Frederic M. Scherer*

In his 1965 study analyzing the relationship between patented inventions and concentration in 48 narrowly defined manufacturing industries, Scherer concluded that "if structural market power has a beneficial effect on the output of patented inventions, it is a very modest effect indeed." [26]

In his 1967 study of 56 more broadly defined industries (mostly at the 3-digit S.I.C. level) — using alternatively the number of scientists employed in R&D (S), number of scientists and number of engineers employed in R&D (S + E), and company-financed R&D expenditures as measures of innovational effort — Scherer reached conclusions more supportive of the Schumpeterian hypothesis. He attempted carefully to take into account the interindustry differences in scientific and technological opportunity and whether industries were in essentially producer or consumer goods (Cf. regression model described above).

Scherer concluded that "using one specification of the model, Schumpeter's hypothesis is sustained with flying colors. Using the alternative and theoretically preferred specification, the support is weaker but not entirely absent." [27]

Additionally, Scherer used his data to test out a "threshold" theory I had suggested in an earlier assessment of the "state of the arts" in this area of inquiry.[28] Briefly, the threshold theory postulates that R&D is positively related to concentration up to a certain critical level of concentration, but once the structure is such that oligopolists will tend to behave as true oligopolists, additional increases in concentration do not matter. Scherer found some support for the theory:

> Technological vigor appears to increase with concentration mainly at the relatively low levels of concentration. When the four-firm concentration ratio exceeds 50% or 55%, additional market power is probably not conducive to more vigorous technological efforts and may be downright stultifying.[29]

*William S. Comanor*

Comanor analyzed the impact of concentration on the employment of professional research personnel for 21 industry groups after adjusting for, among other factors, company size and product differentiation. He included the latter on the grounds that R&D fosters a rapid rate of new product introduction which in turn serves to facilitate product differentiation. Since, he argues, product differentiation is a means of repulsing the competitive thrusts of rivals, R&D should be higher in industries where products are differentiable. He separately analyzed industries falling in groups of consumer nondurables,

26. F. M. Scherer, "Firm Size, Market Structure, Opportunity, and the Output of Patented Inventions," *American Economic Review,* 55 (December 1965), p. 1120.

27. F. M. Scherer, "Market Structure and the Employment of Scientists and Engineers," *American Economic Review,* 57 (June 1967), p. 529.

28. Jesse W. Markham, "Market Structure, Business Conduct, and Innovation," *American Economic Review,* 55 (May 1965), pp. 323-332.

29. Scherer, *supra* n. 27, at 530.

consumer durables, material inputs, and investment goods. Comanor concluded:

> From these findings, it appears that there may be an important interaction between concentration and product differentiation in their influence on research spending. In industries where products are differentiable, and where as a result, competitiveness in research is an important element of market behavior it may be that concentration is not a significant factor. Where, however, product differentiation is less important, concentration is more likely to play a major role.[30]

### Grabowski and Baxter

The objective of this study was to test out a particular variation of the concentration–innovation hypothesis. The authors postulated that if oligopolists employed innovational effort as a strategy more forcefully than competitive firms, then the higher the level of concentration the less should be the variation in research intensity. They tested this hypothesis by running rank correlations between the concentration ratios and the coefficients of variation in the R&D/sales ratios for twenty-nine 3-digit S.I.C. industries. The results tended to confirm their thesis.

> This correlation had the expected negative sign and is equal to −.33 which is significant at the five percent level.[31]

They also found that the correlation between concentration and research intensity was positive but not statistically significant.

## COMPANY SIZE AND INNOVATION

The application of similar research techniques to the relationship between company size and innovational effort has yielded even less consistent results but, on the whole, makes a weaker case for size than for at least moderate concentration. Aside from the questionable relevance of firm size and innovational vigor to public policy, the research results are themselves not susceptible to unambivalent interpretation.

Those studies based on a large number of observations have typically been confined to a universe consisting of the largest 500 companies. Since Scherer (see below) has calculated that about three-quarters of the firms on the list of the largest 500 also fall in the National Science Foundation's largest company group of 5,000 and over employees that account for 80 to 90 percent of all company-financed R&D, the calculated relationships pertain almost exclusively to that very small percent of all corporations generally considered to be "large." In general, these studies sustain the conclusion that among large

---

30. W. S. Comanor, "Market Structure, Product Differentiation and Industrial Research," *Quarterly Journal of Economics,* 81 (November 1967), p. 651.

31. Henry G. Grabowski and Nevins D. Baxter, "Rivalry in Industry Research and Development: An Empirical Study," *Journal of Industrial Economics,* 21 (July 1973), p. 321.

firms innovational effort does not increase, and may very well decrease, in proportion to firm size. However, such results fail to distinguish between inter-industry differences among the largest 500. Scherer has calculated that about 42 percentage points in the overall variance in corporate patenting is attributable to this source, leading him to conclude that such "interindustry differences unrelated to mere sales volume [size] account for a major portion of the variance in corporate patenting." [32]

When the effect of interindustry differences are reduced [33] by analyzing industry groups separately, the results form a mixed pattern.

### James Worley

In one of the first attempts to apply regression techniques to company size and innovational activity, Worley analyzed eight 2-digit industries. He found that in six of the eight, R&D personnel per 1,000 employees increased with size as measured in terms of total employment. However, in only two of these industries were the results considered statistically significant (by application of the 95 percent confidence rule).

### Daniel Hamberg

Hamberg applied techniques similar to those used by Worley to a mixture of seventeen 2-digit and 3-digit S.I.C. industries, and found that R&D intensity increased with firm size in sixteen, with textiles and apparel the only exceptions.[34] His results were consistent with Worley's in all of the seven 2-digit S.I.C. industries common to both studies. However, Hamberg concluded that:

> If the reader will accept as "weak" correlations of less than .70, and as "fairly strong" correlations of .70-.79, then in nine industry groups (6 two-digit and 3 three-digit) the association between employment size and R&D may be characterized as weak and in four groups (3 two-digit and 1 three-digit) as fairly strong.

32. F. M. Scherer, "Firm Size, Market Structure, Opportunity, and the Output of Patented Inventions," *American Economic Review,* 55 (December 1965), p. 1103. Elsewhere, Scherer has demonstrated that the relationships between company size and innovational effort as measured by patents depends very much upon (1) the measure of size used; and (2) whether companies with zero patents are included or excluded. The matter of zero-patent firms arises because of the logarithmic specification of the model:

Log $Y_i = $ log $a + b$ log $X_i + E_i$, where $Y_i = $ number of patents and $X_i = $ size of the $i$th firm. In all regressions where zero-patent firms were excluded, patents did not increase in proportion to firm size; with zero-patent firms arbitrarily counted as having obtained 0.5 patents so that the logarithmic expression would permit their inclusion, patents increased somewhat more than proportionally with firm size, especially when size was measured in terms of total employment. Cf. his "Size of Firm, Oligopoly and Research: Comment," *Canadian Journal of Economics and Political Science,* 31 (May 1965), pp. 256-266.

33. Since such analyses pertain to aggregations at the 2-digit and/or 3-digit S.I.C. industry level, the interindustry differences are obviously not entirely eliminated.

34. Hamberg, *supra* n. 25.

### Edwin Mansfield

Mansfield surveyed the steel, petroleum refining, and bituminous coal industries to identify the most important process and product innovations introduced between 1918 and 1963. He was able to identify the company making 80 percent of the identified innovations. His analysis showed that the largest four firms in petroleum and coal accounted for a larger percentage of the innovations made in their respective industries than of their market shares. He found the reverse to be true in steel.[35] In another study[36] he found that the largest companies in the petroleum, drug, and glass industries spent a smaller percentage of their sales on R&D than did "somewhat smaller companies"; that in the chemicals industry they spend relatively more; and that in steel they spend less, but the computed difference was insignificant.

Mansfield's studies were confined to a relatively few industries, most of which are oligopolistic in character. His results are, broadly speaking, consistent with those of Grabowski and Baxter. Mansfield found interindustry differences, but no clear-cut pattern that large firms in oligopolies were more innovative than their somewhat smaller rivals; Grabowski and Baxter found that the variation in innovational intensity among firms decreased as concentration increased. These studies suggest, but only suggest, that among true oligopolists in the same industry, the relative size of company may be a neutral factor.

Studies such as those cited above have sought to determine the statistical relationships between company size and quantitative measures of innovational effort. Others have addressed the same policy issue by use of the "history of inventions" approach. The latter method is direct and straightforward: each invention appearing on a selected list of inventions is traced back to its origins to ascertain the relative importance of large, medium, and small corporations and number of individuals in the inventive process.[37]

Since the focus of these studies is almost exclusively on inventions rather than innovation, this may be an appropriate place to distinguish between the two. *Invention* is usually defined as a prescription for a producible product or operable process so new as not to have been "obvious to one skilled in the art"; *innovation*, on the other hand, is generally defined broadly enough to encompass all meaningful changes actually incorporated in the productive process, of which an invention and its adaptation to production is only one.

The tally sheets summarizing the results of these historical inquiries indicate

35. Edwin Mansfield, *Industrial Research and Technological Innovation* (W. W. Norton 1968), p. 41.

36. Edwin Mansfield, "Industrial Research and Development Expenditures: Determinants, Prospects, and Relation of Size of Firm and Inventive Output," *Journal of Political Economy*, 72 (August 1964), pp. 319-340.

37. For one of the more comprehensive of such studies, cf. John Jewkes, David Sawers, and Richard Stillerman, *The Sources of Invention* (rev. ed., Macmillan 1969). For a summary of this and other historical studies see John M. Blair, *Economic Concentration: Structure, Behavior and Public Policy* (Harcourt Brace, Jovanovich 1972), pp. 207-254.

that less than half of the important inventions made in the twentieth century originated in the research laboratories of large corporations. Of the 71 inventions they studied, Jewkes and his associates traced the origin of only 19 to such corporate research, while they attributed over half to individual inventors.[38] Invention, properly defined, apparently still remains a matter of individual genius, and the few who are inventive are not heavily concentrated in large corporate research laboratories.

A critical shortcoming of the above empirical studies is that the data used are either highly aggregated or pertain to relatively few observations; some of them suffer from both deficiencies. Recent research results of the Marketing Science Institute's Profit Impact of Marketing Strategies[39] (PIMS) project are based on much more specific data and have a high potential for shedding considerably more light on the issue of firm size, market concentration, and innovational activity. Analysis of data pertaining to some six hundred individual businesses (defined to be approximately equivalent to a 7-digit S.I.C. industry or narrower) indicate that R&D spending has a significantly different profits impact on firms according to their size, market share, and, among other things, degree of vertical integration. While the results must still be considered as tentative, they indicate that:

1. R&D outlays have significantly higher payout in profits for integrated than for nonintegrated companies;
2. R&D is more profitable for companies having large than small market shares. In fact, R&D spending is negatively associated with profits for companies having small relative market shares;
3. The profitability of R&D is higher for large than for small companies.

If, as economists assume, business outlays are at least in some sense governed by their demonstrated and prospective profitability, data are beginning to suggest that large vertically integrated companies with large relative market shares have a greater incentive to invest in R&D than other firms have. However, the really important question of *why* R&D spending appears to be more profitable for such firms is as yet unanswered, except for perhaps suggesting the hypothesis that firms having these characteristics have a strategic advantage when it comes to exploiting the results of industrial R&D.

## CONCLUSIONS AND POLICY IMPLICATIONS

The conclusions we may justifiably draw from empirical studies such as those summarized above depend very largely upon the purposes to which the conclusions will be put. At a purely academic level, no professor of industrial organization could justify dismissing lightly the Schumpeterian alternative

38. Jewkes et al., *supra* n. 37, at 208-209. See also Blair, *supra* n. 37, at 209, 215.

39. S. Schoeffler, R. Buzzell, and D. Heany, "Impact of Strategic Planning on Profit Performance," *Harvard Business Review*, 52 (March/April 1974), pp. 137-145.

theory of industrial behavior on the grounds that it flies in the face of the available factual evidence. On the contrary, at a high level of generalization the theory has met the test of factual analysis in precisely the terms he offered it — it *is* a plausible alternative to the traditional competitive hypothesis.

Further, while I do not agree with the recent contention of Fisher and Temin[40] that Schumpeter's hypothesis has never been tested, it is clear that such quantitative data as those confined to R&D expenditures and scientific R&D employees do not adequately capture all the innovational activity Schumpeter had in mind. Nevertheless, even the restricted nature of the tests, conducted as they were in a highly imperfect data world, surely bestow on the theory at least modest credibility. If technological change and innovational activity are, as we generally assume, in some important way a product of organized R&D activities financed and executed by business companies, it is clear that the welfare payoffs that flow from them can to some measurable extent be traced to the doorsteps of large firms operating in oligopolistic markets.

Even if all could agree with this general conclusion, however, it is not clear that this would argue for a significant reorientation of antitrust policy goals or modification of the present standards for attaining them. As the factual analyses indicate, invention apparently remains largely a matter of individual genius, while innovational effort, however measured, appears to be disproportionately centered in the largest several hundred manufacturing corporations, and these large companies qualify (more frequently than not) as oligopolists in from one to a dozen or so industries. Although this may indeed call for an antitrust policy falling considerably short of wholesale dissolution of market concentration and of the largest one hundred or so corporations, the past and present thrust of antitrust renders this argument virtually superfluous. Moreover, the evidence confirms that innovational effort is not spread throughout American industry in neat proportion to the concentration indexes for those industries. In fact, such effort appears to increase with concentration only up to a certain threshold level, and much of it seems to be centered in a relatively small number of oligopolistic industries where the technological opportunities are unusually large. For many industries, therefore, the level of concentration exists independently of innovational activities. That is, the problem of trade-offs between technological progress and deadweight welfare losses described earlier either does not arise or disappears after a certain level of concentration is attained.

This leaves us with the question of whether, in view of the empirical evidence, innovational efforts on the part of defendants should enter as important desiderata in specific antimonopoly cases. Curiously enough, in spite of the debate that the issue of concentration and innovational effort has generated, cases in which it has played even a subordinate role are surprisingly few in number. Only the *United Shoe* [United States v. United Shoe Machinery

40. Franklin M. Fisher and Peter Temin, "Return to Scale in Research and Development: What Does the Schumpeterian Hypothesis Imply?," *Journal of Political Economy*, 81 (January/February 1973), pp. 56-70.

TABLE 15
Sources and Uses of R&D Funds, Selected Years, 1953-1970

**SOURCES**

| | 1953 | | 1956 | | 1959 | | 1960 | | 1970 | |
|---|---|---|---|---|---|---|---|---|---|---|
| | % | $ | % | $ | % | $ | % | $ | % | $ |
| Federal Government | 52.4 | 2810 | 62.1 | 5234 | 60.0 | 7200 | 63.7 | 8920 | 55.0 | 15130 |
| Industry | 44.2 | 2370 | 34.4 | 2900 | 38.0 | 4500 | 32.8 | 4590 | 40.0 | 11000 |
| School & Other | 3.4 | 180 | 3.6 | 300 | 2.5 | 300 | 3.4 | 480 | 5.0 | 1380 |
| Totals: | | 5360 | | 8434 | | 12000 | | 13990 | | 27510 |

**USES**

| | 1953 | | 1956 | | 1959 | | 1960 | | 1970 | |
|---|---|---|---|---|---|---|---|---|---|---|
| | % | $ | % | $ | % | $ | % | $ | % | $ |
| Federal Government | 18.1 | 970 | 16.7 | 1400 | 13.3 | 1600 | 12.6 | 1760 | 13.4 | 3690 |
| Industry | 72.1 | 3870 | 71.4 | 6000 | 75.8 | 9100 | 76.5 | 10710 | 70.6 | 19420 |
| School & Other | 10.0 | 530 | 11.9 | 1000 | 10.8 | 1300 | 10.9 | 1526 | 16.0 | 4400 |
| Totals: | | 5370 | | 8400 | | 12000 | | 13996 | | 27510 |

Source: Data prior to 1960, National Science Foundation. Data after 1960, Lucie R. Blau, "R&D: Still a Growth Industry," The Conference Board Record, Vol. 7, No. 5 (May 1970), pp. 38-40.

TABLE 16

Company-Financed Research and Development, by Industry and Size of Company, 1961

(millions of dollars)

| Industry | Total | Companies with total employment of— | | |
| | | Less than 1,000 | 1,000 to 4,999 | 5,000 or more |
| --- | --- | --- | --- | --- |
| Total | $4,631 | (a) | $591 | $3,728 |
| Food and kindred products | 106 | | 19 | 83 |
| Textiles and apparel | (a) | (a) | (a) | 13 |
| Lumber, wood products, and furniture | (a) | (a) | (a) | 3 |
| Paper and allied products | 63 | (a) | 14 | 41 |
| Chemicals and allied products | 877 | (a) | 158 | 665 |
| Industrial chemicals | 561 | (a) | 54 | 487 |
| Drugs and medicines | 192 | (a) | 61 | 119 |
| Other chemicals | 124 | (a) | 43 | 59 |
| Petroleum refining and extraction | 286 | (a) | 9 | 258 |
| Rubber products | 88 | (a) | 6 | 76 |
| Stone, clay, and glass products | 95 | (a) | 11 | 80 |
| Primary metals | 151 | (a) | 21 | 128 |
| Primary ferrous products | 95 | (a) | 5 | 90 |
| Nonferrous and other metal products | 55 | (a) | 16 | 38 |
| Fabricated metal products | 90 | (a) | 20 | 52 |
| Machinery | 610 | (a) | 105 | 431 |
| Electrical equipment and communication | 871 | (a) | 103 | 708 |
| Communication equipment and electronic components | 399 | | 39 | 343 |
| Other electrical equipment | 472 | 43 | 64 | 365 |
| Motor vehicles and other transportation equipment | 628 | (a) | 11 | 606 |
| Aircraft and missiles | 392 | (a) | 18 | 363 |
| Professional and scientific instruments | 212 | 19 | 41 | 152 |
| Scientific and mechanical measuring instruments | 82 | 13 | 15 | 54 |
| Optical, surgical, photographic, and other instruments | 130 | (a) | 26 | 98 |
| Other manufacturing industries | 62 | (a) | 13 | 40 |
| Nonmanufacturing industries | 65 | (a) | 28 | 28 |

## TABLE 17
### Full-Time-Equivalent Number of R&D Scientists and Engineers, by Industry, January 1957-1971

| Industry | 1957 | 1958 | 1959 | 1960 | 1961 | 1962 | 1963 | 1964 | 1965 | 1966 | 1967 | 1968 | 1969 | 1970 | 1971 |
|---|---|---|---|---|---|---|---|---|---|---|---|---|---|---|---|
| Total | 229,400 | 243,800 | 268,400 | 292,000 | 312,100 | 312,000 | 327,300 | 340,200 | 343,600 | 353,200 | 367,200 | 376,700 | 387,100 | 384,100 | 359,300 |
| Chemical and allied products | 29,400 | 31,000 | 33,500 | 36,100 | 37,000 | 36,500 | 38,300 | 37,800 | 40,000 | 40,000 | 38,700 | 40,800 | 42,200 | 42,100 | 42,500 |
| Petroleum refining and extraction | 6,900 | 7,400 | 7,700 | 9,200 | 9,000 | 9,100 | 8,900 | 9,000 | 9,700 | 10,200 | 10,400 | 11,200 | 11,900 | 11,500 | 10,800 |
| Rubber products | 4,700 | 4,700 | 4,800 | 5,300 | 5,500 | 5,600 | 5,800 | 6,000 | 5,800 | 5,700 | 5,800 | 6,100 | 6,300 | 6,800 | 6,600 |
| Stone, clay, and glass products | (a) | (a) | (a) | (a) | 3,600 | 3,700 | 3,800 | 3,900 | 4,300 | 4,200 | 4,500 | 5,400 | 5,500 | 5,900 | 5,700 |
| Primary metals | 5,100 | 5,200 | 5,700 | 6,900 | 6,900 | 6,000 | 5,200 | 5,100 | 5,500 | 5,500 | 5,900 | 5,900 | 6,200 | 6,300 | 6,200 |
| Electrical equipment and communication | 42,900 | 47,900 | 54,800 | 72,100 | 79,200 | 82,300 | 85,800 | 87,700 | 86,000 | 90,600 | 96,000 | 97,800 | 100,500 | 101,500 | 94,300 |
| Motor vehicles and other transportation equipment | 13,600 | 15,000 | 16,800 | 17,800 | 19,100 | 20,800 | 21,100 | 23,000 | 23,900 | 24,600 | 25,000 | 24,000 | 24,700 | 25,100 | 24,900 |
| Aircraft and missiles | 58,700 | 58,600 | 65,900 | 72,400 | 78,500 | 79,400 | 90,700 | 99,400 | 97,400 | 97,200 | 98,300 | 98,700 | 97,600 | 90,600 | 76,500 |
| Professional and scientific instruments | 10,200 | 11,000 | 12,000 | 10,000 | 11,100 | 9,800 | 9,400 | 9,700 | 10,300 | 11,200 | 11,400 | 12,500 | 13,400 | 13,400 | 13,800 |
| Other manufacturing industries | b57,900 | b63,000 | b67,200 | b62,100 | 54,500 | 50,600 | 50,100 | 49,100 | 51,400 | 52,500 | 57,600 | 59,800 | 64,300 | 64,900 | 62,900 |
| Nonmanufacturing industries | | | | | 7,500 | 7,000 | 8,200 | 9,600 | 9,400 | 11,300 | 13,600 | 14,500 | 14,500 | 16,000 | 15,200 |

Source: National Science Foundation.

a. Data included in the "other manufacturing" group.

b. For years 1957-60, manufacturing and nonmanufacturing combined — also includes food and kindred products; textiles and apparel; lumber and wood products; paper and allied products; fabricated metal products; and machinery.

Corp., 110 F. Supp. 295 (D. Mass. 1953), aff'd, 347 U.S. 521 (1954)], *du Pont,* and *Cellophane* cases come to mind, and we may assume it will arise in the *IBM* trial [scheduled to begin in late 1974 or early 1975 in the United States District Court for the Southern District of New York]. And in view of the heavy concentration of R&D in those industries singled out for special study if the proposed Industrial Reorganization Act becomes law, it will surely not go unattended in these studies. Nor do the facts suggest that it should.

But even though the possible reduction in industrial progress has rarely entered as a factor in merger or dissolution proceedings, one would be hard put to document a case where the prescribed remedy sacrificed past or prospective innovational intensity in the interests of greater allocative efficiency. After all, Schumpeter only argued that any indiscriminate assault on bigness and market power, taken out of their evolutionary context, would deprive the capitalistic process of its source of progress. No such assault has been mounted, nor does one appear to be imminent. Perhaps the antitrust agencies and the courts, mindful of the issue and of the broad contours of the empirical data underlying recent studies of it, have subconsciously been good Schumpeterians all along.

In conclusion then, until such time as antitrust policy contemplates a much more comprehensive dissolution program for industry generally than it traditionally has, the factual evidence suggests that instances where conventional antitrust remedies conflict with the goal of industrial progress are likely to be extremely rare. In fact, the evidence suggests that antitrust policy could move a discernible distance in this direction before such a conflict would arise. As to the critical question of how far, the factual studies have yet to provide guidelines that can be applied with slide rule accuracy.

# Dialogue*

*John Blair:* The works that Professor Markham has summarized are what we would refer to as the statistical studies of the sources or origins of invention and innovation. There is another type of study which obviously, because of its very nature, almost defies summarization. I have just noted down some fifty-seven different historical studies, done by some fifteen economists, in which the authors do the very difficult work of tracing a particular technology back to its origins. Where did it come from? Who really had the idea first? Who pioneered it? Who developed it?

Anybody who is really interested in this general subject matter would profit from a perusal of some of these remarkably well-done studies, particularly those which have been done by members of the economics profession who happen to be present here. Studies by Professors Adams and Dirlam on

* The session was chaired by John M. Blair, Professor of Economics, University of South Florida. For further biographical information, see Appendix D.

the origins of oxygen conversion in the production of steel, and by Professor Mueller on the role played by the large companies in the development of certain synthetic fibers, are of special interest.

*Eleanor Fox:* Professor Markham, can we properly consider quantitative technological change without considering qualitative change? In other words, if we are to consider massive change that revises technology — introduces quite new technology — what is the correlation between such change and concentration?

*Markham:* Well, one of the real difficulties is to deal quantitatively with qualitative impressions. In short, I think John Blair is quite right, and I wouldn't for a moment attempt to ignore that literature he cites. You can pick almost any author and find evidence that inventions, or what you would call massive technological improvements, at least in their origin, can be dated back to individuals and to very small companies. And no one would deny this.

I did mention contributions to the gross national product in terms of technological change. To the best of my knowledge, no one has yet designed a very good way of incorporating into that product any improvements, which I assume you would agree would be a qualitative change.

*Fox:* I am really suggesting the following proposition: Does not a company having a very big stake in the market have much less reason to come out with a change that will revise its own technology? And the converse is, doesn't a small company, trying to make its way into the market, have much more of an incentive to introduce such technology?

*Markham:* No, I don't think one could really draw that conclusion. I think if you have a monopolistic position the answer is quite clear. All one has to do is look at the Bell Telephone System to get some confirmation of this.

If you have monopoly over the market, the rate of introduction is not completely arbitrary, but there are all kinds of reasons why you would consider, as part of the cost of introducing an innovation, the accelerated rate at which you would have to depreciate your present capital.

As soon as you get into the area of oligopoly — and by that I mean the more typical case encountered in the U.S. economy, where the four largest firms account for about 40 percent or thereabouts of the total market — I don't think one can carry the monopoly argument into oligopoly that far. It is perfectly obvious that there are three or ten others that this particular innovator has to be very mindful of; after all, there is a premium on being there first with the new technology. This is especially true if you view the situation as one in which there are a limited number of competitive strategies that you can play, and if there is any validity to the argument that in a small way, at least, new processes and products get substituted in part for the more vigorous kind of price competition. I don't think that I would be prepared to conclude that oligopoly is an inhibitor to the introduction of new and better processes and new and better products.

*Fox:* If you speak in terms of incentive to discover new technology, is your answer different?

*Markham:* That is subsumed, I'm afraid, in the factual evidence I gave.

Now, I have absolutely no way of removing doubts that you would have, as I do about whether or not research and development and the employment of scientists is a good indication of the importance that oligopolists attach to technological change. But I would argue that that point is covered in the quantitative data that I just gave you. And whatever one may say, I don't think anybody has found a negative correlation between levels of concentration and this kind of effort.

*Louis Schwartz:* Jesse Markham's brave and quite plausible confession of ignorance suggests that we ought to have, from a philosopher, some view of how you make decisions when you are ignorant. Most of the decisions we are called upon to make in the legislature are made in the presence of vast deficiencies of controlling information. I look at R&D as a deceptive or crude measure of significant innovation. I am sure that everybody here looks at concentration ratios similarly as sort of a shot in the dark. And then you make regression analyses with regard to these. I really would like to know the range of error which you will concede to the policymakers in connection with these figures.

*Markham:* It depends on which regression model one is talking about, Lou. They usually do include the pertinent statistics for judging the margin of error. In general, the coefficients spill out to be reliable at a fairly high level of significance.

You are raising, however, I think, a much more fundamental question. I have had some real reservations about the applicability of regression analysis to this whole problem. I am reminded of a statement that Wassily Leontief made when he was putting together his economic input-output tables: "As a practical person, one can sit on his duff and claim that the data aren't good, or you can go ahead and make the best of what facts you have." All I can say is that with all these reservations, I think you finally get around to asking yourself, "Well, if you'd remove all of it, would you be as informed as you presently are?" My own conclusion is that I think I have learned a little by going through all of these studies and, indeed, in a very mild way participating in one of them myself.

*Walter Adams:* I think the questions raised by Professor Schwartz and by Ms. Fox really are methodological questions. I think they reflect a certain amount of dissatisfaction with the cross-section analysis approach. And the question is whether we could learn more by adding up the individual case studies, such as the one done by Mueller and the one that Dirlam and I tried to do with steel. In the steel industry, our evidence — at least to our satisfaction — was pretty clear that in both invention and innovation the giant companies lagged and did not lead. All the major inventions in basic steelmaking came from abroad. They were not the products of American industry.

On the basis of the cross-section analysis, would the correlation be *not* between the structure of the industry and the degree of inventiveness and innovativeness, but rather between the science on which the industry is based and the rate of inventiveness and innovativeness? For example, could it be argued that the explanation for the lethargy of steel was the backwardness of metallurgy as the basic science, rather than the structure of the industry?

Could we explain the progressiveness of chemicals in terms of the explosive nature of chemistry as the basic science, and so on?

*Markham:* Yes. One of the models is Scherer's in which he took account of the technological frontier that industries faced. And I think it is a real issue.

It may very well be that irrespective of what the level of concentration would be in chemicals and in electrical machinery, high R&D goes on because these happen to be industries where the technological frontier is distant and broad and because of the underlying sciences.

I'd like to come back to the question of whether special studies are fruitful. You almost never can erect a reliable generalization by that approach unless you do many of them. The number of very good industry studies, when you try to put them together, is quite small. You need more of them. I would not deny that special studies present an extremely important approach.

*Adams:* If we went through such industry studies simply for the seven industries listed in the Hart bill, would be further ahead than we are now with the cross-section studies? Could we come up with reliable evidence at least for those seven industries and then proceed?

*Markham:* It has been my understanding that if that bill gets passed, that is precisely what will happen. Interestingly, though, while economies of scale are mentioned rather prominently as something that is looked for in these industries, there is no explicit reference to the rate of technological change. Those industries account for 75 percent of all the privately financed R&D that goes on in the U.S. economy, and I would consider that a pretty large sample.

*Richard Posner:* You said that the field had made a lot of progress in some unspecified period of time. But my impression is that the field is in complete intellectual disarray. On the one hand, there is evidence of two sorts. One is cross-sectional analyses, which seem to be largely vitiated or at least largely undermined, not by any problems of statistical steps of significance but because patents and research and development are used as very crude proxies for invention and innovation output, which is what you are interested in.

And then there are case studies. I haven't read Walter Adams' study. As he described it, however, the study consists of positing that Americans are always the first to invent a process, and therefore, if a European invents the oxygen process of making steel before Americans do, there must be some monopolistic deformity in the American industry.

I know you stated that oligopolies had an incentive to innovate. I don't quarrel with that at all. I want you to advance the theory that firms, whether monopolies or competing firms or oligopolies, regardless of structure, have a strong incentive to innovate because they increase their profits by successful innovation; this would seem to be a classical theory. I thought you were searching for a theory that attached different rates of innovation to different market structures, that would imply a difference between monopoly, oligopoly, and atomistic industries. It is that differentiation that I didn't hear.

*Markham:* What I tried to say was: if you are a monopolist and a secure monopolist, there is some reason to believe that you are not under the gun. Sure, you are interested in profits, but you can exploit what you have got.

If you are a small competitive firm, you just don't have the funds to make that kind of a venturesome investment. If you go to a banker and say, "I have reasonable hope that with a certain amount of funds I can come up with a process that, if successful, will have a high-profit payout," funds will not be obtained. Further, competitive companies that operate at about their 6 or 7 percent rate of return are not in the position to make the R&D outlays that oligopolists can.

Now, this is not my theory. There has been a quarter of a century of writings making that particular distinction between monopoly, highly deconcentrated industries, and oligopoly.

*Victor Kramer:* I want to ask Mr. Markham whether he believes that technological innovation produces concentration or whether he believes concentration produces technological innovation.

*Markham:* I am not sure.

*Kramer:* Or neither?

*Markham:* I am not sure. They are associated with each other.

*Keith Clearwaters:* I gather you have compared a cross-section of industries indicating that a concentrated industry spends more money on R&D than an atomized industry. Can you extend that argument and say that since Western Electric spends more money in R&D, it is the most innovative producer in the communications industry?

*Markham:* No, you can't say that.

*Clearwaters:* Why?

*Markham:* It is very curious that we use R&D, a cost factor, as an index of R&D output. Suppose you find in this relationship that R&D is very positively associated with high concentration. Does this reflect something in the way of diseconomies of attaining a certain innovational level?

*William Baxter:* Professor Markham, I am surprised you didn't mention one theory that has appealed to me. The very problems to which our patent laws are addressed is the capturing of private gains that go along with innovation. One might suppose therefore that incentive to innovate was pretty strongly correlated with the scope of the enterprise with respect to the potential applications of the invention. If your enterprise embraces a very large fraction of possible applications of an invention, one can dispense pretty well with the patent system. That is much less true if you are in a highly competitive industry.

*Markham:* I did have that in the paper. There are some statistical results, coming out of a project being conducted at Harvard now, that show there is a very close association between the degree of market occupancy and the innovations that come about pertaining to those markets. The managerial people would tell us in an instant the reason why. After all, the total sales volume involved here, the total market that you encompass, gives you an opportunity to have a tremendously bigger payoff than if you are sitting around with 1 or 2 percent of such a market.

*Michael Mann:* I am sympathetic to Bain's position that the best we have is some sort of comment on what relationship may exist between concentration and size and actual records of progress measured somehow, either by R&D

or patent output. But what we don't know is what that record might have been, or how to compare that record with what might have been or could have been. I don't think all the quantitative evidence that we have brought to bear has given us a basis for a judgment on performance in relation to potentials.

*Markham:* Economists simply don't have the opportunity as physicists do to conduct a controlled experiment. I would simply say, ask yourself: where were we on this issue in 1950, and where are we on March 1, 1974? The productivity of these intervening efforts has certainly narrowed considerably the range of the debate, and perhaps that is the best one can hope for in that short a time, given the nature of the problem.

*Robert Kamenshine:* Do you have any notion how significant this discussion of private investment in R&D is in light of the fact that the government provides the bulk of the R&D expenditure in this country? Is there any assessment of the relative importance of the private expenditures versus the governmental expenditures?

*Markham:* Everything I have reported to you tonight was based on outlays by private companies having eliminated outlays by nonprofit institutions and the government. If you want to know what the statistical picture was — up until a relatively short time ago, by far the larger half of all R&D was federally supported, and you know in what industries they were largely centered. It has just been very recently that private firms' outlays have gone above the 50 percent level. But everything that I have said pertained to privately financed, corporately financed R&D.

## SELECTED BIBLIOGRAPHY

Comanor, William S. "Market Structure, Product Differentiation and Industrial Research." *Quarterly Journal of Economics,* 81 (November 1967), 639-657.

Comanor, William S. and Scherer, F. M. "Patent Statistics as a Measure of Technical Change." *Journal of Political Economy,* 77 (May/June 1969), 392-398.

Fisher, Franklin M., and Temin, Peter. "Return to Scale in Research and Development: What Does the Schumpeterian Hypothesis Imply?" *Journal of Political Economy,* 81 (January/February 1973), 56-70.

Grabowski, Henry G. "The Determinants of Industrial Research and Development." *Journal of Political Economy,* 76 (March/April 1968), 292-306.

Hamberg, Daniel. "Size of Firm, Oligopoly, and Research: The Evidence." *Canadian Journal of Economics and Political Science,* 30 (February 1964), 62-75.

Jewkes, John; Sawers, David; and Stillerman, Richard. *The Source of Invention.* Macmillan, 1969.

Mansfield, Edwin W. "Size of Firm, Market Structure and Innovation." *Journal of Political Economy,* 71 (December 1973), 556-576.

————. *Industrial Research and Technological Innovation.* W. W. Norton, 1968.

Nelson, Richard R. "The Simple Economics of Basic Scientific Research." *Journal of Political Economy,* 67 (June 1959), 297-306.

Scherer, F. M. "Firm Size, Market Structure, Opportunity, and the Output of Patented Inventions." *American Economic Review,* 55 (December 1965), 1097-1125.

————. "Market Structure and the Employment of Scientists and Engineers." *American Economic Review,* 57 (June 1967), 524-531.

Schumpeter, Joseph A. *Capitalism, Socialism and Democracy.* Harper, 1942.

Solow, Robert M. "Technical Change and the Aggregate Production Function." *Review of Economics and Statistics,* 41 (August 1959), 312-320.

Terleckyj, N. E. *Research and Development: Its Growth and Composition.* National Bureau of Economic Research, 1963.

Villard, Henry. "Competition, Oligopoly and Research." *Journal of Political Economy,* 66 (December 1958), 483-497.

6

# The Theory and Evidence
# Inflation and Concentration:

## Editors' Note

At a time when the economy is experiencing a rapid inflation, it is particularly appropriate to examine the role of market concentration as a causal force. Interest in this issue arose from the experience of the late 1950s when it appeared that prices steadily rose in concentrated industries, most notably steel, despite the presence of substantial amounts of excess capacity and a generally soft economy overall. There seems to be agreement that these years represented a catching-up process: oligopolists, because they had not obtained the price levels called for by earlier increases in demand, were still raising prices. Where the price increase was occurring simultaneously with the existence of excess capacity, one interpretation is that the oligopolists mistimated where the optimal price was, went too high, and were effectively penalized by the market.*

There is disagreement over whether the lag in the price behavior of concentrated industries generates persistent upward pressure on the price level and creates an inflationary bias in the sense that inflation occurs when the economy is less than fully employed. Professor Mueller believes so, arguing that the high profits associated with high market concentration encourage large wage increases. The result is an upward push on costs which creates pressure for price increases. If the economy is experiencing rapid increases in aggregate demand, the cost-pressure adds to the force of demand-pull to push prices up. If monetary and fiscal policy dampen demand, prices continue to rise in concentrated markets because the cost increases can be passed along.

Professors Weston and Lustgarten dispute this scenario. They marshal evi-

* M. A. Adelman, "Steel, Administered Prices and Inflation," *Quarterly Journal of Economics,* 75 (February 1961), pp. 16-40.

dence which demonstrates, to their minds, that there is no relationship between concentration and changes in price levels or in wage levels through time, after account is taken of changes in labor productivity. If anything, concentrated industries moderate the inflation because higher wages can be absorbed by greater labor productivity, thereby alleviating the need for price increases.

If, as many economists now believe, our economy is prone to an inflationary bias, it is important to discern whether industrial concentration plays a role. If it does, the effectiveness of monetary and fiscal tools is weakened, and our ability to cope with inflation is thereby diminished.

# Industrial Concentration:
# An Important Inflationary Force

## Willard F. Mueller*

The unfolding of events, rather than a priori theories, fathered the belief that market power creates an inflationary bias and excessive unemployment in a market economy. According to orthodox economic doctrine, changes in the price level were caused by changes in the quantity of money. Simply put, the price level rose (i.e., inflation occurred) only when the supply of money expanded more rapidly than the supply of goods. According to this theory, then, all inflation was of the *demand-pull* variety, as too much money chased too few goods. On the other hand, decreases in the quantity of money caused a fall in the level of prices and wages.

This theory was first seriously challenged during the Great Depression, when those relying on it failed miserably in explaining the events of the day. Since then, the continuing failure of demand-pull theory to explain observed events, improved knowledge of the competitive structure of the economy, and the development and testing of new economic theory have resulted in the growing acceptance of the view that, in addition to demand-pull inflation, there exists a form of *cost-* or *seller-push* inflation, where prices are *pushed up* even in the absence of excess demand.

## THE CLASSIC DOCTRINE CHALLENGED, 1930-1950

In 1933 two theoretical works challenged the classical conception of our industrial structure. These were the pioneering works of Joan Robinson, *The*

* William F. Vilas Research Professor of Agricultural Economics, Professor of Economics and Law, University of Wisconsin. For further biographical information, see Appendix D.

The author wishes to express his thanks to his research colleague, Mr. Brian W. Pekham, for his generous assistance and thoughtful suggestions in the preparation of this paper.

*Economics of Imperfect Competition,* and Edward Chamberlin, *The Theory of Monopolistic Competition.* These works departed from the classical tradition by creating models explaining industrial behavior within a framework that assumed imperfectly competitive markets were the rule rather than the exception.

A second challenge appeared in an influential memorandum prepared by Gardiner Means for the Secretary of Agriculture and published in 1935 as a Senate Document entitled, *Industrial Prices and Their Relative Inflexibility.*[1] It was in this document that Means first coined the term "administered pricing," which he defined as "a price held constant for a period of time and a series of transactions."

Beginning in the early 1930s, several studies provided empirical evidence of growing concentration within American industry. Berle and Means, *The Modern Corporation and Private Property* (1932), National Resources Committee, *The Structure of the American Economy* (1939),[2] and Crowder and Thorp, *The Structure of Industry* (1941)[3] all furnished the first comprehensive empirical documentation of the pervasiveness of high market concentration within the manufacturing sector;[4] in addition, the second work also provided evidence for Means's administered price thesis, while the third provided evidence against it. As a result of these several studies many became convinced of the importance of oligopoly in the American economy and of the value of the Robinson/Chamberlin models which were clearly more realistic than the old Marshallian models restricted to the polar extremes of perfect competition and monopoly.

These various works were not directly related, nor had the theoretical works of Robinson and Chamberlin been empirically tested by the end of the 1930s. Moreover, the latter theories did not, nor were they intended to, provide any direct support for the view that market power had anything to do with the business cycle or inflation; rather, they merely attempted to demonstrate that at any given level of "industry" demand, output would be less and prices higher under a monopolistic or monopolistically competitive structure than under a competitive one.[5] Despite this, these theories contributed to a wide-

1. Senate Document No. 13, 74th Congress, 1st Session (1935).

2. Gardiner Means headed the technical staff preparing the National Resources Committee report.

3. Crowder and Thorp, *The Structure of Industry* (U.S. Temporary National Economic Committee Monograph No. 27, 1941).

4. Berle and Means's work dealt only with so-called aggregate concentration, i.e., the share of total nonfinancial resources controlled by the two hundred largest corporations. However, they also generalized that market concentration had reached such high levels that "the principles of duopoly have become more important than those of free competition." *The Modern Corporation and Private Property* (Macmillan 1933), p. 45. The other two studies cited provided extensive data on market concentration for 1935 and 1937.

5. And while some embraced these models as proof that monopoly caused inflation and unemployment, this was clearly an inappropriate deduction. Neither Robinson nor Chamberlin attempted to explain why prices remained "inflexible" with changes in

spread feeling that somehow excessive market concentration was related to, if not directly responsible for, the depression of the 1930s.

Means's concept of administered prices was in sharp contradiction to classical theory, as well as to the new theories of Chamberlin and Robinson, for it suggested, unlike the others, why prices should become inflexible when industries became concentrated. Means's doctrine, initially at least, was based on empirical observation rather than on any explicit theory. Although his early works were sharply criticized on empirical grounds, in retrospect it appears that they successfully withstood the early attacks,[6] despite the excessively vulnerable terms in which he initially had cast his thesis.[7] Nor has the most recent and comprehensive attack succeeded in disproving Means's basic thesis.[8]

The most famous economic work of the 1930s was John Maynard Keynes's

---

demand, an effect described by Means, nor to show how firms with market power could create a persistent inflationary bias and unemployment. However, Chamberlin did lay down the foundation for future administered pricing theories with his recognition that traditional concepts of rational economic behavior in competitive markets, such as the equation of marginal revenue with marginal cost, were of little value in understanding the actions of a few firms in an oligopolistic industry. Having to set prices and output in an environment of pervasive uncertainty shaped in part by the interdependence of their cost and revenue functions, oligopolistic firms could not necessarily be expected to conform to the behavioral rules of classical price theory.

6. See Scherer's summary of the literature criticizing and supporting Means's early work. F. M. Scherer, *Industrial Market Structure and Economic Performance* (Rand McNally 1970), pp. 294-296.

7. Means's early work was cast almost exclusively in terms of flexible versus rigid prices. He apparently did so because of his preoccupation with explaining the differences in industrial and agricultural pricing behavior during the early years of the Depression.

8. The most ambitious attack was launched by Stigler and Kindahl, who sought to demonstrate that the administered pricing phenomenon is an illusion created by bad economic data. They alleged that the empirical support for this concept was based on wholesale price indices composed of seller list prices rather than actual transaction prices. They therefore obtained from a sample of broadly defined industries the prices actually paid by buyers. G. J. Stigler and J. K. Kindahl, *The Behavior of Industrial Prices* (National Bureau of Economic Research 1970). Although Stigler and Kindahl claimed to have destroyed the administered price thesis, in actual fact they may have strengthened it. Indeed, Means's careful dissection of their study demonstrates that the underlying data support his views. G. C. Means, "The Administered Price Thesis Reconfirmed," *American Economic Review*, 62 (June 1972), pp. 292-306. For Stigler and Kindahl's reply, see "Industrial Prices, as Administered by Dr. Means," *American Economic Review*, 63 (September 1973), pp. 717-721. Perhaps the most devastating critique of Stigler and Kindahl, however, is that of Milton Moore in "Stigler on Inflexible Prices," *Canadian Journal of Economics*, 5 (November 1972), pp. 486-493. For other criticisms of the study, see S. A. Ross and Michael Wachter, "Wage Determination, Inflation and Industrial Structure," *American Economic Review*, 63 (September 1973), p. 677; and John M. Blair, *Economic Concentration* (Harcourt Brace 1972), pp. 461ff.

*The General Theory of Employment, Interest and Money* (1936). As Robinson and Chamberlin contributed to the modification of traditional understandings of behavior in *individual* industries (so-called microeconomics), so Keynes contributed to the modification, at least at the time, of traditional understanding of macroeconomics. Keynes provided a persuasive theory demonstrating that, because of inadequate demand, the economy could stagnate at a low-level equilibrium, one with excessive unemployment. Keynes recognized the assumption that wages and prices were set in perfectly competitive markets was not universally met in the real world, but he believed the exceptions to it were relatively unimportant to his basic thesis. While agreeing that businesses and trade unions could have "considerable practical significance," he viewed them as creating "positions of semi-inflation" as contrasted to "the absolute inflation which ensues on an increase in effective demand in circumstances of full employment." [9] We must recall that Keynes was writing in the depths of a great depression and that he was concerned with putting people back to work. When 10 percent to 15 percent of the labor force is idle and a large part of the industrial machine is silent, getting the economy going again overshadows the potential problem of premature inflation.

But priorities change once the industrial machine is humming again. Whereas prewar Keynesians ignored or said little of the role market power played in "Keynesian economics," thinking changed after the war, especially when the bizarre pricing behavior of certain industries was aired in public congressional hearings during the 1950s.[10]

Events once again proved that even cherished economic theories must ultimately yield — or at least be recast — when they fail to explain reality, despite the mighty efforts of those committed to orthodox views to mold fact to fit theory. Because so much of the "belief" in the market power–inflation relationship is the product of observed experience, this is a case where, in Oliver Wendell Holmes's apt expression, "a page of history is worth volumes of

9. Keynes, *The General Theory of Employment, Interest and Money* (Macmillan 1936), pp. 301-302. Keynes also referred to "administered" prices. *Id.* at 268.

10. Martin Brofenbrenner and Franklin D. Holzman observe that whereas Keynes had made a distinction between excess demand and cost "induced" inflation in his *Treatise on Money* (Harcourt Brace 1930), his failure to expand upon this concept in *The General Theory* led many professed Keynesians to question the very existence of cost-push inflation. "A Survey of Inflation Theory," in *Surveys of Economic Theory,* vol. 1 (1967), p. 64. However, many Keynesian interpreters of the postwar period did nonetheless recognize the possibility of conflicts between full employment and price stability arising from the institutional structure of the economy. For a typical early postwar work by a Keynesian, see Kenneth K. Kurihara, *Monetary Theory and Public Policy* (W. W. Norton 1950), with its many references to problems created by monopoly power of labor and business. Roy Harrod, an old friend and close associate of Keynes, observed in 1972: "I am convinced that Keynes, who was continually adjusting his views in the light of current experience, would, were he alive, firmly repudiate the doctrine that cost-push inflation can be terminated by reducing aggregate demand." R. Harrod, "Imperfect Competition, Aggregate Demand, and Inflation," *Economic Journal,* 82 (March 1972 Supplement), p. 401.

logic." I therefore propose to review briefly some of the critical events and empirical analyses of them that played a central role in developing economic thought in this area. John Blair captured the mood of those searching for theories that could better explain reality in the title of his 1959 paper before the American Economic Association, "Administered Prices: A Phenomenon in Search of a Theory." [11]

## THE CLASSIC DOCTRINE IN RETREAT

The 1950s were a unique interlude in American economic and political history. They marked neither the beginning nor the end of an era, but rather a pause during which policymakers ignored the events of the preceding two decades. Historians may ultimately label the 1950s as an attempted second "return to normalcy." Americans were exhausted with the sacrifices demanded by World War II and the Korean War, and were frustrated with a federal government rendered ineffective by continuing conflicts between legislative and executive branches controlled by opposing parties. Not surprisingly, therefore, most Americans welcomed the kindly and benign leadership of President Eisenhower as the first nonactivist president since 1932. The result was the near total neglect by the federal government of many social and economic problems that swept in the New Deal but which had not been solved by it — indeed, efforts at solution were largely abandoned with the advent of World War II.

For macroeconomic policy the 1950s marked essentially a return to laissez-faire, as epitomized by Eisenhower's near repudiation of the Employment Act of 1946, which charged the federal government with the responsibility of maintaining maximum employment and rapid economic growth. Eisenhower hesitated in activating the Council of Economic Advisors, and months passed before he fully staffed the CEA under its new chairman, Arthur F. Burns, who seemed eminently qualified to play the noninterventionist role expected of him. Many economists agree that the resulting dismal economic record of three recessions in eight years is largely attributable to the essentially passive role of the executive branch in the period.[12]

It is against this background that we must view the behavior of business and labor during the 1950s, a background wholly different from that of the preceding two decades and most of the following one. I emphasize this point because these differences in institutional settings make hazardous any comparisons between the 1950s and subsequent periods, especially when the comparisons involve empirical tests that cannot include variables that adequately explain differences in the institutional environment.

The price inflation accompanying the Korean War was the garden variety excess demand inflation — where too many dollars chased too few goods.

11. John M. Blair, "Administered Prices: A Phenomenon in Search of a Theory," *American Economic Review,* 49 (May 1959), pp. 431-450.

12. Macroeconomic policy was left primarily to the monetary policy pursued by the Federal Reserve Board.

With the return of peace, the general inflation abated. However, whereas the critical wholesale price index actually fell between 1951 and 1953, thereafter it rose steadily, though modestly. This overall price movement obscured significant differences within the index. Most apparent was the contrast between agricultural and industrial prices, a phenomenon that had sparked Means's original interest in "administered" prices. Whereas farm products declined by 2.5 percent between 1953 and 1959, industrial prices rose by 12.3 percent. The rather substantial rise in industrial product prices occurred despite two recessions in 1954-1955 and 1957-1958. This bizarre price behavior did not receive much attention until the late 1950s when Senator Estes Kefauver's Antitrust Subcommittee held its hearings on administered pricing; Senator Paul H. Douglas' Joint Economic Committee held hearings on the effects of monopolistic practices on employment, growth, and price levels; and several researchers, including Gardiner Means, examined carefully the pricing behavior of the steel industry because it seemed to defy the conventional wisdom.

The story bears retelling. What happened in steel, more than anything else, explains why so many economists, some of whom were soon to become key policymakers in the 1960s, came to believe that there was indeed a phenomenon of cost-push, sellers', or administered inflation, and came to reject the conventional view that inflation can only arise because of excess aggregate demand.[13]

13. The manner in which events of the 1950s and since have shaped economists' views toward the inflationary process is perhaps best illustrated by the gradual conversion of Paul Samuelson, Nobel Laureate in Economics. Samuelson, an ardent Keynesian, for over twenty-five years has been recording the development of economic knowledge in the successive editions of his extremely successful textbook, *Economics*. One trend definitely reflected in its pages is the increasing recognition, within the economics fraternity, of the operation of market power in the genesis of inflation. In writing the first edition of 1948, Professor Samuelson depicted inflation as the result of excess demand forces, but hinted in a few sentences that there was an ominous possibility that at times "prices may begin to shoot up *long before* full employment is reached," though he did not relate this problem explicitly to market power. Ten years later and after his exposure to the curious inflation of the 1955-1958 period, Samuelson was no longer so sure that inflation was solely an excess demand phenomenon. Devoting one page to the subject, "A New Kind of Inflation?," he recognized the possibility that the combined exercise of the market power of corporations and unions could lead to a "wage-push" inflation in which wages would be rising faster than productivity, prices would be rising in response, and the monetary-fiscal authorities, anxious to avoid high unemployment, would be ratifying the wage-price spiral by appropriately expansionary policies. Finally, three years ago in his eighth edition of *Economics*, Professor Samuelson granted full diplomatic recognition to administered or so-called sellers' inflation, citing the 1959 hearings of the Joint Economic Committee which disclosed the importance of administered steel prices in the steady rise of the wholesale price index during the late 1950s. Not one to try to pour new wine into old wineskins, he acknowledged that the persistent concurrence of high unemployment and inflation in almost all industrial countries during the postwar era called for "new analytical tools of descriptions, interpretation, understanding

## PRICING BEHAVIOR IN STEEL

Steel prices played a major role in the increases in the wholesale price index (WPI) following the Korean War. Between 1953 and 1959 finished-steel prices rose by 36 percent, in contrast to an 8.5 percent increase for all wholesale prices. In fact, wholesale prices exclusive of those of metals and metals manufacturers were only 1.5 percent higher in 1959 than they had been in 1953.[14] Quite clearly, then, steel provided the mainspring for the price increases during that period.

The persistent increases in steel prices during 1953-1959 simply cannot be explained by the theory of demand-pull inflation. Not only was demand *not* pulling up steel prices, but at times prices were *raised* in the face of *falling* demand and the presence of substantial excess capacity. For example, steel prices were increased in 1954 despite the fact that capacity utilization fell from 95 percent in 1953 to 71 percent in 1954. The 1958 increases, when overall capacity utilization dropped from 85 percent in 1957 to 61 percent in 1958, were especially perverse if viewed in terms of the demand-pull theory.

These sharp price increases resulted in a widening in steel producers' margins after 1953. Gardiner Means's careful analysis shows that producer margins at a standard rate of production about doubled between 1953 and 1959. His analysis reveals that steel prices rose much more rapidly than per unit operating expenses — 36 percent versus 14 percent.[15]

By increasing margins the industry was able to operate profitably at a very low rate of capacity utilization.[16] For example, Means estimates that because of the widening operating margins, in 1959 United States Steel would have been able to break even at an operating rate of 30 percent of capacity. In fact, during the first six months of 1960, while operations were at only 47 percent of capacity, the company enjoyed a net income of $111 million after taxes. In contrast, if it had maintained only the operating margin prevailing

---

and prediction." Inflation is a hybrid of both excess demand and market power, he argued, and although there is a tendency for prices to rise even before full employment is reached, there is also a tendency for high levels of unemployment to dampen wage increases in excess of productivity gains. The Phillips curve (discussed below), in other words, is neither perfectly flat nor perfectly vertical, but a sloping function subject to shifts arising from changing expectations and institutional evolution.

14. G. C. Means, *Steel Prices and Administered Inflation* (Harper, 1962), p. 113.

15. G. C. Means, *Pricing Power and the Public Interest* (Harper & Row 1962), p. 137.

16. Weston and Lustgarten (this volume, this chapter) argue that the below-average profits of steel companies during the 1950s deny the allegations that the steel industry manipulated prices to maintain their profit rates. Of course, the test is not whether the steel industry earned less than many others, but whether an effectively competitive industry could have a break-even point at a 30 percent rate of capacity utilization. This could not have happened unless the industry had the power to widen greatly its operating margins, something a more competitively structured industry could not do in the face of falling demand.

in 1953, it would have made no net income at this rate of capacity utilization.[17]

Steel price inflation between 1953 and 1959 thus cannot be explained by the traditional theory of demand-pull inflation. Otto Eckstein and Gary Fromm conclude that "the wage and price behavior of the steel industry represents an important instance of inflation caused to a substantial degree by the exercise of market power. . . . This type of inflation cannot be controlled by policies aimed at restricting total demand." [18] They estimated the WPI would have risen by 40 percent less between 1947 and 1958 had steel prices risen at the same rate as other wholesale prices.

During most of the 1960s steel prices followed a distinctly different pattern than during the 1950s. From 1960 to January 1966, all metal and metal product prices rose less than 1 percent per year. During the next three years of strong *demand-pull* inflation, metal and metal products prices rose just over 2 percent annually. For the entire 8-year period of 1960-1968, metal and metal products rose an average of only 1.4 percent a year.

The picture changed radically after January 1969, however. Between then and January 1971 metal and metal products prices soared 12 percent. In contrast, wholesale prices of products sold in quite competitive markets rose only modestly, or even declined: farm products, up 3.5 percent; textiles, up 1.5 percent; lumber and wood products, down 14.2 percent (see Table 18).

TABLE 18

Weighted Average Price Change in 296 Manufacturing and Farm Products
Between December 1969 and December 1971

| 4-Firm Concentration Ratio | Number of Products | Weighted Average Price Change |
|---|---|---|
| | | Dec. 1969 to Dec. 1970 |
| 50% and Over | 137 | 5.9% |
| 25-49% | 110 | −1.0 |
| Under 25% | 49 | −6.1 |
| Total | 296 | 1.6% |
| | | Dec. 1970 to Dec. 1971 |
| 50% and Over | 137 | 2.7% |
| 25-49% | 110 | 6.0 |
| Under 25% | 49 | 7.8 |
| Total | 296 | 4.7% |

Source: J. M. Blair, "Market Power and Inflation: A Short-Run Target Return Model," *Journal of Economic Issues,* Vol. 8, No. 2 (June 1974), p. 453.

17. Means, *supra* n. 15, at 148.

18. Otto Eckstein and Gary Fromm, "Steel and the Post-War Inflation" (Joint Economic Committee Study Paper No. 2, 86th Congress, 1st Session, November 6, 1959), p. 34.

How to explain these differing patterns of price behavior in the steel industry over the past two decades? The answer is to be found largely in differences in public policy. During the 1950s, wage and price decisions in steel were made entirely in the "free" market. Government took an essentially hands-off attitude, except for the late Senator Kefauver's persistent investigations of price behavior in the late 1950s. In sharp contrast, the President's Council of Economic Advisors initiated in 1962 a wage-price "guidepost" policy. Although this policy fell far short of complete success in many cases, it was applied quite persistently in steel and other metal products. In essence, the Council's "guideposts for noninflationary wage and price behavior" called for the kinds of wages and prices generated by competitive markets. The Council guideposts were initially designed mainly to educate and mobilize public opinion as to how wages and prices should behave in order to avoid seller-induced inflation. Essentially, wages were to be geared to overall productivity increases, which the Council estimated at 3.2 percent annually, and prices were to decline in industries with high productivity so as to offset price increases in those with low productivity. No mechanism was established to enforce the guideposts. However, events soon conspired to transform the guideposts from mere educational tools into an activist new approach to controlling seller-induced inflation.

Predictably, events in the steel industry provided the impetus to the new policy. As already noted, steel pricing behavior had played a major role in the seller-induced inflation of the 1950s. And significantly, some of the leading students of that problem were now with the Council of Economic Advisors.

In early April 1962, the Steelworkers' Union accepted a wage settlement calling for an increase in hourly wages of about 2.5 percent, a "noninflationary" settlement that fell well within the guideposts and which had been urged upon the union by the Kennedy administration.[19] The week following the settlement, United States Steel announced a general price increase of 3.5 percent. The next day, Bethlehem (the second largest steel producer) and five other companies followed suit with identical price increases, an action reminiscent of the behavior of the 1950s, since the industry was again operating well below two-thirds of capacity. These price increases represented a clearcut use of discretionary pricing power and posed a direct threat to the administration's effort to accelerate economic growth without inflation.

What followed is familiar history. President Kennedy announced that the price increases were in direct conflict with the wage-price guideposts, reminded the industry that the recent wage settlement could be offset by productivity increases and urged those steel companies that had not yet increased their prices — notably Inland, Armco, and Kaiser — not to follow United States Steel's lead. Shortly thereafter, Inland and Kaiser publicly announced that they would not follow the lead. Bethlehem — and shortly United States Steel — then withdrew their own price increases.

19. John Sheahan, The Wage-Price Guideposts (Brookings Institution 1967), pp. 33 ff.

While the episode was all over in three days, bitter memories lingered. At first, much of the business community resented the presidential intervention, but these reactions soon subsided and — perhaps most important — steel prices remained reasonably stable over the next four years, paralleling the behavior of the overall wholesale price index until January 1969.

Although the Kennedy-Johnson guidepost policy was never fully implemented and broke down almost completely during the demand-pull inflation of 1966-1968, it continued to be applied in the steel industry through 1968 with some significant successes. For example, when in July 1968 the steel industry announced a proposed price increase of about 5 percent, President Johnson's Cabinet Committee on Price Stability succeeded in persuading the industry to raise prices by less than one-half the increase originally announced.

The most dramatic proof that guidepost policy influenced steel prices are the events following President Nixon's announcement shortly after his inauguration that he would not use "guideposts," "jawboning," or any other "artificial" device calling for wage and price restraints in industry. Instead, he promised to bring about price stability without significantly increasing unemployment, by retarding the growth in aggregate demand through a balanced budget and a curtailment of monetary growth. Under this so-called game plan, "free markets" would solve what had been diagnosed as a purely demand-pull inflation. The expectation was that as aggregate demand slowed, prices would stop rising. The adjustment process predicted by the Nixon game plan rested on a heroic assumption: businessmen would respond to slackening demand by not raising prices, or better still, by reducing prices, and labor would settle for smaller wage increases as prices moderated and the demand for labor slackened "modestly." For 31 months the President did not interfere with a single wage or price decision, except for a few instances in the construction industry. The experiment ended abruptly in August 1971 and the "free market" was temporarily abandoned in favor of a system of rigid price and wage controls.

The results of this historic experiment with free markets are now familiar to everyone. For 31 months the nation experienced both inflation and rising unemployment. Not too surprisingly, steel was an important contributor to this inflation. When in early 1969 the industry once again felt free to administer its prices as it saw fit, it went on what has been aptly characterized as a post-Johnson price orgy, this despite the fact that during most of 1969-1971 the industry operated with substantial excess capacity. Obviously this behavior was in direct contradiction to the basic assumptions of the President's game plan that "free" markets would restrain price increases once the forces of demand-pull inflation had been quelled.

I recite the steel pricing experience because it illustrates in indisputable fashion that an individual industry with market power, in this case responding in part to the behavior of a powerful union, can bring about price increases in the face of falling demand. The behavior of steel simply cannot be explained by conventional demand-pull theories of inflation. A question still remains, of course, as to whether steel is unique, and therefore whether, as

Markham has argued, market-power-induced inflation is a particular rather than a general problem.[20] Answering this question requires looking beyond case studies to analyses that cut across a number of industries with varying market structures.

## CROSS-SECTIONAL AND AGGREGATE STUDIES

A number of economists have tested statistically the hypothesis that market power influences wage and price behavior. Some of these studies measure the impact of market power of corporations, others that of unions, and some the interacting of powerful corporations and unions.

Although the evidence is somewhat mixed, several conclusions are possible. The first is that during the 1950s prices in concentrated manufacturing industries rose more rapidly than in less concentrated ones.[21] The major critics of this conclusion are DePodwin and Selden.[22] Although they believed their findings sufficiently conclusive to "put the administered inflation hypotheses to rest," [23] careful examination of certain biases in their procedures demonstrated that they had given the hypothesis a premature burial.[24]

In the most comprehensive and sophisticated cross-sectional statistical study of pricing behavior between 1953 and 1959, Leonard Weiss found that prices rose most rapidly in the more concentrated industries.[25] However, when he repeated his analysis for 1959-1963, he found no statistically significant re-

20. Jesse Markham, "Administered Prices and the Recent Inflation," in Joseph W. Conard et al., eds., *Inflation, Growth and Employment* (Prentice-Hall 1964).

21. Two major studies are H. M. Levinson, "Postwar Movement of Prices and Wages in Manufacturing Industries" in *Study of Employment, Growth and Price Levels* (Joint Economic Committee Study Paper No. 21, 1960); and L. W. Weiss, "Business Pricing Policies and Inflation Reconsidered," *Journal of Political Economy,* 74 (April 1966), pp. 177-187.

22. H. J. DePodwin and R. T. Selden, "Business Pricing Policies and Inflation," *Journal of Political Economy,* 71 (April 1963), pp. 116-127.

23. *Id.* at 126.

24. See Gardiner Means's insightful examination of the DePodwin and Selden study, "Business Pricing Policies and Inflation: A Comment," in Hearings on Economic Concentration, Subcommittee on Antitrust and Monopoly, Senate Committee on the Judiciary, pt. 1, at 489-496 (1964). Scherer concluded, after reviewing the "devastating" Means critique of the DePodwin-Selden study, that the latter in fact "supported the original Means conjecture, instead of refuting it." Scherer, *supra* n. 6, at 296-297. J. M. Clark also criticized the DePodwin-Selden position because they hypothesized that inflation must consist entirely of either demand-pull or seller-push. Thus whenever they uncover evidence of demand-pull during the period studied, 1953-1959, they believe it destroys the seller-push hypothesis. Clark believes, on the other hand, that there may be elements of both present over the course of years examined. J. M. Clark, *The Wage-Price Problem* (American Bankers Association 1960), pp. 4, 5 ff.

25. L. W. Weiss, "Business Pricing Policies and Inflation Reconsidered," *Journal of Political Economy,* 74 (April 1966), pp. 177-187.

lationship between concentration and the degree of price increases. Weiss concluded that the administered inflation of the 1950s had largely ended by 1959 and that perhaps it was "simply a *delayed* portion of the inflation of the 1940's." [26]

In another interesting study, Weiss found that for 1967-1969 there existed a statistically *negative* relationship between the degree of industry concentration and price changes — i.e., prices rose less in more concentrated than in less concentrated industries.[27]

Weiss's various findings have been embraced by the demand-pull Chicago School as evidence that market power presents no real problem because it merely creates "lagged inflation." [28]

Care must be exercised in interpreting Weiss's findings. Even if one accepts the Chicago School interpretation that industrial concentration supports a "lagged" theory of seller-induced inflation, the latter still undermines the traditional theory of demand-pull inflation and creates special problems for monetary and fiscal policy. The "lagged" inflation of 1953-1959, when the economy experienced inflation despite the absence of excess demand, resulted in the application of improper monetary and fiscal policies. We had a record three recessions in eight years during 1953-1960. On the other hand, the tendency of concentrated industries to lag (relative to competitive industries which presumably were already operating near capacity), as Weiss suggests they did during the period of true demand-pull inflation in the late 1960s, may mislead public policy officials as to the true magnitude of the demand-pull inflation, thereby delaying prompt application of appropriate monetary and fiscal policies. Moreover, if concentrated industries decide to catch up after monetary and fiscal policy is applied, they cause inflation in the face of falling demand.[29]

Weiss's findings of a difference in behavior between 1953-1959 and 1959-1963 hardly warrant the optimistic conclusion that seller-push inflation does not create a tendency for "continuously creeping" inflation. The observed differences in behavior in these two periods may well be attributable to changes in public policy toward those with market power. As I mentioned earlier, the Kennedy administration's wage-price guidepost policies that began in early 1962 changed significantly wage and price determination in several industries contributing to the seller-push inflation of the 1950s. Several

26. *Id.* at 186 (emphasis added).

27. L. W. Weiss, "The Role of Concentration in Recent Inflation," appendix to testimony of Richard W. McLaren in *The 1970 Midyear Review of the State of the Economy*, Hearings Before the Joint Economic Committee, 91st Congress, 2nd Session, pt. 1 (1970).

28. T. G. Moore, "Incomes Policy, Its Rationale and Development," in *Economic Policy and Inflation in the Sixties* (American Enterprise Institute, April 1972), pp. 204-205.

29. S. A. Ross and M. L. Wachter, "Wage Determination, Inflation, and the Industrial Structure," *American Economic Review*, 63 (September 1973), pp. 690-691.

studies have found that the guideposts did significantly reduce wage and price demands during 1962-1966.[30] Perhaps more importantly, careful examination of particular industries, most notably steel, reveals neither that they were merely practicing "catch up" during the 1950s, nor that they would have voluntarily stopped increasing prices in the 1960s. Rather, the latter behavior was imposed upon them by guidepost policies.[31]

Recent price experience has followed the contrasting patterns of early periods: prices rising in concentrated industries in the face of declining demand, while rising less rapidly than those in competitive industries during periods of rapidly expanding aggregate demand. John Blair has summarized the price behavior in differently structured industries during two years of President Nixon's grand "game plan" for maintaining full employment without inflation by relying solely on monetary and fiscal policy.[32] Table 18 shows the price behavior for 1969-1970, when aggregate demand was contracted. Despite this, during the 12-month period of December 1969 to January 1970, average prices rose 5.9 percent in industries with 4-firm concentration ratios of 50 percent or more; in contrast, average prices declined 6.1 percent in industries with concentration ratios below 25 percent.[33] Because prices rose

30. George L. Perry, "Wages and Guideposts," *American Economic Review, 57* (September 1967), pp. 897-904. For a criticism of this study, see "Comments" on Perry by P. S. Anderson, M. L. Wachter, and A. W. Thorp, as well as Perry's "Reply," in the *American Economic Review, 59* (June 1969). A recent study confirms Perry's earlier work. Otto Eckstein and Roger Brinner, *The Inflationary Process in the United States,* Study for the Joint Economic Committee, 92nd Congress, 2nd Session, February 22, 1972. It found that the guideposts reduced annual wage inflation by 0.7 percent and price inflation by 1.4 percent during 1962-1966. Eckstein and Brinner's formulation expanded upon a study by R. J. Gordon that had found no relationship. "Inflation in Recession and Recovery" (*Brookings Papers on Economic Activity No. 1,* 1971). Also finding that the wage-price guideposts had a significant effect are G. Pierson, "The Effects of Union Strength on the U.S. Phillips' Curve," *American Economic Review, 58* (June 1968), pp. 456-467; S. Wallack, "Wage-Price Guidelines and the Rate of Wage Changes in U.S. Manufacturing, 1951-66," *Southern Economic Journal,* 38 (July 1971), pp. 33-47; Gary Fromm, *The Wage-Price Issue: The Need for Guideposts,* Hearings Before the Joint Economic Committee, 90th Congress, 2nd Session, at 3 (1968).

31. A recent study of Canadian experience supports the administered price theses that in the absence of controls, concentrated industries increase prices in the face of falling demand. W. Sellekaerts and R. Lesage, "A Reformulation and Empirical Verification of the Administered Prices Inflation Hypothesis: The Canadian Case," *Southern Economic Journal,* 39 (June 1973), pp. 345-360.

32. See Fromm, n. 30 *supra,* at 13-14 for discussion of the President's "game plan."

33. Blair made certain additions and deletions to the basic Bureau of Labor Statistics data upon which he relied. J. M. Blair, "Market Power and Inflation: A Short-Run Target Return Model," *Journal of Economic Issues,* Vol. 8, No. 2 (June 1974), p. 453. In his paper, Blair also makes a much less aggregative comparison of price behavior than appears in Tables 1 and 2. He does so to compare behavior in "major product groups having generally similar product characteristics and probably affected

more rapidly than aggregate demand, unemployment climbed from 3.5 percent in December 1969 to 6.0 percent in December 1970. Faced with both rising prices and rising unemployment, the administration reversed its game plan by expanding aggregate demand, thereby introducing demand-pull as well as cost-push forces, with a consequent change in pricing behavior. During the next 12 months the most concentrated industries increased prices less than did the less concentrated ones (Table 18). This confirms the findings of Weiss and others that the pricing behavior of concentrated and unconcentrated industries differs during periods of cost-push and demand-pull inflation.[34]

In addition to studies of industrial concentration and price behavior, an impressive body of research demonstrates that when labor possesses bargaining power it is able to achieve higher wages. A variety of empirical works provides abundant evidence (1) that the economic power of unions has indeed enabled them to obtain greater wage increases than unorganized laborers and (2) that when powerful unions bargain with employers with market power the unions fare even better.[35]

Several other studies approach the problem somewhat differently. Instead of correlating wages with concentration, they correlate wages with corporate profits directly, on the theory that higher oligopolistic profits entice labor to demand, and management to accept, larger wage settlements. These studies, too, have found that wages and prices tend to increase more in industries with the highest profit rates.[36] Not surprisingly, these relationships generally do not hold up during periods of demand-pull inflation, when competitively structured segments of the labor market tend to rise more rapidly than do those in concentrated industries.[37]

---

by similar . . . cost changes." His findings for these major groups are consistent with his combined results for all industries.

34. Blair's findings are confirmed by a staff study of the Kansas City Federal Reserve, which used a larger sample of 347 industries. S. W. Stahl and C. E. Harshbarger, "Economic Concentration: Some Further Observations," *Monthly Review* (Federal Reserve Bank of Kansas City, January 1974), pp. 3-11.

35. J. Garbarino, "Unions and the National Wage Level," *American Economic Review*, 40 (December 1950), pp. 893-896, and "A Theory of Interindustry Wage Structure Variation," *Quarterly Journal of Economics*, 64 (May 1950), pp. 282-305; A. M. Ross and W. Goldner, "Forces Affecting Interindustry Wage Structure," *Quarterly Journal of Economics*, 64 (May 1950), pp. 254-281; H. M. Levinson, *supra* n. 21; L. W. Weiss "Concentration and Labor Earnings," *American Economic Review*, Vol. 56, No. 1 (March 1966), pp. 96-117; Frank P. Stafford, "Concentration and Labor Earnings: Comment," *American Economic Review*, Vol. 58, No. 1 (March 1968), pp. 174-181; W. G. Bowen, *Wage Behavior in the Postwar Period* (Princeton Univ. Press 1960), pp. 55-85.

36. W. G. Bowen, *supra* n. 35; R. J. Bhatia, "Profits and the Rate of Change in Money Earnings in the United States, 1935-59," *Economica*, 29 New Series (August 1962), pp. 255-262; and George L. Perry, *Unemployment, Money Wage Rates, and Inflation* (MIT Press 1966).

37. M. W. Reder, "Wage Differentials: Theory and Measurement," in National Bureau of Economic Research, *Aspects of Labor Economics* (Princeton Univ. Press

In conclusion, there is a growing body of empirical evidence supporting the hypothesis that both wages and prices are related to the degree of market power. Although mixed, the weight of the evidence supports the hypothesis that market power in labor and industrial markets create an inflationary bias in our economy. That is to say, even in the absence of excess aggregate demand, the economy is inflation-prone at less than full employment.

As observed at the outset, the concern with seller-push inflation grew out of experience rather than theory. Similarly, many of the empirical studies cited above have no well articulated theory of seller-push inflation. It is therefore appropriate to set forth briefly a conceptual framework useful for evaluating the phenomenon.

## THE PHILLIPS CURVE AND MARKET POWER

Perhaps the major postwar innovation in studying inflation is the so-called Phillips curve, developed by the British economist A. W. Phillips. Nobel Prize winner Paul Samuelson has called it "one of the most important concepts of our time." [38] In his original formulation Phillips attempted to measure statistically the relationship between the rate of unemployment and changes in the wage rate.[39] He reasoned that there exists a trade-off between the rate of unemployment and wage rates. Because wage rates are such an important part of costs, higher wages also usually mean higher prices.

It has become commonplace to express the relationship more directly as the unemployment–inflation relationship. We shall therefore simply use the short-hand expression, the U-I relationship or U-I curve.

Figure 6 depicts two hypothetical U-I curves. For example, point A on curve #1 would yield an unemployment rate of 5 percent and an annual inflation price increase of 1 percent. The respective figures for point B are 3 percent and 5 percent. Thus with this curve we must "trade-off" a 2 percent decrease in the rate of unemployment for a 4 percent increase in the rate of inflation.

Obviously, a nation would be better off if its U-I curve could be shifted to the left, thereby permitting the nation to experience a lower inflation rate for a given unemployment rate. The crucial issues are: (1) what determines the shape of a nation's U-I curve and (2) how can it be shifted to the left?

1962), pp. 291-296; H. G. Lewis, *Unionism and Relative Wages in the United States* (Univ. of Chicago Press 1963), p. 159; L. G. Reynolds, "The Impact of Collective Bargaining on the Wage Structure of the United States," in J. T. Dunlop, ed., *The Theory of Wage Determination* (Macmillan 1957); M. Segal, "Unionism and Wage Movements," *Southern Economic Journal*, 28 (October 1961), pp. 174-181.

38. Paul A. Samuelson, in P. A. Samuelson and A. F. Burns, *Full Employment, Guideposts and Economic Stability* (American Enterprise Institute for Public Policy Research 1967), p. 54.

39. A. W. Phillips, "The Relationship between Unemployment and the Change of Money Wage Rates in the United Kingdom, 1862-1957," *Economica*, 25 New Series (November 1958), pp. 283-299.

### Figure 6
### Hypothetical U-I Curves

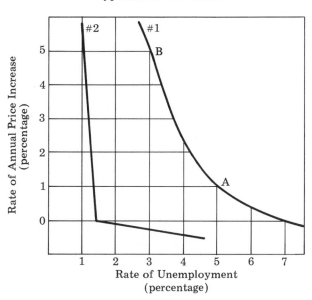

In his pioneering work, Phillips used a monocausal approach wherein changes in money wage rates were caused solely by changes in the level of employment. Both economic theory and experience suggest that wages and inflation rates are caused by a variety of factors, including the competitive structure of labor and industrial markets.

If a nation's wages and prices were perfectly flexible and determined in perfectly competitive markets, its U-I curve might look like #2 in Figure 6.[40] In perfectly functioning markets, labor, materials and capital would respond immediately to small changes in price. Under these assumptions, the only impediments to simultaneous achievement of full employment without inflation would be faulty monetary and fiscal policy that pushed output beyond full employment, or the 1 percent figure shown in curve #2. As Samuelson has put it, a country could then "engineer fiscal and monetary expansion just up to the point of full employment. Prior to that point, the general price level would not rise and average wages would grow automatically with productivity."[41] Samuelson adds: "In this ideal world, which differs dramatically from every mixed economy that now exists, the problem would be merely

40. Samuelson and Burns, *supra* n. 38, at 53-56.
41. *Id.* at 53-54.

one of the macro-economic dosage, and there would be no dilemmas of policy." [42]

But unhappily, in the real world various market imperfections may adversely affect the shape and location of the U-I curve, causing it to resemble #1 more than #2. Of these imperfections, we shall here concern ourselves only with labor and corporate market power. [43]

The most obvious structural factor generating "bad" U-I curves is the interaction between firms and labor unions with discretionary power in setting wages and prices. While powerful labor unions may always seek wage increases exceeding productivity gains, they are especially encouraged to do so when they deal with powerful firms enjoying large profits. Moreover, firms with market power may more readily grant excessive wage demands because they have the discretion to pass forward their higher labor costs to their customers. As we noted earlier, empirical findings support the hypotheses that wages are likely to be greater in industries where labor bargains with powerful corporations and where profits are high. This situation tends to worsen the U-I curve, and presumably the greater the share of the economy characterized by such wage and price behavior, the worse its U-I curve. [44]

Many empirical studies have been conducted to identify the shape of the U-I curve in the United States and other nations. Although a debate continues, it appears that the U-I curve of the United States is shaped more like curve #2 than #1 in Figure 6. Important for our purposes, empirical studies suggest that it is possible to shift the U-I curve by changes in the underlying forces responsible for its shape. Suggestive of the possibilities of shifting the U-I curve are the findings of a prominent econometric study by George Perry, one of several researchers mentioned earlier as having found a statistically significant relationship between industry profits, wages and inflation. Perry identified profits as entering the inflation process in two ways:

> First, in the product market, profits are the goal of pricing policies. Price increases may be initiated to restore profit margins (or maximize profits) in the face of cost increases; or may be initiated to augment (or maximize) profits independently of cost changes. Second, in the labor market, profit rates have been identified as a major determinant of wage increases. [45]

---

42. *Ibid.*

43. For a discussion of other factors that may result in "bad" U-I curves, see the discussion in "The Unemployment-Inflation Problem," Study Paper No. 4, prepared by the Staff of the Cabinet Committee on Price Stability, January 1969, and appearing in *Market Efficiency and Inflation* (Arno Press and The New York Times 1969), pp. 125-150.

44. Other structural factors contributing to a "bad" U-I curve are wage and price rigidities to upward or downward pressures on demand. Such rigidities prevent appropriate response to either an expansion or contraction in aggregate demand, thereby frustrating effective monetary and fiscal policy.

45. Perry, *Unemployment, Money Wage Rates, and Inflation* (MIT Press 1966), p. 112.

Although Perry has "identified" statistically that profit rates are a major "determinant" of wage increases, he has not developed a complete theory explaining this relationship.[46] He relies primarily on the many studies cited above, plus others, demonstrating that both corporations in concentrated industries and powerful unions possess considerable discretionary power in making price and wage decisions. However, there is as yet no complete theory linking the possession of discretionary power and its use. Such a theory requires looking beyond the limited parameters of orthodox economics to the institutional setting of the decision-making process in contemporary America. A growing number of economists believe the behavioral link between profits and wage demands is to be found in the struggle over income distribution.[47]

46. Nor is Perry unique in this respect. Although the authors of the empirical studies reviewed do generally agree that orthodox theory of price and wage determination is inadequate, they do not all embrace the same theory of "administered" pricing, nor do they all even accept the term. Many implicitly or explicitly adopt some variant of the markup inflationary theses, wherein firms sell on the bases of some standard markup over costs, and price so as to protect such markups in the face of falling demand. This concept had its origins in the early work of R. L. Hall and C. J. Hitch, "Price Theory and Economic Behavior," *Oxford Economic Papers*, 2 (May 1939), which challenged traditional marginal cost pricing. An early application of markup pricing to inflation was F. D. Holzman, "Income Determination in Open Inflation," *Review of Economics and Statistics*, 32 (May 1950), pp. 150-158, and J. Duesenberry, "The Mechanics of Inflation," *Review of Economics and Statistics*, 32 (May 1950), pp. 144-149. G. Ackley incorporated this concept in his influential textbook, *Macro-economic Theory* (Macmillan 1961), pp. 421-459. A refinement of the markup theory is the target rate of return pricing formulation of the way in which discretionary power is used. G. C. Means uses this concept in his exhaustive analysis of pricing behavior in the steel industry during the 1950s, *Pricing Power and the Public Interest* (Harper 1962). Means credits Donaldson Brown for having formalized this pricing procedure in 1924 when he was a vice president of DuPont. *Id.* at 236. Other writers developing explanations of the administered price process include W. Adams and R. F. Lanzillotti, "The Reality of Administered Prices," in *Administered Prices: A Compendium on Public Policy*, Antitrust Subcommittee, Senate Committee on the Judiciary, Committee Print (1963). Other noted economists contributing to this classic compendium who gave their views as to how administered prices worked were J. M. Clark, A. E. Kahn, A. P. Lerner, G. C. Means, and E. G. Nourse. Other formulations include the authors conducting the empirical work cited above. Recently John Blair attempted to develop a partial model designed to contribute to a more "general theory" of the pricing behavior of oligopolists over the business cycle. Blair, *supra* n. 33. This is by no means a complete list of those who have formulated theories explaining how firms use their discretionary power. The common thread running through all formulations is: orthodox theory which assumes that firms equate marginal costs and marginal revenue, especially in the short run, does a poor job in explaining how firms behave in the real world.

47. Although this hypothesis does not necessarily conflict with those discussed earlier, which relate wages to industry structure, it envisions a broader view of the problem. According to it, labor unions are not concerned solely with profits and salary income of the corporations with which they bargain, but rather with labor's relative income position in the economy as a whole. If labor perceives an economic

This view is especially common among individuals who actually have dealt with, and observed at first hand, business and labor behavior during the 1960s and 1970s. Gardiner Ackley, a member of the Council of Economic Advisors during 1962-1968, sums up his position as follows:

> My vision of the type of inflationary process which now concerns us sees it as essentially the byproduct of a struggle over income distribution, occurring in a society in which most sellers of goods and services possess some degree of market power over their own wages or prices (in money terms). The extent of each firm's or union's power at any given time is affected by structural and market factors; the manner in which the power is used is affected by perceptions of what is happening, and by political attitudes and social norms. . . . In my view, this model of an inflation-generating struggle to increase or protect income shares . . . provides a substantially meaningful description of wage and price behavior in a modern industrial economy.[48]

Murray L. Weidenbaum, Assistant Secretary of the Treasury in the Nixon administration expresses a similar theme:

> The concern with income distribution can be a powerful mechanism for motivating greater use of potential influence over wage and price decisions. After all, why should a blue collar worker really worry about his wage increases exceeding the growth of productivity . . . when he believes that management is being overpaid, that white collar workers "loaf," and that stockholders are obtaining too large a share of the proceeds both at current income and capital gains? [49]

If these and other economists[50] are correct, they have provided an explanation for Perry's econometric findings that inflation and unemployment are significantly determined by profit rates. The nature of Perry's findings can best be illustrated by reproducing the U-I curves associated with different profit rates. This is done in Figure 7, which is derived from one of Perry's equations. What emerges is not one, but a family of U-I curves, each identified with a particular profit rate. The horizontal axis measures the rate of unemployment ($U$), the left hand vertical axis measures changes in wage ($W$) rates, and the right hand vertical axis measures percentage changes ($C$) in prices. Curve $R = 12.5$ traces the U-I relationship when profits equal 12.5 percent of net worth, and $R = 10$ shows the U-I relationship when profits are 10 percent

---

system which is stacked against the working man, powerful unions will use their power to the fullest. In this event, we would not necessarily expect close correlations between wages and market structure of particular industries.

48. G. Ackley, "An Incomes Policy for the 1970's," *Review of Economics and Statistics*, 54 (August 1972), p. 218.

49. M. L. Weidenbaum, "New Initiatives in National Wage and Price Policy," *Review of Economics and Statistics*, 54 (August 1972), p. 213.

50. Similar views have been expressed by W. F. Mueller, "Monopoly and the Unemployment Problem," *Antitrust Law & Economics Review*, Vol. 5, No. 4 (Summer 1972), pp. 31-32; and W. A. Peterson, "The Corporate State, Economic Performance, and Social Control," *Journal of Economic Issues*, 8 (June 1974), pp. 483-507.

**Figure 7**

Wage-Unemployment-Inflation Curves Associated with Four Profit Rates, with Annual Productivity Rate of 3 Percent

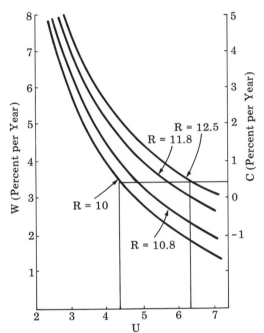

Source: George L. Perry, *Unemployment, Money Wage Rates, and Inflation* (MIT Press 1966), p. 63.

of net worth. U-I curve $R = 10$ is clearly preferable to $R = 12.5$. Whereas $R = 12.5$ yields an inflation rate of 0.5 percent and unemployment of 6.4 percent, $R = 10$ yields an inflation rate of 0.5 percent and an unemployment rate of 4.4 percent.

Perry's empirical findings are used for illustrative purposes.[51] Economists disagree as to the precise shape of U-I curves, their stability, and the factors determining their shape. But there is considerable evidence that they are of the general shape depicted in Figure 7.[52] The implications of these findings are clear: society would benefit greatly if such curves could be shifted to the left.

Thus, the Phillips or U-I curve provides a useful conceptual framework for

51. Perry recommends a number of policy measures to improve the U-I curve including "increases in competition." Perry, *supra* n. 45, at 124.

52. See, e.g., the recent study by Otto Eckstein and Roger Brinner, *The Inflation Process in the United States*, a study prepared for the Joint Economic Committee, 92nd Congress, 2nd Session (1972).

interpreting the impact of market power on the unemployment–inflation problem. The empirical evidence reviewed above which indicates that market power creates wage and price distortions may be interpreted as contributing to "bad" U-I curves. In various ways these distortions result in departures from the perfect market conditions required to yield a U-I curve like #2 in Figure 6. Although many questions remain unanswered, the weight of the evidence supports the hypotheses that the market power in parts of labor and industry does indeed play an important role in creating "bad" U-I curves, i.e., curves which make it impossible to achieve simultaneously full employment and price stability.

The import of this for economic welfare is enormous. Even small improvements in a nation's U-I curve may have a large impact on national wealth. Shifting a U-I curve to the left by 2 percentage points would enable a nation to pursue monetary and fiscal policies that reduce unemployment by an additional 2 percent without increasing inflation. According to "Okun's law," reducing unemployment from, say, 6 percent to 4 percent, would increase United States annual gross national product by about $80 billion in real dollars.[53] Thus the stakes are high indeed, which gives a special urgency to efforts to improve the competitive performance of our economy.

## THE "EITHER/OR" FALLACY

A common fallacy running through the literature critical of the market power–inflation hypothesis is the assumption that all inflation must be explained *either* by excess demand (demand-pull) or by market power. An increasing number of economists have come to believe that much of recent inflation experienced by the United States and other western nations involves a complicated interaction of demand-pull and market power forces.[54]

---

53. A. M. Okun, "Potential GNP: Its Measurement and Significance," in *Papers and Proceedings of the Business and Economics Statistics Section of the American Statistical Association* (1962), pp. 98-104.

54. The British economist Sir Alec Cairncross observes that while at times inflation may be caused "predominantly by demand and price, and at other times *predominantly* by wages and costs, there is a rather confusing mixture of the two, particularly in the neighborhood of full employment." A. Cairncross, "Income Policy: Retrospective and Prospect," in *The Three Banks Review* (published by National and Commercial Banking Group Ltd., London, December 1973), p. 15. Even President Nixon's Council of Economic Advisers recognized that the two sources of inflation "are not necessarily exclusive," observing: "It may be that the economic power structure, though it is not radically different from that of two decades ago and would not on its own cause persistent inflation, does tend to prolong a high rate of inflation, once such a movement is generated by excessive demand. Reduction in the rate of inflation would still be achievable in the face of that type of structure, but it would come faster *if the economic system were more competitive.*" *Economic Report of the President* (February 1971), pp. 61-62 (emphasis added). Peter Fortune of the Boston Federal Reserve states the problem succinctly: "Over long periods of time the primary source of inflation is demand-pull, but over short periods both demand-pull and cost-

Weston and Lustgarten's failure to recognize this possibility of multiple causes mars their entire discussion, renders meaningless their empirical studies, and leads them to interpret improperly the works of others. As discussed above, the most sophisticated study of the relationship between concentration and price behavior was done by Weiss.[55] Whereas Weiss covered the period 1953-1959, Weston and Lustgarten reran the analysis for the entire period 1954-1970, for which they find that concentration is not statistically significant. Their analysis lumps together observations from periods in which market power factors were predominant (1953-1959), periods in which guidepost policy was exerting a strong deterrent to the use of market power by powerful unions and firms (1962-1965), and periods in which excess demand were predominant (1966-1970). This approach inevitably biases the results toward insignificance, since it fails to take into account the fact that different forces were at work over the period.[56] Similarly, their criticism[57] of Perry's study reported above[58] is based on a failure to recognize that the period of the 1960s represented a different economic episode than the period covered by Perry.

I emphasize the fallacy of taking an "either/or" view of inflation to make explicit that market power is only one cause of a complicated multicausal problem. Certainly, demand-pull inflation caused by monetary and fiscal policies has been the major culprit historically, but we should also recognize that existence of excess market power makes it impossible to rely solely on monetary and fiscal policy in coping with inflation. The bizarre pricing behavior of concentrated industries has rendered obsolete policies relying solely on monetary and fiscal policy to manage the economy. As I noted earlier, some economists take comfort from the fact that over long periods prices and wages in the administered price sectors may not diverge greatly, relative to those in the competitor sectors. They would dismiss the problem by calling the aberrant behavior of administered price sectors "delayed inflation." To them, our "competitive" system is working satisfactorily because they believe everything will work out in the long run. But as Lord Keynes so aptly remarked, "in the long run we are all dead." Similarly, the battle against inflation requires adopting appropriate tactics in the short run. But when prices and wages are

---

push factors exist with the weights attached to each varying over time." P. Fortune, "An Evaluation of Anti-Inflation Policies in the United States," *New England Economic Review* (January-February 1974), p. 4.

55. See Weiss, "The Concentration—Profits Relationship and Antitrust," in this volume, Chapter 4.

56. The statistical results appearing in their Tables 1 and 2 are simple comparisons between two variables, thereby ignoring the differences among industries. For example, their finding in Table 2 that concentrated industries did not increase more rapidly than others during 1954-1958 is contradicted by their own regression analysis of this period, as reported in equation 2 in Table 5.

57. Weston and Lustgarten, "Concentration and Inflation," in this volume, this chapter.

58. *Ibid.*

not responsive to demand in the short run, the rules of the game are changed. First, officials may mistakenly interpret seller-push inflation as signalling the onset of demand-pull inflation, as apparently happened in the 1950s. Second, price rigidities in concentrated industries during the early stages of demand-pull inflation may mislead officials into underestimating the true magnitude of demand-pull pressures, thereby delaying timely application of appropriate monetary and fiscal policies. Thus, at any given time inflationary pressures may involve a complicated admixture of seller-push and demand-pull forces that are difficult to combat. As a result, when traditional policies are applied to a demand-pull inflation, they simply do not work. I believe Sellekaerts and Lesage speak for most economists today when they concluded their empirical study of the effects of seller-inflation with the following observation:

> Monetary and fiscal policy, designed to eliminate inflation by reducing aggregate demand below potential output will be relatively unsuccessful if, *in concentrated industries, prices continue to rise in the face of a 10 to 20% fall in all manufacturing capacity utilization.* The major consequence of a traditional *anti*-inflationary policy is an increase in the unemployment rate above what can be considered as socially and politically acceptable, rather than a fall in the rate of inflation.[59]

To sum up, the presence of unrestrained market power creates an inflationary bias in contemporary America. And, significantly, such power creates inflationary pressures even in the absence of strong demand-pull forces. Perhaps the most vexing problem is that efforts to control seller- or cost-push inflation with monetary and fiscal policies, alone, inevitably end up with unacceptably high levels of unemployment or both unemployment and inflation. Hence, to achieve the twin goals of full employment and reasonable price stability requires that restraint be placed on the use of discretionary economic power.

## POLICIES TO CONTROL SELLER-PUSH INFLATION

What, then, are the alternative methods of dealing with the problem of market-power-induced inflation? The alternatives fall into four general categories: (1) comprehensive wage and price controls; (2) a direct attack on the citadels of market power with the objective of dissipating existing power; (3) some form of wage and price guideposts or incomes policy of an essentially voluntary or semivoluntary nature designed to limit the exercise of power where it contributes to inflation; or (4) a comprehensive form of prices and incomes policy that would incorporate a broad mix of measures designed to perfect the functioning of our market economy. Let us consider briefly these alternatives.

I begin with the assumption that the first alternative, comprehensive direct wage and price controls, is an unnecessary and unacceptable solution except as a stopgap measure under the most pressing circumstances.

---

59. Sellekaerts and Lesage, *supra* n. 31, at 356. Emphasis in original.

The second alternative, the dissipation of existing market power, is an essentially long-run approach and therefore is not an adequate solution standing alone. But as discussed below, it is a promising and essential ingredient in a comprehensive approach designed to cope with market-power-induced inflation.

### Wage and Price Guidepost Policy

Samuelson, Perry, Eckstein, and others may be correct that the Kennedy-Johnson guideposts policy shifted the U-I curve during 1962-1966. But such a policy, insofar as it is a mere replay of the wage and price guideposts approach pursued in the 1960s does not offer a viable long-run alternative. First, in the past the policy functioned without a clear legislative mandate, thus depending upon the whims of each occupant of the White House or his staff.

Second, in practice the guideposts were applied arbitrarily and inconsistently. They were too much of a hit-or-miss operation, and as a result a few industries received most of the attention. Although these were important industries, others with equally offensive behavior were left untouched. Such a discriminatory policy is not only inequitable, but eventually becomes politically intolerable.

Third, the policy focused primarily on wages and prices. By neglecting profits, salaries, and other kinds of professional incomes the policy was inherently inequitable. So long as policy focuses solely on wage incomes, labor will ultimately find the program unacceptable.

Fourth, except for the last years of the Johnson administration, scant attention was paid to other measures that might supplement guidepost policy in restraining the use of market power.[60] As a result, an unnecessarily heavy burden was placed on guidepost policy, a burden that could have been lightened had complementary policies been used.

For the above reasons, the simple jawboning approach of the 1960s will not prove adequate for the future. What, then, are the other alternatives? Time permits only the briefest outline of these.

In all that follows I shall assume that every effort will be made to pursue an optimum mix of monetary and fiscal policies. Other policies cannot serve as a *substitute* for appropriate policies that match overall demand with supply and that provide an expansionary environment encouraging economic growth. On the other hand, because monetary and fiscal policies cannot do the job alone, the following are essential complements to such policies.

### Prices and Incomes Policy

To begin, an explicit legislative mandate should be given to any future public policy to influence the prices and incomes[61] of those with market power.

---

60. Cabinet Committee on Price Stability, *Report to the President on the Committee's Activities With Recommendations for Future Action*, December 28, 1968.

61. The term "incomes" is used rather than "wages" to emphasize the need for concern with forms of income other than wages, which had been the sole focus of the 1960 guideposts.

The issues involved are too important to be left solely to the discretion of the temporary occupants of the White House. This mandate should emphasize the "incomes" aspect of the policy and not focus simply on prices and wages.

As indicated, a serious flaw in the guidepost policy of the 1960s was its single-minded emphasis on wages and prices. In the future, profits, salaries, and other professional income must also be considered. It is both inequitable and unrealistic to expect labor to go along with a program that ignores all but wage incomes. This, of course, raises questions regarding the redistribution of income, a subject that received scant attention even in polite liberal circles during the 1960s. Something must be done to reform our inequitable tax structure. Laborers and other salaried employees will find unacceptable a policy that asks them to exercise restraint when so many others enjoy vast incomes on which they pay only small taxes. Relatedly, an incomes policy cannot work if concentrated industries enjoy persistently high profits, a subject to which we will return shortly.

What sort of mechanism should be created to implement this policy? Personally, I favor an independent agency created by the Congress. Its members would be appointed by the President and confirmed by the Senate. The agency would systematically review wage and price decisions in *those industries where labor and business have substantial discretionary power.* I emphasize that the agency should *not* become involved in every wage and price decision in the country. Fortunately, most of the economy is still effectively competitive. The Congress should, therefore, spell out the areas to be covered by the policy.

It would probably be necessary to permit the agency to impose direct price and wage controls in some industries but, hopefully, primary reliance could be placed on the power of publicity in encouraging responsible behavior.

This is not to imply that sole, or even primary, reliance should be placed on a price and incomes policy to improve our U-I curve. Rather, the congressional mandate authorizing such a policy should also make it manifestly clear that a coordinated approach be pursued, involving a panoply of complementary programs that will improve the basic functioning of our market economy.[62]

### The Special Role of Competition Policy

Time does not permit elaboration of these complementary policies. Their primary thrust, however, is to make our market system work efficiently and thereby shift the U-I curve to the left without more direct government intervention into business and labor decision-making. Procompetition policy plays a

---

62. President Johnson's Cabinet Committee on Price Stability outlined some essential ingredients of such a complementary policy, including (1) manpower policies, (2) programs to promote competition, (3) freer international trade, (4) close surveillance and coordination of government procurement programs to avoid unnecessary market disruptions, and (5) special programs to improve productivity and institutional arrangements that created an inflationary bias in particular industries, especially the construction and the health care fields. Cabinet Committee on Price Stability, *Report to the President on the Committee's Activities with Recommendations for Future Action,* December 28, 1968.

central role among these complementary policies. Not only is there growing empirical evidence supporting such a policy, but an increasing number of key public policymakers have come to this conclusion. For example, in its final report President Johnson's Cabinet Committee on Price Stability concluded:

> We recommend vigorous enforcement of the antitrust laws as essential for reducing further the inflationary effects of discretionary power. Only to the extent that we maintain effective market competition can we continue to place primary reliance on private decision-makers in our quest for high employment, rapid economic growth and price stability.[63]

This expression reflected the views of men who had come to this conclusion after having struggled with the market-power-inflation problem for years. Another recent convert to this view is Arthur F. Burns, chairman of the Federal Reserve System and earlier an advisor to the President when he embarked on his famous return to laissez-faire in January 1969. Burns recently testified:

> Improved policies of managing aggregate demand, important though they be, will not of themselves suffice to assure prosperity without inflation. Structural reforms are also needed. Not a few of our corporations and trade unions now have the power to exact rewards that exceed what could be achieved under conditions of active competition. As a result, substantial upward pressure on costs and prices may emerge long before excess aggregate demand has become a problem.[64]

Similarly, Murray L. Weidenbaum, assistant secretary of the treasury, stated explicitly that the existence of market power was responsible for the adoption of wage and price controls in recent years:

> We need to recognize that income policies have been introduced because market imperfections have substantially weakened the ability of monetary and fiscal policy to achieve desired levels of economic growth and price stability.[65]

It cannot be emphasized too strongly, therefore, that the extent of government involvement in price and wage decisions is directly related to the extent that competition restrains the discretionary power of key decision-makers. We therefore have a choice: either enlarge the area of competitive markets or enlarge the area of government involvement in business pricing decisions. Moreover, we have seen that the extent of market power in business bears directly on the extent and use of power by labor. Market power in business begets market power in labor, as well as encourages maximum use of that power. But perhaps even more importantly, where firms enjoy persistently exorbitant profits, as in the drug industry, such excess profits must be eliminated if we are to expect labor unions not to exercise their full power. It is not convincing to argue, as have many economists, that eliminating

63. *Id.* at 7.
64. Testimony of Arthur F. Burns before the Joint Economic Committee, February 20, 1973.
65. M. L. Weidenbaum, *supra* n. 49, at 214.

monopoly profits in a particular industry is not really very important because it will not improve significantly the allocation of resources or the distribution of income in the economy, much less have any effect on seller-push inflation. The critical point missed by this argument is that it is unreasonable to expect some persons in the economy to exercise restraint in the use of discretionary market power unless we adopt an explicit national policy designed to place limits on market power in all segments of the economy. As noted earlier, a persuasive case has been made that much of the current behavior of those with market power involves a struggle over the distribution of income. Thus, increasing competition in an industry aids in the fight against inflation on two fronts. First, it diminishes the inflationary bias created by those with discretionary power. Second, by reducing excess profits it encourages others in the economy to behave responsibly in using their powers.[66]

This immediately raises the question of how best we may increase competition in our problem industries. Our over eighty years of experience with the enforcement of the Sherman Act makes clear that the traditional antitrust approach is not adequate to cope with the task before us.[67] Indeed, there is a serious question whether the antitrust agencies have the capacity to do the job even if they have the will.[68] Others at this conference have the responsibility for determining how we may overcome past failures in maintaining or restoring competition. But, quite clearly, America is at one of those unique crossroads in history when, by inaction or action, it must decide which road to travel — the road of more controls or that of more competition — in pursuing our national objective of full employment with reasonable price stability.

66. Comanor recently estimated that market power has had a substantial impact on the unequal distribution of wealth in America. See W. S. Comanor, "Monopoly and Inequality," a paper presented at the People's Policy Center Conference on Wealth Distribution, Washington D.C., September 22, 1973. This paper summarizes a more comprehensive econometric study by W. S. Comanor and R. S. Smiley, "Monopoly and the Distribution of Wealth," in J. A. Dalton and S. L. Levin, *The Antitrust Dilemma* (forthcoming, Lexington Books).

67. The individuals cited in this article who believe that market power creates a problem in dealing with inflation differ as to whether antitrust or other procompetition policies can play a significant role in improving the trade-off between unemployment and inflation. For example, Means, the father of the administered price concept, has never held out much hope for antitrust, proposing instead mainly greater controls. Among those believing that the procompetition policy may have a salutary effect are Eckstein, Weidenbaum, Burns, Blair, Perry, and Fromm.

68. See testimony of W. F. Mueller in the hearings on Senator Hart's Industrial Reorganization Act, Subcommittee on Antitrust and Monopoly, Senate Committee on the Judiciary, 93rd Congress, 1st Session (March 27, 1973).

# Concentration and Wage—Price Changes

## J. Fred Weston* and Steven H. Lustgarten †

The most general position of economists on the relation between concentration and inflation has been set forth clearly by George Stigler. He stated: "The traditional economic theory argues that oligopoly and monopoly prices have no special relevance to inflation." [1]

There are several reasons for this conclusion. First, the general price level is determined by the interaction of aggregate demand and aggregate supply, modified by pervasive influences such as the grain sales and oil embargo. While there is disagreement on the relative importance of monetary policy versus fiscal policy, there is less disagreement with the proposition that the two together have a major responsibility for movements in general price levels.

A second reason why concentration cannot be appropriately linked with inflation is that pricing and other decision areas in concentrated industries (oligopolies) reflect competitive forces and competitive results of the kind that atomistic industry structures are supposed to produce. [For an elaboration see Weston.] [2] But even if arguments may remain on whether price levels in oligopoly are competitive price levels, a third consideration rejects a positive relation between concentration and inflation. If inflation results from an imbalance between aggregate demand and supply, a rise in demand conditions and/or costs in individual industries and firms will take place. A rise in prices is likely to result, but there is no basis for generalizing that this price increase will be higher in concentrated industries than in less concentrated industries.

But opposing views have been set forth. These include the concepts of "seller's inflation" by Blair and Lerner,[3] "unliquidated monopoly gains" by Galbraith,[4] and "administrative inflation" by Means.[5]

* Professor of Business Economics and Finance, School of Business, University of California, Los Angeles. For further biographical information, see Appendix D.

† Professor of Economics and Finance, City University of New York. For further biographical information, see Appendix D.

1. George J. Stigler, *The Organization of Industry*, (R. D. Irwin 1968), p. 244.

2. J. F. Weston, "Pricing Behavior of Large Firms," *Western Economic Journal*, 4 (March 1972), pp. 1-18.

3. J. M. Blair, "Price and Wage Flexibility — Economic Concentration and Depression Rigidity," *American Economic Review*, 45 (May 1955), pp. 566-604; and A. Lerner, "Sellers Inflation and Administered Depression," in *Administered Prices: A Compendium on Public Policy*, Senate Committee on the Judiciary, 88th Congress, 1st Session (1963).

4. J. K. Galbraith, presentation to the Hearings on Administered Prices, Subcommittee on Antitrust and Monopoly, Senate Committee on the Judiciary, pt. 1 (1957), 85th Congress, 1st Session, and pt. 10 (1959), 86th Congress, 2nd Session.

5. G. C. Means, *Administrative Inflation and Public Policy* (Anderson Kramer Associates 1959).

## THEORIES OF SELLERS INFLATION — WAGE IMPACT

The argument presented by Blair[6] and by Lerner[7] is that the tendency of oligopolistic firms to earn high profits provides a target for union wage demands, leading to an upward wage–price spiral. They reasoned further that firms in concentrated industries will resist these demands less strenuously because they feel that increases in cost due to higher wages can be passed on to consumers in higher prices. Profit levels are thus maintained.

The issue is an empirical one and can be tested by the evidence. The average annual percentage changes in three series of data have been calculated. The data are percentage changes in production worker wages per man hour (WMH), output per production man-hour (QMH), and total labor costs per unit of output (WSQ). The computations are made for four-digit Standard Industrial Classification (S.I.C.) industries and summarized in four concentration groups as set forth in Table 19. The concentration ratio employed is the generally used share of shipments accounted for by the four largest firms in each industry.

Table 19 shows that wages per man hour increase faster in the more concentrated industries as compared with the less concentrated industries. But productivity also rises faster in the more concentrated industries. The net result is that unit labor costs rise less rapidly in the more concentrated industries.

We do not claim that this result occurs because managers of firms in concentrated industries possess some special virtues. Rather it reflects the technological and economic forces that explain why these industries are concentrated. The greater use of capital produces concentrated industries and also contributes to their greater productivity. But the facts do not appear to support the basic arguments of the proponents of the theory that prices increase faster in concentrated industries because their wage costs go up faster.

Greater capital intensity would explain a differentially higher rate of labor productivity in concentrated industries as compared with less concentrated industries at some point in time. However, when analyzing changes in productivity over time, differentially higher capital intensity is not a sufficient explanation. Such a result — that is, an increase in output per man-hour or a differentially higher rate of productivity improvement in more concentrated industries over time as all of the industries are growing — would indicate (1) a greater degree of economies of scale in concentrated industries as compared with less concentrated industries; (2) increasing capital intensity in concentrated industries relative to less concentrated industries, or (3) an increasing degree of disembodied technological improvement in concentrated industries relative to less concentrated. In fact, the data on differentially higher productivity increases over time in concentrated industries lend support to the thesis

6. J. M. Blair, "Administered Prices: A Phenomenon in Search of a Theory," *American Economic Review*, 49 (May 1959), pp. 431-450.

7. See n. 3 *supra*.

TABLE 19

Average Annual Percentage Change* in Wages, Productivity and Unit Labor Cost for 1954-1970 by Level of Industry Concentration

| Period | CR4 < 25 N = 138 | | | 25 < CR4 < 50 N = 157 | | | 50 < CR4 ≤ 75 N = 78 | | | CR4 > 75 N = 24 | | |
|---|---|---|---|---|---|---|---|---|---|---|---|---|
| | WMH | QMH | WSQ | WMH | QMH | WSQ | WMH | QMH | WSQ | WMH | QMH | WSQ |
| (1) 1954-1958 | NA | 4.05 (.34) | 1.57 (.26) | NA | 4.59 (.29) | 1.52 (.27) | NA | 4.88 (.54) | 1.52 (.48) | NA | 6.16 (1.13) | 0.70 (.83) |
| (2) 1958-1963 | 2.69 (.08) | 3.27 (.18) | −0.48 (.12) | 3.03 (.11) | 4.35 (.23) | −0.99 (.15) | 3.35 (.16) | 5.14 (.44) | −1.01 (.25) | 3.73 (.13) | 5.82 (.54) | −1.38 (.47) |
| (3) 1963-1966 | 2.97 (.14) | 3.99 (.38) | −0.16 (.34) | 3.05 (.14) | 3.68 (.45) | 0.43 (.44) | 3.57 (.31) | 4.48 (.58) | −0.59 (.40) | 3.05 (.26) | 4.59 (1.60) | −0.73 (1.21) |
| (4) 1958-1965 | 2.75 (.08) | 3.68 (.21) | −0.54 (.14) | 3.00 (.09) | 4.46 (.28) | −0.72 (.19) | 3.47 (.10) | 5.56 (.50) | −1.00 (.24) | 3.72 (.15) | 6.38 (1.03) | −1.42 (.53) |
| (5) 1966-1969 | 6.24 (.20) | 2.95 (.45) | 3.95 (.49) | 5.86 (.22) | 4.26 (.53) | 2.86 (.56) | 5.15 (.22) | 2.61 (.51) | 2.92 (.53) | 5.65 (.25) | 4.59 (.87) | 1.51 (.82) |
| (6) 1969-1970 | 4.67 (.62) | 2.45 (.97) | 4.37 (.97) | 5.17 (.53) | 0.78 (.87) | 6.62 (.86) | 6.49 (.84) | 2.16 (.83) | 5.82 (.95) | 5.85 (.77) | −0.45 (1.63) | 7.76 (1.83) |

Sources: Output from Federal Reserve Board, Indexes of Industrial Production. Wages and hours from Industry Profiles Annual Surveys of Manufactures, 1970, M70(AS) = 10. The 1954 and 1958 data from 1963 Census of Manufactures.

* Standard errors in parentheses.

that the existing degree of concentration is productive of continuing differential benefits from economies of scale.

## THEORIES OF SELLERS INFLATION — DISCRETION OVER PRICE

Another formulation of the sellers inflation theory is that firms in concentrated industries are "insulated from competitive pressures," so that management is less likely to seek out and institute cost-saving techniques of production. Cost increases can be passed on through higher prices since the large firms possess discretionary power in setting prices.

The basic argument here is that while prices in competitive industries are set by impersonal market forces, firms in concentrated industries can exercise discretion over the prices that they announce. Discretion over price is equated to control over price and is said to permit sellers to raise prices as desired.

This argument has also been expressed in the concept of target return pricing.[8] Oligopolistic firms are said to start with some target rate of return on investments which they consider satisfactory, and then set a price which will enable them to earn that return when plant utilization is at some standard rate (say, 80 percent of capacity). The firm is said to determine its standard labor and materials cost at this volume to which is added a percentage return on capital. Prices are viewed as not responding to changes in operating rates or to changes in demand. Prices are said to change only in response to changes in standard unit costs of labor and materials [Hall and Hitch,[9] Eckstein and Fromm,[10] and Ackley[11]].

At the theoretical level, the target return pricing concept is inconsistent with the basic economic proposition that rational firm behavior calls for profit maximization. Our own interview studies, which covered the same ground that provides the basis for the target return pricing ideas, revealed that the target return concept involves a lack of understanding of accounting and financial planning and control processes.

Financial planning and control processes in firms seek to allocate funds to investments that will earn the industry and firm's estimated cost of capital. Investment opportunities are ranked, and investments that promise returns above the firm's cost of capital will receive high priorities; those that do not will either not be undertaken or will be eliminated on some appropriate time-phasing basis. If longer-run criteria suggest that projects may have more favorable prospects, efforts will be made to bring them to profitability as soon as possible. Such planning is utilized to attempt to forecast prospective

8. R. F. Lanzillotti, "Pricing Objectives in Large Companies," *American Economic Review,* 48 (December 1958), pp. 921-940.

9. R. L. Hall, and C. J. Hitch, "Price Theory and Business Behavior," *Oxford Economic Papers,* Old Series (May 1939), pp. 12-45.

10. O. Eckstein and G. Fromm, "The Price Equation," *American Economic Review,* 58 (December 1968), pp. 1159-1183.

11. G. Ackley, "Administered Prices and the Inflationary Process," *American Economic Review,* 49 (May 1959), pp. 419-461.

volume, and standards are utilized to help achieve the cost control necessary for the firm to earn its cost of capital. The target return is a screening test in choosing among alternative allocations of funds. The use of a target objective provides no assurance that opportunities to earn these targets can be found. The targets do not determine profit levels; opportunities and managerial quality determine profits realized.

Another error among economists in interpreting their interviews with businessmen is to confuse cost standards and standard costs. Cost standards are developed in the effort to be as cost-efficient as possible. Standard volumes and standard costs are used for short-run accounting and financial budgetary purposes. Economists have failed to recognize that standard costs are used primarily as the basis for analyzing variances from such standards as a guide to improving cost efficiency. They also fail to recognize that the variances are carried over into actual costs at each period accounting reports are drawn up, generally quarterly or monthly. Thus, the lags between changes in cost and adjustments to such new information by the business firm, assumed by the economist, represent a misunderstanding. In fact, the emphasis is the opposite; the effort is to make the adjustments to changes before they occur and not afterwards, let alone with long lags.

Indeed, the more appropriate conclusion to be drawn from an analysis of the relation of planning and control processes of business firms and their pricing behavior is just the opposite from that suggested by target return pricing. The main objective of planning and control processes is to speed the firm's reaction time to prospective changes, and to make day-to-day decisions consistent with long-term goals. Furthermore, the areas over which planning and control studies are made include many factors other than pricing decisions: investment decisions, research and development efforts and directions, quality of product, alternative forms of promotion and distribution, development of the requisite marketing and service organizations, financing aids to purchasers, etc.

These planning and control processes in business firms represent the organizational processes by which the abstractions of economic theory are implemented in reality. This is true in small firms and large firms alike. One of the advantages that larger firms have reaped from the improvement of managerial technology since the middle 1950s has been to add important managerial economies of scale to plant economies of scale, effectively implementing planning and control processes, which are increasingly necessary in a dynamically changing world.

## FACTUAL EVIDENCE ON CONCENTRATION AND INFLATION

The argument to this point has proceeded on a theoretical level. It may therefore be useful to evaluate these two alternative theoretical explanations of how businessmen set prices by reference to the facts. The contrasting arguments about the relation among pricing, concentrated industries, and inflationary trends are confronted with the relevant data.

The basic factual evidence on price changes in industries of low versus

TABLE 20

Average Annual Percentage Price Change* for Selected Time Periods
Between 1954 and September 1973 by Level of Industry Concentration

| Period | (1)<br>CR4 ≤ 25 | (2)<br>25 < CR4 ≤ 50 | (3)<br>50 < CR4 ≤ 75 | (4)<br>CR4 > 75 | (5)<br>ALL |
|---|---|---|---|---|---|
| | N = 132 | N = 150 | N = 76 | N = 23 | N = 381 |
| (1) 1954-1958 | 1.70 | 1.79 | 1.77 | 1.58 | 1.74 |
| | (.23) | (.22) | (.29) | (.67) | (.14) |
| | N = 65 | N = 89 | N = 59 | N = 22 | N = 235 |
| (2) 1958-1963 | 0.28 | 0.40 | 0.39 | −0.24 | 0.31 |
| | (.20) | (.16) | (.29) | (.42) | (.12) |
| (3) 1963-1966 | 1.98 | 1.56 | 0.86 | −0.28 | 1.33 |
| | (.29) | (.29) | (.27) | (.71) | (.17) |
| (4) 1958-1965 | 0.51 | 0.54 | 0.42 | −0.35 | 0.42 |
| | (.15) | (.14) | (.22) | (.45) | (.10) |
| (5) 1966-1969 | 2.89 | 2.40 | 2.59 | 1.85 | 2.53 |
| | (.33) | (.26) | (.36) | (.75) | (.18) |
| (6) 1969-1970 | 2.81 | 4.22 | 4.03 | 4.39 | 3.80 |
| | (.72) | (.48) | (.58) | (1.29) | (.32) |
| | N = 14 | N = 31 | N = 32 | N = 14 | N = 91 |
| (7) 1970-1973 | 12.56 | 9.58 | 4.86 | 2.86 | 7.34 |
| | (3.25) | (1.82) | (.55) | (.86) | (.87) |
| (8) 1966-1973 | 7.47 | 5.83 | 4.33 | 2.54 | 5.05 |
| | (1.42) | (.70) | (.44) | (.73) | (.40) |

Sources:

Price Change 1970-1973: U.S. Bureau of Labor Statistics, *Wholesale Price Index,* Industry Sector Price Indexes.

Price Change 1958-1970: U.S. Bureau of Labor Statistics, *Wholesale Price Index,* compiled for four-digit S.I.C. industries by U.S. Department of Commerce Bureau of Economic Analysis and Federal Reserve Board.

Price Change 1954-1958: Census Unit Value Indexes, *Census of Manufactures 1963,* Vol. 4.

Concentration Ratios (CR4): U.S. Bureau of Census, *Concentration Ratios in Manufacturing,* MC67(S)-2.1.

* Standard error shown in parentheses.

high concentration for the period between 1954 and September 1973 is set forth in Table 20. Utilizing the compilations of concentration ratios based on the percentage of sales accounted for by the four largest sellers in an industry, industries are placed into four groups by concentration ratios ranging from 0 to 25 through 75 and above. The average price change for each industry was calculated by taking the ratio of the annual price index at the ending year to the price index at the beginning year for each time period, expressing the change as a percent, and dividing by the number of years in the period.

The most striking feature of Table 20 is that for all but one period, 1969-1970, the average percentage price rise for the highest concentration group (column 4) was less than that for the lowest concentration group (column 1). Thus, both for extended periods of years or relatively short periods of years, generally, the higher the concentration, the smaller the extent of price change.

Of particular significance is the data for the period 1958-1965, when prices rose by less than 0.5 percent per year. This contrasts sharply with the period since 1966, the onset of the Vietnam escalation, when prices rose by more than 5 percent a year (at 10 times the rate). These data provide important evidence relevant to another current argument: that it will not be possible to bring the current inflation under control unless fundamental changes in the strength of labor unions and in industry structures are made. There have been no significant changes either in the strength of labor unions or in industry structures between the 1958-1965 period and the 1966-1973 period. What changed were government spending policies with regard to escalation of hostilities in Southeast Asia, carried on simultaneously with increases in government outlays related to domestic programs. The fundamental difference that has taken place is a change in the character of government fiscal and monetary policies. It is acknowledged that having had seven years of inflation aggravated by such individual episodes as the large grain sales abroad and more recently the oil embargo, government fiscal and monetary policies may need to be supplemented by other actions to achieve a greater degree of price stability. But deconcentration of concentrated industries would place a greater burden on government fiscal and monetary policies and other actions aimed towards reducing the rate of inflation. The evidence as shown in Table 20 is that industries of higher concentration have moderated the rate of inflation rather than the opposite.

In fact, the difference in the rate of price increases among industries with different levels of concentration is the most dramatic for the recent inflationary years. From 1970 to September 1973, the average annual rate of price increase was 12.56 percent and 9.6 percent for the two lowest concentration groups, compared to 2.9 percent and 4.9 percent for the two highest concentration groups.

How do we explain the superior performance of concentrated industries in achieving lower levels of price increase? Indeed, it will be observed that industries with the highest levels of concentration actually achieved price decreases during 1958-1963, 1963-1966, and 1958-1965. The explanation relates to the data in Table 19, in which it was shown that productivity rates were higher in the most concentrated industries than in the least concentrated industries. Thus, the labor-cost-per-unit increases of the firms in the most concentrated industries were smaller than in the less concentrated industries. This, in turn, results from the greater capital intensity of the concentrated industries and the increasing benefits achieved from the enlarged scope of managerial economies of scale that were particularly pronounced beginning in the late 1950s in the United States.

But even with the potential for lower prices, if the firms in concentrated industries have the degree of discretion alleged by some schools of thought, why were these lower costs passed on into lower prices by the concentrated industry? In our judgment, this is strong evidence in support of the proposition that competitive processes between a small number of large firms in concentrated industries are equivalent to the textbook descriptions of the kind of competitive forces that are supposed to be operative only in atomistic industries. [Weston, *supra* n. 2.] These results are consistent with our interpretation that, due to the large number of variables with virtually infinite gradations on which business decisions are made, competition is alive and thriving in oligopolistic or concentrated industries.

This is not to preclude that special circumstances associated with individual years may be operating. For example, the extreme differences between the low price increases among concentrated industries since 1970 and the price increases of the less concentrated industries are probably influenced by other factors as well. These wide differences are probably attributable largely to the differential effects of the government-waged price control program instituted in August 1971. Government wage and price controls have operated more stringently against large firms in concentrated industries. As these controls are relaxed, and prices in concentrated industries reflect more fully the prevailing demand and supply conditions in these industries, price rises in concentrated industries may approach price increases in less concentrated industries. A similar adjustment took place in the period 1954-1958 following the relaxation of the price controls imposed during the Korean War. In fact, the so-called administered price inflation of the mid-1950s represented in part this kind of lagged adjustment to free market forces of demand and supply after the artificial influences of price control during 1950-1953.

These data provide a perspective on Galbraith's theory of "unliquidated monopoly gains" which he set forth in presentations to the Kefauver Committee in 1957 and 1959. [Kefauver Hearings, parts 1 and 10, *supra* n. 4.] Galbraith, using the evidence during the mid-1950s, was attempting to develop a general theory on the basis of the special characteristics of a limited number of years. In fact, in presenting his theory, Galbraith starts by assuming that an inflation is under way, so that "the demand curves of the firm and industry are moving persistently to the right. Under these circumstances there will normally be an incomplete adaptation of oligopoly prices." Stigler has rightly observed that Galbraith is inconsistent in explaining inflation by the behavior of oligopolists when his explanation begins with an assumption that an inflation is already under way.[12] Stigler also observes correctly that Galbraith presented his case (as he has presented his more general theories of how the economy operates) by arguing from a small number of selected examples rather than by systematic, statistical evidence.

## THE ADMINISTERED PRICE THESIS REVIEWED

The third theory which asserts an undesirable influence of concentration on price behavior is the administered price thesis. The administered price thesis

12. G. Stigler, "Administered Prices and Oligopolistic Inflation," *Journal of Business*, 35 (January 1962), pp. 1-13.

of Gardiner Means holds that administered prices are inflexible relative to other prices, tending to fall by less during recession and rise by less during recovery. An explanation of why prices were relatively inflexible has not been made clear by Means. At one time Means wrote that "the dominant factor making for depression insensitivity of prices is the administrative control over prices which results from the relatively small number of concerns dominating a particular market." [13] However, at another place he confused readers by stating: "The presence of administered prices does not indicate the presence of monopoly, nor do market prices indicate the absence of monopoly." [14]

The administered price thesis is essentially an empirical proposition.[15] In his first study, after computing the frequency of price changes for 447 commodities in the Wholesale Price Indexes for 1926-1932, Means identified two groups of prices. Those with a high frequency of change were considered market prices while those with a low frequency of change were labeled administered prices. Means then argued that the relatively infrequent changes in "administered prices" were due to their control by business firms. At a later date Means emphasized an inverse correlation between the amplitude of price decline for 1926-1932, and the industry concentration ratio.

In his earlier work, Means used two criteria to identify administered prices: (1) frequency of price change, and (2) industry concentration. Later he used additional criteria. There have also been shifts as to what type of economic phenomena administered prices were causing. Originally it was depression;[16] later it was administrative inflation;[17] and more recently it was simultaneous recession and inflation.[18]

The significance of administered prices has been questioned on a number of grounds. Means claimed that he discovered a phenomenon which seemed "incapable of explanation by textbook theories of classical economics." However, studies by Thorp and Crowder[19] observed that differences in the amplitude of price movements during the depression were explained by differences

13. See U.S. National Resources Committee Report, *The Structure of the American Economy* (1939), p. 143 (prepared under the direction of Gardiner Means).

14. See Means, n. 16 *infra*.

15. The thesis was later given theoretical justification in the writings of Lerner, n. 3 *supra*; J. K. Galbraith, "Market Structure and the Stabilization Policy," *Review of Economics and Statistics*, 39 (May 1957), pp. 124-133; and Ackley, n. 11 *supra*.

16. G. C. Means, "Industrial Prices and Their Relative Inflexibility," Senate Document No. 13, 74th Congress, 1st Session (1935), reproduced in Means, *The Corporate Revolution in America* (Crowell-Collier 1962).

17. G. C. Means, *Hearings on Economic Concentration*, Subcommittee on Antitrust and Monopoly, Senate Committee on the Judiciary, 88th Congress, 2nd Session, pt. 1, at 22 (1964).

18. G. C. Means, "The Administered Price Thesis Reconfirmed," *American Economic Review*, 62 (June 1972), pp. 292-306.

19. W. F. Crowder and W. L. Thorp, "The Structure of Industry," in *Investigation of Concentration of Economic Power* (U.S. Temporary National Economic Committee Monograph No. 27, 1941), pp. 350-365.

in durability of goods and in types of purchasers, which were reflected in differential shifts in demand. Alfred C. Neal [20] found that differences in price changes were related to differences in direct labor and materials costs rather than to industry concentration.

A major criticism of the literature on price flexibility is that the Wholesale Price Index, used in studies by Means and others, does not reflect the differences between list prices or reported prices and actual transaction prices. Discounting and variations in extras are known to be widespread, so that real prices fluctuate by more than the WPI indexes. In order to deal with this problem, Stigler and Kindahl [21] compiled actual transaction prices by surveying buyers of goods that had been earlier identified by Means as administered price commodities, and analyzed the transaction price behavior during business expansions and contractions. Stigler and Kindahl found that transaction price movements during the cycle generally conformed with expectations based on classical microeconomic theory. That is, prices tended to rise during expansions and fall during contractions.

Means[22] had two major objections to the work of Stigler and Kindahl: one, that their sample contained many commodities which he would now classify as competitive; two, that they tested the absolute changes in administered prices (rather than relative changes) which allowed conclusions only on a "truncated" form of the administered price thesis.

We have retested the administered price thesis using the Stigler and Kindahl data in a manner to meet Means's two criticisms. The confusion as to which prices are administered and which are competitive results from Means shifting criteria from frequency to concentration to other factors. Initially, we use seller concentration because (1) it is the criterion used by Means until his most recent article, and (2) the concentration criterion provides "objective" (although not unambiguous) measures, in contrast to the additional subjective considerations of Means that cannot be put to the usual scientific tests of repeating the experiment by others. Means [*supra* n. 17] himself had previously suggested that concentration alone had produced administrative inflation, as Blair has emphasized. "But concentration in industry has brought a new type of inflation. . . ." [23] Accordingly, the relation between concentration and absolute price changes is studied using four-firm concentration ratios to place the 63

20. A. C. Neal, *Industrial Concentration and Price Inflexibility* (American Council on Public Affairs 1942).

21. G. Stigler and J. Kindahl, *The Behavior of Industrial Prices* (National Bureau of Economic Research 1970).

22. Means, *supra* n. 18.

23. J. M. Blair, "Administered Prices and Oligopolistic Inflation: A Reply," *Journal of Business*, 37 (January 1964), pp. 68-81, emphasized the same point in defending Means's position. "Stigler implies that the basis of Means's classification was frequency of change — a basis which he then goes on to characterize, in the first of a series of colorful adjectives, as 'whimsical.' Actually the primary basis was concentration. . . ." *Id.* at 70.

industries into three groupings suggested by the tests set forth in the "Merger Guidelines" of the Department of Justice (1968).[24]

In Table 21, we use the same time periods employed by Means in his most recent publication, grouping industries by concentration ratios to test whether the direction of price changes in contractions and expansions conforms to the administered-price doctrine. Each panel contains two classifications of price changes which follow from the (truncated) administered price thesis prediction of no change or increase during contractions, and no change or decrease during expansion. For each of the periods we test whether the pattern of the behavior of price changes is affected by the level of concentration. The differences between the groups are not significant for any of the four individual periods; the administered price thesis thus falls short of support by usual statistical significance tests. Further, combining the five periods into a single test also gives results which contradict the administered price thesis.

Means's time periods are panels 1 through 4 in Table 21. The most recent contraction, November 1969–November 1970, provides an additional opportunity to test the administered price thesis. In fact, Means claims that during the 1970 recession "the BLS index of industrial prices has risen substantially and administration-dominated prices have risen even more," but he presents no supporting data.[25] The data for the recent recession (in panel 5 of Table 21) utilizing the WPI industry sector price indexes for four-digit S.I.C. industries, show no significant differences between the groups in terms of the percentage of industries in which prices increased.[26] Nor do the average levels of price increase for these groups — 2.7 percent, 5.1 percent, and 3.6 percent, for low, medium, and high concentration respectively — support Means's claim.[27]

Means argues that Stigler and Kindahl inappropriately tested only a truncated version of his administered price thesis. He emphasizes that the administered price thesis focuses on *relative* price behavior. We therefore tested the "full" version in Table 22.[28] Additionally, since the results in Table 21 may be

24. The full version of the administered price thesis deals with the movement of administered prices relative to competitive prices. The tests in Table 20 are performed for a more restricted thesis, labeled by Means as the "truncated" version, which considers absolute changes in price.

25. Means, n. 18 *supra*, at 292.

26. The difference between the lowest and the mid-range of concentration is statistically significant, but the difference between the lowest and the highest concentration group is not. Further, the difference between the less than 50 percent concentration group and the over 50 percent concentration group is not significant.

27. We also attempted further variations of the analysis to determine whether the test might be sensitive to the classification systems utilized. We also performed the analysis for the two contractions, the two expansions, and for the two cycles combined. None of the applicable statistical tests were close to being significant.

28. Because the 1970 contraction data in Table 20 were taken from the BLS Industry Sector Prices comprising a different set of industries than the Stigler-Kindahl series, in Table 21 we were limited to the time periods covered in Means's article.

TABLE 21

Tests of the Administered Prices Hypothesis for 63 National Bureau Price Indexes,
July 1957 to March 1962, and 90 WPI Industry Sector Price Indexes,
November 1969 to November 1970

|  | Concentration Level * | | | Chi-Square Value ** | Degrees of Freedom |
|---|---|---|---|---|---|
|  | Less than 40% | 40% to 60% | Over 60% | | |
|  | N = 16 | N = 29 | N = 18 | | |
| 1. Contraction 7/57 to 4/58 | | | | 3.12 | 2 |
| Increase or No Change | 37.5 | 58.6 | 66.7 | | |
| Decrease | 62.5 | 41.4 | 33.3 | | |
| 2. Expansion 4/58 to 6/59 | | | | 2.47 | 2 |
| Decrease or No Change | 56.2 | 62.1 | 38.9 | | |
| Increase | 43.8 | 37.9 | 61.1 | | |
| 3. Contraction 1/60 to 1/61 | | | | 0.42 | 2 |
| Increase or No Change | 50.0 | 44.8 | 38.9 | | |
| Decrease | 50.0 | 55.2 | 61.1 | | |
| 4. Expansion 1/61 to 3/62 | | | | 1.15 | 2 |
| Decrease or No Change | 75.0 | 79.3 | 88.9 | | |
| Increase | 25.0 | 20.7 | 11.1 | | |
| 5. Contraction 11/69 to 11/70 | N = 38 | N = 27 | N = 25 | 0.16 | 2 |
| Increase or No Change | 81.6 | 85.2 | 84.0 | | |
| Decrease | 18.4 | 14.8 | 16.0 | | |
| Combined 5 periods | | | | 7.32 | 10 |

Sources:

G. J. Stigler and J. K. Kendahl, *The Behavior of Industrial Prices* (National Bureau of Economic Research, 1970).

*Concentration Ratios in Manufacturing Industry.* Report prepared by the Bureau of the Census for the Subcommittee on Antitrust and Monopoly, Senate Committee on the Judiciary, 90th Congress, 1st Session, pt. 1, table 4 (1967).

U.S. Bureau of Census, *Census of Manufactures* (1967). *Concentration Ratios in Manufacturing*, MC67(s)-2.1 (U.S.G.P.O. 1970).

U.S. Bureau of Labor Statistics, *Wholesale Prices and Price Indexes.*

* Four-firm concentration for 5-digit S.I.C. product classes; 4-digit S.I.C. industries in last panel only.

** For 2 degrees of freedom, the chi-square value at the 5% level is 5.99; at the 1% level, 9.21. For 10 degrees of freedom, the respective values are 18.31 and 23.91.

argued to be influenced by our use of Means's concentration criterion for identifying administered price industries, we adopted his present designation of 50 administered price industries in the Table 22 tests. For the competitive price deflator required, we used the Wholesale Price Index for individual

TABLE 22

Frequency of Price Change for 50 Administered Prices, Relative to Competitive Prices, July 1957 to March 1962

|  | 7/57–4/58 | 4/58–6/59 | 1/60–1/61 | 1/61–3/62 |
|---|---|---|---|---|
|  | Contraction | Expansion | Contraction | Expansion |
| Decrease | 45 | 13 | 45 | 43 |
| No Change | 1 | 8 | 3 | 6 |
| Increase | 4 | 29 | 2 | 1 |
|  | 50 | 50 | 50 | 50 |

Sources: Same as Table 21.

commodity groups which Means had earlier identified as competitively priced during his testimony before the Kefauver Committee in 1958.[29] Those identified as competitive were processed food, hides and leather, lumber and wood, textiles and apparel, and farm products. The average price changes in these five categories were used as the deflator to the National Bureau (Stigler-Kindahl) price series for the 50 industries characterized by administered prices by Means.

The relative price movements of the 50 administered prices designated by Means are shown in Table 22. During both contractions, 90 percent of the relative price changes were decreases, overwhelmingly in disagreement with the Means thesis. During the 1958-1959 expansion, increases took place in 58 percent of the commodities, which also contradicts the thesis. During the 1961-1962 expansion, the relative price increases were only 2 percent. Thus, the data in three of four periods covered by Means in his most recent study demonstrate that "administered prices" were generally more cyclically flexible than the average of competitive prices. In the one period, the 1961-1962 expansion, when only 2 percent of the "administered price industries" exhibited price increases relative to the "competitive price industries," this indicates that in 98 percent of the "administered price industries" relative prices declined. Furthermore, during the two contraction periods, relative prices in the "administered price industries" also declined. Thus, even the one contraction period in which Means asserts that administered prices should have risen relative to competitive prices to deny his thesis, the concentrated industries are shown to have made a contribution to blunting the secular rise in prices.

The evidence therefore points to the conclusion that in concentrated industries, or industries which Means defined as concentrated-plus-other-characteristics, there is in fact no evidence of "administered-price behavior." The

29. See testimony of Gardiner C. Means, Hearings on Administered Prices, Subcommittee on Antitrust and Monopoly, Senate Committee on the Judiciary, 86th Congress, 2nd Session, at 4745-4760 (1959).

conclusion which follows is that the administered price thesis remains a theory in search of a phenomenon.[30]

The factual evidence to this point has established that (1) price increases have been smaller in concentrated industries than in less concentrated industries, and (2) the timing and direction of price movements in concentrated industries behave not significantly differently from the timing and direction of price movements in less concentrated industries. These results are consistent with the analysis and the reasoning [Weston, *supra* n. 2] employed to argue that concentrated industries exhibit competitive behavior similar to the result reached in atomistic industries.

But another rejoinder must be taken into account. At this point the structuralists take recognition of the fact that concentrated industries are concentrated because of their greater capital intensity, which enables them to absorb large wage increases and achieve price *reductions*. So now the argument becomes the following: because concentrated industries are more capital intensive, they could contribute even more than they have to the achievement of price stability. The concentrated industries are thus confronted with the "what have you done for me lately?" argument and the "why haven't you done even more?" criticism. To address ourselves to these queries, we must employ a statistical methodology which seeks to measure the net effects of a number of influences simultaneously.

## REGRESSION ANALYSIS OF CONCENTRATION AND PRICES

While the simple averages in Tables 19 and 20 consider each variable separately, regression analysis is capable of evaluating the interrelationships of several variables simultaneously. It also enables the investigator to consider a continuous relation between variables rather than the discrete relationship implied in the quartile averages. Consideration of several variables together is necessary because the rate of price change is primarily a function of the rate of change in unit materials and unit labor cost and only secondarily related to concentration, if at all. It may also be the case that these unit cost variables are themselves a function of concentration. For example, if the hypothesis that prices rise faster in concentrated industries because costs go up faster is valid, then a simple regression between concentration and price change should produce a positive coefficient for concentration. Thus both simple and multiple regressions are useful techniques of investigation.

Simple two-variable regressions of price change on concentration were computed by DePodwin and Selden,[31] using a sample of 155 four-digit S.I.C. manufacturing industries for the 1953-1959 period of supposed administrative inflation. These authors observed a weak positive relationship between price change and concentration which was not statistically significant.

30. M. J. Bailey, "Administered Prices Reconsidered — Discussion," *American Economic Review*, 49 (May 1959), pp. 459-461.

31. H. J. De Podwin and R. T. Selden, "Business Pricing Policies and Inflation," *Journal of Political Economy*, 71 (April 1963), pp. 116-127.

Leonard Weiss,[32] building on DePodwin and Selden's work, computed multiple regression equations for the same time period, 1953-1959, by adding changes in unit labor and unit materials cost as additional explanatory variables. His sample contained 81 industries used by DePodwin and Selden which were not affected by the 1957 S.I.C. revision. When Weiss computed the regressions introducing materials costs and measuring unit labor cost by its components (hourly wages and productivity) he found that concentration was not a statistically significant variable. However, when unit labor costs were used in his regression instead of its components (hourly wages and productivity) concentration was significantly related to price changes during the 1953-1959 period.

By the latter method, Weiss also computed the regression equation for a later period 1959-1963, in which he found no effect for concentration. Since the positive effect of concentration remained for the combined period 1953-1963, he believed that the gains made by concentrated industries during 1953-1959 were not lost during the following period. Weiss concluded that the administrative inflation of the 1953-1959 period was actually a delayed response on the part of concentrated industries to the excess demand of the 1940s. The implication was that concentrated industries had lagged in responding to initial increases in industry demand and were catching up during the 1950s.

In Table 23, the latter methodology used by Weiss is applied to an enlarged sample and longer time period. It contains 224 four-digit S.I.C. industries which had complete data for all time periods between 1954 and 1970. For the periods 1954-1958 and 1958-1965, the results with respect to concentration are the same as those observed by Weiss. That is, concentration is positive and statistically significant in the multiple regression for the early period, but insignificant in the later period. For the period 1966-1969 concentration is negative in both simple and multiple regression. However, it is statistically significant above .05 only in the multiple regression. The negative effects for concentration during 1966-1969 are consistent with the lag hypothesis since this was a period of excess demand, for which oligopolistic industries are expected to fall behind in price increases. However, the period 1969-1970 was a contraction period during which the lag hypothesis predicts concentrated industries will accelerate in price increase. Equations 7 and 8 of Table 23 which cover this period do not confirm this prediction. Neither simple nor multiple regressions are positive and statistically significant.

The combined period 1954-1970 is covered by equations 9 and 10 of Table 23. A statistically significant negative effect for concentration appears in the simple regression. However, concentration becomes insignificant when unit labor and materials cost are added. This suggests that concentrated industries have increased prices at a significantly lower rate than the unconcentrated industries. The reason is that material and labor costs have gone up more slowly in these industries. Rather than allowing costs to go up more

32. L. W. Weiss, "Business Pricing Policies and Inflation Reconsidered," *Journal of Political Economy*, 74 (April 1966), pp. 77-87.

TABLE 23

Regression Equations† with $P^1/P^0$ as Dependent Variable, for 1954-1970 and Subperiods

| Period | Constant | $\dfrac{Q^1}{Q^0}$ | $\dfrac{W^1/W^0}{Q^1/Q^0}$ | $\dfrac{MAT^1/MAT^0}{Q^1/Q^0}$ | CR4 | $R^2$ |
|---|---|---|---|---|---|---|
| (1) 1954-1958 | 1.940 | | | | −0.0056 (.0082) | .002 |
| (2) 1954-1958 | 0.109 | 0.0024 (.0184) | 0.3411** (.0321) | 0.4296** (.0285) | 0.0108* (.0043) | .780 |
| (3) 1958-1965 | 0.932 | | | | −0.0115* (.0045) | .029 |
| (4) 1958-1965 | 0.832 | −0.0065 (.0140) | 0.0527 (.0556) | 0.3861** (.0471) | −0.0058 (.0037) | .353 |
| (5) 1966-1969 | 3.034 | | | | −0.0126 (.0081) | .011 |
| (6) 1966-1969 | 2.914 | −0.0519 (.0343) | −0.0688 (.0505) | 0.3285** (.0407) | −0.0139* (.0068) | .330 |
| (7) 1969-1970 | 2.827 | | | | 0.0238 (.0151) | .011 |
| (8) 1969-1970 | 2.563 | −0.0139 (.0273) | 0.0550 (.0370) | 0.3825** (.0331) | −0.0085 (.0112) | .487 |
| (9) 1954-1970 | 1.912 | | | | −0.0113* (.0055) | .019 |
| (10) 1954-1970 | −1.782 | −0.0159 (.0099) | −0.1858** (.0591) | 0.4435** (.0573) | −0.0028 (.0041) | .469 |

Source: See Table 19 and Table 20.

† Standard error in parentheses.

* Significant at .05

** Significant at .01

rapidly and raising prices to compensate, the data for 1954-1970 demonstrate that concentrated industries have controlled costs and passed the savings on to consumers in the form of lower prices.

## REGRESSION ANALYSIS OF WAGE CHANGES AND CONCENTRATION

As outlined above, several authors argue that wage rates rise faster in concentrated industries, and that the price rise which follows the wage increase is generally more than enough to compensate. It is argued further that wage settlements provide a signal for coordinating price increases among oligopolists so as not to disturb the collusive structure of prices. For the period 1958-1970 the coefficient of correlation between hourly wage change for production workers $(W^1/MH^1)/(W^0/MH^0)$ and CR4 was $r = .201$. However, in that same period the correlation between labor productivity $(Q^1/MH^1)/(Q^0/MH^0)$ and CR4 was $r = .180$, which indicates that wages rose faster in the concentrated industries because productivity rose faster.

In order to further test the proposition regarding oligopolistic response to wages, the following relationship is considered.

(1)     $$P = f\left[\frac{WS^0}{VS^0},\ \left(\frac{WS^1}{TMH^1}\Big/\frac{WS^0}{TMH^0}\right),\ \left(\frac{Q^1}{TMH^1}\Big/\frac{Q^0}{TMH^0}\right)\right]$$

TMH is total manhours of all employees. According to (1), the change in price is a function of the importance of labor in total cost, the increase in hourly wages, and the increase in productivity. The relationship between the variables on the right side of (1) is multiplicative. This is verified by observing that when the second term within the brackets is divided by the third, the expression becomes:

$$\frac{WS^0}{VS^0} \cdot \frac{WS^1}{WS^0}\Big/\frac{Q^1}{Q^0}$$

This makes price change a function of the change in unit labor cost and the share of value of shipments accounted for by labor cost. The logic of this relationship is that a given percentage increase in unit labor cost will have the greatest impact on price change where the industry is more labor intensive.

In order to test price flexibility with respect to wages, annual changes in prices, wages, productivity, and labor's share $(WS/VS)$ were computed for 1958-1970 for 296 four-digit S.I.C. industries. This produced twelve observations for each industry, or 3552 observations in total. Each was treated as an independent observation on price, wages, productivity, and labor's share. A regression equation with a logarithmic specification was fitted to equation (1), allowing a different impact (i.e., slope) for different levels of industry concentration. A log specification follows from the multiplicative relation to equation (1) above. Since man-hours is available only for production workers, the variables $MH$ and $W$ were substituted for $TMH$ and $WS$ in computing productivity and wages. The following regression equation was computed:

(2)

$$\ln(P^1/P^0) = .0170 + \underset{(.0014)}{.0035}\ \ln\left(\frac{WS^0}{VS^0}\right) - \underset{(.0088)}{.2232}\ \ln\left(\frac{Q^1}{MH^1}\Big/\frac{Q^0}{MH^0}\right)$$

$$+ \underset{(.0232)}{.2367}\ D1 \cdot \ln\left(\frac{W^1}{MH^1}\Big/\frac{W^0}{MH^0}\right) + \underset{(.0244)}{.2444}\ D2 \cdot \ln\left(\frac{W^1}{MH^1}\Big/\frac{W^0}{MH^0}\right)$$

$$+ \underset{(.0280)}{.2941}\ D3 \cdot \ln\left(\frac{W^1}{MH^1}\Big/\frac{W^0}{MH^0}\right) \qquad R^2 = .174 \quad N = 3456$$

D1, D2, D3 take on value 1 when concentration is high (CR4 > 50), medium (25 ≤ CR4 ≤ 50), or low (CR4 < 25), respectively, and zero otherwise. The standard error is shown in parentheses.

If wage rates are a more important variable in the concentrated than non-concentrated industries, this should be reflected in the magnitude and significance of coefficients for the different slope dummies. However, equation

(2) above does not support this hypothesis. The coefficients of the wage change variables are similar for the three levels of concentration. In fact, the coefficient for the low concentration group is actually slightly higher than the others.

A recent paper by Ripley and Segal [33] analyzed price change in 395 manufacturing industries using a data base similar to the one used here. One of their major findings was that changes in unit labor cost had a lesser impact on price change in the concentrated than in the unconcentrated industries. Although the authors do not provide an explicit theoretical justification for their finding, they conclude that since prices are less responsive to unit labor cost in concentrated industries, an optimum incomes policy should rely on controlling prices in the concentrated industries and wages in the unconcentrated industries.

Equation (1) provides an explanation for the relationship observed by Ripley and Segal. The impact of changing unit labor cost $(WS^1/WS^0)/(Q^1/Q^0)$ is a function of the share of labor in total cost $(WS^0/VS^0)$. This share is lower for concentrated industries which are more capital intensive. The response of price to wage rates can be equal for both groups (as in equation (2)), while the response to unit labor cost differs, because labor productivity and labor's share are different. With respect to an incomes policy, it should be noted that the differential response to unit labor cost is related to capital intensity, not to the number of sellers. Thus if one wishes to accept Ripley and Segal's logic for an incomes policy, a criterion for differential treatment should be the industry's capital/labor ratio rather than its concentration ratio.

Our findings on the relationship between concentration and wages are confirmed by other studies. Leonard Weiss concluded as follows:

> Once personal characteristics are introduced, the relationship between concentration and earnings is no longer significant and is negative about as often as it is positive. The monopolistic industries do get superior "quality" for the incomes they offer. Moreover, a substantial portion of the relationship between the earnings of labor in concentrated industries and their quality is due to a relationship of both variables with the number of weeks worked. The laborers in concentrated industries seem to receive no more for their services than they might in alternative employments for persons with similar personal characteristics. Their earnings contain little or no monopoly rent. . . . The conclusion with respect to the effect of unionism on labor earnings is more equivocal than the results for concentration. The relationship between unionism and earnings does not decline greatly when personal characteristics are introduced for nonregulated industries. Unions that organize their entire jurisdictions seemed to raise earnings by 7 to 8 per cent for craftsmen and 6 to 8 per cent for operatives, compared with poorly organized industries. The relationship between unionism and earnings is often nonsignificant after personal characteristics are introduced, but this may well be the result of measurement errors.[34]

33. F. C. Ripley and L. Segal, "Price Determination in 395 Manufacturing Industries," Review of Economics and Statistics, 55 (August 1973), pp. 263-271.

34. L. W. Weiss, "Concentration and Labor Earnings," American Economic Review, 56 (March 1966), p. 115.

A. W. Throop obtained similar results as conveyed by the following brief summary statement:

> Concentration has a statistically insignificant influence for the full decade in contrast to the positive influence observed by Bowen in certain subperiods. But when the rate of change of the index of skill level is introduced, only the coefficient of the degree of unionization exceeds its standard error.[35]

In a more recent study Haworth and Rasmussen carried the analysis in the earlier work further by seeking to take into account worker quality more fully by analyzing in greater depth the measurement of human capital. They observe that the most commonly used measure of human capital, median years of education completed, is not a satisfactory index. They use a measure of human capital that seeks to take into account educational level adjusted for quality, and an index of the skills level of the labor force. They conclude as follows:

> The variables representing (C) concentration and (U) degree of unionization have the expected sign also, but are not significantly different from zero. The failure of industry concentration to be a significant determinant of wages after labor quality considered is consistent with the findings of Masters and other work. . . .
> These results indicate that when worker characteristics are included in a specification, unionism has no additional effect upon wages. This is not equivalent to saying unions have no effect upon wages. The higher union wages might lead employers to hire workers with desirable characteristics even if the job did not require these characteristics. . . .
> Using a model based on the assumption of competitive markets, six variables could explain over 72 percent of the inter-industry wage variations. The addition of variables reflecting market imperfections did not improve the explanatory power of the model.[36]

Thus, the most recent empirical studies establish that when other variables, particularly differences in the quality of the work force, are taken into account, the net effect of concentration on wage levels is not significant. Indeed, in the broad perspective, market forces result in the finding that the net influence of unionization on wage levels is not statistically significant. Both of these findings are subject to the qualification that initially higher wages may result in a reshuffling of the labor force so that the higher wages in concentrated industries or in unionized industries result in the selection of the higher quality of work force. Hence, after the economic adjustments are made, the net relation between concentration or unionization on wages adjusted for worker quality is no longer statistically significant.

35. A. W. Throop, "The Union-Nonunion Wage Differential and Cost-Push Inflation," *American Economic Review*, 58 (March 1968), p. 92.
36. C. T. Haworth and D. W. Dasmussen, "Human Capital and Inter-Industry Wages in Manufacturing," *Review of Economics and Statistics*, 53 (November 1971), pp. 378-379.

## IMPLICATIONS OF THE PHILLIPS CURVE RELATIONS

Another theory which asserts that concentration exerts an undesirable influence on prices has drawn upon the concept of the Phillips Curve. It posits a relation between wages, profits, and inflation. Particularly, equation 3.8 on page 50 of Perry's study,[37] is used to set forth a family of unemployment–inflation curves. One such figure set forth on page 63 of the Perry book is repeated as Figure 7 in Professor Mueller's paper.[38] The presumed link is that concentration produces higher wages and profits and hence creates "bad unemployment-inflation (U-I) curves." The empirical findings reported by Perry in his book have been used to support this position.

However, an updating of the Perry study provides counter evidence. The newer findings are contained in Table 24. Row 1 repeats the Perry study for the years 1948-1960. The same results were obtained. In row 2, the study is repeated for the subsequent decade, 1960-1970. The influence of profits on wage change was negative, not positive, and the influence of profit change was no longer significant. For the decade of the 1960s, (as shown by row 4), Ratajczak obtained a higher percentage of explanation of wage change without the profit and change in profit variables than Perry had obtained for the 1948-1960 period, including them.[39] When Ratajczak includes profit, but not the change in profit (as shown in row 6 for the decade of the 1960s), she obtains a still higher degree of explanation of wage change, but the influence of profit is now negative rather than positive.

Without a full evaluation of the Phillips Curve approach as utilized by Samuelson and Perry and adopted by Mueller, meeting the argument on its own grounds, the updating of the analysis is consistent with "good U-I curves" produced by the role of profit. And again, these results are consistent with the newer evidence which shows no significant net relationship between concentration and profits or concentration and wages and a favorable relationship between concentration and price change.

### THE STEEL INDUSTRY EVIDENCE

Some writers seeking to establish that an undesirable relationship exists between concentration and prices cite as their primary evidence the steel industry during the mid-1950s. A full appraisal of the steel industry would require analysis of many factors too detailed for coverage in a paper dealing with patterns in the economy as a whole. Some factual evidence for perspective, however, may be usefully reviewed.

---

37. G. L. Perry, *Unemployment, Money Wage Rates, and Inflation,* (MIT Press 1966).

38. See W. Mueller, "Industrial Concentration: An Important Inflationary Force," in this volume, this chapter.

39. See Rosalinda Ratajczak, "Disaggregate Participation Equations and the Phillips Curve" (ms. 1973).

TABLE 24

Relation Between Wages, Prices, Unemployment, and Profits, 1948-1970

| | Regression Results for w Dependent Variable (Perry) | | | | | |
|---|---|---|---|---|---|---|
| Period | Constant | CPI t-1 | U | R t-1 | RDELTA | $R^2$ |
| 1. 48-3 to 60-3 | −4.421 | .385 | 14.611 | +.434 | .832 | .867 |
| | (5.2) | (6.9) | (6.7) | (6.3) | (4.7) | |
| 2. 60-3 to 70-4 | +2.122 | .474 | 28.198 | −.503 | .318 | .930 |
| | (4.0) | (5.5) | (6.0) | (4.9) | (1.3) | |
| 3. 48-3 to 60-3 | +0.483 | .473 | 14.146 | | | .691 |
| | (0.7) | (6.8) | (4.4) | | | |
| 4. 60-3 to 70-4 | +0.371 | .671 | 8.41 | | | .882 |
| | (0.8) | (8.6) | (3.0) | | | |
| 5. 48-3 to 60-3 | −3.86 | .317 | 13.470 | +.412 | | .799 |
| | (3.6) | (4.9) | (5.1) | (4.9) | | |
| 6. 60-3 to 70-4 | +2.11 | .431 | 28.182 | −.492 | | .927 |
| | (3.9) | (5.4) | (6.0) | (4.7) | | |

Source: R. Ratajczak, "Disaggregate Participation Equations and the Phillips Curve" (ms. 1973), pp. 7-9.

*Variables in Table 6:*

Wages (w): Straight time average hourly earnings of production workers, current dollars, not adjusted for interindustry shifts, total manufacturing. From Perry; *Survey of Current Business;* and *Monthly Labor Review.*

$$w_t = \frac{w_t}{w_{t-1}} - 1$$

Unemployment (U): Unemployment rate for the civilian labor force, seasonally adjusted, averaged and inverted. From Perry and *Survey of Current Business.*

$$U_t = \frac{4}{U_t + U_{t-1} + U_{t-2} + U_{t-3}}$$

Prices (CPI): Consumer Price Index, 1958 = 100. From Perry and *Monthly Labor Review.*

$$CPI_t = \frac{CPI_t - CPI_{t-1}}{CPI_{t-1}} + \ldots + \frac{CPI_{t-3} - CPI_{t-4}}{CPI_{t-4}}$$

Profits (R): After-tax profits as a percentage of stockholder equity in manufacturing corporations. From Perry and Federal Trade Commission.

$$R_t = \frac{R_t + R_{t-1} + R_{t-2} + R_{t-3}}{4}$$

Change in profits (RDELTA): $RDELTA = R_t - R_{t-1}$

Table 25 provides a framework for analyzing price changes over a number of time periods. During the years 1926-1945, farm products rose 28.2 percent while prices in the iron and steel industry declined 1 percent. Indeed, during this period, wholesale prices in the rubber and rubber products industries declined by 38 percent, and the prices of industrial chemicals declined by 3.8 percent. Encompassing a downward swing in prices into 1933 and a rise thereafter, the overall trend of price movements for the wholesale price

TABLE 25

Percentage Price Changes for Various Time Periods
and Wholesale Price Index Components, 1926-1945

| Time Period | All Commodities | Iron and Steel | Farm Products | Industrial Chemicals | Rubber and Rubber Products |
|---|---|---|---|---|---|
| 1926-1945 | 5.7% | −1.0% | 28.2% | −3.8% | −38.0% |
| 1945-1950 | 49.9 | 66.9 | 35.6 | 24.4 | 21.89 |
| 1951-(1957-1959) | 3.4 | 37.2 | −19.2 | 2.5 | 7.5 |
| (1957-1959)-1966 | 5.9 | 2.3 | 5.6 | −4.3 | −5.2 |
| 1967 to October 1973 | 39.5 | 38.6 | 88.4 | 5.3 | 20.2 |

Source: *Handbook of Labor Statistics* (1969), Table 117, pp. 313-318. *Monthly Labor Review* (December 1973), Table 27, pp. 113-114.

index as a whole was 5.7 percent for the 19-year period, representing a rise of .3 percent per annum.

The price increases during the 1945-1950 period represent the varying influences of the removal of World War II price controls, price pressures during the period of "refilling the pipelines of product flows," and the initial impact of the Korean War.

The rise in prices after the start of hostilities in Korea through the 1957-1959 period was 3.4 percent for the wholesale price index as a whole. But during this period, iron and steel prices rose by 37.2 percent. It was this large rise in prices in the iron and steel industry that has been the basis for the argument that the iron and steel industry (and concentrated industries generally) have been the major contributory cause of price increases following World War II. During the seven years following 1951, farm product prices declined by 19.2 percent while prices of industrial chemicals, and rubber and rubber products, rose moderately. It may be noted in passing that during the 1951-(1957-1959) period, when the iron and steel industry was alleged to be a major cause of inflation in the United States economy, the price change per annum in the wholesale price index was less than .5 percent per year. After our recent price experiences, we can look back with some nostalgia for this moderate degree of price movements.

During the next eight years through 1966 the wholesale price index as a whole rose by 5.9 percent. Prices in the iron and steel industry rose only 2.3 percent while farm products rose 5.6 percent. It is of interest that prices of both industrial chemicals as well as rubber and rubber products declined by 4 to 5 percent during this period.

The last time period covered by Table 25, 1967 through October 1973, represents the period of substantial inflation. During this period, farm products rose by 88.4 percent, more than double the increase in iron and steel prices. The overall wholesale price index rose by 39.5 percent while iron and steel prices rose 38.6 percent. Again, it is of interest to note that during this period of a high rate of inflation the prices of industrial chemicals rose only moderately while the prices of rubber and rubber products rose at a rate about half that of the overall wholesale price index.

With regard to prices, the data demonstrate that any conclusions are highly dependent upon the time period chosen and the concentrated industries selected. During the period 1926-1945 the rubber industry was a hero, while the rise in farm products was out of line with the other price trends. From 1951 through 1958 prices in the steel industry were in the same relation to the overall wholesale price index as farm product price trends during the earlier period. From 1958 through 1966, steel prices rose at cne half the rate of the WPI.

Table 26 presents data on profitability. During the years 1947-1959, the steel industry had an average rate of profit on equity approximately 1 percentage point below that of all manufacturing. (This is somewhat more than 8 percent lower in profitability.) During the 1960-1971 period, the profit rate of the steel industry was 3.70 percent lower than for all manufacturing, or lower by a factor of ⅓ the profit rate of all manufacturing.

These data alone deny the allegations that the steel industry manipulated prices to maintain their profit rates. The factual evidence is that they did not maintain their profit rates. Of course, these data do not defend the steel industry against the charge of inefficiency — although some have also argued that if there is a problem of efficiency in the United States steel industry, it is because the United States steel industry is not sufficiently concentrated rather than the opposite. They point out that the 1972 total assets of Nippon Steel of $8.6 billion are over 30 percent higher than the total assets of U.S. Steel at $6.8 billion. The 1966 prices in the steel industry rose at half the rate of price increases in the wholesale price index and in farm products.

These data alone suggest that more detailed analysis is required to achieve a balanced evaluation of the role of the steel industry. Even if one were to attach great weight to the comparative price behavior of the steel industry during the one period, 1951-1958, this still would not support criticism of the price behavior of the steel industry in any of the other periods covered in the time period 1926-1973. Furthermore, even if the data demonstrated that the steel industry had an influence on prices that could be justifiably criticized

TABLE 26
Comparative Profitability Rates of All Manufacturing Compared with
Primary Iron and Steel Industries, 1947-1971
(measured by net income after taxes to stockholders' equity)

| Time Period | All Manufacturing | Primary Iron and Steel Industries | Primary Iron and Steel Industries less All Manufacturing |
|---|---|---|---|
| 1947-1954 | 12.02 | 11.03 | −0.99 |
| 1960-1971 | 10.88 | 7.18 | −3.70 |

Source: *Economic Report of the President* (1967, 1973).

(and the data are at best moot), this would provide no basis for the sweeping generalization, frequently made by reference to selected years during the 1950s for the steel industry alone, that all concentrated industries could be appropriately tarred with the same brush (assuming that the brush really has any tar on it).

## CONCLUSIONS

This topic of concentration and prices is one which standard microeconomic theory states should not seriously have been raised in the first place. The simple relations between concentration and prices indicate that the higher the concentration the smaller the price changes over a period of time. But other influences must be taken into account. The simple result follows from the greater labor productivity in concentrated industries because of the greater capital intensity. After adjusting for further influences, as economic theory predicts, there is no relationship between concentration and either wage levels or price levels or changes in wage levels or changes in price levels over time.

On the basis of the facts developed in the tables of this paper many of the popular generalizations about the positive relation between concentration and price increases are demonstrated to be false. Much folklore has been promulgated about the relation between concentration and prices primarily through the forum of congressional hearings. When these presentations have been subjected to scholarly appraisal, they have not stood up against the facts.

Yet in recent periods it has been possible to cite government officials and economists responsible for policy in the early years of the escalation of Viet Nam hostilities, that failures of monetary and fiscal policy cannot be held accountable as factors in the inflation that began to get underway in 1966. These officials have also sometimes asserted that success in controlling inflation will require restructuring industry. These have been general statements without revealing or demonstrating the basis for such recommendations and conclusions. The evidence is all to the contrary.

An important contribution has been made to controlling inflation by concentrated industries because of their greater labor productivity and efficiency in realizing more of the potentials of advances in technology and managerial practices since the end of World War II. Furthermore, evidence of the 1958-1965 period is one of general price stability and of price decreases in concentrated industries. Admittedly for the last two years the tasks of fiscal and monetary policy, in seeking both to correct for its past mistakes and at the same time to encompass new developments, have been formidable. The changes in food prices were transmitted through an atomistic industry. The consequences of energy shortages are being transmitted through a concentrated industry. The basic causal forces are not related to the happenstance of the degree of concentration of the industry through which the price changes are being transmitted, nor is the evidence of recent years proof of the failure of monetary and fiscal policy. Rather, the evidence is more of the lack of application of the monetary and fiscal tools than of their inability to deal with the problem.

A broad survey paper necessarily omits considerable detail and considerable evidence that are related to the problems at hand. Particularly, the international influences on domestic inflation and the contributions of United States policies to international inflationary forces involve much greater complexities than covered in this paper. The determination to follow diplomatic and military policies abroad and at the same time pursue domestic programs that involved large outlays could not be carried off without making the necessary adjustments in monetary and fiscal policies to avoid inflationary pressures. Furthermore, sound long-range policies were inaugurated without making the appropriate short-run adjustments to carry out the long-range policies.

Perhaps this topic is most useful for its by-products, in delineating more clearly why some industries are concentrated in their economic role. Greater concentration generally reflects greater capital intensity. The greater capital intensity and technological complexity of industries interact with managerial factors to produce both larger sized firms and greater concentration in some industries.

The greater role of the use of capital, including managerial technology, in the concentrated industries also contributes at least a partial explanation of the greater degree of unionization which appears to be found in concentrated industries. With a relatively greater role of capital and managerial technology, there is a greater ability to set wages related to the job rather than to individuals. This provides a basis for collective bargaining at the firm level as well as at the industry level, because of the relatively greater uniformity of jobs given the greater relative role of capital. However, industry-wide collective bargaining has other effects not pursued in the present analysis.

The foregoing evidence on concentration and prices is consistent with the arguments made that in standard oligopoly industries intense competition continues. There is, in addition, international competition as well as domestic competition. In the few dominant-firm industries where one firm has a large market share compared to other firms, the complaint is that competition from the dominant firm with respect to all other firms is too tough rather than having the quality of forebearance.

But most of us have predilections for pluralism in our society and a preference for decentralization of power. In this connection the preoccupation with concentrated industries is both a bogey and a false issue. The power of the federal government and federal agencies compared to the efforts of many individual firms striving at various points of competition is a great contrast. The recent evidence of political giving is more evidence of the use of the strong position of the executive office to bring pressure to bear on individual firms than vice versa.

The share of the top 200 firms in value added in manufacturing is about 42 percent, and manufacturing is less than 30 percent of the economy. Thus, the share in the total economy of the top 200 manufacturing firms is on the order of magnitude of 12 percent. In addition, whatever increase in the position of the top 200 firms is due to the increased size of some 40 newcomers who grew primarily through conglomerate type merger activity. Their aspirations and interests were different from the remaining 160 firms as well as from the 40 firms that they displaced in the top 200. These data are consistent with evidence of decentralized economic power.

Other derivative evidence is corroborative. Let us apply some of the tests of a pluralistic society. There is substantial evidence that social and economic mobility in our society remains high.[40] While there is inequality of both income and wealth distribution, the inequality has decreased over time. In addition, there is a relatively equitable distribution of opportunity for achieving upward social and economic mobility. The expanded protest movements and increased criticism of our institutions also constitute evidence of a pluralistic society. Social protest groups have had easy entry, and have had the ability to attract a following, to thrive, and to exert considerable influence. By these and related tests our society can, with the present levels of both macroconcentration and microconcentration, score high as a pluralistic society.

But if these observations on the degree of pluralism and mobility in our society are not satisfactory to some, the evidence of this paper on the relation between concentration and price changes suggests that trade-offs are involved if our industrial structure is to be changed. The evidence in this paper is consistent with the conclusion that in standard oligopolistic industries competition is vigorous and efficiency is high, and that these efficiencies are elements of competition that result in benefits to consumers and society at large. But if the degree of concentration is still regarded as undesirable in some industries, deconcentration would involve efficiency losses.

# Dialogue*

*Leonard Weiss:* I think the crucial evidence that Weston and Lustgarten present are a set of regressions of a form that I originated. I essentially get the same results in the same periods. I interpreted them a little bit differently.

What they are saying, as I understand it, is that during the 1960s if there were increases in price-cost margins everywhere, they increased less in the concentrated than unconcentrated industries.

With respect to the statement that it makes no sense for a monopolist to raise prices continually, I thoroughly agree, but I have observed that monopolists do not at every point in time have their optimum prices. In particular, during inflations, they raise prices relatively slowly for a number of reasons — partly because they are easy to control. At the end of a period of open inflation the prices of monopolists are in disequilibrium; monopolists are not

40. Neil H. Jacoby, *Corporate Power and Social Responsibility* (Macmillan 1973).

* The session was chaired by John M. Blair, Professor of Economics, University of South Florida. For further biographical information, see Appendix D.

taking full advantage of their position. This would imply a rise in price for a short period such as the 1950s.

I obtained the same regression results as Weston-Lustgarten in the 1950s, in the early 1960s, and in 1967-1969. During the latter period of accelerating inflation, the concentrated industries' prices rose more slowly than prices in unconcentrated industries, once you allowed for changes in direct cost. But when I got that result four years ago, I made the prediction that when open inflation ends we ought to see a period of continuing inflation in concentrated industries as these firms recoup. At that time I could only make a prediction about 1970-1972. When you looked at these years, what did you find?

*Lustgarten:* We examined the period 1969 to 1970, which was a recession period since a peak occurred in November 1969 and a trough occurred in November 1970. We did not find that your prediction was confirmed. We then looked at 1970 to 1973, although we didn't have data on wage changes at the time. We found that the relationship between price change and concentration was the same as in the 1960s, but it was even more pronounced during this period. We attributed this partly to the imposition of wage and price controls in August 1971, which may have been more effective in concentrated industries. This would explain why the concentrated industries were increasing their prices even more slowly than ever before.

*Mueller:* There is a common fallacy running through the Weston-Lustgarten paper which I call the "either/or" philosophy, the assumption that all inflation must be explained in terms of excess aggregate demand or by structural factors. Their failure to recognize this mars their entire discussion and renders meaningless all the empirical studies. Their own empirical studies haven't yet stood the test of peer review and professional journals, in contrast to the authorities I cited. Most of their analyses are simply wrong. For example, they make some comparisons in price behavior of concentrated and unconcentrated industries. But unless productivity is taken into account, such comparisons are meaningless except for very short periods. In their short-period analysis, for 1969-1970, their results differ not only from John Blair's study for the same period, but also from a study by the staff of the Kansas City Federal Reserve, which, using a larger sample, comes to conclusions similar to Blair's.

Similarly, Weston and Lustgarten redid George Perry's study that I cited. I talked with George about this earlier this week, and he agreed that the reason for their differing results is very simple. Perry was dealing with an earlier period in which cost-push inflation was a factor. The authors apply their analyses to a period in which demand-pull factors are at work, specifically in the late 1960s, to try to distinguish the separate influences of structural forces and excess demand forces.

This is closely related to the findings of Weiss's study. It isn't just that firms with market power necessarily experience low profits during periods of rapid demand-pull inflations. It is just that in the short run competitive industries — which are always operating where marginal cost is equal to price — experience a surge in profits during a period of rapidly increasing aggregate demand. And, at least in a short period of time, where they can't make immediate capacity adjustments, you get that kind of price and profit behavior.

The same things mar their various statistical studies. They just don't admit to the possibility that there are two different kinds of forces at work that create an inflationary problem in the economy.

*Weston:* With regard to the either/or question of whether there was cost-push going on during the 1960s, our multiple regression analysis shows that there wasn't. But the multiple regression analysis shows that there was during the 1953 to 1958 period. A significant point here is that even if there were, until 1966 we experienced price increase of an order of magnitude of less than 1 percent per year. And that is a kind of influence on price we could live with.

With regard to the 1969-1970 period, I should comment that our results are the same as Professor Blair's, and the Kansas City Federal Reserve. But during 1968-1969 there was a run-up in prices in the less concentrated industries, and the data for 1969-1970 simply indicate they were falling back into line.

*Victor Kramer:* Is there any consensus among economists on whether in times of deflation there is a relationship between stabilized prices and concentration?

*Weston:* We presented evidence on that in our paper, and our evidence was that in 1969-1970, using our multiple regression analysis, the role of concentration was insignificant. There was no relationship between the price change and concentration.

*Milton Handler:* On the assumption that in the current year, 1974, we have a two-digit rate of inflation, could Professor Mueller quantify the amount of inflation that he would ascribe to concentration during the current year as distinguished from the other causes of inflation, so that we could have some measure of the significance of the relationship which he finds.

*John Blair:* Nobody can do that with existing data.

*Mueller:* I agree. The people who are devoting all of their time to this particular subject haven't been able to do so. The complex problem facing policy-makers today is that monetary-fiscal policy alone is incapable of dealing with this inflation. The present inflation is not primarily cost-push. I am not making that argument. But in trying to deal with the inflation of the last four years, I am satisfied that it has been a serious problem. The precise theory underlying it isn't clear. But it reminds me of the woman who said, "I can't prove that someone watered my milk, but how else can I explain the fish in the milk can?"

*Donald Dewey:* There seems to be a consensus among the speakers to avoid saying the obvious about this problem. The trouble is that the obvious is often the most important. Many years ago Henry Simons argued that business monopoly was essentially a skin disease — there were fairly easy remedies — and the really serious problem was labor monopoly. When you look at the data, the most obvious thing is that by and large the concentrated industries are the highly unionized industries. If you have industry-wide collective bargaining agreements, and if you have inflationary expectations written into these agreements running over periods of two or three years, then obviously the fiscal authorities have to increase the money supply to make good on these agreements. If you don't, you get very substantial unemployment.

So you come down to the problem: how can you manage to get inflationary expectations written out of collective bargaining agreements? It is a problem which is very easy to formulate. Devising remedies, of course, is much more difficult.

*Weston:* There are some elements of theoretical validity in that, but I think the facts are also very important. With regard to the labor monopoly problem, we would argue that that is not the prime cause. Our data show that in the concentrated industries, because of greater capital intensity, etc., unit costs rise less because of the productivity factor than in less concentrated industries.

During the period 1958 to 1965 we had the so-called labor monopoly problem, and we didn't have the inflation problem.

Also, when we look at the facts during the 1966 to 1969 period, during the first three years of the inflationary period the real income of workers was declining. It was beginning in 1970, when we had the strong thrust of the efforts of the labor unions to maintain real income, that we began to have that added into the picture. But that wasn't the prime cause. It was a reinforcing factor from 1970 on. The heart of the problem was the basic fiscal-monetary policy, particularly in 1966 and 1967.

*Mueller:* Professor Lustgarten pointed out correctly what inflation is: an increase in the overall price level. Their evidence about higher labor productivity in these industries where labor and firms happen to have market power is beside the point. Merely because these industries don't cause prices to increase as rapidly as industries with lower productivity misses the point. In order to have price stability, these high productivity industries must experience price decreases in order to offset the inevitable price increases that occur in low-productivity industries.

I think the problem of the power of labor unions is very complex. There is an interrelationship here between the market power of firms and of labor. They happen to be, in most cases, in the same industries. My paper points out, and it is becoming increasingly accepted by economists as part of the explanation, that the struggle between labor and corporations is becoming a struggle over income share. I think the monopoly problem is an essential ingredient in this struggle. I don't see any simple way to control the use of power by unions — certainly you can't break them up and have individuals bargaining with large firms. So I think there must be some kind of institutional device used to encourage the responsible use of their power. We attempted that with the wage-price guideposts in the 1960s, and I think we are going to continue, as are other Western nations, experimenting with alternative methods of control. But in my view, the only way a just society can reasonably expect labor and other segments of the economy not to exercise their full discretionary power is if we implement a number of institutional reforms in our system.

Let me illustrate from my government experience. When I was executive director of President Johnson's Cabinet Committee on Price Stability, this was frequently brought home to me. If you asked labor to exercise restraint, they'd say, "What about the excess profits in the drug industry?" It turned out they had been asking this question all during the wage-price guidepost era. The point is that unless labor is convinced that our system is run fairly — and this goes to other things affecting income distribution — we are going to have increased militancy on the part of labor unions and others with market power. This is showing up in other Western nations, perhaps most bitterly today in England.

The other alternative, of course, is simply unacceptable. You can discipline labor by having 10 percent unemployment. That is just not acceptable today as far as the American public is concerned. You may disagree with that, but no modern economy is going to take that alternative.

*Frederick Scherer:* Inflation at present is not just a United States phenomenon; it is a world phenomenon. The nub of the present problem seems to be overcoming inflationary expectations. As long as people feel that the rise of prices is going to continue, they want to stay at least even in this race, and this, of course, simply makes the race continue and perhaps even accelerate.

The experience in Germany is illustrative. The Germans, who are terribly sensitive about inflation because of their very bad postwar experiences, are experiencing inflation of about 8 percent this year, probably about 12 or 13 percent this coming year.

About ten years ago, when wage negotiation rounds came up, Konrad Adenauer and Ludwig Erhard would go before the people and read them the riot act and say, "Okay, you want price stability. All of us are going to have to make some sacrifices." And people really listened and believed. During the present inflation, Willy Brandt has made no effort to exert moral leadership to break these inflationary expectations.

I think there is a real problem. Unless Western statesmen exert political-moral leadership, or unless they try to suppress inflation by all sorts of controls, we are not going to break these inflationary expectations. How can we get the kind of moral leadership we need?

*Weston:* I think it is absolutely the wrong diagnosis. Moral suasion and guideposts work in a framework of the appropriate monetary-fiscal policy, and absent that, they don't work. It is immoral to come out and tell people to behave irrationally in the face of monetary-fiscal policy that created the problem in the first place and prolongs and aggravates it.

*Dewey:* Do you favor Milton Friedman's solution?

*Weston:* No, I depart from the Chicago School in that area. I believe in authority rather than rules in the monetary-fiscal area. The world is too complex for rules.

*Dewey:* Would you run unemployment up to 8 or 9 percent for six months to break inflationary expectations?

*Weston:* That didn't occur in 1965.

*Dewey:* It is a different ball game.

*Weston:* It is a different ball game, right; but after the inflationary period had been generated by a number of factors, primarily the presentation of really a dishonest budget message in 1966, which suggested that the Vietnam War would be over in the autumn. This was done so that the Great Society programs would be financed by the Congress. The Viet Nam War continued, and a great income redistribution was taking place through the Great Society program, so that the real income position of both labor and the profit sector deteriorated.

There was a possibility for a solution when the new administration came in, because the problem had been created by the previous one. But the new administration, in announcing its policies, said no one was going to be hurt. There would be a recession, but it would be very minor in amplitude and of very short duration. You don't kill off inflationary expectations that way, because that added up to, "We are not really going to do anything." My point is that in the area of macropolicy, mistakes have repeatedly been made.

The other problem is that you have immense cash balances that were built up all over the world, and it is difficult to soak those up and to make overall monetary-fiscal policy in a particular year work. Since the problem is world-wide — and Professor Scherer is certainly correct on this — there has to be coordination among policies of the leading nations to make any such program effective. If you have this coordination among nations, or even a leaning in the direction, you could cure the problem over a three-, four-, or five-year period of time.

*Mueller:* Professor Weston has rewritten a little history. In January 1969 our monetary and fiscal house was in order. We were running a fiscal surplus, and we followed a restrictive monetary policy for a period of about one year. Only four days after he was sworn in, President Nixon announced that he was going to achieve simultaneously a return to price stability without any significant increase in inflation. It was during this period that the price behavior of the industrial sector, which he called catch up, occurred. In other sectors prices declined or increased moderately.

This policy failed as unemployment increased, since we had constricted aggregate demand, yet prices were going up. Then we returned to this policy of validating the price increases, thereby expanding aggregate demand. The result is the problem that Don Dewey posed. Admittedly, it is extremely difficult to unravel the factors that were at work.

## SELECTED BIBLIOGRAPHY

Adelman, Morris A. "Steel, Administered Prices and Inflation." *Quarterly Journal of Economics,* 75 (February 1961), 16-40.
De Podwin, H. J., and Selden, R. T. "Business Pricing Policies and Inflation." *Journal of Political Economy,* 71 (April 1963), 116-127.
Eckstein, Otto. "A Theory of the Wage-Price Process in Modern Industry." *Review of Economic Studies,* 31 (October 1964), 267-286.
Perry, G. L. *Unemployment, Money Wage Rates, and Inflation.* MIT Press, 1966.
Phlips, L. "Business Pricing Policies and Inflation — Some Evidence from E.E.C."

*Journal of Industrial Economics,* 18 (November 1969), 1-14.

Ripley, F. C. and Segal, L. "Price Determination in 395 Manufacturing Industries." *Review of Economics and Statistics,* 55 (August 1973), 263-271.

Ross, S. A., and Wachter, M. L. "Wage Determination, Inflation, and the Industrial Structure." *American Economic Review,* 63 (September 1963), 677.

Schultze, C. L. *Recent Inflation in the United States.* Joint Economic Committee Study Paper No. 1, 86th Congress, 1st Session, 1959.

Sellekaerts, W. and Lesage, R. "A Reformulation and Empirical Verification of the Administered Prices and Inflation Hypothesis: The Canadian Case." *Southern Economic Journal,* 39 (June 1973), 345-360.

Stigler, George J. "Administered Prices and Oligopolistic Inflation." *Journal of Business* (University of Chicago), 35 (January 1962), 1-13.

Weiss, Leonard W. "Business Pricing Policies and Inflation Reconsidered." *Journal of Political Economy,* 74 (April 1966), 177-187.

_____. "The Role of Concentration in Recent Inflation." Appendix to testimony of R. W. McLaren in *1970 Mid-Year Review of the State of the Economy,* Hearings before the Joint Economic Committee, 91st Congress, 2nd Session, Part 1, 1970.

# 7

# Public Policy Implications
# of the New Learning

## Editors' Note

To a considerable degree, one's view of the policy implications of the "new learning" turns on one's reaction to the underlying substantive issues now in debate. If the economic costs of deconcentration are high (due to, for example, lost economies of scale or hindered innovative activity), few would be willing to pay the price of generic legislation. On the other hand, if net economic benefits are likely to result from such a policy (due to, for example, the elimination of the so-called x-inefficiency factor) or even if deconcentration could be accomplished at little or no cost, then a "Brandeisian bias in favor of human-sized institutions," as one commentator put it, would incline many towards a deconcentration statute.

Professor Donald F. Turner, who chaired the dialogue on policy alternatives, wisely and wittily set forth the following precis of the debate:

A good many years ago, Thomas Reed Powell, a famous professor at the Harvard Law School, was asked to review a book by two sociologists on the subject of crime in the United States. His review started out as follows: "In this book the authors tell us that the rate of crime in this country is excessive, but at no point do they give us any indication as to what rate they think would be adequate."

I think our discussion of concentration is a little better off than that, for clearly the critical issues are in dispute. I would summarize them in this way. First, most studies show a positive relationship between profits and concentration, but not all people are satisfied with the evidence, and there is some question as to the durability of that relationship. Second, even if concentration, at least at rather high levels, carries with it monopoly power (which persistent abnormally high profits indicate), there is a dispute as to how much of this is attributable to economies of scale or to other large-scale efficiencies that would be reduced with deconcentration.

Then there is a contrary point, namely that even if the concentration—profit relationship is modest, there is a common belief, which Professor Scherer gave ✓ some evidence to support, that firms with market power are less cost conscious and hence less efficient than they would be if there were effective competition. But some people are very dubious about this theory. Finally, insofar as concentration and innovation are concerned, the evidence seems to indicate that we should have some oligopoly but not too much. And so we are now prepared to move to policy alternatives.

# A. AN ANALYSIS OF THE
# PRINCIPAL LEGISLATIVE PROPOSALS

# Legislative Proposals for Industrial Deconcentration
## Harlan M. Blake*

Although Senator Philip A. Hart's Industrial Reorganization Act [1] is the focus of current discussion concerning deconcentration of industry, two other fairly recent and somewhat similar proposals have attracted support, at least in scholarly circles, and merit comparison. In 1959, Carl Kaysen and Donald F. Turner elaborated a legislative program for industrial deconcentration.[2] And in 1968 the White House Task Force on Antitrust Policy (the "Neal committee") drafted and proposed a new "Concentrated Industries Act." [3]

Since proposals for industrial deconcentration, even though they may adopt a cautious approach, are widely regarded as hopelessly utopian or irresponsibly radical, it is worth noting that the ideas they embody are neither new nor exclusively the province of ivory-towered intellectuals. Indeed, op-

---

* Professor of Law, Columbia University Law School. For further biographical information, see Appendix D.

1. S. 1167, 93rd Congress, 1st Session (1973) (hereinafter "the Hart Bill"), originally introduced as S. 3832, 92nd Congress, 2nd Session (1972). The Hart Bill is reproduced in Appendix B. See also Hearings on S. 1167 Before the Subcommittee on Antitrust and Monopoly of the Senate Committee on the Judiciary, 93rd Congress, 1st Session (1973).

2. Carl Kaysen and Donald F. Turner, *Antitrust Policy* (Harvard Univ. Press 1959), pp. 265-272 (hereinafter "Kaysen-Turner").

3. "Report, Comments and Separate Statements," reprinted in *Antitrust Law and Economics Review*, 2 (Winter 1968-1969), pp. 11-52 (hereinafter "Neal committee report"). The Concentrated Industries Act is reproduced in Appendix C.

position to the growth of economic concentration, with its real or supposed evils, is one of a few basic tenets about which there has been a wide and continuing consensus in the Congress at least since the passage of the Sherman Act [4] nearly eighty-five years ago. That first antitrust statute was surely an urgent mandate to the attorney general and the courts to "deconcentrate" the American economic system by, among other things, dissolving the trusts.[5] The more modest Clayton[6] and Federal Trade Commission Acts,[7] twenty-four years later, were anticoncentration measures in that they sought to assure that the new judicial "rule of reason"[8] would not open the floodgates to a tide of business practices which it was thought might lead to additional concentration.[9] The Celler-Kefauver Act's[10] strengthening of the Clayton Act in 1950 was directed at renewed and accelerated industrial concentration brought about through a particularly potent device — the merger.[11] And numerous pieces of legislation peripheral to antitrust, including the Public Utilities Holding Company Act,[12] the Bank Holding Company Act,[13] and statutes authorizing postwar disposition of government assets,[14] have directly or indirectly manifested Congress' deeply held belief that most forms of economic power should be dispersed.

It is, of course, easier to oppose evil in general terms than to devise and win consensus on a specific program for its extirpation. Thus the Sherman Act's draftsmen preferred the posture that their use of common law concepts as the core of the statute provided prosecutors and courts with the certain and specific guidance of traditional legal wisdom.[15] In fact, of course, the old concepts enabled Congress to avoid facing up to specific decisions, and provided very little guidance on how specifically to deal with new problems in industrial structure. In part for this reason the Harrison, Cleveland, and Mc-

---

4. 26 Stat. 209-210 (1890), 15 U.S.C.A. §§1-7.

5. See, e.g., H. M. Blake, "Conglomerate Mergers and the Antitrust Laws," 73 *Colum. L. Rev.* 555, 575-579 (1973), and sources cited.

6. 38 Stat. 731 (1914), 15 U.S.C.A. §13.

7. 38 Stat. 717 (1914), 15 U.S.C.A. §45.

8. Standard Oil Co. of New Jersey v. United States, 221 U.S. 1 (1911).

9. See, e.g., D. Martin, *Mergers and the Clayton Act* (Univ. of California Press 1959), pp. 46-49, and sources cited.

10. 64 Stat. 1125 (1950), 15 U.S.C.A. §18.

11. See, e.g., Handler and Robinson, "A Decade of Administration of the Cellar-Kefauver Antimerger Act," 61 *Colum. L. Rev.* 629 (1961); Bok, "Section 7 of the Clayton Act and the Merger of Law and Economics," 74 *Harv. L. Rev.* 226 (1960).

12. 49 Stat. 803 et seq. (1935), 15 U.S.C.A. §79.

13. 70 Stat. 133 (1956), 12 U.S.C.A. §1842. See Edwards, "The One-Bank Holding Company Conglomerate," 22 *Vand. L. Rev.* 1275 (1969).

14. 58 Stat. 765 et seq. (1944), 50 U.S.C.A. App. §§1611 et seq.; 63 Stat. 378 et seq. (1949), 40 U.S.C.A. §§471 et seq.

15. See, e.g., D. Dewey, *Monopoly in Economics and Law* (Rand McNally 1959), pp. 142-144; H. Thorelli, *The Federal Antitrust Policy* (Stockholm: P. A. Norstedt & Söner 1954).

Kinley administrations were understandably slow to begin carrying out the desired deconcentration program.[16] And before the task was completed a conservative Supreme Court, largely uninterested and untutored in problems of industrial structure and performance, seized upon the ambiguity of the statutory language effectively to call a halt before remedial action could be extended to the steel trust [17] and other industries which would today be described as oligopolistic.[18] Subsequent administrations have by and large been pleased to leave well enough alone, in part doubtless because big business support has been increasingly necessary to finance inordinately costly political campaigns.

By the mid-1930s economic theories had been devised and were widely used to explain that firms in concentrated markets were likely to collude or to engage in noncollusive practices resulting in industry performance more nearly monopolistic than competitive.[19] Although there was dispute as to trends and their magnitudes, new economic investigation demonstrated that more than half of the United States' industrial and mining industries were concentrated, and that the concentrated sectors were larger in total size and more importantly positioned in the economy than the unconcentrated.[20]

In a new round of antitrust cases aimed consciously at industry structure, some important substantive and remedial victories were won.[21] Yet it also became apparent that the legal theories on which a renewed deconcentration program might have been based were far from satisfactory; the *United States Steel* case[21a] and other early decisions had not been fully overcome. Poor market performance resulting from noncollusive oligopolistic behavior could obviously not be reached by injunctive relief.[22] True, by 1957 the Supreme Court had made it clear that antitrust laws could be made to "reach back" to

16. See, e.g., W. Letwin, *Law and Economic Policy in America* (Random House 1965), ch. 4.

17. United States v. United States Steel Corp., 251 U.S. 417 (1920).

18. E.g., United States v. International Harvester Co., 274 U.S. 693 (1927). See Blake and Jones, "In Defense of Antitrust," 65 *Colum. L. Rev.* 377, 387-389 (1965).

19. J. Robinson, *The Economics of Imperfect Competition* (Macmillan 1933); E. Chamberlin, *The Theory of Monopolistic Competition* (Harvard Univ. Press 1933). These works are placed in historical context, discussed, analyzed, and built upon in D. Dewey, *The Theory of Imperfect Competition: A Radical Reconstruction* (Columbia Univ. Press 1969).

20. Temporary National Economic Committee, Final Report and Recommendations, S. Doc. No. 35, 77th Congress, 1st Session (1941).

21. See, e.g., American Tobacco Co. v. United States, 328 U.S. 781 (1946), discussed inter alia in Levi, "The Antitrust Laws and Monopoly," 14 *U. Chi. L. Rev.* 153 (1947); Rostow, "The New Sherman Act: A Positive Instrument of Progress, 14 *U. Chi. L. Rev.* 567 (1947); United States v. Paramount Pictures, Inc., 334 U.S. 131 (1948); United States v. Crescent Amusement Co., 323 U.S. 173 (1944).

21a. See n. 17 *supra*.

22. See, e.g., Turner, "The Definition of Agreement Under the Sherman Act," 75 *Harv. L. Rev.* 655 (1962).

undo the results of mergers carried out as long ago as 1914,[23] or probably even 1890,[24] even though their anticompetitive potential is not seen until much later. However, no aggressive antitrust prosecutors accepted the challenge. Moreover, some influential commentators argued that the Supreme Court should not be encouraged to approve new interpretations of the antitrust laws which would operate more strongly against oligopoly in the absence of a further and more specific manifestation of congressional purpose.[25]

Thus, the passage of time has made it increasingly clear that neither the law enforcement agencies nor unaided Schumpeterian gales of innovation were likely to impose satisfactory limits on the extent or duration of oligopoly power. The social costs of the failure in the *United States Steel* case, attenuated only at a glacial pace, have extended beyond a half-century.[26] The failure of the automobile industry, once the shining centerpiece of American industry, to hold its own in domestic markets, or (except through acquisition or joint venture) to penetrate foreign markets, or to anticipate environmental or energy developments, has demonstrated even more dramatically that size and market share are not highly correlated with adaptability, imagination, and

---

23. United States v. E. I. du Pont de Nemours & Co. (General Motors), 353 U.S. 586 (1957).

24. United States v. First National Bank & Trust Co. of Lexington, 376 U.S. 665 (1964).

25. See, e.g., Kaysen and Turner, *supra* n. 2, at 111-112. This view, it seems to me, misapprehends the necessary relative roles of Congress and the executive branch in the antitrust field. Repeated congressional expressions of legislative policies supporting competition and opposing tendencies towards monopoly reflect fairly the public's generalized desire to be free of the threat inherent in discretionary power in the hands of a financial or industrial elite. Yet each industry, striving to serve its own interests, seeks to avoid the rigors of competition. Thus, as proposals for legislation to inhibit economic power become more specific, and are perceived to have important consequences in individual industries, the pressures from those special interests easily come to overwhelm generalized concern for the public weal.

The reverse is not true. If the executive branch or the courts go too far in expanding the reach of antitrust at the expense of any firm, industry, or group, Congress finds little difficulty in passing redressing legislation. Cf. the Newspaper Preservation Act, 84 Stat. 466 (1970), 15 U.S.C.A. §§1801 et seq.; the two Bank Merger statutes, 64 Stat. 891 (1950), 12 U.S.C.A. §1828, and 70 Stat. 134 (1956), 12 U.S.C.A. §1842; the McGuire Act, 66 Stat. 632 (1952), 15 U.S.C.A. §45; the Patent Act of 1952, 66 Stat. 797 et seq. (1952), 35 U.S.C.A. §§101 et seq.; the bill dealing with the El Paso Natural Gas case, S. 2404, 92nd Congress, 1st Session (1971). Given the enormous breadth and fundamental drive of the Sherman Act, I believe that the burden is on the executive to explore and reexplore its limits by imaginative antitrust prosecutions rather than on the legislature to reiterate its commands in impossible detail. Of course, where new administrative machinery or detailed criteria for action are desired, legislation is necessary.

26. See, e.g., W. Adams, *The Structure of American Industry* (4th ed., Macmillan 1970), ch. 5; S. Whitney, *Antitrust Policies* (Twentieth Century Fund 1958), ch. 5.

social performance.[27] And the recent disastrous social performance of the international oil oligopoly has suggested to many that its decades of privileged antitrust treatment have been less than clearly in the public interest.[28] In any event, the past fifteen years have produced the first carefully elaborated proposals for industrial deconcentration and may be providing some of the political fuel to get them seriously considered.

## THE PROPOSALS AND THEIR STATED PREMISES

The preamble of Senator Hart's bill, and his statements to the Senate on its introduction, provide an account of its underlying premises. The Neal committee's report and its "Comments to Accompany the Concentrated Industries Act," and relevant sections of the Kaysen-Turner book, provide similar summaries of their respective approaches.

Senator Hart's statement of objectives is by far the most far-reaching, possibly because its primary audience, legislators, are thought to be in need of, or responsive to, a "hard sell"; this fact also makes it the most controversial. Its stated premises are that:

(1) too much power lies in too few hands, and this concentration of power is bad for social, political and economic reasons;

(2) industry is becoming increasingly concentrated and government by private corporations is replacing public government;

(3) market concentration chills competition, produces high prices unresponsive to demand (and thus inflation), and causes unemployment, inefficiency, underutilization of economic capacity, and a decline in exports;

(4) the present antitrust laws have not been broadly enough interpreted or enforced, nor have remedies been sufficiently innovative, to undo the concentration that has already taken place; absent a new congressional mandate, the existing laws will probably not be applied to restructure oligopoly industries.

The Neal committee report and the Kaysen-Turner rationale are each narrower, giving major emphasis to adverse industry performance consequences of oligopolistic market structure; both point to inefficient resource allocation and reduced pressure for cost reduction and innovation. Each is concerned with perfecting the self-regulating mechanism of the market, as opposed to relying extensively on government ownership or direct regulation, and each recognizes a preference for a large number and variety of decision-making units in the economy, for reasons not exclusively economic.

Hart parts company with the Neal committee, and far outdistances Kaysen-Turner, in giving major emphasis to inflation, unemployment, and foreign

---

27. See, e.g., "The Energy Crisis Spurs Demand for Small Cars and Detroit Responds — With Big Car Prices," *N.Y. Times*, April 7, 1974, §11, at 1.
28. But see FTC Complaint, Exxon et al., Docket No. 8934 (filed July 17, 1973).

trade balances as reasons for deconcentration. This greater emphasis on broad social and political reasons for concern with concentration of economic power is reflected in the more stringent substantive and procedural provision of his proposed bill. All would presumably agree, however, with Hart's fourth premise — that existing antitrust laws "will probably not be applied to restructure oligopoly industries." The other two proposals do not join Hart in identifying specific industries or groups as requiring special attention.

## THE OFFENSE AND STRUCTURE OF REMEDY

The Hart Bill declares unlawful possession by a corporation or corporations of "monopoly power in any line of commerce in any section of the country or with foreign nations." Although "monopoly power" is nct defined in the statute, a rebuttable presumption of monopoly power arises if:

> (1) the corporation has an average rate of return on net worth after taxes in excess of 15 percent over five consecutive years out of the most recent seven, or
>
> (2) there has been no substantial price competition among two or more corporations in any line of commerce in any section of the country for three consecutive years out of the most recent five, or
>
> (3) four or fewer corporations account for 50 percent or more of sales in any line of commerce in any section of the country in any year out of the most recent three.

It is not clear how the presumption would be rebutted, since monopoly power is not defined; nor is it clear whether or how monopoly power might be shown other than through the presumptions. The bill requires divestiture of "monopoly power" except where it is attributable solely to valid patents or would result in loss of substantial economies. This remedy would be available against a single-firm monopoly, or even against a firm or firms in an unconcentrated industry which fell within a presumption, as well as against firms in concentrated industries. An Industrial Reorganization Commission would prosecute violations before a special Industrial Reorganization Court.

The Neal group's proposed statute is more specific and much more limited in reach. Its provisions apply only to "oligopoly industr[ies]" in which

> (1) any four or fewer firms have accounted for 70 percent or more of aggregate market shares (based on industry sales) during at least seven of the ten and four of the most recent five base years,
>
> (2) industry sales and the aggregate market shares of the oligopoly group are not in substantial decline,
>
> (3) the identity of the four largest firms has not substantially changed in recent years, and
>
> (4) aggregate sales have amounted to more than $500 million in at least four of the five most recent years.

The proposal provides that when the attorney general determines that a market appears to be an "oligopoly industry," and subject to relief, he will bring a proceeding in equity before a Special Antitrust Court for the reduction of concentration, making parties all "oligopoly firms" (those with market shares of 15 percent or more during two out of three base years). During a one-year period following an affirmative decision by the new court, the parties are provided an opportunity to take voluntary steps toward reduction of concentration. After that time, necessary further relief will be provided with the objective of reducing the market share of each oligopoly firm within four years to no more than 12 percent. No remedy may entail substantial losses of economies of scale.

The Kaysen-Turner proposal takes a middle ground. It makes "possession of unreasonable market power" the offense and defines "market power" as

> the persistent ability of a person, or of a group of persons whether or not acting pursuant to agreement or conspiracy, to restrict output or determine prices without losing a substantial share of the market, or without losing substantial profits or incurring heavier losses, because of the increased output or lower prices of rivals.

Evidence of market power may include, but is not limited to:

> (1) persistent failure of prices to reflect substantial declines of demand or costs, or to reflect substantial excess capacity;
> (2) persistence of profits that are abnormally high, taking into account such factors as risks and excess capacity; or
> (3) failure of new rivals to enter the market during prolonged periods of abnormally high profits or of persistent or recurring rationing.

Market power, furthermore, is conclusively presumed where, for five years, one company has accounted for 50 percent of sales in the market, or four or fewer companies have accounted for 80 percent of sales.[29]

Market power is deemed "unreasonable" unless created and maintained by reason of economies of size, lawful patents, low prices or superior products attributable to innovation, or extraordinary efficiency.

29. In testimony before Senator Hart's Antitrust Subcommittee on March 30, 1973 (Hearings on S. 1167 Before the Subcommittee on Antitrust and Monopoly of the Senate Committee on the Judiciary, 93rd Congress, 1st Session, pt. 1, at 279 (1973)), Professor Turner said that he was no longer sure about the suitability of this presumption: "It may well be reasonable to presume some degree of monopoly power in such circumstances, but unless there are no serious questions about market definition (no close substitution, and no other producers who can quickly enter the market if there are minor price increases), I do not believe that such figures provide an adequate basis for establishing a substantial degree of monopoly power."

A showing of substantial persistent monopoly power will normally require, in his new formulation, a finding of one of the following: (1) substantial persistent profits in excess of cost of capital; (2) substantial persistent differences between prices and marginal costs; or (3) substantial persistent price discrimination (which shows monopoly in the higher-priced market).

Kaysen-Turner's proposal declares the possession of unreasonable market power to be injurious to trade and commerce, and provides for an Industrial Reorganization Commission to institute proceedings in equity before a new Economic Court to prevent and restrain such injuries. After a judgment that unreasonable market power is possessed, the court may order division of assets, divestiture or other relief, limited by defendant's right to show that its own plan is more appropriate.

## AFFIRMATIVE DEFENSES AND LIMITATIONS ON RELIEF

The Hart Bill sets forth two conditions under either of which a defendant will not be required to divest monopoly power. (Nonetheless, the firm would still technically possess illegal monopoly power; the conditions are not expressed as defenses.) They are:

> (1) if the power is due solely to the ownership of valid patents, lawfully acquired and lawfully used [30] or
>
> (2) if divestiture of monopoly power would result in a loss of substantial economies.

Similarly, the Neal committee's plan does not provide affirmative defenses. It vests in its Special Antitrust Court the widest possible powers to frame relief, including the removal of even otherwise valid patents and contractual arrangements as barriers to entry, but provides that the decree may not require that a firm "take any steps which such firm established would result in substantial loss of economies of scale."

The Kaysen-Turner approach is more complex. Once "market power" is shown, it is deemed unreasonable unless shown by defendant or defendants to have been created and maintained entirely or almost entirely, by one or more of the following:

> (1) such economies as are dependent upon size in relation to the market;
>
> (2) ownership of valid patents, lawfully acquired and lawfully used; provided that, on a showing that market power has been created and maintained by patents, the government shall have the burden of showing invalidity, unlawful acquisition, or unlawful use;
>
> (3) low prices or superior products attributable to the introduction of new processes, product improvements or marketing methods, or to extraordinary efficiency of a single firm in comparison with that of other firms having a substantial share of the market.

Even if none of these defenses is made, the Economic Court may only provide "feasible" relief, such as division or divestiture of assets, to eliminate unreasonable market power, subject to important limitations:

---

30. Although the bill's language is confusing, the burden of proof here lies with the commission.

(1) the assets of a single plant may not be divided;

(2) any probable permanent loss of substantial economies intrinsic to the defendant may be taken into account in deciding the "feasibility" of division or divestiture;

(3) defendant may defeat a divestiture order by showing that other relief suggested by it would provide materially equivalent competitive conditions; and

(4) defendant may show that one or more companies resulting from a divestiture order would lack reasonable prospects for survival under the competitive conditions likely to prevail.

## ADMINISTRATIVE AND PROCEDURAL PROVISIONS

The Hart Bill's Industrial Reorganization Commission would be an independent agency supervised by a commissioner appointed by the President, with the advice and consent of the Senate, for a 7 ½ -year term. Fifteen years after enactment of the statute, the commission's existence would be terminated and its functions transferred to the Federal Trade Commission.

In addition to prosecuting monopoly power cases, it would be required to study each of seven broad industries, to develop a plan for reorganization of each (whether or not any firm is determined to be in possession of monopoly power), to report to Congress each such plan with recommendations, including recommendations for legislation deemed necessary, and to study the collective bargaining practices within each such industry and determine their effect on competition. The industry groupings are: (a) chemicals and drugs; (b) electrical machinery and equipment; (c) electronic computing and communication equipment; (d) energy; (e) iron and steel; (f) motor vehicles; and (g) nonferrous metals. In addition, it would make recommendations for amendments to the antitrust laws, the Internal Revenue Code, the patent laws, and the National Labor Relations Act; it would report to Congress on the effect on competition of the policies of executive or regulatory agencies of the government, with any recommendations for legislation deemed necessary.

The commission would have the power to conduct industry studies and to require the filing of periodic and special reports necessary to carry out the provisions of the Act. It would have the power to require the filing of registration statements by corporations or persons in or affecting any of the seven specified industries. The Act would impose on persons and corporations required by the commission to file data with it the duty to do so, punishable by substantial fines or imprisonment.

The Hart Bill's new Industrial Reorganization Court would have a chief judge and fourteen associate judges, appointed by the President with advice and consent of the Senate. Appeal would lie only to the Supreme Court of the United States. The scope of review would be limited to whether or not the court proceeded correctly and whether or not its findings of fact are supported by substantial evidence.

The Neal committee's proposal relies on the attorney general to initiate proceedings, based on his own or Federal Trade Commission investigations.

Its Special Antitrust Court is composed of an indeterminate number of regular district court and circuit court judges designated by the Chief Justice of the Supreme Court to serve for one or more proceedings or for a period of time. The Chief Justice also designates a chief judge, who may in turn designate panels of one or more judges to conduct proceedings, in accordance with the Federal Rules of Civil Procedure and such special rules as the Special Antitrust Court may adopt. The court may designate and call economists or others to serve as special witnesses, and they would have access to evidence, might offer testimony and analyses of issues, would be subject to cross-examination, and would recommend appropriate provisions for decrees.

Appeals either from a judgment or decree of the Special Antitrust Court may be appealed directly to the Supreme Court. Between four and five years after the entry or affirmance of a decree, proceedings would be conducted to determine whether the decree has achieved the required reduction in concentration. If not, a further decree ordering additional measures is mandated. Proceedings involving regulated industries, and resulting divestiture orders, are subject to a veto in the concerned federal or local regulatory body.

The Kaysen-Turner proposal, since it is not cast in definitive statutory terms, provides less detail concerning the organization of its Industrial Reorganization Commission and Economic Court, but does offer an analysis of their respective functions. The commission would be a new independent agency, hopefully enabling it to attract superior personnel; this would also permit it to achieve economies of specialization and would increase its immunity from politics. A system of close coordination of activities with the Antitrust Division and FTC is spelled out. The commission's first function in any proceeding would be to carry out an exhaustive staff investigation of a potentially covered industry and prepare a full and reasoned study. Next, it would seek to negotiate a voluntary reorganization with the industry. If this failed, a complaint would be filed with the Economic Court.

Final decisions of the Economic Court (as to whether defendants possess undue market power, or incorporating a remedial decree) would be reviewed by direct appeal to the Supreme Court, but only as to the correctness of procedures (including questions whether the Economic Court followed statutory mandates), and whether the critical fact finding rested on substantial evidence.

## SOME COMPARISONS IN THE LIGHT OF NEW DATA

In general, the common elements of the three proposals are more significant than their considerable differences. Each relies decisively on economic theory and data tending to demonstrate that tight oligopoly markets perform less efficiently than markets served by, say, eight or more firms.[31] Each seeks

31. In large part the material on economic theory and empirical data which follows is derived from the papers delivered at this Conference, particularly those of Professors Dewey, Weiss, Demsetz, and Edwards. I have also reexamined Stigler, *The Theory of Price* (3rd ed., Macmillan 1966), esp. ch. 12, and his "A Theory of

to achieve, among other things, greater efficiency in such industries by taking such steps to increase the number of competitors as is thought to be consistent with, in varying degrees, preserving or not impeding future realization of economies of scale.

The economic theory thus relied upon asserts that, in general, the larger the number of firms in a market the more difficulty they will have in maintaining collusive behavior and the more readily any collusive behavior will be detected. Even where collusion is absent, effects equivalent to collusion may arise from the imperatives of market structure. Under such market conditions, antitrust law cannot produce competitive performance by ordering the oligopoly firms to ignore each others' existence. To avoid economic inefficency, either direct regulation of price or an improvement of the competitive structure of the market is required.

Industries so unconcentrated that collusion (tacit or explicit) is impossible are expected to yield only opportunity costs to all factors, plus random dynamic deviations. Profit rates are expected to increase with concentration as collusion becomes more successful, approaching a limit set by given demand, cost, and entry conditions. These theories of the social costs of oligopoly have found empirical support in numerous studies that have found a significant association between high levels of concentration and persistent high rates of return on capital, particularly in industries where the largest four firms account for more than 60 percent of sales.

Until recently there was very little serious dispute about these structural theories. Recently, however, Harold Demsetz and others have begun to challenge their adequacy.[32] Demsetz argues that inadequate attention has been paid to entry and potential competition. If entry is easy, firms in even a tightly concentrated oligopoly market may be impelled to hold prices at or near competitive levels and otherwise to perform competitively. If only the largest firms in concentrated markets show supranormal profit levels, the proper inference may be that they are simply more efficient; this inference may find support in theory which argues that firms in concentrated industries are more fully able to exploit economies of scale and are more capital intensive and innovative than smaller firms. And even if firms in a concentrated industry are able to collude as to price, they may still exhaust all but normal profits through rivalry as to product quality or variety, services, guarantees, and the like.

Obviously, insofar as the new attack on hitherto generally accepted theory is successful in undermining the postulate that deconcentration will substantially improve industry performance, the underpinnings of the proposals are weakened. Attention might better be turned toward efforts to eliminate kinds of governmental intervention in the economic system which constitute a major source of monopoly power; this at least would channel action in a direction in which economists, lawyers, and businessmen could come closest to consensus.

Oligopoly," *Journal of Political Economy*, 72 (February 1964), pp. 44-61, as well as Dewey, *supra* n. 6.

32. See, e.g., Demsetz, *The Market Concentration Doctrine* (AEI-Hoover Policies Studies 1973).

But agreement on the usefulness of vigorous attack on regulatory sources of market power need not imply abandonment of the position that theory and empirical work are adequate to support a policy directed at reducing its structural sources. Leonard Weiss's useful review of the evolution of oligopoly theory properly concludes, in my view, that — Demsetz's arguments and those of some of his fellow neo-Chicagoans to the contrary notwithstanding — "the mainlines of oligopoly theory point pretty consistently to higher prices in more concentrated industries." [33]

Furthermore, Demsetz's data do not necessarily challenge directly the modern theory of profit–concentration relationship, but seem only to suggest that some part of the frequently observed and understated statistical correlation may be due to lower costs (stemming from greater efficiency, including scale economies) rather than to higher prices (stemming from collusion). Other researchers who have reached similar results have not leaped to Demsetz's conclusions.

To my mind, the papers of Dewey, Weiss, and Edwards indicate that the underlying core of economic theory and data on which deconcentration proposals rely has not been basically shaken. Or, more accurately, the general economic case for social benefits associated with less highly concentrated industries remains unshaken; the case for overriding social costs remains to be considered.

## MARKET DEFINITION AND CONCENTRATION MEASURES

Weiss reminds us that a major problem in all studies involving profit–concentration correlations has been the inadequacy both of concentration data and of profit data.[34] Census industries often do not correspond to economically meaningful markets (most obviously as to local or regional markets), data often do not reflect significant noncompeting subproducts (as in many distinct drugs of the pharmaceutical industry), interindustry competition is frequently not accounted for (as in treating cane and beet sugars as separate industries), and foreign trade is not reflected as imposing constraints where products are traded in international markets.

Where market shares trigger deconcentration procedures, such problems in market definition and data may be critical. This is especially true of the Neal committee's proposal, which excludes all other criteria and adopts a fairly high critical percentage (70 percent); an inappropriate market definition would in effect provide an exemption from the statute or, conversely, impose unwarranted burdens on an industry which is performing efficiently.[35] The com-

33. L. W. Weiss, "The Concentration–Profits Relationship and Antitrust," this volume, Chapter 4.

34. See Comments of Dr. Betty Bock on Line of Business Category System for Proposed FTC Annual Line of Business Report, submitted to Office of Management and Budget, November 7, 1973.

35. The proposal's time and continuity requirements provide some insurance against inappropriate market definitions, and will also screen out some industries in which entry is easy.

mittee's Comments note that in departing from the Clayton Act "line of commerce" language (which has been blown up into a market definition requirement in many cases and in the Department of Justice "Merger Guidelines") it hopes to encourage the trier "to make sound determinations free of the distortions which have arisen in some Clayton Act cases." The Kaysen-Turner proposal is similarly general; however, in it market shares play only a supplementary role to simplify proceedings in cases of obvious and very "tight" oligopoly.

The Hart Bill, however, accepts the "line of commerce" language as the market definition rule, thus inviting not only the market "gerrymandering" in which the Supreme Court has acquiesced,[36] but a lawyer's field day which would almost surely be burdensome to proceedings and next to useless in arriving at a sound result.[37] Defining industries or markets in a dynamic world of multiproduct firms with scattered geographical operations and somewhat differentiated outputs — and lacking adequate statistical data — is difficult enough, even starting with a clean slate.

In addition, the Hart Bill adopts a low "trigger" concentration ratio. Kaysen-Turner's "conclusive presumption" comes into play only where one company has 50 percent of sales in the market or four or fewer account for 80 percent. The Neal committee selects a four-firm concentration trigger of 70 percent. In contrast, the Hart Bill would create a presumption of illegality on the basis of four firms occupying only 50 percent of the market. Skepticism about the bill stems in large part from the fact that such a figure is low enough to involve a large proportion of our major firms (and minor firms, one might add, since the Hart Bill contains no minimum size limitation, either as to small firms in concentrated markets or as to size of market). The Neal committee proposal limits deconcentration proceedings to markets which currently and regularly account for sales of over $500 million, sensibly focussing attention and resources on most important cases and limiting administrative discretion; it also excludes from deconcentration proceedings firms with less than 15 percent of the market.

The primary merit of the use of concentration data, in the clearest cases, rather than other indices of monopoly power, is that in those cases it would simplify proof by not subjecting to the litigation process all elements of the underlying studies which have concluded that monopoly power exists.

However, even the most careful and sophisticated market definition — looking to substitution possibilities in both consumption and production, not overlooking locational considerations — only begins to solve the practical and theoretical problems inherent in employment of critical concentration measures as a surrogate for oligopoly market power. Not only are existing data imperfect, but — as discussions of the Federal Trade Commission's new "line of business" report program have suggested — often the several firms in an in-

---

36. See, e.g., United States v. Pabst Brewing Co., 384 U.S. 546 (1966) (geographic market definition); United States v. Grinnell Corp., 384 U.S. 563 (1966) (product and geographical market definitions).

37. Blake, *supra* n. 5, at 564, and sources there cited.

dustry do not structure their internal operational and financial reporting in the same manner, nor in any manner consistent with providing clear answers to economists' questions relevant to market power.[38] Indeed, recognition of this fact of life is one of the reasons that Census data remain inadequate. Presumably, the investigative agencies which the proposals envisage — the new Industrial Reorganization Commission provided for by Hart's bill and by the Kaysen-Turner proposal, or the Federal Trade Commission, active pursuant to the Neal committee's plan — if they were fully armed with powers to require new methods of data-keeping and reporting, could in time repair such deficiencies. And it is likely that such systematization should be carried out in any event, in the general interest of better understanding the functioning of the economy.[39] Nonetheless, the fact is that adequate data for general implementation of any plan based on concentration measures alone are not currently at hand, although for some industries, of course, present data may provide an adequate approximation.

Papers in this volume call attention to at least two related theoretical difficulties. First, what is probably a relatively minor one: Weiss notes that the four-firm concentration ratios incorporated into the critical measurements of each of the three proposals (doubtless because that is the manner in which Census data are available) are "only crude proxies" for likelihood of oligopoly performance in models such as Stigler's. The index most appropriate to such theories would probably be the Herfindahl index, which gives weighted independent value to the relative market share of each firm in the market.[40] But Herfindahl indices have not been regularly developed, probably in large part because underlying data are recognized to be generally too crude to support so discriminating an index measurement.

A more fundamental difficulty is suggested by Professor Demsetz's observations: where entry is easy, concentration measures may bear little relationship to market power, since entry threats may disrupt collusive conduct or at

---

38. See, e.g., Comments on Behalf of the Trade Regulation Committee of the Association of the Bar of the City of New York, to the Federal Trade Commission, February 6, 1974.

39. The Neal committee report explicitly recognizes that its proposal would require better data than are now available. The report recommends the establishment of an "interagency group" — including the Census Bureau, SEC, IRS, FTC, and Department of Justice, among others — to deal with this and related problems. The proposed act itself, however, does not deal with the problem; neither does the Kaysen-Turner proposal, but the Hart Bill provides that the commission may require reports "necessary to carry out the provisions of this Act, including but not limited to reports by product or line of commerce."

40. Professor Scherer notes that the Herfindahl index tends to skew toward low values, which may not be desirable; this effect can, however, be eliminated by a single logarithmic transformation. Scherer also questions whether the differences between concentration indices would be of great practical importance. F. M. Scherer, *Industrial Market Structure and Economic Performance* (Rand McNally 1973), pp. 51-52.

least impose a low ceiling on the range of noncompetitive prices which it can make effective. Occasionally this problem can be adequately handled, at least in theory, through careful attention to production flexibility aspects of market definition. But often effective entry may be threatened by firms whose current output is not closely related in terms of either consumption or production substitutability.

Partial answers to this objection may be of two kinds. First, one may doubt that, given sufficient attention to basic structural and technological supply conditions in defining the market, forces outside the market, as so defined, will often be sufficiently strong and reliably continuing to insure efficient performance in the market. And second, the market share test in the proposals is ultimately a judicial criterion, and perhaps as complex a one as the litigation process can effectively deal with. Entry conditions and other considerations could and should be examined during the industry study which must precede any prosecution; nothing in any of the proposals (except for the Hart Bill's seven specified industries) requires or suggests that the challenging agency may not exercise sound discretion in deciding whether to institute a proceeding or, at the very least, in establishing decisive orders of priority.

## DEFINITION OF THE VIOLATION — CRITERIA AND PRESUMPTIONS

Title I, §101(a) of the Hart Bill declares the violation to be possession of "monopoly power." Although the term is not defined, the Bill's preamble and other provisions make it clear that the term includes oligopoly power. The use of the word "monopoly" might lead courts or others to misunderstand that a violation requires proof of monopoly as defined in *Alcoa*,[41] *du Pont* (*Cellophane*),[42] and related cases. The term "oligopoly power," however, is even more ambiguous, and its use would introduce opportunity for fruitless disputation on economic theory and for judicial misunderstanding. As indicated earlier, Kaysen and Turner suggested a preferable approach, defining the prima facie offense in terms of clear and explicit market performance characteristics of oligopoly which virtually all economists regard as undesirable; their definition also directs attention to entry as a constraining factor, thus avoiding much of the criticism which can be levelled both at the severity and ambiguity of the Hart presumptions and at the Neal committee's total reliance on the structure–performance hypothesis. It is, perhaps, also less open to criticism as too elusive for judicial efficiency than are the approaches necessitating market definition, since the issues of proof would usually be less abstract. Although antitrust courts are often asked to engage in market definition, judicial determinations in deconcentration proceedings must surely be more economically defensible than the results they have achieved in many merger cases.

The Hart Bill both makes use of more arbitrary criteria and spreads its net

---

41. United States v. Aluminum Co. of America, 148 F.2d 416 (2d Cir. 1945).
42. United States v. E. I. du Pont de Nemours & Co., 351 U.S. 377 (1956).

more broadly than does the Kaysen-Turner proposal.[43] The existence of persistent and unreasonably high profits is a criterion used by both proposals. Kaysen-Turner settle for the lesser guidance but greater flexibility of the general terms "persistence" and "abnormally high profits," further directing that "such factors as risk and excess capacity" be taken into account. For example, "a firm or group of firms persistently earning positive profits during a long period of excess capacity" would be a clear case of persistent abnormal profits, without regard to what "normal profits" might be. The Hart Bill, on the other hand, is highly specific, calling for a rebuttable presumption of monopoly power where there is "an average rate of return on net worth after taxes in excess of 15% over five consecutive years out of the most recent seven." Since the fair use of presumptions requires, at the least, that they reflect realistic probabilities in all but aberrant cases, there is reason to doubt the suitability of a single rate of return criterion applicable to all industries, regardless of inherent differences in risks or of the newness or declining nature of the industry, or its technology or capital needs. Even over five out of seven years, 15 percent may be a not unreasonable rate of return for some industries, though grossly excessive for others. Furthermore, since rate of return on net worth is directly affected by debt—equity ratios, significantly within the control of a company, some other denominator — perhaps return on capital investment — seems preferable if a specific rate is to be designated.

A second "evidence" of market power, for Kaysen-Turner, is "persistent failure of prices to reflect substantial declines of demand or costs, or to reflect substantial excess capacity." The nearest counterpart in the Hart Bill appears to be the presumption of monopoly power if for three consecutive years out of the most recent five "there has been no substantial price competition among two or more corporations" in the market. Although probably the two approaches would usually come to the same thing, the Kaysen-Turner formulation is not only more careful in terms of theory but also guides investigation towards the best evidence. In the absence of the price rigidities set forth by Kaysen-Turner, the fact of the absence of different price patterns (if that is what the Hart criterion comes down to) is, after all, consistent with highly competitive market conditions.

Some lawyers will surely be concerned about the use of presumptions of any kind — even when most carefully formulated — in this kind of case. They argue that the proponent of major structural change should need to show less than a fully demonstrated case only where probabilities of underlying causal connections are almost beyond dispute or where, in general, the social benefits of the kinds of change involved substantially outweigh social costs of such kinds of change. Donald Dewey reads the evidence strongly to suggest that the latter is not the case; Demsetz and Brozen — although they have probably not persuaded the less-than-faithful that the traditional wisdom

43. The Neal committee, it will be recalled, eschews entirely such statutory "rebuttable presumptions" (Hart) or evidentiary guidelines (Kaysen-Turner) other than market concentration ratios.

is really mythology — do persuade that considerable caution should be exercised in employing procedural shortcuts based on theorems not yet shown to be laws. True, the Supreme Court has been willing to devise per se rules in some classes of antitrust cases[44] and to employ strong presumptions in suits to prevent mergers.[45] But there are important differences between using the device as a shield and using it as a sword, in the absence of consensus concerning the social costs and benefits of change.

## THE DEFENSES TO DIVESTITURE

The Neal committee proposal flatly bars any remedy which would "require a firm to take steps which would result in loss of substantial economies of scale," providing only that the oligopoly firms must bear the burden of proof on this issue. The committee's Comments point as an example to "divestiture reducing a firm below minimum efficient size," but give little guidance on how to deal with the endless variety of lesser claims which will surely be made, except to note that the minimum size of "viable competitors" in the industry may set a floor. Although the Comments speak of "*net* loss of economies of scale beyond the plant level" — suggesting that the commission might introduce evidence of possible *dis*economies — its proposed statutory language is ambiguous.

The Hart Bill bars any divestiture which would result in "loss of substantial economies"; this will doubtless come to the same thing. Unlike the Neal proposal, the Hart Bill contains an explicit patents defense, substantially coextensive with Kaysen-Turner's,[46] but it contains no specific efficiency defense comparable to their item (3).

Kaysen-Turner are not quite so solicitous of claims of efficiency, although their list of "justifications" of market power is broad: (1) economies of "size in relation to the market," (2) lawful patents (with the burden on the government to show invalidity, illegality, or unlawful use),or (3) low prices or superior products attributable to innovation or comparative efficiency of a firm. To these must be added the four requirements which must be satisfied in the granting of relief,[47] the most important of which for this discussion is the provision that in a divestiture order "any probable permanent loss of substantial economies intrinsic to the defendant be taken into account." The total approach, then, is that even substantial economies of scale do not justify market

---

44. The most recent is United States v. Topco Associates, Inc., 405 U.S. 596 (1972) (division of territories).

45. United States v. Philadelphia National Bank, 374 U.S. 321 (1963).

46. The Hart Bill is internally inconsistent. In one sentence it provides that the defense is available "if [defendant] can show . . . valid patents, lawfully acquired and lawfully used." In succeeding sentences it provides that the burden of showing invalidity, unlawful acquisition, or unlawful use of patents is on the commission. It also provides that only power "solely" due to such patents is defensible, while Kaysen-Turner provides that "power . . . created or maintained, entirely or almost entirely" by such patents is protected.

47. See pp. 347-348 *supra*.

power unless they (along with patents and innovative superiority) are "entirely or almost entirely" its cause. Thus, in the usual case — in the light of Scherer's finding that high levels of concentration are seldom necessitated by economies of scale — they will not bar a deconcentration proceeding, but rather simply be taken into account — presumably, balanced against probable gains — in deciding on divestiture as a remedy. Complex though the formula indeed is, it gives a more limited role to claims of "economies" than do the other two proposals. However, the additional Kaysen-Turner "low prices–superior products" efficiency defense (item (3)) may produce substantially the same result. Quite possibly the narrow distinctions drawn in the Kaysen-Turner proposal, interesting and defensible though they may be, would serve to make the judicial proceedings overly complex; still it is hard to conclude that either the Neal committee proposal or the Hart Bill have succeeded in greatly reducing the problem.

It seems pointless to speculate further on what differences, if any, these three somewhat different formulations of the "economies" defense would produce in actual result. The important fact is that each—except, perhaps, for the (overly elaborate) Kaysen-Turner approach — is so far-reaching as quite conceivably to defeat most attempts to implement the proposal of which it is a part. That this is the case is supported by divergent views presented in this volume. McGee may not have persuaded everyone that the domestic automobile industry could plan for an efficient future only if the "Big Three" were permitted to merge at least their press-plant operations,[48] but he clearly demonstrated both the differences among economists in defining "economies" and "minimum optimum scale," and the disagreement about how to measure (or estimate) their dimensions. McGee's definitions of these concepts would provide an arguable defense to relief to virtually any firm in any industry subject to such proceedings, and we might confidently expect his expertise to be promulgated from many a witness box if any such proposal as these were to become law.

Scherer's study and Dewey's appraisal, on the other hand, are reassuring to proponents of deconcentration. Implicit in Scherer's approach is a narrower, more "engineering-oriented" concept of economies and optimal scale than McGee's. But none of the proposals goes very far in equipping the court with guidance on whether to adopt a "hard" (and perhaps somewhat backward-looking) or more expansive (and arguably more dynamic) view of these concepts.

Each of the three proposals is open to criticism — perhaps in differing degrees — for failing fully to work out how its "economies" defense should be applied. Kaysen-Turner in part avoid the problem by providing that "economies" *justify* market power only in unusual cases, and that they be only "taken into account" in devising relief. The other two proposals make substantial economies a flat bar to relief. In either approach, surely all concerned are entitled to know explicitly whether they may, or must, consider: (1) *disecono-*

48. See J. S. McGee, "Economies of Size in Auto Body Manufacture," *Journal of Law & Economics,* Vol. 16, No. 2 (October 1973), p. 239.

mies or probable "x-inefficiency" considerations as to any one or more firms, (2) anticipated industry-wide improvements in performance (such as through a remedy providing for a more efficient arrangement of functions, skills, or resources), and (3) the attainability of a more nearly self-regulating market and a greater number and variety of decision-making units.

None of the three proposals is clear enough on how, if at all, these considerations should be handled. All are probably overgenerous to the "economies" defense, perhaps because of doubts about advocating legislation that the business community could attack as ingenuous or wasteful. McGee's highly civilized discourse on early nineteenth-century political philosophy is, of course, designed to exacerbate those self-doubts, but Scherer's more extensive empirical work suggests strongly that "economies" defense loopholes could be tightened down with a large spanning wrench without substantial danger of social waste. Although Neal indicated that he was made more comfortable by Scherer's studies,[49] perhaps he should have been made less comfortable, since that work suggests that his committee might well have been less solicitous of claims of economies. The same criticism may be made of the Hart Bill's "economies" provisions; but as to it, at least an overbroad limitation on relief has the modest merit of balancing overbroad presumptions of illegality.

One further observation is in order on the question of judicial competence to deal with the "economies" defenses, as well as market structure data and probable industry performance. Posner and others warn us that many such questions of fact or probability are often intractable both to empirical work and to judicial analysis. The point is well taken. But, paradoxically, an approach such as Kaysen-Turner's — requiring the court to undertake the apparently more complex (or impossible) task of balancing claimed economies against other factors — may be more amenable to judicial process than approaches which require that it define, more or less in the abstract, relevant market boundaries or the substantiality of economies. Judges are accustomed to balancing "equities" to arrive at a workable result, even though they would be unable accurately to quantify any of them. Similarly, in the context of a specific and well-thought-out approach to industrial restructuring in a divestiture plan, it may become clear that a claimed loss of economies is not "substantial," even though not trivial, although there are doubts as to its exact dimensions. And in the same context an "abstract" question as to appropriateness of a market definition might also disappear. A good case can thus be made for providing both the commission and the court with more flexible rather than unduly rigid criteria for illegality and for remedy; a good case can also be made that the two should be dealt with simultaneously.

This implies, of course, need for a clear directive that proceedings be undertaken at first only in those few cases in which the likelihood of net social gain seems likely to be greatest, defined largely by industry and firm size, and by studies of performance and likely responsiveness to deconcentration measures. It also argues against the Neal committee's proposal that substan-

49. See Phil C. Neal, "On Implementing A Policy of Deconcentration," this volume, Chapter 7.

tive questions and remedies be dealt with in two separate proceedings. Proposed remedies and alternative proposals should be dealt with, as in Kaysen-Turner, in the principal proceeding.

## CONCLUSION

Although the particular approach or detailed provisions of each of the current deconcentration proposals can be criticized — the Hart Bill most seriously — they have stimulated interest in industrial organization research and have helped focus attention on specific problems which require continuing work. Even though the moment for basic new legislation may not yet have arrived, recent events seem to be combining with deepening problems related to the United States position in the world economy to produce a political climate more hospitable to proposals looking towards improving the competitive posture of domestic industry in all markets. Unless much of traditional economic thought is archaic, such plans should surely include legislative action directed towards introducing new competitive vigor into our economic system. Industrial deconcentration remains one of the more promising alternatives.

Although the Hart Bill courageously responds to an urgent economic problem, it has failed to win the full and unanimous support of lawyers and economists most concerned with industrial organization. Many of their doubts would be removed if the critical measurement of four-firm concentration were raised to 70 percent, and minimum sizes for industry and oligopoly firms were set. Others would ask that its presumptions in general be reconsidered and that the "seven designated industry" provision be eliminated. My proposal to deal with claims of efficiency as only one consideration in evaluating the restructuring proposals is perhaps more controversial.

However, the basic problem of the Hart Bill seems to be not in the specifics of its provisions, but that it is too technical an "economists' bill" to appeal to its natural political constituency in sufficient degree to surmount the enormous pressures which will be brought against it. The same is true of the Kaysen-Turner and Neal committee proposals. How can those who favor a basic reexamination of the role and performance of business rally around a bill whose efficiency loopholes are so cautiously commodious as to likely defeat most of the deconcentration proceedings it promises? What broad appeal can be found for a restructuring program too loosely drawn to subject the oil or drug industries, for example, to scrutiny, or to provide an occasion to examine the performance of I.T.T., a company which has come to symbolize much of what is worst in American "big business"? (The Hart Bill proceedings might even have the side effect of promoting I.T.T. from number nine on the *Fortune* list to a rank of second or third.)

I have attempted to show elsewhere that both conglomerate firms[50] and vertical integration[51] in some circumstances should be the subjects of serious

---

50. See n. 5 *supra*.

51. H. M. Blake and W. K. Jones, "Toward a Three-Dimensional Antitrust Policy," 65 *Colum. L. Rev.* 422 (1965).

antitrust concern. If this is the case, the simplest, most defensible (in terms of traditional antitrust policy), and most politically potent approach to the concentration problem would be to bring under close scrutiny, for possible deconcentration, in rank order of their sales, the largest 20, 50, or 200 firms in the economy. Of course, the proceeding as to Exxon or General Motors, for example, would join the other major firms in its industry. The objective would not be exclusively to reduce industry concentration — although that might be the central result in appropriate cases — but to seek any and all appropriate and feasible antitrust kinds of relief (including vertical and conglomerate deintegration), with the burden on the industry or large firm to show why the public interest is better served by a high degree of integration than by the antitrust law's traditional presumption in favor of an "open" economy with greater dispersal of decision-making centers and economic power.

## B. THE POLICY ALTERNATIVES DEBATE

## Corporate Power and Economic Apologetics: A Public Policy Perspective

### Walter Adams*

I take as my text for today a chapter from both ecclesiastical and profane history. The date is 1610. Galileo Galilei, armed with his telescope, has scanned the heavens and discovered the Jupiter satellites. But a learned professor, articulating the orthodoxy and wisdom of his time, rejects what Galileo has seen:

> We know — he said — that there are seven planets and only seven, because there are seven openings in the human head to let in the light and air: two eyes, two ears, two nostrils, and a mouth. And the seven metals and various other examples also show that there have to be seven. Besides, the stars are invisible to the naked eye; therefore they do not influence human events; therefore they are useless; therefore they do not exist. (*Quod erat demonstrandum.*) [1]

Not unlike that Padua professor, economists today also profess a conventional orthodoxy. Be they neoclassicists or Keynesians, they theorize on the assumptions that (1) the consumer is king in the marketplace, and (2) the citizenry controls its government. They generally conclude that, except for

---

* Distinguished University Professor and Professor of Economics, Michigan State University. For further biographical information, see Appendix D.
    1. Quoted in Frank H. Knight, *Intelligence and Democratic Action* (Harvard Univ. Press 1960), p. 57.

minor abberations and imperfections, free markets and democratic political institutions add up to an effective system of social control.

## APOLOGETICS I: HORIZONTAL POWER

Having changed the name of our discipline from political economy to economics, the purveyors of the current orthodoxy pretend that power does not exist or that, at worst, it causes only minor and transitory distortions in an otherwise workable system. There is one exception. Even orthodox economists accord scientific recognition to monopoly or horizontal market power, i.e., the influence exercised by a single seller or a group of dominant sellers over price and output decisions in the marketplace.

But horizontal market power, they are quick to point out, is a problem more troublesome in theory than in practice. After all, in most markets there are mitigating forces — notably interindustry or substitute competition, countervailing power, and the Schumpeterian gales of creative destruction — which tend to neutralize the effectiveness of horizontal power combinations. Thus, the theory of interindustry competition[2] tells us that a high concentration level in the tin can industry is reduced to practical insignificance by the substitute competition of glass bottles, paper cartons, and plastic containers. The dominance of the major oil companies is neutralized by the availability of such substitute fuels as coal, nuclear energy, oil shales, tar sands, and nuclear, solar, and geothermal energy. Similarly according to the theory of countervailing power, the real restraints on a firm's dominance are not vested in its competitors, but in its suppliers and customers; they are imposed, not from the same side of the market but from the opposite side.[3] Hence industrial concentration is no cause for concern; monopolistic exploitation is more conjecture than reality. Finally, according to Professor Schumpeter, the capitalist process is rooted not in classical price competition, but rather the competition from the new commodity, the new technology, the new source of supply, the new type of organization — competition which commands a decisive cost or quality advantage and which strikes not at the margin of the profits and outputs of existing firms, but at their very foundations and their very lives. The very essence of capitalism, according to Schumpeter, is the perennial gale of creative destruction in which existing power positions and entrenched advantage are constantly displaced by new organizations and new power complexes. This gale of creative destruction is not only the harbinger of progress, but also the built-in safeguard against the vices of monopoly and privilege.[4]

These apologetics, of course, are based on the rather arrogant assumption that only economists understand the mitigating forces which limit a firm's

2. See, e.g., Clair Wilcox, "On the Alleged Ubiquity of Oligopoly," *American Economic Review Proceedings*, 40 (May 1950), pp. 67-73.

3. J. K. Galbraith, *American Capitalism: The Concept of Countervailing Power* (Houghton Mifflin 1952).

4. Joseph A. Schumpeter, *Capitalism, Socialism, and Democracy* (Harper Bros. 1942).

market power. The presumption is that monopolists or oligopolists are either unaware of these forces or, more importantly, that they accept them with passive resignation. The reverse is true. Businessmen are quite sensitive to their power position, and constantly strive to liberate themselves from the forces which limit their discretion and confine their freedom of action. Thus, on the interindustry competition front, the tin can oligopolists appreciate the desirability of market extension mergers into glass, paper, and plastic containers. The major oil companies, as Table 27 indicates, are fully cognizant of the

TABLE 27
Diversification in the Energy Industries by the 25 Largest Petroleum Companies, Ranked by Assets, 1970

| Petroleum Company | Rank in Assets | Energy Industry | | | | |
|---|---|---|---|---|---|---|
| | | Gas | Oil Shale | Coal | Uranium | Tar Sands |
| Standard Oil (N.J.) | 1 | X | X | X | X | X |
| Texaco | 2 | X | X | X | X | |
| Gulf | 3 | X | X | X | X | X |
| Mobil | 4 | X | X | | X | |
| Standard Oil of Cal. | 5 | X | X | | | |
| Standard Oil (Indiana) | 6 | X | X | | X | X |
| Shell | 7 | X | X | X | X | X |
| Atlantic Richfield | 8 | X | X | X | X | X |
| Phillips Petroleum | 9 | X | X | | X | X |
| Continental Oil | 10 | X | X | X | X | |
| Sun Oil | 11 | X | X | X | X | X |
| Union Oil of Cal. | 12 | X | X | | X | |
| Occidental [1] | 13 | X | | X | | |
| Cities Service | 14 | X | X | | X | X |
| Getty [2] | 15 | X | X | | X | |
| Standard Oil (Ohio) [3] | 16 | X | X | X | X | |
| Pennzoil United, Inc. | 17 | X | | | X | |
| Signal | 18 | X | | | | |
| Marathon | 19 | X | X | | | |
| Amerada-Hess | 20 | X | | | X | |
| Ashland | 21 | X | X | X | X | |
| Kerr-McGee | 22 | X | | X | X | |
| Superior Oil | 23 | X | X | | | |
| Coastal States Gas Producing | 24 | X | | | | |
| Murphy Oil | 25 | X | | | | |

Source: National Economic Research Associates, Washington, D.C.
1. Includes Hooker Chemical Company.
2. Includes Skelly and Tidewater.
3. Includes reported British Petroleum assets.

advantages derived from control over such substitute fuels as coal, oil shale, and nuclear energy, and are merging into these fields with remarkable success. (According to a House of Representatives Small Business Subcommittee, the majors already control approximately 84 percent of United States oil refining capacity; about 72 percent of the natural gas production and reserve ownership; 30 percent of domestic coal reserves and 20 percent of the domestic production capacity; and over 50 percent of the uranium reserves and 25 percent of the uranium milling capacity.[5] While there are no reliable data on control over oil shales, the majors have already begun their apparently successful campaign to invade the government's multitrillion barrel domain by organizing joint ventures to lease federal shale lands.[6]) In short, firms subject to interindustry competition fully understand its potential danger, the need to subvert it, and the action required to accomplish that objective.

Similarly, with respect to countervailing power, dominant firms are not unaware of the discipline to which it subjects them. They proceed, therefore, with such strategies as vertical integration, top-level financial control, and tacit vertical collusion to blend the opposite sides of the market into one — to combine "original" and "countervailing" power into a framework of coalescing power.[7] In doing so, they once again neutralize one of the forces which ostensibly makes horizontal concentration compatible with the public interest.

Finally, with respect to the gale of creative destruction, it is quite apparent that firms with market power appreciate the danger of the gale and the damage it might cause. Instinctively, they understand that storm shelters have to be built to protect themselves against this destructive force, because the mechanism which is of undoubted public benefit carries with it exorbitant private costs. And so they build private storm shelters wherever possible within the parameters of benign neglect by the antitrust authorities; and, where private monopolies and cartels are patently unlawful, unfeasible, or inadequate, they increasingly turn to the government for succor and support. Those who possess entrenched power need not be told that manipulating the state for private ends is perhaps the most felicitous instrument for insulating themselves against, and immunizing themselves from, the Schumpeterian gale.

In sum, the market forces on which orthodox economists seem to rely as an amelioration and mitigation of horizontal power concentrations do not constitute what can reasonably be called an effective control mechanism. These forces may operate in the right direction, but they provide no systematic structural safeguards, nor do they compel conduct which in any predictable sense will serve the public interest.

---

5. *Concentration by Competing Raw Fuel Industries in the Energy Market and Its Impact on Small Business,* 92nd Congress, 2nd Session (1972).

6. See, e.g., *Wall Street Journal,* February 13, 1974.

7. For an extended critique of the countervailing power theory, see W. Adams, "Competition, Monopoly, and Countervailing Power," *Quarterly Journal of Economics,* 67 (November 1953), pp. 469-492.

## APOLOGETICS II: VERTICAL POWER

Vertical power, orthodox economists assure us, has no economic significance except as an extension of preexisting horizontal market control. If restraint of trade exists, it is the horizontal elements that need to be singled out for remedial treatment, not the vertical structure.[8] Robert Bork, before he became solicitor general, explained the issue as follows: monopoly power is the power to alter market price; such power depends on percentage control of the market and ease of entry; vertical integration does not change either the degree of market control or the ease of entry; *vertical integration does not affect price policy because an integrated firm will maximize profits at each level and set output as though each level at which it operates were independent from all other levels* (except in the bilateral monopoly case); the vertical squeeze, therefore, is an optical illusion — representing nothing more than price cutting at one level in the vertical chain.[9] Bork's policy conclusion was that "in the antitrust context the law should not concern itself at all with vertical integration by acquisition, growth, or contract. This is to say that there should be no antitrust law about vertical mergers, exclusive dealing contracts, resale price maintenance or dealer market division by individual manufacturers or suppliers, or any other vertical relationships."[10] Or as Sam Peltzman put it more succinctly, "the appropriate vertical integration policy is, in fact, no policy at all."[11]

This begs the question. It is undoubtedly true that vertical integration, absent horizontal power, poses no policy problem; but it is also true that vertical integration is a mechanism for harnessing market power and transmitting it through successive stages of production and distribution. As Corwin Edwards points out:

> [S]o long as the vertically integrated concern is self-contained, its occupancy of successive stages in the process of production and distribution does not accord it additional power beyond that which springs from its proportion of the market at a particular stage or from its aggregate size. But where such a concern has been disproportionately integrated, so that at one or more stages of production or distribution it acts as supplier or customer for enterprises with which it is in competition at later stages, the existence of vertical integration may become the basis for a special type of power. If a disproportionately integrated concern is big enough to be important to its competitors, it has the power to squeeze them.[12]

8. J. J. Spengler, "Vertical Integration and Antitrust Policy," *Journal of Political Economy,* 58 (August 1950), pp. 347-352.

9. Robert Bork, "Vertical Integration and the Sherman Act: The Legal History of a Misconception," 22 *U. Chi. L. Rev.,* 194-201 (1954), italics supplied.

10. "Vertical Integration and Competitive Processes," in Weston and Peltzman, eds., *Public Policy Toward Mergers* (Goodyear Publ. Co. 1969), p. 149.

11. "Issues in Vertical Integration Policy," in Weston and Peltzman, *supra* n. 10, at 176.

12. Corwin D. Edwards, *Maintaining Competition* (McGraw-Hill 1949), p. 98.

A firm so integrated can discipline its nonintegrated competitors through a foreclosure of access to markets, denial of supplies, or manipulation of relative prices so as to effect a simple or double squeeze. Vertical integration, therefore, when it is combined with elements of horizontal power and dual distribution, can be made a formidable barrier to entry. It becomes a structural obstacle to workable competition and tends to relegate competition to the interstices and fringes of an industry.

The petroleum industry is a case in point. Consider, for example, the combined effect of vertical integration and the depletion allowance on independent refiners. The depletion allowance encourages the integrated companies to report their profits at the crude oil stage rather than at the refining or marketing stage. The majors have an incentive, therefore, to post a high price on crude oil which they then "sell" to their own refineries as well as to independents. For the vertically integrated companies, the high price for crude is simply a bookkeeping transaction. Its effect is to increase profits on crude, reduce tax payments, and (in spite of lower profits at the refining stage) to increase total profits for the integrated concern. For the independent refiner, by contrast, the increase in crude prices means a decrease in both refining profits and total profits; being nonintegrated, he cannot recoup the narrowed margins in refining at some other stage of operations.

By way of illustration, assuming a 27½ percent depletion allowance, an integrated concern that can supply 77 percent of its refinery needs with its own crude oil production stands to gain from an increase in crude prices even if the increase is *not* passed on at the refining stage. If the integrated company has a self-sufficiency ratio in excess of 38.5 percent, it stands to gain even if it passes on only one-half of the crude oil price increase.[13] In other words, an integrated company could decide to operate its refineries at zero or subnormal profits and thus discipline, squeeze, or bankrupt the nonintegrated refiners who are both its customers for crude and its competitors in the sale of refined products. (Incidentally, fifteen of the top seventeen refiners in the United States have a crude oil self-sufficiency ratio in excess of 38.5 percent.)[14]

As the FTC concluded in its recent petroleum report, "The [vertical integration] system contained all the elements essential to a squeeze on refining profits and could be overcome only if the potential refining entrant could enter [the industry] on a vertically integrated basis."[15] By thus raising the cost of entry at the refining stage, vertical integration in and of itself becomes a formidable entry barrier which few newcomers can afford to hurdle. It is also a barrier to the established independent refiners, many of whom eventually give up the battle for survival and sell out to their integrated rivals.

---

13. Cf. M. de Chazeau and A. E. Kahn, *Integration and Competition in the Petroleum Industry* (Yale Univ. Press 1959), pp. 221-222.

14. FTC Preliminary Staff Report, *Investigation of the Petroleum Industry* (1973), p. 20.

15. *Id.* at 26.

(Acquisitions of independent refiners accounted for 40.7 percent of the increase in refining capacity among the top twenty oil companies between 1959 and 1969.)

The control of pipelines by the vertically integrated majors poses a similar problem. If the pipeline sets a rate well above the competitive cost of transporting crude oil, for example, this imposes no burden on the majors who own the pipeline. To them, it is a bookkeeping transaction involving a transfer of funds from the refinery operation to the pipeline operation. But to the non-integrated refiner, an excessive pipeline charge is a real cost increase which he cannot recoup elsewhere and which places him at a competitive disadvantage vis-à-vis his integrated competitors.

The integrated majors can also use their control of pipelines as an entry barrier if they choose to exclude or limit flows of crude oil to the independents. According to the FTC report,

> this can be done by (1) requiring shipments of minimum size, (2) granting independents irregular shipping dates, (3) limiting available storage at the pipeline terminal, (4) imposing unreasonable product standards upon independent customers of pipelines, and (5) employing other harassing or delaying tactics.[16]

Thus, in petroleum as elsewhere,[17] vertical integration can be used as an instrument for parlaying horizontal power at one stage into strategic leverage over another. Such power is not, as orthodox economists would have us believe, an "optical illusion." It is the very real power to decide whether non-integrated competitors shall be tolerated, disciplined, coerced, or excluded. It is the power to determine the conditions for entry and the rules for survival in an industry. *A vertical oligopoly has this power, because its members are not constrained to play the economist's game of short-run profit maximization and are free, therefore, to pursue the more important long-run goal of protecting themselves and the entire industry structure from competitive erosion.*

## APOLOGETICS III: CONGLOMERATE POWER

Conglomerate power, according to the conventional wisdom, has even less significance than vertical power. As Donald Turner puts it:

16. *Ibid.*

17. See, e.g., W. Adams and J. B. Dirlam, "Steel Imports and Vertical Oligopoly Power," *American Economic Review*, 54 (September 1964), pp. 626-655. In the public utility sector, a monopolist like AT&T may extend its power from the service field, where it is subject to regulation, into the field of equipment manufacture, in which there are no corresponding checks and balances. FCC, *Report of the Investigation of the Telephone Industry in the United States* (1939), cited in Edwards, *supra* n. 12, at 98-99. A patent holder may also try to use his legal monopoly power in one field to gain dominance in another totally different market by exploiting vertical leverage in a buyer–seller relationship. See, e.g., International Salt Co., Inc. v. United States, 332 U.S. 392 (1947).

The rules developed for determining the validity of horizontal and vertical mergers clearly will not do for conglomerate acquisitions generally. In the familiar types of horizontal and vertical merger cases, the Supreme Court has come to place important if not decisive weight on the share of the relevant markets controlled by the acquiring and acquired companies. . . . But whatever significance can be attached to market shares in these cases, quite clearly the significance becomes less when we deal with conglomerate mergers, and indeed may vanish altogether.[18]

Why? Because in a conglomerate merger, it is hard to imagine a substantial lessening of competition resulting from the joinder of two firms operating in different geographical areas (market extension mergers) or in different product lines (product extension mergers) or in altogether dissimilar industries (pure conglomerates). How can there be a lessening of competition if none existed between acquirer and acquired to begin with?

Take a specific case: I.T.T., a multinational conglomerate giant, acquires O. M. Scott, a producer of grass seed with a significant but not dominant share of the grass seed market. Conventional theory attaches no significance to this merger, since I.T.T. was not even remotely involved in the production of grass seed prior to the merger. Since I.T.T.-Scott has no larger share of the market than the independent O. M. Scott had before the merger, and therefore presumably no greater control over price, the conventional theorist sees no need to be concerned. Indeed, if a hundred companies in different fields were to merge into one, the theorist would see no accretion of power in such an amalgamation, because no change could be observed in the respective market shares of the formerly independent firms. Their horizontal market power — i.e., their monopoly power — would be no greater after than it was before the merger. In short, so the argument runs, absolute size is absolutely irrelevant.[19]

To those untutored in the mystery and esoterica of economics, it might seem relevant that the newcomer to the grass seed business happens to be I.T.T.; that this vast international organization, with assets of more than $8 billion and 400,000 employees, "is constantly working around the clock — in 67 nations on six continents, in activities extending from the Arctic to the Antarctic and quite literally from the bottom of the sea to the moon;"[20] that I.T.T.'s list of officers and directors has included such luminaries as a former secretary general of the United Nations, a former premier of Belgium, two members of the British House of Lords, a member of the French National Assembly, a former president of the International Bank for Reconstruction and Development, and a former director of the C.I.A.;[21] that the newcomer happens to be a corporation which has sufficient access to the corridors of gov-

18. Donald F. Turner, "Conglomerate Mergers and Section 7 of the Clayton Act," 48 *Harv. L. Rev.*, 1315-1316 (1965).

19. *Report of the Attorney General's National Committee to Study the Antitrust Laws* (1955), p. 325.

20. I.T.T., *Annual Report* (1968), p. 7.

21. See testimony by W. F. Mueller, Senate Small Business Committee, Hearings, *Role of Giant Corporations*, Part 2, 1971, pp. 1097-1098.

ernment power to offer the C.I.A. and the National Security Council a grant of $1 million to assist in the overthrow of a constitutional Latin American republic;[22] that it is a political-economic entity which can propose a $400,000 donation to finance the Republican National Convention, and then miraculously persuade the Justice Department to forego an appeal of three I.T.T. merger cases to the Supreme Court and settle instead for an amiable consent decree.[23]

Pretending that a firm with I.T.T.'s absolute size and aggregate power is a run-of-the-mill newcomer to the grass seed business is not unlike the suggestion that injecting Kareem Abdul Jabbar into a grade school basketball game would have no impact on preexisting power relationships or the probable outcome of the contest. As Kenneth Elzinga, counsel to former Antitrust Chief Richard McLaren, explains:

> The Scott seed company, under the aegis of I.T.T., will find the federal government far more approachable than it ever did in its independent status. And Scott is more likely to use this position to gain favors regarding taxes, import competition, government contracts, and other amenities which give it an advantage over its rivals, thereby lessening competition in the grass seed industry. . . . Note also that I.T.T.-Scott will probably not have to pummel competing grass seed companies, in a manner reminiscent of John D. Rockefeller, to persuade them to shun aggressive, competitive behavior. The rival managers need not be graduates of the Wharton School to realize that their old adversary Scott must now command more respect. And common sense tells us that potential competitors, possibly willing to spar with an independent Scott, will look elsewhere before entering the ring with an I.T.T.-Scott.[24]

In short, conglomerate power does make a difference. It derives not from monopoly or oligopoly control of a particular market, but from diversification over a whole range of markets. It enables a firm, endowed with absolute size and the deep purse, to "outbid, outspend, and outlose" its smaller rivals,[25] and thus to insure its survival almost irrespective of its performance. Finally, as recent events have demonstrated, it conveys a unique access to political power and the opportunity to transform the state into an instrument of privilege creation and protection.

22. See Subcommittee on Multinational Corporations of the Senate Committee on Foreign Relations, *Report, The International Telephone and Telegraph Company and Chile, 1970-71*, 93rd Congress, 1st Session, at 4-5 (June 21, 1973). See also *N.Y. Times*, February 28, 1974.

23. W. F. Mueller, "The I.T.T. Settlement: A Deal With Justice?," *Industrial Organization Review*, 1 (1973), pp. 67-86; Harlan M. Blake, "Beyond the I.T.T. Case," *Harper's Magazine* June 1972, pp. 74-78.

24. W. Adams, "Politics, Power and the Large Corporation," (forthcoming).

25. C. D. Edwards, "Conglomerate Business as a Source of Power," in National Bureau for Economic Research, ed., *Business Concentration and Price Policy* (Princeton Univ. Press 1955); see also Harlan M. Blake, "Conglomerate Mergers and the Antitrust Laws," 73 *Colum. L. Rev.* 555-592 (1973).

## THE PUBLIC POLICY QUESTION

The essence of a firm's economic power is the ability to insulate itself from the social control mechanism imposed by the market or by government or by both. It is the capacity "to avoid market or political sanctions for poor performance." [26] The basic elements of such power are the ability (1) to exploit mutual interdependence, and (2) to erect barriers against new competition, and thus stifle the emergence of alternative sources of supply. The manifestations of this power may occur in a horizontal, vertical, or conglomerate structural context.

If this be so, what is the appropriate social control mechanism to deal with economic power? Demsetz gives us a Hobson's choice:

> Should our efforts be directed to the task of reducing the degree of government intervention, or should we seek to restructure industries and to modify the competitive tactics used by firms? Those who subscribe to the belief that self-sufficient monopoly is the main problem will answer this question by seeking more intervention, while those who see the source of monopoly in government intervention will seek to reduce the role of government in our economy. [27]

Demsetz himself clearly opts for the latter course of action, but feels that its implementation "is hardly the province of the economist."

I find part of Demsetz' argument highly persuasive. Indeed, some twenty years ago, in *Monopoly in America: The Government as Promoter*, Horace Gray and I concluded that the great aggregations of power in this country are not the will of God. They do not conform to some inexorable law of nature. They are not a response to technological or economic imperatives. We found that, in large measure, these power aggregations are the result of unwise, discriminatory, and privilege-creating actions of government. They are the creatures of political power exercised as a reflection of, and on behalf of, private economic power. [28]

Conceding, therefore, that government is a promoter of monopoly, the political economist still faces two additional questions. First, is the government the *only* villain or is it probable that, even in the absence of government intervention, private interests will succeed in forging conspiracies, mergers, and monopolies which are immune from public control and contrary to the public interest? Second, if the government is indeed the *only* culprit, is this not largely a reflection of the power distribution in the economy? Is it not imperative to strive for a decentralization of the power structure precisely in order to reduce the likelihood that government will become an Elizabethan handmaiden of private interests? I submit that both these questions must be

---

26. W. J. Adams, "Market Structure and Corporate Power," 74 *Colum. L. Rev.* —
(1974).

27. "Two Systems of Belief About Monopoly," this volume, Chapter 4.

28. W. Adams and H. M. Gray, *Monopoly in America: The Government as Promoter* (Macmillan 1955).

answered in the affirmative. As political economists and heirs of Adam Smith, and as a gesture to empirical relevance, we simply cannot afford to assume that politics and economics operate in separate, hermetically sealed spheres.[29]

Let me illustrate this proposition — again by reference to the petroleum industry. Here, government has certainly played the role described by Demsetz and others. In the name of conservation and national defense, it has provided the indispensable legal underpinnings for an industrywide cartel. It has done for the oil companies what they could not legally do for themselves without violating the per se prohibitions of the antitrust laws against price-fixing and market allocations.

The process is familiar, although for the moment it may be of only historical interest. The Bureau of Mines in the Department of the Interior publishes monthly estimates of the market demand for petroleum (at desired prices, of course), thus establishing a national production quota. Under the Interstate Oil Compact, approved by Congress, these estimates are broken down into quotas for each of the oil-producing states which, in turn, through various prorationing devices, allocate "allowable production" to individual wells. Oil produced in violation of these prorationing regulations is branded as "hot oil," and the federal government prohibits its shipment in interstate commerce. Also, to buttress this output-restriction and price-maintenance scheme against potential competition, the government protects the industry with a tariff of 10.5 cents per barrel on crude oil and with import quotas (belatedly suspended in May 1973). Finally, to top off these indirect subsidies with more visible favors, the government authorizes oil companies to charge off a 22 percent depletion allowance against their gross income, to "expense" their intangible drilling costs, and to apply their foreign tax and royalty payments as an offset against their obligations to the United States Treasury.

The absurdity of these government restrictions hardly requires detailed comment. For example, it is incontrovertible that the import quotas — originally justified by national self-sufficiency and national defense considerations — had the following deleterious effects:[30] (1) supply was artificially limited and domestic prices were artificially raised; (2) domestic reserves were utilized at an accelerated rate while foreign production was artificially kept out of the American market; (3) the United States was less self-sufficient in 1974 than it was when the import restraints were first imposed; (4) the construction of domestic refinery capacity — a key factor in the current energy crisis — was inhibited by the systematic exclusion of foreign crude oil; and (5) the taxpayer was forced to subsidize overseas operations which yielded no benefits to him.

29. See, e.g., J. K. Galbraith's presidential address to the American Economic Association, "Power and the Useful Economist," *American Economic Review*, 63 (March 1973), pp. 1-11.

30. See, e.g., testimony by Jesse Markham and A. E. Kahn before the Special Subcommittee on Integrated Oil Operations of the Senate Committee on the Interior and Insular Affairs, 93rd Congress, 1st Session (December 12, 1973 and November 28, 1973, respectively).

The only tangible result of the government's policy of restrictionism, protectionism, and subsidization was to entrench the control of the multinational oil giants, and to enable them to run the industry as a government-sanctioned cartel.

This type of governmental intervention in the market mechanism, however, is only part of the explanation for the industry's structure, conduct, and performance. Private action played a quite significant role. Thus, not content with the storm shelters built by the government to protect them from competition, the major oil companies have used their government-subsidized cash flows (roughly $10 billion annually) as a war chest to finance an aggressive horizontal, vertical, and conglomerate acquisition program. Between 1956 and 1968, the 20 majors negotiated a total of 226 mergers to solidify their dominance over crude, refining, and natural gas; to acquire control over such substitute fuels as coal and atomic energy; to integrate vertically into such fields as fertilizers, plastics, and other chemicals; and to expand in purely conglomerate directions such as crushed stone, sand and gravel, foods, paper, brooms and brushes, and automatic vending machines. Most dramatic, perhaps, were the mergers between fully integrated majors — each representing hundreds of millions of dollars in assets — consummated during the last decade (see Table 28). Consolidation of control proceeded undisturbed by the entry of newcomers, the threat of potential entry, or serious efforts by the government to attack along the antitrust front. Indeed, throughout this period, the government seemed to be a policeman looking the other way.[31]

In addition to outright mergers, the major oil companies have used joint ventures as a convenient and expedient method for implementing their market control. Table 29 shows the prevalence of joint ventures in bidding for federal

TABLE 28
Mergers Between Major Integrated Oil Companies, 1961-1970

| Date | Acquiring Company | Assets ($ Mil.) | Acquired Company | Assets ($ Mil.) |
|---|---|---|---|---|
| 1961 | Standard of Cal. | $2,782.3 | Standard of Ky. | $ 141.9 |
| 1965 | Union Oil of Cal. | 916.5 | Pure Oil | 766.1 |
| 1966 | Atlantic Refining | 960.4 | Richfield Oil | 499.6 |
| 1967 | Getty Oil Co. | 659.2 | Tidewater Oil Co. | 1,011.1 |
| 1968 | Sun Oil Co. | 1,598.5 | Sunray DX Oil Co. | 749.0 |
| 1969 | Amerada Petrol. | 471.1 | Hess Oil | 491.5 |
| 1969 | Atlantic Richfield | 2,450.9 | Sinclair Oil | 1,851.3 |
| 1970 | Standard of Ohio | 772.7 | British Petrol. Corp.* | 627.3 |

* Partial acquisition involving less than 100 percent of acquired firm's total assets.

31. See the testimony of Mark J. Green before the Senate Subcommittee, *supra* n. 30 (November 29, 1973), detailing the futility of antitrust action against the petroleum industry.

TABLE 29
Joint Bidding in Federal Offshore Lease Sales, 1970-1972

| Company | Number of Independent Bids | Number of Joint Bids |
|---|---|---|
| Amerada-Hess | 0 | 168 |
| Amoco | 6 | 321 |
| Atlantic Richfield | 12 | 293 |
| Chevron | 79 | 108 |
| Cities Service | 7 | 372 |
| Continental | 27 | 384 |
| Exxon | 80 | 0 |
| Getty | 0 | 281 |
| Gulf | 17 | 32 |
| Marathon | 24 | 214 |
| Mobil | 8 | 103 |
| Phillips | 0 | 169 |
| Shell | 59 | 93 |
| Sun | 115 | 2 |
| Texaco | 15 | 32 |
| Union | 0 | 245 |

offshore lease sales. Their effect on competition, as Walter Mead has demonstrated, is tantamount to rigging bids:

> In any given sale, it is obvious that when four firms . . . , each able to bid independently, combine to submit a single bid, three interested, potential bidders have been eliminated; i.e., the combination has restrained trade. This situation does not differ materially from one of explicit collusion in which four firms meet in advance of a given sale and decide who among them should bid (which three should refrain from bidding) for specific leases and, instead of competing among themselves, attempt to rotate the winning bids. The principal difference is that explicit collusion is illegal.[32]

Similar joint ventures are employed by the major oil companies in their control of interstate pipelines (see Table 30) and their overseas dominion (see Table 31). Reinforced by top-level financial interlocks,[33] and apparently immune from successful antitrust attack, they are the cement which binds together a loose-knit cartel into a cozy system of mutual interdependence.

In short, as the case of the petroleum industry so dramatically illustrates,

32. Walter J. Mead, "The Competitive Significance of Joint Ventures," *Antitrust Bulletin,* 12 (Fall 1967), p. 839. One would suppose that this practice is clearly proscribed by the per se rule under Section 1 of the Sherman Act, as articulated by the Supreme Court in United States v. Socony-Vacuum Oil Co., 310 U.S. 150, 224 n. 59. (1940).

33. Stanley H. Ruttenberg, *The American Oil Industry: A Failure of Antitrust Policy* (Marine Engineers' Beneficial Assn. 1973).

TABLE 30
Typical Joint Ventures in the Oil Pipeline Industry

| Pipeline Company | Co-Owners | Percent Held by Each |
|---|---|---|
| Colonial Pipeline Co. | Amoco | 14.3 |
| (assets = $480.2 mil.) | Atlantic Richfield | 1.6 |
| | Cities Service | 14.0 |
| | Continental | 7.5 |
| | Phillips | 7.1 |
| | Texaco | 14.3 |
| | Gulf | 16.8 |
| | Sohio | 9.0 |
| | Mobil | 11.5 |
| | Union Oil | 4.0 |
| Olympic Pipeline Co. | Shell | 43.5 |
| (assets = $30.7 mil.) | Mobil | 29.5 |
| | Texaco | 27.0 |
| West Texas Gulf | Gulf | 57.7 |
| Pipeline Co. | Cities Service | 11.4 |
| (assets = $19.8 mil.) | Sun | 12.6 |
| | Union Oil | 9.0 |
| | Sohio | 9.2 |
| Texas-New Mexico | Texaco | 45.0 |
| Pipeline Co. | Atlantic Richfield | 35.0 |
| (assets = $30.5 mil.) | Cities Service | 10.0 |
| | Getty | 10.0 |

public policy must come to grips with private action to restrain trade and to entrench power *as well as* with governmental policies of restrictionism, protectionism, and subsidization. It is not an either/or choice. If the ultimate objective is free markets and a decentralized economic power structure, we have no alternative but to attack on both fronts.

## PUBLIC POLICY RECOMMENDATIONS

If it is our objective to control the behavior and performance of large corporations through a system of competitive markets and a decentralized power structure, our agenda for action should include the following public policies:

*First,* and probably most important, the government must refrain from intervening in markets which, in the absence of such interference, would be workably competitive. In the words of Adam Smith, it may be difficult to "prevent people of the same trade from sometimes assembling together," but government "ought to do nothing to facilitate such assemblies; much less to render them necessary." Government should abjure the role of the mercantilist state in sanctioning and legitimizing private privilege.

An initial step might be to reexamine the role of the so-called independent

TABLE 31

Selected Major International Joint Ventures of
Large Integrated Petroleum Companies

---

Arabian American Oil Co.

| | |
|---|---|
| Texaco | 30.00% |
| Exxon | 30.00 |
| Chevron | 30.00 |
| Mobil | 10.00 |

1971 crude production = 1,449.05 mil. bbls.

Iranian Oil Participants, Inc.

| | |
|---|---|
| Mobil | 7.00% |
| Exxon | 7.00 |
| Chevron | 7.00 |
| Texaco | 7.00 |
| Gulf | 7.00 |
| B. P. | 40.00 |
| Shell | 14.00 |
| Atlantic | 1.67 |
| Signal | .83 |
| Getty | .83 |

1971 crude production = 1.3 bil. bbls.

Iraq Petroleum Co.

| | |
|---|---|
| B. P. | 23.750% |
| Shell | 23.750 |
| Exxon | 11.875 |
| Mobil | 11.875 |

Kuwait Oil Co., Ltd.

| | |
|---|---|
| Gulf | 50.00% |
| B.P. | 50.00 |

1971 crude production = 1.27 bil. bbls.

---

regulatory commissions, which probably represent the least felicitous experiment in American economic statecraft. The history of these commissions shows that what starts as regulation almost inevitably winds up as protection. The power to license becomes the power to exclude; the regulation of rates, a system of price supports; the surveillance of mergers, an instrument of concentration; and the supervision of business practices, a pretext for harassing the weak, unorganized, and politically underprivileged.[34]

In some industries which are inherently competitive and where there are no substantial economies of scale (e.g., trucking), gradual but total deregulation is both feasible and desirable. In other industries (e.g., airlines, television, communications) where competition cannot be allowed full sway or where government cannot avoid active participation in the economic game, the basic

34. See, e.g., W. Adams, "The Role of Competition in the Regulated Industries, *American Economic Review Proceedings,* 48 (May 1958), pp. 527-543.

guidelines should militate toward maximum possible decentralization. In most cases, the technological constraints are so broad as to permit infinitely more competition than the regulatory bureaucracies have shown a willingness to tolerate. Congress should compel them by legislative mandate to utilize competition and diversification, wherever possible, as the *paramount* instrument for promoting the public interest,[35] and the Antitrust Division should continue to wage its unceasing battle against the neomercantilist restrictionism which is the hallmark of these commissions.

Another step forward would be the repeal of tariffs, import quotas (mandatory and "voluntary"), "anti-dumping" statutes, "Buy American" regulations, and similar devices to exclude foreign competition. Not only are they a tax on domestic consumers and a subsidy to the sheltered industries, but the capstone of any policy to protect entrenched economic power. It is time to recognize the wisdom of Gottfried Haberler's observation that "free international trade is probably the best anti-monopoly policy."

These examples are merely suggestive of the many areas in which a reorientation in the role of government can contribute mightily to a deconcentration of economic power. They illustrate how a government can govern best by governing least.

*Second,* as a short-run alternative to a comprehensive restructuring of major concentrated industries, Congress should enact a new antitrust law to control the *conduct* of giant firms — especially those types of conduct which entail serious structural consequences. Under this law, drafted along lines suggested by Louis B. Schwartz,[36] any corporation with assets in excess of $250 million, or any corporation which ranks among the top eight producers in an industry where the eight-firm concentration ratio is 70 percent or higher, shall be prohibited from:

35. In McLean Trucking Co. v. United States, 321 U.S. 67 (1944), which involved a trucking merger under Section 5 of the Transportation Act, Mr. Justice Douglas stated the proper standard for accommodating antitrust policy and regulatory policy: "[S]ince the 'public interest' includes the principles of free enterprise, which have long distinguished our economy, I can hardly believe that Congress intended them to be swept aside unless they were in fact obstacles to the realization of the national transportation policy. But so far as we know from the present record that policy may be as readily achieved on a competitive basis as through the present type of consolidation. At least such a powerful combination of competitors as is presently projected is not shown to be necessary for that purpose. . . . [A]dministrative authority to replace the competitive system with a cartel should be strictly construed. I would read §5 of the Transportation Act so as to make for the greatest possible accommodation between the principles of competition and the national transportation policy. The occasions for the exercise of the administrative authority to grant exemptions from the anti-trust laws should be closely confined to those where the transportation need is clear." *Id.* at 94 (dissenting opinion).

36. Louis B. Schwartz, "Monopoly, Monopolizing, and Concentration of Market Power: A Proposal," in A. Phillips, ed., *Perspectives on Antitrust Policy* (Princeton Univ. Press 1965), pp. 117-128.

1. acquiring the stock, assets, or property of another company;
2. granting or receiving any discrimination in price, service, or allowance, except where such discrimination can be demonstrated to be justified by savings in cost;
3. engaging in any tie-in arrangements or exclusive dealerships; and
4. participating in any scheme of interlocking control over any other corporation.

In addition, such firms shall be obligated to:

5. perform the duties of a common carrier by serving all customers on reasonable and nondiscriminatory terms;
6. license patents and know-how to other firms on a reasonable royalty basis; and
7. pursue pricing and product policies calculated to achieve capacity production and full employment.

Note that the foregoing provisos do not limit the growth of giant firms on the basis of superior efficiency, technological innovation, or market success. They are designed only to limit growth artificially induced via merger, and to prevent the extension of existing market power by means of selected restrictive practices. As such, these provisos are a forthright recognition of the fact that industrial giantism has social and economic consequences of pervasive impact. As in the case of public utilities, decisions which profoundly affect the public interest should not be entrusted to a private industrial oligarchy.

*Third,* Congress should undertake a major amendment of the antitrust laws to accomplish basic structural reform along the lines suggested in the Neal report (see Appendix C) and Senator Hart's Industrial Reorganization Act (see Appendix B). The new law should be based on the explicit recognition that industries which do not have a competitive structure are not likely to evidence competitive behavior nor to perform competitively in the public interest.

*Finally,* to promote institutional or yardstick competition, the Congress might as a last resort create public corporations in selected industries which over time have exhibited high and persistent levels of concentration. The goal here would not be to eliminate private enterprise by nationalization, but to subject a noncompetitive industry to the challenge of a T.V.A.-style competitor.

Whatever policy or combination of policies we finally adopt should, in the final analysis, be determined by the kind of society we want. As Allyn A. Young said long ago:

Most of the more weighty discussion of the economic advantages of monopoly have to do with the effect of monopoly upon the aggregate production of wealth measured in terms either of subjective satisfaction or of objective commodity units. Even from this point of view the case for monopoly is exceedingly dubious and, at best, has a validity that is restricted and conditioned in many ways. Moreover, such considerations are relatively unimportant compared with matters like the effect of monopoly upon distribution, upon the scope for individual initiative, upon economic opportunity in general, and upon a host of social and political relations. In short, it is a question less of the relative "economy" of monopoly or competition than of the kind of economic organization best calculated to give us the kind of society we want. Until our general social ideals are radically changed, it will take more than economic analysis to prove that it would be sound public policy to permit monopoly in that part of the industrial field where competition is possible." [37]

# On Implementing a Policy of Deconcentration

## Phil Caldwell Neal*

In considering policy alternatives as to deconcentration we move inescapably from economic analysis to political judgment. Describing the problem as political does not mean abandoning reasoned analysis or abdicating to the prejudices of voters or congressmen. I merely mean that, as in most problems of policy, a choice must be made in the face of uncertainty about outcomes and on the basis of highly subjective estimates of possible gains and costs. Although I remain persuaded that there is a strong case for new legislation dealing directly with concentration, I shall add little to the familiar arguments on that side of the ultimate question. Instead, I will devote myself mainly to some questions about the form such a policy might take and the difficulties of executing it.

On the broad question of whether to do something or do nothing about concentration, the assumptions a policymaker must start with seem little changed by the analysis and data presented in this volume. First, both economic theory and the empirical literature provide substantial foundation for thinking that reduction of concentration would have benefits akin to preventing collusion. In short, it would increase competition. Second, there is some basis for fearing that the policy would reduce efficiency. Third, we can scarcely hope to have any reliable predictions of the values associated with these potential gains and losses. Fourth, when measured against total productivity of the economy, both the potential gains and potential costs are probably fairly modest. Perhaps there is a greater risk of major losses of efficiency than there is a possibility of great economic benefit, but that danger, if it exists, is one than can be somewhat minimized in the administration of the policy.

In this state of uncertainty a policy judgment may well turn importantly on

---

37. Allyn A. Young, "The Sherman Act and the New Antitrust Legislation," *Journal of Political Economy*, 23 (1915), p. 214.

* Dean and Professor of Law, University of Chicago Law School. For further biographical information, see Appendix D.

factors other than the economic calculus. One such factor might be the possibility of increasing public confidence in the competitive character of the economy and willingness to rely on competition as an alternative to regulation. Widely held beliefs are realities with which public policy must be concerned, and there is a widespread view that much of American industry is dominated by a few giant concerns which are not held in close check by competitive forces. This impression has consequences for other public policies, and contributes to the climate of interventionism that many who, though opposed to deconcentration, would like to reverse. The amount of deconcentration that would be produced under any reasonably cautious policy might not greatly change the prevailing image of American industry; but we should not altogether discount the possibility that a clearly enunciated and firmly enforced limit on concentration would help us move toward a less regulated economy.

One reason this might be so is that a program for deconcentration would complete the present framework of the antitrust laws and enable us to say that we have a comprehensive policy for preserving competition. As matters now stand, there is an undeniable gap. The tightening of the law on mergers has reduced a previous gap, but at the same time has made more conspicuous the failure to deal with other paths to concentration. It can be argued, of course, that a stringent policy on mergers is tolerable only because it leaves open the possibility of unlimited internal growth. On the other hand, there is an anomaly in a policy that manifests great concern over even slight tendencies toward concentration where mergers are concerned, while largely ignoring the same presumed evil where it already exists on a large scale or can come about by other means. There are relevant differences between mergers and nonmerger concentration; they call for different policies, but they do not obviously support having a strict policy as to one and no policy as to the other. Rectifying that discrepancy, even in a cautious way, would contribute to a general belief in the continuing significance and efficacy of the antitrust laws.

From a narrower perspective, a declared policy on concentration might have salutary effects on the administration of the rest of the antitrust laws. The failure of the antitrust laws to deal directly with oligopoly exerts its influence on decisions dealing with business practices. The existence of what the courts perceive to be monopoly power, even though not itself unlawful, is an invitation to find exclusionary or otherwise harmful practices where none exist and to warp the antitrust laws in the direction of greater regulation of business behavior. The adoption of a statutory definition of undue concentration and the application of structural remedies would undermine the case for finding monopoly power everywhere and attempting to control it indirectly.

Whether it is worth taking steps to reduce concentration will also turn in part on judgments about the feasibility of stating a sound policy and the difficulties of executing it. These questions were much in the minds of the Task Force which proposed the Concentrated Industries Act. None who joined in the proposal would regard that draft as a finished or perfect solution. It was meant to exemplify the main lines of what appeared to the committee a sound approach to the problem. As among alternative approaches that have been suggested, including particularly the bill sponsored by Senator Hart, the Task Force approach still seems to me much closer to an acceptable and workable measure.

The theory of the Concentrated Industries Act is simple and clear. It proposes that oligopoly industries and oligopoly firms be identified in purely structural terms, based on concentration ratios and market shares in an economically meaningful market. It defines the objectives of relief in similar terms. The test of undue concentration in monopoly cases thus cuts loose from the Sherman Act's main tradition that associates illegal power with bad practices or wrongful intent. It rejects inquiry into such matters as behavior and performance, as the earlier Kaysen-Turner proposal would have required, or the presence or absence of price competition, which is one test under the Hart proposal. Nor does it make profits relevant, as the Hart Bill would do.

Although there is an element of arbitrariness in such a straightforward structural test, we felt that this was both justified by the principle underlying the policy and warranted by considerations of enforcement. It is sound in principle because the policy rests on a structural theory. The theory says that markets with concentration will tend to behave in certain ways because of their structure, even though the undesirable behavior cannot be readily identified or its consequences clearly measured. The remedy should lessen the probabilities, rather than depend upon or regulate the behavior. A clear-cut structural test also promotes workability because it greatly narrows the range of inquiry required in proceedings to enforce the policy. Although such proceedings may still be complex and protracted, they should be significantly simpler than those required under approaches like the Keysen-Turner and Hart proposals. Indeed, the question of remedy aside, such proceedings should not be inherently more difficult and complicated than many Section 7 cases. There is also a sense in which a relatively simple structural test reduces arbitrariness: by narrowing the criteria of judgment, it removes the problem from a wide-ranging discretion of judges or an administrative agency and subjects all potential defendants to a uniform standard defined by Congress.

An important advantage of the simple market-share approach taken by the Concentrated Industries Act is that its somewhat Draconian character can be tempered by the choice of numbers to be inserted in the definitions. It permits confining the policy of deconcentration to extreme cases and thus embarking on such a policy with the caution that the uncertain state of the evidence suggests. The Task Force somewhat arbitrarily proposed use of a four-firm, 70 percent concentration ratio, stable over a ten-year period, in markets exceeding $500 million annual sales. It also proposed deconcentration in a four-firm, 50 percent concentration as the target of remedial steps. These criteria seemed to the committee to represent a conservative policy; but there is obviously room for debate about the appropriate boundaries, and any of these measures could be moved up or down without impairing the general principle. That approach seems preferable to open-ended definitions of market power that would potentially encompass a vast range of industries and firms, and preferable, on the other hand, to an industry-by-industry approach without the benefit of general criteria. There remains the possibility, of course, that any proposed target for deconcentration (such as a four-firm, 50 percent target) will be inappropriate for a particular industry because of scale economies. But that question seems best examined in connection with the problem of relief, to which I will come in a moment.

Although one cannot minimize the administrative problems associated with any deconcentration program, I am not quite so pessimistic as some of the critics. In particular, that phase of the proceeding which is to set the stage for remedial measures — what might loosely be called the "liability" phase — does not seem to me to present the prospect of unusually formidable litigation. The purpose of that stage is to determine whether an industry is an oligopoly, as defined, and which firms in it are oligopoly firms. This turns entirely on delineating the relevant market and ascertaining market shares over time. Definition of a relevant economic market is, indeed, an elusive matter but it is a problem with which, in one way or another, courts have often had to cope in antitrust cases. The Task Force recommendation in this respect does not inject a novel concept but merely tries to make clear that the search is for an economically meaningful definition of the market as opposed to spurious geographic lines or product classifications. A strong mandate to conduct such a search, in contrast with the cavalier dismissal of the problem in the *Pabst* case,[1] might hasten the development of accepted techniques or guides for market definition.[2] Endless argument about the precise boundaries of an economically significant market is always possible; but one suspects that this is an issue on which, in any given case, a fairly strong consensus of judgment among disinterested economists might be reached. One aspect of the Task Force proposal sought to encourage the use of court-appointed economic experts. The market-definition issue is a place where the device of neutral experts might be especially fruitful.

A virtue of the Task Force proposal is that it would shift most of the complexities of litigation from the determination of liability to the framing of appropriate relief. Once the determination of an oligopoly industry and oligopoly firms is made, there is a mandate for relief; the only questions are the form the relief should take. Those are complex questions, to be sure, but their resolution would take place in the more informal and flexible procedural setting that characterizes the framing of an equitable decree, rather than by the adversary presentation of evidence on every conceivable issue. There would be a heavy burden on the parties to come forward with proposals; much would be left to negotiation; and the trial judge's principal task would be to choose between alternative plans or alternative features of proposed plans, informed by argument and whatever written submissions the parties chose to offer. The incentive of the defendants to maximize the values preserved for their shareholders would, in itself, be a considerable assurance that the surviving and new firms resulting from the decree would be economically viable

---

1. United States v. Pabst Brewing Co., 384 U.S. 546 (1966).
2. See, e.g., Elzinga and Hogarty, "The Problem of Geographic Market Delineation in Antimerger Suits," 18 *Antitrust Bull.* 45 (1973).

and efficient units. As George Hale has pointed out,[3] the experience with dissolutions carried out in earlier major cases — such as those against the Standard Oil, American Tobacco, harvester, powder, and photographic equipment trusts — suggests that "commercial triumphs among the successor units are almost universal."[4] As Hale also notes, "whatever doubts may be entertained as to the efficacy of dissolutions of the past, it seems clear that the mechanics of separating monopolistic combinations, in the degree of 'atomization' heretofore attained, has not presented insuperable problems."[5]

The most difficult problem is what to do about economies of scale, and it is on this point that the papers presented in this volume have given me greatest pause about the adequacy of the Task Force proposal. Those papers make clear both the great complexity of tracing efficiencies and the strong likelihood that persuasive efficiency considerations can be advanced against almost any proposed dissolution. Seen in their light, the attention given the problem in the Concentrated Industries Act may seem oversimplified and unduly optimistic.

It is well to note, however, that the Task Force proposal does not exactly create a "defense" of economies of scale, as Professor Posner's strictures might imply. That is, a deconcentration proceeding is not to be defeated by a general defense that reduction of concentration would impair the efficiency of a firm. The question of efficiency arises, rather, as part of the relief proceedings and is addressed to whether a particular remedial meaure will result in the loss of substantial economies of scale. There is warrant for Professor Posner's concern, however, in the language of a comment in the Task Force Report which speaks of placing the burden of proof on the defendant to establish such loss of economies. Injecting the notion of burden of proof into the relief proceedings might indeed be an invitation to additional prolonged litigation.

A preferable solution would be to leave the question of economies of scale simply as one of the factors guiding the court's discretion in framing or approving a plan of dissolution. The problem is how to define the limits of discretion. How far is the court to be permitted to depart from the stated target of deconcentration (the four-firm, 50 percent measure, as proposed in the Concentrated Industries Act) in the interest of preserving possible or probable efficiencies?

One approach might start from recognition that the decision to embark on a policy of deconcentration is itself a decision to risk loss of efficiencies for the sake of other gains. On this view even the limited "defense" proposed by the Task Force is too absolute: although the court should do what it can to maximize efficiencies in the plan it adopts, even the loss of substantial econ-

---

3. George Ellery Hale, "Trust Dissolution: 'Atomizing' Business Units of Monopolistic Size," 40 *Colum. L. Rev.* 615 (1940).

4. *Id.* at 623.

5. *Id.* at 631.

omies should (under this program) be no bar to a decree that achieves the required deconcentration.

A modified version of this approach might merely attempt to give the court some leeway, but not too much, in applying the stated target for deconcentration. The statute might, for example, require the judge to enter a decree that approximates the four-firm, 50 percent measure "as near as may be practicable, having regard to preventing the loss of substantial efficiencies, etc." It is difficult, however, to open the door without having it swing too wide. An important objective of an effective deconcentration statute should be to prescribe a definite goal for deconcentration decrees in lieu of vague formulations such as "restoring workable competition." Rather than sacrifice this objective, it might be better to accept whatever losses of efficiency are associated with the marginal cases.

There remains the hard case where a court is persuaded that any reduction in a firm's size that comes even close to the required level of deconcentration will result in much higher costs of production. The single-plant firm would be the clearest case, and an exception must obviously be provided for such a case. Whether other such cases exist has yet to be demonstrated. I agree with Professor Posner's argument that a test which looks to the size of viable smaller firms in an industry must be used with caution, but it is not irrelevant, particularly if one assumes that some loss of efficiency is a price worth paying for reduction of concentration. Still, a prudent statute should afford some escape hatch for the extreme case convincingly demonstrated. The form such an escape hatch should take appears to be the most difficult problem of devising an acceptable policy. One possibility might be to require the defendants in such a case to seek an express exemption from Congress, or a designated agency, after a judicial finding that a plan of reorganization conforming to the statute would impose substantial losses of efficiency. To allow for such an application for exemption, entry of a final decree could be stayed during a specified period. Such a mechanism would have the merit of inviting a legislative or quasi-legislative judgment based on a well-developed record of the facts of the particular industry and firm, and would permit consideration of possible conditions that might be attached to the granting of an exemption. The very fact that such an application would be an invitation to special regulation might itself deter undue or exaggerated claims of economies of scale; it might also provide an incentive to devise plans of reorganization compatible with a minimum loss of efficiencies.

There is good ground for hesitancy about measures that call for major surgery on our economic arrangements without certainty about outcomes. It is tempting to say that the burden is on those who propose change, and that we should not tamper until convinced beyond a reasonable doubt that the benefits will exceed possible costs. But there are costs in inaction, too, and to demand too much certainty could paralyze policy on many fronts. For those whose conservative nature shrinks from a policy of deconcentration, it is worth recalling that such proposals have an impeccable conservative ancestry. Over thirty years ago Henry Simons's classic tract, *A Positive Program for*

*Laissez-Faire,* urged deconcentration as an indispensable feature of any program to preserve free enterprise.

> Even if the much-advertised economies of gigantic financial combinations were real, sound policy would wisely sacrifice these economies to preservation of more economic freedom and equality. . . . Few of our gigantic corporations can be defended on the ground that their present size is necessary to reasonably full exploitation of production economies: their existence is to be explained in terms of opportunities for promoter profits, personal ambitions of industrial and financial "Napoleons," and advantages of monopoly power. We should look toward a situation in which the size of ownership units in every industry is limited by the minimum size of operating plant requisite to efficient, but highly specialized, production—and even more narrowly limited, if ever necessary to the maintenance of freedom of enterprise." [6]

It would be interesting to know how far Simons's views would have been altered by developments since he wrote, and by the additional economic evidence and analysis reported in this volume. Others better versed in Simons's thought may care to speculate on that question. A noneconomist must confess that the issues, as illuminated by the papers herein, appear much more complex than Simons's treatment of them suggested. In the light of that complexity, the quite different form of laissez-faire represented by John McGee's views has strong attraction. But it seems also true that the evidence fails to dispel the concerns that underlay Simons's policy preference, or to warrant abandonment of the search for a viable policy of deconcentration.

# Industrial Concentration and Public Policy: A Middle Ground
## Almarin Phillips*

## I.   INTRODUCTION

The formation of appropriate public policies is relatively easy — indeed, even largely noncontroversial — in two circumstances. One occurs when there is substantial knowledge about the underlying nature of the system to which the policies are to be applied. More precisely, if the goals of the system are known and agreed to, and if the interrelations among the parts of the system and the external constraints can be specified, public policy is little other than

---

6. Henry C. Simons, *Economic Policy for a Free Society* (Univ. of Chicago Press 1948), pp. 52, 59.

* Professor of Economics and Law, University of Pennsylvania. For further biographical information, see Appendix D.

the exercise of certain control variables so as to maximize goal attainment in the system. The other occurs when, despite a lack of knowledge about the nature of the system, everyone shares the same values and faith.

Unhappily, policy towards industrial concentration cannot proceed in an easy fashion. Neither circumstance applies. Goals are not and cannot be clearly defined. They involve economic, political, and social considerations — the values of which cannot be quantified even for individuals. Because goals are multidimensional and the system operates so that "better" performance in one respect often means "poorer" performance in another, trade-offs in goal attainment are involved. In addition, there is no unanimity among individuals in their evaluation of the relative importance of the several dimensions of goals, and often no market is possible for individuals to exchange goal achievements so as to maximize their individual satisfaction.

Even if the problems of goal definition were not present, the interrelations among the component parts of the market system are not very well understood. The system is complex; what occurs when a particular control variable is pushed is just not known. Thus, despite the confidence with which a given "expert" may espouse particular politics, it is wise to proceed on the assumption that all experts are fallible. It might even be suggested that not only are the experts fallible, but that they sometimes — consciously or unconsciously — use different basic concepts of the market process which reflect their own subjective economic, political, and social values.

## II.   THE STATE OF ECONOMIC UNDERSTANDING ON ISSUES RELATING TO CONCENTRATION

There is a temptation to compare explicitly the papers in this volume to illustrate the differences in concepts and analytic approaches. To do so, however, would elicit more acrimonious debate and more cries of misinterpretation than would be productive of better understanding. Beyond this, hyperbole not really representative of the papers will be used for emphasis.

What do we not know? First, we know little about systematic relations between market concentration and other measures of market structure and market performance. The continuing debate concerning concentration ratios and profitability is illustrative. Part of the problem is that there is no generally accepted theory as to why there should be a relationship; part of the problem is also that data ostensibly measuring both concentration and profits are not close counterparts to the underlying economic concepts. But, theory and data problems aside, some argue that a positive and continuous relationship has been demonstrated. Others find that there is a threshold point beyond which a positive relation exists, with no consistent effects below the threshold. Another variant is that concentration has an effect only when accompanied by high barriers to entry. Nonlinear relations have been reported, including negative partial effects of concentration on profitability when the former is high. Some have produced evidence to show that the relationship is, at least, transitory and, at worst, something of a statistical artifact. None has found the relationship to be so strong that, with problems of statistical method considered, a high proportion of the variance in profits can be accounted for by measures of market structure. What guidance for public policy can come from this?

A not dissimilar state characterizes knowledge of relations between market structure — concentration and barriers to entry, in particular — and technological change. There exists a body of theory and some empirical support to the effect that innovations will be adopted more rapidly in competitive than in monopolistic markets. But that theory is silent with respect to the production of the technical knowledge required to make innovation possible.

Theory with respect to R&D and investment in knowledge is far more mixed. At one extreme, there is the theory — or perhaps it should be called just a view — that the incentive of the rewards of monopoly stimulates progress. The Schumpeterian vision and the somewhat similar Galbraithian position run in this vein, though both of these place considerable importance on oligopolistic nonprice rivalry. It is not difficult to find literature suggesting that competitively structured markets are the ones most conducive to technical progress. A few recent studies — theoretical and empirical — support the position that there is an optimal degree of concentration, with technological change being first positively and later negatively associated with concentration. Again, concentration has not been shown to explain a large proportion of the variance in any of the measures of technological change. Even the direction of causation in the relationship, if there is one, has been questioned. What guidance for public policy can come from this?

Advertising and its effects on market performance have been investigated but hardly resolved. Since advertising occurs in markets which are definitionally less than purely competitive, economists have not generally been charitable in their a priori approaches. Demand curves (it is said by some) become less elastic due to advertising, and entry barriers are increased. Hence the public suffers from greater monopoly power, because it leads to high concentration — or because high concentration leads to advertising? But does advertising perform an educational role instrumental in improving consumer choice? Does advertising permit and encourage product differentiation which adds to the range of products from which consumers may select? Does advertising, rather than increasing entry barriers, somehow reduce them? Does advertising increase the elasticities of demand? Some economists would answer at least some of these questions affirmatively. What guidance for public policy can come from this?

The standard industrial organization text lays out possible explanations for the extent of market concentration. Economies of scale, other barriers to entry (including governmental actions), mergers motivated by collective desires for higher profits, and stochastic processes are discussed. Which, if any, of these is relevant for particular industries is for the most part unknown. The idea that concentration arises from random events offends some who like to think the world is more of a cause-and-effect, deterministic system. If the debate here is less heated than that surrounding other issues, it may well be because — given the background of microtheory on which economists are reared — most are prepared to take structure as given exogenously. But is it? Could structure be endogenous to the market system? What guidelines for public policy can be confidently offered?

The economics of regulation, and connections between regulation and the exercise of monopoly power, are no less confused. On one side, there are those who see little danger from the exercise of private monopoly power in the absence of abetting government regulations. Government regulation is seen as the device to turn otherwise ineffective private actions into full-fledged monopoly behavior. On the other side, some persist in the view that regulation is an administrative substitute for competition in markets where, for one reason or another, competition cannot be relied upon to produce efficient results. There is a growing literature detailing different types of regulation, stemming from different kinds of problems, with different effects on the regulated firms and their customers. Even behavioral theories are being developed which deal with regulators' responses to those with whom they interact in varieties of organizational contexts. But again, what guidance for public policy can be gained?

Finally, there is the concentration–inflation problem. Aided — or blinded — by the now famous "45 degree" diagram approach to macroeconomics, an important element in the profession sees inflation as a problem relating only to aggregate demand. A few tend to neglect the aggregate demand problem, since that can be controlled through prudent monetary and fiscal policies, and point exclusively to "wage push" inflation originating from concentrations of market power in key unions. Alternatively a critical role is given to concentrated industries, sometimes acting in conjunction with strong unions and sometimes acting without. Approaches emphasizing interrelations between aggregate supply and aggregate demand exist — that, after all, was fairly clearly explained in *The General Theory* — and there is evidence that microaspects of macrotheories will get increasing attention in the future. In the interim, is there clear guidance for appropriate micropolicies in our present knowledge?

## III.   THE AMBIT OF POLICY ALTERNATIVES

The state of economic knowledge on issues relating to concentration obviously offers little precise guidance for policy. Rather than causing a paucity of policy alternatives, however, this state of knowledge appears to have led to a plethora of alternatives.

The ostensibly demonstrated positive relationship between profitability and concentration has been the foundation for a number of policy approaches. The Antitrust Division's merger guidelines bear the imprint of regression coefficients showing the positive relationship. Senator Hart's proposal to deconcentrate selected industries and to shift the burden of proof when concentration or profits reach particular levels are similarly based. And the Federal Trade Commission has attempted — unsuccessfully thus far — to obtain summary judgments of violations of Section 7 based on the effects of a merger on four-firm, eight-firm, and twenty-firm concentration ratios alone.

Alternative policy suggestions, implicit or explicit, range to a defense of large firms and concentrated markets based on neo-Social Darwinian views.

Large firms get that way because of some kind of superiority over their rivals. To deconcentrate via new applications of the Sherman Act or through new legislation and, presumably, to prevent "superiority-inducing" mergers by application of Section 7 would be an attack on efficiency. Those who advocate these policies seem to deny that there can be such things as monopoly in the economic sense or monopolization and a lessening of competition in the legal sense.

Much the same dichotomy of possible policies exists with respect to concentration and technological change. The patent system is thought by some to be sacrosanct, immune from changes which might improve market performance. On the other hand, policies are suggested to discriminate on the degree of patent protection based on differences in the market power of the patentee, the social importance of the patent, and related matters. Compulsory licensing, controls over royalties, and reduced periods of patent protection are promulgated as general statutory reform or as reforms for special industries such as ethical pharmaceuticals.

Aside from the question of the legal monopoly of the patent, there is the direct question of whether a vigorous antitrust policy with respect to industrial concentration would stifle technological progress. Some propose policies consistent with Judge Hand's position in *Alcoa*: "Immunity from competition is a narcotic, rivalry is a stimulant, to industrial progress . . . the spur of constant stress is necessary to counteract an inevitable disposition to let well enough alone." [1] Along these lines, serious students of technological change have contended, for example, that innovation in the iron and steel industry would have been more rapid had the largest companies been broken up. To the contrary, others argue that it is just the superiority of particular firms in technology which causes market concentration and that to attack the latter would be to discourage progress.

Policy alternatives with respect to advertising are similarly disparate. Some would impose limits on advertising expenditures; some would regulate "truth" in advertising, with requirements to "counteradvertise" when lack of truth was discovered; some would regulate the use of brand and generic names for certain industries (and again, ethical pharmaceuticals is a prime target); some would discourage advertising by revisions in Internal Revenue tax treatments; some would insist that there should be no controls over advertising in any circumstances.

Policy toward economic regulation has extreme alternatives, too. Those who see regulation as doing nothing other than effectuating monopoly argue for its elimination. The Interstate Commerce Commission, the Federal Power Commission, the Federal Communications Commission, the Civil Aeronautics Board, the Securities and Exchange Commission, perhaps the Federal Reserve Board and related regulators of financial institutions, state utility commissions, milk commissions, and the gamut of licensing agencies — all would simply be abolished. Intermediate approaches favoring less regulation and revisions of

---

1. United States v. Aluminum Co. of America, 148 F.2d 416, 427 (2d Cir. 1945).

regulations in particular cases are pressed. And it is clear that more regulation is favored, quite often by advocates of "consumerism."

Regulation and deregulation are suggested policies for the concentration—inflation problem. Strict wage–price controls, loose wage–price guidelines, application of antitrust principles to unions, the breaking up of oligopolies, and just taking "hands off" are all policy alternatives.

## IV.   THE LIMITS OF GENERALITIES AND THE DANGERS OF EXTREMES IN PUBLIC POLICY

Undoubtedly, the extreme differences in policy positions can be accounted for by the unsatisfactory state of generalized economic knowledge about the effects of concentration on various dimensions of market performance, about the causes of concentration, and about relations between concentration, efficiency, firm behavior, and directions of causality. One is tempted to say that we know nothing of what the proper policy approach to questions of concentration should be, and that economics really offers no help at all.

This conclusion would be wrong. While neither theory nor empirical studies have yielded unequivocal generalizations on which to base reformulations of policy applicable to all situations, microeconomics remains a powerful tool when used in an unimpassioned way to analyze particular market circumstances. It is not the answer to all questions, and different practitioners may reach different conclusions, but economics is useful in delineating the way markets operate, the ways firms behave, the effects of structure and conduct on performance, and the effects of performance on structure and conduct. The relationships are complex, however, and require an understanding of the details of the markets under consideration. There are no counterparts of neat Newtonian or Einsteinian physics in economics.

The implications of these truths for policy should be clear. Good policy requires less doctrine and more analysis. Good policy — at least until the time empirical studies with no identification, specification, and basic data problems yield explanations of variance much closer to unity than those now relied upon — depends on a case-by-case, industry-by-industry, problem-by-problem approach.

It would be unfortunate if concentration ratios, by themselves, gained increased relevance in the enforcement of Section 7 of the Clayton Act or Section 2 of the Sherman Act. On this count, extremists on both sides are wrong. A policy to deconcentrate any time when the four-firm or eight-firm concentration ratios reach arbitrary levels is as wrong as a policy which ignores or excuses concentration regardless of its level. Considered in conjunction with other characteristics of given markets — technology, firm behavior, governmental influences, etc. — the level of concentration is helpful in understanding how markets operate. Extremists to the contrary, relatively high concentration is not always the result of superiority and better performance. High concentration is sometimes the result of socially costly monopolistic practices and sometimes the cause of economic inefficiency and social inequities. On the other hand, relatively high concentration does not always signal a concomitant lack of rivalry, of inefficiency, of high entry barriers, and monopoly.

Section 7 of the Clayton Act and Section 2 of the Sherman Act require continued, but reasoned, enforcement. Tendencies for Section 7 enforcement to become per se based on concentration alone, and legislation which shifts burdens of proof based on concentration or profit performance, have only weak foundations in economics. But analysis of particular cases often shows that concentration has *no* justification in terms of efficiency and *does* have adverse effects on the public. Not always — just sometimes. After all, the usual multiple regression coefficients are in the .20 to .40 range. There is a great deal of unexplained variance which study of particular cases can unravel.

If there is an inadequate policy in the present law with respect to concentration, it can be found in the Sherman Act. The need to show intent and improper behavior in monopolization cases thwarts the restructuring of industries with the behavior of the so-called "good trust." Monopoly, in the economic sense, does exist, even without government regulation, and it would be useful to be able to attack it when it appears. Similarly, it would be useful to be able to attack mutually self-benefiting oligopolistic firms in various dimensions of behavior — price, advertising, market areas, technology — without the cumbersome and unrewarding legal approach of having to infer agreement and then applying per se rules. "Per se" leaves a great deal of economically collusive behavior and concentrated market power immune from antitrust action.

Policy with respect to concentration and technological change requires a similar disavowal of generalization. If we know anything about industrial R&D, invention and innovation, it is that there are enormous differences in the behavior of firms in different industries which are largely unrelated to differences in market structures. Whether the differences are due to different scientific opportunities which arise exogenous to market processes is more debatable, but for policy purposes the fact remains that case-by-case attention is necessary. Concentration in the aerospace, electronic, pharmaceutical, and steel industries very probably has different effects and different causes in each. It is conceivable that technology considerations would lead to no action under Section 7 in, say, a McDonald-Douglas merger despite market share consequences, while a merger involving much smaller market shares in steel would have no technological justification. Similarly, patents are likely to have different consequences in the aerospace industry than they have in steel. With knowledge of the particulars in given circumstances, economic analysis can be helpful, but general information on concentration and its relationships to technical change is, alone, no guide.

The same is true of advertising and promotional expenditures. The performance of the ethical pharmaceutical industry is probably quite insensitive to changes in the conventional measures of industry structure. Peculiar characteristics in the distribution of drugs, the role of prescribing physicians, the requirements of the Federal Drug Administration, and the use of patents and trade names are undoubtedly more consequential in determining performance than is the fact that the largest four firms have 25 or 35 percent of the sales of a four-digit Census industry classification. Policy appropriate for the pharmaceutical industry — whether to increase price competition or to foster technological change — is almost certainly different from the policy appropriate for the electronic computer industry. Good sense and understanding of the particulars, not generalizations that advertising and promotion are "good" or "bad," are needed.

There are also policy weaknesses inherent in the total approach to competitive policy. Cases are brought against one or a group of firms for alleged violations of specific statutory provisions, with too little attention to the full complex of structural, behavioral, and performance aspects of the markets in which the firms operate. A good illustration of this is the 1920 *United States Steel* case,[2] in which what most economists would regard as a history of tight collusive behavior was disregarded in a case focusing on structural conditions. The *Columbia Steel* case,[3] though rather thoroughly upset by subsequent legislation, illustrates the same problem. Behavior, not structure, should have been the prime concern.

Advertising and promotion — behavioral elements in market analysis — need to be considered in the full context of how markets function. It may be true that prices are negatively related to some kinds of advertising in some markets; it may be true that in some cases advertising is an aid to entry; but it may also be true that advertising and promotion in other cases are indeed critical entry barriers and the most important deterrents to competition. Can there be question that advertising and promotion in the pharmaceutical industry has different effects from advertising and promotion for eyeglasses, liquor, and gasoline?

Economic regulation also defies simple, generalized policy. Monopoly does not come in two distinguishable systems, which a lack of regulation always consonant with the maximization of social welfare and the existence of regulation always consonant with the achievement of monopolistic gains. Neither do all facets of regulation work to the public advantage: industries which might properly be defined as natural monopolies are regulated; so are other industries with none of the claims to natural monopoly. Regulation sometimes bears directly on prices (with little regard for rates of return), sometimes on rates of return (with little regard for relative prices), and it sometimes controls entry and little else. Regulation in some instances goes only to product quality; in others, product quality is largely left unregulated. Regulation affects employer–employee relations. Regulation appears by designated commissions, and regulation exists through tax and subsidy schemes. Regulation is sometimes designed to correct for externalities and sometimes to protect the affected industries from "competitive excesses." Some industries are permitted considerable "self-regulation" of prices, product quality, and entry; others are denied "self-regulation."

2. United States v. United States Steel Corp., 251 U.S. 417 (1920).
3. United States v. Columbia Steel Co., 334 U.S. 495 (1948).

Overall, there can hardly be a question that a good deal of regulation is supported by and beneficial to the regulated firms. To acknowledge this, however, is far from supporting the view that all regulation is unnecessary. Conditions of natural monopoly may exist in the real world. Regulation or public ownership is not, prima facie, an unreasonable alternative to private ownership and control in such cases. And there probably are other valid reasons for regulation, such as health, safety, and soundness of financial institutions, though these, too, seem to have been frequently used to the advantage of the regulated.

Some experimentation on deregulation seems worthwhile. It cannot be done, however, simply on the basis of a system of belief. Knowledge of the industry is essential so that one has some predictive ability concerning the effects of regulatory changes in specific situations. Moreover, deregulation, as suggested here, does not imply the total absence of governmental control. The regulatory framework for deposit financial institutions, for example, is a prime candidate for some deregulation. Yet it would seem foolhardy to suggest that there should be no regulation of these institutions.

Beyond deregulation, policy changes which "re-regulate" are possible. Rate-of-return rate-making quite certainly causes inefficiencies of several kinds. Experimentation in marginal cost pricing has been used abroad with some success. Its application in the United States, especially for the distribution of electricity, water, gas, and telephone services, deserves further attention.

And beyond deregulation and re-regulation, de novo regulations for some currently unregulated activities may be justified. It is not offensive to the beliefs of some to think that environmental and ecological factors require additional and novel interferences with market forces. Perhaps tax-subsidy arrangements are sufficient in many cases, but the possibility of other kinds of regulation can hardly be dismissed out of hand. The need for de novo regulation extends beyond corrections for externalities, however. It is not clear that the mix of present regulations — including a good deal of self-regulation — and no regulation in the medical profession, for example, is ideal. Perhaps a blend of deregulation and new regulation would be in the public interest. Similarly, some regulation of advertising and promotional practices in some industries may be needed. But, to repeat, the policy choices should be based on knowledge of the cases, not on visceral feelings.

Finally, what can be said of policy towards the concentration-inflation problem? That concentrations of power are involved in the inflation problem can hardly be denied. But it is also true that the more fundamental, underlying problem is in a political system which uses fiscal policy in economically irresponsible ways. In recent years the burden put on monetary policy has been so large that deconcentrations of power would have cured few, if any, of the problems of the inflation problem.

There is, however, a built-in, institutional bias toward inflation which, in a loose sense, is related to economic power. Suppose, for illustration's sake, the economy had only an agricultural sector and a manufacturing sector. Suppose controls were instituted to give the agricultural sector "parity prices" based on the cost of goods purchased from manufacturing. Suppose that manufacturing prices were controlled to provide constant cost-price markups, and that wage controls were used to keep real labor incomes constant. Then add a full-employment goal for the government.

The functioning of the economy in this scenario is inflationary. If any segment of the economy were dissatisfied with its position and succeeded in getting an adjustment, the rest would roll up with it. Thus, if manufacturers got an upward price adjustment, agricultural prices would rise, the cost of living would increase, upward wage changes would be in order, and the next round of price change for manufacturing would be needed. The full-employment policy would necessitate increases in aggregate demand to fuel the inflation.

This is not what we have, but an analogy is not farfetched. Market power in key industries, both manufacturing and nonmanufacturing, permits cost-plus pricing. Market power in key labor unions — not necessarily on a year-by-year basis — permits wage-setting strongly affected by the cost of living. Prices of basic agricultural commodities do have parity pricing influences. In the real economy, however, there are some "left outs" — some segments with little market power where real income declines in the inflationary process.

New policies are needed to alter this inflationary bias. New directions for antitrust and the deconcentration of market power would ideally be part of the policies, but it is difficult to be sanguine about the prospects. Antitrust policy would have to be altered drastically. Oligopolistic, conscious parallelism in pricing and output would have to be attacked on new grounds. A number of per se legalities — that is, exemptions from antitrust — would have to be removed. And to do this would require a restructuring of the body politic to make it less responsive to blocks of economic power.

## V. CONCLUSION

It must be acknowledged that the policy approach being suggested lacks the apparent consistency and coherence of an approach based more closely on an unambiguous set of categorical imperatives. This is not just because of disbelief that truth exists, but rather because truth is so elusive. The policy suggested here involves reasonable men using reasonable judgments, and it smacks of pragmatism. The alternative approaches are internally consistent but extreme. Neither a total abandonment of concern about concentration nor full concern about concentration alone is the proper direction for policy; the middle ground is.

# Problems of a Policy of Deconcentration
## Richard A. Posner*

I

I want to point out what seem to me the strong objections to a policy of deconcentrating concentrated (even highly concentrated) industries. To indicate the precise character of my objections, let me declare at the outset my belief that effective deconcentration might have some good effects. This belief is based not on the extensive but ambiguous and in some important respects unsatisfactory statistical evidence demonstrating a positive correlation between concentration and profitability, but on the simple theoretical point that price-fixing, whether tacit (call it "oligopolistic interdependence" if you like) or express, is facilitated by fewness of competing firms.[1] Other things being equal, the costs of reaching agreement are lower with fewer parties to the agreement. The likelihood of cheating — the bane of cartels — is also reduced since it is easier to identify a defector from a small group. To be sure, other factors — such as the elasticity of demand for the industry's product and the speed at which new entry can be effected — also bear importantly on the feasibility and attractiveness of collusion. These factors may in particular cases dominate the effect of concentration. Still, it seems plausible that if concentration were substantially reduced, the costs of collusion would be higher and its incidence therefore lower.

The benefits of an effective policy of deconcentration are those that result from any measure to eliminate monopolies. Since monopoly pricing induces purchasers to substitute less valuable (or more costly) products for the monopolized good, its elimination increases the value of the economy's output. Also, opportunities for monopoly gains induce firms to expend resources on monopolizing;[2] these expenditures, which from a social standpoint are wasteful, are reduced by any measure that makes monopolizing a more costly activity. Imperfect collusion can generate other economic losses, such as

---

* Professor of Law, University of Chicago Law School. For further biographical information, see Appendix D.

Phil C. Neal commented helpfully on a previous draft.

1. See, e.g., my "Oligopoly and the Antitrust Laws: A Suggested Approach," 21 *Stan. L. Rev.* 1562, 1569-1574 (1969).

2. This is why the traditional "deadweight loss" of monopoly (the difference in net value, to those consumers who cease to purchase the monopolized product because of the monopoly price, between that product and the substitutes to which they switch) understates the social costs of monopoly. Monopoly profits will induce expenditures on monopolizing until the return to the activity is bid down to the normal return. These expenditures are valueless socially.

wasteful service competition;[3] these losses are reduced by measures that diminish the attractiveness and hence amount of collusion. Insofar as wealth equalization is considered a social goal (it is not an economic goal), the elimination of monopoly can be expected to promote it by transferring wealth from a relatively more affluent group (stockholders) to a relatively less affluent one (consumers).

Some people believe that monopolistic or concentrated industries are less progressive technologically, or less concerned with (or effective at) minimizing the costs of the resources that they employ, than are competitive industries. But theory and evidence are hopelessly inconclusive on this point, so it cannot count in favor of a policy of deconcentration.

Deconcentration is sometimes supported on political grounds, as reducing the power of an industry to procure legislation favorable to it but harmful to the public interest. The argument has some force. If one accepts the proposition stated earlier that concentration facilitates the formation and maintenance of cartels (price-fixing agreements) by reducing the costs of agreement among the competing firms and the likelihood of defection, then it would seem to follow that the costs to the firms of pursuing a common lobbying program will also be lower. To be sure, other factors are relevant to the ability to manipulate the political process effectively, such as the number of votes that can be mobilized in support of a candidate who favors an industry's legislative goals; the other factors may be much more important than concentration;[4] but it remains a plausible speculation — though no more — that, *other things being equal*, a concentrated industry is more likely to obtain favorable legislation.

The political case against concentration is not sharply different from the economic one. The legislation sought by the industry — a tariff, a tax on a substitute product, control of entry — will usually have economic effects similar or identical to those of a private cartel agreement. The argument is that concentration facilitates monopolization indirectly through the legislative process (as well as directly through cartelization).

## II

Although a policy of deconcentration would confer some benefits on society, in my opinion it would not be a wise policy to pursue at this time. It is unlikely that it would be effective. And if it were effective it might well cost more than the benefits it conferred.

### A

A proceeding to deconcentrate an industry by reorganizing the major firms into smaller units would inevitably take many years to complete. This would

3. If competition is prevented in price but not in service, firms will increase their expenditures on improving their service. The service improvement will be carried beyond the point at which the costs of improvement are offset by the benefits to the consumer. It will be carried to the point where the monopoly price yields only a normal return.

4. See my "Theories of Economic Regulation," *Bell Journal of Economics and Management Science* (Fall 1974), for a more complete discussion.

be true, I believe, whatever the precise configuration of the prima facie case and defenses in such a proceeding.

It is difficult to devise an acceptable theory on which to base such a proceeding if brought under one of the existing antitrust statutes. I have argued elsewhere for an interpretation of Section 1 of the Sherman Act as forbidding tacit collusion, but this form of attack would require actual proof of noncompetitive behavior and the appropriate relief would be injunctive (or, after the principle became established, criminal), rather than the dismemberment of the leading firms.[5] One could perhaps extend the logic of the *Alcoa* case[6] to the situation where a group of firms, jointly occupying a monopoly position, are acting as if they were a single monopolist. But again, proof of actual anticompetitive behavior would be necessary (it would be a bit much to argue that, because there are only a few firms in a market, they *must* be behaving like a single firm, i.e., charging the monopoly price); and again, it would be necessary to establish to the court's satisfaction that no less drastic relief than divestiture would be sufficient to restore competition. The most facile route to divestiture would be a proceeding under Section 5 of the Federal Trade Commission Act, where it could be argued that the leading firms in a highly concentrated industry should be dismembered because there is some probability that otherwise the industry would behave monopolistically.

Under any of these approaches, deconcentration would be the work of many years. The government would have to offer evidence of the anticompetitive effect of concentration which the defendants would be free to rebut (even in a Section 5 proceeding, the defendants could hardly be prevented from trying to prove that concentration in *their* industry was unlikely to lead to monopoly pricing). The issue of possible loss of efficiency from changing the structure of the industry would be fully, and endlessly, litigable.

One can understand why most proponents of deconcentration propose a statutory approach. The thrust of such proposals — for example, of the Concentrated Industries Act appended to the Neal report[7] — is to avoid an unwieldy "Rule of Reason" type of inquiry by (1) presuming anticompetitive effect conclusively from proof of specified concentration levels, and (2) placing on the defendants the burden of proof as to whether deconcentration would reduce the efficiency of the industry. But the authors of the Neal report are, I suggest, deceived if they expect such a statutory proceeding to be manageable. While eliminating proof of anticompetitive effect, the report introduces a complexity that is probably no longer a part of existing antitrust law by requiring that concentration be demonstrated in an economically meaningful market.[8] And shifting the burden of proof is unlikely to reduce the

5. See n. 1 *supra.*
6. United States v. Aluminum Co. of America, 148 F.2d 416 (2d Cir. 1945).
7. Report of President Johnson's White House Task Force on Antitrust Policy (1968); see Appendix C. I discuss the Neal report's proposal because it is the most carefully conceived and articulated of the recent deconcentration proposals.
8. The report is critical of the market definitions that the courts have used in merger cases (and presumably would use in an "oligopolizing" case). On the difficulties of

resources devoted to litigating the efficiency question. Moreover, even if there were no legal issues *at all* in a deconcentration proceeding, the process of reorganizing an industry — deciding what assets to divest and to whom — would be enormously complicated and time-consuming, as any student of corporate reorganization will appreciate. Experience with divestiture in antitrust cases, unhappy as that has been,[9] cannot prepare us for the type of corporate restructuring that would be required in a deconcentration proceeding. Divestiture under the antimerger law has involved recent acquisitions; divestiture in the old monopolization cases was usually limited to the dissolution of a holding company. The case against Standard Oil is an example: its 34 subsidiaries were simply spun off to its shareholders. We have no good precedent for proceedings to dissolve General Motors, Ford, IBM, Eastman Kodak, Western Electric, and the other probable targets of the Concentrated Industries Act.

I do not know how long it would take to complete the average deconcentration proceeding. It would be reckless to assume, however, that it would take less time than the classical "big" cases of antitrust such as the *Standard Oil* case and the *Alcoa* case.[10] And the implementation of the final decree might take longer. The striking thing about the "big" antitrust case is how, again and again, by the time the case is completed the conditions of the industry have so changed as to make the case an irrelevance. This was true in the aluminum case; the final decree was almost equivalent to a dismissal. It was largely although not entirely true in the Standard Oil case (a case also marred by a bad decree, but that is an occupational hazard of ambitious antitrust proceedings). Industrial markets do not stand still. Foreign competition has effectively deconcentrated the American automobile industry. Steel has long since ceased to be highly concentrated. Monopolization in the motion picture history has been undone by the growth of television. The sleeping-car monopoly fell apart with the decline of railroad passenger transportation. I doubt that the lumbering processes of the law can have much effect on the concentration of industry, because any *responsible* proposal for deconcentration (such as the model statute of the Neal report) is bound to furnish numerous opportunities for protracting a deconcentration proceeding indefinitely.

### B

Now assume that what I have just said is incorrect and that a deconcentration proceeding could be completed expeditiously. Then I would be concerned

---

establishing economically meaningful markets, see my *Economic Analysis of Law* (Little, Brown 1972), pp. 121-123.

9. See Kenneth G. Elzinga, "The Antimerger Law: Pyrrhic Victories?," *Journal of Law & Economics,* 12 (1969), p. 43; Malcolm R. Pfunder, Daniel J. Plaine, and Anne Marie G. Whittemore, "Compliance With Divestiture Orders Under Section 7 of the Clayton Act: An Analysis of the Relief Obtained," 17 *Antitrust Bull.* 19 (1972).

10. Standard Oil Co. of New Jersey v. United States, 221 U.S. 1 (1911); United States v. Aluminum Co. of America, 148 F.2d 416 (2d Cir. 1945). Some statistics on the duration of monopolization cases are presented in my "Statistical Study of Antitrust Enforcement," *Journal of Law & Economics,* 13 (1970), p. 406, Table 29.

that a deconcentration policy might impose heavy costs on society by requiring industries to operate with higher costs than before they had been deconcentrated. This possibility led the authors of the Neal report to include in the Concentrated Industries Act a provision relating to economies of scale, which they explain in the following words: [11]

> A decree cannot require a firm to take steps which would result in substantial loss of economies of scale. This provision would, for example, preclude divestiture reducing a firm below minimum efficient size or creating new entities below minimum efficient size. The burden of proof is on the firm, and the possible loss of economies is not a defense to the issuance of a judgment. . . . Division of a single plant would ordinarily result in substantial loss of economies of scale, and the Act permits a firm to establish that a decree would result in a net loss of economies of scale beyond the plant level. Net loss of economies of scale beyond the plant level might be established directly or by considering the minimum size of viable competitors in an industry. Thus, the court would not ordinarily divide an oligopoly firm into firms smaller than that indicated by experience to be necessary to survival in the industry. We are not unaware of efficiencies other than economies of scale; other efficiencies will generally reflect scarce resources such as unique management talent. These resources may be transferred pursuant to a deconcentration decree without significant loss.

The quoted discussion is unsatisfactory. There is no reliable method of establishing "directly" the existence of economies of scale at either the plant or the firm level. The methods discussed in Scherer's paper suffer from grave conceptual shortcomings, pointed out by McGee and others,[12] and are in any event insufficiently developed to generate evidence assimilable in a legal proceeding. The indirect method suggested by the Neal report, which is to consider the minimum size of viable competitors, is inappropriate in the context of a deconcentration proceeding. By assumption, the industry under scrutiny in such a proceeding is one in which the major firms are maintaining supracompetitive prices; this is the fundamental premise of a policy of deconcentration. Such prices will attract into the industry firms that may have higher costs than the existing firms and that may be "viable" only because of the umbrella of the monopoly price. The method proposed by the Neal report thus consists of observing a fringe of possibly inefficient small firms and improperly inferring from their existence that the reorganization of major firms in the industry into firms of that size would not raise the total costs of the industry. The relevant "survival" is survival under competitive conditions, that is, under conditions where market price is equal to cost (including a reasonable profit). The survival one observes in a noncompetitive industry is survival under conditions where price is above cost and where, therefore, firms can survive and prosper even if they are smaller than the efficient scale for the industry.

---

11. See n. 7 *supra.*
12. See, e.g., Caleb A. Smith, "Survey of the Empirical Evidence on Economies of Scale," in *Business Concentration and Price Policy* (Universities–Natl. Bur. Comm. for Econ. Res. ed., 1955), p. 213.

The quoted passage also states that the only proper concern in a deconcentration proceeding is with the economies of scale. This is incorrect too. The reason offered for dismissing sources of efficiency besides scale, such as managerial skill, is that such resources can be transferred pursuant to a deconcentration decree without significant loss. A simple example will show that this need not be so. Suppose that one firm has a 50 percent market share because of its very talented president [13] who has enlarged the firm's market share by lowering its costs and undercutting competitors. The industry is deconcentrated and the firm's market share is reduced to, say, 12 percent. The industry's costs will now be higher, because by assumption the cost of production is now higher for the 38 percent of the industry's output that has been shifted to the firms having inferior management. The larger the market share controlled by "unique management talent" (the Neal report's expression), the lower the costs of the industry.

This conclusion is independent of how much of the increased revenues of the firm due to the president's special abilities are captured by him in the form of higher salary or other compensation. That question relates solely to the distribution of the social gains from lower costs. Those gains are reduced if his ability to lower the industry's costs is limited by a measure that withdraws from his control a large portion of the assets over which he had previously exercised his talent for cost reduction.

I do not think that the Neal report solved the problem of reducing concentration without sacrificing possible efficiencies, scale and otherwise, with which concentration might be associated. Nor can the problem be swept under the rug by assuming that efficiency is not an important cause of concentration. Theory suggests that it is quite important in explaining *persistently* high concentration — the only kind the Concentrated Industries Act would affect.[14] Ask yourself how it is that an industry becomes, and remains, highly concentrated, notwithstanding that it is presumed to be charging supracompetitive prices (otherwise the foundation of a deconcentration policy collapses). It could become concentrated as a result of mergers designed to facilitate monopoly pricing; this was the basis of the dominant position long enjoyed by United States Steel in the steel industry. Over time, however, we would expect concentration so achieved to erode as the monopoly price charged by the leading firms induced the entry of new competitors and a resulting expansion of the industry's output and reduction of the market shares of the existing firms — just what happened in the steel industry.[15] If this does not happen, if concentration persists, where are we to seek an explanation? One (unlikely) possibility is exclusionary practices — but if they are the explanation, deconcentration is unlikely to be a suitable remedy; the practices can be enjoined or punished. Another possibility is that valid patents or some other govern-

13. Or a management team that would be less effective if split up.

14. The act is limited to markets in which high levels of concentration have persisted for at least ten years.

15. See George J. Stigler, "The Dominant Firm and the Inverted Umbrella," in *The Organization of Industry* (R. D. Irwin 1962), ch. 9, p. 108.

mental grant of monopoly power prevents new competition — but this would provide no basis for deconcentration either, unless (as Phil C. Neal has suggested to me) the members of the industry obtained their patents by acquisitions that were not scrutinized under appropriate legal standards designed to prevent monopolization by the acquisition of competing patents.

Still another possibility is that there are barriers to entry: new firms would have higher costs than existing firms. That this is an unlikely explanation can be shown by considering, as a type of prospective entrant, an existing but very small firm in an industry (almost every industry, however concentrated, has a fringe of small firms). If the leading firms are charging monopoly prices, one or more small firms will have an incentive to shade the monopoly price and thereby expand their output and profits.[16] If there is some "barrier" that prevents the small firm from doing this, it must be something that makes the small firm's costs as high as the monopoly price charged by the leading firms, so that it cannot make money by shading that price. But why should its costs be higher than those of the leading firms unless there are economies of scale that it is too small to exploit, or unless the leading firms are protected by valid patents, engage in exclusionary practices, or have superior management? On a close analysis the barrier to entry question dissolves into the other possible reasons for concentration that we have considered, and rejected, as appropriate bases for a policy of deconcentration. Thus, in those cases where concentration is persistent, it is likely that deconcentration would be an inappropriate remedy for dealing with the situation.

### C

There is another respect in which a policy of deconcentration is apt to create significant social costs. As a firm's market share approaches the level at which the commencement of a deconcentration proceeding becomes likely, the firm will have an incentive to reduce its market share, or stabilize it, or retard the rate of its increase. The logical way to do this is by increasing price. The result is to bring about the very thing that a policy of deconcentration is intended to prevent — supracompetitive pricing.

The Neal report rejected this concern by pointing out that the remedies provided for in the Concentrated Industries Act are not punitive. But the issue is not how the legal system characterizes the proceeding; it is whether a deconcentration proceeding would impose costs on the defendants. If so, firms will be willing to incur some costs to avoid being subjected to such a proceeding. And obviously it would impose costs, if for no other reason than that the Neal report's proposal assumes that the leading firms in concentrated industries enjoy supracompetitive profits before, but not after, deconcentration; the loss of such profits would be costs to the firms involved.

It is true that the application of the statute is triggered by industry, rather than firm, concentration levels. But it does not follow that a firm will take no

---

16. Suppose the market price is $10 and the unit cost of a firm producing anywhere from 10 to 50 units is $5. If the firm sells 10 units at $10, its profit is $50. If by reducing price to $9 it can sell 20 units, its profit will increase to $80.

steps to prevent its market share from growing because its action will not significantly affect the likelihood of the industry's reaching the forbidden level. First, if it is a large firm, its market share will significantly affect the four-firm concentration ratio on which the application of the statute turns. Second, even if the industry concentration ratio is at or above the triggering level, no firm need fear being the target of a deconcentration proceeding unless its market share is at least 15 percent, and so it will have an incentive to prevent its share from reaching that level. Third, and most important, the basic premise of the Neal report is that leading firms in highly concentrated markets are capable of a form of undetectable collusion, and if that is so, they will collude to avoid market-share increases that bring them to the forbidden level.

---

I conclude that the costs of a deconcentration policy probably outweigh the benefits. The benefits are more conjectural. We do not know by how much the probability of collusive pricing is altered by marginal changes in concentration ratios. We do know that the administrative costs of deconcentration proceedings will be great and we have theoretical grounds for concern that a policy of deconcentration will lead to higher costs in a significant fraction of concentrated industries.

# Commentary
## Senator Philip A. Hart*

I would like to suggest that no theory of industrial organization has yet reached the state of perfection that it alone can tell us whether there is workable competition in any marketplace. We must, I submit, reexamine the tools used to determine whether our marketplace is really serving the public interest.

Industrial organization economists have done a good job in isolating many factors which make up a competitive marketplace. But I must question if there yet has been developed a method for laying these standards against life in the real world and being sure that the results are worthwhile. Too often it seems that the neat econometric model is really only the beginning in our search for the whys and wherefores of the marketplace. And what do four-digit, four-firm concentration ratios tell us about the ability of industry to respond to the needs of the community?

After all, concentration ratios were adopted as a substitute for good direct evidence on the viability of the marketplace. Yet, too often, we become fascinated with them and ignore the direct evidence that is available.

Consider the oil industry. Lay the concentration ratios beside the figures on the makeup of this industry and you would feel confident that all was well,

* United States Senator, Democrat, Michigan. For further biographical information, see Appendix D.

and that in this sector — at least — we have competition. But look at the evidence of joint ventures, banking interlocks, vertical integration, joint ownership of facilities, joint production, absence of real price competition, and lockstep decision-making and one must wonder. If it looks like a monopoly, walks like a monopoly, and talks like a monopoly, maybe the simple fact that concentration ratios say it is not a monopoly is deceiving.

Every once in a while we get an insight into the industry which seems to tell more about its competitiveness than all the theoretical, congressional, and economic studies combined. In 1971, Robert E. Yancey, president of Ashland Oil, Inc., came before the Senate Antitrust and Monopoly Subcommittee. The subject was gasoline marketing practices. He counseled us not to overlook the industry's vertical integration — especially when trying to make sense of the role of the independent. To understand the private brand marketer, he said, we must have a full understanding of his supplier, the "independent refiner" — of which Ashland is the biggest. "Here," he reminded us, "the term 'independent' may not be apt at all, because the refiner is truly dependent, dependent upon others for his source of crude oil supply." He pointed out that at each increase in the crude price, the independent refiner worried as to whether it would carry through to the retail price. The major integrated companies make this choice, he said. He continued:

> The market for refined products need not support recovery of the cost of the crude advance through higher product prices in the case of the integrated company. However, in the case of the independent, it is a matter of survival that the product prices must support the crude oil advance, else his competitive position erodes significantly.

That seems, at least to me, a description of market dominance. But it would not show up on any concentration ratio table.

There are other questions raised by the oil industry today. We see an ever-constricting market — with increasing prices and unmet demands. To many, this seems to be a normal result of a competitive market. After all, even I know that in a time when demand outstrips production, prices will go up.

But if this were a truly competitive market, would we even have the shortages? No one can deny that only two years ago refineries were putting out as much product as the market could absorb. Independent refiners and marketers were having a field day, competing for the consumer's dollar. The consumer had the benefits of competition.

But what was happening to our refinery capacity? Between 1960 and 1973, we added 4 million barrels daily of capacity. At the same time, demand was increasing by 8 million barrels daily. The truth of the matter is that if we were awash in either Mideast or domestic crude today, we would still have a refinery shortfall of between 4 to 5 million barrels a day. In reality, we are running shorter than that because the independent refineries cannot lay hands on sufficient crude to run at capacity. Why weren't the new refineries built? The oil companies tell us that environmental and governmental policies are to blame. Well, certainly Machiasport was not killed by the environmentalists.

The major oil companies bitterly opposed the plan. According to some reports, they made visits to the White House to make sure this opposition was fully understood.

Among others, the *Oil and Gas Journal*, an industry-oriented publication, began warning of the impending shortage in 1970. In an editorial in March 1972, it said:

> The conviction of many refiners — who point to widespread price-warring and distress gasoline — is that a lull in construction is needed for demand to catch up a bit. That sounds reasonable — if the lull doesn't last too long. At this point, it appears there's a definite danger of this.

What the editorial did not mention — there was no need to do so for its readers understood fully — was that price wars and distress gasoline came because of the participation of independents in the market. And it is entirely possible that when the oil companies spoke of "letting demand catch up" they were talking about demand from their own outlets — excluding the independents. This type of thinking and behavior seldom shows up in econometric models either.

Another type of activity doesn't show up in such models or in concentration ratios. Professor Demsetz discussed it in his paper — that is, the impact of government intervention. Certainly, I agree that government gets into the act and distorts the market. And I would agree that in those industries with workable competition, we should get the government out. But I think to blame the government and then retire, confident that we have pinned the tail on the right donkey, ignores other facts of the real world.

Government action sometimes is taken simply in the name of the public good. But it also is taken — at times — because certain segments of the business community see the action as being in their own best interests.

Certainly, it is clear that the major integrated steel producers were responsible for the promulgation of the voluntary steel import agreements. It is clear that the oil industry was responsible for import quotas, foreign depletion allowance, and royalty tax credits.

Not only is much of what government does the result of business power, but also much of what business does is really governmental in nature. In this category, I would put the reported ITT efforts to topple the government of Chile and the joint negotiations of our oil companies with the OPEC nations.

I have a great fear that if we place no constraints on the use of corporate power, and if we give up government regulation, we may simply be turning things over to private government.

There is a thread running through many of the papers in this volume that "we know so little, so we should do nothing." Frankly, the idea is bound to have some appeal. One of my colleagues on the House side has been quoted: "You never lose an election because of the speech you didn't make." But while we who believe that competition should be given one more chance do nothing, those with opposite views may *not* sit on their hands.

If Congress does nothing at all, the trends will continue toward merger of government and business. But I doubt that Congress will do nothing. The people, including the business community, have a way of forcing congressional action to help them cope with their economic problems whenever they reach the crisis state. At such times, the policy alternatives that require years to accomplish are pushed aside in favor of quick and easy attempts at solution.

Already in the midst of long lines at the gasoline stations, we hear talk about nationalization or public utility regulation for oil. Senator Jackson has notified us that he is drafting a regulation-type bill, which would get the government squarely into the basic business decisions of the oil industry.

Therein lies a problem. Should the government move in because of evident failure of the existing structure and abandon hope of a competitive market solution? Or should we create an orderly process with which to accomplish restructuring wherever feasible?

My vote, of course, has been registered with the introduction of the Industrial Reorganization Act. If enacted, the government would intervene, but only on a one-shot basis. It would restructure industries where this would not sacrifice efficiencies. Then it would get out of the market.

It is this bill that caused my earlier request for help. We need better tools to measure concentration. But, I warn again, time may not be on our side; we must not still be arguing about how many angels can dance on the head of a pin, when others move us permanently away from the idea of a competitively structured economy.

# Commentary

## Senator Roman Hruska*

The subject of economic concentration is not new to the Senate Antitrust and Monopoly Subcommittee. In 1964, our subcommittee undertook a series of hearings on concentration in industry. At that time, the late Senator Dirksen and I joined in an opening statement in which we said:

> These hearings . . . are based on a faulty assumption; namely, that economic concentration is a growing menace in America.
> The facts show otherwise.
> The inquiry is based on the report entitled, "Concentration Ratios in Manufacturing Industry, 1958," issued by the Subcommittee two years ago. The statistics in that report indicate *less* concentration, not more. . . .[1]

---

* United States Senator, Republican, Nebraska. For further biographical information, see Appendix D.

1. Hearings pursuant to S. Res. 262 Before the Subcommittee on Antitrust and Monopoly of the Senate Committee on the Judiciary, 88th Congress, 2nd Session (1964).

At that time, Chairman Hart ventured the opinion that that series of hearings might cover as much as two years. Now, that was in 1964, ten years ago, and we are still at it, 14 volumes, 7500 printed pages later, and the end is not yet in sight. That tunnel has no glimpse of the blue sky at its far end. And the hearings, of course, continue to be churned out in a seemingly never-ending stream; the subcommittee's staff continues to grow.

What you and what other taxpayers are entitled to know is what we have learned, if anything, in ten years and at the expenditure of about $8 million. I submit that we have learned a great deal. I submit that we have learned that industrial concentration is not a subject which permits facile generalization; that "taking care of it" will not remove the crucial problems that plague us. And we have learned that those who, as an article of faith, assert that industrial concentration is an evil which must be eradicated have yet to prove their case.

Clearly, there is no agreement — no substantial consensus — on the effects, if any, of industrial concentration, or on its policy implications. Indeed, we cannot even agree upon *what* concentration may be, or *how* it is measured, and whether, in fact, it is either increasing or decreasing. And if I understand your discussion of the past few days, there has been a wide difference of opinion on these issues reflected here.

As you know, Congress sometimes moves to solve dilemmas and settle issues by legislative fiat. That is what my esteemed colleague, Senator Hart, seeks to do in the bill which he has proposed — a bill which would drastically revise the structures of our major industries by fragmenting or dissolving the companies in those industries.

That bill, which ignores the substantial disagreements among economists and the absence of a sound factual or theoretical basis for these dire remedies, would simply proclaim industrial concentration and permit industrial reorganization in designated instances. Where a company is too successful a competitor, where it decides to compete on a basis other than price, or even where it competes so effectively that the prices it charges are the same prices that its competitors charge, it would be threatened with dissolution.

I must confess that these proposals are a complete riddle to me. I have great difficulty understanding how we can profess a profit incentive system — a system where profits are the anticipated reward for excellence in meeting consumer needs, where we expect profits to attract new entrants into the markets which are prospering and thereby to increase the supply of products and services consumers demand — and at the same time make profits of a legislatively prescribed degree a signal for the destruction of those who make such profits. Nor do I understand how, in a system which assumes that price competition will often lead to price uniformity, we can infer the absence of competition from uniform prices.

I know that there are some who argue that it is not important that there is lack of agreement among economists and that there is insufficient information with which to appraise the economic issues relating to our industrial structure. I recognize that there are those who argue on philosophical and sociological grounds that we should break up big companies and return to a very finely-phrased state of being, "human-sized institutions."

Let me assure you, I believe in human-sized institutions as much as any man. I also, however, believe in institutions and systems which are responsive and are responding to human needs and desires, not merely to human measurements. Unfortunately, the complexities of our economy and society confront us at times with the necessity of choosing between alternatives. And that is not easy. If, however, we make a social judgment that bigness is bad, if we decide as a matter of *social* policy that we want to break up companies and restructure industries, then we should — we must — at least be honest about it and admit that we are engaging in a project of social engineering, and not try to justify that concept on economic grounds. Because if we have learned anything in these ten long years, it is that this dogma is not justifiable on economic grounds.

As a legislator, I have come to these debates and these considerations with a very specific inquiry. It is simply this: is the statutory and regulatory framework which Congress has established to attain our competitive and economic objectives one which, for the most part, is succeeding in achieving those objectives? Do we need something more, or something less? Is legislation required to correct the problems or protect the benefits of our industrial structure? These are not easy questions to answer; in the last analysis the answers, whatever they are, will require trade-offs. So for us, the question is how to balance those trade-offs.

When Professor Donald Turner appeared before our subcommittee last year, he suggested a standard by which to make such judgments — one which I think makes a good deal of sense. He advised us that any "relief designed to increase competition [should] have promise of yielding *substantial economic gains*." [2] In other words, when the costs and risks of making a change are weighed against the benefits that accrue as a result of that change, the benefits must clearly predominate. That simply cannot be said of the industrial reorganization proposal now in Congress. I object to it on a number of grounds.

First of all, it is too simplistic a way of going about things — destroy bigness and you have got the millennium.

Secondly, it is far too narrow. It moves against one small circumstance in a multifaceted problem.

Third, its theoretical basis is unsubstantiated, and it mandates remedies without regard to their propriety, necessity, or effect in varying circumstances. It discards the need for analysis; it calls for no judgment — and indeed provides no opportunity for a fully documented judgment — that the proposed action promises to yield substantial net economic gains; it dispenses with the necessity of weighing costs and risks against anticipated benefits. This bill sub-

2. Hearings on S. 1167 Before the Subcommittee on Antitrust and Monopoly of the Senate Committee on the Judiciary, 93rd Congress, 1st Session, 276 (1973) (emphasis added).

stitutes legislative edict in advance on an inflexible mathematical and mechanical scale for analysis and reasoned judgment. What Congress would really do by enacting this bill would be to eliminate the burden of proving in each case that on the basis of the particular facts and surrounding circumstances, there is some reason to expect that the remedy would alter conditions for the better — that, in Turner's words, the proposed action would yield net economic gains.

And, of course, it will not do away with bigness — it cannot do away with it even temporarily. Because industrial bigness as it affects the United States economy is not a matter which is wholly within the jurisdiction of Congress. When Professor J. Fred Weston was before us a year ago, he analyzed the growth of foreign firms. They, you can be sure, are not heeding the so-called ground swell for breaking up big combinations that is supposed to exist in this country. Not at all. They are emulating our biggest companies; they are working hard at it; and they are making good progress.

Professor Weston told us:

> Recent developments, including the encouragement of mergers by foreign governments, have resulted in increases in the size of foreign firms compared to those in the United States. The growth rates of the largest foreign firms during the past 5 years have been roughly double the growth rates of the largest U.S. firms. . . . If the growth rate in assets of the top 100 foreign firms continues to exceed the growth rate of the large U.S. firms as during the last 5 years, in 4 years the top 100 foreign firms would exceed the total assets of the largest 100 U.S. firms.[3]

Now, then, putting aside for a moment its other deficiencies, will the functioning of the Hart Bill reduce size? Or will it just reduce size here in America? At a time when many of the barriers to foreign trade are finally coming down and when the truly relevant markets are increasingly international markets, what will be the effect on our balance of payments, our employment, and our independence, if we restructure industries solely to reduce size, when foreign companies are increasing size at a furious pace? The passage of Senate Bill 1167 will not reduce the size or impede the continued functioning of OPEC, the Organization of Petroleum Exporting Countries. And how will we deal with OPEC — by sending a combination of neighborhood filling station owners over there to deal with the empire of the OPEC countries? These are factors which have not been adequately considered in our examination of Senate Bill 1167.

All of that is not to suggest that improvements cannot be made in our competitive regulatory scheme. There are no doubt legislative programs which can do much to promote competition and confer economic benefits. But to legislate on industrial concentration in the abstract seems to me a useless and even risky exercise. Can we realistically expect that simply by deconcentrating manufacturing industries we will improve competition?

What about those industries which ship and distribute their products through transportation industries, which are concentrated by law? What about those

3. *Id.* at 240.

businesses which communicate with consumers and customers through media which are concentrated by law? What about those industries for which the major element of product cost is labor, whose concentrated structures and preferences are protected by law — and deeply and firmly entrenched there? What about those manufacturers whose biggest customer is the law, the United States government? And finally, what about our competition with companies abroad that have been nationalized or are government-subsidized in their home countries?

These questions are rough ones. How, then, are we to proceed? What are we going to do, sit by and do nothing? And the answer is no, not at all. But first we must abandon the piecemeal, scatter-gun approaches which have characterized the last ten or fifteen years, most of them meeting with fruitless results.

Last year I joined with Senators Javits, McGee, and Tower in proposing the establishment of an Antitrust Review and Revision Commission.[4] This Commission would review all legislation affecting competition, whether it be in the area of taxation, international trade, labor, agriculture, antitrust, banking, or other. It would bring together economic experts, as well as experts in other spheres of concern to our national well-being, to consider whether different legislative programs are required to preserve and encourage competition and to protect its rewards. If industrial concentration is to be the subject of legislative consideration, it seems to me it is only in that kind of very broad context that our competitive framework can realistically be acted upon.

Too often the government singles out one element, one circumstance of the economic picture with which it is dissatisfied. It seeks to treat the one aspect without regard to the factors surrounding it, and hopes by such action to change the whole picture. The results have sometimes been disastrous. We have very low rates on natural gas, haven't we? We have had since 1955. Now, true, we don't have much natural gas, but that is irrelevant because one can go back to one's constituents and say, "I voted to regulate the price of that gas so that you wouldn't have to pay too much for it." And the poor fellow shivering in his living room says, "What gas?"

In the area of industrial concentration I hope we will learn that these simplistic solutions backfire more often than they succeed. If we are going to treat this subject, let us not deal with the ailment in the horse's ear and forget that he might have bronchitis. Let us undertake for once a comprehensive diagnosis and a comprehensive treatment.

---

4. S. 1196, 93rd Congress, 1st Session (1973).

# Commentary
## Phil Caldwell Neal

This is a quotation from the George Stigler of 1952:

> No such drastic and ominous a remedy as the central direction of economic life is necessary to deal with the problems raised by big business. The obvious and economical solution, as I have already amply implied, is to break up the giant companies. This, I would emphasize, is the minimum program and it is essentially a conservative program. Dissolution of big businesses is a once-and-for-all measure in each industry if the recent merger amendment to the Clayton Act is adequately enforced, and continuing interference by government in the operation of private business is relatively unnecessary. One dissolves three or four big steel companies and leaves the many smaller companies completely alone.
>
> The dissolution of big businesses is only part of the program necessary to increase the support for a private competitive enterprise economy and reverse the drift toward government control. But it is an essential part of this program, and the place for courage and imagination. Those conservatives who cling to the status quo do not realize that the status quo is a state of change and that the changes are coming fast. If these changes were to include the dissolution of a few score of our giant companies, however, we shall have done much to preserve private enterprise and the liberal individualistic society of which it is an integral part.

It is now no great breach of confidence to relate that the members of the White House Task Force in 1968 thought they heard very similar views, although more mildly expressed, when discussing deficiencies in the antitrust laws with Professor Stigler. Now, of course, our views on such difficult and doubtful problems may well shift with more knowledge, and perhaps also as a result of the very fact of thinking concretely about what such a policy would look like if one tried to write it down and put it into practice. So, actually, I think one of the objectives of our Task Force was to help bring the issue to a head and provoke closer examination of the policy question. And if there is any correlation between our report and the fact that, for example, such a conference as this is being held — if there is any such correlation, weak though it may be — I think most of us on the Task Force would feel some sense of accomplishment. But it does leave one wondering a bit at what can account for such a wide difference of view as between, let us say, the George Stigler of 1952 and the Harold Demsetz of 1974 — or perhaps even the George Stigler of 1974.

I was for a time somewhat shaken by what I understood from Yale Brozen's revisionist work, but my present impression is that such studies as the Weiss and Scherer papers in this volume have considerably rehabilitated or reinforced the premises on which our Task Force was operating in making its recommendations.

As I now read over the Task Force report in the light of this conference, I do not see very much that I would be inclined to change, partly because that report was couched in appropriately cautious and hesitant terms. So for the moment, at any rate, I am left very much where I was: prepared to support, although not with any evangelistic fervor, a reasonably conservative policy of deconcentration.

I would also put some emphasis on the possible benefits of a deconcentration policy in cleaning up and making more coherent other aspects of antitrust law. I think that a good many aspects of the antitrust laws that tend toward controlling behavior, and doing things that are essentially anticompetitive, rest on a lack of confidence in the competitive structure of the industries concerned, and on a tendency to use assumed market power or monopoly power as a point of reference, even though it is not explicitly illegal under the antitrust laws.

# Commentary

## Almarin Phillips

The arguments in my paper boil down to this: first, the papers represent extreme positions; second, the papers are based on what I would call simple models of market processes. The range of policy conclusions in this session reflect both of these characteristics. But, third, I argue that despite the diversity here, economics can be useful in policy matters, if it is recognized that markets are indeed very complex things. Simple models do not capture the complexity.

My paper also indicates my own opposition to general deconcentration of industry, particularly deconcentration that involves the shifting of the burden of proof. It notes that I am in favor of a retention of the corpus of present antitrust policy and, indeed, that I would advocate its strengthening in several respects. The paper shows, too, that I agree that in some cases there is a need for deregulation; but rather than total deregulation, it acknowledges the possibility of some re-regulation of existing regulated industries and a need for de novo regulation in some instances.

Now, what I'd like to do is to look first at the models implicit in the views we have heard here, and then move from those to what I regard as a more realistic picture of the way markets operate.

One of the approaches is represented in the Mann and Markham papers. Model I in Figure 8 says that industries have various structural characteristics, S — the number of firms, size of firms, entry conditions, cost conditions, what demand looks like, and things of that sort. The model says that (somehow or other) out of structure the conduct of firms, C, is determined. Conduct covers the degree of collusiveness, R&D behavior, behavior relating to broad innovation, price—output policies, advertising, and so forth. Market performance, P, ultimately depends on structure alone, since conduct is itself seen as uniquely

**Figure 8**
Structural Models of the Market

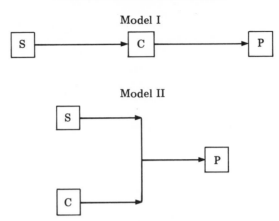

related to structure. This is certainly in the tradition of conventional economics.

Cournot was the first clearly to employ it. George Stigler's theory of oligopoly is similarly based. Structure determines the degree to which firms stick to collusive agreements, and hence the kind of performance that comes out of the market. We have heard a good deal of that here.

Model II also assigns a key role to structural considerations and to considerations of conduct, but the two need not go hand in hand. We can have a concentrated industry with particular characteristics of conduct — collusiveness and so forth — or we can have various degrees of concentration with different kinds of conduct possible. The argument is that there is an interaction between the structural characteristics and the conduct characteristics, and it is this interaction, if you will, that determines the performance of markets.

In a sense, it is this model that underlies the Hart Bill, particularly if you look at the Hart Bill in terms of a symptomatic approach to the world. It says there are certain structural conditions that may exist that will bring forth public policy; that is the concentration ratio part. It says there are certain conduct aspects that will bring forth public policy actions; that is the question of whether there has been price competition. And there are performance aspects of the bill; this is the standard concern with the level of profits.

But, nonetheless, structure remains paramount. If any of these symptoms is violated, it will bring forth an attack on the structure of the industry and moves toward industrial deconcentration. The control variable that people are looking to is the structure of the industry.

I would next like to model what has been referred to as the Chicago School approach. It seems to me there are two models involved here. One is Model III(a). In III(a), there is just something about the way firms behave, implicitly behaving as individuals to maximize something or other, that leads them to forms of conduct, C. And the forms of conduct lead to different sorts of per-

### Figure 9
### Conduct Models of the Market

Model III (a)

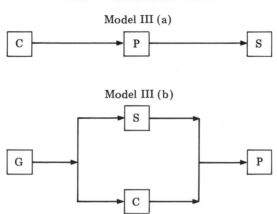

Model III (b)

formances among firms, *P*, and the different performances among firms lead to market structure, *S*. Model III(a) is really the nongovernmental model.

Model III(b) says if you put government, *G*, into the picture, and let it affect or control structure, and do some things to control conduct, you will get interactions between structure and conduct, as the earlier models said. However, the interactions will produce a performance which in some characteristics, in some dimensions, is antisocial.

As we go into real markets, all of the above models are naive and not very realistic pictures of the market processes. I suggest instead Model IV, but it too is simplified.

At its core, Model IV retains *S*, *C*, and *P*. There are structural characteristics to industries, and there are conduct characteristics to industries; and following from traditional microtheory and Model II, some aspects of performance can be explained in terms of the structure and conduct variables. But the system is much more complicated. Various dimensions of performance are perceived from the point of view of the managers of the firms in the industry, of the stockholders, of workers, of consumers, of Congress, and of regulatory bodies. In the more realistic market system, different people respond or adapt to performances of industries in one way or another: there is feedback.

One kind of adaptive response is entry of new firms — and exits and mergers. Thus, performance produces feedback effects which induce firms to enter the industry, to leave the industry, or to merge. The effects will be to influence structure over time, as shown by the dotted lines in the diagram.

This system is very different from those represented in the other models. In my system, structure just doesn't appear from nowhere. Economies of scale and other factors may, of course, influence structure. But markets operate in ways which change structure. This concept is in accord with some of the views stated in John McGee's paper.

**Figure 10**
A Realistic Model of the Market

Model IV

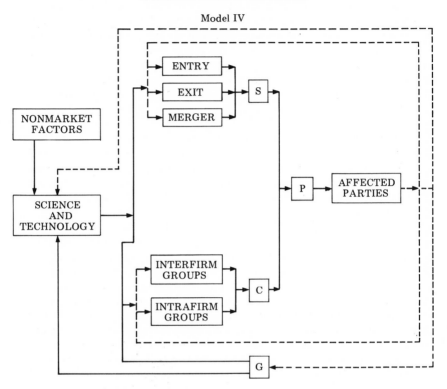

It also is true that conduct is affected by performance. Conduct may reflect coalescences among firms. This is collusion. Coalescences also take place within firms, leading to independent firm profit maximization. Conduct may also reflect some things we have not talked much about here, especially what goes on internal to the firm with respect to managerial discretion and organizational processes. Lawyers who have been involved in Section 1 (Sherman Act) cases often find that something has happened in markets that leads firms to collude. The point is that conduct, too, can be studied as a response — a feedback — to various aspects of performance.

Performance brings forth other factors affecting structure and conduct, especially governmental intervention, the G of Model III(b). Now again, G can come in lots of dimensions. It can come because of Ralph Nader or because of the worries of the owners or managers of the companies. It could possibly come because consumers are upset and do something about it. Out of the process comes government control of entry, exit, mergers, prices, output, advertising, and so forth. The antitrust laws themselves are part of this picture as they affect the degree of collusion and other patterns of firm behavior.

Now let me make it just a bit more complicated. Jesse Markham's discussion of structure, conduct, and performance with respect to technological change emphasizes just the Model II part of the relationship. Model IV includes as a partially exogenous factor the basic bodies of science and technology. One of the things I think has great importance in the economics of technological change is the effect of different states of the sciences and of technology on the conduct of firms, the kind of R&D they do, and their attitude towards innovation.

Model IV also recognizes that performance characteristics may lead government to become involved, through R&D contracts and other devices, in altering the state of technology. Firms themselves may also make contributions to basic science and technology. Whatever the source of the contributions, changes in technology are going to influence cost and demand functions and, indirectly through performance differences, affect structure.

It would be very nice if, with this simultaneously determined system, we could capture all the relationships and make great generalizations. Unhappily, at this point we really do not know how different configurations of S, C, and P get the process working and how the different feedbacks work. It is because of this ignorance that I argue in my paper that if economics is going to be useful for policy purposes, it is not going to be so because of a regression equation that explains 20 to 40 percent of the variance in some measure of performance. The system is complicated; this is why the regression results — nearly all of which pay no attention to simultaneity — are typically so poor.

If one pays attention to particular cases — whether it is the petroleum industry or the pharmaceutical industry — and to particular forms of government regulation, a study of particular markets can give us guidance as to what we ought to do with respect to government policy. This model avoids categorical generalizations. It does not say that all advertising is good or that all advertising is bad. It does not say that all R&D is good or that all R&D is bad. It does not say that all mergers are good or that all mergers are bad or that all increases in concentration are bad. It says: look at all these characteristics simultaneously, find out how particular markets operate, and move into those markets with appropriate public policy. In this way we can find those instances where this government has interposed itself in ways contrary to the public good. It also permits consideration of new regulations consistent with the public good. These are the reasons for my iconoclastic, if not middle-ground, approach to public policy questions.

# Commentary

## Richard Posner

The debate over concentration is largely a history of recantation. Professor Stigler's famous article in *Fortune* magazine in 1952, where he urged deconcentration, was repudiated by Professor Stigler in 1969. In *Antitrust Policy* (1959), Professors Kaysen and Turner had proposed deconcentration, and their book, along with the Stigler article, was prominently cited in the Neal report as support for its recommendation. Unbeknownst, apparently, to the authors of the Neal report, Professor Kaysen had recanted his views in testimony in 1965 before the Senate Subcommittee on Monopoly, where he had described the proposal as academic and speculative. Professor Turner repudiated his support for the proposal in testimony before the same Subcommittee in March 1973.

Dean Neal issued what I take to be a partial retraction of his support for his Task Force's proposals in his paper. He made such statements (nowhere to be found or alluded to in the Neal report itself) as: there is substantial basis for fearing that a policy of deconcentration would reduce efficiency; we can scarcely hope to have any reliable predictions of the values associated with these potential gains and losses; when measured against the total productivity of the economy, both the potential gains and potential costs of such a policy are probably fairly modest. And he indicated that perhaps there is a greater risk of major losses of efficiency than there is a possibility of great economic benefit. He went on, however, to suggest that maybe the danger could be reduced in the administration of the policy. He then concluded that in this state of uncertainty, a policy judgment may well turn importantly on factors other than the economic calculus.

That is, finding the economic reasoning no longer compelling, he attempts to shift discussion to a different plane and proposes a political reason to support what had formerly been an economic proposal.

Dean Neal stated in his commentary, "It is now no great breach of confidence to relate that the members of the White House Task Force in 1968 thought they heard very similar views, although more mildly expressed, when discussing deficiencies in the antitrust laws with Professor Stigler." But this is a position which Professor Stigler has since repudiated. I can understand why Dean Neal and the other authors of the Task Force report would feel disappointed and chagrined at having the rug pulled out from under their feet. If the rug has been pulled out, one may have remedies against the person who pulled the rug; nonetheless, the rug is no longer there.

That leaves Professor Simons, whose proposal for deconcentration, in the 1930s, remains a principal intellectual pillar of the deconcentration movement. Unfortunately, Professor Simons died prematurely in 1948 and had no opportunity to modify his views.

One thing that is very significant in Dean Neal's paper is a much greater sensitivity to the costs of a policy of deconcentration than can be found in the Neal report itself, where those costs are said to be very low. I want to stress briefly what seemed to me to be the major costs of such a policy and to suggest that the Neal report analyzed those costs incorrectly.

First, we are talking about deconcentration proceedings for which nothing in the history of the antitrust laws, or even Section 11 of the Public Utility Holding Company Act, prepares us in terms of complexity, protraction, cost, and likely futility. Those people — including Professor Adams — who have studied the history of structural remedies under the antitrust laws have found repeated failure to implement effective relief. In this connection, Dean Neal's reference to George Hale's study of some of these decrees may have created a somewhat misleading impression. It is true, as Hale found, that the firms emerging from the remedial process were able to thrive commercially. But that was because the remedial proceedings were in most cases perfunctory. An example is the Standard Oil decree, where, because the court was content with simply dissolving a holding company and not altering the underlying structure of the Standard Oil enterprise, the result of the decree was to create a set of regional monopolists who ever since have been hindered from competing with each other by the fact that the Standard Oil Trust had parcelled out the exclusive rights to the Standard Oil trademark among the regional firms, so that they couldn't use the trademark in each other's territories. The lesson of the Hale study is that while it is true than antitrust remedial proceedings may not create firms that are deformed and incapable of survival, this is primarily because antitrust remedial proceedings have never seriously attempted to alter the structure of industry.

It would have been instructive in this regard if the Neal report had listed the companies that would be dissolved under its proposal. At a guess, they would include such firms as General Motors, Ford, Alcoa, General Electric, Xerox, IBM, Procter and Gamble, Western Electric, and Eastman Kodak. There has never been an antitrust decree quite comparable to what would be involved in trying to dissolve any of these firms.

Growing concern with the costs of a deconcentration policy and its questionable benefits has, as I suggested earlier, led Dean Neal to shift discussion to a new ground and to propose a political reason for deconcentration. He offers in fact several reasons, but I will limit myself to his major one. He says that deconcentration would restore public confidence in a competitive economy. What underlies that suggestion, I suppose, is some notion that there are people in this country with problems — high prices, or crime, or whatever — who blame those problems on big business.

If that is so, we can be confident that when deconcentration is completed, their problems will not be solved. Therefore, they will demand some other solution — some further solution. They will come to recognize that deconcentration was a fraud perpetrated on them by their intellectual superiors as a way of distracting them from whatever actual conditions are the source of their miseries and of their desire to place blame on big business.

To adopt policies simply to pander to popular misunderstanding is a recipe for creating new demands for further restrictions on business. To repeat, once big business is identified by means of a deconcentration statute as a source of major social problems, and after deconcentration fails to remove those problems, the pressure will become irresistible for further legislation aimed at these villains who have somehow escaped the punishment that we had attempted to mete out by a policy of deconcentration. If the policy of deconcentration cannot be justified on rational grounds, in terms of its intrinsic merits, then it seems to me a serious mistake to urge it on grounds of warding off lesser evils in the future.

# Dialogue*

*Turner:* Dick Posner suggested that I had recanted the position Carl Kaysen and I took some years back. That is somewhat of an exaggeration. The position I took in testifying on the Hart Bill was that I believed a deconcentration statute was appropriate, but one considerably more confined than the bill that had been proposed. And specifically I said that it seemed to me that any legislative proposal should confine itself to relatively serious cases: those evidencing not only substantial market power, but substantial market power that has persisted for a long enough period of time to indicate that market forces are not likely, within a reasonable future period, to eradicate it. A reorganization program should, of course, further be limited to cases in which feasible relief gives promise of distinctly improving matters.

There were two respects in which I think I changed my view from what Kaysen and I originally proposed. In the original proposal we suggested market share percentage tests as a presumptive indication of market power. I have lost considerable faith in that, and I no longer adhere to it. Second, adopting a principle that was contained in the Neal Task Force report, I would limit any statute to fairly large markets. The suggested limitation was $500 million gross sales.

*Leonard Weiss:* Mr. Neal, would you compare the Neal proposal and the Hart Bill for us?

*Neal:* Aside from the four-firm concentration test of 50 percent in the Hart Bill (versus 70 percent in the Task Force proposal), there are a number of other differences. In the Hart Bill there is the profits test. There is also the test of observing whether there is price competition, which, it seems to me, would be a very difficult exercise. And then the structure of the Hart Bill creates a presumption of monopoly power. There is no definition of monopoly power. It says that a rebuttable presumption of monopoly power is created by any of these three tests, but there is nothing to tell you what you are looking for apart from those three tests, and it doesn't tell you how it can be rebutted. It seems

---

* The session was chaired by Donald F. Turner, Professor of Law, Harvard University School of Law. For further biographical information, see Appendix D.

to me the Hart Bill throws you into the litigation morass that our draft statute tried very hard to avoid.

One further point I would make is that the Hart Bill is a single-firm test, or has a confusion between a single-firm and an industry test. Ours was beamed at the industry as a whole, or the set of oligopoly firms, and that seems to be preferable.

*Victor Kramer:* Do you think the Antitrust Division is doing all it can do with existing law to enforce our national antitrust policy?

*Phillips:* My answer can only be an impression, because I have never been privy to the inner workings of the Antitrust Division. If you are asking whether the division is doing all that it can with its present budget constraints and other constraining factors considered, I really don't have much basis for criticism of the Justice Department. On the other hand, if you are asking whether with a larger budget there are other things that they might be doing, whether they should do more experimenting with particular cases to see if there weren't some ways of attacking particular problems, I guess I'd urge them to try it. But I feel favorably disposed in general towards the efforts of the Antitrust Division to enforce the existing laws.

*Adams:* No, I don't think the Antitrust Division is doing all it might. For example, I find it terribly perplexing that the Division does not seem to have moved effectively against joint ventures in bidding on federal oil leases. To me, the factual situation is reminiscent of bid-rigging in the *Addyston Pipe* case,[1] and if we can have a per se rule that governs that situation, I cannot see why, for example, the kind of joint ventures in the bidding on federal oil leases are not a rather obvious restraint that the division could move against.

*Weiss:* What about the small independents who do this as a means of attaining economies of scale?

*Adams:* I am not much concerned about the strawberry growers of Louisiana, who were once sued by the Antitrust Division. I always believe in going elephant hunting rather than rabbit hunting.

*Neal:* If the suggestion is, as sometimes advanced, that the division might be more adventurous in trying to press the borders of Section 2 of the Sherman Act, and to pick off some large test cases in the area that we are talking about, I don't have any great enthusiasm for that myself. It seems to me it is asking a lot of the courts to wrestle with the present crude instrument of Section 2 for dealing with problems of concentration. I think their reluctance in the past cases has been understandable. It seems to me it would be much preferable in the whole field to have a fresh and clear kind of mandate from Congress rather than to try to determine in what ways the concepts of Section 1 and Section 2 can be bent and pulled to do something that is really quite novel.

*Donald Baker:* It seems to me, looking at the world from a somewhat different perspective of the day-to-day business of enforcement, that one has to think in terms of ease of enforceability. And that really raises the question of

---

1. United States v. Addyston Pipe & Steel Co., 85 F. 271 (6th Cir. 1898), aff'd, 175 U.S. 211 (1899).

whether you should have any statute at all. In the end, the only kind of statute that is workable is going to end up on a sort of per se justification. It is going to have to work very much the way our price-fixing rules do. A lot more attention is needed to the mechanics of litigating the thing, because this kind of litigation is like war on the western front. If you create a presumption, as in the Hart Bill, and the defendant rebuts it with a little evidence, you may have another *Alcoa* or *Socony Vacuum* case.[2]

*Turner:* I don't think I am all that pessimistic — or not as pessimistic as Phil Neal and his colleagues were — about the ability to establish monopoly power. I assume that you attempt to establish it primarily by looking at substantial price–cost differentials. Substantial price discrimination will also indicate monopoly power in a high price market. In some cases you will get a fairly clear profit showing. I think the *du Pont* (*Cellophane*) case[3] is a good illustration of that. In other words, I don't think it is all that unmanageable a problem. It takes data gathering and analysis.

*Baker:* You are looking at it as a one-shot statute based on an industry's past performance so you don't get into the problem of affecting its future performance?

*Turner:* Yes. And my view is that it should be really severely limited, if for no other reason than what we should be doing is one experimental try. Take one industry that seems to fit the bill, and see what happens when you get done with it.

I would have to concede that the recognition of an efficiency defense, if it were recognized in a court proceeding, would pose extremely serious problems. The ideal solution would be rather tough presumptions in the statute, but an enforcing agency would come to its conclusion that a case should be brought only after very careful evaluation of the evidence. That raises some problems that lawyers should be concerned about — at a minimum. The possibility of a combination of rather tough rules with enforcement discretion, it seems to me, deserves further exploration. It puts a heavy demand on the enforcement agency to be sensible.

I would be fairly certain that an enforcement agency operating under a statute of this kind would behave rather conservatively. The political pressures, as I see them, are going to be against bringing proceedings of this kind anyway.

But on the other hand, I am not sure; and I think Phil Neal's defense of the other approach is a very strong one. I think, when it comes down to it, the choice between the two rests on some estimate of what the comparative costs are.

Clearly, Phil Neal's program contemplates more extensive restructuring than I think I would be inclined to do, but it may be that his statute would sort of fit my bill. That is, you would get the rules that are relatively simple to enforce, but the enforcement agency would be very careful in using them.

2. United States v. Aluminum Co. of America, 148 F.2d 416 (2d Cir. 1945); United States v. Socony-Vacuum Oil Co., 310 U.S. 150 (1940).

3. United States v. E. I. du Pont de Nemours & Co., 351 U.S. 377 (1956).

But if what he contemplates is a systematic restructuring — and I think it is — I would be concerned that the efficiency costs would exceed the gains. I'd be much more cautious.

*Baker:* So basically you end up with the government making the judgment as to efficiency.

*Turner:* That is right. Ideally that is what I would like to see.

*Phillips:* There are a couple of things in Professor Turner's remarks that I'd like to comment on. The first is the question of whether per se, despite its apparent simplicity, really shortens trials. In some cases it does and in some cases it doesn't. *Socony Vacuum* was tried as a per se case and it certainly was a voluminous record. It took a long time for the court to decide whether or not the offense that was per se had, in fact, occurred.

I question your statement that a per se rule on price-fixing, for example, always leads to better results. Remember my Model IV and the many different responses that can be involved. In the *Addyston Pipe* case, after they were found guilty of price-fixing, they merged into the United States Pipe Iron and Foundry Company, which for many years was probably one of the nation's worst monopolies. There are a lot of feedbacks that can appear as alternatives, some of which may fall into per se areas and some of which don't. Merger is one of the latter alternatives.

The alternative that Harold Demsetz keeps pressing on us here, one with which I agree in large measure, is the alternative of using the feedback loop through government and letting the government do the kind of price-fixing which you deny through the per se rule. If the application of per se means that the industries that are affected — and they tend to be the large-number, unconcentrated industries — run off and get the government to create a regulatory commission, it is not clear that net benefit results. And there are lots of such commissions at the state and federal level that have sprung into being because without them the firms would be found guilty of per se violations. Does per se always lead to better results?

*Baker:* There are a couple of points. First of all, *Socony* is a huge case and it's a huge case because it came after *Appalachian Coals;*[4] it wasn't clear at the time that it was a per se case. The argument for a per se rule is the *Socony* record.

Second, the pleas for special regulatory schemes do not turn on whether the rule is per se or not. They turn on the fact that firms don't like to compete. If the decision is going to be made that they shouldn't have to compete, it is probably better made as a legislative decision.

Third, the justification for the per se rule is not that it works better all the time, but that it works better in the bulk of the cases. Proving the conspiracies is complicated, but if we allowed a full economic inquiry, those records would be fifteen times as long.

*Wesley J. Liebeler:* Most comments so far have focused primarily on the ''monopoly power'' created by the federal government. The problem is at least

---

4. Appalachian Coals, Inc. v. United States, 288 U.S. 344 (1933).

as serious on the state level. To my mind, *Parker v. Brown*,[5] which shields state sanctioned monopoly from antitrust scrutiny, should be reversed and replaced by some kind of balancing test.

At the same time, I think the Federal Trade Commission could interest itself in this problem, and under Section 5 of the Federal Trade Commission Act could do things that would improve competition to a considerable extent on the state level.

As to a deconcentration bill, what I want to know about is the relationship between efficiency and size. If we are going to bring an efficiency defense into the merger area, where market shares are small, we could see how economists, lawyers, and judges would handle the trade-offs between efficiency and increased concentration. Then, in future merger cases, we'd learn how institutions like the Trade Commission and the courts can deal with these issues in a context similar to that of the deconcentration bill.

*Posner:* I don't think economies or efficiencies are litigable issues, especially in a merger case, where the issue is not whether, as a result of the merger, there will be efficiency, but how long would it have taken the firms to obtain the same efficiencies by internal growth. It is the loss in time as a result of forcing them to expand internally rather than merge that provides the measure of the actual cost. And even if one came up with a figure for sacrificed efficiencies, with what would one compare it? We have no information on the costs in monopoly pricing of any given horizontal merger, unless it is a United States Steel type of merger.

On the more general point that Professor Liebeler raises — and it is also implicit in Professor Turner's remark — I don't think the answer to our ignorance on many empirical questions is to increase the scope of legal proceedings. We have had a long history of attempts, in merger proceedings in the regulated industries, to measure the economies of scale, and I believe those proceedings have not advanced our knowledge about economies of scale by an iota.

*Liebeler:* Phil Neal and Senator Hart seem to think this question of efficiency is litigable. Given this, I wonder if we could learn something about how our institutions could handle the issue by permitting an efficiency defense.

*Posner:* You can go back and read the record of the *United Shoe Machinery* case[6] and see how distinguished economists and a judge fall on their faces trying to evaluate the efficiency and monopolistic behavior of a relatively simple, rather small industry.

*Turner:* I think I come closer to Professor Posner's point of view than others, but there, again, the economists may correct me. My understanding is that the establishment of plant-scale economies is not an impossible task. I would suppose every time a company is going to build a plant and decides what plant to build, it gets a blend of engineering and cost data which gives the firm some estimate of what the best size is.

---

5. Parker v. Brown, 317 U.S. 341 (1943).

6. United States v. United Shoe Machinery Corp., 110 F. Supp. 295 (D. Mass. 1953), aff'd per curiam, 347 U.S. 521 (1954).

But that doesn't constitute an efficiency defense. As Professor Posner said, one of the problems is that for the defense to really make sense it has to accelerate the achievement of efficiencies.

That isn't the only problem. Just take a plain horizontal merger between two companies, each one of which has a concededly inefficiently small plant. The question is: Assuming that you have established that both firms are inefficiently small, how is the merger going to make any difference? The immediate consequence of the merger is that instead of having two inefficient plants individually held, there are now two inefficient plants commonly held.

About the only respect in which I can see the merger does very much is that if the companies are quite substantial, is may be that the replacement of the two inefficient plants by one efficient plant will have less of a capacity effect, and hence less of a depressant effect on the market, than if each replaced its inefficient plant individually. But still there is a question: If they don't merge, maybe one of them will build the efficient plant anyway, so it doesn't make any difference.

In short, when you get into the question of whether an efficiency defense should be recognized, wholly apart from the question of whether the companies are inefficient, there are highly speculative questions as to whether the merger will really make any difference.

*Harold Demsetz:* What you are asking people to demonstrate is that two parties to an exchange, which is the way I would interpret a merger, are both better off because of the merger, quite aside from the monopoly power. That is a very difficult technical thing to do, and you can't make something like plant economies the sole measure of merger efficiency.

I think that Professor Posner has too simple a notion of the kinds of savings that might be involved in a merger. For example, if you take the inefficient management of one company and the efficient management of another company, and the efficient management says, "Let's merge with that company and make it more efficient by virtue of our management," and it is able to do this through a merger route that does not involve bringing new capacity in under its own ownership and forcing the other firm's capacity out of the industry, it seems to me this could be a considerable social savings.

*Turner:* If one takes that proposition seriously, you sound the death knell to any meaningful merger law. It seems to me that at any given time in any industry some firms are more efficient than other firms: some firms, if they took over the less efficient firms, could run them more efficiently. Your approach would rapidly concentrate everything.

What our supposition is — and experience tends to bear this out — is that most of the time the firm that is temporarily managed inefficiently will pull up its socks before it exits by the bankruptcy route. And this, indeed, is the process of competition that you anticipate.

*Demsetz:* There are all sorts and kinds of competition. I think the one factual prediction you made is one I'd emphatically disagree with: that in the absence of an antimerger law, which many Western countries have suffered under, you'd get a great deal of monopolization. I just don't believe that is factual.

*Milton Handler:* As I understand it, the genesis of a program for deconcentration came about because certain economists, on the basis of their studies, concluded that there was a positive correlation between concentration and profitability, and that the degree of profitability was excessive. Now, we have heard from the very talented people here that in the 50 or more studies that have been made, the positive correlation has been found on the basis of data which is admitted to be imperfect. And the correlations have been described as being on the weak side.

On the basis of this evidence, we propose to alter the structure of American industry. And the reorganization is to take the form of substituting eight companies where you had four before. I asked Weiss yesterday whether there was any evidence that the profitability of the eight companies would be any different from the profitability of the four companies, and he said there was no such evidence.

Then, economists suggest that inflation alters the significance of the evidence, and perhaps over a long period of inflation you would find that concentrated industries did not maintain an excessive level of prices and profits in comparison with the others. Thus, inflation introduces a factor that casts a cloud over the studies.

So I ask the proponents of deconcentration what do they discern as the social benefits that would flow from the measures that they propose?

*Neal:* I would not have thought that the case for deconcentration rested solely on the correlation between profits and concentration. I think that was taken rather to be some confirmation of a fairly wide consensus of theory about the likelihood of highly concentrated industries acting in less than an optimum competitive way. And if you want a short statement of the case for such a bill, I think it's very well set forth in the first part of Professor Posner's paper, all of which I agree with.

I think the differences come down to estimates about the probable losses in efficiency that such a measure would produce and the difficulty of devising a scheme that would enable you to make a reasonable determination of those efficiencies, either in general or in a particular case.

It seems to me that any steps one takes in this area are bound to be somewhat crude and rough-and-ready, and therefore a judgment about their desirability is going to turn very largely on how much of a gamble you are willing to take in the face of what evidence is available about the probable losses. For myself — and I don't pretend to have an expert appraisal of the value of the evidence — the kind of thing that Professor Scherer has adduced here seems to me to be somewhat reassuring on the broad question that substantial measures could be taken without catastrophic effects.

*Adams:* My answer, Professor Handler, is that every society must have some mechanism to deal effectively with the power problem. And there are just so many alternatives available. One is competition and competitive markets. The other is government regulation. A third is government ownership.

Obviously there are a lot of hybrids, but you must assure the people who compose a society that power is under control. That is the great gain of a deconcentration statute, especially if you can show that this decentralization of power does not carry with it substantial losses in terms of economies of scale.

*Handler:* Well, do you think that you have a deconcentration of power when you substitute eight for four?

*Adams:* Yes.

*Handler:* What is the evidence for that?

*Adams:* That there are eight instead of four.

*Turner:* Well, I think there is no way of resolving this dispute.

*Scherer:* On the question of some of the social-political benefits of deconcentration, I think Professors Turner and Kaysen have stated this case very well in the first chapters of their book, with which I suspect most of us are familiar.

Another point is this: Professor Posner seems to be concerned with the fact that courts are not able to cope very well with the complexities of determining whether or not economies of scale would be sacrificed as a result of deconcentration. I would tend to agree with his historical judgment. I would add, however, that one of the reasons is that we have lacked an adequate theory of economies of scale.

I say with some arrogance that one of the purposes of my research during the past four or five years has been to provide us with such a theory. To be sure, the theory is far from perfect. I hope others will continue this work and improve it. But I think as a result of this kind of work the courts will be able to do a much better job of asking the right kinds of questions if, indeed, they do proceed into this sort of investigation.

*Phillips:* Up to this point there has been some tendency in the discussion to equate political and social power with high concentration ratios. And I think there is some evidence in history that that is really not true. The milk farming industry is not especially concentrated by any kind of measure you'd want to use for market purposes. On the other hand, it seems to be able to wield considerable power. So do teachers. So do varieties of labor unions. So do banks which may have a lot of local market power but are nationally not highly concentrated. They have great power because of the way they associate.

*Turner:* Retail druggists.

*Phillips:* Yes, and you could go down the list. They also happen to be the ones who have been given some sort of exemption from the antitrust laws because of structural and performance problems.

*William Baxter:* We must then be talking about some other kind of unease which Don Dewey referred to this morning. Why are we so uneasy? To me, reliance on political-social values seems largely a matter of mystery and folk superstition. Is there really any reason to believe that a far-flung, worldwide, diversified conglomerate has any more political clout than a trade association made up of dairy farmers? Recent evidence is not conclusive. There are apparently fairly low costs of cooperation in matters such as that.

Those who refer vaguely to "predatory practices" and to amorphous social gains that might be achieved by deconcentration should present their evidence for the existence of such.

*Posner:* I am sure that if Professor Scherer were the judge in a case in which Professor Scherer's study of economies of scale was introduced by way of expert testimony, there would be little difficulty in using that economic work to come to a legal conclusion. But experience with the use of economics and economic evidence in the litigation process does not suggest that the growing complexity and sophistication of economists' quantitative tools has helped courts to decide issues in a correct fashion. There is a way to test this proposition. We don't have to leave it to speculation. We can ask if the performance of courts in deciding antitrust cases improved in, let us say, the last 30 years, which has seen a considerable improvement in econometrics and in mathematical economic theorization. I'd be willing to bet very confidently that the answer will be that there has been no improvement in the rationality of antitrust decision-making.

*Donald Dewey:* Professor Posner, do you believe the present level of concentration in the economy is about right? If not, what measures would you recommend to increase it?

*Posner:* I don't think the antitrust laws, as so far administered, have seriously inhibited the growth of companies. There is recent and pending antitrust litigation which, depending on its outcome, might have some such effect. Of course, there were the few cases in which very early monopolies like the Standard Oil Trust were dissolved, but it seems to me quite plausible that the concentration involved in those proceedings was the result of monopolization rather than efficiencies.

*Joseph Brodley:* It seems to me the distrust of power is everywhere, but it is distrust of centralized power. And Professor Phillips' presentation has given me a thought of a way of responding to that without some of the risks that have been pointed out, because he has suggested that the number of variables is so great that only a full-blown investigation into those variables would be adequate. This would, no doubt, cause prolonged and extensive proceedings, but it might serve the essential purpose that centralized power could occasionally be called to justify itself before a forum established by the Hart Bill to provide scrutiny and review.

*Phillips:* You are suggesting that a full-blown review within the context of the Hart Bill would be possible. That is what I am looking for, but I have the feeling that the way the bill is now drawn — and even the title of it — puts an importance on structural aspects of the market which I really don't feel is correct. I think structure will become the dominant test, and I don't think it should be. Further, I don't like the aspect of it that shifts the burden of proof.

Somewhere in the Bible is the passage, "In my Father's house there are many mansions. If it were not so I would have told you."

What this suggests is that someone is capable of enumerating all the things that aren't true. There are an infinite number of things that aren't true. If you put an industry or firm in the context of going through and disproving the whole gamut of things that could lead to monopoly power, you'd wonder if you would ever exhaust the list. I'd have more confidence in somebody having looked at the industry and saying, "This is bad, and we are going to accept the burden that it is bad and has bad results." The opposite burden is too great.

In addition to that, while I can pick out some cases I dislike, by and large I think the existing judicial system has done a fair job with the existing antitrust laws.

*Mark Green:* I thought Professor Posner acknowledged that there are economies of lobbying for a large firm. Therefore, a large firm, a leading firm in a concentrated market, does have more political power than do smaller firms. Professor Posner, are you recanting your position?

*Posner:* If you increased the number of firms in an industry, you would increase their costs of coordinating, and that might be either costs of fixing prices or costs of mounting a joint lobbying program. So concentration might have some relationship to the ability to mobilize political power. On the other hand, that effect is obviously dominated by other factors, because when you look around you find little correlation between the degree of concentration of an industry and the amount of its political power. The politically powerful industries include, for example, the agricultural industry, the retail druggists, many other retail segments, the medical profession, and the banking industry.

*Phillips:* Home builders.

*Posner:* In contrast, it seems that many of the concentrated industries are relatively impotent politically. It is my strong impression that network television, which is a concentrated industry, has less political influence than the broadcast stations, which are smaller and more numerous. On balance, therefore, it doesn't seem that a reduction in concentration would markedly reduce the influence that business and other occupational groups have in the political process.

*Green:* If we go from economic concentration to conglomeration, do you think that absolute size is absolutely political, that an I.T.T. can do things that other firms cannot because it has plants in many states and therefore can influence Senators and Congressmen more than smaller firms?

*Posner:* That doesn't seem to me to be an obvious proposition at all. A firm that is highly diversified is going to have multiple interests. If a firm that is, say, both an exporter and an importer takes a position on tariffs, which position will that be?

I.T.T. is a firm with such diversified interests that it would often find it difficult to identify the policy that it ought to favor. I.T.T. is a good example, along with the other conglomerate firms, of companies that have been largely impotent in the political process. If you ask yourself how conglomerate firms have fared in the last five years, the answer is that they have fared very badly. Their stock values have collapsed. Their growth through acquisition has been prevented by the antitrust laws. They have been unable to ward off adverse changes in accounting conventions. They have, in short, failed to mobilize political power effectively.

*Robert Pitofsky:* I think our policy discussion is in the process of being overtaken by events. It always seems to me that one of the things that led to the Neal report was an understandable feeling that Section 2 has been a dead letter since 1945. But look what has happened since Senator Hart's bill was first introduced.

I was interested in Professor Posner's list of the likely targets. IBM was one.

It has been challenged under a Section 2 philosophy. So have Xerox, GE and Westinghouse, Eastman Kodak, and Firestone and Goodyear. And the whole question of advertising and its relation to concentration has been raised by the FTC's cereal cases.

In light of doubts about the advantages to be derived from a deconcentration statute, wouldn't it make sense to await the results of the litigation underway?

*Neal:* I think it's a good point. If these cases go to a conclusion in favor of the government, it tends to undermine the case for a new statute. I would still personally prefer to have this kind of surgery on the economy, if it is to be done, come about as the result of a quite explicit legislative mandate.

## SELECTED BIBLIOGRAPHY

Bain, Joe S. *Industrial Organization.* Wiley & Sons, 2nd ed., 1968.

Blair, John M. *Economic Concentration: Structure, Behavior and Public Policy.* Harcourt, Brace, Jovanovich, Inc., 1972.

Bock, Betty. *Concentration, Oligopoly and Profit: Concepts vs. Data.* The Conference Board, 1972.

Brozen, Yale. "The Antitrust Task Force Deconcentration Recommendation." *Journal of Law and Economics,* 13 (1970), 279.

———. "Bain's Concentration and Rates of Return Revisited." *Journal of Law and Economics,* 14 (1971), 351.

The Conference Board. *An Anthology of Studies of Industrial Concentration: 1958-72.* 1973.

Dewey, Donald J. *Monopoly in Economics and Law.* Rand McNally, 1959.

Handler, Milton. *Twenty-Five Years of Antitrust.* Matthew Bender, 1973.

Kaysen, Carl, and Turner, Donald F. *Antitrust Policy: An Economic and Legal Analysis.* Harvard University Press, 1959.

MacAvoy, Paul W.; McKie, James W.; and Preston, Lee E. "High and Stable Concentration Levels, Profitability and Public Policy: A Response." *Journal of Law and Economics,* 14 (1971), 493.

McGee, John. *In Defense of Industrial Concentration.* Praeger, 1971.

Mueller, Willard F. *A Primer on Monopoly and Competition.* Random House, 1970.

Posner, Richard. "Oligopoly and the Antitrust Laws: A Suggested Approach." 21 *Stan. L. Rev.* 1562 (1969).

———. "A Program for the Antitrust Division." 38 *U. Chi. L. Rev.* 500 (1971).

Scherer, F. M. *Industrial Market Structure and Economic Performance.* Rand McNally, 1970.

Shepherd, W. G. *Market Power and Economic Welfare.* Random House, 1970.

Simons, Henry C. *Economic Policy for a Free Society.* University of Chicago Press, 1948.

Stigler, George J. *The Organization of Industry.* R. D. Irwin, 1968.

Turner, Donald. "The Scope of Antitrust and Other Regulatory Policies." 82 *Harv. L. Rev.* 1207 (1969).

Weston, J. Fred. "Implications of Recent Research for the Structural Approach to Oligopoly." 41 *A.B.A. Antitrust L.J.* 623 (1972).

# 8

# Issues for Further Study: Where Does the Researcher Go from Here?

## Concentration, Monopoly, and Industrial Performance: One Man's Assessment

### Franklin R. Edwards*

## I.   DISAGREEMENT AS THE THEME OF THIS VOLUME

In surveying the history of economic analysis, Joseph Schumpeter astutely observed:

> [T]he motives of the analyst are not relevant to the question whether his facts or arguments are or are not true, valuable or not valuable, and the presence of "interested motive," however effective its revelation may be in popular discussion, no more invalidates the reasoning that proceeds from it than its absence avails to validate a man's reasoning. For us, the special pleader's facts and argument are just as good or bad as those of the "detached philosopher," even if he exists.[1]

This observation is particularly applicable to this volume, which pits one economist against another in debate. The advocacy format is, of course, not accidental. Rather, its adoption represents a conscious attempt to isolate areas of

---

* Associate Professor of Business, Graduate School of Business, Columbia University. For further biographical information, see Appendix D.

1. J. Schumpeter, *History of Economic Analysis* (Oxford Univ. Press 1968), p. 154.

clear agreement and disagreement among economists so that we might, for example, uncover the areas where additional research would be especially valuable. In this paper I attempt to assess the outcome of the debates about the economic effects of concentration and monopoly and to highlight the areas where additional research is needed.

## II. THE DEBATES

### The Concentration, Economies of Scale, and Profits Debates

If there are any areas of industrial organization where economists have arrived at a consensus, it is on these issues. We generally agree that:

1. there are economies of scale in almost every industry up to at least some fairly substantial size of firm or plant; and
2. there is a repeatedly observed positive relationship between profits and market concentration across industries.

These areas of agreement do not carry unambiguous policy implications, but their importance should not be minimized. The existence of economies of scale suggests that free markets left to themselves will not remain atomistically competitive but will evolve towards some form of oligopolistic interdependence. Even Scherer, who strongly leans towards minimizing the importance of economies of scale as a determinant of market structure, obliquely admits this inevitability. He says, "at least in the huge United States market, *plant scale economies* alone seldom mandate extremely high seller concentration — i.e., with four-firm concentration ratios exceeding 80. . . . If there is a plant scale imperative toward oligopoly, it is for the most part an imperative toward loose oligopoly." [2] In addition, Scherer grudgingly acknowledges that the existence of "product-specific" scale economies, capital-raising economies, and procurement economies increases the likelihood of an oligopolistic market structure. Thus, even for United States markets, which are large in comparison to those of other countries, economists agree that at least loose oligopoly is probably inevitable in most markets.

Given the remote likelihood of atomistically competitive markets, the positive relationship observed between profits and concentration — our second area of agreement — is subject to alternative interpretations. If no economies of scale existed, of course, such a relationship would clearly suggest that high market concentration results in firms acquiring monopoly power. How else could firms in concentrated markets consistently earn abnormally high profits? If, on the other hand, economies of scale exist and are responsible for creating high concentration, the relationship between concentration and profitability will be due partly to superior cost efficiency in concentrated industries. This is not to say that firms in concentrated markets do not exercise some degree of monopoly power. If these firms consistently earn abnormally high

2. F. M. Scherer, "Economies of Scale and Industrial Organization," this volume, Chapter 2.

profits, they clearly do exercise monopoly power. The crucial issue, however, is whether their monopoly power is derived partly from superior efficiency due to economies of scale, or whether this power stems solely from their ability to successfully collude because of their "fewness." If the former is true, a policy of preventing or eliminating high market concentration will reduce monopoly power at the cost of sacrificing the efficiency benefits of economies of scale. This is the policy dilemma that now confronts us.

Economists have tried to extricate us from the horns of this dilemma in two ways. First, by direct measurement of firm cost curves they have sought to show that economies of scale are generally not extensive enough to warrant high concentration.[3] In other words, economies of scale are exhausted long before concentration is high enough to make collusive behavior among firms either easy or successful. This contention, however, has been hotly contested. Dissidents argue, to begin with, that because of the difficult conceptual and measurement problems involved in the *direct* measurement of scale economies, there is no way that we can ever hope to derive precise and meaningful estimates of them by direct measurement.[4] Consequently, empirical work which shows only limited scale economies, such as Scherer's, is not convincing. Secondly, dissenters note that studies of the concentration–profits relationship *by size of firm* indirectly suggest that economies of scale are extensive in highly concentrated industries: Demsetz finds that the positive concentration–profitability relationship we observe across industries holds only for very large firms, and not for small and medium-sized firms.[5] If there were no economies of scale, or if both large and small firms in an industry had identical average cost curves, a collusive price in a highly concentrated industry would result in both large and small firms in that industry earning similarly high profits. Consequently, the observation that only very large firms in concentrated industries earn abnormally high profits suggests that there must be substantial economies of scale in such industries. (Small and medium-sized firms in these industries, having higher average costs, earn only normal profits.) Present evidence on economies of scale, therefore, is not convincing enough to provide an answer to the policy dilemma we are facing.

The second argument used to extricate us from the efficiency–conspiracy dilemma is the contention that the relationship observed between concentration and profitability is not a permanent one. Rather, what we have observed is a temporary, or disequilibrium, phenomenon which, given sufficient time, will disappear.[6] Thus, there is no long-run monopoly power associated with high concentration, and therefore no policy dilemma after all. Because of the paucity of good (or comparable) time series data on concentration and industry profitability, this disequilibrium hypothesis has not yet received serious

3. *Ibid.*

4. See J. S. McGee, "Efficiency and Economies of Scale," this volume, Chapter 2.

5. H. Demsetz, *The Market Concentration Doctrine* (Washington: American Enterprise Institute 1973).

6. Y. Brozen, "The Persistence of 'High Rates of Return' in High-Stable Concentration Industries," *Journal of Law & Economics*, 14 (October 1971), pp. 501-512.

empirical testing. Nevertheless, it clearly has a certain amount of plausibility and cannot be ignored. It should be noted, however, that empirical verification of the hypothesis will still not successfully extricate us from our policy dilemma unless it can also be shown that "equilibrium" is the normal state of affairs in industrial markets. If "disequilibrium" is the rule, there will always be an association between concentration and monopoly power, and our policy dilemma will continue to exist.

What kinds of research will help us to resolve this dilemma? First, it is clear that we need to arrive at some consensus about the general feasibility of measuring scale economies. What methodology should we use and what types of data must we have? Second, we need to develop a greater understanding of the behavioral mechanism through which market concentration affects firm behavior. Exactly how do collusive arrangements develop in concentrated industries? What causes them to persist or not persist through time? What is the interrelationship between concentration and barriers to entry? Would concentration, even high concentration, have any effect on performance in the absence of barriers to entry? In other words, we need a conceptual breakthrough in oligopoly theory before we can feel completely secure about how the issues we are debating should be resolved. This is not to say we should dismantle our computers and wait for this bolt of originality to strike. On the contrary, theoretical breakthroughs frequently flow from, or are suggested by, the regularities we observe in empirical work.

Aside from their role as a stimulant to theoretical development, more empirical studies can also help to resolve our dilemma in other ways. In particular, we have barely begun the study of "product-specific" scale economies, capital-raising economies, and procurement economies. Perhaps more evidence on these factors will lead to the conclusion that high concentration is inevitable after all. Perhaps not. In any case, economies of scale are just part of the larger question: what are the determinants of market concentration? A better understanding of the relative roles that economies of scale, innovation, and pure chance play in creating market concentration will help us to understand how concentration interrelates with firm performance.

Finally, additional studies of the concentration–profits relationship using individual firm data along the lines of Demsetz's study would be useful. Indeed, if these studies were done with time series as well as cross-section data, they would also aid us in appraising Brozen's disequilibrium hypothesis. In the past the availability of an adequate data base has been the primary obstacle to studies of this kind. Hopefully, this too is a disequilibrium condition that will disappear in time.

### The Advertising Debate

The main issue in this debate is whether extensive advertising enables firms to erect a barrier to entry which thereafter permits them to earn monopoly profits. Alternatively, is advertising a weapon used to foster monopoly, or is it the by-product of competitive struggle? Economists disagree about almost every aspect of this debate. Yet, I believe this question may prove to be one of the most susceptible to additional study.

The main issues of controversy are the following.

1. Is there an empirical relationship among advertising intensity, concentration, and profitability? Here the issues are: (a) How should advertising expenses be capitalized? (b) How should the value of capitalized past advertising be depreciated? (c) Should firm or industry data be used? (d) What is the relationship between profit rates and advertising over time versus at a moment in time (cross-section evidence)? At present, we have very little evidence on these issues, but I see no reason why with additional study they cannot be settled with a fair degree of unanimity.

2. What is the causal explanation for the relationship (if it exists) between advertising and either concentration or profitability (or both)? Does high advertising intensity cause high concentration which results in high profits? Or, do high profits cause high advertising intensity? Alternatively, does high concentration result in high profitability which results in high advertising intensity? Finally, does high advertising intensity alone (or in unconcentrated industries) enable firms to earn high profits?

The study of these interrelationships has just begun. Only now are we beginning to develop the kinds of empirical models capable of answering these questions. Deciphering causal relationships is, after all, not a new problem for economists. Tools do exist with which to attack the problem. In particular, it is probable that in future work economists will treat both profitability and advertising as endogenous variables, and will begin to estimate multi-equation simultaneous models to explain the advertising–concentration–profits relationship. (Indeed, it is conceivable that concentration may also be treated as an endogenous variable.) In short, we are a long way from exhausting the tools of our trade in the resolution of these questions, and until that time comes, I see no reason to be pessimistic.

Before leaving the subject of advertising, I should mention another issue — the contention that advertising expenditures are socially wasteful. More nakedly, if advertising is completely exonerated of the charge that it creates a barrier to entry (and the consequent excess profits), is it not, nevertheless, a socially wasteful expenditure, at least in excess of some "reasonable" volume? Those who hold this view argue that advertising is a form of nonprice competition, and that oligopoly generally results in "excessive" nonprice competition.[7] The notion that advertising is wasteful, therefore, is not so much an advertising issue as it is a nonprice competition issue. Any "excessive" expenditures on nonprice rivalry — not only advertising, but such expenditures as those associated with model changes, service and sales systems, and even possibly research and development — qualify for such concern. Further research on this aspect of advertising, therefore, should be addressed directly to the broader question of the relationship between concentration and nonprice rivalry, rather than to the narrower issue of the concentration–advertising relationship. In particular, we need answers to such questions as: Why does oligopoly result in *excessive* nonprice competition? Are nonprice rivalry ex-

7. H. M. Mann, "Advertising, Concentration and Profitability: The State of Knowledge and Directions for Public Policy," this volume, Chapter 3.

penditures higher in "loose-knit" or "tight-knit" oligopolies? These issues have gone almost completely unexplored by economists, either theoretically or empirically.[8] It is time we tackled them.

### Concentration and Innovation

If high concentration brought with it substantially greater innovation and technological change, most of our misgivings about its adverse effects would fade. Nobody, to my knowledge, seriously questions the immense social value of innovation and technological change.

Economists generally agree that there exists a positive relationship between concentration and innovation (measured in a variety of imperfect ways). We do not agree about whether this relationship is linear, or whether an increase in concentration above a certain level (such as a four-firm concentration ratio of 50 percent) will result in a further increase in innovational activity. Thus, the situation is much like the economies of scale debate. Just as we know there are economies of scale associated with concentration, we know that innovational activity tends to increase with concentration. The question is whether the pace of innovation and technological change continues to increase after moderate levels of concentration are reached, and, if so, whether the benefits associated with it are sufficient to offset the adverse monopoly effects of high concentration.

Can further research help? Here the obstacles are undoubtedly as formidable as in any area of economics; yet, the potential gains from this information are great. I believe two avenues are open to us: more and better work on the theoretical underpinnings of the concentration–innovation relationship, and painstaking efforts to collect better data on innovational activity, especially on an industry-by-industry basis. So little is presently understood about the determinants of innovational activity in an industry that our singling out market structure as an important determinant seems highly arbitrary. With more and better data on innovational activity — of the grubby kind that most economists eschew collecting — we will hopefully learn more about why innovation occurs in some industries but not in others; and this in turn will help us to construct better models with which to test the concentration–innovation hypothesis. In summary, solid empirical and theoretical work on this topic is in its early stages, and it will probably be many years before we are able to resolve the major issues in this debate.

### Concentration and Inflation

The question of whether high concentration increases the rate of inflation is, in my opinion, the least understood subject covered by the conference. Questions about the relationship of concentration to profits, economies of

---

8. But see G. Archibald, "Profit-Maximization and Nonprice Competition," *Economica,* 31 New Series (February 1964), pp. 13-22; and G. Stigler, "Price and Non-Price Competition," *Journal of Political Economy,* 76 (January/February 1968), pp. 149-154.

scale, advertising, and innovation all have one thing in common: they have clear welfare implications. What exactly are the welfare implications of a higher rate of inflation brought about by greater industrial concentration? Would the result be serious allocative inefficiencies? Or, are we concerned about its having important distributive effects on personal income and wealth? Thus, before we examine the issue of whether high concentration increases the inflation rate, some discussion of the welfare implications of such a relationship seems appropriate. Perhaps the issue is not worth debating.

Those who contend that a concentration-inflation relationship exists appear to argue that if all industries were suddenly transformed from low to high concentration, the result would be a higher rate of inflation. Or, that firms would raise prices by more in response to given changes in either demand or unit costs, and that over time these price responses would result in a higher (equilibrium) rate of inflation. What, therefore, are the allocative inefficiencies which stem from a higher equilibrium rate of inflation? Will the rate of economic growth diminish? Will the unemployment rate rise? Neither result seems inevitable or even likely, and I see no reason to assume that government policymakers (e.g., the Federal Reserve Board) will pursue a policy which forcibly brings about such a result. In addition, even if policymakers consciously pursue a vigorous anti-inflation policy, both the theoretical and empirical underpinnings of the "Phillips curve" are such that the long-run trade-offs between inflation, unemployment, and economic growth are far from clear. Thus, unlike the other topics covered by this volume, the concentration—inflation relationship does not have clear allocative (or welfare) implications. Finally, I should point out, for the sake of completeness, that even the most ardent supporters of the concentration-inflation hypothesis do not, to my knowledge, suggest that an increase in concentration will result in a continuously *accelerating* rate of inflation. Such a result would, of course, have quite different welfare implications.

Is it the adverse distributive effects on income and wealth that concern proponents of the concentration—inflation relationship? Typically, economists ignore such effects in assessing the welfare costs of monopoly,[9] since, from the perspective of economic theory, it is impossible to show that one income distribution is superior to any other. Nevertheless, what can we actually say about the distributive effects of a (concentration-induced) higher rate of inflation? Again, the answer is "not much." Measuring such effects is always a tricky empirical task, and in the case of inflation it is doubly difficult. Are we, for instance, talking about a higher inflation rate that is fully anticipated by everyone, or an inflation rate that always takes everyone by surprise? Despite

---

9. See A. Harberger, "Monopoly and Resource Allocation," *American Economic Review Proceedings*, 44 (May 1954), pp. 78–87; D. Schwartzmann, "The Burden of Monopoly," *Journal of Political Economy*, 68 (December 1960), pp. 627–630; D. Kamerschen, "Welfare Losses from Monopoly," *Western Economic Journal*, 4 (Summer 1966), pp. 24-36; and A. Bergson, "On Monopoly Welfare Losses," *American Economic Review*, 63 (December 1973), pp. 853-870.

considerable rhetoric on the distributive effects of inflation, we know very little about it. Further, the little evidence we do have suggests that inflation does
not have substantial distributive effects.[10]

In summary, before becoming too deeply involved with the questions of
whether there exists a relationship between concentration and inflation, I believe we should explore more fully the welfare implications of such a relationship. These implications are certainly not very obvious to us at the present
time.

Is there in fact a positive relationship between concentration and inflation
rates? One of the striking features of empirical studies of this question is that
they frequently find a *negative* relationship between concentration and the
rate of price change. Moreover, results from one time period often contradict
those from another, and the addition or omission of certain independent variables sometimes makes the concentration coefficient significantly positive,
sometimes significantly negative, and sometimes not significant at all, depending upon the time period studied. Nevertheless, there does seem to be an in-
triguing relationship between firms' cyclical price behavior and concentration,
although we do not know exactly what this relationship is or why it should
exist. Are we observing that firms in concentrated markets have different equilibrium responses to a given change in demand or cost conditions, or are we
simply observing different dynamic (or cyclical) response patterns where equilibrium responses are the same?

It is abundantly clear that both more theoretical and more empirical work
on this issue is needed. Our most pressing need is to develop testable models
of dynamic pricing. The heart of the concentration–inflation relationship involves the problem of how firms adjust to a new equilibrium induced by an
exogenous change in demand and/or costs. Which firms change price and
why, at what speed, and with what time path? What are the behavioral rules
that firms follow when a market is out of equilibrium and why should these differ in concentrated versus unconcentrated markets? What exactly are the costs
associated with a change in price, and are these costs higher or lower in concentrated industries? I think it is fair to say that empirical work in this area has
not been able to distinguish between firms having different adjustment paths
to equilibrium and having different equilibrium responses to a given exogenous shock. While we are developing these models of price behavior, we
should, of course, continue to search out empirically all possible explanations
for the observed concentration–pricing relationships. In particular, by further
study of different phases of the business cycle we may be able to learn more
about the dynamics of price behavior in concentrated versus unconcentrated
industries.

Before leaving this subject, one additional comment seems required. The
emotional aura surrounding the concentration–inflation debate is such that
quick legislative action in this area is not inconceivable. This would, in my
opinion, be both premature and unwise. We possess neither sound theoretical reasons nor even remotely convincing empirical evidence to justify such

10. See G. L. Bach, *The New Inflation* (Prentice-Hall 1973), ch. 2, pp. 9-38.

action. Moreover, legislative action will more than likely take the form of wage and price constraints in concentrated industries (or in industries with high profit margins),[11] and such constraints will themselves almost surely be the cause of serious resource misallocations. No one who has studied government price regulation (in public utilities, taxis, interest rates, etc.), or who has tried to buy gasoline recently, can deny the perverse effects of this kind of government intervention.

## III. SOME OMITTED ISSUES

There are two issues relevant to market concentration and monopoly power which were touched on in the dialogues in this volume but which deserve even more attention. These are the distributive consequences of monopoly and the problem of cost inefficiency on the part of firms with monopoly power. (The latter is often referred to as "X-inefficiency.")

### Distributive Consequences of Monopoly

As I indicated earlier, the income and wealth distribution consequences of monopoly power are typically ignored by economists who examine the economic impact of monopoly. In contrast, legislators and consumer advocates almost always focus on the distributive consequences of monopoly, typically ignoring the traditional welfare factors that occupy economists. For example, a recent study (1972) by the FTC on the impact of concentration in some 100 manufacturing industries is widely cited (although it has never been released) as showing that monopoly pricing in manufacturing industries "costs the consumer" more than $15 billion a year, or results in consumers being "overcharged" by $15 billion a year.[12] Nobody cites the "deadweight" or "allocative" loss implied by this study (which, of course, is only a fraction of this magnitude).

Legislators and consumers have always been more concerned about the distributive consequences of monopoly than about its economic costs, and I do not expect this to change. Should not, therefore, economists also study this issue in order to ascertain the magnitude and directions of these distributive effects? We have, after all, been quite willing to study the distributive consequences of government programs, such as taxation, education, and welfare programs. Why should the distributive effects of monopoly escape our analytic net?

To date, there have been very few systematic studies of these effects. Knowledge of the concentration–profits relationship is not sufficient. We must also examine the income and wealth distributions of those who benefit from monopoly profits relative to those who pay monopoly prices to determine the

11. See W. F. Mueller, "Industrial Concentration: An Important Inflationary Force," this volume, Chapter 6.

12. See "McGovern Asks Price Freeze," *Washington Post,* April 24, 1972, p. A-2; and "Proxmire Seeks FTC Report on $15-Billion Overcharge," *Washington Evening Star,* April 24, 1972, p. A-11.

total distributive impact. In addition, it is well known that over time monopoly profits are capitalized into the value of the firm. What impact does this have? [13] The issue of the distributive consequences of monopoly are here to stay, whether economists like it or not. Economic research can make an important contribution to this debate.

### The Monopoly–Costs Inefficiency Issue

This topic has many guises and has been with us in one form or another for a long time. Put succinctly, it can be stated as follows: firms not under the gun of keen competition become inefficient and wasteful, permitting their costs to rise well above what they would be under competition.[14] In other words, for one reason or another we should expect monopolistic industries to be characterized by a higher cost per unit of output, everything else equal. Or, from still another perspective, the potential benefits of economies of scale in concentrated industries must be weighed against the cost inefficiency and waste associated with the lack of competition. It is possible that these inefficiencies may be great enough to offset whatever benefits there are from scale economies.

Like many issues in industrial organization, the theoretical and empirical foundations of this thesis are insecure. This has not, however, retarded its rise to a position of prominence in today's literature. In a recent textbook on industrial organization, for example, Scherer attributes a third of the total welfare losses in the United States due to monopoly to monopoly-induced cost inefficiency.[15] He also suggests that the welfare loss from such cost inefficiency is more than twice as great as the "deadweight" or "allocative" loss due to monopolistic pricing. He declares: "How typical it is for firms insulated from competition to operate with copious layers of fat can only be guessed. My own belief is that padding as high as 10 per cent of costs is not at all uncommon." [16]

The idea that monopoly breeds cost inefficiency has also not been exclusive to the community of scholars. In a "confidential" FTC study of monopoly power in manufacturing, the authors say: "We expect both waste and deception to be relatively more serious the higher the concentration. . . . As concentration increases, the opportunity for waste . . . increase[s], since the true profit margin increases." [17] Consumer advocates also argue that lack of com-

---

13. For an innovative study of this question, see W. Comanor and R. Smiley, *Monopoly and Distribution* (Stanford Univ. Grad. Sch. of Bus. Research Paper No. 156, May 1973).

14. See H. Leibenstein, "Allocative Efficiency vs. 'X-Efficiency,'" *American Economic Review*, 56 (June 1966), pp. 392-415; and Oliver E. Williamson, "Managerial Discretion and Business Behavior," *American Economic Review*, 53 (December 1963), pp. 1032-1057.

15. F. M. Scherer, *Industrial Market Structure and Economic Performance* (Rand McNally 1970), p. 408.

16. *Id.* at 405.

17. "Inefficiency Cited in Industry Study," *Washington Post*, April 26, 1972.

petition leads to excessive executive compensation and internal inefficiency.[18]

In sum, the notion that concentration results in cost inefficiency appears to be well entrenched in the minds of academics, government officials, and consumer advocates. Moreover, if Scherer's guess-estimate of the waste that results from this inefficiency is anywhere close to being correct, the concentration–cost inefficency problem may truly represent the submerged part of the monopoly iceberg.

What evidence do we have to support these claims? Aside from the bits and pieces of scattered evidence drawn together by Liebenstein and a little statistical work by Williamson, we have almost none. Indeed, in the perspective of the evidence we have marshaled on other issues, we have practically no evidence. Clearly, the claim that high concentration results in cost inefficiency has slipped into its position of prominence almost unnoticed by industrial organization economists. It seems time we put the claim under searching inquiry.

## IV. GOVERNMENT AS SOURCE OF MONOPOLY POWER

This volume focuses on only one dimension of the monopoly problem — whether high market concentration is an important source of monopoly power. However, concentration may represent only a secondary source of monopoly in our economy. The primary factor may be government intervention in the form of myriad protective regulations. Although government regulation of industry and markets occurs for many reasons, its effect is frequently to circumscribe competition. In many instances the scope of regulation is much broader than that required to accomplish its intended purpose. In other cases regulation is typically used to foster and protect cartels or trade associations. Business-instigated government intervention is often the most effective and least costly way for an industry to monopolize. All this is not to say that market concentration is not an important source of monopoly power, but only that government regulation may be an equal or more important source of such power.

Examples of regulation resulting in the diminishment of competition are not difficult to find. Can anyone doubt that the result of the extensive regulation of taxicabs common to most cities is to eliminate all significant competition in the industry? Due to severe entry restrictions in Chicago, for example, two taxi companies control more than 80 percent of the market.[19] In New York and Chicago, taxicab medallions sell for fifteen to thirty thousand dollars. Or, take the Webb-Pomerene Act, which permits (by exemption from the antitrust laws) firms in an industry to export through a single sales agency. A recent study of our experience with the act concludes that, contrary to original inten-

18. See testimony of Ralph Nader before the Subcommittee on Monopolies and Commercial Law of the House Judiciary Committee, 93rd Congress, 1st Session (July 17, 1973).

19. See Kitch, Isaacson, and Kasper, "The Regulation of Taxicabs in Chicago," *Journal of Law & Economics,* 14 (October 1971), pp. 285-350.

tion, Webb-Pomerene export associations have had important anticompetitive effects in *domestic* markets.[20] Even consumer protection legislation as seemingly innocuous as whiskey labelling laws have been found to have had significant anticompetitive effects.[21] Finally, it seems too obvious to even point out that price-fixing regulations or agreements that are exempt from the antitrust laws, such as interest rate ceilings on bank deposits, or, until recently, brokerage commission rate and bar association fee schedules, are far more effective restraints on competition than those that are likely to result from high concentration.

In summary, further study of regulation and its role in creating and sustaining monopoly in private markets would be immensely instructive. Where regulation has anticompetitive effects and is not necessary to achieve some higher social purpose, it should clearly be attacked and eliminated. Surprising as it may seem, much of the regulation we now have is of this kind. Alternatively, where regulation is successful in achieving some higher social objective, we should continuously evaluate it so that it does not prevent competition where competition is possible. All too frequently regulation which served a useful function at one point in our history becomes a fossilized barrier to competition in subsequent periods. Finally, we should study the desirability of granting fewer explicit exemptions from the antitrust laws and of aggressively applying our antitrust laws to "regulated" industries not so exempted.

## V. CONCLUDING REMARKS

This volume does not settle the issue of whether the net economic impact of high concentration is beneficial or harmful. Do the possible benefits of economies of scale and more rapid technological change offset the harmful effects of collusive behavior in concentrated markets? Does advertising increase or decrease competition? Do firms not under the gun of keen competition have higher costs per unit of output? How severe are the distributive consequences of monopoly? These questions will continue to be debated.

Nonetheless, this volume unquestionably projects into sharper relief the essential issues of the monopoly question. No word in the English language is surrounded with as much misunderstanding and resentful distrust as is "monopoly," and both laymen and economists have quite naturally come to associate "big business" and "concentrated markets" with the whole range of monopolistic abuses, both real and mythical. An important function of economists, therefore, is to keep the debate over monopoly from being sidetracked by emotion and irrelevancy.

What are the prospects of being able to resolve some of the important

20. See D. Larson, "An Economic Analysis of the Webb-Pomerene Act," *Journal of Law & Economics*, 13 (October 1970), pp. 461-500.

21. See Urban and Manche, "Federal Regulation of Whiskey Labelling: From the Repeal of Prohibition to the Present," *Journal of Law & Economics*, 15 (October 1972), pp. 411-426.

questions raised herein? I believe they are great. Serious and extensive work on these questions has only just begun. Ten years ago the evidence that economists could have mustered for this volume would have looked frail by comparison. Ten years from now today's evidence may look equally thin. If there is any hope of our developing wise and objective policies toward "big business," surely it rests with the spirit of inquiry exhibited here.

# Appendix A

## The Principal Antitrust Statutes Applicable to Monopolies and Mergers

### THE SHERMAN ACT [1]

*Section 1.* Every contract, combination in the form of trust or otherwise, or conspiracy, in restraint of trade or commerce among the several States, or with foreign nations, is hereby declared to be illegal. . . . Every person who shall make any contract or engage in any combination or conspiracy hereby declared to be illegal shall be deemed guilty of a misdemeanor, and, on conviction thereof, shall be punished by fine not exceeding fifty thousand dollars, or by imprisonment not exceeding one year, or by both said punishments, in the discretion of the court.

*Section 2.* Every person who shall monopolize, or attempt to monopolize, or combine or conspire with any other person or persons, to monopolize any part of the trade or commerce among the several States, or with foreign nations, shall be deemed guilty of a misdemeanor, and, on conviction thereof, shall be punished by fine not exceeding fifty thousand dollars, or by imprisonment not exceeding one year, or by both said punishments, in the discretion of the court.

### THE CLAYTON ACT [2]

*Section 7.* That no corporation engaged in commerce shall acquire, directly or indirectly, the whole or any part of the stock or other share capital and no corporation subject to the jurisdiction of the Federal Trade Commission shall acquire the whole or any part of the assets of another corporation engaged also in commerce, where in any line of commerce in any section of the country, the effect of such acquisition may be substantially to lessen competition, or to tend to create a monopoly.

No corporation shall acquire, directly or indirectly, the whole or any part of the stock or other share capital and no corporation subject to the jurisdiction of the Federal Trade Commission shall acquire the whole or any part of the assets of one or more corporations engaged in commerce, where in any line of commerce in any section of the country, the effect of such acquisition, of such stocks or assets, or of the use of such stock by the voting or granting

1. 26 Stat. 209 (1890), 15 U.S.C.A. §§1, 2.
2. 38 Stat. 731 (1914), 15 U.S.C.A. §18. This section contains the provisions of the Celler-Kefauver Act of December 29, 1950, 64 Stat. 1125 (1950).

of proxies or otherwise, may be substantially to lessen competition, or to tend to create a monopoly.

This section shall not apply to corporations purchasing such stock solely for investment and not using the same by voting or otherwise to bring about, or in attempting to bring about, the substantial lessening of competition. Nor shall anything contained in this section prevent a corporation engaged in commerce from causing the formation of subsidiary corporations for the actual carrying on of their immediate lawful business, or the natural and legitimate branches or extensions thereof, or from owning and holding all or a part of the stock of such subsidiary corporations, when the effect of such formation is not to substantially lessen competition.

Nor shall anything herein contained be construed to prohibit any common carrier subject to the laws to regulate commerce from aiding in the construction of branches or short lines so located as to become feeders to the main line of the company so aiding in such construction or from acquiring or owning all or any part of the stock of such branch lines, nor to prevent any such common carrier from acquiring and owning all or any part of the stock of a branch or short line constructed by an independent company where there is no substantial competition between the company owning the branch line so constructed and the company owning the main line acquiring the property or an interest therein, nor to prevent such common carrier from extending any of its lines through the medium of the acquisition of stock or otherwise of any other common carrier where there is no substantial competition between the company extending its lines and the company whose stock, property, or an interest therein is so acquired.

Nothing contained in this section shall be held to affect or impair any right heretofore legally acquired: *Provided,* That nothing in this section shall be held or construed to authorize or make lawful anything heretofore prohibited or made illegal by the antitrust laws, nor to exempt any person from the penal provisions thereof or the civil remedies therein provided.

Nothing contained in this section shall apply to transactions duly consummated pursuant to authority given by the Civil Aeronautics Board, Federal Communications Commission, Federal Power Commission, Interstate Commerce Commission, the Securities and Exchange Commission in the exercise of its jurisdiction under section 10 of the Public Utility Holding Company Act of 1935, the United States Maritime Commission, or the Secretary of Agriculture under any statutory provision vesting such power in such Commission, Secretary or Board.

## THE FEDERAL TRADE COMMISSION ACT [3]

*Section 5.* (a) (1) Unfair methods of competition in commerce, and unfair or deceptive acts or practices in commerce, are hereby declared unlawful. . . .

3. 38 Stat. 719 (1914), 15 U.S.C.A. §45. The phrase "and unfair or deceptive acts or practices of commerce" was added by the Wheeler-Lea Act, 52 Stat. 111 (1938).

(b) Whenever the Commission shall have reason to believe that any such person, partnership, or corporation has been or is using any unfair method of competition or unfair or deceptive act or practice in commerce, and if it shall appear to the Commission that a proceeding by it in respect thereof would be in the interest of the public, it shall issue and serve upon such person, partnership, or corporation a complaint stating its charges in that respect and containing a notice of a hearing upon a day and at a place therein fixed at least thirty days after the service of said complaint. The person, partnership, or corporation so complained of shall have the right to appear at the place and time so fixed and show cause why an order should not be entered by the Commission requiring such person, partnership, or corporation to cease and desist from the violation of the law so charged in said complaint. . . . If upon such hearing the Commission shall be of the opinion that the method of competition or the act or practice in question is prohibited by this Act, it shall make a report in writing in which it shall state its findings as to the facts and shall issue and cause to be served on such person, partnership, or corporation an order requiring such person, partnership, or corporation to cease and desist from using such method of competition or such act or practice. . . .

# Appendix B
## The Industrial Reorganization Act
## (The Hart Bill, S. 1167)

. . . The Congress finds and declares that (1) the United States of America is committed to a private enterprise system and a free market economy, in the belief that competition spurs innovation, promotes productivity, preserves a democratic society; and provides an opportunity for a more equitable distribution of wealth while avoiding the undue concentration of economic, social, and political power; (2) the decline of competition in industries with oligopoly or monopoly power has contributed to unemployment, inflation, inefficiency, and underutilization of economic capacity, and the decline of exports, thereby rendering monetary and fiscal policies inadequate and necessitating Government market controls subverting our basic commitment to a free market economy; (3) the preservation of a private enterprise system, a free market economy, and a democratic society in the United States of America requires legislation to supplement the policy of the antitrust laws through new enforcement mechanisms designed to responsibly restructure industries dominated by oligopoly or monopoly power; (4) the powers vested in these new enforcement mechanisms are to be exercised to promote competition throughout the economy to the maximum extent feasible, and to protect trade and commerce against oligopoly or monopoly power.

### TITLE I — POSSESSION OF MONOPOLY POWER

*Section 101.* (a) It is hereby declared to be unlawful for any corporation or two or more corporations, whether by agreement or not, to possess monopoly power in any line of commerce in any section of the country or with foreign nations.

(b) There shall be a rebuttable presumption that monopoly power is possessed —

(1) by any corporation if the average rate of return on net worth after taxes is in excess of 15 percentum over a period of five consecutive years out of the most recent seven years preceding the filing of the complaint, or

(2) if there has been no substantial price competition among two or more corporations in any line of commerce in any section of the country for a period of three consecutive years out of the most recent five years preceding the filing of the complaint, or

(3) if any four or fewer corporations account for 50 percentum (or more) of sales in any line of commerce in any section of the country in any year out of the most recent three years preceding the filing of the complaint.

In all other instances, the burden shall lie on the Industrial Reorganization Commission established under title II of this Act to prove the possession of monopoly power.

(c) A corporation shall not be required to divest monopoly power if it can show —

(1) such power is due solely to the ownership of valid patents, lawfully acquired and lawfully used, or

(2) such a divestiture would result in a loss of substantial economies.

The burden shall be upon the corporation or corporations to prove that monopoly power should not be divested pursuant to paragraphs (1) and (2) of the above subsection: *Provided, however,* That upon a showing of the possession of monopoly power pursuant to paragraph (1), the burden shall be upon the Industrial Reorganization Commission to show the invalidity, unlawful acquisition, or unlawful use of a patent or patents.

## TITLE II — INDUSTRIAL REORGANIZATION COMMISSION

*Definitions*

Section 201. As used in this title, the term —

(1) "industry" means all extractive, processing, smelting, refining, transporting, manufacturing, assembling, fabricating, constructing, financing, distributing or other economic activity carried on in closely related parts of commerce;

(2) "registered corporation" means a firm required by the Commission to file a registration statement under section 205;

(3) "Commission" means the Industrial Reorganization Commission established under section 202;

(4) "Commissioner" means the Commissioner of the Commission;

(5) "person" means an individual, a corporation, a partnership, an association, a joint stock company, a business trust, or an unincorporated organization; and

(6) "security" means any note, stock, Treasury stock, bond, debenture, evidence of indebtedness, certificate of interest or participation in any profit-sharing agreement, collateral-trust certificate, preorganization certificate or subscription, transferable share, investment contract, voting-trust certificate, certificate of deposit for a security, fractional undivided interest in oil gas, or other mineral rights, or, in general, any interest or instrument commonly known as a "security," or any certificate of interest or participation in, temporary or interim certificate for, receipt for, guarantee of, or warrant or right to subscribe to or purchase, any of the foregoing.

*Establishment of Commission*

Section 202. (a) There is an independent agency to be known as the Industrial Reorganization Commission.

(b) The Commission shall be under the direction and supervision of a Commissioner, who shall be appointed by the President, by and with the advice and consent of the Senate, for a term of seven and one-half years. . . .

(c) The Commissioner shall appoint and fix the compensation of an Executive Director and such other officers, agents, and employees as he deems necessary to assist him in carrying out the duties of the Commission. The Executive Director shall be the chief administrative officer of the Commission, and he shall perform his duties under the direction and supervision of the Commissioner. The Commissioner may delegate any of his functions, other than the making of regulations, to the Executive Director. . . .

(h) The Commission shall terminate its operations fifteen years after the date of enactment of this Act, and the functions, jurisdiction, powers, and duties of the Commission shall be transferred to the Federal Trade Commission. Upon transfer, the Federal Trade Commission shall succeed the Commission as a party in any legal proceedings, and any judgment or decree of any court of the United States applicable to the Commission shall, at the discretion of that court, be applicable to the Federal Trade Commission.

*Duties of the Commission*

Section 203. (a) (1) In order to determine whether or not any corporation, or two or more corporations, are in violation of title I of this Act, and develop a plan of reorganization to make competition more effective within each industry, the Commission shall study the structure, performance, and control of each of the following industries:

(A) chemicals and drugs;
(B) electrical machinery and equipment;
(C) electronic computing and communication equipment;
(D) energy;
(E) iron and steel;
(F) motor vehicles; and
(G) nonferrous metals.

(2) The Commission shall develop a plan of reorganization for each such industry whether or not any corporation is determined to be in violation of title I. In developing a plan of reorganization for any industry, the Commission shall determine for each such industry—

(A) the maximum feasible number of competitors at every level without the loss of substantial economies;
(B) the minimum feasible degree of vertical integration without the loss of substantial economies; and
(C) the maximum feasible degree of ease of entry at every level.

(3) The Commission shall study the collective-bargaining practices within each industry named in paragraph (1), and determine the effect of those practices on competition within that industry.

(4) The Commission shall report to the Congress not later than June 30 in each odd-numbered year with respect to the status of each study undertaken

under paragraph (1), (2), or (3) and each plan to be developed under paragraph (2), together with such recommendations, including recommendations for legislation as it deems necessary. Such legislative recommendations may include, but are not limited to, amendments to the antitrust laws, the Internal Revenue Code, the patent laws, and the National Labor Relations Act. The Commission may also report to Congress upon the effect on competition of the policies of executive or regulatory agencies of Government together with such recommendations, including recommendations for legislation, as it deems necessary.

(5) The Commission shall prosecute violations of title I of this Act.

(b) The Commission shall enforce the provisions of title I of this Act by filing a complaint and proposed order of reorganization with the Industrial Reorganization Court, established under title III of this Act, in accordance with the provisions of that title.

(c) Whenever the Commission obtains information under this title which furnishes a reasonable basis for inferring that any corporation or person has acted in violation of any law of the United States other than title I or of any State relating to trade or commerce, it shall notify the appropriate law enforcement official.

### Powers of the Commission

Section 204. (a) The Commission shall have power—

(1) to conduct studies of the structure, performance, and control of any industry and its collective-bargaining practices directly or by contract or other arrangement;

(2) to require corporations in industries named in section 203(a), or any person who the Commission shall have reason to believe affects the structure, performance or control of any such industry, to file registration statements in such form as the Commission may require in order to carry out the provisions of section 203(a);

(3) to require periodic and special reports and such other information of corporations, from time to time, as may be necessary to carry out the provisions of this Act, including but not limited to reports by product or line of commerce;

(4) to inspect and examine accounts, procedures, correspondence, memorandums, papers, books, and other records under section 205;

(5) to require interlocking relationship reports and securities control reports by officers directors, or persons, directly or indirectly, controlling, exercising, or executing the right to vote of 1 percentum or more of any class of securities for any registered corporation under section 206; . . .

### Penalties

Section 208. Any person who violates any provision of this title shall be deemed guilty of a misdemeanor, and upon conviction thereof, shall be punished by a fine not exceeding $500,000, if not a natural person, or if a natural person, $100,000, or by imprisonment not exceeding one year or both. . . .

## TITLE III — ESTABLISHMENT OF
## INDUSTRIAL REORGANIZATION COURT

### Appointment and Number of Judges

[Section 301.] The President shall appoint, by and with the advice and consent of the Senate, a chief judge and 14 associate judges who shall constitute a court of record known as the United States Industrial Reorganization Court. Such court is hereby declared to be established under article III of the Constitution of the United States. . . .

### Review of Industrial Reorganization Court Orders

[Sec. 304.] (a) In any proceeding brought in the Industrial Reorganization Court, an appeal from the final order of the Industrial Reorganization Court will lie only to the Supreme Court.

(b) The scope of review on appeal of any Industrial Reorganization Court order to the Supreme Court under this section shall be limited to: (1) whether or not the Industrial Reorganization Court proceeded correctly under the provisions of this title; and (2) whether or not the findings of fact of the Industrial Reorganization Court are supported by substantial evidence.

# Appendix C
## The Concentrated Industries Act
## (The Neal Report)*

Section 1. *Reduction of Industrial Concentration*

(a) It shall be the duty of the Attorney General and the Federal Trade Commission to investigate the structure of markets which appear to be oligopoly industries.

(b) When, as a result of such investigation, the Attorney General determines that a market appears to be an oligopoly industry and that effective relief is likely to be available under this Act, he shall institute a proceeding in equity for the reduction of concentration, to which all firms which appear to be oligopoly firms in such oligopoly industry shall be made parties.

(c) The court shall enter a judgment determining whether one or more markets are oligopoly industries and, if so, which of the parties are oligopoly firms in such oligopoly industries. Any party to the proceeding may appeal such judgment directly to the Supreme Court.

(d) In order to provide an opportunity for voluntary steps looking toward reduction of concentration, no affirmative relief shall be ordered against such oligopoly firms for a period of one year following entry or affirmance of such judgment.

(e) After such one-year period, further proceedings shall be conducted and a decree entered providing such further relief as may be appropriate, in light of steps taken or initiated during the one-year period, to achieve, within a reasonable period of time not in excess of four years, a reduction of concentration such that the market share of each oligopoly firm in such oligopoly industry does not exceed 12%. Such decree may include provisions requiring a party (i) to modify its contractual relationships and/or methods of distribution; (ii) to grant licenses (which may, in the discretion of the court, provide for payment of royalties) under and/or dispose of any patents, technical information, copyrights and/or trademarks; and (iii) to divest itself of assets, whether or not such assets are used in an oligopoly industry, including tangible assets, cash, stock or securities (including securities in existing firms or firms to be informed), accounts receivable and such other obligations as are appropriate for the conduct of business. The decree may also make such other provisions and require such other actions, not inconsistent with the purposes of this Act and the antitrust laws, as the court shall deem appropriate, in-

* Prepared by the White House Task Force on Antitrust Policy, submitted July 5, 1968.

cluding any provisions which would be appropriate in a decree pursuant to the antitrust laws. Such decree shall not require that a firm take any steps which such firm establishes would result in substantial loss of economies of scale.

(f) Any decree entered pursuant to subsection (e) may be appealed directly to the Supreme Court.

(g) Between four and five years after entry or affirmance of a decree pursuant to subsection (e) or a further decree pursuant to this subsection (g), proceedings shall be conducted to determine whether the decree has achieved the reduction of concentration referred to in subsection (e). If the court determines that it has not attained such end, it shall enter a further decree ordering additional steps to be taken. Such decree may be appealed directly to the Supreme Court.

(h) Any decree entered pursuant to this section 1 shall be subject to modification on the motion of any party according to the usual principles governing decrees in equity.

### Section 2. Regulated Industries

No action may be brought pursuant to section 1 of this Act with respect to any market which is subject to regulation under [specify federal regulatory statutes], unless, prior to the commencement of such action, a copy of the proposed complaint in such action shall have been furnished to the agency, commission, board or body vested with regulatory power pursuant to any of the Acts enumerated, and such agency, commission, board or body shall not have disapproved the commencement of such action within 90 days after receipt of such proposed complaint or shall have waived disapproval. No decree in any action pursuant to section 1 of this Act may require divestiture of any assets used in any such regulated market, unless such agency, commission, board or body shall have been served with a copy of the proposed decree and shall not have objected thereto within 90 days after such service or shall have waived objection. No such disapproval or objection or the withholding or waiver thereof shall be considered to be either an adjudication or a rule-making proceeding for purposes of the Administrative Procedure Act or any Act of Congress establishing procedural requirements for determinations by any agency, commission, board or body.

(b) No action may be brought pursuant to section 1 of this Act with respect to a market (i) in which maximum prices or rates are subject to direct public utility regulation by any state, municipal, District of Columbia or territorial agency, commission, board or other body, and (ii) which consists of the furnishing of electricity, gas, water or telephone services, without the consent of each such agency, commission, board or body.

### Section 3. Procedure

(a) All proceedings under this Act shall be conducted by the Special Antitrust Court established pursuant to subsection (b) of this section 3. Such proceedings shall be conducted in a judicial district or districts determined by the court or pursuant to rules established by the court.

(b) The Chief Justice shall designate not more than —————— circuit judges and district judges to serve on the Special Antitrust Court for purposes of a specified proceeding or proceedings or for such period or periods of time as may be specified by the Chief Justice. The Chief Justice shall designate one such judge as Chief Judge of the Special Antitrust Court. Proceedings under this Act shall be conducted by panels consisting of one or more judges of the Special Antitrust Court designated by the Chief Judge of the Special Antitrust Court or by a judge or judges designated by the Chief Justice for the purpose. Such proceedings shall be conducted pursuant to the Federal Rules of Civil Procedure in effect at the time, subject to such additional rules (which may supersede or supplement the Federal Rules of Civil Procedure) as shall be adopted by the Special Antitrust Court for the purposes of proceedings under this Act.

(c) In any proceeding under this Act, the Special Antitrust Court may designate one or more economists or other persons to serve as expert witnesses to be called by the court. Such witness or witnesses

(i) shall be furnished with all evidence introduced by any party;

(ii) may offer additional evidence subject to objection by any party;

(iii) shall offer analyses of the issues, with particular reference to relevant markets;

(iv) shall recommend appropriate provisions for decrees;

(v) shall be subject to cross-examination and rebuttal.

Section 4. Definitions

As used in this Act

(a) The term "oligopoly industry" shall mean a market in which

(i) any four or fewer firms had an aggregate market share of 70% or more during at least seven of the ten and four of the most recent five base years; and

(ii) the average aggregate market share during the five most recent base years of the four firms with the largest average market shares during those base years amounted to at least 80% of the average aggregate market share of those same four firms during the five preceding base years, but shall not include any market in which the average aggregate sales of all firms during the five most recent base years declined by 20% or more from such average sales during the preceding five base years.

(b) The term "oligopoly firm" shall mean a firm engaged in commerce whose market share in an oligopoly industry during at least two of the three most recent base years exceeded 15%.

(c) The term "firm" shall include corporations and associations existing under or authorized by the laws of the United States, any of the Territories, any State, or any foreign country, and shall include any firm controlling, controlled by, or under common control with a firm.

(d) The term "market" shall mean a relevant economic market, appropriately defined with reference to geographic area (which may be the United States or another geographic area) and product or service, including sales within such market by firms located outside the geographic area, *provided* that aggregate sales in the market amounted to more than $500 million during each of at least four out of the five most recent base years.

(e) The term "market share" shall mean the proportion of a firm's sales in a relevant market to all sales in such market.

(f) The term "sales" shall mean annual gross sales, gross income, gross receipts, or, if no such amount is applicable, the corresponding amount, whichever is largest, as set forth in reports filed by a firm with the Securities and Exchange Commission pursuant to section 13 or section 15(d) of the Securities Exchange Act of 1934, or the largest such amount which would have been reported if section 13 or section 15(d) of the Securities Exchange Act of 1934 were applicable to require reporting by such firm for a base year of its gross sales, gross income, gross receipts, or a corresponding amount, in a market, and sales in a market shall include amounts which would have been reported but for the fact that goods or services were both produced and consumed by the same firm.

(g) The term "base year" shall mean one of the ten calendar years, the most recent of which ended more than six months and not more than eighteen months prior to the date on which any proceeding is instituted pursuant to subsection (b) of section 1 of this Act.

(h) The term "antitrust laws" shall mean the Act entitled "An Act To protect trade and commerce against unlawful restraints and monopolies," approved July 2, 1890, as amended, and section 7 of the Act entitled "An Act To supplement existing laws against unlawful restraints and monopolies, and for other purposes," approved October 15, 1914, as amended.

(i) The term "commerce" shall mean trade or commerce among the several States and with foreign nations, or between the District of Columbia or any Territory of the United States and any State, Territory, or foreign nation, or between any insular possessions or other places under the jurisdiction of the United States, or between any such possession or place and any State or Territory of the United States or the District of Columbia or any foreign nation, or within the District of Columbia or any Territory or any insular possession or other place under the jurisdiction of the United States.

## COMMENTS TO ACCOMPANY
## CONCENTRATED INDUSTRIES ACT

*Section 1. Reduction of Industrial Concentration*

(a) The Attorney General and the Federal Trade Commission are under a duty to investigate market structures of lines of commerce which appear to be oligopoly industries. Since the Attorney General and the FTC do not have unlimited resources at their disposal, they would necessarily have discretion in establishing priorities. In exercising this discretion, it is assumed that they would first investigate those industries which are of most fundamental importance in the economy and in which concentrated market structure, not dictated by economies of scale, has had the most pronounced effect in producing market behavior at variance with competitive norms.

(b) Enforcement authority is vested solely in the Attorney General, but he would often proceed on the basis of an FTC investigation. This would require improved cooperation between the FTC and the Department of Justice.

(c) The first step in a proceeding under the Act is a determination of oligopoly firms and oligopoly industries. The sole questions for determination would be relevant markets and market shares.

(d) There is a mandatory one-year waiting period after a determination that an industry is an oligopoly industry and parties are oligopoly firms. The purpose of this waiting period is to permit an oligopoly firm to take or initiate steps to reduce its market share in a manner most advantageous to its stockholders. The Act imposes no penalties and, until entry of a decree pursuant to subsection (e), provides for no relief against oligopoly firms. Therefore, it is not expected to influence firms to reduce their market shares by simply restricting their output without disposing of assets. Artificial restriction of output would be undesirable from an economic point of view.

(e) After the waiting period, the court is to determine what steps are to be taken to reduce the four-firm concentration ratio below 50% and the market shares of individual firms below 12%. The statutory language recognizes that this objective will not always be feasible. In entering its decree, the court is to take account of steps taken or initiated during the waiting period. The decree may use a variety of techniques short of divestiture if they promise to bring about the desired reduction in market share. These steps would include the removal of such barriers to entry as contractual arrangements and patents. The Act does not specifically authorize the court simply to restrict output or advertising expenditures, since restrictions of this nature would come very close to direct regulation of business and would seldom produce desirable economic results. Such restrictions might, however, be used in unusual situations and would be justified by the general reference to provisions appropriate in an antitrust decree.

A decree cannot require a firm to take steps which would result in substantial loss of economies of scale. This provision would, for example, preclude divestiture reducing a firm below minimum efficient size or creating new entities below minimum efficient size. The burden of proof is on the firm, and the possible loss of economies is not a defense to the issuance of a judgment under subsection (c). Division of a single plant would ordinarily result in substantial loss of economies of scale, and the Act permits a firm to establish that a decree would result in a net loss of economies of scale beyond the plant level. Net loss of economies of scale beyond the plant level might be established directly or by considering the minimum size of viable competitors in an industry. Thus, the court would not ordinarily divide an oligopoly firm into firms smaller than that indicated by experience to be necessary to survival in the industry. We are not unaware of efficiencies other than economies of scale; other efficiencies will generally reflect scarce resources such as unique management talent. These resources may be transferred pursuant to a deconcentration decree without significant loss.

(f) This subsection provides for immediate Supreme Court review of a decree.

(g) This subsection provides for a mandatory "second look" every four to five years after the entry or affirmance of the original decree until concentration is reduced to the extent described in subsection (e). If relief granted in a decree has not had the desired effect, more drastic relief would generally be in order. This procedure is not unlike the procedure in a monopolization case under section 2 of the Sherman Act. See *United States v. United Shoe Machinery Corp.*, Supreme Court, May 20, 1968.

(h) A decree is subject to modification pursuant to usual equity principles. Thus, the "second look" provision of subsection (g) does not exclude additional modification of a decree.

Tariffs and import quotas often serve as an important barrier to entry and may serve to restrict the relevant market. If such barriers were dropped, competition would, in many cases, immediately improve. The Act contains no provisions for reducing or eliminating such barriers in oligopoly industries. Such a procedure might harm small firms as much as or more than oligopoly firms. The participation of courts in an area so closely linked to foreign affairs might be regarded as an inappropriate incursion on the powers of the executive and might upset delicate and sensitive trade and treaty relationships. But in establishing and negotiating tariffs and import quotas, it would clearly be appropriate for the President and Congress to take account of concentration in domestic industries.

### Section 2. Regulated Industries

In general, this section provides that an action may not be brought with respect to markets regulated under specified federal statutes. The decision as to which statutes to specify would reflect the fact that remedies under the Act are not limited to divestiture and might interfere with statutory regulatory patterns. The Act also excludes divestiture of part of the assets used by a public utility whose maximum rates are regulated by a state commission. A State could not exempt its industries from the Act by unusual expansion of the scope of public utility regulation. Our recommendation of this provision does not mean that we approve existing statutory provisions for exemption, but simply that we do not believe that the Act should be at cross-purposes with other statutes.

### Section 3. Procedure

Proceedings under the Act will require judges with special expertise, and this expertise is not likely to be acquired unless all litigation is directed to a small number of judges with special qualifications. There is ample precedent in 28 U.S.C. section 1407 for the use of specially selected judges to handle litigation no matter where it arises. The Act should be supplemented by amendments to title 28 to provide nationwide service of process and to ensure that venue in the Special Antitrust Court will be proper.

Subsection (c) allows the use of court-appointed economic experts. In many cases, the Attorney General and the defendants may confine their arguments to those best supporting their position in particular cases. Impartial economic experts could present additional arguments, as well as helping the court to sift and evaluate arguments made by the parties.

### Section 4. Definitions

(a) The definition of "oligopoly industry" is limited to markets in which the four-firm concentration ratio has been both high and stable. The first clause of the definition requires that the concentration ratio have been at least 70% during four out of the five most recent base years and seven out of the ten base years. In the judgment of the members, this is a conservative figure, at the upper end of the range in which direct action to reduce concentration would be justified. The second clause excludes industries in which there have been substantial changes in the identity of the four largest firms. If the situation stabilizes, a proceeding may be brought at a later date. The language after the second clause excludes industries with declining sales. This reflects our views of the appropriate limits on the use of the remedies of the Act and of appropriate priorities in the use of enforcement resources. An industry which is presently not an oligopoly industry because of a sales decline may become an oligopoly industry later on if the decline in sales is arrested.

(b) An "oligopoly firm" is a firm with a market share in excess of 15% during at least two of the three most recent base years. Unless the top four firms have exactly 70% and there are only two other firms with exactly 15% each, there will not be more than five oligopoly firms in an oligopoly industry, and there will generally be four or fewer, depending on how market shares are distributed among the largest firms.

(c) The definition of "firm" is very similar to the definition of "person" in the Clayton Act. Unlike the Clayton Act term, it does not include individuals. It includes firms controlling, controlled by, or under common control with a firm. Thus, in determining whether a firm is an oligopoly firm, the market shares of its subsidiaries would be considered.

(d) The term "market" has been substituted for Clayton Act term "line of commerce" in order to permit the court to make sound determinations free of the distortions which have arisen in some Clayton cases. In order to exclude extremely narrow market definitions and to restrict the operation of the Act to industries of substantial importance in the economy as a whole, the Act is limited to markets with annual sales of at least $500 million.

(e) A firm's "market share" is defined as its proportion of sales in a market.

(f) "Sales" as defined by reference to amounts which would be reported pursuant to the Securities Exchange Act of 1934. Some elaboration is necessary, since the Securities Exchange Act does not, and even with additional divisional reporting requirements would not, require reporting of sales in every conceivable market. Language is added at the end to indicate that the definition of sales is not limited to goods or services sold outside an enterprise. Thus, differences in the degree of vertical integration would not affect sales or market shares.

(g) There are ten "base years," determined by reference to the date a proceeding is instituted. The most recent base year will have ended at least six months prior to the date as of which figures must be known for the base year. This takes account of necessary delays in gathering and reporting figures.

(h) The term "antitrust laws" is used only in section 1(e), which permits the court to include in its decree any provisions which would be appropriate in a decree pursuant to the antitrust laws. For this purpose, the antitrust laws include the Sherman Act and section 7 of the Clayton Act, but do not include section 2 of the Robinson-Patman Act and various miscellaneous antitrust laws referred to in the Clayton Act definition of the same term.

(i) "Commerce" is defined substantially in the same terms as in the Clayton Act, and is designed to exhaust congressional power under the Commerce Clause.

# Appendix D
# Biographical Information on Conference
# Authors, Chairmen, and Editors

**Adams, Walter,** Distinguished University Professor and Professor of Economics, Michigan State University. Ph.D. 1947, M.A. 1946, Yale; B.A. 1942, Brooklyn College.

Economist, teacher, and university administrator (president of Michigan State University 1969-1970). Member, Advisory Committee on International Education and Cultural Affairs; member, Attorney General's Committee to Study the Antitrust Laws (1953-1955); consultant, Small Business Committees of the Senate and House, and Senate Judiciary Committee.

**Adelman, Morris A.,** Professor of Economics, MIT. Ph.D. 1948, Harvard; B.S.S. 1938, College of the City of New York.

Member, advisory committees to the Federal Power Commission, the National Research Council, and the American Petroleum Institute; editor, *Journal of Industrial Economics* (1958-1968); member, Attorney General's Committee to Study the Antitrust Laws (1953-1955); member, Universities-National Bureau Committee (1950-1962).

**Blair, John M.,** Professor of Economics, University of South Florida. Ph.D. 1941, American University; B.A. 1936, Tulane.

Chief economist, Subcommittee on Antitrust and Monopoly of the Senate Judiciary Committee (1957-1970); assistant chief economist, FTC (1946-1957); chief, Office of Regional Economics, Dept. of Commerce (1946); director, Office of Reports, Smaller War Plants Corp. (1944-1946); economist, War Production Board (1938-1944).

**Blake, Harlan M.,** Professor of Law, Columbia University School of Law. J.D. 1954, M.A. 1947, B.A. 1946, Chicago.

Director, European Common Market Antitrust Project of the New York City Bar Association (1964–); consultant, Inter-American Law Center, Columbia (1967–); author, *Cases and Materials on Antitrust Law* (1967) (with Pitofsky) and other works.

**Brozen, Yale,** Professor of Business Economics, Graduate School of Business, University of Chicago. Ph.D. 1942, Chicago; B.S. 1939, MIT.

Head of program on recent developments in applied economics for professors of economics, and adjunct scholar at the American Enterprise Institute for Public Policy Research at Chicago. Consultant to business and government; member, NSF Advisory Board. Served the President's Material

Policy Commission, the State's Attorney Office in Illinois, the Antitrust Division of Dept. of Justice, and the National Association of Manufacturers.

**Coase, Ronald H.,** Clifton R. Musser Professor of Economics, University of Chicago Law School. Ph.D. 1931, London School of Economics.

Director, law and economics program at Chicago Law School; editor, *Journal of Law and Economics* (1964–). Taught at several universities and served the British government as an economist before coming to the United States in 1951. Well known for work on social cost in which he reconstructed the problem of efficient markets and launched the theory of transaction cost.

**Demsetz, Harold,** Professor of Economics, UCLA, Ph.D. and M.A. 1959, M.B.A. 1954, Northwestern; B.S. 1953, Illinois.

Testified on behalf of the Justice Dept. on the desirability of adopting market-determined commissions for the organized trading of securities. Consultant, Rand Corp. (1961-1962); scientific analyst, Center for Naval Analyses (1963); author of numerous articles on competition and concentration.

**Dewey, Donald J.,** Professor of Economics and Chairman of the Department, Columbia University. Chicago, 1949-1950; London School of Economics, 1948-1949; Cambridge University, 1947-1948; M.A. 1947, Iowa; A.B. 1943, Chicago.

Recipient of many academic awards including Ford Fellowship in Economics (1966-1967); invited to Institute for Advanced Study in the Behavioral Sciences (1956-1957); Distinguished Article Award, *Journal of Political Economy* (1949); Senior Fulbright Research Scholar (1956-1957); research associate, National Planning Association (1950-1952).

**Edwards, Franklin R.,** Associate Professor of Business, Graduate School of Business, Columbia University. J.D. 1968, New York University; Ph.D. 1964, Harvard; M.A. 1960, B.A. 1958, Bucknell.

Served as senior economist and editor, *National Banking Review* (1964-1966); worked at the Federal Reserve Board. Current areas of research include banking and financial structure, monetary theory, and regulation; author of numerous articles in these areas.

**Goldschmid, Harvey J.,** Professor of Law, Columbia University School of Law. J.D. 1965, B.A. 1962, Columbia.

Chairman, Committee on Trade Regulation of the Association of the Bar of the City of New York (1971-1974); consultant, Administrative Conference of the United States (1971-1973), Investor Responsibility Research Center (1973-), and other public and private groups. Author of a number of articles on antitrust and corporate law.

**Hart, Philip A.,** United States Senator (D. Mich.). J.D. 1937, Michigan; A.B. 1934, Georgetown.

Chairman, Subcommittee on Antitrust and Monopoly of the Senate Judiciary Committee; elected to United States Senate in 1970, 1964, and 1958; elected as lieutenant governor of Michigan in 1954 and 1956. Legal advisor to Governor Williams (1953-1954); United States attorney for eastern

Michigan (1952); director, OPS (1951); Michigan Corporations and Securities Commissioner (1949-1950).

**Hruska, Roman L.,** United States Senator (R. Neb.). J.D. 1929, Creighton; University of Omaha and Chicago Law School, 1927-1928.

Ranking minority member, Subcommittee on Antitrust and Monopoly of the Senate Judiciary Committee; elected to United States Senate in 1970, 1964, 1958, and 1954; elected to Eighty-third Congress in 1952. Chairman, National Commission on Revision of the Federal Court Appellate System (1972-); member, National Commissions on Causes and Prevention of Violence (1968), Reform of Federal Criminal Laws (1967-1971), and Food Marketing (1964). General law practice, Omaha (1929-1952).

**Lustgarten, Steven,** Assistant Professor of Economics and Finance, City University of New York, Baruch College. Ph.D. 1971, M.S. 1967, UCLA; B.A. 1966 CCNY.

Recipient of several research grants; author, "The Administered Price Thesis Denied: Comment," *American Economic Review* (March 1974) (with Weston and Grottke), and "The Impact of Buyer Concentration in Manufacturing Industries," *Review of Economics and Statistics* (forthcoming).

**Mann, H. Michael,** Professor of Economics, Boston College. Ph.D. 1962, Cornell; B.A. 1956, Haverford.

Director, Bureau of Economics, FTC (1971-1973); special economic assistant and consultant, Antitrust Division, Dept. of Justice (1968-1970). Recipent, NSF grant to study the stability of oligopolistic market structure (1967-1968). Has given frequent testimony on various aspects of industrial concentration before Senate and House committees; presentations at economics conferences and before the SEC.

**Markham, Jesse,** Charles E. Wilson Professor of Business Administration, Harvard Business School. Ph.D. 1949, M.A. 1947, Harvard; A.B. 1941, University of Richmond.

Chief economist, FTC (1953-1955); member, ABA Commission to Study the FTC (1969); consultant, Federal Reserve Board; senior economist, FCC Network Study Staff; chairman, Dept. of Commerce Task Force on Marketing and Competition; U.S. delegate to the Organization for European Cooperation and Development (1956-1963); economics editor, Houghton Mifflin (1961-).

**McGee, John S.,** Professor of Economics, University of Washington, Seattle. Ph.D. 1952, Vanderbilt; A.B. 1947, Texas.

Current research and writing on economics of exploiting reproducible resources, economies of size in engine manufacture, and economics of style. Consultant in economics, marketing, and antitrust matters for leading companies in major industries and for various law firms. Recipient of Guggenheim, NSF, Rockefeller, and Ford Foundation research fellowships.

**Mueller, Willard F.,** William F. Vilas Research Professor of Agricultural Economics, Professor of Economics and Law, University of Wisconsin. Ph.D. 1955, Vanderbilt; M.S. 1951, B.S. 1950, Wisconsin.

Consultant on antitrust matters to staffs of various congressional committees, federal independent agencies, and executive departments. Executive director, President's Cabinet Committee on Price Stability (1968-1969); director, Bureau of Economics and chief economist, FTC (1961-1968); chief economist, House Select Committee on Small Business (1961).

**Neal, Phil Caldwell,** Dean and Professor of Law, University of Chicago School of Law. LL.B. 1943, A.B. 1940, Harvard.

Chairman, President Johnson's Task Force on Antitrust Laws (1968); executive secretary, Coordinating Committee for Multiple Litigation of the United States District Courts (1962-1966); member and chairman, Pacific Regional Enforcement Commission, Wage Stabilization Board (1950-1952). Worked for Dept. of Justice (1945) and in private law practice before becoming a professor of law.

**Phillips, Almarin,** Professor of Economics and Law, University of Pennsylvania. Ph.D. 1953, Harvard; M.A. 1949, B.S. 1948, Pennsylvania.

Advisor/consultant to the Secretary of the Treasury, C.E.D. committees, and private research organizations and companies. Director, National Bureau of Economic Research (1971–); member, Board of Governors of the Federal Reserve System (1962-1973); Senior Fellow, Brookings Institution (1971–). Codirector, President's Commission on Financial Structure and Regulation (1970-1971); Ford Foundation Faculty Research Fellow (1967-1968); editor of various economic journals.

**Posner, Richard A.,** Professor of Law, University of Chicago School of Law. LL.B. 1962, Harvard; A.B. 1959, Yale.

Research associate, National Bureau of Economic Research; editor, *Journal of Legal Studies.* Member, Research Committee of American Bar Foundation; President's Task Force on Competition and Productivity (1969); ABA Commission To Study the FTC (1969). General counsel, President's Task Force on Communications Policy (1967-1968); assistant to the solicitor general (1965-1967); assistant to Commissioner Philip Elman at the FTC (1963-1965).

**Scherer, Frederic M.,** Director of the Bureau of Economics, Federal Trade Commission. Ph.D. 1963, M.B.A. 1958, Harvard; A.B. 1954, Michigan.

Senior Research Fellow, International Institute of Management, Berlin (1972-1974); principal investigator in a study of "The Economics of Multi-Plant Operation: An International Comparisons Study" (1969); recipient, F. W. Lanchester Prize, Operations Research Society of America (1964); consultant on defense, arms control, patent policy, and antitrust matters.

**Turner, Donald F.,** Professor of Law, Harvard University School of Law. LL.B. 1950, Yale; Ph.D. 1947, Harvard; B.A. 1941, Northwestern.

Assistant attorney general, Antitrust Division, Dept. of Justice (1965-1968). Private law practice before becoming a professor of law.

**Weiss, Leonard W.,** Professor of Economics, University of Wisconsin. Ph.D. 1954, Columbia; B.S. 1945, Northwestern.

Member, Brookings Institution Advisory Committee on Studies of Regulation of Economic Activity; Universities-National Bureau Committee. Expert witness in AEP-CSOE electric holding company case before SEC (1971);

special advisor to the assistant attorney general, Antitrust Division (1969 1970); author of numerous articles and monographs.

**Weston, J. Fred,** Professor of Business Economics and Finance, School of Business, UCLA. Ph.D. 1948, M.B.A. 1943, B.A. 1937, Chicago.

Member, American Economics Association Census Advisory Board; president, American Finance Association (1966); president, Western Economic Association (1959-1960); associate editor (1948-1955) and on editorial board (1958-1959), *Journal of Finance.*

# Appendix E
# Conference Participants

**Adams, Arlin**
Circuit Judge, United States Court of Appeals, Philadelphia, Pa.
**Ariga, Michiko**
Visiting Lecturer in Japanese Law, Columbia
**Baker, Donald I.**
Deputy Assistant Attorney General, Antitrust, Dept. of Justice
**Baxter, William Francis**
Professor of Law, Stanford
**Blake, Harlan**
Professor of Law, Columbia
**Bock, Betty**
Director of Antitrust Research, The Conference Board
**Bork, Robert H.**
Solicitor General of the United States
**Brodley, Joseph F.**
Professor of Law, Indiana
**Butzner, John D., Jr.**
Circuit Judge, United States Court of Appeals, Richmond, Va.
**Clearwaters, Keith I.**
Deputy Assistant Attorney General, Antitrust, Dept. of Justice
**Collier, Calvin J.**
General Counsel, FTC
**Corash, Michele**
Wilmer, Cutler & Pickering, Washington, D.C.
**Dam, Kenneth**
Professor of Law, Chicago
**Day, Richard E.**
Professor of Law, Ohio State
**Engman, Lewis**
Chairman, FTC
**Falco, James F.**
Chief Counsel, House Antitrust Subcommittee
**Feinberg, Wilfred**
Circuit Judge, United States Court of Appeals, New York, N.Y.
**Flynn, John J.**
Professor of Law, Utah

**Fox, Eleanor**
Simpson, Thacker & Bartlett, New York, N.Y.
**Gellhorn, Ernest**
Professor of Law, Virginia
**Ginsburg, David**
Ginsburg, Feldman & Bress, Washington, D.C.
**Green, Mark**
Corporate Accountability Research Group, Washington, D.C.
**Grunschlag, Dov M.**
Professor of Law, California (Davis)
**Halverson, James T.**
Director, Bureau of Competition, FTC
**Handler, Milton**
Professor of Law, Columbia
**Hay, George A.**
Director, Office of Economic Policy, Dept. of Justice
**Holmes, Allen**
Jones, Day, Cockley & Reavis, Cleveland, Ohio
**Jones, W. Kenneth**
Professor of Law, Columbia
**Jones, Mary Gardner**
Professor of Law, Illinois
**Kamenshine, Robert D.**
Professor of Law, Vanderbilt
**Kirkpatrick, Miles W.**
Morgan, Lewis & Bockius, Washington, D.C.
**Kramer, Victor H.**
Professor of Law, Georgetown
**Liebeler, Wesley J.**
Director, Office of Policy Planning and Evaluation, FTC
**Martin, David**
Chief Economist, Senate Antitrust and Monopoly Subcommittee
**McWilliams, Robert H.**
Circuit Judge, United States Court of Appeals, Denver, Colo.
**Meeks, James E.**
Professor of Law, Iowa
**Millstein, Ira**
Weil, Gotshal & Manges, New York, N.Y.
**Pitofsky, Robert**
Professor of Law, Georgetown
**Posner, Paul S.**
Professor of Law, NYU
**Rahl, James A.**
Dean and Professor of Law, Northwestern
**Rose, Jonathan**
Professor of Law, Arizona State

**Ross, Leonard**
Professor of Law, Columbia
**Schwartz, Louis B.**
Professor of Law, Pennsylvania
**Schwartz, Warren F.**
Professor of Law, Virginia
**Weston, Glen E.**
Professor of Law, George Washington

## Appendix F
## Conference Sponsors*

Alcoa Foundation
Amoco Foundation
Bethlehem Steel Corporation
Computer Industry Association
Deere & Company
Eastman Kodak Company
Exxon Corporation
General Electric Foundation
General Motors Corporation
Gordon F. Hampton, Esq.
IBM Corporation
International Paper Company
Johnson & Johnson Company
Kraftco Corporation
Mobil Oil Corporation
PPG Industries Foundation
Union Carbide Corporation
Xerox Corporation

* One corporate donor contributed anonymously to the Conference.

# Index*

* In preparing this index, the editors have had the invaluable assistance of Steven
E. Harbour and Robert M. Stokes, two students at the Columbia University School of
Law. We acknowledge our debt to them for their most important contributions.